1900 do c... ...a

n. Ba ḋlí...

-ċabrac. Is cuiṁin liom

ċonnaic mé é. Bí

ni, Éadbárd Máirtín

luaiġ móir daoine bail-

g Glinn, an áit ar

innneacán ar Raiftiri

(litreacaib óir.

agus Sgríbinn ~~beirri~~ λ

n bróáin —— óir do

anta aca —— agus

an Bpobal i nGaedilg

do bí ionnam, nuair

eon, uasal, caol, árd, ina

...ur é

eirseacht liom ar a ḋíceall

ċ isteac ar an ċnocán,

MY AMERICAN JOURNEY

BY
DOUGLAS HYDE

EDITED BY
LIAM MAC MATHÚNA, BRIAN Ó CONCHUBHAIR,
NIALL COMER, CUAN Ó SEIREADÁIN
& MÁIRE NIC AN BHAIRD

Published by
UNIVERSITY COLLEGE DUBLIN PRESS
PREAS CHOLÁISTE OLLSCOILE BHAILE ÁTHA CLIATH
2019

First published 2019
by University College Dublin Press
UCD Humanities Institute, Room H103,
Belfield,
Dublin 4
www.ucdpress.ie

Irish text first published as *Mo Thurus go hAmerice*
by *Oifig Díolta Foillseacháin Rialtais* in 1937

ISBN 978-1-910820-48-3 hb

CIP data available from the British Library

Design by iota (www.iota-books.com)
Typeset in Granjon with Norwester display titling by Ryan Shiels
Map design by Timothy O'Neill
Printed in England on acid-free paper by CPI Antony Rowe, Chippenham, Wiltshire

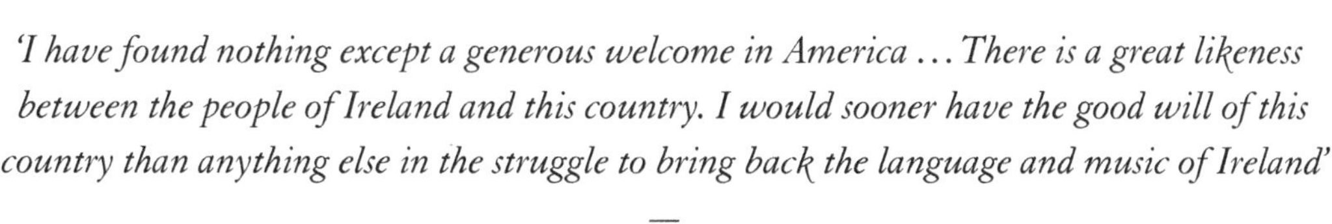

'I have found nothing except a generous welcome in America ... There is a great likeness between the people of Ireland and this country. I would sooner have the good will of this country than anything else in the struggle to bring back the language and music of Ireland'

—

Douglas Hyde

CONTENTS

ACKNOWLEDGEMENTS

This book has been many years in the making. It has, like Hyde's journey, been a transatlantic effort, and we are grateful to a community of supporters and assistants who came together to make it a reality. We would especially like to mention Mary Broderick at the National Library of Ireland, to whom special thanks is due for her invaluable assistance in tracing sources relating to Prof. Douglas Hyde. Warm thanks is also due to Micheál Mahon of Frenchpark, whose parents worked for the Hydes, and to Kevin Flynn, who now lives in Ratra House, Frenchpark, Co. Roscommon. The late Michael Carty, of Frenchpark, and Galway, and Mrs Mary Sealy, Howth, Co. Dublin, widow of Douglas Hyde's grandson Douglas Sealy, represent our living link to Hyde. The support of Dr Aodhán Mac Cormaic and Micheál Ó Conaire at Roinn na Gaeltachta, Niall Burgess, Eugene Downes, and Feargal Ó Maolagáin at the Department of Foreign Affairs and Trade, and funding from those departments was crucial to the book's realisation.

We would like to thank Conor Graham, Noelle Moran and Clare Appezzato at UCD Press for copyediting, proofreading, and project managing the production, Caoimhe Ní Bhraonáin for copyediting and proofreading the Irish text, Ryan Shiels for typesetting and internal layout design, Daniel Morehead at Origin Design for the cover design, Cormac Kinsella for organising publicity, Nicole Cuskeran, Séamus Mac Conmidhe, and Gabhán Ó Dochartaigh for their help with the text, and Seosamh Ó Murchú at An Gúm - Foras na Gaeilge for his assistance with copyright for the original text. Paula O'Dornan at Westmeath Co. Library, and Dr Críostóir Mac Cárthaigh at the National Folklore Collection, UCD, helped source the postcards which illustrate this book.

We would also like to thank Julian de Spáinn at Conradh na Gaeilge, Dr Maxim Fomin at Ulster University, Jennifer Frankola Crawford, Seán Crowley, Domhnall Ó Catháin, Micheala Fallon, Keith Farrell, Crystal Fisher, Eimear Friel (Deputy Consul General of Ireland – New York), Patrick Griffin (University of Notre Dame), Susan Guibert (University of Chicago), James Harte (National Library of Ireland), Nicolle Ho, Cynthia Harris (Jersey City Free Public Library), Gerard Kavanagh (National Library of Ireland), Mary Kinahan-Ockay (St Peter's University, Jersey City, NJ), Prof. J. J. Lee, (Glucksman Ireland House, NYU), Fiona Lyons (UCD), Tara MacLeod (University of Notre Dame), Dr Tim McMahon (Marquette University), Conall McConagle, Máire Mhic Mhathúna, Hilary Mhic Suibhne, (Glucksman Ireland House, NYU), Tokozile Mlambo (University of Notre Dame), Frances Mulraney (Irish Central), Daniel Mulhall (Ambassador of Ireland to the United States), Dr Brian Murphy (TU Dublin), Dr Miriam Nyhan Grey (Glucksman Ireland House, NYU), Gearóid O'Brien (Westmeath County Library), Robert O'Driscoll (Consul General of Ireland – Western United States), Dr Philip O'Leary (Boston College), Gearóid Ó Lúing (National Library of Ireland), Conor O'Reilly (Áras an Uachtaráin), David O'Sullivan, (US Ireland Council), Selena Ponio, Karen Roberts (Galway), Guieswende Rouamba (University of Notre Dame), Maggie Mello (University of Notre Dame), Patrick Sheridan, Allegra Wallingford, Dr Aoife Whelan (UCD), Mairéad Willis, and Dr Nicholas Wolf (Glucksman Ireland House, NYU).

And finally, our special thanks to President Michael D. Higgins, whose interest in Hyde and his experiences in San Francisco, provided the inspiration for this project.

Ár mbuíochas dóibh ar fad as an gcabhair agus as an gcúnamh.

The Editors
September 2019

LIST OF ILLUSTRATIONS

INTRODUCTION

ENGLISH LANGUAGE TEXT

IRISH LANGUAGE SECTION

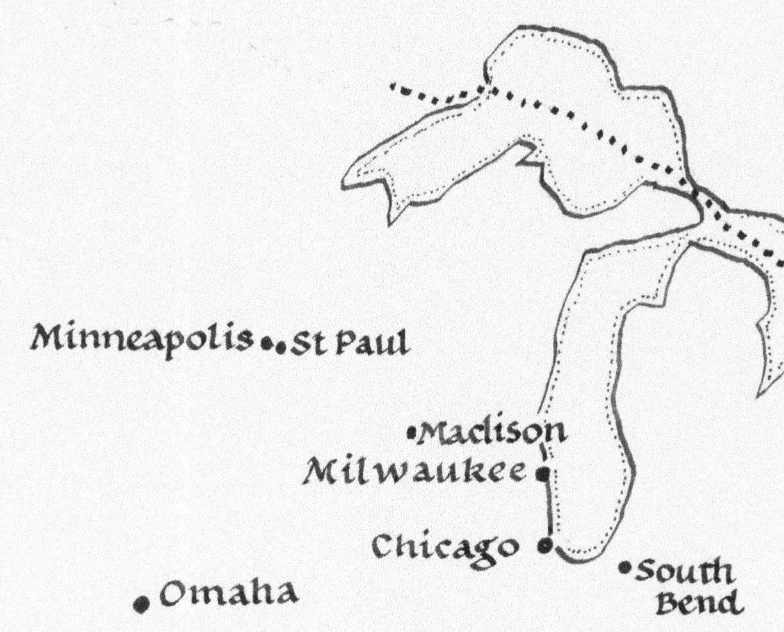
Minneapolis
St Paul
Madison
Milwaukee
Chicago
South Bend
Omaha
Indianapolis
St Louis

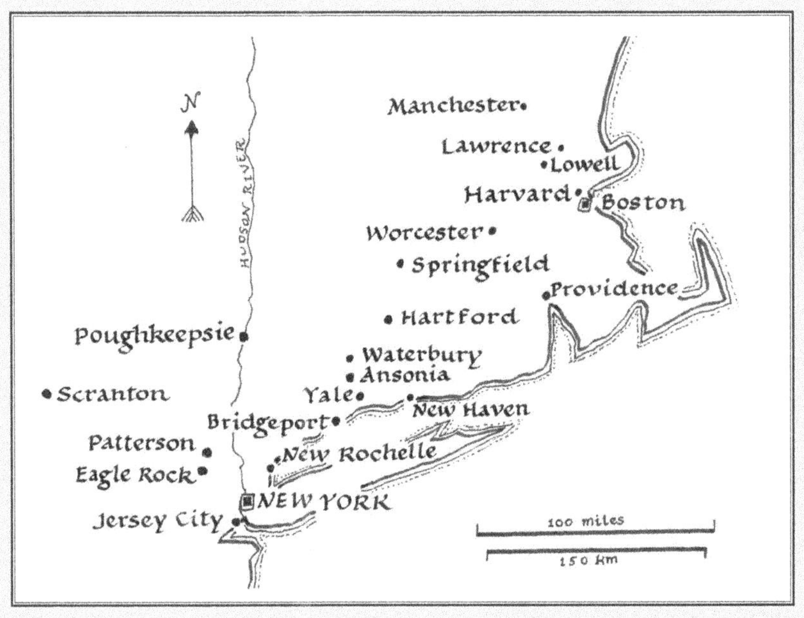
N
HUDSON RIVER
Manchester
Lawrence
Lowell
Harvard
Boston
Worcester
Springfield
Providence
Hartford
Poughkeepsie
Waterbury
Ansonia
Scranton
Yale
New Haven
Bridgeport
Patterson
New Rochelle
Eagle Rock
NEW YORK
Jersey City
100 miles
150 km

Toronto
Rochester
Boston
Buffalo
Brocton
Cornell
Elmira
Cleveland
New York
Pittsburgh
Philadelphia
Columbus
Baltimore
Washington D.C.
Cincinnati
300 miles
500 km

Seattle
Spokane
Portland
Anaconda
Butte
Sacramento
San Francisco
Santa Barbara
Pasadena
Los Angeles
Santa
Catalina Is.

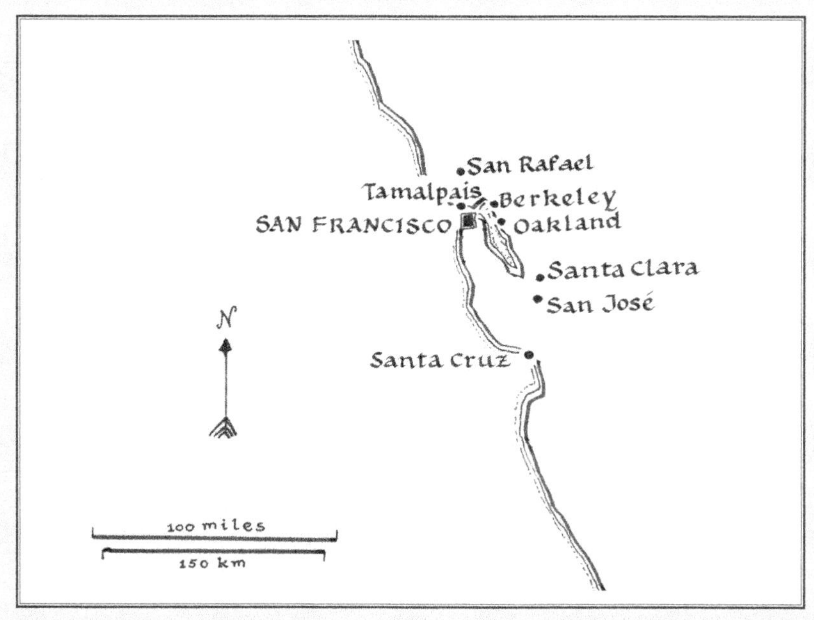
San Rafael
Tamalpais
Berkeley
SAN FRANCISCO
Oakland
Santa Clara
San José
Santa Cruz
N
100 miles
150 km

FOREWORD

by Michael D. Higgins
Uachtarán na hÉireann
President of Ireland

Douglas Hyde is a foundational figure in Ireland's history - an idealist, visionary and scholar. Paradoxically, it is these characteristics that led him to being one of the least studied of Ireland's major figures of the ninteenth and twentieth centuries. He is perhaps best remembered for his work to revive the Irish language, and for becoming the first President of Ireland in 1938. The portrait of Hyde, pictured in front of Áras an Uachtaráin, which featured on Robert Ballagh's beautiful series of Irish banknotes issued in the 1990s best encapsulates the image held in public memory of *An Craoibhín Aoibhinn*: avuncular, gentle, quiet, and perhaps a little eccentric. The neglect of Douglas Hyde may also be related to the decline in enthusiasm for his great life projects by those who would invoke the demands of a pragmatic survival of a new State, as they saw it.

In recent years, a new wave of scholarship has begun to reveal a more complex personality in Hyde, a calculating and sophisticated politician, strategist, and supreme diplomat.

In this new and critical translation of *Mo Thurus go hAmerice*, Hyde's 1937 account of his fundraising lecture tour of the United States from November 1905 to June 1906, we get to share his perspective on an extraordinary moment in Irish, Irish-American, and American-Irish history. Here we observe Hyde at the height of his powers, captivating audiences across the United States with brilliant oratory, building relationships with influential figures, ever conscious of the image of Ireland being projected, and of the potential pitfalls of the factional politics of the Irish-American societies, and, of course, of the need for the careful management of how Ireland and its quest for self-determination was being publicly presented.

The recognition awarded to Hyde during the visit was significant, was that deemed appropriate to a leader of people and a visionary, and had many of the characteristics of a head of state. The visit included not one but two private lunches with the President of the United States, Theodore Roosevelt; receptions by important delegations at each of the stops on the tour; and blanket newspaper coverage in each location, deftly orchestrated by John Quinn and the Douglas Hyde Reception Committees. Hyde was presented and promoted as a representative of all Ireland, and was received as such.

California, and particularly San Francisco, seemed to have gained a special place in Hyde's heart during his time there. The Souvenir booklet issued shortly after the honorary banquet held on his behalf described it as 'the most brilliant social gathering ever held in San Francisco ... Class, creed and politics were laid aside for the occasion, and in consequence the banquet will live forever in San Francisco's memory as the most sincere tribute paid to the representative of a vital, noble and influential movement.' He was deeply shocked at the news of the Great Earthquake in San Francisco on 18 April 1906, and immediately moved to return the funds which had been raised there. This gesture was typical of Hyde: spontaneous, generous, dramatic, and politically astute. He was to travel 19,000 miles, visit over 60 cities and make the case for the Irish language to 80,000 people.

As President of Ireland and as a successor to our first Uachtarán, I am delighted that this wonderful new edition of Hyde's account of his adventures in America has been itself the result of an international cooperation: translated by Brian Ó Conchubhair, Associate Professor of Irish Language & Literature and Director of the Center for the Study of Languages & Cultures at the University of Notre Dame; and edited by Liam Mac Mathúna, Professor Emeritus of Irish at University College Dublin; Niall Comer, President of Conradh na Gaeilge and Lecturer in Irish at Ulster University; Cuan Ó Seireadáin, Curator at Conradh na Gaeilge and Project Director at the Douglas Hyde Foundation; and Máire Nic an Bhaird, Lecturer in Irish Language and Literature in the Froebel Department at Maynooth University.

I trust that this translation of Dr Douglas Hyde's own words will allow many more people to become familiar with his enormous contribution to the Irish nation and to understand the central part that he played in the making of modern Ireland.

Michael. D. Higgins
Uachtarán na hÉireann
President of Ireland
September 2019

INTRODUCTION
MY AMERICAN TOUR

Liam Mac Mathúna

INTRODUCTION: BACKGROUND AND CONTEXT

My American Tour is Dr Douglas Hyde's own day-by-day account of his highly successful eight-month tour of the United States and Canada, which lasted from November 1905 to June 1906. This introduction sets the scene for Dr Hyde's fundraising tour of America and explains the context in which it took place. Dr Hyde went to America as President of the Gaelic League. He had co-founded this organisation with Eoin Mac Néill (Eoin MacNeill) in Dublin in 1893, in order to spread awareness of the Irish-language revival movement and to fundraise in support of its activities. Hyde later became Professor of Modern Irish at University College Dublin (1909–32), and President of Ireland (1938–45). Originally published in Irish as *Mo Thurus go hAmerice* (My Journey to America) in 1937, an English translation of this work is provided now for the first time, together with a new edition of the Irish text, revised in line with *An Caighdeán Oifigiúil*, the official written standard for the Irish language. The 1937 publication included photographs of many of the people centrally involved in the 1905 to 1906 tour and these are reproduced here. In addition, the present volume also contains a selection of the picture postcards that Douglas Hyde and his wife Lucy sent home to their two young daughters, Nuala and Úna, then 11 and 9 years old, respectively, who remained behind in Ireland, being cared for at home in Ratra, Frenchpark, Co. Roscommon. Other postcards were sent to Miss Ethel Chance, a family friend of the Hydes, who lived in Birmingham, England. A range of images drawn from other textual and visual sources provides fascinating insight into the nature of their American journey as undertaken and experienced by the Hydes.

HYDE'S BACKGROUND

Douglas Hyde was born in Longford House, Castlerea, Co. Roscommon on 17 January 1860, when his mother, Elizabeth Oldfield was on a short visit to her original family home. His father, Rev. Arthur Hyde, was a Church of Ireland rector in Kilmactranny, Co. Sligo until 1867 when he was appointed rector of Tibohine, near Frenchpark, also called Dungar, in Co. Roscommon. The young Douglas was schooled at home, and so became acquainted with many of his elderly neighbours, some of whom were Irish speakers. He developed a close friendship with Seamus Hart, Lord French's game-keeper, who became a father-figure for him, as well as John Lavin and Mrs William Connolly, all of whom taught him Irish.

Hyde started a diary in the Irish language in 1874 when he was just 14 years of age, and continued to write entries until 1912. A visit to a meeting of the Society for the Preservation of the Irish Language in Dublin in 1877 and acquaintance with Thomas O'Neill Russell prompted him to think of the language in a national context. He was soon publishing his own poems in Irish under the pseudonym *An Craoibhín Aoibhinn* ('The Pleasant Little Branch') in newspapers such as *The Irishman* and *The Shamrock*, published in Dublin, both of which circulated in Ireland and America. He attended Trinity College Dublin in the 1880s where he had a distinguished career as a student of theology, although he eventually decided against becoming a minister in the Church of Ireland, as his father and grandfather had done before him. He went on to spend the years 1890 to 1891 in Canada, in Fredericton, as Professor of Modern Languages at University of New Brunswick.

Hyde delivered his celebrated lecture 'The necessity for de-anglicising Ireland' to the National Literary Society in Dublin in November 1892. In this thought-provoking address he argued that the Irish people should be true to their own language, literature and culture, rather than copy English values and fashions. This lecture was one of the catalysts that led to Eoin Mac Néill and Hyde himself establishing the Gaelic League (Conradh na Gaeilge) in Dublin in July 1893. In many ways 1893 was a watershed for Hyde as it was also in that year that he published his ground-breaking collection of Connacht folksongs, *Abhráin Grádh Chúige Connacht or Love Songs of Connacht*, and married an Englishwoman of German background, Lucy Cometina Kurtz.

The Gaelic League gradually gathered momentum and began to pursue a vigorous programme of cultural engagement and public agitation, especially in the area of education. Hyde spectacularly faced down Trinity Professors John Pentland Mahaffy and Robert Atkinson at public hearings in 1899, thus ensuring a continuing role for

Mo Ṫuras go hAmerice

An Craoiḃín.

Dust Cover of 1937 1st Edition of *Mo Thurus go hAmerice*. Courtesy of Foras na Gaeilge

Irish in intermediate education in the country's schools. The Gaelic League was also successful in having a bilingual programme of instruction introduced into national or primary schools in Irish-speaking districts in the early 1900s. At the turn of the century Hyde forged alliances with Lady Gregory, W. B. Yeats and Edward Martyn – leading personalities of the Anglo-Irish literary revival. The Gaelic League also made common cause with Horace Plunkett's agricultural reform movement, which advocated the establishment of cooperatives, and spear-headed efforts to promote domestic Irish industries, by organising annual processions supporting both the Irish language and native industries in Dublin from 1902 onwards. There were also specific language-focussed campaigns that centred on activism, such as one to ensure that the Post Office would deliver parcels addressed in Irish, and another to compel the authorities to acknowledge the right of citizens to display their names in Irish on cart vehicles used publicly.

THE IDEA OF THE AMERICAN TOUR

The tour of America arose out of a confluence of impulses. It was masterminded and directed by John Quinn, a wealthy and highly successful Irish-American lawyer who lived in New York. Quinn was a man of boundless energy, enthusiasm and vision. A patron of the arts, he was already commissioning portraits from John Butler Yeats, father of the poet W. B. Yeats and his artist brother, Jack B. Yeats. Quinn first met W. B. Yeats and Hyde when they were guests of Lady Augusta Gregory at her residence at Coole Park, near Gort, Co. Galway at the end of August 1902. They had gathered in order to attend a Gaelic League *Feis* being held beside the cemetery in Killeeneen, east Co. Galway, where the blind itinerant poet Anthony Raftery was buried. There, just two years earlier, Lady Gregory had been primarily responsible for the placing of a headstone on the poet's previously unmarked grave. During his short vacation, Quinn found the intellectual conversations he had with Hyde and Yeats regarding art, culture and language exhilarating. They had a lasting impact on him, inspiring him to organise fund-raising lecture tours of American venues, first for Yeats in 1903, and then for Hyde in 1905 to 1906. By doing so, Quinn hoped to introduce the two men and their ideas on culture to American audiences and to afford the Irish visitors and the linked causes they championed the opportunity to garner badly needed financial and moral support.

John Quinn. Le caoinchead Fhoras na Gaeilge

Such tours were by no means new. The great English Victorian novelist Charles Dickens had been to America first in 1842, and again in 1867 to 1868, conducting tours where he read melodramatic passages from his novels to great acclaim. Aged just 27, Oscar Wilde travelled throughout the United States and Canada in 1882, undertaking some 140 lectures. For Irish politicians too there were many precedents. Michael Davitt had toured on behalf of the Land League in 1878; Parnell for the Land League and famine relief in 1880 and John Redmond, leader of the Irish Parliamentary party, journeyed to the US in 1904, following an earlier visit in 1899. Many a fine parochial church throughout Ireland owed its splendour to the generous Irish-American response to the appeals of travelling Catholic clergymen. Nonetheless, considerable novelty was attached to visits by a lyric poet such as Yeats, who revelled in his creative persona, and a cultural activist such as Hyde, whose message of Irish nationality was not only intellectual as well as emotional, but one that he proclaimed neutral as regards religion and politics.

These were new concepts and emphases, and Hyde in particular found himself having to stake out a space for the Gaelic League among an already crowded field of Irish-American societies, many of which were worried that success for the new organisation would be, literally, at their expense. However, the established interrelationship between efforts in Ireland and America to promote the Irish language in the latter part of the nineteenth century meant that the American dimension was not a new phenomenon. Indeed, the far greater affluence of the Irish in America had actually allowed the New World to play a pioneering role in the rise of Irish-language newspaper columns, bilingual periodicals, and the establishment of societies to promote the language.

As early as 1903 Hyde had been in touch with Quinn on behalf of the Gaelic League, raising the possibility of financial support from America for the movement. Interestingly it had been a bequest of Patrick Mullin, a Donegal-born emigrant to America who died in 1895, that had enabled the League to employ its first organiser – or *timire* –Tomás Bán Ua Concheanainn, in the traditionally Irish-speaking areas of the west and south, later to be known as the *Gaeltacht*. In fact it was the very success of Ua Concheanainn and an increasing number of full-time organisers that was placing severe strain on the League's finances. Quinn proposed that Hyde tour America, fundraising. Hyde held back, however, partly because he wasn't sure that such a trip would be financially successful and partly for family reasons. His wife Lucy was reluctant to leave their two young daughters for an extended period of several months and his father was in failing health.

The Gaelic League itself felt that a tour of America would indeed be worthwhile. However, the organisation's *Coiste Gnótha* (Executive Committee) tended to emphasise the tour's awareness raising potential, placing less stress on the financial aspects. The League decided it would send Ua Concheanainn, its chief organiser, as an advance agent, responsible for making the necessary practical arrangements in cities ahead of Hyde's arrival. Ua Concheanainn, from Inis Meáin in the Aran Islands, had lived in the United States for many years, mostly in California, where he went originally in 1887 to join two older brothers. He had returned to Ireland in 1898 and become a leading supporter of the language movement. Ua Concheanainn was therefore well versed in the ways of the new world. As the Rev. Arthur Hyde passed away at the end of August 1905, there was no longer that family impediment to Douglas's journey. Furthermore, Quinn had assured Hyde that he personally would indemnify both Hyde and the League against any monetary loss. Suitable arrangements were made for the two daughters and Lucy relented.

PREPARATIONS

Detailed planning arrangements were made by John Quinn on his side of the Atlantic. First, he established the Douglas Hyde Reception Committee of New York in order to oversee the financial and operational aspects of the tour. Judge Martin J. Keogh of the New York Supreme Court was nominated President of the Committee, Judge Victor J. Dowling was Treasurer, while Quinn himself acted as Secretary. This body functioned as a national steering committee with satellite reception committees, established by Quinn, in the cities to be visited during the tour. Quinn issued a printed three-page prospectus of the trip to US Universities and Colleges on 1 June 1905 and followed this up with a reminder on 27 September 1905, entitled 'Lectures by Dr Douglas Hyde (President of the Gaelic League) in the United States 1905–1906'. This latter brochure set out Hyde's academic and public service credentials and hailed him as 'a scholar of acknowledged European reputation, a fine lyric poet, a dramatist and a gifted orator, both in the Irish and in the English, and the most respected and beloved man in Ireland today.' Declaring that the Gaelic League owed its chief inspiration to Dr Hyde, Quinn described it as 'the greatest organization in Ireland, the only body in Ireland which at one time appeared to realize the fact that Ireland had a past, had a history, had a literature, and the only body in Ireland which sought to render the present a rational continuation of the past.'

Rather than repeat the same lecture over and over again, it had wisely been agreed to vary the fare. The prospectus explained that Hyde would speak on any one of four given themes, as requested by an institution. Universities were accordingly invited to choose one or more of the following topics: The Gaelic movement: Its origins, importance, philosophy and results; The last three centuries of Irish literature; The folk tale in Ireland; and The poetic literature of Ireland. Quinn set the honorarium for a lecture at $100 and the arrangement was that this money would go to Hyde personally, while the more important addresses to the wider public would raise funds for the League itself. The Coiste Gnótha of the Gaelic League published its own announcement concerning the American trip, laying stress on the aims of the revival movement. It was entitled 'Dr Douglas Hyde's Mission', dated 14 October 1905, and was signed by P. Ó Dálaigh (General Secretary), Stiofán Bairéad (Treasurer), together with Eoin Mac Néill and An tAthair Peadar Ó Laoghaire (Vice-Presidents).[1]

For Quinn, the primary object was to raise money, something he made crystal clear in a letter to Lady Gregory, dated 27 October 1905: 'I am after money for Hyde. Hyde and his work need money. I wouldn't have got Hyde to come out if I thought he couldn't get money and I don't hesitate to say so.'[2] In fact Quinn had never been a member of a Gaelic society in the US. He had two main aims. He wanted the tour to portray Hyde and the Gaelic League movement as a cultural force with the Irish language at its core, and to collect money. On the same date he wrote to Hyde himself: 'I mistrust enthusiasm very much on general principles. Most enthusiasts want to belong to "committees" and go to "banquets."'[3] He had no interest in what he termed 'missionary work', that is, morale boosting and displays of enthusiasm for their own sakes, which he disparagingly associated with the Gaelic societies.[4] His efforts were therefore concentrated on the upper strata of society: judges, industrial magnates, newspaper editors, members of the Catholic hierarchy, and the like. He wanted to steer clear of the various Irish-American societies – with their endless splits and squabbling – as much as possible. Having opted for forming his own ad hoc 'Dr Douglas Hyde Reception Committees' in the places to be visited by Hyde, Ua Concheanainn was left to labour in the more receptive, if less affluent, domain of the Gaelic societies, but a middle way must have been forged eventually, for Hyde was later to note in his diary:

> Now I should state that I had the support of not only the rich, educated Irish – thanks to Quinn – but the AOH[5] who were also with me, or at least, if they were not, then Clan na Gael[6] were with me from day one and some of them were in every section of the AOH; they were 'the tail that wagged the dog.' They, unlike others, understood the essence of the work I was undertaking.

STARTING OUT

It was evident from the very start of his journey that Hyde's mission to America had caught the public imagination on both sides of the Atlantic. As President of the Gaelic League, he already enjoyed wide popularity. A poll of 15,000 readers in *The Irish Independent* on 1 November 1905 had just returned him as the fourth most popular man in Ireland (after John Redmond, Cardinal Logue and Archbishop Walsh of Dublin). From the moment Hyde left Roscommon until he set sail from Cóbh – then known as Queenstown – in Co. Cork, the public crowded around. The entry for 3 November in Hyde's personal diary describes the send-off they were given at the local train station in Ballaghderreen, as they set off for Dublin on the first stage of their momentous journey. The boys of the local Diocesan College, headed by Fr O'Daly, and a great crowd of neighbours were at the station to bid them farewell. A young 19-year-old local man, Fionán Mac Cárthaigh, read a poem he had composed specially for the occasion. The boys sang the traditional Irish song 'An Spailpín Fánach', Hyde gave a short speech, the train blew its whistle a few times and they were off.

In Dublin a great municipal reception involving speeches, toasts and well-wishes was held in the Gresham Hotel on 6 November 1905 to send Hyde on his way. Yeats had agreed that Lady Gregory should present him with flowers on behalf of the Irish National Theatre Society, of which he had once been Vice-President. Hyde sat alongside the city's Lord Mayor in his ceremonial carriage as a large accompanying procession made its noisy way from O'Connell Street to Kingsbridge – now Heuston – Station. In the enthusiastic words of the Gaelic League's own paper, *An Claidheamh Soluis*, there were

> salvoes of cheers and the music of bursting fog signals and the roar that went up from the huge throng in the great thoroughfare proclaimed that the most beloved man in Ireland stood there, and that the democracy of Dublin had no doubts as to the significance of the man and of his work, and more especially of the mission on which he was about to enter.

Complementing this report is an insider's account of the night's events penned by the playwright Seán O'Casey, who was at the time Secretary of the League's Drumcondra branch. Although somewhat cynical in tone, O'Casey recreates the atmosphere of the occasion in the following passage, in which he refers to himself as 'Seán':

> The hurlers of Seán's club were chosen to be the bodyguard around the coach bearing him to Kingsbridge Station, *en route* for Cove in Cork, and thence across the Atlantic to the broad bosom of the sea-divided Gael. And so Seán in full dress of the club's jersey, of hooped bands of alternate dark blue and dark green, walked beside the Protestant Chief of the Gael, in the midst of thousands of flaming torches carried before and behind the carriage, followed by all the hurling and football clubs of the city and its suburbs. Horsemen headed the cavalcade, carrying the Stars and Stripes, the French Tricolour, and the green banner of popular Ireland ... Everywhere the drums beat again their lusty rolls, making the bright stars in the sky quiver, and bands blew Ireland's past into every ear, and called forth the history of the future.[7]

Crowds greeted the train carrying Hyde at every station at which it stopped on its way south, but the largest civic and public gathering to bid him farewell was in Cork city itself. Dr Douglas Hyde and his wife Lucy set sail for America on the *Majestic* liner from Cóbh, Co. Cork on 8 November 1905. A week later on 15 November, they landed in New York, having endured a rough crossing. Here too, a large number of people came to the quay to welcome Hyde to America. The waiting assembly comprised John Quinn himself, Tomás Bán Ua Concheanainn, Judge Keogh and many others. As a mark of respect, Hyde's luggage was not searched by customs and he was allowed to enter the US without any of the usual formalities. For the next eight months Hyde's mission was to publicise the aims and achievements of the Irish language revival movement throughout the length and breadth of the US and to raise funds for the cause in Ireland. Quinn had mapped out a strategic and rather daunting schedule that started with a bang: within just ten days of his arrival in New York, Hyde had been introduced into the highest echelons of American life in the spheres of politics, learning and public discourse.

NEW YORK, WASHINGTON, DC AND CITIES OF NEW ENGLAND

The Hydes spent the first four days of their American tour in the well-appointed Hotel Manhattan. Built just ten years previously in the style of a French chateau, the 14-story Manhattan stood on the corner of Madison Avenue and 42nd Street. Their short stay in what Hyde called the 'gorgeous' Manhattan allowed the couple to recover from the effects of their difficult passage. Many of the city's newspapermen came to interview Hyde about his mission. He was already becoming acquainted with the

120 Broadway, New York, 1906. This building was the location of John Quinn's office and functioned as Hyde's headquarters during the tour. Courtesy of RMP Archive / Irving Underhill

ways of American journalists, as a number of reporters had interviewed him while they were still on-board the ship and not yet disembarked. Hyde had been bemused to read their subsequent reports in which they informed their readers that he had a 'small' moustache and was wearing a 'bottle-green' necktie. On the contrary, he was particularly proud of his large and imposing moustache and was dressed from head to toe in black clothes, as he was still in public mourning following the death of his father, in accordance with the custom of the time. After their short stay, the Hydes left the Manhattan and joined Quinn in his apartment at 120 Broadway.

On 20 November Hyde headed to Cambridge, Massachusetts for his first public engagement, at Harvard University. There he delivered a lecture on 'The folk tale in Ireland' to an audience of some 500 people. Three days later, Yale University, New Haven, Connecticut was the venue when he spoke on 'The Gaelic movement: Its origin, importance, philosophy, and results'. Later that evening in an Irish club in the town he was introduced to elderly Fenians who had fought in the American Civil War, a reminder of the strong ties between nationalist and revolutionary Ireland and the American conflict.

On Saturday 25 November, Quinn and Hyde journeyed together to Washington DC, having been invited to the White House to dine with President Theodore Roosevelt. The President proved to be very knowledgeable about both Irish and Norse mythology and was able to draw comparisons between them. Indeed, Roosevelt told his visitors that he had been brought up by Irish nurses and that Cú Chulainn and Fionn Mac Cumhaill, the leading heroes of traditional Irish tales, had been familiar and vivid figures to him before he ever saw their names in literature. In a letter to Lady Gregory that he penned just four days later, Hyde summarised the first stage of his trip, telling her how on the previous Saturday he had been to lunch with President Roosevelt 'who spoke so nicely about your work and the Irish sagas in general. It was a delightful experience meeting him. There was nobody there except himself and his own family and Mr Quinn and myself.'[8] The President too enjoyed the lunch, as we learn from a letter Quinn sent to Hyde (6 December 1905), in which he passed on word from Professor Maurice Egan of the Catholic University of America in Washington that the President had told him 'that he enjoyed the hour with Dr Hyde very much'. At any rate, Hyde was paid the unusual compliment of being invited back to the White House for a second visit on 21 May 1906.

On the evening following the meeting with the President, Carnegie Hall in New York was the imposing venue for Hyde's crucial debut address to a 3,000-strong metropolitan audience, which included 140 company Vice-Presidents. The meeting was chaired by Judge Martin Keogh. A somewhat lengthy introductory speech was delivered by W. Bourke Cockran, a wealthy Congressman who was held to be the finest orator of his day in the US. Cockran was followed by the tenor, Patrick O'Shea, who sang two Irish folksongs, 'Maidrín Rua' and 'Aililiú na Gamhna'. Judge Dowling spoke next. He proposed a motion in favour of the Irish language and called on Hyde to deliver his lecture. Unusually for one long accustomed to public speaking, Hyde tells us that his heart was throbbing in apprehension as he began to address the large gathering. He started in Irish and continued to speak in this language for five minutes. He tells us that while many of his listeners understood him, others were terrified. However, he then switched to English, delivering a version of his de-anglicisation lecture, something he had done many times before in Ireland. He was soon well into his stride and went on to speak for an hour and a half, winning his audience over, as *The New York Times* confirmed the next day:

> Reverting to English, Dr Hyde reviewed the aims as well as the accomplishments of the League. Time and again he emphasized the non-sectarian and non-political character of the movement, and the cheers rang out lustily when he cried; 'We are moved not by hatred for England, but by love for Ireland.' He told his hearers that it was a struggle for life or death, nevertheless, and that only by preserving its national language could the Irish people preserve its national existence. Too many, he said, had in the past ceased to be Irish without becoming English ... [9]

After the lecture Diarmuid Lynch presented Hyde with an elegant illuminated address scroll on behalf of the Gaelic League of New York.

To Hyde's relief and satisfaction, the city's newspapers carried positive reports of the meeting and were at one in declaring it a resounding success. Knowing that where New York led the papers of the other states would follow Hyde felt reassured, and was ready to face the rest of his long tour with reaffirmed confidence in his ability to sway crowds and raise money. In his letter of 29 November 1905 to Lady Gregory he spoke enthusiastically about New York and his tour's prospects: 'On Sunday we had a huge meeting in Carnegie Hall. It was a great success in every way and will probably net over $4,000 for the League. ... I don't know how my tour will turn out, but my success in New York seems commensurate with the send-off that I got from Ireland.'[10]

With the major initial events successfully behind him, it was now time for Hyde to focus on the hard work and grind of visiting the cities and towns of New England that had large Irish immigrant populations. The following weeks were hectic as he criss-crossed the states of New England, with just a lull between Christmas and the New Year. He had speaking engagements in Hartford, Connecticut, in Boston itself and in Manchester, New Hampshire. In South Hadley, Mass., Hyde addressed the students of Mount Holyoke College, a women's college, the first such institution he had ever visited. Then it was on to Springfield, Mass., Ansonia, Conn., and Lowell, Mass. and Brockton, Mass. In Wellesley, Mass. he spoke at another private women's liberal arts college. In these states he had been using Boston as a base. Now it was the turn of New York City to act as fulcrum as he headed out and back to places such as Waterbury, Conn., although he sometimes stayed away overnight, as he did in both Providence and Philadelphia. He also travelled to Worcester and Lawrence, Mass., but was back in New York on 22 December. His next excursion out of the city did not take place until 31 December, the destination then being New Haven, Conn. In December he had also spoken at Fordham and Manhattan Colleges in New York. When he was using New York and Chicago as hubs from which he travelled out to the neighbouring cities, their practice was for Lucy to stay behind. In New York she was the guest of Quinn himself, while in Chicago, Francis Hackett had arranged for her to stay with the Murphy family at the Virginia Hotel. This had worked out very well, as Hackett apprised Quinn in a letter dated 11 February 1906: 'Mrs Hyde found the Murphys, a nice family living at the Virginia, very attentive to her during her stay. They took her to several concerts and the theatre, and she was very much at home in their suite, with the three girls.'[11]

The general pattern for each city visit was that Hyde would be greeted at the train station by a delegation of dignitaries from the local Reception Committee and brought to his hotel – in New Haven, the President of Yale himself came to meet him. The high point of each occasion was undoubtedly the speech delivered by Hyde, followed by an appeal for funds and the opportunity for him to interact with at least some of the audience afterwards. A more or less formal dinner would usually be arranged, regularly attended by judges, senior clergy and leading officials of the local Irish-American societies. Rather than feel imposed upon, Hyde, who was gregarious by nature, seems to have enjoyed these social occasions. He found the conversation and the fresh American societal environment with its many points of difference from Ireland quite congenial, and often he did not make his way back to his hotel until one-thirty or two o'clock in the morning. Interestingly, while the reader of his diary is kept abreast of the variety of drinks on offer, few details emerge about the food on the menu.

Of course, not everything went according to plan. In fact, Hyde's very first major engagement at Carnegie Hall had been the occasion of a significant sabotage attempt by one Luke J. Finn, apparently at the instigation of colleagues in the United Irish League, which supported the Irish Parliamentary Party led by John Redmond. Finn had arranged to buy a tier of 32 boxes and some 150 other tickets, all of which he returned unsold just before the meeting began. However Quinn's quick thinking saved the day, as he redirected patrons from cheaper seats to the boxes, thus avoiding the embarrassment of a half-empty gallery.

Something similar seems to have happened shortly afterwards in Boston, where there was the added complication of an imminent mayoral election. No sooner had Hyde arrived than he was being tugged in different directions by two rival factions and had to deploy his wide experience to avoid being seen to endorse either side. The situation had not been helped by an element of over-reaction on the part of his advance agent, Tomás Bán Ua Concheanainn.

Interestingly one of the people on the platform listening to Hyde's address, according to *Boston Daily Globe*, 4 November 1905, was none other than Hon. John Fitzgerald, that is John 'Honey Fitz' Fitzgerald, maternal grandfather of President John Fitzgerald Kennedy. In December Honey Fitz was elected mayor of Boston for the following year. In fact, correspondence from John O'Callaghan, national secretary of the United Irish League based in Boston shows him appraising John Redmond, leader of the Irish Parliamentary Party, of Hyde's progress, and betraying evidence of mere tepid support for the Gaelic League's mission. O'Callaghan assures Redmond:

> Of course the one object I have had in mind from the outset is to put it out of the power of anybody, even Dr Hyde himself, to claim when he returns to Ireland that the [United Irish] League here was hostile to him, while to be frank about it, I do not feel like killing myself working for the success of his mission, which I think is a good deal chimerical.[12]

Reporting in a subsequent letter that 'Hyde's meetings in the main are being utilized and run by Clan [i.e. Clan-na-Gael] men', O'Callaghan says that he had ensured that the United Irish League 'was as much identified with his visit in public as the Clan was, while at the same time we of the League did not at all break our hearts in working for his meeting.'[13] Furthermore, O'Callaghan's downbeat and antagonistic assessment of the Boston meeting acts as a foil to the generally enthusiastic and positive accounts of his progress provided by Hyde himself and his circle of supporters. He told Redmond:

> The meeting itself was almost a fiasco. The Boston Theatre, in which yourself, Capt. Donelan and Pat O'Brien spoke was less than half filled when he spoke, and although he

went around for several days himself after the meeting personally soliciting subscriptions, and several of the newspapers gave $100 apiece to the fund, the total amount promised up to date since his meeting a fortnight ago, has not exceeded $1,500, or about 1/6 of the amount paid and pledged on the platform the night of your meeting there last year. Even of that $1,500, Teevens, who is one of the treasurers, announced at the last meeting of the committee that only $400 or $500 had then been subscribed, which will not necessitate Dr Hyde's employing an express messenger to carry back to Ireland.[14]

There were also quite a few occasions when no collection at all was made, thus nullifying the principal purpose of holding the event. In such instances, at first reluctantly and with a rather heavy sense of duty, Hyde allowed himself to be ferried round calling on rich businessmen in an effort to persuade them to part with a few hundred dollars for the cause. As time went on, however, Hyde seems to have got used to this aspect of his role. At any rate, it allowed him to sketch fascinating pen-pictures that give insights into the personality of such hyper-successful figures as Andrew Carnegie. For example, a St Stephen's Day visit in New York to this renowned philanthropist, in the company of Judge Keogh, yielded a vague and ultimately unfulfilled promise of future support, as well as a present of a small book that Carnegie himself had written. The self-absorbed millionaire industrialist insisted on 'making it valuable' for Hyde – by signing his name in it.

While Tomás Bán Ua Concheanainn sent regular reports to the League's own weekly newspaper, *An Claidheamh Soluis*, there were other ways by which information regarding Hyde's busy schedule found its way back to Ireland. For instance, Neilí Ní Bhriain, Secretary of *Craobh na gCúig gCúigí* (The Branch of the Five Provinces) of the Gaelic League, maintained regular correspondence with Hyde while he was touring the States. Anxious to spread the word, she relayed the substance of one of Hyde's early letters to readers of *The Irish Times* via its letters' page. Hyde had written to her on 23 December 1905, summarising his activities during the first three weeks of December, and the newspaper published Ní Bhriain's letter on 9 January 1906. In this way even the predominantly unionist readership of *The Irish Times* was made aware of the American activities of the League's President.

But this was a two-way exchange of letters and not all of the correspondence was destined to be published in *The Irish Times* or anywhere else. Quinn had provided Hyde with a stenographer and his usual practice during the tour was to dictate his letters. However he regularly topped and tailed them with friendly, more personal greetings, many of which were in Irish, as he did in a letter to Neilí Ní Bhriain on 5 December

1905.[15] Neilí kept up her side of the correspondence all through the trip: eight letters she wrote to Hyde between December 1905 and March 1906 are now in the National Library of Ireland.[16] She assured Hyde that his use of the typing medium was not an impediment to communication: 'Beannacht Dé leat a Chraoibhín a chroidhe. (God bless you, dear Craoibhín) You're the only friend I have whose personality can carry even through a type written letter!' (31 January 1906).

Significantly, most of her own letters thank Hyde for cards and letters that she had received from him. For example at the start of the New Year she wrote: 'It was a great joy to me to get your long letter yesterday and also the postcard [of] New York at night. It is splendid to hear of your success but I am filled with sorrow to think that you won't be back for St Patrick's Day' (6 January 1906). In March she reported to him that his name, *An Craoibhín*, was emblazoned on both sides of a cart in the St Patrick's Day Irish-language procession, but she still missed the man himself – no pictures are a substitute, she says, and she is anxious to be told well in advance when he will be returning to Ireland, as she would never forgive herself if she were to miss the occasion by being otherwise engaged.

THE MIDWEST

The start of the 1906 New Year saw the Hydes move westwards as Douglas was to spend the next five to six weeks lecturing in the principal cities of the Midwest. Following his visit to Pittsburgh, Chicago served as the base for brief forays to Milwaukee, Wisconsin, Cleveland and Columbus, Ohio. The Chicago part of the enterprise was overseen by Francis Hackett, a young journalist and literary critic from Co. Kilkenny who had emigrated to America in 1901 and had got to know Quinn in New York. It was then on to Indianapolis, Cincinnati, St Louis, South Bend and the nearby University of Notre Dame, Indiana. Following that, Hyde returned to Chicago, before heading to Madison, Wisconsin, St Paul and its twin city, Minneapolis in Minnesota and a little later to Omaha, Nebraska.

In Chicago itself, Francis O'Neill, Chief of the city's police from 1901 to 1905, and famed collector of Irish traditional music had just retired. Chief O'Neill felt strongly that most of the music being played during Hyde's tour was not authentically Irish and he resolved to right the balance, inviting Hyde to an evening of traditional music and song on 12 January. In particular, O'Neill felt embarrassed that on the previous Sunday, 7 January, when Hyde had addressed an audience of several thousand in the

Chicago Auditorium, he had heard such pieces as Thomas Moore's 'The harp that once through Tara's halls' and the 'Minstrel boy', sung by the Irish Choral society. O'Neill later wrote:

> The programme of music was so disappointing – ludicrous it might be termed – and out of all proportion to the importance of the occasion, that the idea of allowing the great Apostle of the Gaelic Revival to return to Ireland under false impressions of Irish musical talent in Chicago could not be entertained.

O'Neill went on to record the impression that his own choice of repertoire made on the distinguished guest from Ireland as follows:

> The 'Craoibhin Aoibhinn' sat for hours listening to those men of Erin pouring forth an inexhaustible flood of music, songs and melodies of the motherland. On several occasions he was visibly affected. He was moved to ecstasy at the thrill of his own music heard in a foreign land. ... The 'Craoibhin' was astonished at the wonderful proficiency of the players and the inexhaustible extent of their repertoire.

O'Neill says that 'Fr Fielding played that beautiful descriptive tune called the Modhereen Rua (or Fox Chase), which Dr Hyde said an Englishman couldn't even whistle if the Almighty promised to endow him with a sense of humor.'

Hyde's own diary entry recalls the evening: O'Neill 'had gathered dancers, singers, pipers, and other musicians, and they danced and sang and played for two or three hours. Most of them were Irish-speakers and the dancers were top-notch. He presented me with a large book of tunes that he has printed. I returned home at half-past eleven.' However, despite the enthusiasm and fond memories on all sides, it is worth noting that returning home at 11.30 p.m. actually meant that Hyde was having an early night! For example, after a dinner at the Twentieth Century Club in the same city just two nights earlier, where he had been presented with a wreath of lilies of the valley in the shape of a harp, he had not reached his bed until 2.15 a.m.

On 14 January it was the turn of Cleveland, Ohio to hear Hyde speak in the city theatre. In his diary he characterised the event as 'a reasonably successful meeting', with some 800 people in attendance, and 600 dollars collected, most of the money coming from the Ancient Order of Hibernians (AOH) However, as John Quinn's sister, Mrs Anderson, lived in the city, Quinn himself had occasion to visit it regularly and relayed a more positive account of the occasion to Hyde 18 months later in a letter dated 16 August 1907: 'Everybody remembered you with the greatest pleasure; in fact they all said that your visit to Cleveland was the best Irish event that had been there in a generation.' Hyde's charismatic personal impact on behalf of the language revival is further evidenced in Quinn's more general reflection: 'Everybody almost that I meet who keeps in touch with Irish things asks me how you are and when I have heard from you and how you are doing and how the movement is getting on, and so on.' Hyde's interactions clearly made a positive impression throughout the Midwest. For instance, the Vice-President of the State Life Insurance Company informed Quinn how well things had turned out in Indianapolis (22 January 1906):

> Dr Douglas Hyde has come and gone. He won us all with his big heart, superb intellect and splendid good fellowship. We had a magnificent meeting, over two thousand, which is a large audience for Indianapolis. The amount subscribed at the meeting was about $5000.00, and taken by tickets about the same amount. We will probably clear $1000 for the Doctor.

Ó Concheanainn too had 'also done his part nobly': 'The one thing in his mind is collections.'[17]

Francis Hackett spent a month organising the Chicago segment of the tour and was pleased that the Chicagoans had filled the Auditorium. 'Dr Hyde came through as a messenger,' he tells us in his memoir, 'not that he was born to sweep an audience from its moorings, but he did what was in him as a scholar and a teacher; he defined the Gaelic Movement and won accord and support.'[18] Financially Hyde was grateful, assuring Hackett that he had been 'invaluable', but Hackett felt that the outcome in Chicago did not compare favourably with that of San Francisco, which he estimated to have subscribed a full third of the total raised in America. The complexity and ambivalence of Hyde's views on political matters shows through in an interesting vignette recounted by Hackett: 'Hyde kept his mission unpolitical, but when I mentioned in private that my brother Bat was now a doctor at Mountjoy Prison in Dublin where political prisoners were sometimes confined, he looked at me with depth in his black eyes. 'He may be of good use there, some day.' This private observation may be set alongside a public pronouncement of Hyde's, in an interesting eight-page question and answer session that he had with a journalist in Cleveland on 15 January 1906.[19] The interview concludes with a brief discussion of political matters, which illustrates well how warily Hyde treated this subject in public:

Reporter: What do you think of the Clan na Gael?

Hyde: Excuse me, that is getting upon dangerous ground.

Reporter: Then what do you think of the United Irish League?

Hyde: You are asking me to tread upon ground even more dangerous. I am not a politician and the Gaelic League is not a political body, and never has been. We are nothing but a linguistic, educational and industrial movement. We are grateful for the support of the Clan na Gael. We are grateful for the support of the United Irish League ... and beyond that I cannot go.

The diary includes an amusing account of a rather different question and answer session that Hyde had in Cincinnati with the tongue-tied editor of a newspaper entitled *Men and Women*. The editor wanted an interview for the St Patrick's Day edition of his paper and had brought a shorthand writer with him, but in the event he could not think of any questions to ask. Hyde rose to the occasion, however, and tells us: 'Therefore, I composed the questions myself and also answered them. A young German girl recorded the talk.'[20]

THE PACIFIC COAST

By 11 February 1906 the schedule for speaking in the major cities of the Midwest had drawn to a close and it was time for Douglas and Lucy Hyde to take another long-distance train journey through the Rockies, and onto San Francisco and the Pacific Coast, where the redoubtable Fr Peter Yorke, rather than John Quinn, was directing operations. With the able assistance of another priest, Fr Philip O'Ryan, Fr Yorke had put such exceptional effort into the preparations for Hyde's visit that California in general, and San Francisco in particular, proved to be the high-point of the Gaelic League President's great American journey – the devastating earthquake struck San Francisco just a few weeks after Hyde's visit. As the train passed through the town of Rawlins in the State of Wyoming, Hyde observed in his journal that his sister Annette and her husband Cambreth Kane had a large farmstead nearby.

Hyde and Yorke got on superbly in San Francisco, each highly appreciative of the abilities of the other. Hyde recorded in his diary that Yorke was the best speaker he had ever heard and the best Irishman he had ever met. He also noted that Yorke had been so impressed by his lecture on folklore that he had published it in full in his own newspaper, *The Leader*, which had been founded in 1902. In fact, the 1906

St Patrick's day issue of *The Leader* was styled 'Dr Douglas Hyde Edition March 17, 1906' and was printed in green. On the front page, entwined around the masthead of the paper itself were pictures of Douglas Hyde, LLD, Mrs Hyde and Hon. Frank J. Sullivan, attorney and former candidate for mayor of San Francisco, all framing a beguiling image of Glendalough, Co. Wicklow on the top half of the sheet. The lower half of the front page was given over to an imposing photograph of the attendance at the 'Dr Douglas Hyde Banquet. Palace Hotel, Wednesday Evening Feb. 21, 1906' – an all-male audience dressed in formal evening attire. This banquet was widely regarded as the greatest reception ever accorded a private citizen in the city and the occasion was clearly also intended to mark Irish-America's coming of age. The genteel, black-tie congregation of the great and good of San Francisco was a world away from the emaciated, ragged hordes who had flooded into American east-coast ports half a century earlier in a desperate bid to escape from the famine stalking the Emerald Isle.

There had not always been such good rapport between Dr Hyde and Fr Yorke. When Yorke visited Dublin in 1899 to deliver a stirring speech, entitled 'The turning of the tide', Hyde had stayed away. He explained in *Mise agus an Connradh* (The Gaelic League and Me) that he was happy enough with the content of the lecture[21]; he felt Yorke had things to say that were worth saying, but which he as President of the Gaelic League was reluctant to express for fear of losing allies. After all it was not for nothing that a subsequent biographer chose to style Yorke a 'clerical firebrand'. But none of this impinged on the Californian spectacle and experience. Personal accounts by individuals of their initial meeting with Hyde regularly indicate that he possessed a certain charisma, and, in addition, there was evidently an aura of celebrity about him, which had been growing over the years. It can be seen, for instance, in the practice of composing and publicly declaiming poems in his honour. This tendency reached a new level on his America tour. For instance, in September 1905 in advance of his arrival, an Irish night held at Manhattan Beach by the Gaelic League of New York included a pyrotechnic display that projected the face of Douglas Hyde as well as the badge and motto of the Gaelic League, a multi-coloured harp and the features of Robert Emmet, all prefaced with the word 'Welcome'.[22]

In San Francisco, apart from the Douglas Hyde newspaper supplement of *The Leader*, it seems that when he addressed an audience of many thousands in the city all were wearing buttons or badges carrying his image and some words of Irish. We may add to this aspect of the mission, the care that Quinn took to have studio photographs of Hyde taken and then circulated in their thousands. He offered Yorke lithographs in preparation for Hyde's coming:

> I had prepared some good lithographs of Dr Hyde, which we have sent out to all of the towns where he is lecturing. We posted 1,000 in New York and 600 were used in Philadelphia, 500 in Boston, 900 in Chicago and smaller numbers in other cities. I should be glad to express to you as many lithographs as you think could be used on the Coast, even up to 1,500 or 2,000. The sheets on which these lithographs are printed are about 20 x 40. The lithograph occupies the upper half and that leaves a space of about 20 x 20 at the bottom of the lithograph for printing.

This also gives a good idea of Quinn's meticulous, if not indeed obsessive, attention to detail.[23]

The weather was very wet during Hyde's stay in San Francisco and for a few days he suffered from a cold and a hoarse throat. Nonetheless, time was found for sight-seeing and California's tourist attractions proved to be quite varied. First, there was the spectacularly situated Cliff House restaurant to which James Phelan drove Douglas and Lucy in his large 45 horse-power automobile. Perched on a headland, Cliff House afforded a beautiful view of the ocean that stretched out before it. Hyde was amazed at the size of the sea-lions, observing that they were as large as the biggest cows he had ever seen, while the last surviving wild grizzly bear from California was to be found in a park nearby. One afternoon the president of the city police arranged for a detective to take the Hydes on a guided tour of San Francisco's Chinatown to see its contemporary array of wonders, including shops, opium dens, joss-houses and the Palace of Arts, a place of ill repute. They encountered an elderly Chinese man stretched out on a bed of boards, smoking opium, with a cat lying on his chest. The man blew the opium smoke under the cat's nose in order to make it sleepy. He explained that the cat would not give him a moment's peace until it went into an opium-induced sleep.

There was more spectacular sightseeing a few weeks later near Santa Cruz when they were taken to view the famous Red Wood trees. After a tortuous journey, they realised that they would have to cross a footbridge that swayed from side to side to finally reach the trees. The planks were rotten: some gave way beneath their feet and the entire structure shook as if it were to about to collapse into the river far beneath them. It frightened the priest who was with them, Fr Fisher, as well as Hyde himself, although Hyde was too embarrassed to let it show. At first, the unfortunate priest froze midway, afraid to proceed but equally afraid to retreat. However, when he saw the others cross safely, he followed suit. But the trees themselves were declared to be 'truly wonderful' and worth the effort to reach them. Hyde reports that they grow very slowly but once they mature, are very tall. Many of the trees he saw were 45 feet in circumference at their base and 280 feet high. One or two were over 300 feet in height, while it was said that the largest of the trees were probably a couple of thousand years old.

The extent of the sightseeing undertaken in California and the enjoyment that Douglas and Lucy derived from their time there reflected the warm friendships which developed between them and their hosts. Apart from Fr Peter Yorke and Fr Philip O'Ryan, there were James Phelan, one of the richest men in San Francisco and a former mayor, Frank Sullivan, Chair of the Hyde Reception Committee in San Francisco, and his wife Alice, sister of James Phelan. Then there was Dr Benjamin Ide Wheeler, President of the University of California or Berkeley University, as it was also called. Wheeler was extremely friendly, especially as he had studied Old Irish in Europe as a young man under one of the leading continental Celtic scholars, Zimmer or Thurneysen – Hyde could not recall which. He attended all of the four lectures Hyde gave at his University. Indeed, there had been no let-up whatsoever in the lecturing, which entailed many journeys back and forth across San Francisco Bay. The main public meeting was held on 18 February in the Tivoli Opera House. All seats were taken, Hyde had got his voice back and was able to speak for an hour and forty minutes, as was his custom. Financially the evening was a great success, as Fr Philip O'Ryan reported to Quinn in a letter dated 23 February 1906: the proceeds ran to over $3,600 while the expenses were light, about $200.[24] Frank Sullivan contributed $1,200, the largest donation received on his trip, while James Phelan later gave $1,000. In all, San Francisco delivered the impressive sum of $11,500 for the cause.

The 'Dr Hyde Banquet' held in the Palace Hotel on 21 February 1906 was the climax of the visit to San Francisco. There were 450 guests including the State Governor, George Cooper Pardee, Mayor Eugene Schmitz, leading clerics of all religions, university academics, and prominent members of the judiciary. Chief Justice James V. Coffey acted as toastmaster; in all there were 13 toasts. The menu was bilingual, in Irish and English, and a special banquet booklet of 88 pages was published to mark the occasion. It included all of the speeches and toasts along with excellent photographs of the speakers. The last to speak was Fr Yorke and, in Hyde's opinion, he surpassed all the others, although he noted that Dr Benjamin Ide Wheeler, the University President, Dr Frederick W. Clampett, an Episcopalian minister who had studied at Trinity College, Dublin, and Fr Frieden S. J., President of St Ignatius College, also spoke very well. Held on the eve of Washington's Birthday, a federal holiday, the banquet lasted from

7.00 p.m. to 2.00 a.m. 'and very few left before the end', as O'Ryan informed Quinn. He explained that the banquet itself was not intended to raise funds: 'We make no money on the Banquet. It pays expenses, but it was absolutely necessary in order to stir up interest in the mission of Dr Hyde.' In advance, the San Francisco newspapers had heralded the banquet as a major upcoming event, and the editions of the day afterwards, proclaimed it to have been a hugely successful occasion. Hyde felt the banquet in particular and the entire Californian visit to have been a great personal triumph and wrote excitedly to Quinn on 25 February, eagerly passing on his assessment: 'My success in California has been I think unparalleled.'

Although the San Francisco banquet itself had not been organised in order to make a profit, it was viewed as an essential component of the whole west coast enterprise. At any event, for the Gaelic League and its President, money and message were inextricably intertwined in America, no less than in Ireland, even if finance was to the fore on the US tour. After all, if there were no message to proclaim, no cause to advance, there would be no need for money and therefore no need for an American mission. In his letter to Quinn, O'Ryan went on to summarise the impact of Hyde's visit on the city of San Francisco as follows: 'After the University lectures, the public lecture in this City and Banquet, the whole State knows of him, and no man has ever met with such a Reception. Americans and Germans and all nationalities approve of his work, in fact, to talk Gaelic is one of the hall-marks of culture nowadays.' In order words, the Irish were learning not to be ashamed of themselves, thereby realising one of the major aspirations of Hyde in his celebrated 1892 lecture, 'The necessity for de-anglicising Ireland', the lecture that led to the founding of the Gaelic League the following year and energised the Irish cultural revival.[25]

As for the overall high level of activity in California, Quinn was later to complain bitterly in a letter to Hackett, 'They nearly killed Hyde on the Pacific Coast. Contrary to my express request, repeated two or three times over, they had a banquet or a lecture or a dinner or a High Mass or a something every day almost' (10 April 1906). In a way Hyde was his own worst enemy for he never spared himself when called upon to further any aspect of the language revival movement. Family friends maintained that, were it not for the restraining influence of his wife Lucy, he would kill himself working. Lucy for her part is recorded as telling a reporter in San Francisco: 'I didn't marry a man, I married a cause.' Indeed, although prone to frequent bouts of illness and once dismissed by Lady Gregory as 'Hyde's fashionable and rather distant wife', Lucy actually seems to have come into her own during the Californian section of the trip and charmed journalists with her lively repartee. For example, when the couple were faced with reporters on their visit to Los Angeles, Hyde had turned to his wife, saying 'The women are everything in this country, you will notice,' repeating the point for emphasis, 'The women are everything here'. The *Los Angeles Herald*'s account continues: '

> 'Yes,' said the little woman, who smiled at his remark, 'and when we return to Ireland kindly remember that. What is good for the United States should be good enough for Ireland.' The merriment which the remark aroused was of course at the doctor's expense, but it only further cemented the good feeling between the hosts and their guests (10 March 1906).

The Douglas Hyde papers in the National Library of Ireland include 18 handwritten foolscap pages that evidently contain the text of Hyde's generic Gaelic Revival cum de-anglicisation lecture as delivered at a venue in San Francisco. While Hyde varied his stock address somewhat from occasion to occasion, the essence of the message remained the same. He assured his American audiences that it was their moral backing that he really wanted:

> I am not exaggerating when I say that I look upon the moral support of the Irish in America to be the most valuable asset that the Gaelic League at home could have; … I would sooner have the moral support of the Irish in America than a quarter of a million of dollars poured into the Gaelic League to-morrow.[26]

Irish nationality – through the Irish language – was engaged in an existential struggle: 'It is the last possible life and death struggle of the Irish race to preserve not their own language but their national identity.'[27] The rhetoric was lofty, the language high-flown: 'We are like the white dove of peace passing over the land and obliterating the old feuds and hatred and black bad blood of the country. So you see that we are no clique, we are no faction, we are no party. We are above and beyond all politics, all parties, and all factions; offending nobody – except the anti-Irishman.'[28] San Francisco was also the venue for this ringing declaration:

> Well, just remember this; the Irish language, thank God, is neither Protestant nor Catholic. It is neither a landlord nor a tenant; it is neither a unionist nor a separatist and, in taking it for our platform, we have achieved what is to my mind the supreme and crowning glory of the Gaelic League, because for the first time in Ireland within

my recollection Catholic and Protestant, Unionist and Nationalist, landlord and tenant, priest and parson, came together, all working hand in hand, in the interest of Ireland's life and intellectuality and we are realising for the first time, the glorious dreams of Thomas Davis.

> 'How every race and every trade
> Should be by love combined.'

> We are working together in a common cause, in a spirit of good fellowship. Mr Chairman, that word is not strong enough; in a spirit of loving brotherhood which has, of recent years, been unexampled in Ireland, and we are not engaged in doing anything that is impossible, it is perfectly possible, and we know it, and we see it. … We have the sympathy of the scholars of Europe. We have the goodwill of all well-wishers of Ireland, and against us we have only race hatred, anti-Irish bigotry, and Trinity College, Dublin, and the time has gone by when that combination from which nothing constructive ever yet emanated – the time has gone by when they shall win any more battles in Ireland.[29]

However, not everyone was persuaded by Hyde's arguments and the case he declaimed in meeting after meeting, in city after city across America. For instance, John O'Callaghan of the United Irish League in Boston sent John Redmond an out of sympathy summary of the lecture, which Hyde delivered in that city on 3 December 1905:

> His speech of course was a glorification of the work of the Gaelic League, from the establishment of which he dates all progress in Ireland. O'Connell helped to make an anglicised Ireland; Davis and the '48 men did nothing that will live permanently. They simply tried to graft an English bark on an Irish tree; no mention of Parnell, the land league movement, or any lat[t]er day movement or man. But in 1893 the Gaelic league rose up and made a new Ireland which is today the only Ireland worth considering. That is substantially an outline of his two hours' talk.[30]

There is the further sting in the insinuation that Hyde had taken a long time to convey his message. Although, that point can no doubt be countered by acknowledging the need for Hyde's public lectures to provide a satisfying night out for his audience, in addition to their intellectual content.

However, the time eventually came on 26 March for the couple to bid farewell to San Francisco. Hyde's diary eloquently contrasts the pleasure of the welcome they received and the destruction visited on their friends' homes shortly after they had left:

> We are almost six weeks there now and such kindness and generosity I never before encountered. As regards to money, I think I collected as much here as in New York itself and I will never forget the good friends we made here. Little we thought on departing them today that they and their city would, in three weeks, be laid waste; that James Phelan's beautiful house, the house of the most generous Frank Sullivan and many other places in which we experienced such generosity and hospitality would go up in flames and their inhabitants left without a dry crust.

As will be seen later, he reciprocated the city's generosity with the return of the money he had collected in San Francisco.

POSTCARDS: 'AN CRAOIBHÍN' AND 'L. C. H.' WRITE HOME

The early years of the twentieth century were a highpoint for the sending of picture postcards to family and friends while on holiday and away from home.[31] Throughout their trip to America, Douglas and Lucy Hyde sent a steady stream of such greeting cards to their two daughters and to friends. Many of the cards were of a high aesthetic and visual quality, as is shown by the selection of illustrations included in this volume. Almost 60 postcards that were originally sent to the girls and some 30 addressed to Ethel Chance, a family friend, are held in the Aidan Heavey Collection in the public library in Athlone, Co. Westmeath, while two more which Douglas sent to Miss Chance are included in a second collection of Hyde postcards, held in the National Folklore Collection, University College Dublin.[32] As the daughters were frequently reminded to keep the cards it was obviously intended that they would form a pictorial record of the journey. For her part, Ethel must have returned the cards she received to the Hydes at some later date. We know from Neilí Ní Bhriain's correspondence that she too received picture postcards, and other references to the grateful receipt of similar postcards are to be found elsewhere in Hyde's correspondence. For example, Eoin Mac Néill's papers include a greeting card with a picture of seals on Seal Rock, San Francisco, written by Hyde on 3 March 1906.[33]

Postcard sent by Douglas Hyde to his daughters. Courtesy of Westmeath Libraries (Aidan Heavey Collection)

Douglas Hyde's first visit to President Roosevelt in the White House on 25 November 1905 seems to have prompted the initial flurry of cards. At any rate, the first picture postcard to the children available to us was franked on 27 November. Written by Hyde in both Irish and English, it was sent to their eldest daughter, Nuala, informing her that he had dined with the President. Later, Lucy sent Christmas greetings to both Nuala and Úna, with illustrations of the Bunker Hill Monument and the State House in Boston, respectively. These were accompanied by Lucy's usual reminder to keep all cards. Thus, on 16 December she sent each girl the season's greetings with identical messages: 'A Merry Christmas and Happy New Year. Keep this card for me.' The girls also got separate cards in English sent by their parents from Pittsburgh on 9 January 1906, Nuala's sent by Douglas, Úna's by Lucy. Douglas sent a bilingual postcard from Cleveland, Ohio, on 15 January, urging that the area be sought out on a map: 'This is the shore of Lough Erie. Look it up on the map. I'm alive yet! Bhfuil sibh-se go maith? Sgríobh gan mhoill.' (... Are you well? Write soon). Two days later Lucy sent each girl a card from Chicago: Úna was the recipient of a dramatic scene of football being played on ice at Marshall Park, Chicago. Characteristically, the accompanying message began with the direction 'Keep all p.cards', and Lucy finished stating, 'Am writing a long letter to you both', before signing off 'L. C. H.' 'Keep this picture and all the postcards' was the exhortation from 'L. C. H.' to Nuala on the picture of an 1833 Indian settlement in Chicago.

The pattern had now been set and the postcards continued thick and fast, usually sent separately to each of the girls, and frequently penned by Lucy. The daughters received cards from Cleveland, St Louis, St Paul and Minneapolis, Chicago again, then several from Omaha, which took the date as far as 9 February. It is worth recalling that the postal regulations at the time only permitted messages on the side of the card with a picture, the address had to be on its own on the reverse. This left little room for communication, so that the few words written were literally marginalised, penned around the illustration and most often at the bottom. However, on some cards a blank column was available at the right-hand side of the picture, which allowed for a slightly longer message. The positive enlivening effect that California seems to have had on Lucy Hyde is reflected in the postcards: she sent quite a lot from California, variously illustrating a rose tree, residents of Chinatown, an ostrich farm, as well as Indians on reservations and, a little later, a variety of images from the States of Oregon and Washington. The last two cards of the stream of Californian mail, with their pictures of 'Mission San Gabriel, California' for Nuala and 'The Grizzly Giant (world's biggest tree)' for Úna, were actually franked and dated 18 April, the very day that disaster struck the city of San Francisco.

The effects of the earthquake itself are conveyed in the illustrative pictures on two cards dated 7 May: 'What the earthquake did in half a minute / 1906 San Francisco earthquake' to Nuala, 'Earthquake ruins in Mission Street / 1906 San Francisco earthquake' to Úna. The parents must have had a good stock of Californian cards as images from the Pacific Coast continued to wend their way to Ireland through the first half of May, although they were interspersed with a card of President Roosevelt and his family sent to both children on 11 May. Then for the rest of the month the kaleidoscope of images was of Niagara Falls, the city of Toronto, Lake Ontario, Washington's Mansion, Mt. Vernon, Virginia, and finally there is the Bowling Green, New York, which Lucy sent to Nuala. In total the girls were sent 59 cards.

It is interesting to note the contrast in tone between Douglas's messages and those of Lucy. Douglas tended to be light-hearted, playful, occasionally pedagogical, at times writing bilingually, at other times unilingually, in either Irish or English, whereas his wife could be somewhat more serious, even sombre, as well as affectionate. For example, from Cawston Ostrich Farm, Pasadena, California her father sent Nuala a picture of a man in a bowler hat astride an ostrich, with a message in Irish which began 'Nach deas an capall é seo!' (Isn't this a nice horse!). He then continued, stressing the immediacy of the occasion, and managing to link in all family members: 'Chonnaic mé féin é. Tá Mam go maith agus mé féin, buidheachas le Dia. Tá súil agam go bhfuil sibh-se go maith. An Craoibhín' (I saw it myself. Mam is well, and me too, thank God. I hope that you are well. An Craoibhín'). In another card from the same ostrich farm, Lucy assured the girls 'We have got you both real ostrich feathers.' Bilingualism was not always a matter of Irish and English, for on 16 March Douglas combined French and English. The card that Douglas sent the girls ahead of the visit to Toronto, Canada was also bilingual, but again French rather than English accompanied the Irish. On the other hand, Nuala got an Irish/English bilingual card regarding Niagara Falls on 9 May.

Occasionally, both parents wrote jointly on the same card. One such postcard sent from San Francisco on 21 February was bilingual in that Douglas added the Irish sentence 'Nach deas an áit í seo!' (Isn't this a nice place!) to his wife's English message on a card depicting 'Five Idols in Holy of Holies. Joss Temple.' Similarly he added 'Nach árd an crann é seo' (Isn't this a tall tree) to a card from Lucy to Úna, depicting 'The Grizzly Giant', billed as 'The biggest tree in the world' (15 February, from San Francisco), and he made a similar addition on 8 April to Úna about another large tree. In this latter card, Lucy appraised the girls of the danger they had had overcome to see the tree: 'We saw this tree and nearly lost our lives in going to see it as the road there was broken down and precipices at the side' (from Butte, Montana). Her starkest message of all, however, was sent on 26 April following the devastation visited on San Francisco. It accompanied a picture of 'Five Idols in Holy of Holies. Joss Temple':

> The great earthquake and fire swallowed up these idols. We just escaped in time. You never would have seen us again if we had remained on. Everything was burnt up our grand hotel and all Chinese Town all burnt and lots of Chinese too. Save all post-cards all very valuable now. April 26.06. N. York, L. C. H.

Two didactic messages were transmitted by Douglas in a card dated 19 January 1906 showing High Street, Columbus, Ohio: 'Tá mé anseo anois in Ohio. Feuch ar an mapa é. Labhair Gaedheilg le Úna. An Craoibhín' (I am here now in Ohio. Look it up on the map. Speak Irish to Úna. An Craoibhín). Nuala was two years older than her sister Úna, and accordingly was given the responsibility of initiating conversation in Irish, as well as being encouraged to add to her geographical awareness. Explicit expressions of affection are rather infrequent, although Douglas wished the girls 'Beannacht libh' (A blessing to you both) in a card to Úna showing Ohio State University, also posted on 19 January, while 'Beannacht leat.' (A blessing to you.) was also sent to Úna on 13 March. Nonetheless 'grádh' (love) was explicitly mentioned when Douglas wrote to Nuala from St Paul, Minn. on 1 February: 'Tá mé annso anois. Nach deas an áit í! Tabhair mo ghrádh d'Úna. An Craoibhín.' (I am here now. Isn't it a lovely place! Give my love to Úna. An Craoibhín). Sending a card with a picture of George Washington's Mansion at Mt. Vernon, Virginia, Lucy praised Washington himself and urged Nuala to learn about him: 'The house where the great Washington lived. Tell Jane to give you some idea who he was and what he did' (23 May, from Washington DC). Neither parent used a familiar or pet form of their own name when signing the cards to the children. Douglas retained 'An Craoibhín', the Irish-language pen-name by which he was widely known, while Lucy contented herself with the initials 'L. C. H.', standing for Lucy Cometina Hyde. On the other hand, in the text of the cards themselves Lucy referred to the girls' father as 'Poppy', while Douglas calls their mother 'Mam'.

Lucy seems to have been the more serious of the two, stressing repeatedly that all cards should be kept. After the earthquake her message is that the girls' parents could easily have died and they would be bereft. On the other hand, she too had a lighter side, often asking the girls to give her love to Polly – their pet cockatoo, which at one stage was recuperating from an illness. Lucy sent 'Love to Polly' on 1 June. Douglas too was fond of the cockatoo, and sent Polly his affectionate regards from Minneapolis, asking Úna: 'Tabhair póg do Polly uaim.' (Give Polly a kiss from me) (2 February). On one occasion, Lucy asked that Polly be told that they had seen lots of her cousins in lovely houses in Pittsburgh. Lucy also regularly sent her regards to Jane, the governess who was looking after the girls, back at their Ratra home. She requested, for example, that Jane be thanked for letters she had sent: 'Thank Jane for the beautiful letters' was the message from Lucy to Úna in a card which also included the German phrase 'Gott sei Dank' (Thank God) (Butte, Montana, 5 April 1906). When sending a picture of a large rose tree in a Santa Cruz garden to Nuala, Lucy told her that their hotel room was full of flowers, and added, thinking of home, 'I hope the greenhouse is doing well' (14 February).

There is just one card in the Heavey Collection, which Douglas wrote to Lucy. Sent on 1 February from the city of St Paul, Minnesota while she was in the Virginia Hotel in Chicago, Douglas signed off with the German 'Dein' (Your). As it also includes the German phrase 'Gott sei Dank', it adds to the evidence for Lucy's use of that language. Otherwise the card, which was of a view of 'Fort Snelling on the Mississippi River', merely keeps Lucy abreast of Douglas's current speaking engagements: 'A fine meeting last night. 3000 people but admission free and no collection. Speak tonight in Minneapolis 12 miles away. Am very well Gott sei Dank (Thank God). Speak here on Friday night. Hope return either Saturday night or Sunday morning to Chicago.'

The other main recipient of cards from the Hydes during their American tour was their friend Ethel Chance from Birmingham, whom Lucy once described as 'a great favourite of ours and [she] often comes to see us out here and we always go to her when we visit England.'[34] While the chronological and geographical range of the cards sent to Ethel parallels those sent to the girls – indeed on a few occasions they received cards with the same image – the messages to Ethel from Douglas were if anything even more upbeat: he was definitely not hiding his light under a bushel. The first card, that of 25 November 1905, sets both the scene and the tenor: 'Have been at Harvard (largest college in the States), and at Yale, sec. largest. Here's a picture of it! Left Lucy in lap of luxury in Long Island with friends. Am returning to N York today. Am frightfully rushed. Dining with President Roosevelt tomorrow. D. H.' On the picture side of the same card, was written, 'I am writing this on the shaking train en route to N York. D'. It may be noted in passing that the facility to write brief messages on a train, when little else except reading could usefully be undertaken, helps to explain the profusion of postcard correspondence. At any rate, in a second postcard to Ethel, sent a mere two days later, over a picture of the White House, Hyde was able to report two major developments: 'I dined with the President etc yesterday. Most delightfully informal and republican. Had my great meeting last night. Most tiers of boxes for my speech sold at $3240! Unparalleled.' On the bottom was the following reminder: 'Have lectured at Harvard and Yale also.' Interestingly, he signed off with a multilingual flourish: 'Dein Craoibhín'.

In mid-December Hyde wrote to Ethel, saying he was now back in New York, but would be leaving for Chicago on 5 January, and would not return until the end of March. On 1 February a picture of a frozen scene informs Ethel that he is in one of the twin cities, where there is 'great cold' and' everything frozen'. He hopes to head for San Francisco on 8 or 9 February, and signs himself 'Douglas'. From Wisconsin, he tells her 'All well. No time to write. Lots of hard work', and again signs 'Dein Craoibhín', before adding in a different ink, 'Lucy well too.' Other postcards followed from the Midwest. From Omaha, Nebraska on 8 February, he apologises that he cannot get a card of the city, and has to make do with one of the Logan monument in Chicago. Lucy had better luck, and was able to send Ethel a card with a picture of Omaha; she wrote of a blizzard and signed herself 'L. C. H.'.[35] On 12 February beneath a lively scene of seals on rocks and in water, Douglas wrote that they had landed safe and sound in San Francisco that day, where they were welcomed as if to a fairyland by the hedges and flowers, which provided a great contrast to the Rockies through which they had just passed.[36] An atmospheric picture of 'An underground opium den, Chinatown' then followed. It was unsigned but had the note 'Arrived here, Feb. 14 1906'. It was evidently the stop on the tourist trail to which their police guide conducted them, as related in the diary itself; the writing on the address is Hyde's.

The two cards held in UCD were also sent to Ethel Chance from San Francisco, but a little later in the month. The first, a picture of the Music Stand in the fashionable Golden Gate Park, was franked on 27 February 1906. It is in bravura mode, rather like the initial two postcards concerning Harvard, Yale, the White House and Carnegie Hall: 'I have just been given here the biggest banquet ever given anyone in California. The Governor, Mayor, Archbishop, Chief Justice & 500 guests at it! Everything is in flower here. This is the most beautifully situated city in the world I think. I am meeting great success here. An Craoibhín.' The other card posted just a day later, shows the Hotel Vendome, where they were staying in San José. The tone is still dynamic, if slightly more relaxed: 'This is our hotel here. But we return tomorrow I hope. This is one of the gardens of California. We motored here from San Francisco, over 50 miles yesterday. And I spoke in the theatre in the evening. We are both feeling a little acclimatized now! Feb 28.06. D. H.' On 20 April, from Memphis, Douglas sent Ethel a picture of 'the only statue of a Confederate general I have met yet.' He explains 'We are in the heart of the South.' As he was writing just two days after the earthquake, he observes 'What a narrow escape we had from San Francisco. We go to Baltimore tomorrow, 36 hours journey. We came from Chicago here. D. H.'

Two postcards connected with Hyde's second trip to Washington in May 1906 allow us to round off this cycle of cards near where they began six months earlier. Evidently in anticipation of his imminent return visit to the White House, Hyde sent Ethel a postcard of President Roosevelt and his family, dated 6 May and posted in New York on the ninth. The accompanying message informed her they would be leaving for Canada on 12 May and hoped to leave America itself at the end of the month or in early June. Finally, on 20 May, Hyde was able to point out both the hotel where they were staying 'on the left' and 'the Capitol in the distance' in the picture on a postcard he sent to Ethel. After referring to the two-day train journey it had taken to reach Washington and to the heat, Hyde ended his message: 'I go to dine with the President today/ Glück zu. An Craoibhín.' (… Good luck. An Craoibhín). He was back at the centre of American power.

QUINN AND UA CONCHEANAINN

In the background there were certain organisational and interpersonal tensions, which had been increasingly exercising Quinn, and which came to the fore as the tour swung back east. While Hyde had always had a good relationship with Tomás Bán Ua Concheanainn, the same could not be said of Ua Concheanainn's relations with either Quinn or Hyde's wife, Lucy. As Hyde's advance agent, Ua Concheanainn seemed to operate much as he had done in Ireland when establishing branches of the Gaelic League. He liked to liaise personally with local dignitaries and members of Gaelic societies. Quinn, on the other hand, operated mostly by mail, and through the reception committees he had established in the cities Hyde was to visit. Given the vastness of the country, one can understand the validity of this approach.

Quinn's initial impressions of Ua Concheanainn had been positive. On 27 October 1905 he wrote to Hyde: 'O'Concannon is a charming fellow and I like him very much and everybody that meets him likes him and he makes an excellent impression wherever he goes.'[37] By late December, however, doubts had set in. Quinn was now telling Fr Yorke:

> Concannon takes well with Gaelic Societies and those who know of the movement and of the work he has done. But he seems to lack the faculty of that concise and lucid

and brief statement that is necessary to interest the Irish-American who is disposed to give only a little time to appeals for help.[38]

Lucy Hyde was also growing increasingly dissatisfied with Ua Concheanainn. On 15 December 1905 she had written independently of her husband to Úna Ní Fhaircheallaigh, a leading Gaelic League member, in order to complain about Ua Concheanainn, stating: 'We have in plain language brought out *the wrong man*.' She contended that Ua Concheanainn was 'not educated enough for a smart and progressive people', with the result that he could not 'influence the right kind of people'. She also stated that he was not sending appropriate reports and financial accounts back to Dublin.[39] Ní Fhaircheallaigh reacted by writing a 'Private and Confidential' letter to Mac Néill, Vice-President of the Gaelic League, enclosing Lucy's letter, in which she went so far as to propose that Ua Concheanainn be recalled to Ireland.[40] Mac Néill replied on 3 January 1906 that he felt the situation could be adequately dealt with by firstly, having Ó Dálaigh, the General-Secretary, telegraphing Ua Concheanainn to send in his accounts without further delay, and secondly, the Organisation Committee authorising a communication to Dr Hyde to the effect that Ua Concheanainn's services were urgently required in Ireland, if and as soon as he could be dispensed with in America. Mac Néill proceeded however to outline some personal reasons that Mrs Hyde may have had for her unhappiness with Ua Concheanainn's behavior.[41]

By April Quinn himself had had quite enough of Ua Concheanainn and felt he would be no good in Philadelphia, writing to Hyde as follows: 'He is only fit to work among the Gaelic Societies, and money doesn't come from them, as you know. He mussed things very badly in New England. ... I don't want to be bothered with Concannon here. If he is in and around New York he will be hanging around my place and I'm tired of him. I'm too busy to be bothered with him anymore.'[42] He was even more forthright when corresponding with Hackett: 'The egregious Concannon blew in here last Thursday. Concannon is rotten with vanity and conceit.'[43] As Lucy also found Tomás Bán insufferable, she and Quinn made common cause, each complaining to the other about the advance agent. Quinn wrote to Lucy in April, saying 'Nobody can tell me that he is a simple, unspoiled child of nature and a simple peasant and all that stuff. He is one of the most conceited and stubborn men I ever met.'

Throughout this, Ua Concheanainn was assiduously professional, never failing, for instance, to thank the local newspapers for their readiness to spread the word about Hyde's visits, and the effect of their actions, as can be seen in the message he wrote to *The Chronicle* newspaper as he departed Spokane: 'I feel it my bounden duty to thank *The Chronicle* on my own behalf, and on behalf of my learned and eloquent chief, Dr Douglas Hyde, for the great assistance given the Gaelic League Revival since my arrival in Spokane, Washington. *The Chronicle* I feel, realizes the full significance of this revival, it realizes that it is more than a linguistic movement that in fact it is a racial fight, a fight for the nationality of Ireland at the eleventh hour.'[44] In reading this, we need to be mindful that 'race' was used at the time as the equivalent of 'nation'. Ua Concheanainn was reiterating Hyde's oft-repeated assertion that the Irish were on the brink of losing their distinctiveness as a separate people, that they were in the final stages of assimilation to English culture.

At any rate following consultation with Pádraig Ó Dálaigh, the Gaelic League's Secretary General back in Dublin, Hyde wrote several letters to Ua Concheanainn stressing the urgent need for him at home in Ireland, where the work of several newly appointed organisers required to be coordinated. Hyde passed on the word to his advance agent that Ó Dálaigh had written to him to say: 'The Executive Committee hope that you will be able to send Tomás home, as they are in bitter want of organizers.'[45] Ua Concheanainn duly arrived back in Ireland, in Derry, on 26 May 1906, where he was given an enthusiastic welcome. It is not clear that Tomás Bán appreciated the level of Quinn's dissatisfaction with his general approach, nor does he seem to have resented what might well be regarded as the effective foreshortening of his work in America. Indeed, when it came to the time for Ua Concheanainn to report on the American tour at the Gaelic League's Ard-Fheis in autumn 1906, he was fulsome in his praise of Quinn's contribution and expressed his thanks to him unreservedly.

RETURNING EAST

This disquiet was kept in the background, behind the scenes, as it were. Douglas and Lucy continued on their grand tour, retracing their steps as they travelled back to St Paul, Chicago and the Midwest, and then further east. However, there was a certain difference of emphasis this time, as their journey took them to mining towns like Butte and Anaconda in Montana, south to Memphis and north across the Canadian border to Toronto. Quinn wrote to Hyde, 6 April 1906, 'I was especially glad to have you go to Memphis because that is the only town in the South that has held out any encouragement for your meetings. Louisville, with a much larger population of Irish was disorganised and couldn't guarantee anything.' Hyde got a warm welcome and generous financial support in both Butte and Anaconda. In Butte he declined an invitation to go down the mines on the advice of Quinn, who said he had suffered terribly from doing so once. Hyde and Tomás Bán Ua Concheanainn established a branch of the Gaelic League in Anaconda City Hall on 14 April. The new branch promised to send $700 annually to Ireland to support the cause, a promise which was kept for a number of years.

It was on the train to Memphis, late on 18 April that Hyde saw a newspaper placard that announced that San Francisco was burning. However, he had to wait until the following morning before he could read full accounts of the terrible catastrophe of earthquake and fire that had befallen San Francisco the day before. Overwrought though he may have been, Hyde had to continue his tour. Back in Chicago, a Gaelic League branch to serve the Midwest was established on 20 April. Hyde's itinerary directed him eastwards to Baltimore, Cornell, Elmira, Scranton, then a return visit to Philadelphia, and on to Buffalo, Rochester and Toronto. But his thoughts were with the people of San Francisco, and he sent them a telegram shortly after arriving in New York: 'New York, April 24, 1906. Overwhelmed with sorrow at the great calamity. Hope and pray you all have escaped any personal injury. Douglas Hyde.' He consulted the Executive Committee as soon as possible and received their permission for Quinn to cable $5,000 to Fr Yorke for the disaster fund in San Francisco. It had been almost four months since he was last in New York city, and he noticed that Quinn wasn't looking well. In fact, unknown to Hyde, Quinn's brother had recently died.

News gradually came from their friends in the devastated city. James Shehan cabled Hyde, care of Quinn, on 30 April: 'We are safe but the city is destroyed. We have begun the work of rebuilding, Kind regards to Mrs Hyde. Your sympathy is appreciated. Mrs Phelan is well and in the country.'[46] Judge J. V. Coffey wrote to Mrs Hyde on 22 May 1906 from the temporary quarters of the Superior Court at Temple Israel, Office of the Hills of Eternity Cemetery: '… My loss was total in court-room and chambers. My nephews lost all their office effects. We fortunately saved our habitation, once rather remote, now in the centre of the inhabited quarter.' Coffey then proceeded to recall a striking, rather theatrical event that occurred just before the Hydes left San Francisco, a gesture which in retrospect took on greater significance, and one that underlines the celebrity status which Lucy's husband had achieved and in fact assumed:

> I shall write a line to Dr Hyde in a day or two. Meanwhile I cannot help recalling the incident of his departure on the Oakland boat as we were approaching the 'Mole' or pier, towards the train … : As we approached the landing on that night, and Father Yorke and others were conversing with him, Doctor Hyde drew apart for a moment, saying he

JILTED.

JOHN REDMOND, M.P.—Bedad! I see how he's put the com'hether on her—he's earning more nor I am. But wait till I get me new holdin', "Home Rule," an' see if she won't be comin' back.

DOCTOR DOUGLAS HYDE arrived in Dublin from his tour in America bringing with him 50,000 dollars for the Gaelic League Fund.

'Jilted'. From *The Lepracaun Cartoon Monthly*, July 1906. Courtesy of Dublin City Library and Archive

> wanted to take a last look at the city. The night was fair, the scene was grand from the opposite shore, the hills electrically luminous. Taking off his hat, the Doctor, with true feeling, said, saluting the vision, 'San Francisco, I shall never see you again.' We were all affected by his remark. But it is to be hoped that someday we shall have the pleasure of receiving you both in this metropolis, when you will find as cordial a welcome as before.[47]

Hyde himself received some unprompted correspondence, which may best be understood as fan-mail. For instance, one Martan P. Mac an Báird, or Martin P. Ward, evidently unused to some of the conventional spelling norms, wrote to him as follows from Oakland, Cal.: 'Esteemed and learned country man. I thank Heavens. that I live-ed to meet see and hear you. and grasp that *Honest Gaelic Hand* 6.000 miles away from *Ratra*. & Historic old *Dún-Gar*. And say to yourself and Mrs Hyde *Cead Mile Failte*.'[48] A cleric by the name of J. F. Sullivan, wrote enthusiastically from the Holy Name Rectory, Providence, R. I. on 9 August 1906 after Hyde's return to Ireland to tell him: 'Since we met here I have followed closely every line published about your great success in this broad big-hearted country, and rest assured that the greater your success the more joy it gave me.' The writer went on to say that he had composed and translated a 'few simple verses in his honor'.[49]

The same tone pervades much of the correspondence Hyde received. His friend M. J. Henehan or M. I. Ua h-Éidhneacháin wrote from Seattle on 12 July: 'A cara mo Chroidhe. I am sure if your make up had any vanity your head would be turned with the reception you got. There is no doubt but the heart of the Irish people is true to their ideals and I believe you came the nearest to their ideal of any man of the race. … We love you just the same for what you are and what you represent.[50] Nor was Quinn himself immune from these sentiments. He wrote to Francis Hackett, 28 March 1906: 'I have been very much rushed the last two or three months and haven't seen anybody hardly, not even your brother. Between you and me, this has come to be a tiring grind, but I am going to see it through to the end. I have a real affection for Dr Hyde and there are not many men living for whom I would do more.'

Hyde spoke in Toronto on 17 May, and apart from his debut speech in Carnegie Hall, this was the only occasion where he admitted to a certain level of apprehension – due to the large proportion of Orangemen among the Irish population in the city. However, all turned out well. On the day following his lecture the *Toronto Star* reported that Dr Hyde spoke to '1,000 enthusiastic Irishmen of all creeds, religions and politics' in Massey Hall, while the *Toronto Evening Telegram* noted that his speech contrasted the Irish and the English, saying that the Irish 'are distinguished by lightness, wittiness, piety, artistic temperament', while the English are 'marked by intense perseverance, great business faculties, [and] a grand capacity for making money.' This, and Hyde's ambiguous references to 'Gaelic' – not clarifying whether he was referring to the Irish or Scottish variety – evidently kept all sides happy. Hyde's visit raised $1,000 and encouraged the setting up of a Toronto branch of the League.[51]

Hyde visited Washington for the second time from 20 to 25 May. Despite the heat and a bad bout of rheumatism, he completed his programme of addresses – giving one in the National Theater and two in the Catholic University of America. In addition to a second lunch with the President, he had the opportunity of visiting Washington's home at Mt Vernon, and the Smithsonian Institute, the Senate, the House of Representatives and the Library of Congress. However, Hyde's account of his second visit to the nation's capital is perhaps most memorable for its insight into the curative properties of a Mint Julep cocktail, and the beneficial effect it had on his rheumatism: 'After lunch, I returned with Egan to the Cosmos Club and had a Mint Julep. This is a common drink in these parts but not one I encountered anywhere else. Similar to a High Ball, it is poured in a large tall glass and garnished with mint leaves. To drink it, one places their nose and mouth in the mint, and inhales the herb's taste and scent. I was in a bad way with the pain when I took the initial drink but thought the pain lessened afterwards. Either way, I did not leave the club nor did Egan abandon me until we had had four each. Although I barely managed to make it to the White House, I was able to walk back home to the hotel reasonably well.'

FAREWELL AND RETURN TO IRELAND

The tour was now winding down. As the summer temperatures rose, the pace of lecturing slowed and the public meetings were interspersed with ever more frequent valedictory social engagements. Hyde particularly enjoyed a mid-day meal at Delmonico's restaurant in New York on 26 May, where he was joined by John Quinn, Judge Daniel F. Cohalan, Judge Martin J. Keogh, Arthur Brisbane of the *Evening Journal*, later to become the highest paid newspaper writer in the world, and the celebrated journalist and humourist Peter Finley Dunne, known as 'Mr Dooley'. They sat down at one o'clock and did not leave until six. Hyde remembered the occasion fondly, observing with satisfaction, that it would be difficult to bring together another group of six men equal to the six of them at lunch that day. Hyde delivered further lectures at Bridgeport, Long Island, and Paterson, New Jersey, but now also had a little time to engage with the latest technology. On 1 June he visited the premises of the phonographer Hollenbeck, and was presented with audio courses of French, German and Spanish, while he himself was given the opportunity to speak some Irish into a phonograph tube. He also spent a day or two finishing an article on aspects of early Irish culture for *Scribner's Magazine*.

Hyde had heard that his two-volume work, *Abhráin Diadha Chúige Connacht, or Religious Songs of Connacht*, had just been published by Fisher Unwin in London, and collected the large number of copies sent to him at Wessel publishers. In fact, he spent two or three days sending off about a hundred sets of his *Religious Songs of Connacht* to those who had assisted him during his tour. With characteristic thoroughness, this involved Hyde not only signing his own name in every book, but that of the recipient as well, and in most cases he added a personal letter. He stayed indoors on the 8 June, practising on a typewriter which had been presented to him, but typing seems to have been a skill that he never really mastered. Berths were booked with some difficulty on the liner *Celtic*, which set sail for Ireland on 15 June. Hyde's last act of the tour was to finish a farewell letter for New York's newspapers while on board ship, waiting to depart. Quinn himself hand-delivered copies of this letter to the city's newspaper offices, while the final piece of his great organisational *tour de force* was to ensure that the financial accounts were in order, down to the last cent. In all, $64,000 had been collected for the Gaelic League. The *New York Times* of 16 June carried the following farewell message from Douglas Hyde: 'I have found nothing except a generous welcome in America. I travelled 19,000 miles, visited over 60 cities, and explained the cause of the Irish language to perhaps 80,000 people. I have not heard a single word that was not favourable to our cause. I understand now as never before, how great is this country and how numerous, strong, and powerful are the Irish who are in it. ... There is a great likeness between the people of Ireland and this country. I would sooner have the good will of this country than anything else in the struggle to bring back the language, music, of Ireland.' The same newspaper kept an eye on the distinguished visitor, even after his departure. On 23 June it carried a report of his arrival back in Queenstown, Co. Cork and told its readers that numerous deputations had greeted him when he disembarked there earlier that day. The following evening his train pulled into Dublin at Kingsbridge Station, where a large crowd awaited him.

By early summer Quinn could look back with considerable satisfaction on what had been accomplished. In fact, he had already told Maud Gonne in a letter at the end of May that he was very pleased with the way the tour had gone: 'Hyde has had a great

Arrival of Dr. Douglas Hyde at Kingsbridge Station yesterday evening.

'Filleadh an Chraoibhín' (The return of Douglas Hyde), *Irish Independent*, 25 June 1906. Courtesy of the National Library of Ireland trip out here. He has been here seven months and has travelled over 19,000 miles and has spoken to over 75,000 persons. He will take back with him $50,000 net, over and above all expenses and exclusive of the $5,000 which he returned to San Francisco. When you consider the fact that he came here without any organisation and was practically unknown except to a mere handful of insignificant Gaelic Leaguers, I think the results of the tour are marvelous.'[52]

Writing to W. B. Yeats in July, less than two months later, Quinn was now reviewing the bigger picture, surveying the tours he had organised for both Yeats and Hyde, assuring Yeats:

> You did more to make him known here than anyone else and I finished the job that you began. You did it generously and Hyde should never forget it. … Outside of the Irish Societies he was almost unknown here a year ago except to some Irish, who weren't numerous enough to make up a corporal's guard. Today he is almost an international figure.

Quinn had achieved what he set out to do when he envisioned the tours for both Yeats and Hyde:

> You and Hyde have done more for the elevation of the Irish in this country and for the increasing respect with which Irish ideals and aspirations are regarded in this country than any other two men of your day and generation. The people were getting tired of mere politicians, whose sole stock in trade consisted of abuse of Englishmen and promises of the good things they were going to do.[53]

Whatever about being an international figure, by the time Hyde returned to Dublin in June 1906 Dublin Castle was on his case, as is clear from a file now in the National Archives of the United Kingdom (TNA) at Kew, Richmond, Surrey.[54] The authorities had arranged for a number of detectives to attend the gathering at Kingsbridge station and they accompanied the crowd to the Gaelic League's Headquarters in Upper O'Connell St, where Hyde addressed a huge gathering. Significantly, the League's building was situated quite close to the Gresham Hotel from where Hyde had set out for the US the previous November. The police officers' file drew its information from the *Daily Express*, *The Irish Times* and the *Freeman's Journal*, as well as the detectives' own eye-witness accounts. The police officers were anxious to minimise the significance of the proceedings, but the facts were clearly against them. From this official account we learn that Hyde had been welcomed at Kingsbridge station by the Lord Mayor and members of Dublin Corporation, as well as P. O'Daly (Pádraig Ó Dálaigh) and other officials of the Gaelic League itself. The file states: 'A fairly large crowd assembled at Kingsbridge but when the procession moved off it is estimated that only from 4,000 to 5,000 persons marched in it.' However, the gathering soon increased dramatically, for we next learn: 'An enormous crowd collected in Sackville St to hear the address, but only a small proportion succeeded in attaining this object.'[55] The Castle listeners noted that Hyde had emphasised the fact 'that his success in America was mainly due to John Quinn.' This was indeed the case, as Hyde himself relayed directly to Quinn shortly afterwards: 'The whole of O'Connell Street was packed from side to side, and from the Rotunda to below Nelson's Pillar, with one solid mass of people and they all with one accord cheered for John Quinn, as well they might. I left nobody in any doubt as to whom the American success was due.'[56]

In general, the detectives' report laid great stress on the money raised in America. Heavy red pencil marks accompanied the *Daily Express*'s account of Hyde declaring that he had in his pocket a cheque for £10,000 and that it had been agreed that it would be spent over a period of five years. Some of the detectives were disturbed by his statement that 'he was more confident than ever that "Sinn Féin" should be the watchword of the Gaelic League.' In fact, Hyde's use of the words 'Sinn Féin' had been a spur of the moment response to the phrase being shouted by someone in the crowd, and the authorities were in danger of misinterpreting its import. However, the Castle officers eventually realised that Hyde had not been referring to the newly established political party of the same name, but rather to the self-help ethos which underlay the phrase.[57]

Public honours and congratulations were showered on Hyde throughout the country during the rest of the year. On 30 June 1906 *The Irish Times* reported that a special meeting of Dublin Corporation had been held the day before in the City Hall for the purpose of considering a proposal to 'confer the freedom of the city on Dr Douglas Hyde, president of the Gaelic League, on the occasion of his return from America, and in recognition of his magnificent and untiring services on behalf of the restoration of our national language.' The Lord Mayor presided, and there were about two dozen members present. It was noted, however, that none of the Unionist members attended. The resolution was adopted unanimously and the freedom of the city was duly conferred on 'An Craoibhín Aoibhinn' or Douglas Hyde on 7 August 1906. Hyde was also made a freeman of the cities of Cork and Kilkenny in 1906 in recognition of his achievement in America.

Finally, returning to the money trail, it is clear from the last lines of *My American Journey* that the funds raised in America were primarily spent on financing the

An extract from the Dublin Metropolitan Police Intelligence analysis of Hyde's rhetoric on his return from the U. S. Courtesy of the National Archives (UK), ref. CO 904/204/5 momentous and ultimately successful public campaign to have Irish recognised as an essential subject for matriculation in the new National University of Ireland, established in 1909. John Quinn, initiator and chief organiser of Hyde's tour died in 1924 at the age of just 55. Hyde dedicated *My American Journey* to this Irish-American and chose a fine portrait of him by Augustus John as frontispiece of the volume. By doing so, he paid fitting tribute to the man behind his American tour.

MY AMERICAN JOURNEY
OR
AMONG THE IRISH IN THE UNITED STATES

AN CRAOIBHÍN AOIBHINN
(DOUGLAS HYDE)

In memory of John Quinn

MY AMERICAN JOURNEY

I first encountered John Quinn[1], an American lawyer from New York, in August 1902.[2] I clearly remember the first occasion I saw him. Lady Gregory[3], Edward Martyn from Tulira[4], and a large crowd had gathered in Killeeneen Cemetery[5], where a fine inscribed stone memorial had been erected, inscribed with gold letters, in memory of the poet Raftery.[6] I was up on the fine stage that had been erected, speaking as lively as possible in Irish to the audience, when I noticed a tall, slender, and distinguished man standing in the midst of the crowd listening intently. As the crowd encroached on the stage, an elderly local man kept them at bay, saying, ''Back'!' "Go back out of that'!' When the event ended and the speeches concluded, I met the tall man again. We spoke, and he informed me that he was touring Ireland on holidays. I believe he was Lady Gregory's guest, the noble lady responsible for Raftery's fine tomb, and she took him back to her residence at Coole House.[7] I conversed with the American and he enquired about the Irish language in Ireland. He apparently heeded my answers, as I received one or two letters from him once he returned to New York, stating that, if possible, I should come to America where I would receive assistance from him and others. He was very interested in anything concerning the arts and literature, and had already read the books I had written. 'I believe', said Judge Keogh[8], 'that he did something which nobody else in America ever did: he read your *Literary History of Ireland*, twice'!'[9] He was very friendly with the poet Yeats[10] also, and had brought him to America a few years earlier, guiding him from city to city, and from university to university. Maybe that trip minded him to invite me as he had Yeats. I became very friendly with him, but it was pointless for him to invite me until 1905. That year my father[11] died, and his death freed me to travel abroad. The Gaelic League considered the possibility of sending someone to fundraise in America, I alone was available and, as I was President of the League since its establishment, there was, in their opinion, no one more suitable than me.

There followed a long correspondence between Quinn and me. Were I to travel, he promised to arrange matters and pave my way, but an advance man was necessary.

Tomás Bán Ua Concheanainn[12] was selected to travel as the advance man. Born in Inis Meáin, one of the Aran Islands, Tomás had gone to America when he was 17. Like the Americans themselves, he went from place to place; he went to South America and to Mexico after a period, where he learned Spanish. There are many Irish in Argentina and Señor Bulfin[13] told me that a rider could travel for seven days and seven nights without venturing beyond Irish-owned property. Fr O'Growney[14], God rest his soul, informed me that those who lived near him used to travel to South America as people from other places went to the States, and on returning after 20, 30 or 40 years, their speech betrayed no hint that they had ever left Ireland. So different from those who go to the States, if only for a fortnight, to New York or Boston, and find their speech affected. Fr O'Growney recalled often hearing Spanish spoken at fairs in County Westmeath. When Tomás Bán returned home in 1898, he found the Irish-language movement in full flow. He assisted it and was the first *timire* (community language organiser) and he was the finest resource we had. He traversed Ireland, north, south, east, west, organising for us and promoting the Irish-language gospel. As a result, he knew Ireland and the States both well. He was selected, therefore, to travel in advance of me. He was the advance agent for me in many of the cities and states in the US. Were it not for his groundwork, we would not have raised so much money for the Gaelic League.

From the New England states to the mid-western states of that large country as far as Missouri and Minnesota, he followed the schedule John Quinn set out. Quinn arranged every detail in advance and I followed what he set out.

On reaching San Francisco, Tomás operated in California, Oregon, Washington and Montana under the direction of Fr Yorke[15], chief guide and advisor of the Irish in that part of the Western World.

I don't think that any other person in Ireland in the Gaelic League had the ability to affect the task as skilfully as him.

On 29 September 1905, before Tomás departed, John Quinn convened a meeting of influential people in New York and formed a committee to organise my welcome. He identified people of prominence and influence in the city including Chief Justice Martin Keogh, Judge Dowling, Judge Temple Emmet[16], Daniel Cohalan[17] (Daniel's father – he spoke the best, and the most eloquent, and most accurate Irish I heard in

America – told me that Ó Cathalláin was their correct surname and that it came from the word 'cath' i.e. a person who was good at waging battle. But when they spoke English they usually said Co-halon i.e. 'Halon' with the same sound as the name Fallon in English), John Devoy[18], the old Fenian, and involved the presidents of many athletic societies, musical societies and the Gaelic League among many others. He secured letters of invitation and welcome from Judge Fitzgerald[19], Judge Morgan O'Brien[20], Judge O'Gorman[21], Recorder Goff[22], John D. Crimmins, Patrick Ford[23], editor of the *Irish World* and others. I don't believe that anyone else in New York save John Quinn alone had the connections to convene such an assembly.

Tomás came to New York in October, and Quinn hosted him at his home at 120 Broadway. The Gaelic League issued a circular to America announcing my journey and requesting that I be welcomed by the Irish in America. Both Vice-Presidents, Fr Peadar Ó Laoghaire[24] and Eoin Mac Néill[25], as well as Pádraig Ó Dálaigh[26], the Secretary, and Stiofán Bairéad[27], our treasurer, signed the circular.

On seeing such distinguished men advocating for the Irish-language, some people became suspicious; the *Irish World* declared, 'The New York Welcome is a curious affair. It appears that those undertaking such great work were previously alienated from every Irish movement, – they alone know why. If it is true that they are finally paying a small portion of the nationalist debt in which they are in arrears, then it is better now than never. It will greatly please the Gaelic League, as the Leaguers are like the souls of the dead in the heavens above us, i.e. they rejoice sevenfold at the return of those who went astray and they are willing to ignore the rank and file who pass by unnoticed … our readers know well our opinion of those wealthy Irishmen and their neglect, etc., etc.'

Not all my friends knew my purpose in travelling to the States was not only to promote Irish and Irish-language affairs but also to fundraise; and since I wanted money, I had to go to the people who had money and places that had money. I distinctly remember being but three or four days in New York, and still unaware of how things worked, when Quinn placed a paper in my hand telling me that dissatisfied people would visit me to complain; the paper contained his recommended response to such people. However, so occupied was I by other affairs that I pocketed the paper without reading it. That evening six or more men called to the hotel to see me with a long list of complaints. From their appearance, it seemed the end of the world was nigh. Looking as worried as could be, they informed me that the 'Welcome' was not in the hands of the right people, that the Tuxedo (short evening jacket) brigade never did anything worthwhile for Ireland.

120 Broadway,

New York, October 11, 1905.

Francis O'Byrne Hackett, Esq.,
361 Superior Street E.,
Chicago, Ill.

My dear Hackett:

We are making arrangements in New York for the coming of the Craoibhin. He will be here November 15th. Thomas O'Concannon, the chief organizer of the Gaelic League, arrived here Sunday week, and our work for the success of the big New York meeting is now fairly well started.

I have felt more and more since I have thought about the work of the Gaelic League (and I have known about it for some years and have had personal knowledge of it and of the fine work that is being done) that if the language is to be saved at all it is to be saved in Ireland. A great many practical Americans think that Gaelic League is nothing but a mere language movemant and are a little inclined to sneer at it. Of course they are utterly mistaken. The Gaelic movement is much more than a language movement, and is the most powerful and most beneficial movement and the movement most worthy of support in Ireland today. It is badly in need of funds. So far it has been carried on by the contributions of the people in Ireland. Unlike Sir Horace Plunkitt's movement and others of that kind, no fashionable persons have aided the Gaelic League and no persons of power have secured favors for it. Dr. Hyde has given his services for over twelve years to the

Letter from John Quinn to Francis Hackett, 11 October 1905. Courtesy of the National Library of Ireland

At first, I did not know who they were, but then recalled Quinn's note. If I did, however, it was too late; I could hardly pull it out of my pocket in front of them. But after some conversation, I pretended to hear the telephone ring in my bedroom and suddenly said, 'that blasted telephone is ringing again. Gentlemen, please excuse me for a moment until I see to it.' I ran into my room and spoke in a loud voice on the phone, pretending to be in conversation. I pulled out Quinn's note and read it. I then knew who these people were, what they wanted, and who was inciting them. I returned, thanked them heartily and explained that I intended to take every advantage possible of the Tuxedo brigade and their friends; I was on a mission to all the Irish, high and low, and would refuse assistance from no one. I spoke in Irish with one or two of those men who were fluent. I gave them a drink and, after considerable conversation, they departed extremely satisfied. I heard no more of them.

Those men were honest and well meaning. They supported me in other places, the best of the Irish, no doubt, but they did not correctly comprehend the dynamics in New York. I am almost certain that they were jealous and envious when they saw that I was under the wing of Quinn and his friends, and they really thought nothing good would come of it. But if that was the case, they were greatly mistaken. I knew very well what I had to do: raise funds!

My wife[28] and I left Dublin on 6 November 1905 at seven o'clock in the evening surrounded by a large crowd. The Lord Mayor in his official carriage came to the meeting. In his speech, he said, 'There are fourteen parties in Dublin Corporation – and in five or six of them there is only one person and therefore they are always of one opinion – but it is a great honour for An Craoibhín[29] that they are all of one word in bidding him a hearty farewell and they all willingly took time off to come and bid him farewell.' I was presented with numerous addresses, one from the Executive Committee, one from the Maynooth Colmcille Branch, Fingal District Committee, Limerick, Navan, Tirawley [Mayo], Dublin GAA, and Dublin Chamber of Commerce. When called on to respond, I stated that the Lord Mayor was correct when he said that the Gaelic League was not a political organisation. 'That is correct,' I said, 'and that is precisely why it is the strongest political organisation in Ireland. The correct meaning of the word 'politics,' in the Greek is any power that pertains to any citizen, and powerful is the League that has the support of the people and that entices the people of the city to itself, and, therefore, it is a very strong political organisation! But it does not favour one group over another.' I said more about my aim in visiting the United States. We departed the Gresham Hotel[30] then and made our way through the streets which were thronged with people, and a group of hurlers conveying us, singing a song I composed for them years previously. (See p. 154 for note on song.). Countless carriages followed us, and we marched slowly down by the river until we reached Kingsbridge Station.[31] Once we entered the station, those who accompanied me staged a meeting outside. I learned this subsequently from friends, as I only knew that a multitude had followed us. The train departed and people cheered us at every station where we stopped.

It was one o'clock at night when we came to Limerick Junction where there is a good hotel.[32] We spent the night there. In the morning, I received a telegram from my old friend Canon Arthur Ryan, Tipperary [town] Parish Priest, requesting that we lunch with him as Tipperary town is only three miles or so from the Junction. We accepted and had a pleasurable day and received additional addresses from the Gaelic League and the GAA. We returned to the Junction and boarded the Cork train at twenty minutes past six. On reaching Mallow there was a very large crowd and I was compelled to address them.

But on reaching Cork, we encountered a mass gathering. The Lord Mayor[33] himself was present and transported myself, Roche and Horgan[34] in his carriage to the City Hall. Thousands gathered around us; representatives of 24 branches (of the Gaelic League) and six bands were there. I made a speech and received five addresses and my friend Fr Austin delivered as fine a speech as I ever heard. When all was done, I went to my old friend Windle's[35] house, who is the College President. My wife already was already there and I spent the night there. The following day, I stayed at the house and enjoyed the company of my old friends.

The next morning, we ventured to Cobh at 9.50 a.m. and I received another great welcome there, including Bishop Browne[36], the Bishop of Cloyne. We boarded the tender accompanied by a slew of friends and were finally deposited aboard the ship. This concluded our journey out of Ireland, or should I say my triumphant passage out of the country! A senior Protestant minister ferried to the ship with us and I spoke with him as I knew him and his wife, who came from my own county. This gentleman's name appeared in the newspaper the following day as one of those who accompanied my farewell group. The unfortunate man had to write a letter to the paper to deny it, and state that he had travelled to bid farewell to another party altogether, and not to me, which was true. He understood, no doubt, it that it did him little credit to honour the Gaelic League![37]

We made land at New York on 15 November 1905 and even before we disembarked the ship, the journalists visited and interviewed us. The American 'reporter' has to say something and it worries him little, on occasions, if he has to invent it himself. I was taken aback the following morning to read that I had a 'small' moustache and a vivid green necktie. Needless to say, I wore nothing green. I was dressed all in black, jet-black, because of my father's death but the reporter described me as wearing 'bottle green.' These newspaper people are a great irritation. I had discussed them on board ship with a theatre woman, who had spent almost 40 years in America, and asked how best to deal with them. She sagely advised me to 'Go with them, as you would with any other person and you will find that they will be accepting of you.' Travelling America I recalled that counsel and I followed it whenever I was interviewed by a reporter. And they posed the most difficult and vexing questions! Wherever I went, the reporter would ask, 'What are the MPs doing for the Irish language?' and many other questions about the MPs and Parliament. It was my habit, when asked such questions, to pause for a little while, take out my cigarette case, slowly light a cigarette, offer my interviewer a cigarette and at the same time say 'Now, my dear man, I wish to give you all the facts – how do you like my cigarette? But you know, just between us, there are certain questions that I prefer not to be asked, but you know that as well as I do.' I was always very courteous with them and can say that I went across the whole country without any trouble, except for one occasion.

I was in one remote place – I do not recall its name now – and I was exhausted from constant talking. In the middle of the night, I heard a knock, followed by another knock, on the locked door. I paid no attention initially, but my patience waned in the end, and I refused to grant the man entry. I uttered a few words through the door, which of course were less than conciliatory. He vanished and wrote a report that appeared in the following day's paper. Pretending to have interviewed me, he claimed that I said I planned a large meeting of the Irish in that town at the end of the year and that the Irish should begin preparations immediately. I had to telegraph New York denying the claim in that article and advising them to ignore it. If I was cautious before this, I was more mindful than ever afterwards to treat reporters carefully whether in the light of day or the dark of night.

A great number came to the ship to welcome me. Among them were John Quinn who organised and directed the entire operation, Tomás Bán who had been working for a month in the city, Judge Keogh and many others. Out of respect for me, customs declined to search my luggage and allowed me entry without any formalities. Quinn brought me to the large Hotel Manhattan[38] where a suite of rooms awaited us, because as he himself said, 'Nobody is respected here unless he stays in a top place.'

I remained four days in the Manhattan with reporters constantly interviewing me. I had to do my best to earn New York's respect; almost all the papers follow New York's

2006—Whitehall Building New York.
this is called a sky scraper
because it nearly touches the sky.
Keep it for me
Souvenir Post Card Co., New York and Berlin.

Courtesy of Westmeath Libraries (Aidan Heavey Collection)

lead, and if they do not copy them, they certainly pay great attention. Therefore, I had to do my utmost to ensure that the newspapers would be favourable to me.

When I had spent four days in the Manhattan, Quinn took us to his own place at 120 Broadway. Tomás Bán, (who had been staying there), had left a while before. (This was his method of work: on arriving in a city, he went to everyone he knew or knew of and to those whose names he was given as people who were favourable toward the language movement. Among them were bishops, priests, doctors, lawyers, titans of business, newspapermen, and the Irish societies; his role was to convene them to organise the meetings at which I would speak, and to seek financial support, as well as the papers' goodwill and adequate publicity). Quinn had an 'apartment' and it contained a comfortable room for us.

My first engagement was at Harvard, perhaps the most famous university in America, on the 20th of the month. I went from New York to Boston on the train that day, and Dr Robinson[39], Professor of Celtic, and Fr O'Flanagan, met me at the station. Robinson took me to his own home, and I had just enough time to eat dinner and change my clothes before being taken to the University Lecture Hall to speak on Irish folklore. Eliot[40], the University President, was absent, but Dean Briggs[41], the next in charge was present. He was shy and nervous; on ascending the stairs, we were at cross-purposes as to whom should enter the room first; once we entered, he was unsure whether I should sit to his left or right. They are much more circumspect in America about such trivial things than in Ireland. We finally entered the room. There were some 500 in attendance both faculty and students. I made them laugh several times during my lecture, and all agreed that my lecture was 'informal,' which pleased them since they are unaccustomed to such. We all retired to Robinson's home and had a great party, some 70 of us, professors and their wives. I thought those distinguished women were the nicest I had seen until then and that increased my respect for the professors' acumen.

It was very late that night when I went to bed. The next morning, Robinson's brother-in-law called and drove us to Concord, where the first shot in the American War (of Independence) was fired, a shot 'whose echo was heard around the world.' Memorials to the Minute Men dotted the sides of the road. They were the men who said they would rise to fight the English at a minute's notice. Every mile of road housed a memorial in memory of those valiant men, American and Irish, who fell in the struggle with the English. Close to Concord was the house of Hawthorne, the novelist, and I never saw such a dark, desolate house. I also met the daughters of Child[42], the folklore editor, and Longfellow, and spent a considerable period chatting with them. We returned for lunch and who was before us but Eliot, the most famous and respected educationalist in the States, and twelve other professors as well. There was no female among their number. It was Kittridge[43] I found most interesting. He is an American York Powell. He was well versed on numerous topics especially folklore. We sat conversing and drinking until it was time for me to return to Boston.

I reached Boston after an hour's journey in a carriage and when I arrived, Matthew Cummings[44], the president of the AOH (Ancient Order of Hibernians) was waiting for me. Two others accompanied him: O'Connor and Murphy. We chatted until evening when they brought me around the city to the presses, and I had to stay to see them prepare the papers for the morning, inserting pictures and so forth. I penned letters in Irish to three of the largest circulation papers, informing the people of Boston that I would return soon and conveying the Gaelic League's compliments. Facsimiles of the three letters appeared the following day's newspapers. I returned to the hotel between one and two o'clock in the morning. The next morning I returned to New York, a five-hour journey. I dined with Quinn in a city restaurant.

Today I had to visit Yale, possibly the second largest university in America. I boarded the train to New Haven and arrived there after several hours but, when I alighted, there was nobody to greet me! I waited apprehensively, but after a long period, a crowd of Irishmen from the town came to greet and welcome me. I chatted merrily with them until suddenly a strange silence fell upon the group. I looked around and saw a small nervous man approaching. He introduced himself as Mr Hadley[45], the University President. It astonished my Irish companions that this distinguished man came to the station to greet me. They said he had never done so for any other speaker. His manners intimidated the others. When the President departed, I was taken to a hotel where I ate before the President returned to take me to the lecture hall.[46] Since we were too early, we sat chatting and he spent another quarter of an hour questioning me about Ireland. He was very courteous. I then lectured on 'The philosophy and mentality of the Gaelic League.' The President chaired the meeting, sat there for the duration and gave the impression that he was interested in what I had to say. I did not spare the English or the English Educational System but no Englishman was present: as for the professors, I don't think any of them attended except the President and only around 12 students. How different from Harvard. Were it not for the Irish from the town I would not have had any audience at all. They would have filled the hall to overflowing but feared that would not have pleased the college authorities. I was informed that only thirty turned up for the previous lecturer despite his reputation as one of the most renowned speakers in the States. Around one hundred showed up for

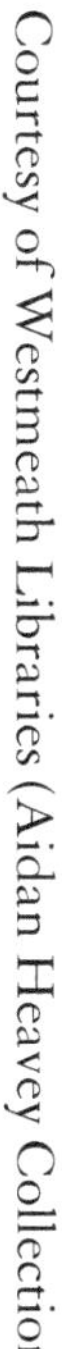

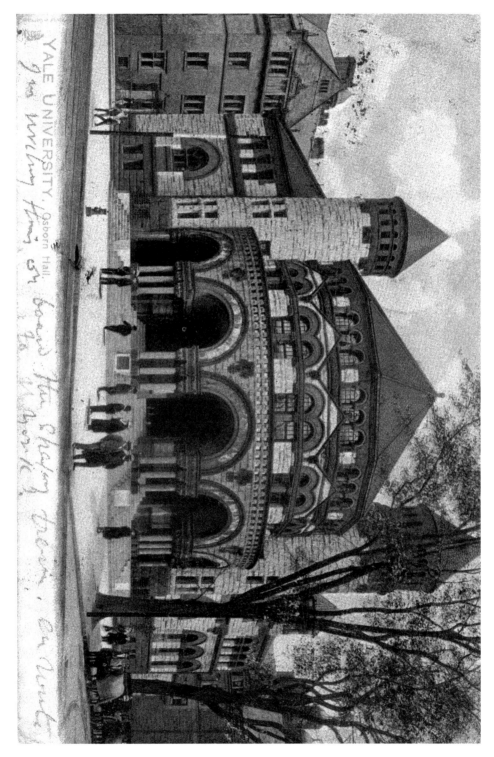

Courtesy of Westmeath Libraries (Aidan Heavey Collection)

me. They were all very grateful to Mr Hadley, the President, for remaining until the end, as he had never previously done so for anyone, they said.

When the lecture was over, the Irish brought me back to their club in town. There I met a lot of fine old warriors and veterans, soldiers who fought in the Civil War. They joined the Fenians after the war and travelled to Ireland in expectation of war. Among them was Captain O'Brien who kept us for an hour recounting his adventures in Ireland and how he was imprisoned in Clonmel Jail and escaped. He said he was responsible for the Prison Governor's death as he claimed it was the Governor himself who released him. I recall him telling us that he hid in the bushes on the first day (of the season) for shooting partridges and how the hounds of a few gunners almost found him. He was very entertaining, and I wished more than anything that I had a gramophone or some equipment to record his stories.

Captain Dunn, whose son succeeded Henebry as Professor of Irish at Washington, was also present. A Madden and an O'Sullivan were also there. There were all veterans who had been in Ireland in the year 1868, or thereabouts, and they were all knowledgeable about mixing drinks! It was past two o'clock when they released me.

I returned to New York on the morrow and on the same night at eleven, Quinn and I boarded a train to Washington DC. We had a sleeper carriage and arrived at the premier state of America at seven or eight the following morning. We had an invitation from President Roosevelt[47] himself to dine with him for lunch. Quinn and I went to the White House at one o'clock and the President welcomed us warmly. He introduced us to his wife, a pleasant lady, to their second daughter (Alice[48], the eldest, known as the princess was not at home), to his sister-in-law, and to the other children, and we sat for lunch with no fuss or ceremony. It was a simple lunch with one black servant waiting on us; a cup of tea and glass of sherry to drink. Apples and green grapes, direct from the barrel, with ashes still on them, for the second course. He was very well-informed about Irish and Norse mythology and compared them. We smoked in each other's company after lunch; he informed us that he had had Irish nurses[49] when he was young and that he had always known the names of Cú Chulainn and Fionn Mac Cumhail long before he saw them written. He also said his own family had Irish nurses too. He was of the opinion that there were still too many 'colonies' in America; it was a nation composed of many nations and since there were so many Irish in their midst, America should accept everything good, worthy or interesting in the life of the Irish and make their own of it. He said he was to write an article for the *North American Review*[50] urging wealthy Irishmen in the United States to establish Irish-language professorships in the colleges. Quinn and I then returned to our hotel[51] and Dunn, the Professor of Irish at Washington was there before us. He cannot converse well in Irish, as he was born and raised in America. We visited the editor of the *National Hibernian*[52] and the President of the AOH in the city. I knew him already as we sat together at the Foyne's *Feis* in Limerick the previous summer. He delivered a very loud address that displeased me at the time though he was very kind today. Quinn and I returned to New York at ten o'clock or so that evening and we had to go around the city to the major papers and instruct them not to publish a story we had previously submitted. That story concerned me presenting a copy of *The Religious Songs of Connacht*[53] to Roosevelt. But on realising that day the type of man the President was, we feared the circulation of such a story would appear to him as self-promotion and self-advancement, and as the proverb says: 'self-praise is no praise.' It took a long time to visit all the newspapers.

Now came the day of reckoning: the great meeting I was to have at Carnegie Hall. It was well publicised in advance. The first-tier box tickets were auctioned in advance at Hoffman House[54] and raised a lot of money thanks to Quinn. He convened the people and appointed Finley Peter Dunne, a man known throughout America as 'Mister Dooley,'[55] to sell the boxes. But when he was not available, they appointed another well-known man to sell them. Some of the boxes went for up to $300. They were 140 Vice-Presidents there, all wealthy and famous people and they were generous with their money when purchasing the boxes. But the second-class boxes were sold to a man who undertook to purchase them for the counties as there is a special society for the Irish counties. This man did not pay in advance since there was no reason to doubt him. On the night of the meeting, however, he reneged on the deal claiming that he had failed to sell the tickets, in addition to returning 150 tickets that he had purchased. This, it appears, was a deliberate effort to sabotage the meeting. The reader will see that a similar ploy was in use against me in Boston. I know well who was responsible in that city and why they did it, but I am not certain who was responsible in New York: was it those who were jealous of the 'Tuxedos', or those who thought the Irish were going astray in following the Gaelic League? The man who purchased the tickets and broke the contract was called 'Finn.' But he was probably only a tool of other people. Either way, it delayed the meeting by some 30 minutes. John Quinn was directing everything; he was standing at the door when the box tickets were, unexpectedly, returned. Fearing that the boxes would be empty and the meeting ruined, what did he do, but went immediately to those who only had standard tickets (which cost a dollar each) and ushered them into the empty boxes. The theatre was now full and none the wiser to what had transpired. The meeting was scheduled to start at eight o'clock, but due to what happened, it was later than eight thirty when it started. Chief Justice Keogh chaired the meeting, and Bourke Cockran[56], a wealthy congressman, and a solid Irishman, introduced me to the crowd. He had been urged beforehand not to speak for more than 15 minutes. He promised and guaranteed that he would not exceed that limit but did not keep his word. He has a fine voice, and he is said to be the finest orator in the States and I believe that. Once he commenced his speech with a large audience listening, he could not control himself, and he spoke for 33 minutes – and speaking all the while on a topic he knew nothing about! When he finished, my friend Patrick O'Shea[57] performed 'Maidrín Rua' and 'Aililiú na Gamhna.' The High-Court Judge Dowling spoke, and proposed a motion in favour of the Irish language and called on me to deliver my lecture.

I began then with my heart throbbing with fear. I commenced in Irish and continued thus for five minutes. Many people understood me, but most were terrified. They thought I intended to continue in Irish for the entire night. I then switched to English and delivered *mutatis mutandis* almost the same lecture I had frequently given at home on the de-anglicisation of Ireland. I spoke for an hour and a half and everyone listened attentively - laughing and praising - to every word I uttered. It was clear that they were of one mind with me, and that encouraged me to deliver my message forcibly. That I did. Commencing in Irish, I said that we were gathered to strike a blow for the poor old woman, but upon my word, I said, she is no longer a poor old woman but a hearty young girl with whom thousands upon thousands are falling in love. While still poor, she is young, beautiful, and attractive. Moreover, there are things worse than poverty. Nevertheless, be she rich or poor, she is our own Ireland, and we are going to raise her. Twelve years ago, we found our country, I said, existing as a province, nay an English county, a small miserable annex; and we are making a nation of her. Tomás Bán and I came here to explain and share what we are accomplishing in Ireland. There is a great difference between Ireland today and Ireland twelve years ago. Then there were but two parties in Ireland; the Lords and the tenants, fighting, knocking and bashing each other. That fight is now almost over, thank God. People are gaining control of the country's land again and the Lords are becoming more Irish since they relinquished their land. At the end of the talk, I said 'I care not a toss for an Ireland with the language, music, sports, dances and manners of the foreigners, she matters little to me as such an Ireland would only be a little English annex, and I'd prefer to live in England proper than in such an annex.' I spoke in English henceforth.

After my lecture, Diarmuid Lynch[58], President of the New York Gaelic League, presented me with an address and it was a lovely scroll. These were the concluding words – I only mention them here as they were prophetic, more or less, thank God - 'May God in all his glory grant you long life and health, O Irish Prince; nor may he call you to Himself until Ireland is free from English oppression.' Who on that occasion would have believed that the English would be gone so soon from the 26 counties and that Irish would be accepted as a national language?

The following day, the newspapers carried accounts of the meeting; they were univocal in their praise and all agreed that no such meeting of Irishmen had occurred in New York since the time of Parnell. If that is true, all credit is due to John Quinn, and to him alone. Tomás Bán and I would never have accomplished it without his help.

Now I should state that I had the support of not only the rich, educated Irish – thanks to Quinn – but the AOH[59] who were also with me, or at least, if they were not, then Clan na Gael[60] were with me from day one and some of them were in every section of the AOH; they were 'the tail that wagged the dog.' They, unlike others, understood the essence of the work I was undertaking.

I was very satisfied the following day with the newspapers and what I heard, as I knew that if I was welcome in New York I would succeed in other locations, for, as I said previously, many of the newspapers in the United States take their lead from New York. But I could not relax. The following day it was on to Hartford, Connecticut.

HARTFORD

Hartford is a big town with some 100,000 people of which some 30,000 are Irish. The meeting was in the Opera House where there was a good-sized crowd but without a collection in the hall after my lecture the League was left in a hole. The event generated $113.85, a small amount, as the only income came from ticket sales. When I was finished, an old Irishman by the name of Cross recited a poem in Irish he had written for me. On realising that the funds collected were so pitiful, I undertook to pay a personal visit on the town's richest individuals the following day. I started with Colonel Donohue[61], a beer manufacturer who promised to assist me; Miss Linehan, and a man named McGovern, an insurance broker. He promised me 200 dollars. Another man, Garvan, also promised assistance. But the colonel plied me with a bottle of champagne until the train arrived and I only had three or four minutes to drink it! I left the matter in the hands of Miss Linehan and Mr Hagerty, the secretary. (Not a penny of this promised money ever materialized!) I returned that evening to New York, hoarse and with a cold, and did not stray from the hotel the following day. My dinner was sent into me. The next day was Thanksgiving, the biggest festival in America, and even if I were able, I could not have accomplished any work.

Boston

A day or two later my wife and I departed New York in the early morning to travel to Boston. I was due to attend a luncheon hosted by the acting mayor[62] on behalf of the corporation and in the name of the city. I received, on the train, a telegram from him, instructing me to alight at Back Bay station[63], as there are two stations in Boston. I acted accordingly and met the mayor's secretary, who brought me to the hotel[64], where I met the mayor himself[65], some 20 of the most prominent educators in the city, and newspaper editors etc., etc. I was about to sit for lunch, quite happy and content, when Tomás Bán telephoned. He urged me at all costs not to have lunch unless I secured an assurance from the mayor that this was strictly an unofficial visit. Boston's Gaelic League, Tomás said, was already divided over my lunch with the mayor and people were very displeased. I was naturally very upset and at a loss on the heel of this news from Tomás. I took the mayor aside and, in private, informed him that I hoped that he was not under any misapprehension that I was involving myself in city politics through lunching with him, as I was well aware of the contest to become city mayor. 'I learned my lesson long ago not to allow anyone to present me as endorsing him over another.' The mayor laughed and told me that he had not invited anyone other than educators and newspapermen. Nonetheless, I derived no enjoyment from the lunch: whatever appetite I had, it was spoiled. Thinking back on the event, I suspect Tomás Bán was unnecessarily alarmed. I think the real concern was the mayor not inviting a certain AOH person to the lunch, who was the President of the Boston Welcoming Committee. He considered it an insult and he vexed Tomás Bán, who in turn vexed me! I later learned that the welcoming committee was waiting for me at the other Boston station, and they considered it a cheap trick to have me alight at the first station. I never fully understood the ins and outs of this, but later learned from reliable people that some of those waiting for me at the other station were of a strong political party and that Toomey[66], the owner of *Donahoe's Magazine*[67], devised the plan to intercept me at Back Bay and thus avoid any potential conflict.

My friend Robinson, the Harvardian, and numerous other educators were at the lunch. I had to deliver a short talk after lunch in both languages but I did not speak well, given my anxious state.

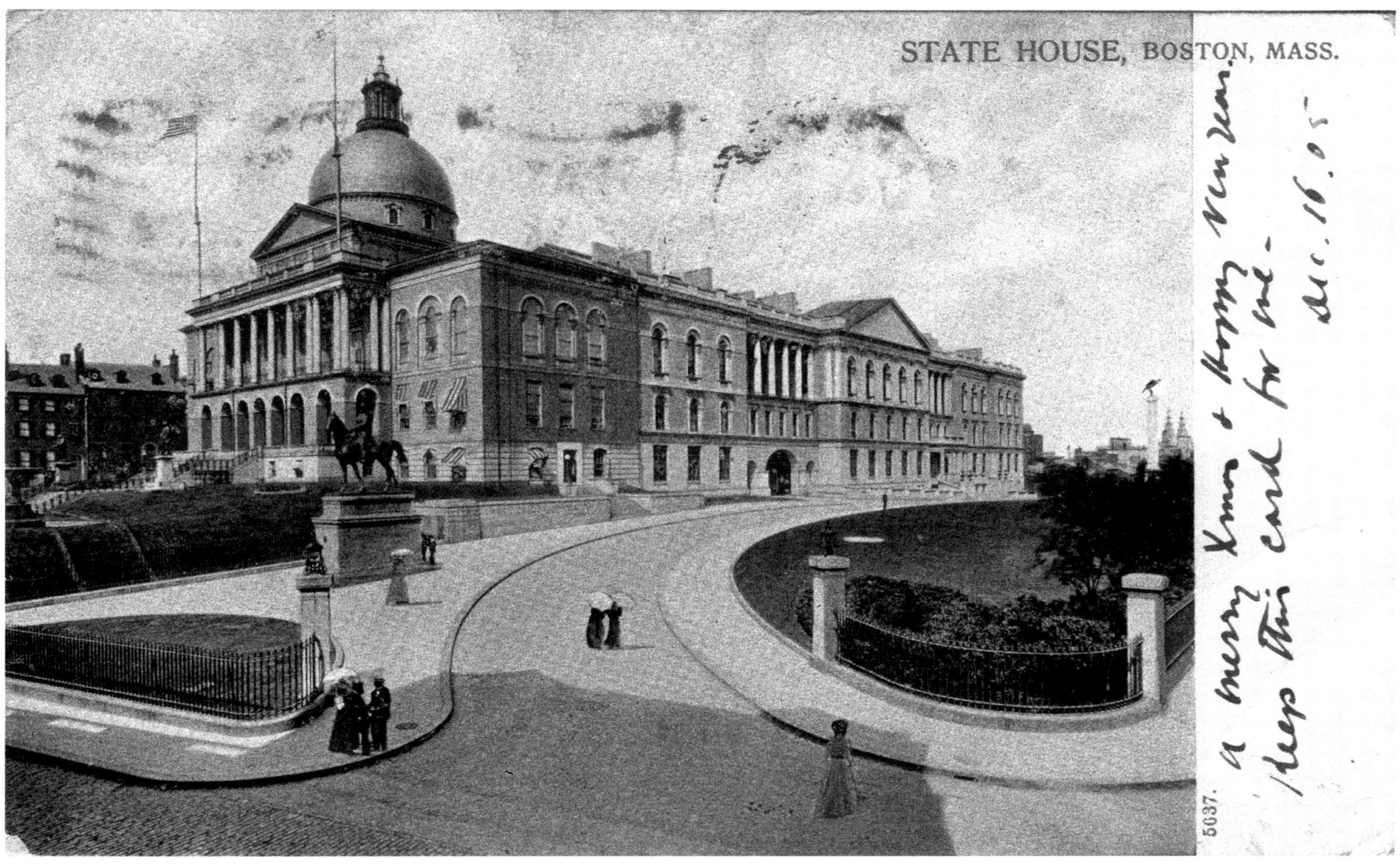
STATE HOUSE, BOSTON, MASS.
5637.
a merry Xmas & Happy New Year.
Keep this card for me -
Dec. 16. 05

Courtesy of Westmeath Libraries (Aidan Heavey Collection)

I was brought to the Touraine[68] afterwards, the most old-fashioned and comfortable hotel in which I have yet been, and I sat until the small hours with the scores of people who welcomed me.

The following day the famous old lawyer, named Doherty, called and brought me to the Protestant Church and introduced me to the Bishop. My wife and I lunched with Toomey and his wife! Tomás Bán was also there and a man from my own county named Galvin. The large meeting was scheduled for four o'clock in the Boston Theatre. It was a terrible day with torrential rain. Nonetheless, the theatre was much more than three-quarters full and would probably have been packed to the doors had not a notice appeared in one or two morning papers stating that the event was slated not for that Theatre but for another Theatre and scheduled for the evening rather than the afternoon. That occurred neither by accident or mischance, it was definitely a deliberate effort to jeopardise the meeting. Numerous people told me who was responsible: the UIL (United Irish League) secretary. Appointed to the committee charged with welcoming me, he was appointed as president of the publicity committee, in order to afford him some status. I learned that from start to finish, he did his utmost to undermine everything and he certainly succeeded that morning. He ensured that the wrong notice did not appear in his own newspaper! That is the version of events I received and I presume it to be correct but in case it is not, I will not name him. I met him myself and I did not care for him.

Silence is golden! I never let on that such a trick like that was played on me. I travelled through all of America and I never told that story to a living soul. It was very similar to the trick played on me in New York when the box tickets were returned after being purchased. I was informed that this man in Boston was jealous lest my meeting would be a greater success that those of his own party.

I spoke for an hour and forty minutes, and I think my words went over well with the audience. All the newspapers were very well disposed toward me. They astonished me when they opened their columns to subscriptions for me before I even arrived, and each of them gave me $100 themselves! Despite this, the event was not a financial success. An envelope was left on each seat for the audience to put their money in it to be collected and then transferred to the stage. We would have succeeded much better had three or four people on the stage stood up and announced that they would give subscriptions. Then the chairperson could have asked the audience to bring up their own subscriptions. But I did not have John Quinn in Boston, and since the financial matters were not better managed, the amount collected was only half of what could have been collected. ($1,783.83 was procured in Boston, but $9,303.53 in total in New York. See Appendix, p. 155).

When the meeting concluded, I was all but overwhelmed by the swarm of people who came to shake my hand and I remained until it was late into the night greeting those who visited me at the hotel.

MANCHESTER

The following day, I went to Manchester, New Hampshire, a large town about a three-hour's journey from Boston. After a hard frost snow blanketed the ground. O'Dowd, an old Gael with an intimate knowledge of Irish-language books and all things to do with Irish, greeted me at the station. There was also a man from Lough Talt in County Sligo with excellent Irish and a vast collection of songs. They were a very enthusiastic pair. There were others, also. They brought me to the Bishop's house, Dr Delaney.[69] He is the Bishop of New Hampshire, and his diocese is as large as Ireland in its entirety. He was a young man, very kind and very generous without any airs or graces. I met him the following day on the train wearing a billycock - a common hat - and smoking a cigar. As the people said: 'The Bishop's a good citizen.' They did not refer to him as 'Lord' either. Bishop was what they always said. I dined with him and then we went to the Opera House. Manchester is a great cotton city. I heard that it boasts some of the world's largest cotton mills. Those mills attracted thousands of French people from Canada. I also heard that there were at least 18,000 French and a little more Irish there. We had a fine escort en route to the Opera House. The Foresters, finely dressed, the Friendly Sons, some of the AOH, and a battalion of the State militia, as well as torchbearers and bringing up the rear, the bishop and myself. I spoke for an hour and forty minutes. My talk fared better than in Hartford. I got $150.

I returned to Boston the following day and went around the city to five of the largest and richest trading houses seeking subscriptions for the Gaelic League. I was refused in one establishment but the others informed me that they would consider the request. I do not think anything came of it. Today, my wife went to the Fitzpatrick family home. Fitzpatrick[70] has one of the largest places in Boston. I left Touraine and went by train to South Hadley, Mass., to Mount Holyoke College.[71] It is a women's college and I was particularly curious never having been to such an establishment before. A female professor met me at the station and without losing a moment, swept me into a

MARSHALL FIELD & COMPANY

STATE, WASHINGTON, RANDOLPH AND WABASH

CHICAGO WHOLESALE, ADAMS, QUINCY, FRANKLIN, FIFTH AVE.
CHICAGO RETAIL, STATE, WASHINGTON, RANDOLPH & WABASH.
NEW YORK, 104 WORTH STREET.
MANCHESTER, 38 GEORGE STREET.
NOTTINGHAM, 20 A FLETCHER GATE.
BRADFORD, 49 PEEL PLACE.
PARIS, 22 & 24 RUE ST GEORGES.
CALAIS, 20 PLACE DE LA REPUBLIQUE.
LYONS, 15 RUE D'ALSACE.
CHEMNITZ, 17 LOH STRASSE.
ST GALL, 34 ROSENBERG STRASSE.

CHICAGO

December 13, 1905.

Thomas V. Concannon, Esq.

New York City.

My dear sir:

As a part of our publicity campaign for the reception of Dr. Douglas Hyde we have arranged to have Dr. Hyde's message to the Gaels of Chicago printed here on the day of his arrival, in the Daily News, both in Irish and in English. As we shall have to make a plate of this message in the Irish language some time in advance, will you not kindly communicate with Dr. Hyde and let him know what we desire. It is necessary that we have the message and the English translation at your earliest possible convenience.

Very truly yours,

J. J. Stokes.

Chairman Publicity Committee.

Letter to Tomás Bán Ua Concheanainn from James J. Stokes, Advertising Manager for Marshall Field & Company. Stokes was also Chairman of the Publicity Committee of the Gaelic Association for the Reception of Dr Douglas Hyde in Chicago. Courtesy of National Library of Ireland carriage and brought me to the college. I had dinner with Miss Woolley[72], the College President. I was unable to see the college that night but I toured it the following day. There is, I think, 100 acres attached to it with large houses here and there in which the female students live. That area is referred to as the 'campus.' They heat one large stove every day that warms each house even though they are reasonably far removed from each other. The stove consumes six tons of coal daily. The place also contains a library, museum, classrooms, lecture halls, etc.

After dinner, all the girls, some 700, came into the great hall and I lectured them on 'The poetic literature of Ireland.' I have often given better lectures but I think the girls were very satisfied with it and gave me a warm round of applause. At the start I made them laugh. 'Ladies,' I said, and then I stopped, and continued, 'I normally start with gentlemen after ladies, but as there is no gentleman here, I will say ladies and Miss Woolley.' On hearing that, an old man at the back, who travelled from Lowell to hear me, shouted aloud, 'I am present.' That amused them further. Once the lecture concluded, the old man would not leave without conversing with me and he presented me a stick he had cut in Florida as a present. On receiving the stick, I mistook it for my umbrella and left that behind, taking instead the stick. The old man was Connor O'Sullivan from County Kerry.

Early in the morning the following day, my breakfast was brought to my room; at eight or half past eight I had to go to the college chapel to see the girls, all gathered together, the majority wearing college hats and dresses with Miss Woolley, as a high priest or bishop in a long black robe, reading a service to them. It struck me, never having seen anything like it before, as quite funny.

Miss Woolley left me in the care of two of the nicest female professors in the college to escort me around. Each spent an hour guiding me around. They showed me every inch of the campus and it was well worth it. I lunched with Miss Woolley and all the girls. The girls themselves served us. I never saw, and I never thought that I would see, anything so similar to what I read, long ago, in Tennyson's 'Princess.'

SPRINGFIELD

After lunch, I departed for Springfield, which is not far from Holyoke. There I met Ó hÉigeartaigh (Hagerty)[73] the finest Irishman I encountered anywhere.[74] I had a good meeting[75] in the afternoon – some 500 people attended – and I accumulated $292 as a result.

After the lecture, three Irishman and a Scottish man accompanied me to their club. These Irish disgusted me but of course I hid my disdain. None of them deserved to be called Irish other than the Scotsman and the others teased, tormented, and mocked him. It was as if they were embarrassed to have any drop of Irish blood in them and I am certain that only the Scotsman understood the League's gospel. That was my impression that night, at any rate. It shook me but maybe I was mistaken. In my opinion they were the worst Irishmen I had yet met.

The following day I visited Ó hÉigeartaigh's house. He has a family and Irish is the language they speak with their father and mother.[76] I fear that they are in straitened circumstances. Springfield is a major armoury producer and generates much of the city's wealth. Labourers only toil for eight hours per day. Ó hÉigeartaigh informs me that there is plenty of poverty in the city despite the surface appearance of prosperity. But thanks be to God, he has his own house and everyone strives to purchase their own house. I regretted parting with this noble Gael.

ANSONIA

That afternoon, I journeyed to Ansonia, Connecticut, a place full of iron and brass works. The majority of the 28,000 people are Irish. The mayor is a Farrell.[77] He met me at the station and brought me to his house. He is a young, cultured, educated, and a very gentle man to boot. He informed me that his people had been in the country since 1640 or thereabouts but he did not believe that he boasted any blood other than New-England or Yankee. I explained to him who the Uí Fhearghaill (Farrells) were originally. He has a large iron works employing 800 people. He has a very beautiful home. He has travelled throughout the American continent, England, and much of Europe, and overall he was the most cultured man that I had yet met. The meeting that evening was reasonable and brought in $101.

Farrell drove me around that countryside in his motor-car. It has beautiful hill-sides, streams or rivers flowing through it, and every hillock is a real hive of every kind of industry. Mills were placed on the rivers originally, and even now, when they are being operated by steam rather than water, the mills and the work remained in the self-same spot.

I returned to Boston that evening as John Quinn was to join me and we were both to visit Fitzpatrick's house where my wife was. I was standing alone on the station platform in the city, unaware of where I was or where to go and obviously lost. An old

511. BUNKER HILL MONUMENT, BOSTON, MASS.
COPYRIGHT 1905 BY METROPOLITAN NEWS CO., BOSTON.
A Merry Christmas & Happy New Year
Keep this card for me
Dec. 16.05

Courtesy of Westmeath Libraries (Aidan Heavey Collection)

Irishman addressed me and told me that he recognised me and that he would direct me. He was born in County Cork, near to Castle Hyde (or Carraig an Éide[78] to give it its correct name in Irish). He then proceeded to sing the entire song, from start to end! (see note, p. 156). After that, he gave me the directions.

Quinn found me and we both went to Fitzpatrick's home. A far-seeing taciturn man and the only Irishman I saw in Boston that I would consider a 'wealthy man' even though more than half of the people of Boston is Irish. He sells ribbons and haberdashery and has a wonderful store. He is an excellent Irishman, ever ready to assist any movement in Ireland. Nevertheless, he was somewhat intimidated by me. He did not know precisely what political views I held. He feared that I was against him, or that the Gaelic League opposed the Parliamentarians in some way. When I explained that we were not in conflict with them in any way, he changed his attitude and gifted me $100. I fear that many people, especially the wealthy, share similar reservations and are suspicious of us; and everywhere I went, I attempted to undo that negative perception. He has a nice house, a wife, family, and a gold medal from the Pope. After lunch, I departed Boston again for Lowell, an hour's journey from Boston.

LOWELL

The snow was deep on the ground. Joe Smith[79], the Chief of Police, met me and brought me to a hotel where we drank a bottle of wine and enjoyed a good meal together. I believe him to be the most ardent hater of the English that I encountered in America. He was lame due a bullet in his foot. It occurred in the American West. He told me how he escaped by stooping in a ditch from where the bullet came until he located a gun and fired a lump of lead through the man who shot him, killing him. We then went to the meeting.[80] There were about 500 people there. He was unsatisfied, however, as he thought the attendance should have been greater. We had supper, and when the others departed, a Gallagher man remained to inform me that it was Smith himself who had sabotaged the meeting; had it been the responsibility of all the Irish Societies or Gallagher himself, it would have been a much bigger meeting. I did not believe him. I received $716 because of my talk.

I returned to Boston the following day to go to Wellesley College,[81] another women's college. Not an hour's journey from Boston, I was there just in time for the 'welcome' Miss Hazard[82], the College President, afforded me. I think this place is slightly larger than Holyoke and in just as nice of a location. I was introduced to a large group and

I had to perform a recitation for them! I dined in the company of Miss Hazard, six women professors, and one man. Among a staff of 110 professors, all are women other than some 12. It differs from Holyoke where there are no men at all. I had a large meeting of the female students, more than 700 of them, and I gave the same lecture about the Gaelic League as I had given at Yale. I didn't spare the English politicians but of course, my audience did not care about that.

One lady told me she was always in favour of Ireland but that she didn't believe there was any value in the language until she heard me and that I altered her attitude. The amount of information they had about Ireland and their interest in our country was astonishing. I think Yeats's visit a few years previously was responsible.

BROCKTON

After breakfast, I returned to Boston and lunched with the Fitzpatrick family. I then went to Brockton, a large shoe-manufacturing town. There is no other place in the States that produces so many shoes. Good wages are available for making shoes, and as shoes were then in great demand, everyone was well satisfied. Some 800 attended my lecture. The city boasts approximately 40,000 inhabitants, many of them being Irish. A doctor Sweeney from Macroom, a fine Irish-speaker, is the heart and soul of the movement there, but I had little opportunity to converse with him. Alderman Gilmore[83], directed the meeting. As it was a dry town, he could not offer me a drink after the lecture. There is a ban on alcohol in the town but he secured a drink in a chemist's shop, and I drank it in my bedroom! It is peculiar to prohibit alcohol in this town while the people of Boston, less than an hour away can drink as they wish. It is a case of the 'local option.' Boston chose drink and this place did not. I liked the people of Brockton very much. I thought them to be the most cheerful Irish I met to date. My talk generated $176.

I returned to Boston early in the morning, and my wife and I departed the city to journey to New York. We went to Quinn's home, as was our habit, and dined with him in the Manhattan Hotel. Mr Brisbane[84] and his sister Mrs Thursby[85], a charming woman whom I met in London previously, joined us also. She wore a widow's dress today, and I surmise, therefore, that her husband had died in the interval. Brisbane is the *Evening Journal*'s editor and a powerful man among the media moguls. He is reputed to be the confidant and adviser of W. R. Hearst[86], the man who controls so many American newspapers. After dinner, we all journeyed to Fordham College, a

Form No. 1.

THE WESTERN UNION TELEGRAPH COMPANY.

INCORPORATED

23,000 OFFICES IN AMERICA. CABLE SERVICE TO ALL THE WORLD.

This Company TRANSMITS and DELIVERS messages only on conditions limiting its liability, which have been assented to by the sender of the following message. Errors can be guarded against only by repeating a message back to the sending station for comparison, and the Company will not hold itself liable for errors or delays in transmission or delivery of Unrepeated Messages, beyond the amount of tolls paid thereon, nor in any case where the claim is not presented in writing within sixty days after the message is filed with the Company for transmission.

This is an UNREPEATED MESSAGE, and is delivered by request of the sender, under the conditions named above.

ROBERT C. CLOWRY, President and General Manager.

NUMBER	SENT BY	REC'D BY		CHECK
345 Ex	Kg	XX	26 paid	120p

RECEIVED at 16 BROAD ST. Dec 14 190

Dated Sx Chicago Ills 14

To John Quinn

120 Bway NyC

Lithographs not here must have them at once also few photographs of Hyde can use Oconcannon any time this month. In Chicago to advantage rush lithographs.

John a McGary

Telegram to John Quinn from John McGarry urgently requesting lithographs and photographs in Chicago, 14 December 1905. Courtesy of the National Library of Ireland

Jesuit university.[87] While Fr Collins[88] is the President, Fr Mahony[89] was most in charge of my lecture. I had intended to discuss Irish poets, but on seeing the number of priests altogether, I decided it better to speak on the Gaelic League, and that is what I did. I did not reach Quinn's home until after one o'clock that night.

WATERBURY

The following day I went to Waterbury, Connecticut, the home of watch-making and every type of jewellery and ornament. I was expected at three o'clock and there was a reception ready for me but I did not arrive until the time the lecture was scheduled to commence in the auditorium. Consequently, they postponed the reception until after the lecture.[90] It was a very enjoyable reception. Some 20 of us stayed up until three o'clock drinking, telling stories, and making speeches.[91] With plenty to drink, eat and smoke, every one of us was more cheerful than the next. A man named Luddy[92] is the heart and soul of the movement here. He is very similar to Ó hÉigeartaigh (Hagerty) in Springfield and O'Dowd in Manchester but he lacks O'Dowd's strange habits. A pleasant little priest named Brennan[93] and the high-school President Wilby[94] were present. Wilby is a gentle humorous man and very Irish in his attitude despite not having a drop of Irish blood in him. He was by my side throughout the reception. There was also an undertaker present, the funniest and most entertaining such man I ever met. He was the master of ceremonies. Everyone present donated a dollar and became Gaelic League members. They were the most educated, most mannerly, and nicest group I encountered since I came to America. I accrued $237.

The following day was very cold. I rode through the town with Luddy and Fr Brennan and we paid a visit on Wilby, the High School President. I returned to New York that afternoon and the following day Quinn and I ventured to the Lawyers' Club[95], where he hosted a lunch for Judge Dowling and Daniel Cohalan. I sharply requested that they send a Christmas present of 1,000 pounds back to the League and they agreed to do so; 'It will prove to the people,' I said, 'that I am working!' I took the day off, and we all went to the theatre to see Sarah Bernhardt[96] in a piece entitled *Femme de Claude*. She was as graceful and light-footed as ever, and the venue was full. I met a man of my own surname who was in the news since I arrived in this country on account of some insurance scandal.[97] He is very interested in French education. He introduced the *Alliance Française* to America. He is a reasonable young man and very rich. We had supper at Beaux Arts[98], and it was two in the morning when we arrived home.

PROVIDENCE

I had to be in Providence, Rhode Island, a large town some five-hour's journey from New York, the following day. Before leaving New York, I visited a throat specialist who washed my throat with some substance and applied an electrical apparatus. I feared my voice would fail, as I had to speak in Providence tonight and in Philadelphia tomorrow.

I reached Providence at six o'clock in the evening and dined with a man named O'Gorman. More than 12 of the most distinguished people in the city attended the dinner. We then drove to the Opera House. The venue was full to capacity. Some 1,200 or 1,300 people attended and they gave good subscriptions as well. I believe this was the best meeting I had outside of Boston and New York. I returned to O'Gorman's house in the company of Fr Walsh. He is a good Irishman, but a better cleric! We had drinks and slept the night there.

I was working in New England among the Yanks, in the towns north of New York until now, but today for the first time, I had to venture south to Philadelphia. Before leaving Providence, Fr Walsh came in O'Gorman's carriage to bring me to a doctor's house, a Sullivan who is a millionaire. The doctor did not attend the previous night's meeting, and I suppose he has no interest in Irish-language affairs despite being a good Irish-speaker. He has a beautiful house, and everything spoke of money. We did not request a subscription, but if a collection is undertaken here in the future, it appears he will give a generous subscription. I have since learned that – from both the meeting and subscriptions – we collected $680 in Providence.

PHILADELPHIA

I departed Providence at eleven o'clock and reached New York at a quarter past three. Quinn met me and straight away drove me to the station. I was just in time. I arrived in Philadelphia at six or thereabout, where some 30 or so of the most prominent Irishmen in the city greeted me. They conveyed me to the Bellevue Hotel.[99] In my opinion, it is as fine as any hotel of its type in New York. They provided dinner then. The company for dinner was very strange. On one side was a minister of the Dutch Protestant Church, or Dutch Reformed Church, as it is called in English; opposite me was another minister – somewhat dour and bitter – with what I considered to be an English accent. This man was connected to the Episcopalian Church. On my other side was Fr Coghlan[100], a gentle old priest from Foxford, County Mayo. In the middle of dinner, the Dutch minister startled me when he announced that he believed that he was the only American who had fired naval cannons at an English warship. He was almost correct in that, as I later learned. He was captain of the guns aboard the 'Jackmel'[101] and had circumnavigated Ireland three times, thus fulfilling Colmcille's prophecy. He did not say why the English war ships did not send him to Davy Jones's locker. Maybe he evaded them in the fog (*The Cruise of the Jacknell*, published in the year 1868 does not describe this incident.[102] They spent 107 days on the sea, 24 days circumventing Ireland and sailed 9,265 miles in total. After nine days at sea they hoisted a new flag, 'the sun beam' and fired their guns in honour of it. I think this is what the minister was thinking of.) I never heard of Colmcille's prophecy but did not say this to him. The sour Minister opposite me who answered to the name Dr Page was the son of John Mitchel's daughter[103], and he bore England the same loathing as his grandfather. Fr Coghlan was another Fenian. There was also a man called Daly present, our treasurer – a rich man, involved in insurance – I believe.

After dinner, we all went to the Music Academy where we had an extremely large meeting, some 2,600 or 2,700 people. After my lecture, $400 in subscriptions was collected, not counting the income from ticket sales. The elderly Archbishop Ryan[104] was in one of the boxes, in addition to the City Mayor[105], an Englishman, and many other city notables. This was the best meeting I had had yet, outside New York. My photograph appeared in the most prestigious city newspaper the following day, and all the papers were favourable.

I was very busy the following day. Dr Coghlan, Garretty, Dr Page (John Mitchel's grandson), our treasurer Daly, and six or seven others brought me around the city in two carriages. We commenced with the Archbishop, who was kind and mannerly while only offering a small subscription. Others had earlier intervened in case he would reduce his subscription to the UIL. After half an hour, we went to the high school where Dr Thompson presides. Several thousand people attend this school and some one hundred and fifty proceed to some university every year. The boys at this school have every facility. They have no cause for complaint! We then went to the Catholic high school[106] that has 400 boys enrolled. I addressed them first in English, said a little then in Irish, and then addressed the German boys in German.[107] I had heard of Pennsylvanian Dutch, but do not believe it is spoken in the city. It was obvious my companions did not understand when the Irish stopped and the German began! I convinced the president to award the boys a half-day holiday. Regarding [the president] Ellis Thompson[108], he is a man who favours freedom for every

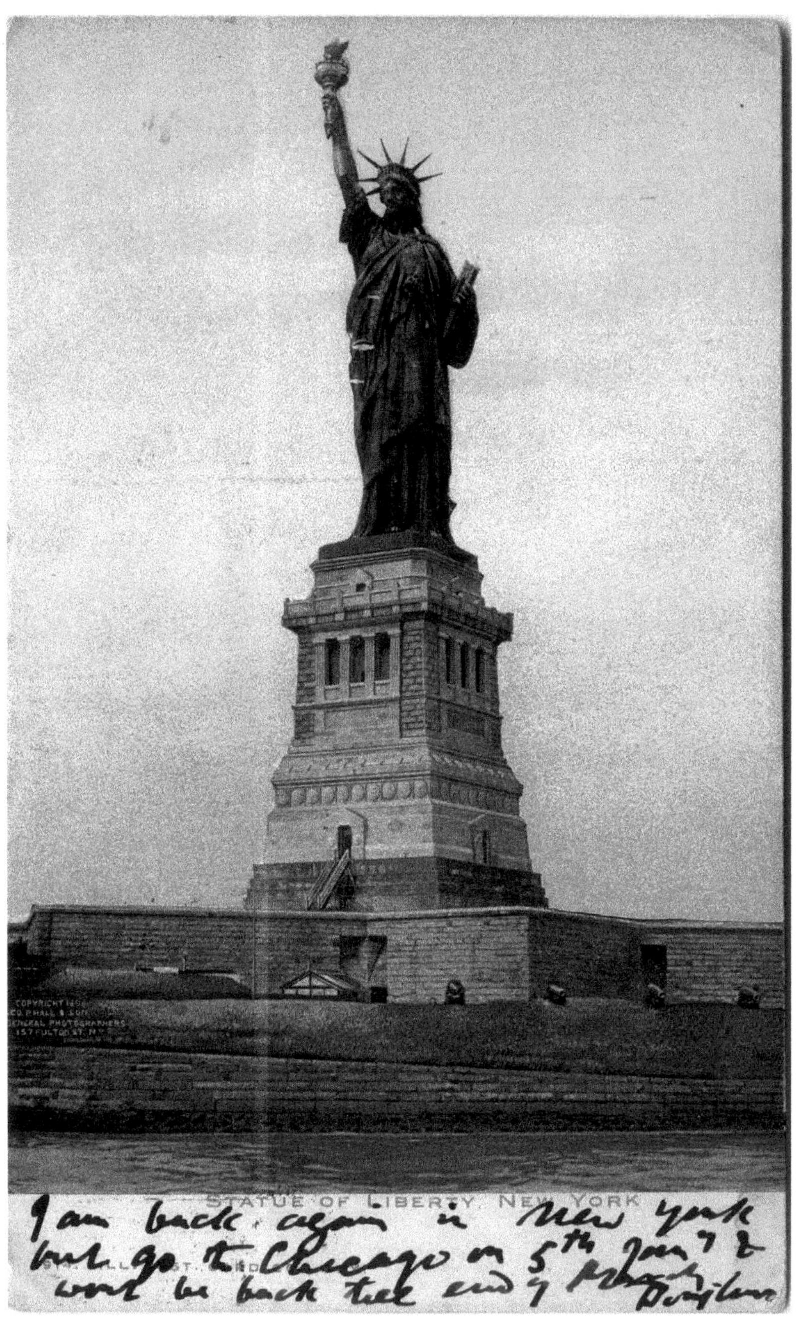

Courtesy of Westmeath Libraries (Aidan Heavey Collection)

country, and he wrote and accomplished much for the cause of Ireland. (He often wrote long articles in the *Irish World*). We then proceeded to the Irish-American Club, Clan na Gael's primary institution in the city. They treated me very well and showed us the entire building. There was an old lad from Roscommon there, Daly was his name I think, who performed a recitation in which he addressed a portrait of Thomas Francis Meaghar that hung on the wall and he shed tears during the speech. But Crossin, is the heart and leader of the Clan na Gael here. He is known as 'Old-Man-Crossin,' and is the finest Irishman, intellectual, and shrewd, without any airs and graces.[109] Very similar to John Devoy in New York. They were all of one mind with me that the Irish language had to be preserved and revived. After spending an hour or two there, we visited Fr Coghlan, a relation of my old friend Coghlan from Foxford, County Mayo. We dined in his house and Mrs Page, John Mitchell's daughter, was present, and we toasted her. Some twelve others were also present. Fr Coghlan is the Gaelic League's heart and soul in Philadelphia. He barely allowed me to depart his home in time for the train that was to return me to New York. Garretty accompanied me the entire journey to New York. He talked the entire journey, describing among other things his own life, how he came to be in America without a penny in his pocket, how he carried a bag for a gentleman from the ship to the railway station and how the gentleman enquired where he was headed. On hearing that he was penniless without the price of a ticket, the gentleman purchased the ticket for him. He has a large liquor store now and is doing very well. He is well respected within Clan na Gael and he gave me a $500 subscription expecting that others would follow his example but alas, they did not! Clan na Gael worked diligently on my behalf while I was in America, and were it not for their support in Philadelphia I fear I would have fared poorly. An effort was made there, as had been made in New York, when tickets were returned at the last moment but Garretty and his friends were alert to the situation and thwarted the saboteurs. While some ten or twelve members of the executive committee were richer than Garretty, none were as generous. We spoke until we reached New York, where Tomás Bán was waiting, at midnight and he took Garretty to his hotel.

WORCESTER

The next day, 20 December, I departed New York again and went to Worcester, something of a five-hour train journey from New York. My old friend Duff, a Canadian from Scotland or a Scotsman from Canada, met me and took me to his own house. He had been in my company long ago in New Brunswick. We went to the theatre where I was to lecture. An AOH group arrived and marched past with their guns and swords. Nonetheless, the theatre was only half-full. After the lecture, I was brought to the Waldo managed by a Mr Rogers and his wife. I had received letters from them before departing for America, and many people came there to pay their respects. I returned to Duff's house at midnight.

It was incredibly cold today, and I liked it, as I was not bothered at all, which left me free to relax and chinwag with Duff. I left Duff at half past two and visited my old friend from the Decies in Waterford, Richard O'Flynn.[110] The poor fellow was on his deathbed when I reached the house, and his son informed me, 'when you were coming, my father commenced speaking in Irish, something he had not done in years and he did not know you were in this city at all.' The poor man willed me his musical pipes, as I have heard, but I never saw them! I bade farewell then to Duff and my friends on the executive committee and departed for Lawrence.

LAWRENCE

To go to Lawrence required going back through Boston again. I shared my carriage with four priests journeying to Lawrence in order to attend the funeral of an Augustinian priest. One of them, Fr Mahony, attended my lecture. My lecture did not benefit from the priest's funeral. Fr O'Reilly presided at the meeting. He was the head of the Augustinian order in the city. He spoke well, following me, and on requesting subscriptions, received a good amount. We collected $215 in this town.

After the meeting, Dr Michael O'Sullivan[111] took me home. Lawrence has five doctors named O'Sullivan, and I was told that there are some fifty doctors and forty Irish-American lawyers in this town. Medicine and law are mainly practiced by the Irish, but the Irish are not faring well in the mills. The English are doing better in those places. Dr O'Sullivan hosted a lovely party and among those present was a doctor named McGovern from County Cavan who spoke Irish well. There was also a man named Coakley, who had attended my first meeting in Cork, twelve years ago and who is now a highly respected Gaelic Leaguer in Lawrence. It was later than two o'clock when I got to my bed.

I returned to New York the following day, travelling through Boston and barely had time to change my suit before I delivered a lecture at Manhattan College,[112] which is governed by the Christian Brothers. I spoke on the topic of Irish-language literature for the past three hundred years. I noticed Thomas Kelly[113], the son of Eugene Kelly[114], the deceased banker in the audience. He is a very rich man. His father, the banker, made his fortune in California when things were starting there. Risking death, he and a handful of others scaled the mountains until they reached that area in which gold was first discovered. There was only a trifling number of people in San Francisco at that time, mainly gold prospectors. He opened a store or a shop and thrived. The houses were all timber made then and people were fond of drink, gambling and every sort of vice. Kelly recognized that the town would burn before long and said to himself that he would go East and return with iron windows and doors to put in his store, in case it burned if a fire came. He and some 12 others left the town with a few Indian guides to cross back over the mountains. All went well until ten or so days into the journey. They noticed that the Indians were very anxious and ill at ease. On investigating, they learned that they feared it was about to snow, 'and if it snows,' they said, 'our footprints will remain on the track and the wild Indians will follow and kill us.' Thus it happened; the snow came and a cloak of snow covered the entire plain. They all huddled around a fire and decided to divide into two groups each taking a different route. They reckoned that if the Indians discovered and followed the trail one group left, they would follow that and the other party would survive. That is what happened. They split up and took different paths. The party containing Kelly survived but neither hide nor hair was ever heard of the other party. Presumably, the Indians murdered them.

Kelly purchased the iron windows and doors, placed them on mules, and traversed the mountains again. He built a stone house and installed new windows and doors. Not long after, what he predicted occurred. A fire broke out and burned the entire town, other than his house. Afterwards, his was the only store and all the miners purchased their supplies from him. He raked money in and soon became prosperous. He purchased some of the land across the bay, which is now called Oakland. It was only wasteland then. Years later, however, as San Francisco grew, he set about laying out streets and erecting houses in Oakland; he discovered that poor people had already occupied the place and had constructed small wooden huts there and he failed to evict them. He had left them there too long in their shanties and that entitled them to a claim on the land. Only for that, he would be a millionaire two or three times over. He returned to New York and became a banker. He was very wealthy and very generous to any movement connected with Ireland. He was the Land League's treasurer until his death. He left two sons after him, one of whom, Thomas, attended my lecture.

Fr Chadwick[115] took us to supper. He had been the chaplin on the war ship the *Maine*[116] when it was blown to pieces but he survived the disaster. He was a fine conversationalist and raconteur. He was entertaining also, and even if a few of his stories called Rabelais to mind, that did not lessen our interest in them! I was very thirsty, there was a nice sweet wine on the table and I believe I consumed much of it. I went to my bed around twelve as I was worn out after the long journey from Lawrence and the exertions of my lecture.

The next day I dined at the Players' Club.[117] John Quinn and a man named Graham hosted the dinner for us and 15 or 16 people in total attended. No speeches were made, but there was plenty of conversation. Everyone had to tell a story. I had to tell the story of the Gaelic League and what it had achieved. The group contained several newspaper people: Paul Elmer Moore[118], editor of the *Evening Post*[119]; Arthur Brisbane, editor of the *Evening Journal*; J. I. C. Clarke, editor of the *Sunday Herald* (who recited his new poem, 'Kelly and Burke and Shea'[120]); Witter Bynner[121] from *McClure's Magazine*, and Richard Watson Gilder, editor of *The Century*. Also present was Munroe, a man who followed Tolstoy as a guide, Malone - an old drama producer - and Van Thorne, my own former student, who now works for a New York newspaper. We passed the time pleasantly chatting, reminiscing until three in the morning. I smoked more cigars than I had for a long time and drank some of what in this country are called 'high balls.' I went home about half past three.

Today is Sunday and we attended the closest chapel. But it resembled more of a meeting place than a place of worship. There was little devotion evident. The only trace of a chapel was the plate that was circulated and the large pile of dollars placed on it. At half-past three I accompanied my old friend Diarmuid Lynch to his own society, the Philo-Celtic.[122] I delivered a long speech in Irish. There were about 100 people present. From there I went to the St Brendan branch (of the Gaelic League). There were more impressive Irish-speakers there than anywhere else I had visited. In particular, there was an old man by the name of Ferriter.[123] He had neither gestures nor a loud voice, but he uttered the sweetest and purest Irish one could possibly hear. I addressed them again in Irish. Then I visited the County Sligo Society, in the same building as the Philo-Celtic. I also made a brief address there. Every county has its own society in America and I am not sure if that is a good or a bad thing. Some argue that it prevents members from uniting as Irishmen and that it divides the good Irish from each other. The Maynooth students in Ireland have the same habit, where each diocese has its own organisation. Moreover, those distinct dioceses do not intermingle. Lynch and four or five others then brought me to a restaurant and provided me with dinner and then we all headed off to Brooklyn. We reached that place between eight and nine o'clock. I visited three other societies and spoke in English and Irish at each and shook hands with all those present, some four or 500 people. It was one o'clock in the morning by the time I was home. I enjoy nothing more than meeting with these Irish-speakers, honest, decent, kind people, the real Irish on whom one could depend despite what jealousy or treachery exists among their leaders from time to time. But, I only meet them on Sundays.

Today is Christmas Day. We were so tired that we did not leave the house until seven in the evening, when my wife and I went to dinner with Thomas Kelly and his wife. As I said previously, we had met Thomas a long time ago in Ireland. Quinn would not come with us and it was only the two of us. It was this Eugene Kelly, the brother of Thomas, who hosted the Metropolitan Club dinner. This Eugene is a generous, kind man. He's married to a Spanish woman from South America but she wasn't with him. It was only the two Kellys, Thomas's wife – a lady from Brittany in France who graduated from Vassar – a beautiful young woman well versed in Greek. Regarding the Christmas pudding, Eugene brought it over from the Orleans Club in London, England, the previous Fall. It was not a great pudding, in my opinion, but he thought it superb given the trouble it took, I suppose! After dinner, we all retired to Eugene's rooms where there was a Christmas tree. He did have a very good punch that he named 'Barbadoes Punch.' He brewed it himself after years of mixing and tasting! That punch was as good to drink cold out of the bottle as it was heated. I had the after-effects the following morning, at any rate. There was only the five of us.

This was the Thomas Kelly who gave a room free of rent to the School of Irish Learning[124] for a long while in Dublin and encouraged Pádraic Colum to persist with literature. Nevertheless, I think his subscription to me was on the small side.

Today is St Stephen's Day but there is no talk of wrens here! Chief Justice Keogh took me to visit Andrew Carnegie. We thought we might be able to convince him to take an interest in the Gaelic League. He is reputed to be one of the two richest men in America. On reaching his house, we were unable to see him for a quite a while, as he was tied up resolving some trading issue. Once that task was resolved, he came and warmly welcomed the judge, a man for whom everyone has the highest regard. He was very cordial toward me as well. He is a small short man with a little grey beard, and of course, he is not at all attractive. Nor is there any limit to his own sense of self-importance. He told us many stories about himself. Here is one of them. He told us that he had received a letter from a missionary in Japan. He was very pleased with the letter and read it aloud for us. The letter writer said that he was sitting in the shade of a tall tree when a young Japanese person approached him and in order to practice his English, commenced thus in English: 'You are a Christian.' 'I am,' said the missionary. 'That is not a good religion,' says the Japanese person. 'Never mind that,' said the missionary, 'would you not agree that there are good decent people in places other than your country?' 'I agree with that,' said the Japanese person. 'Very well,' said the missionary, 'There never was anyone better or greater than Jesus Christ, and I say this even though he was not born in my country but in Palestine.' 'But', says the Japanese person, 'I also have a big great man and he doesn't come from my country either.' 'And who is that?' asked the missionary. 'Andrew Carnegie,' the Japanese man answered.

'Oh ho,' exclaimed the judge and slapped his thigh, 'I know why he said that' and I thought the reason the judge said that was because of Carnegie's large subscriptions to libraries and public education. But that was not Carnegie's interpretation. 'Well yes,' he said, 'but when the last book I wrote was translated into Japanese it sold better than any book ever translated into that language.'

We had a long chat and he gave me a small book with a paper cover that he had written as I was leaving. I was about to put it in my pocket when he said, 'Allow me to make it valuable for you,' and he signed it! He displayed no interest in the Gaelic League until Horace Plunkett's name cropped up. He listened then. He accompanied us to the large door and asked me to call again once I returned from the West. 'Maybe,' I said to myself, 'some good will come of this yet if I'm lucky.' But I never again saw him.

The following day I lunched with the Judge and Charles DeKay[125] at the Delmonico Hotel.[126] DeKay, the president of the Arts Club, wrote a scholarly book to prove that the Greek gods were originally birds![127] Fionn Mac Cumhaill was a bird also, as was Cú Chulainn, and that Fionn was the same as Faunus! He claimed to have found traces of the gods who were birds in Greece, in Ireland, and in Finland, but all traces of this evidence were destroyed in other Aryan countries in Europe. We discussed this thesis, and we spent several hours in debate. We had small little crabs for lunch none of which was larger than a big bee. The crabs live inside oysters and are only to be found in live oysters. When roasted, it is food of considerable interest to Americans. I never heard of, nor saw, them until now.

NEW JERSEY

Today is the twenty-eighth of December (1905). I accompanied my wife to the 'Battery' to view the Statue of Liberty, but I did not venture out to it in a boat. In the afternoon,

I went to Jersey City with Quinn. That city sits on the other city of the Hudson. While close to New York, it is in a different state. Patrick O'Mara, a good man over there and a Clan na Gael man, organised this meeting with little if any assistance from anyone.[128] This was the smallest meeting thus far. Some 250 attended. Nonetheless, Fr McLaughlin[129], the chairperson, asked for subscriptions after my speech and they were generous and forthcoming. $250 made its way up to the stage. I had supper with O'Mara and he crossed the river back to New York with me. It was well after midnight when I reached my bed.

The following day I did not leave the house until evening when Quinn and I went to dinner with John D. Crimmins. He has a nice house and some valuable treasures, including some interesting old letters, one written by George Washington himself. He was writing about a wolf hound. This letter was written in 1788, and the Irishman who answered it, said he knew there was a female hound in the south of Ireland, and a male hound in the north of Ireland but did not know if both would be found together. I believe that Lafayette wanted the hounds and wrote to Washington on the matter and Washington wrote to someone in Ireland. This person mentioned some noble who had these hounds to scare the wolves and drive them out of the area. But I doubt if there were too many wolves in Ireland around the year 1788. He also had two valuable letters by Burns, the Scottish poet. Burns was roundly damning one of the mothers of his many sweethearts. He also had several Irish-language manuscripts. His daughter is married to a Jennings. We attended a large dance at his house. Wealthy Catholic girls were present. Collectively they were said to be worth 30,000,000 dollars; they were all dressed fashionably, but there was none among them that could be described as beautiful. Crimmins's daughter was the pick of the lot. It was after one o'clock when we returned.

NEW HAVEN

The next day I stayed in the house answering correspondence and the following day, the last day of the year, I left New York at four o'clock to travel to New Haven, a journey of a few hours from New York. 120,000 reside here and I suppose 40,000 of them are Irish. A crowd greeted me at the station and brought me to a hotel managed by an Irish-speaker. His mother's Irish was far superior to her English. She was an old woman from County Kerry who had once been Daniel O'Connell's tenant and as a child often spoke with him. We had a good meeting in the Theatre, some 500, but they were the cream of the city. I never spoke better since I came to this country, my strength and energy had returned having relaxed slightly over Christmas. But no subscription was collected from the audience and I fear that the night was wasted. I later learned that the meeting generated $300.

I returned to the hotel, my pockets brimming with cigars that people gifted me! A fine dinner awaited us with some 30 people in attendance. I sat at the head of the table with the city mayor on one side and John Moriarty on the other. He (Moriarty) travelled from Waterbury to hear me a second time having heard me previously. Old Captain O'Brien[130], who escaped from Clonmel Prison in Ireland, came to hear me again also. He had been a rider under Sheridan, sweeping through Shenandoah in the Civil War. Captain Dunn, the father of the Celtic Professor[131], came twice as well. There was one other person but I failed to catch his name. He was from County Mayo but had spent 18 years in prison in England for attempting to blow up the House of Commons.[132] There were plenty of doctors and professional people present. At midnight, they leaped up and welcomed the new year, singing a song I believed to be about Yale. They sang plenty of songs – but songs more concerned with Yale than Ireland! The poor fellow who had been imprisoned in England made a short speech in Irish and then in English. He was pitiful in appearance, broken and beaten down, as if he had lost part of his mind. I heard that the mayor had secured him a job in the city in return for what he suffered. There was a Sullivan present, a lawyer and he was the soul of the gathering. He promised much assistance, but no subscription was collected. Nonetheless, everything succeeded perfectly and I thought it a wonderful meeting given that it was New Year's Eve. It was after half-past two when I reached my bed.

1906 – NEW YEAR'S DAY

I returned to New York, and Captain O'Brien accompanied me to the station. In the afternoon, Quinn and I attended a large party thrown by Charles DeKay. As I said earlier, he is the president of the Arts Club and married to a sister[133] of Gilder, the editor of *Century*.[134] There was a large container full of a liquid known as eggnog and a large wreath surrounding it, in the middle of the table. The hostess was busy filling glasses for everyone in the room. There was a large crowd present, all connected in some way or other with literature or the arts. Nobody interested me other than Mrs Worthington, a woman I had known previously. This party was like none I had ever attended before on account of that there was neither music nor song, and because of the eggnog!

The following day I stayed at home working until evening when we all went to dinner at Byrne's, the lawyer, and his wife. Young Emmet, his wife, and a girl by the name of Mitchell was there and we had a very pleasurable dinner. We returned home about midnight.

It rained heavily the following day. I lunched with Mrs Thursby, a woman I knew previously in London, England. I did not put my nose outside the door in the evening.

I wrote, packed, and prepared to leave today, as the time had come to go west and bid farewell to John Quinn, as I would not see him again until I returned in the Spring. Nonetheless, he had scheduled everything and arranged everywhere I was to speak. I was under his direction and care until I crossed the mountains into California, several thousand miles from New York. John Quinn was the sponsor and architect of my journey; he arranged everything, he scheduled everything, he forgot nothing, he gave generously of his time and resources, and he did all in a spirit of friendliness. I cannot express my gratitude. It was in his home that my wife and I stayed when we arrived in America, and it was with him that we dined every night. He introduced me to the most famous and wealthiest people in the city. Now we were departing, heading west, not knowing what lay before us.

PITTSBURGH

My wife and I left New York on the fourth of January and spent the entire night on the train. A corridor extended the length of the train with beds on the side and light curtains hanging in front of them. There are two beds in each recess, one above the other; the person in the upper bed has to ascend by means of a ladder. It is possible, on occasions, for a woman to be in the top bed and a man in the lower. In the morning, when the train's servants – they are all black men – wake the people, they are certainly the worse for wear. If they could see themselves, they would be ashamed of their unkempt appearance!

Pittsburgh is in the state of Pennsylvania, but it is about 300 miles from the city of Philadelphia. It is the dirtiest and blackest city in America, in my opinion, as it contains large iron and steel works. It is located between two rivers, the Allegany and the Monongahela, and it is in the valleys on the banks of the rivers that the large iron

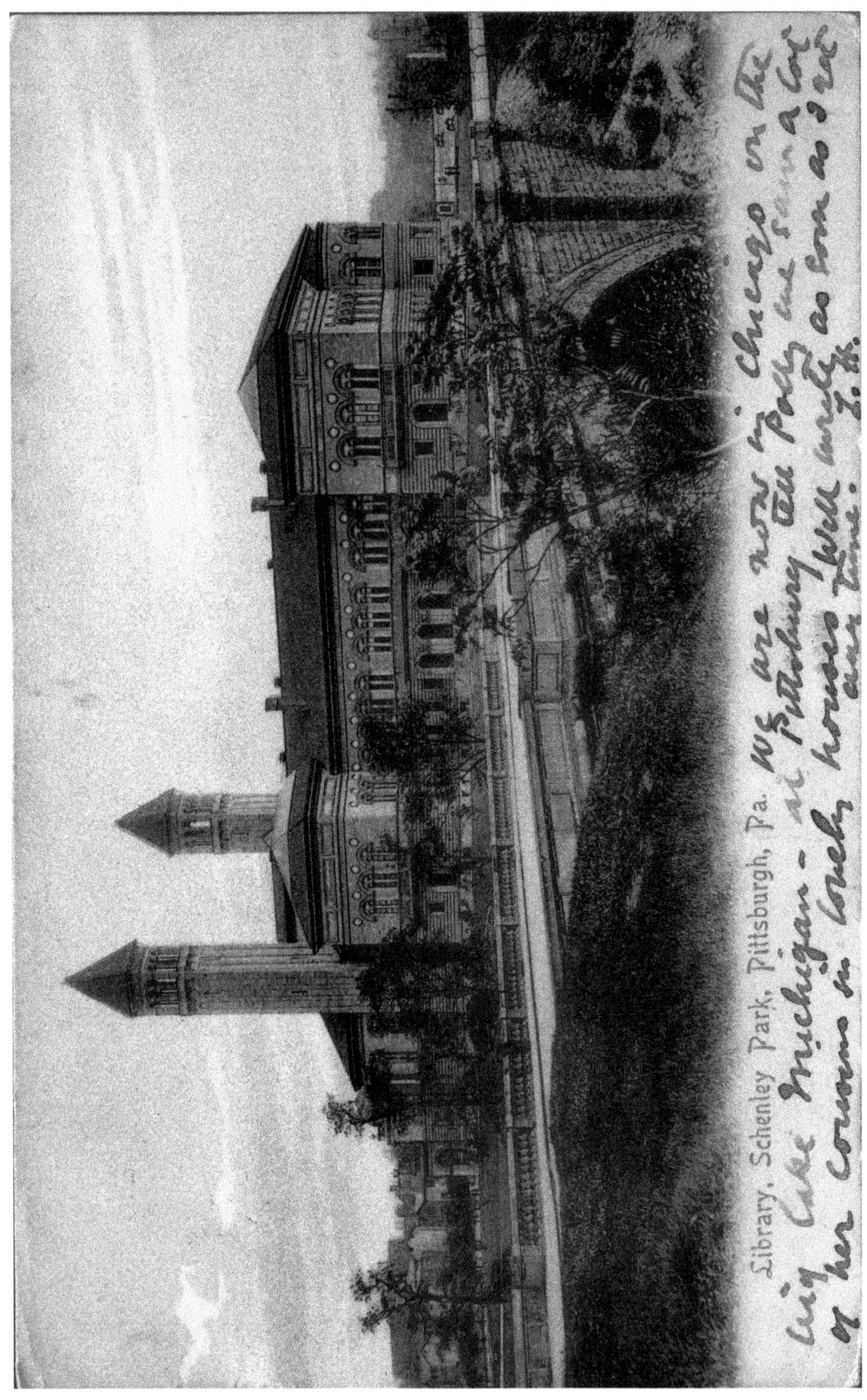

Courtesy of Westmeath Libraries (Aidan Heavey Collection)

works are to be seen. Smoke rises in great clouds and when the sun shines as it sets, it appears as if a flame. I never saw anything comparable. A Frenchman, on seeing it, commented that it was 'hell uncovered.' This is where Carnegie made his money. The city holds some 300,000 people. I do not know how many are Irish, but 50,000 are Slovakians. Anyone from Croatia, Lithuania, and others I never heard of such as the Kreimers, are called Slovakians. Dr Canevin[135], the Bishop, informed me that the gospel is preached in 13 languages in the city every Sunday.

A crowd came to greet me at the station: John McCarthy, Alderman Martin[136], a one-handed justice, and Michael O'Malley, a fine Irish-language speaker. I enjoyed McCarthy greatly. They brought me to the hotel and I stayed there all day, greeting those who came to welcome me. Five newspapermen arrived to interview me. Afterwards, a delegation from 'The Sons of Patrick' presented me with a scroll. They are 300 members in the 'Sons of Patrick', and Patrick is the Christian name of each of them. There is no shame in being named Patrick, they are proud of it and they formed a club. This is the first sign I have seen that the Irish respect themselves, as I do not believe that you would see anything similar among the Yankees in the East.

I dined with a man named Haverty and another called O'Loughlin. One of them is a young lawyer, the other man is connected with Clan na Gael and he invested great effort in preparing for my arrival.

The following day I spent the morning greeting those who came to welcome me. I was then brought onto a tram – or a trolley car as they are called here – which the Tram Company provided free of charge for us. The Organising Committee had arranged for me and some of the wealthiest Irishmen to ride this tram and view significant city sites in each other's company. It did not succeed as a plan. The wealthy Irish, like the crowd in the gospel, began making excuses. In my opinion, they did not have time to waste touring the city in a tram. At any rate, they did not show up. But Fr Toler, Fr Price, Fr Hehir, Miss Hogan and some 12 others accompanied me. The weather was very cold and the wind would cut your nose off. We visited the zoo, where we saw some fine lions but almost froze walking to them! They brought me to the ice rink, the largest rink of its kind in America.[137] There were some 1,800 people skating on ice all under one roof with a band playing music. As soon as I entered, the band struck up 'The Wearing of the Green.'

I was chatting with the Justice, 'Squire Martin' as he is known. He is paid for the basis of the amount of work he does, per 'job.' Sometimes he has up to 4,000 cases per year.

We had a very large meeting in the afternoon, but I never saw a worse venue than the long narrow hall. Some 2,500 people attended but all were seated on the same level.

I was only slightly higher than them, and the back-row seats appeared 50 yards away. I raised my voice, I shouted, I screamed in an effort to make myself heard. I exaggerated, I kicked the stage, I did everything possible to attract attention to what I was saying. Dr Canevin, the Bishop chaired the meeting and spoke as well. Nonetheless we only collected $350. (I did not speak for free. Pittsburgh gave $972 in total).

I almost died in Pittsburgh. I went out in a car with Mr Gaughan, president of the AOH, with a man called Nugent driving the car. He was going far too fast, maybe 40 miles an hour, when we met a horse and buggy. I myself thought there was only an inch or two between the kerb stones on one side, and the buggy on the other side. In Pittsburgh I made my acquaintance with a new drink which they call 'rock and rye,' i.e. rye whiskey, with candy in it. It gave me heartburn.

CHICAGO

The seventh of January. We travelled overnight by train and reached Chicago at eight fifty. A smart welcoming committee greeted me including Tomás Ua Concheanainn, John Dillon's brother William, John McGarry, Dr Crowe, John T. Keating, Barry and many others. They brought me to the hotel, the Auditorium[138], above the lake and kindly allowed us to rest until four o'clock. Then more than 12 reporters and Fr Judge, who used be a professor at Maynooth, called. The meeting was scheduled for eight o'clock in the Auditorium. It was almost as successful as the large New York meeting. I was certain that I would have no voice left after the previous night in Pittsburgh, but thanks be to God, having been allowed to rest in the morning my voice had returned, and I spoke for an hour and forty minutes. The Auditorium was almost full.[139] The papers reported that prelates, scholars, businessmen, and representatives from the Irish Societies were present in the house and when I appeared all jumped to their feet, waving their handkerchiefs and shouting joyously. Dr Quigley[140], Archbishop of Chicago, and Dunne[141], the Mayor of Chicago chaired the meeting. The paper stated that when I spoke in Irish, I laid my finger on the pulse of the old Irish present and when I switched to English, I was called upon from all sides of the theatre to continue in Irish, which received a great round of applause. In the midst of my speech I said that English newspapers were turning the people's brains into mules, and my old friend Fr Fielding rose in his box and called out 'Here's a $100 to fight the mule,' and I believe he received a large subscription – between $10 to $50 – from every priest in Chicago, almost. The Mayor appealed to people to be generous with subscriptions, and he spoke passionately. This is what the newspapers reported the next day. 'At the conclusion of the speech, Mayor Edward F. Dunne did not adhere strictly to the program and invited the audience to contribute to the cause. Men and women rose to their feet in every section of the auditorium and promised subscriptions, ranging from one to a hundred dollars. Some envelopes were circulated among the audience and hundreds of them were stuffed with paper bills. $4,488 came from those envelopes counted on stage and not all were opened. Written on one envelope was 'Ó Chailín Éireannach,'[142] which elicited a happy cry from the crowd.'

Fr Fielding and others returned with me and I went to my bed between one and two, fully satisfied with my labours. Chicago will now be my centre of operations, and I will visit the large towns in its vicinity exactly as I did in New York. I am fortunate, therefore, that I succeeded so well in Chicago and that the papers were well disposed toward me.

The eighth of January. I spent the morning with people who photographed me for the newspapers and greeting those who came to welcome me. In the afternoon, Dr Crowe took us out in his carriage. He brought us in to see a fire extinguishing apparatus. We were inspecting the horses when the bell rang to indicate there was a fire somewhere. The harnesses fell automatically on the horses, the men were seated and the engines out of their stalls within half a minute from whence the bell rang. I never saw anything so swift. As the majority of the houses in the States are made of wood, they must have very good equipment to fight fires. It is no surprise that they are very proud of their equipment. Nine of every ten firefighters are Irish and they are the only department, more or less, not under political control. The Government usually appoints the Chief Superintendent but the others remain without rotation, regardless of who is in government. In the afternoon Fr Thomas Judge[143], editor of the *New World*[144], brought with him a man to record my answers to his questions in shorthand. He spent some two hours questioning me. The conversation was printed in his paper and some of the other papers, word for word both questions and answers. This priest is a capable intellectual man and an excellent speaker. He hails from Ballymote. He spoke well at the meeting in the Auditorium seeking money on my behalf. When I had done with Fr Judge, Fr Fielding, McGarry, Keating and others arrived, some of whom stayed until twelve at night.

MILWAUKEE

The ninth day of January. I departed Chicago to go to Milwaukee in Wisconsin. I reached the town in the afternoon, and a group came to welcome me. Among them was O'Kelly, Rohan and O'Connor. They traveled thirty miles outside the city to welcome me. When we arrived in Milwaukee proper, the state governor was waiting for me. He is a Scandinavian from Norway by the name of Davidson.[145] The city sheriff was also present and an old man named Quinn[146], who was a Fenian in his youth and who never forgave the Church for their treatment of the Fenian movement. I spoke in the theatre in the afternoon.[147] Archbishop Messmer[148] from Switzerland, the State Governor and some 800 people attended.

Wisconsin, where I am at present, is a half-Scandinavian State. It is said that there are 40 Scandinavians for every 100 persons in the State. Nonetheless, it is not as Scandinavian as the state to the north, Minnesota, where a little more than half the people are Scandinavian. I was informed that nobody but a Scandinavian would be governor of either of these two states in future, for if a Scandinavian is nominated for governor, that man would get not only the votes of his own party, but a lot of votes from the other parties because he is a Scandinavian. Therefore both parties have to nominate a Scandinavian. The Scandinavians elected a senator specifically to speak on their behalf. But any Irishman in the Senate is elected not as an Irishman but as an American. Milwaukee is a big city with some 350,000 inhabitants. Almost half are German. It is a major brewing centre and Pabst is the chief brewer. The beer they produce is more similar to the German lager than the beer produced in England or Ireland. German is taught in every school in the city. Many of those who visited me spoke German with me once they realised I knew that language. Many Irish can also speak it. Nevertheless, it is destined to die and I would say that it will soon be finished as when I paid attention to which language the young people spoke among themselves on the street, it was all English. But I was told that German is the primary language of the home.

Kelly and Rohan took me out in a carriage and we paid a visit to the Archbishop but did not see him as he was paying me a visit at the same time. My speech last night so impressed him that he contributed $50. Maybe I won him over by speaking some German and praising the Germans in my lecture. While he is Swiss, he was far more generous than the Archbishop of Pittsburgh, Dr Canevin. However, Dr Messmer is known far and wide for his big heart and generosity.

The tenth day of January. I returned to Chicago in the afternoon and spoke at the Twentieth Century Club at the house of a man named Dr Turck.[149] There were some

120 people present and I spoke about Ireland for an hour. We enjoyed a fine supper afterwards, and they presented me with a wreath of lilies of the valley in the shape of a harp. I reached my bed at a quarter past two.

The eleventh of January. Dr Crowe took us out in his carriage. But it was cold beyond description. Large mounds of ice lay on the shore of Lake Michigan and the lake itself was frozen. The glass[150] was several degrees below zero, and the cold entered our marrow. In the evening, a man named Barry hosted a large dinner at the Union League Club, the finest club in the West, from all accounts. Cudahy[151], the wealthy meat packer from Chicago was due to be there, but sent his apologies after we were seated. He feared, I suppose, that I would lighten his pocket as none of the Cudahy family met with me in any city thus far. Yet there were many other wealthy people there. One of them, named Lynch, promised me 500 dollars after this dinner. He is the president of a city bank here. The dinner was very fancy with plenty of speeches. I recall one. A man named Kavanaugh proposed that the judge deliver a speech, and after the same man proposed that the Attorney General give a speech. I believe the Attorney General was an O'Donnell, and he said at the same time that O'Donnell deserved to be a judge as well. I believe that greatly displeased him as I heard he was an important lawyer earning good money. This is how he commenced his speech: 'Does anyone know how a lawyer resembles a baseball player?' The answer: '*When he fails to make a hit, he's sent to the bench!*' If you saw the Judge's face! However, everyone else in the company roared laughing.

The twelfth day of January. A gentleman named Payne[152] took me out to the university[153] which is some eight miles from here. I gave a lecture to some 800 or 900 students on Irish poets. I spoke for an hour and a quarter.[154] The attendance would have been larger had not the president, Dr Harper died the previous day.[155] He was an interesting man. He and I had corresponded for 14 years.

I spent the afternoon with O'Neill[156], once the Chief of Police, now on pension. It was Fr Fielding who took me out. Every piper, fiddler or musician from Ireland that came to Chicago, O'Neill cornered them and recruited them into the police and in due course collected their music and tunes from them. He produced several large books of the tunes he gathered from these Irish musicians. Tonight, he had gathered dancers, singers, pipers, and other musicians, and they danced and sang and played for two or three hours. Most of them were Irish-speakers and the dancers were top-notch. He presented me with a large book of tunes that he has printed. I returned home at half-past eleven.

The thirteenth day of January. I delivered a lecture to the university group again on Irish folklore. Some 300 attended. I spoke for an hour and 20 minutes. My lecture had barely concluded when I was taken to Sherman House[157] for a Memorial Luncheon of the Fellowship Club. Some 70 people were in attendance with much conversation. I spoke for 20 minutes myself!

I returned, left the auditorium and took my wife and our luggage to the Virginia Hotel[158], where she would remain while I toured the large towns. I boarded the train to go to Cleveland, Ohio, at half-past ten at night.

CLEVELAND

After spending the night on the train, I arrived in Cleveland at eight o'clock in the morning. A crowd welcomed me and brought me to the Hollenden House.[159] Cleveland is a large city with approximately half a million people. Maybe some 50,000 are Irish but they are widely scattered. This is a coal and iron city and there is very little that is not manufactured here. It is a great place for making every kind of object. I met many people who once lived near my own place in County Roscommon. Similarly, I met a man named Maddigan. He has the second-best office in the city, the best being the mayor's office. When he spoke, he thought that I was exaggerating in saying that Ireland was becoming Irish as I claimed. 'And where in Ireland do you come from?' I asked him. 'I'm from Foynes, Limerick,' he said. 'You know the Mounteagles then,' I said. 'Of course, why wouldn't I,' he said. 'Well, I said, were I to show you a letter written in Irish, a letter I received from Mary Spring Rice[160], the Lord's daughter, would you believe that the country was undergoing a change?' I pulled the letter out of my pocket that I had received from her the previous day. Fortunately, the name of the house, Mount Trenchard[161] was printed on the letterhead as he attempted to read Mary Spring Rice's name in Irish. His face coloured and he said, 'That struck my heart; whatever you say from now on, I'll believe you.'

We had a reasonably successful meeting in the theatre[162], with some 800 people in attendance, and collected 600 dollars, but I believe most of the money came from the AOH.

Bishop Horstmann was there and Fr McHale[163] chaired the meeting. In the American fashion, first the chairperson is introduced, then the chair introduces the lecturer or speaker to the audience and says a little about him. Fr McHale had prepared a nice little speech, but the Bishop's introduction was too long and left no time for the poor priest to deliver what he had prepared. He returned the favour to the Bishop at the end of the night. Once I had concluded and while he was seeking subscriptions from the audience, he reduced everyone to tears of laughter by faulting the Bishop. 'That's the second time, he's done that to me,' he said, 'but this time he took the words out of my mouth, it was the best speech I was to ever deliver.' That humoured the audience – other than the Bishop, I suppose – but he enticed people through humour to be more generous with donations.

I often observed that thing: there is no better way to gather subscriptions than to make people laugh while collecting.

The fifteenth day of January. I spent the morning letter writing, greeting those who came to meet me and dined with Fr McHale in the evening. Maddigan and nine priests were in attendance. I felt I was back at home again! There was a young priest, a Power, who was very enthusiastic about the Irish language, and he sang several fine songs for us.

I heard much, while in the city, about an organisation called the Knights of Equity.[164] It was, I understood, a society to concentrate Irish trading and shopping among the Irish themselves. I heard that it achieved much good as long as it lasted but that the knights fell out among themselves and the society dispersed. Their headquarters was located in Cleveland but is now in another city. Politics was at the root of the problem. It is very difficult to keep politics out of any such business! Every ship, eventually, runs aground on the rock of politics!

The sixteenth day of January. I visited the Bishop this morning and he donated fifty dollars. I then departed Cleveland and came to Oberlin in the afternoon. This is a large, famous college with some 1,800 students.[165] No other university in the country is as rigid or as strict: humour and drink are forbidden. The Rev. Mr King[166] is the president and he hosted me in his own home. He brought me to hear four musicians playing some stringed 'smetano' and in case people did not understand it, the meaning of the music was available in a printed leaflet on each seat. According to this leaflet, every note had a special meaning, a far more significant meaning than that of Lord Burleigh in Sheridan's play. I spoke on the topic of folklore in the afternoon, and some 700, both students and professors, attended. Afterwards I greeted those who came to shake my hand. I addressed the faculty on the Gaelic League and answered many questions put to me. I returned, very tired, between eleven and twelve o'clock. The president placed a lit candle in my hand and asked, 'Would you care for anything?' I had often been asked that question previously, and it always had but one meaning: what would you like to drink? I totally forgot the college's reputation and, without thinking, said bluntly 'Well, a small drop of rye, if you have some,' (Whiskey is made from rye in this country. There is also a type of whiskey know as Bourbon, made of Indian grain, but I never liked it, even though O'Neill Russell[167] told me (and he understood the matter) that it was superior.) I did not realise my error until I saw his face. But then he said that his mother-in-law or somebody else in the house was taking it as a remedy, and that he would get some for me, which he did.

COLUMBUS

The president and his wife were very kind to me and allowed me to sleep in until between nine and ten o'clock in the morning. Such an event is rare in this country. As far as I can tell everyone is up and working by seven o'clock. I bid them farewell, and he sent his secretary to accompany me as far as Wellington, and he did not leave me until he ensured I boarded the train for Columbus, the capital of Ohio. I reached Ohio late in the afternoon and lodged with Dr Thompson[168], the University President there. I soon discovered that he was an Irishman, but nobody in the city knew until my arrival. I believed he originated in Ulster. There are some 150,000 inhabitants in the city and some 15,000 are Irish. At 20-yard intervals, an iron arch spans the main street; hundreds of small electrical lanterns are attached to these arches. When lit at night one would think that they were hundreds of burning bridges along a couple of miles of the street. I never saw anything like it elsewhere and it adds greatly to the city at night.

We had a large meeting in the theatre with up to 1,000 people present. The city bishop, Dr Hartley[169], Colonel Kilburn, a war veteran, and many others attended. Dr Thompson spoke well and he humorously introduced me to the audience but no collection was conducted.

The eighteenth day of January. Today, I was shown the Capitol and the Assembly house. In most of the States I visited, Congress only convenes once every two years and even then only sits for a few months. Fear and uncertainty strikes most people in the state when congress sits, as they do not know what tomfoolery they will undertake, or what misfortune will result! They long for them to be adjourned again. That is not, I think, how it would be in Ireland. Were we to have a parliament and freedom of speech, does anyone think a few months every second year would suffice? But, there is no respect for speech in the New World; they are too busy trying to make money and that is not achieved by talk.

Dr Thompson's daughter, who had just graduated, showed me around the university. There are 1,800 students, 300 of whom are women. There is a fine agricultural college as part of the university where sweets are made from the maple trees. One tree

Courtesy of Westmeath Libraries (Aidan Heavey Collection)

supplies roughly one pint of syrup. One pint of syrup requires 40 pints of sap. First, the tree is pierced in multiple places with holes no deeper than an inch, and then the sap seeps from these.

Dr Thompson hosted a lunch for me at some club and invited Bishop Hartley, Colonel Kilburn, Ryan[170], once the Secretary of State, a man of the Joyces, and some ten others. We were all eating, drinking and conversing to our contentment, until somehow the topic of the Gaelic League's opposition to drink cropped up; I said that few people in the Gaelic League drank even a drop other than myself. 'Ah!' said the Colonel – without any trace of an American accent, and dressed like someone who strolled out of a London club – 'That reminds me of a story.' Now I believe that I was drinking less than anyone else was at the table, but as misfortune would have it at that moment, most of the bottles were in front of me. The Colonel looked at the bottles and winked. 'That reminds me of a story that occurred in the small town in which I was born and raised. Cigars were rare then and when a man smoked one, he threw the butt on the street and one of the urchins, that sold newspapers, would seize on it and light it for himself. But in time, that no longer satisfied them, and they decided to form their own club to buy a proper cigar in order to know what the real thing tasted like. Twelve banded together, contributed two cents each, and with that money, they purchased a good cigar. They elected a president, placed him in a chair and put the cigar in his mouth so he would have the first puff. After three or four puffs, they said it was time for the next child to have an opportunity. 'That was not the deal,' said the president. 'The deal was the president would smoke the cigar and the rest of you could spit!' With that, the Colonel winked again at the bottles before me. He left me speechless. I had no response but to stammer, 'I was not one of those people.' When I later returned to New York, I recounted the story to the Knights of St Patrick, when in their company, and they enjoyed it.

After lunch, I visited the *Catholic Columbian*[171] of which Carroll[172] is the editor. Carroll is the Secretary of the AOH in America. A Mayo man named Varley accompanied him. I did my utmost to explain to Carroll how effective and energetic the Gaelic League was, the need for it, and the great national work it was undertaking. I knew that few men in America could do as much for us as he could should he wish to. He was well-inclined and promised help. I have to state here that the AOH were supportive in most of the states, especially, I think, in the central and the western states.

INDIANAPOLIS

I departed Columbus at half past five and arrived in Indianapolis, Indiana between eleven and twelve o'clock at night. People met me and took me to the hotel.

The nineteenth day. This morning I visited Wolf[173], the Methodist minister from Skibbereen, a friend of Irish professor Goodman[174] at Trinity. I believe Sweeney to be the strongest proponent of the Irish language in this city. He was previously a teacher, but is now a wealthy man. He has a German wife and speaks German very well. He was at death's door a few years ago. His digestion was terrible, but he cured himself and regained his strength by eating a few mouthfuls of bran every morning before breakfast. The quantity of saliva created in the mouth before the throat can swallow the bran cures the worst infection. He told me that he cured many people in that manner. Two others who were strong advocates were also present: Quinn, an insurance man, and a man named Donnelly who has a hotel. There was a fine Irish-speaker from the Creggs in South Roscommon who told me that there were 5,000 people, both young and old, a short distance outside Indianapolis who speak Irish, but alas, I did not have time to visit them.

There was another good Irish-speaker there O'Mahony, a member of Clan na Gael but unlike the others, he was not wealthy. I met another wealthy Irishman who I had previously encountered in Dublin. A big tall man who married a woman from Gort. But, as wealthy as he is, he only gave me $10.

People paid their respects throughout the day and we had a large meeting in the afternoon but it was a truly terrible place to speak in.[175] I shouted and roared as loud as I could for two hours to two or 2,500 people. But, I think they were satisfied. I did not go to bed until two o'clock in the morning.

The twentieth day. I stayed in all morning and all sorts and types came to pay their respects. The executive committee arranged a party in my honour that lasted from half past two to half past five in the evening. Thirteen attended and everyone delivered a speech. Sweeney was the best of them.

All, or most of us, visited the great poet James Whitcomb Riley[176], as when I arrived at my hotel the day before yesterday, I found a bouquet of lovely roses awaiting me. He had sent them as a present. The people on the stage last night had presented me with a harp of roses. The harp was more than four feet high and lilies of the valley were interspersed through the roses. I told the committee that the bouquet should be given to him. We placed the harp in the carriage and went in search of the poet. We found him in bed with a large cigar in his mouth and his doctor with him. He had returned from visiting relations in the South and I believe that they had welcomed him royally! Either way, I told him that I brought the harp for him, as no other man in Indianapolis but he could play it. His father or grandfather, I am not sure which, was Irish and there is a drop of Dutch blood mixed with the Irish. He is a gentle, simple, decent man who is very funny. Nevertheless, he is shrewd businessman and is rumoured to have invested much money in houses and property. He regularly received money from the humorous lectures he gave.

Once we left him, I barely had time to return to the hotel, change into evening dress and go to the Athenaeum Club[177], where I was to lecture on folklore. Many of the Irish attended, Sweeney, Quinn, and others, to hear me. A 'reception,' followed at the club afterwards and refreshments, ice-cream, tea, and more were provided.

Lynchehaun[178] is in Indianapolis. The English attempted everything to catch him, but all the Irish combined and thwarted the effort to extradite him. They did so out of spite and hatred for England, but it appears they failed to comprehend the cowardly villain he is. The scoundrel himself said, 'When I die, Indianapolis will be etched on my heart.' He has reason to be grateful to the people of that city. He was on the platform when I spoke and he came to shake my hand, while somewhat embarrassed about approaching. Initially I did not realise exactly who he was but said to him in Irish 'chuala mé caint ortsa roimhe seo'[179] and turned away from him.

It was after eleven when we came back to the hotel: myself, Quinn, Sweeney, Donnelly and O'Mahony. We smoked and drank when someone said – I do not know why – the word 'ghost.' That was a thing that had not entered my head since arriving in America, and I never again heard the word for the remainder of my stay. The States is not for ghosts or spirits! I was amazed, therefore, when I discovered that each of the Irishmen present had had some experience of the other world. And each man was so firm in his belief that there was no point debating it. Nor were their experiences similar. O'Mahony said he rose early one morning in his youth when he and another boy walked four miles to catch rabbits between the cliff and the sea at daybreak. They separated: one of them went to be between the rabbits and the cliff, and the other was to drive the rabbits. When O'Mahony was walking through the tall bracken, he startled a rabbit that according to him, was as large as a horse. The animal ran to the sea and leaped in. He almost passed out. He was ill for a long time afterwards.

Quinn said that he was standing one afternoon outside the door of his mother's house watching the night and saw a heifer or a white cow near him. He paid no attention until he saw it elevate in the air and disappear from sight.

Sweeney saw a white woman before him on the road. She jumped over the ditch and disappeared from sight. He said that other people often saw her in the same spot.

Donnelly had a strange story. In his youth, a gentleman was dying in the neighbourhood, whose family was said to have a banshee. Donnelly and five or six other boys planned to observe the house to establish if the banshee would appear. He hid in the middle of a laurel hedge on the path to the house's main door. The other boys hid in various places around the house. Not long afterwards, they clearly heard the banshee approaching the door, weeping, crying, and striking her palms. He himself heard her as she passed him, and her clothes almost touched him as she swept in the doorway. Terrified, he ran to his companions who, when they gathered, each swore they heard the banshee going out past them in the same way. That was the very moment the ill man expired. During my time in America, I never heard any such stories other than those on this night. It was a strange thing, I thought, as I never expected to find one in a hundred in this country who would believe in such things. Nevertheless, here were four men, businessmen, far-sighted men, rich men – including two millionaires - who believed.

CINCINNATI

I greatly regretted leaving Indianapolis today and went to Cincinnati, Ohio. I arrived there at four in the afternoon. Captain Sweeney, Conroy and a few others came to greet me. I dined with a man named Cavanaugh and I spoke that night in a large theatre. Some 2- or 2,500 attended. I spoke for two hours and when I finished, I received a large bouquet of roses.

Cincinnati can be termed a German city. It has 400,000 inhabitants and 300,000 are German. It was no misjudgement on my part, therefore, to praise the Germans for their traits, scholarship and more. Were the Germans and the Irish to bond together (they both benefit and suffer from the same things), they would burst the Anglo-Saxon bubble in a short period. They are very friendly with one another in this city; they often intermarry and have wonderful families. But I heard a woman say that she would not like her daughter to marry a German as, she said, he might kill himself. Suicide is seven times more prevalent among Germans than other groups. But such is rare among the Irish. Chamberlain sent an intelligent young man to this country to spread his own political beliefs, and Murphy met him in Buffalo. 'Give up,' he said, 'there is no point seeking to develop the Anglo-Saxon relationship or passing laws to render every controversy under the arbitration of certain people. We'll beat you every time.' 'And how will you accomplish that?' asked the Englishman. 'It is easy,' said Murphy, 'We tried it and it is true. Scratch a German and you'll find an opponent of England.' I doubt that myself!

The twenty-second day. I was brought across the river today to Kentucky, which is on the far side. Kentucky in the Indian language is said to mean, 'the dark bloody land.' On my return, I was brought to the Chamber of Commerce and had to speak to the members.[180] The room contained some 100 people, mostly old men and, I suspected, mostly German. I praised their race and their city, I praised their boats, I praised their great river, I compared their land to the 'dark bloody land' I had visited that morning, and I even spoke some German with them. That satisfied them, and I heard that men who had not spoken German aloud for many years, were heard conversing (in German) with each other as soon as I left the room.

When I left these businessmen, three Irishman, Kenney, Cavanaugh and Conroy brought me to the University.[181] A beautiful comely woman welcomed me on behalf of the university and sat at the head of the table. I heard afterwards that she was Polish, but her English was so fluent that I thought her Irish. They had a lovely party, and I was thoroughly welcomed. There was a Frenchman – I do not recall his name – who had come to lecture on behalf of the *Alliance Française*, who was also a guest of honour at the reception.

When we returned from the university, we all went to Conroy's beautiful house. He is a furniture dealer, and also has a big shop in St Louis. He is among the best and most intelligent Irishmen I have met here so far, but that is not to say that he cannot be slightly contrary. He provided wine, and on taking our leave, we went to my hotel, where a party was held for me. The party did not conclude until after nine o'clock, when I had to leave them to go to St Louis. The editor of a newspaper entitled *Men and Women* wanted an interview for the St Patrick's Day edition and brought a shorthand writer with him, but he did not know what questions to ask and could not think of any. Therefore, I composed the questions myself and also answered them. A young German girl recorded the talk and she spoke German well. I asked her if she spoke the language at home. She replied not, other than when her mother or father spoke it to her. I met some other good Irishmen here, Mitchell, Taylor, Mulveyhill, and Hart. It is peculiar that the weather is so soft here this time of the year, and I saw people today working without jackets.

ST LOUIS

The twenty-third. I slept on the train and arrived in St Louis, Missouri at eight in the morning. It is a large city with a population of around 700,000, of which some 200,000 are German and some 100,000 Irish. The ground was covered in snow and the glass read forty degrees lower than Cincinnati yesterday! I was brought to the Hotel Jefferson[182] and given fine rooms. Doyle, a dentist, was the chief-organiser of my welcome. Br Bernardine chaired the welcome committee. I spoke that afternoon in the Odeon.[183] Archbishop Glennon[184] chaired and spoke well. Some $500 was collected but that was poor in a city as large as St Louis. I saw many people from my own district in County Roscommon, from Cloggarnagh, Lisaherca, Carrowgarve, and Ballaghaderreen. A relative of my own, Oldfield Cubbage came from Moberly, a 100 miles away, to hear me. It was two o'clock when I reached my bed.

The twenty-fourth day. Dr Doyle, the dentist, took me out in a car and we visited four people. Then I lunched with the Archbishop, the youngest archbishop, I believe, in America. He is only 43, a tall, handsome man, and very funny. I did not have much conversation with him. He told me that his real name was Mac Ghiolla Fhionnáin. He is famous in St Louis and he is very popular with everyone in the city. It is fashionable to be acquainted with him.

When I departed the Archbishop, I went to the Wednesday Club[185], as it is called, to address 400 ladies about folklore, and when I returned there was a party for me in the hotel. Ninety-four people sat at the table. Many toasts were raised, and as the toasts were given to particular speakers beforehand, the toasts themselves – as usual – were very good. I sat between Br Bernardine and Judge O'Neill Ryan. The judge spoke fiercely and bitterly against the English, and I feared his language would prove detrimental. I discretely asked the chairman to call on me again to speak when the toasts were concluded. He complied, and I acted surprised when called on to speak for a second time. Maybe it occurred to allow me bid farewell to my friends. I used the opportunity to address the issue of politics and explained that all shades of politics co-existed in the Gaelic League and, whatever our political differences, we were united on the issue of the Irish language. I did so without upsetting anyone. The judge noticed nothing. He is a very small man, clean-shaven with a round head and tightly pursed lips. He is a vigorous speaker and the most powerful man in Clan na Gael on this side of the country. He is renowned for his generosity and intellect, and all are well disposed toward him.

The twenty-fifth day. Dr Doyle, the dentist, arranged a special lunch for me in Hotel Jefferson[186], and invited six or seven of the wealthiest people in the city. Among them was Wade, Drew, Nugent, Walsh, and a couple of Germans. None of the company apart from the Germans were interested in anything. If Doyle believed anything good would come from the lunch, he was misled, as he botched it himself. He broached the railways as a topic of conversation, a matter on which the Germans had far more knowledge than him. He proceeded to criticize England and the English in such a gruff and unreasonable manner that his conversation lost all currency. His words betrayed his mind, and that frightens, and even repulses, people on occasions. He is a very peculiar man, and I did not understand him.

When the lunch concluded, I went to Mrs Bailley's house to meet my old friend Mrs Worthington and from there I went to dinner with Judge O'Neill Ryan at his club. Dr Kane, the old Fenian, Br Bernardine[187], and the dentist were there. When the dinner was over, I went to the Christian Brothers' College[188] and gave a lecture to some 500 people on Irish-language literature during the past 300 years. It was after two o'clock when I was in my bed.

The twenty-sixth day. I departed St Louis at nine o'clock in the morning and the judge came to the station to bid me farewell. When conversing I said that I had done my best to bring the Irish and the Germans together. 'O!' he said 'You are a Talleyrand!'[189] With that, a whistle sounded and the train began to shunt, and I did not have an opportunity to tell him that Talleyrand was related to me and my family on my grandmother's side. I did not have the opportunity then or since but I sent word via a friend, if it ever reached him.

I had a high-speed train and was back in Chicago in only nine hours. The terrain is flat, with neither hill nor mount, between the two places. Nothing is hidden from view due to the lack of elevation on either side of the railroad. It is ideal land for Indian corn! The entire land, almost, is under cultivation. The roads, however, are in terrible condition, even in the towns. They are like cattle tracks. The roads, I believe, are the worst aspect of America.

On approaching Chicago, I saw, as I thought, on the left-hand side the first hills since leaving St Louis. Initially I took them for mountains, as the land was so flat, but that was not so. It was piles of the rubble, earth, stone, and shattered rocks excavated during the construction of the great dyke through which Chicago's refuse and sewerage flows. Quarried from rock, this amazingly large ditch remained open, uncovered for some 40 years, and it all flows into a small river; I think it all eventually enters the Mississippi, but I believe most of the dirt filters out and evaporates before then. The damp earth through which it flows along its course absorbs much. Reputed to be the finest piece of drainage in the world, they had little option but to undertake it; they could not pollute Lake Michigan which supplies their drinking water. On the other side of the city lay bare sandy fields, which are worthless. But Rockefeller acquired some of them where he constructed large oil tanks.[190]

On returning to Chicago, I dined with the Murphy family.[191] They were most kind to my wife while I was absent. He is a whiskey maker and is very rich. He has three daughters, lovely girls. My wife was out when I arrived. She was visiting with Miss Adams[192], the woman who performs the most charity in the city. The Englishman John Burns claimed that the two finest things he found in America were Miss Adams and their apple pies.

SOUTH BEND, INDIANA

I had to leave the city again and go to South Bend, Indiana which is some eighty miles from Chicago. Hugh O'Neill, a professor there, met me, along with McGarry and another man, a Sullivan from the province of Munster who speaks a lot of Irish. I went to St Mary's Academy[193], run by the Sisters of the Holy Cross, where I spoke to 500 girls on Irish-language literature. I had not eaten since morning and was weak with hunger. It was after six when I finished and the sisters provided a light snack before I hurried to Notre Dame to lecture on folklore to 500 boys. Once finished, I had a long chat with the president, Fr Cavanaugh[194], and some of the professors. I was exhausted after delivering two lectures – each an hour and a half in duration – and only a few hours between them, all while fasting.

Fr Cavanaugh provided a bed in the college and allowed me to sleep until eleven o'clock. I lunched at one o'clock and was then brought to meet Fr Zahm[195], who probably holds the largest Dante collection in America. The priest is a gentle old man who gifted me a nice small copy of Dante and pleaded with me to translate some of it into Irish. Dante, he said, was translated into almost every language other than Irish. I promised to do so, if I could. (I accomplished that crossing the Rockies when I had a few days to myself on the train).

The Priests of the Holy Cross manage the University of Notre Dame and the Sisters of the Holy Cross manage St Mary's Academy. While only three miles apart they are not linked other than in name. Indians[196] were here 60 years ago, and, I presume, some of their descendants are still here. In the evening, I lectured in South Bend, the town where the University of Notre Dame is located. 50,000 people live there and it is the leading centre for the manufacture of ploughs and sewing machines. The ploughs are called 'Oliver'[197], and I saw them throughout America. The university serves approximately 700 students, many of whom are Protestants, but they often attend mass with the other students. My meeting in South Bend was the smallest thus far. There were no more than 200 present and no collection.

The twenty-ninth day. I returned to Chicago today. I had a severe headache all day. Murphy served a fine dinner today so that I would baptise his new house that he has constructed outside the city. I named it 'Cúl na Craoibhe' ['Coolnacreeva', lit. 'The Nook of Branch']. Fr Riordan[198], the Archbishop's brother[199], Dr Gueron, who knew Fiona MacLeod (i.e. William Sharp), the Egans, Miss Moran, and others were present.

MADISON, WISCONSIN

The thirtieth day. I departed Chicago at nine in the morning to go to Madison, Wisconsin, via Milwaukee. I reached there at three. The clerk in the hotel misled me as he directed me the long way around, and if not for that, I would have been there long before three. This is a city of 50,000 people. There are many Germans, but even more Norwegians. There is only one university in the state and it is here. I met Professor Brown[200], Dr Robinson's former student. We had corresponded about Arthurian stories when I was home. I lunched with him, before he brought me to President Van Hise's house.[201] Nobody was at home but a servant girl showed me the guest room; I threw myself on the bed and fell asleep. I did not wake until late at night. I left my room and encountered the president's daughter on the stairs; she was unaware of anyone else in the house and took me for a thief! The household dined and I joined them. Van Hise informed me that the people of the state were ready and willing to donate money to the university as its teaching of tillage and related matters offers more to the inhabitants of the state than they spend on it. He stated that he continually strove to unite the people and the university to create a truly democratic college. Dr Mahaffy[202], from Dublin, had visited a short while before me, but nobody liked him. He had nothing good to say about anything in America. This is a fine example of a national university. I lectured on folklore to about 600 people and strolled back to Brown's rooms with him where some of his friends waited. The night was very cold and a fine dry snow blew in the wind; I had to leave Brown's comfortable rooms at one o'clock in the morning. With neither a car nor a coach available, I had to walk and carry my own bag. Poor Brown accompanied me. The station was a few miles' trek and the wind and the snow never abated. It entered my ears and deafened me. I am not certain if I ever fully regained my hearing ability. When I reached the station (or the 'depot' as it is called here), there was no train available and I had to wait several hours until one arrived.

ST PAUL

The train was several hours delayed in arriving at St Paul. I expected to arrive at nine o'clock and did not eat on the train, but it was half past eleven when we reached the city. I looked around at the station but recognized nobody. I hailed a carriage and instructed the driver to take me to a quality hotel, but instead, he brought me to a filthy dark inn. A group came to welcome me and took me to the Ryan Hotel.[203] They would not allow me to eat until they took a photograph, but by then the restaurant had closed and would not reopen for several hours! The cold here is beyond description, the glass is at zero or below and there are two feet of ice on the Mississippi. Yet I am told that this is the mildest winter for years!

This is a large city, with some 200,000 people. Many are German and three-quarters are Catholic. There are 25,000 or 30,000 Irish among them. There are two cities side-by-side here, St Paul and Minneapolis. Only four or five miles separate them and they should be one city but they are very jealous of each other. St Paul is at the head of the Mississippi, where the shipping commences, and that advantage made it a thriving city. A boat can travel from St Paul to the mouth of the Mississippi in Orleans. But Minneapolis contains large flour mills and is the flour capital of America. There are many Scandinavians here. Slightly more than half of the people in the State of Minnesota are Scandinavians. At least three-quarters or two-thirds of the women seen in the city have hair the colour of ash.

We had a wonderfully big meeting in the afternoon.[204] There was hardly any standing room and I would estimate that at least 2,800 people were present. Archbishop De Irleont i.e. Ireland[205] was on stage and, by right, should have chaired the meeting, but J. Regan[206], president of the AOH chaired it. He is from Boyle. Quinn wanted the Archbishop to chair it, but that intention, as I heard, created a furore among the AOH's political factions.

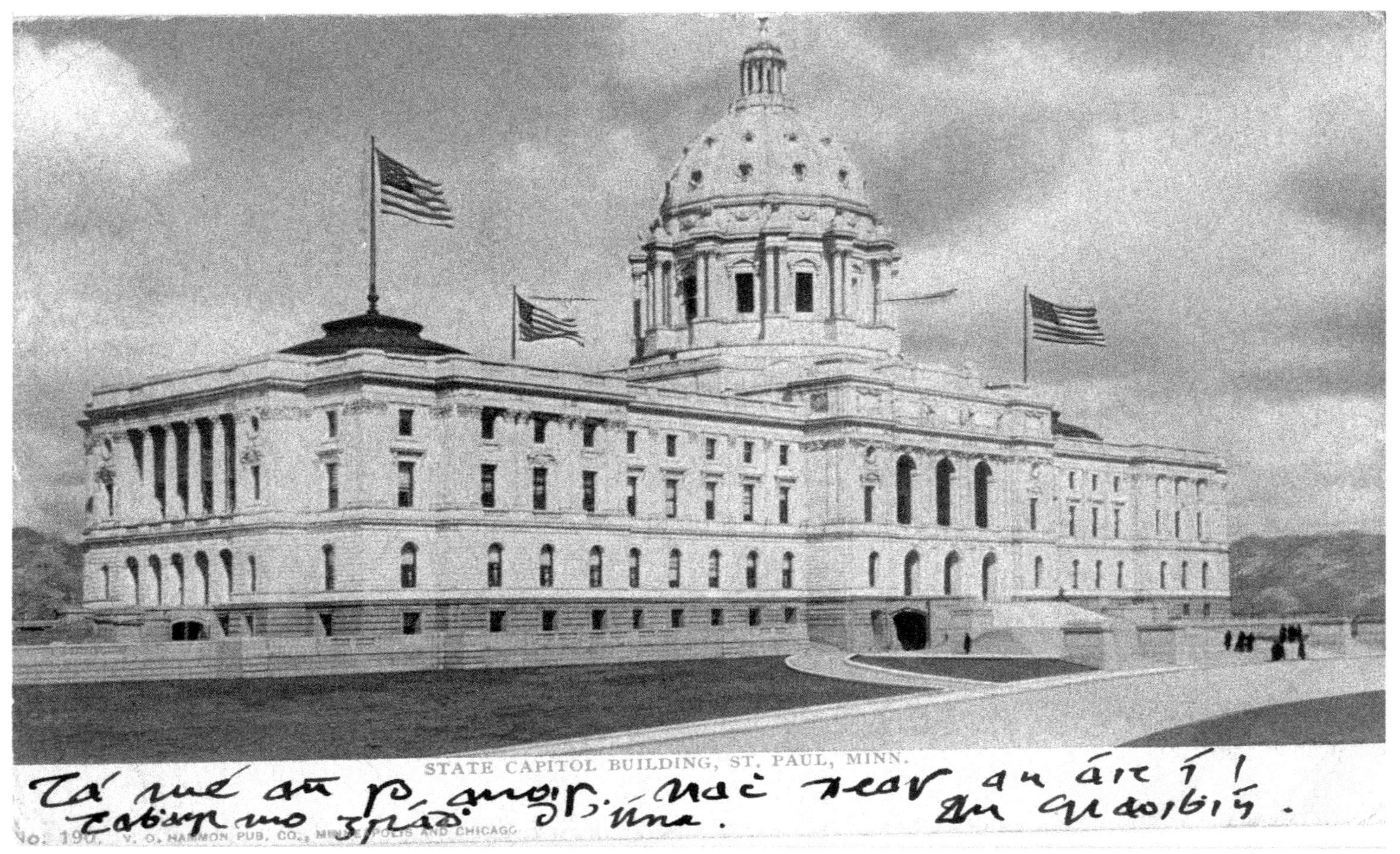

Courtesy of Westmeath Libraries (Aidan Heavey Collection)

The event was free to the public, but without a collection. I spoke for more than two hours.

I met people from my own abode in County Roscommon, from Cartron and Rathkeery, but John O'Brien was the finest among them and the man I most enjoyed meeting. He was the only man I ever met who would hunt wild ducks with a bow and arrow. The arrowhead was dull rather than a sharp point. Now a lawyer, he was born and raised on an island among the Indians on one of the Great Lakes, and he spoke *Chippewa*[207] fluently. He brought me to his own house where we conversed at length. He was very astute. He received *The Leader*, Moran's[208] newspaper weekly. As he did not speak Irish, he asked me to translate an Irish-language essay in it (*The Leader*) by Fr Dinneen.[209] Typical of Dinneen, the essay was both intriguing and intelligent; that surprised O'Brien as he had thought the Irish language a sham! He could recall a time in Minnesota when there were only 2,200 people in the entire state. In his youth, he was post-master in St Paul and he was able to place the entire city's letters in one cart.

The first of February. I lunched with Archbishop Ireland and some nine or ten others. The Archbishop is very kind and humorous, and numerous amusing stories were told. He is a fine, open-minded American, so liberal that he is disliked by those more narrow-minded than him. He did his best to entice the Irish westwards, when land was available almost free at that time.[210] Had he succeeded, the Irish would now have three or four large states to themselves. But the priests in the East opposed the plan as did the Democrats. They wanted the Irish vote since every Irishman was a Democrat; they, and the clergy, wished the Irish to remain in the large cities once they landed in America. The Archbishop told me of two colonies he had established: one for the Irish, another for Yankees.[211] The Irish colony he named 'Avondale.'[212] When strangers visited to consider if it was a good place to settle, the Irish – ashamed and abashed – would denigrate it and present it in the worst possible light. When the stranger asked why they remained if conditions were so wretched, they replied, 'O! I don't know, I was cursed to come here the first day.' But if the stranger ventured a little further to the Yankee colony and posed the same questions, he would be told 'Can't you see with your own eyes the sort of place it is, it is God's paradise. See the fields, the soil, the view. If you don't settle here, you will regret it forever.' 'That,' said the Archbishop 'is the difference, or part of the difference, between the Irishman and the Yankee.'

Around 1866, a serious effort was made, I was told, to direct the Irish who were flowing in their scores of thousands, to the Western states. A great meeting was convened in New York to discuss the effort; most of the bishops and Irish leaders favoured it. Archbishop Hughes[213] made a powerful speech opposing the venture for fear the Irish would lose their nationality and religion were they to be 'planted.' I think this was a great pity. A great many lost their race and religion, not to mention their health, in the Eastern cities; had they moved then to the large Western plains, they would now possess a great part of six states and would be rich and independent. Archbishop Ireland and Archbishop Spalding[214] did their utmost but did not succeed very well. At that time, much of the Western States were considered unproductive wastelands, while now the opposite is true. When the land was broken – at a rate of some four and half miles per year – the rain followed. That is the version I heard, but what I presume to be true is that, once ploughed, the land absorbed the rain as it had not prior to cultivation; it transformed into good land rather than bad land, which had been its reputation. John O'Brien strongly criticized the error in not enticing the Irish westwards. I heard, although I cannot recall if it was from John O'Brien I heard it, that Rome wanted to condemn the Knights of Labour[215] as a secret organisation. Archbishop Ireland, Archbishop Riordan[216] and Bishop Spalding[217] went to Cardinal Gibbons[218] in Baltimore and asked him to lend his name along with theirs against the society's condemnation. He was not happy, but when pressure was put on him, he signed while saying 'Gentlemen, I'm ruined by you all.' Rather than damage him, however, it earned him the people's respect and love and he became more powerful than ever. A Cardinal from Rome is currently in America specially attending Church affairs in the country.

MINNEAPOLIS

On returning from lunch with the Archbishop, a Fitzgerald and another man took me to Minneapolis on a trolley car. If the St Paul meeting was large, the Minneapolis meeting was larger still. I believe there were in excess of 3,000 people here. I spoke for two hours and ten minutes but the acoustics were poor and I had to shout at the top of my voice. Fr Harrington, a young priest, and also a good Irishman, chaired the meeting. The elder Fitzgerald did well also. Just before I commenced my speech, I was handed a letter from 'Frederick Stuart,' offering me $25,000 for the Gaelic League. He said it had proved difficult to find a trustee, but that eventually Carnegie had agreed to serve in that capacity. I enquired after this gentleman and was told that a man, calling himself 'Frederick Stuart' had waited for me for a considerable period before I arrived. If he wished to speak with me, he had many opportunities as I remained

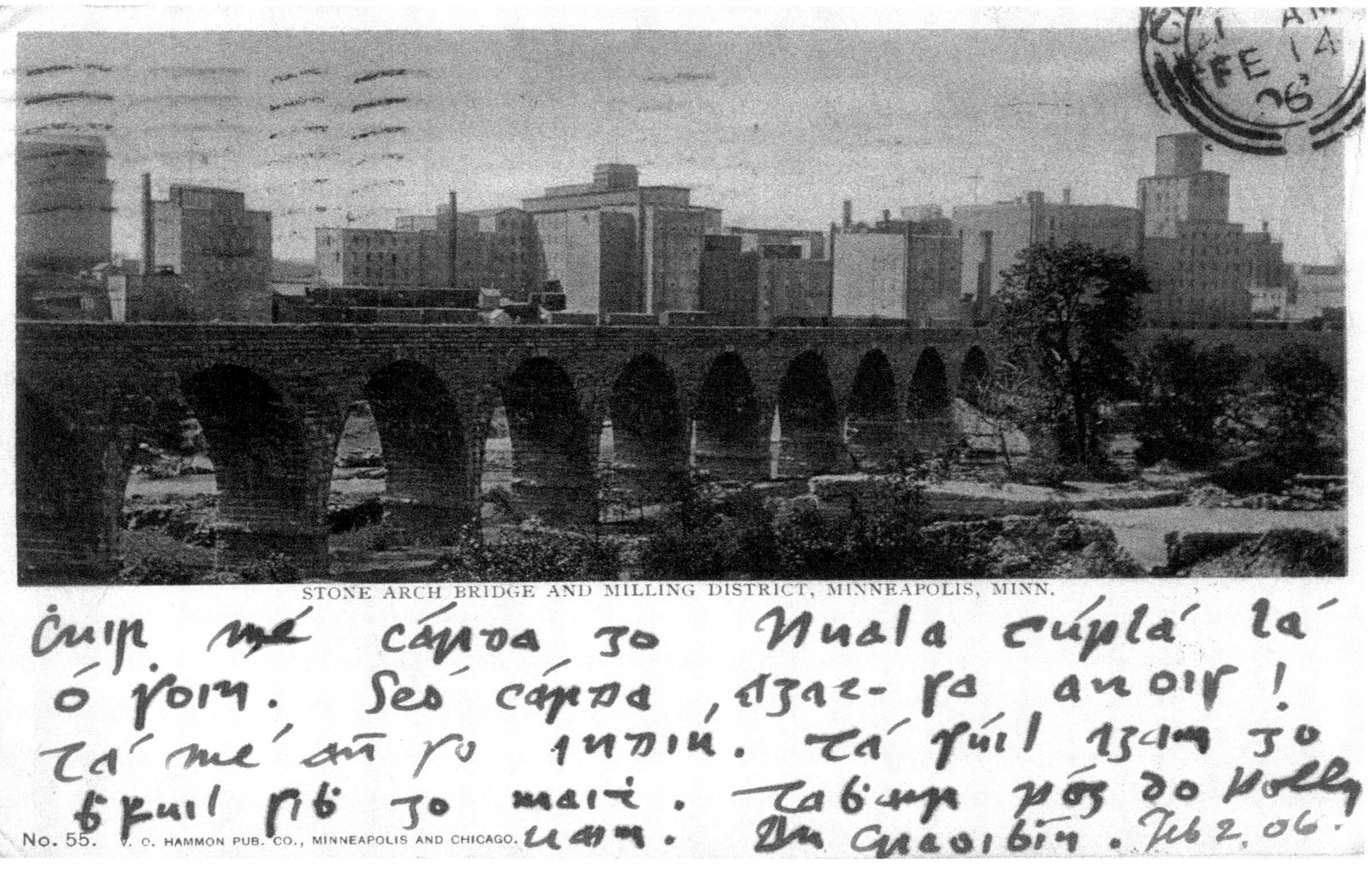

Courtesy of Westmeath Libraries (Aidan Heavey Collection)

on stage a long time after the lecture shaking hands. He could have spoken with me had he wished. I searched the *Directory*[219] but found nobody by that name. I conclude, therefore that it was 'a pipe dream,' an expression used here for such delusions. It was twelve o'clock when I returned to the hotel in Minneapolis.

I spent a good portion of the morning with a tailor, a German or Scandinavian, who has a shop in the hotel at street level. Two Kerrymen, a Lenihan and a Casey, worked there. Casey has a few Irish-language songs that I collected from him. He then provided a piece in English describing Irish-language poetry that I have often used since. (see note on p. 158).

I returned to St Paul at four o'clock and went to John O'Brien's house for dinner. He has a nice wife and two beautiful daughters. By chance, I saw a notice some storekeeper sent to the eldest girl. Entitled, 'The responsibility of beauty,' the notice stated that it was the duty of anyone who was beautiful to have similar paper and envelopes, and such items where only available from the advertiser! Such is how business is conducted in America!

After dinner, I went to St Luke's School where I lectured on folklore. The Archbishop was on stage, as well as three or four judges and other distinguished people. Fr Turner[220] is in charge of the school and he is a brother of my old friend, the Redemptorist, in Ireland.

I returned to O'Brien's house feeling very cold. I made myself a glass of punch for fear I would catch cold. I had not tasted punch since coming to America. It is not drunk in this country and they do not know how to make it!

The fifth day of February. The next day was another cold day and seldom was I as cold. I walked with O'Brien to Fort Shelling[221] (sic.) at the source of the Mississippi. I left to return to Chicago at half past seven in the evening, even though I was reluctant to part with the O'Briens. I slept on the train and arrived in Chicago safe and sound; I stayed the night with the Murphy family. This was the first free day I had in a long time.

The next day was my final day in Chicago and I spent it mostly answering correspondence. Miss Murphy and Francis Hackett[222] typed some letters for me. Hackett is a young man and has done his utmost for me since I arrived. I think he is the editor of an evening paper. His family hail from Kilkenny. He is very kind. We left Chicago to go to Omaha, on our way to San Francisco. Fr Fielding purchased half-price tickets for us. He and Hackett accompanied us to the train. We now depart to the centre of America.

Courtesy of Westmeath Libraries (Aidan Heavey Collection)

OMAHA, NEBRASKA

We arrived in Omaha at eleven in the morning. Before us at the station was T. P. Redmond, a handsome clean-shaven man who has one of the largest places in the city, and C. S. Smyth[223] another handsome whitehaired man. Although young, he had been the Attorney General for the State of Nebraska. Heafey[224], the undertaker, was there as well as Miss Hayden. We went for dinner than evening with the Haydens. Count Creighton[225], a fine old warrior with a white beard and an excellent storyteller was there. He erected the first telegraph between Salt Lake City and Omaha when the Indians controlled the country. He is a wonderful proponent of public endeavours. He built a college, a hospital and God knows how many other things in Omaha. He is very rich. He told stories and sang songs. We had a fine dinner.

The eight day of February. My wife and I dined with Bishop Scannell[226], a Corkman with plenty of Irish. (They say Scan-ell in English, with a stress on the second vowel, the same applied to Mor-an). We went there in the company of Mr Smyth. Then the pair of us went to the convent and from there to the college founded by Count Creighton.[227] The college is managed by the Jesuits. The Count greeted and offered us drinks, and placed a sugar lump in each glass. Such is a habit in this country. I lectured the girls in the convent[228] in Irish and then the Bishop translated it into English! I had a long conversation with the priests. There was a man among them, Stritch[229] who came from the neighbourhood around Ballaghaderreen. There are some 150,000 people in Omaha and some 25,000 are Irish. I met a man named Con O'Donovan and he showed me a large Irish-language book, a manuscript that contained some 80 sermons. I told the bishop that the book should be preserved by some means lest it be lost. I do not know what happened to it. O'Donovan would not part with it. There was another man, Holmes[230], a lawyer. He was born and raised in this country but had excellent Irish. In the afternoon, we had a fine meeting in the Theatre.[231] The Bishop spoke very well in Irish and English. Smyth, who was once the Attorney General, chaired.

When the meeting concluded, we went to a hotel; some thirty people, both ladies and gentlemen and had supper. They then started to tell stories. They are wonderful raconteurs, and are more inclined to tell stories the further west you travel.

The ninth day of February. Heafey took us out in his carriage, driven by a pair of black, spirited horses. Before departing, he gave us a book in which was printed every letter and telegram he had received when his wife died. It is a reasonably large book. I never saw anything like it as a memorial to the dead! He, or his father, was General Hickey's tenant in County Tipperary, I believe. He greatly praised his former

Courtesy of Westmeath Libraries (Aidan Heavey Collection)

landlord. He was very kind to us and then, the Chief Attorney brought us into a court that was in session. A significant case was in progress. My wife and I were admitted as distinguished visitors and seated near the judges, of whom they were two. The jury of twelve were sworn in and I was amazed that there were two black jurors. A man of ill repute, as I learned, named Crow stood accused of kidnapping a twelve-year old boy and detaining him in a miserable cabin until paid so many dollars – 30,000 I think.[232] Nothing in this court resembles a court in Ireland or England. People walked in and out the large door. I believe they also smoked. The jury consisted of very common people. They all appeared poor. Crow himself was dressed better, and more decently, that most of them. It was clear to me, after a while, that he would be acquitted regardless of the evidence against him as everyone, both jury and spectators, appeared happy that anyone secured that amount of money from the millionaire, who was one of those wealthy Cudahy brothers in Chicago. He was, indeed, acquitted.

We have now reached the very centre of America; Omaha is midway between the two oceans, between San Francisco and New York. I had visited the major Eastern cities and had spoken everywhere I was invited and everywhere Quinn and Tomás Bán had arranged for me to go. But the States between Omaha and California are new states without either cities or large concentrations of people. Therefore, we now had to go straight to California, to San Francisco, where Fr Yorke, rather than Quinn, directed operations. Tomás Bán Ua Concheanainn had already departed from St Louis to relax for a few days with his brother and to assist Fr Yorke on that side of the country. We were to follow him having left Omaha. We left Omaha today, therefore, the tenth of February to go to the ocean on the far side of America. Heafey and several others came to the station to bid us farewell and nothing would satisfy Heafey but to purchase chair car tickets for us.[233] That day we passed through terrain in which they were large farmhouses here and there, but they were scarce. The farms were very large. This is part of the land where the Irish should be. There are some few Irish, as I heard, among these farms but even in the places where they had good farms they are not as plentiful now as previously since they sold the farmsteads to return to the big cities. During the night, I presume, we travelled through more of the same kind of territory.

The eleventh day. The following day we crossed the Rocky Mountains, where desert, wilderness and cold ruled on all sides.[234] Small sage thickets grew through the alkaline soil and a few horsemen were to be seen. White alkaline clay dominated the landscape and neither house nor home nor tillage were visible. This was my first day of relaxation, and I spent the day translating the canto Dante had written about Paolo and Francesca, as I promised Fr Zahm.[235] I wrote it in an Irish *terzetti* and believe that

Courtesy of Westmeath Libraries (Aidan Heavey Collection)

rhyme was never used previously in Irish. We spent the day passing through the State of Wyoming; including Rawlins where my sister[236] has a large farmstead. Upon leaving Wyoming, we entered Utah, the Mormon created state. I was greatly displeased in the afternoon on reaching Ogden[237], on the bank of the Great Salt Lake[238], when two journalists from San Francisco newspapers joined me. Their papers dispatched them 1,000 miles to interview me and telegraph ahead what I intended to do and say. One, Miss Jolliffe[239], was a wealthy lady who chose journalism as a hobby. The other was an elderly man known as Pop Cahill [pronounced Pop Kail here]. The train crossed Salt Lake on a causeway[240], constructed on posts and piles driven into the sand. This causeway stretches some 60 miles across the lake. We crossed very slowly, at walking pace.

The following day, the twelfth day of February, we arrived in the State of Nevada and passed through the Sierra Nevada. These mountains are much grander than the Rocky Mountains. Snow surrounded us on all sides. In case a snow avalanche would damage the track or halt the train journey, a shelter, or defence-wall, made of posts and wood, had been constructed at the highest point of the road, which meant we would not see the best views. This roof continued for scores and scores of miles so that it appeared at times that we were travelling through a hole.[241]

Now trees appeared on the side of the track again and after another while, we arrived in a place with fine trees. We immediately went along by the richest mines in the world, until finally we arrived in Sacramento. This is a journey of some two hours from San Francisco. Sacramento is California's principal city and claims the parliament and the courts, despite being a small place. Similarly, New York is not the State capital, rather it is Albany, a small town further up the Hudson. Fr Yorke and Frank Sullivan[242] came to Sacramento to greet us. Shortly afterwards the great lengthy train on which we were boarded a type of vessel – said to be the largest of its kind in the world – and the vessel and train crossed the bay until we reached the city of San Francisco.[243] There was a great welcome for us there, photographs and portraits were taken until we were exhausted. We were then taken to the St Francis,[244] one of the finest hotels in America.

The thirteenth day. Numerous newspaper people, lots of visitors and photographers called. They continued even into the night; they came and lit some type of powder to provide light for themselves until the room was dark with smoke. We had a reception in the afternoon and we welcomed those who came. Some 200 were present including, Archbishop Montgomery[245] and many ladies were present. James Phelan[246], once the city mayor and one of the richest men in the city, introduced me and then I spoke for a quarter of an hour or thereabouts in response. The O'Growney Gaelic League branch and AOH delegates were also present.

The fourteenth day of February. Frank Sullivan brought me across the bay to the house[247] of Dr Benjamin Ide Wheeler[248], the President of the University of California or Berkeley University, as it is known by both names. It is said that those who named the university were debating what to call it when one of them recited the verse from 'Westward the course of empire takes its way,' composed by Berkeley[249], the famous Irishman, and Bishop of Cloyne. They all agreed to name the university, Berkeley. The president hosted a reception in my honour. Some 120 people attended and it included a large bowl of the finest cold punch I ever tasted. He requested that I make a note in his autograph book and, spontaneously, I wrote a verse from *Laoi Oisín*.[250]

Is í an tír is aoibhne le fáil,
Is mó cáil anois faoin ngréin,
Crainn ag cromadh fá thorthaí a's bláth,
A's duilliúr ag fás go barr na ngéag.

(It is the most pleasant land of all,
The most famous now under the sun,
With trees bending under fruit and flower,
And leaves growing to the top of the branches.)

And it was also true. We had passed from winter to summer when we journeyed through the Sierra Nevada. Leaves on the trees, roses in bloom, thousands of flowers of ever type were visible; it was magical the way winter gave way to summer within a few days. Dr Wheeler was very friendly, especially as he had studied Old Irish on the European continent when he was younger with Zimmer[251] or Thurneysen[252], I cannot recall which. I dined with him and then spoke on the topic of 'The Educational Ideas of the Gaelic League' before some 600 or so people. It poured rain for the remainder of the day and that night I had to cross the bay alone. As my clothes were wet, I developed a cold.

The following day, James Phelan brought us out in his large 45 horse-power automobile to Cliff House at the edge of the sea.[253] This house is perched on a large rock with a beautiful view of the ocean that stretches out before it. About a half-mile or a mile beyond Cliff House, lie bare rocks, rising out of the sea consisting of an acre or two, covered in the most extraordinary animals. Some big seals rested there but the sea

HON. JAMES D. PHELAN

HON. FRANK J. SULLIVAN

DR. BENJAMIN IDE WHEELER

MOST REV. GEORGE MONTGOMERY

lions amazed me most. Some of the lions were as large as the biggest cow I had ever seen. It was amusing to observe them, attempting to come ashore and climb the rocks. We had binoculars and could see them clearly. They may have been further away than we thought but we clearly heard them barking. There were seven or eight lions on the rock with large seals interspersed. We lunched at Cliff House and then went around the Park to see the large grizzly bear.[254] Captured by some large newspaper, it was given to the Park to promote the newspaper.

Once evening arrived, I crossed the bay again. They call this sea inlet the Golden Gate. It extends 40 miles inland; Oakland, the university, and much more rests on the far shore, but San Francisco is on this side. When the English fleet sailed past, looking to plunder the Spanish settlements, in Elizabeth's time, they failed to see this bay and cruised by without any booty.

I dined with Professor Schilling[255] and his wife, both lovely people. He himself is a German and told me that he did his best to unite the Germans so they would not lose their language, literature and culture.[256] He succeeded, for a while, but was then accused of playing politics and his efforts failed. He told me that most of those Germans who accumulated vast fortunes in America were ignorant, uneducated men such as Claus Spreckels[257] in San Francisco. They cared little for literature, language, or anything other than money.

After dinner, I spoke to 1,200 people on 'The last three centuries of Irish literature'. I returned home at midnight, crossing the bay on my own again. It is three or four miles, I believe, from shore to shore.

The following day, my wife and I crossed the bay again and dined with Professor Gayley[258] and his wife. He is an Irishman and worked diligently for Parnell in his youth. After dinner, I lectured to more than 1,000 people, mainly Irish from Oakland on 'The Irish Bards.' When the lecture was over, I was taken to the Faculty Club[259] where beer was provided. No other drink is permitted in the club. I returned home across the bay at midnight with a bad sore throat.

The seventeenth day. I had intended to cross over the bay and speak again at Berkeley today, but I was apprehensive. It poured rain all day and my throat was so bad that I had to stay indoors and station myself above a bowl of boiling water allowing the steam to enter my throat. I did everything in my power to ensure that I was ready for the big meeting scheduled for tomorrow – the first time I would speak in San Francisco itself.

The eighteenth day. Sunday. The day of the great meeting. Thanks be to God my voice returned reasonably well. I spoke for an hour and forty minutes. I had a meeting at a quarter past two in the Tivoli Opera House.[260] No seat remained empty or unsold. Boxes sold for $1,400; the parquet – every single seat – two dollars per seat – and the upper galleries a dollar per seat. Frank Sullivan presented the largest subscription I received prior to this or afterwards, in America –1,200 dollars; and before I departed California, I received $1,000 from James Phelan. But, Phelan did not have the same degree of interest in Irish affairs as Sullivan. We lunched with Phelan before the lecture and Mrs Brooks, a lady who is married to an English Colonel. She is descended from George III, the English king and his wife, Mrs Fitzherbert. She had a wonderful voice. I met her afterwards in London, England. Frank Sullivan chaired the meeting and Archbishop Montgomery was on the stage. The audience was the heartiest I ever addressed. In the afternoon, my wife and I went to a large dinner hosted by Frank Sullivan.

The nineteenth day. I was very happy that my voice had recovered and that I had succeeded so well yesterday. Many of the newspapermen and other people called on me in the morning. After lunch, I accompanied Fr O'Ryan[261], a genial young Irishman who is Fr Yorke's assistant and of the same opinion as regards the Irish language. We went in an automobile to visit Mayor Schmitz and toured around so I could view some of the city. This city was very Irish until shortly before I arrived. Most of the large stores on the main street have Irish names. But the young generation did not care for their fathers' labour, and consequently the stores and even the streets were passing out of Irish hands and into Jewish hands.

In the evening, the Archbishop hosted a grand, lavish dinner for me, something, I was informed, he had not done for anyone else. Some 20 people attended the dinner and, collectively, they were worth half a million dollars. I was seated next to Michael Cudahy, one of the four brothers I was keen to meet as he and his brothers had cleverly evaded me in Chicago, St Louis, and Milwaukee. I think it was his brother's son, who had been kidnapped in Omaha. I believe he is a close friend of the Archbishop and hence he could not refuse the invitation to attend. He is believed to be the cleverest of all the Cudahies and I believe that, as he spoke very well on all matters. He hailed, he informed me, from Callan, County Kilkenny. They came first to America fleeing the famine during the 40s. He was not a bit ashamed to admit it. I benefited from conversing with him, for when I came to Los Angeles where he has a house, he donated 500 dollars for my collection.

The twentieth day. I went to the Christian Brothers' College[262], Brothers of the Sacred Heart, and spoke for over two hours on 'The last three centuries of Irish literature.' There was a huge attendance, more than 2,000 people and numerous rounds of applause. The Brothers brought me home and plied me with food and drink. I

HON. JAMES V. COFFEY

HON. GEORGE C. PARDEE

HON. W. H. BEATTY

VERY REV. JOHN P. FRIEDEN, S. J.

returned half an hour after midnight; the Brothers were most generous and would not release me any sooner.

The twenty-first day. The largest reception ever accorded to a private person (or to anyone, I would say) on the coast was afforded to me tonight. I took this extract from the large daily paper, the *Cronicle*, the following day. 'Seated last night with Douglas Hyde, at the Palace Hotel, were more than 450 of San Francisco's best citizens and it was in all likelihood the largest reception for a private individual ever accorded in the city. There was no nation, class or religion which was not represented at the reception, and all with but one objective: to revive Irish self-respect and to be proud in the knowledge that the land of their ancestors was squarely behind them, similar to the Germans, the French and other nations. Seated at the same table were Archbishop George Montgomery and other clerics, the Reverend F. W. Clampett, of Trinity Episcopal Church, Rabbi Jacob Voorsanger[263] and Rabbi Nerto, Governor Pardee[264], Mayor Schmitz[265], Dr Benjamin Ide Wheeler from Berkeley, Dr David Starr Jordan[266], from Stanford (University), Chief Justice Beatty[267] from the High Court and some other judges. Throughout the hall sat distinguished men, scholars, financers and merchants; all cheered every word uttered about the resurrection of Ireland. The Germans, unable to wrap their tongues around the phrase 'Sláinte na nGael,' replied with 'Gut Heil!' and all clinked their glasses. Chief-Justice James V. Coffey[268] served as toastmaster, as the stars and stripes and the Irish flag hung behind him. The musicians played Irish tunes throughout the evening and, from time to time, the entire gathering joined in the chorus. To the toastmaster's right sat the guest of honour, Doctor Douglas Hyde; next to James Phelan, and next to him sat Governor Pardee. To the toastmaster's left, sat Frank S. Sullivan, Chief Justice Beatty, the Lord Mayor and Benjamin Ide Wheeler. The menu was printed in English and Irish and after each toast there was an Irish-language quotation and the master of ceremonies read these in English.' All the papers praised the banquet and lauded the project.

One thing was amiss with the party. I often observed the same shortcoming at other parties. At the start of the night, the wine flows and drink is plentiful, but later in the night when people are thirsty from talking or smoking, the waiters leave them parched, without as much as a drop. That was a great mistake as the company only wanted a bottle of cheap wine, white or red, to wet their whistle from time to time, but such was not to be.

There were 13 toasts and 13 toasters, and Chief Justice Coffey spoke before every single toast. This judge is a very gentle, noble man and loved by all in San Francisco – except the lawyers! However, he has a low, thin voice and none, other than those near

BANQUET SCENE

The Dr Hyde Banquet held in the Palace Hotel, San Francisco, 21 February 1906

DR. HYDE. BANQUET

sláintí — TOASTS.

HON. JAMES V. COFFEY — *Chairman*

Fallsaċt dlíġ' do ċlaoiḋ go cuṁaċtaċ,
Seáraṁ i dteanntaḋ fann a's faon-lag.
'S caiṫfeaḋ an teann beiṫ ceannsa daona,
Caiṫfeaḋ an neart do'n ċeart so stríocaḋ.

The Midnight Court.

DR. DOUGLAS HYDE

A Ċraoiḃín Aoiḃinn áluinn óig
Is leaṫan do ċroiḋe, is deas do póg;
Mo leun! gan mise leat féin go deo,
'S go dtéiḋ tú a ṁúirnín, slán.

An Craoibhin.

MOST REV. ARCHBISHOP MONTGOMERY — *Civil and Religious Liberty*

D'á ḃríġ sin tugaiġ do Ċaesar na neiṫe is
le Caesar agus tugaiġ do Ḋia na neiṫe is le· ,
Dia.

Naomh Matha xxii.

HON. JAMES D. PHELAN — *The United States*

Foscerd iarsin inaraile indsimór.
Conactar eclaismbic agus dún and.
Senoir clerig leiṫ isandeclais.
Imcomaircis Maeldúin dó:
"Can duit!" ol se.
" Meisse an coiceḋ fer déc di muintir
Brenaind Birra.
Dodeacnomar diar nailithri isinnocian
Condotarrla isaminnsise."

The Voyage of Maelduin.

HON. GEO. C. PARDEE — *The State of California*

'Sí 'n tír as aoiḃne ar biṫ le fáġail,
An tír 's mó cáil anois fá'n ngréin,
Na crainn ag cromaḋ le toraḋ a's bláṫ
As duilleaḃar ag fás go bárr na ngeug.

The Lay of Oisian.

HON. EUGENE E. SCHMITZ — *The City of San Francisco*

Cia an dún ríoġḋa, ró ḃreaġ,
As fós is áilne d' a ḃfaca súil,
'Na ḃfuilmid ag triall 'na ḋáil,
No cia is árd-ḟlaiṫ ós an dún?

The Lay of Oisian.

2

Toasts given at Hyde Banquet at Palace Hotel, San Francisco, 21 February 1906

HON. W. H. BEATTY — *The Judiciary*

Ní cúirt gan aċt, gan reaċt, gan riaġail í,
Ná cúirt na gcreaċ mar ċleaċt tu riaṁ í,
An ċúirt so ġluais ó ṡluaiġte féiṁe,
Aċt cúirt na dtruaġ, na mbuaḋ 's na mbéiṫe.

The Midnight Court.

HON. FRANK J. SULLIVAN — *The Exiles of Erin*

Is fuar í an ġaoṫ orm, cruaḋ-lá Márta
Éire mo ṁúirnín, slán leat go bráċ;
Agus mise ag triall anonn ṫar an tsáile,
Anonn ṫar an tsáile, mo ċreaċ! mo ċraḋ!
Ó tá mé ag triall uait, a ṁúirnín dílis,
Beannaċt agus síṫe ort, a rúin óm' ċroiḋe 'stiġ.
Beannaċt ort go buan, oċ! beannaċt agus míle,
'S Éire 's a ṁúirnín slán leat go bráċ.

An Craoibhín.

JOHN McNAUGHT — *The Press*

Níor ċómráḋ leaṁais ná dubartam bréige é,
Ná dubairt bean liom go ndubairt bean léi é.

The Midnight Court.

DR. BENJAMIN IDE WHEELER — *A People's Heritage*

Is é deir saoṫar Páḋruig ḋaoiṁ,
A's léir-ġuṫ léiġeannta dáiṁ' a's naoiṁ,
Is é deir méin na gcáiṫ-ḃan min—
Go mairiḋ ár nGaeḋilig slán!

Dermott O Foley.

THE VERY REV. JOHN P. FRIEDEN, S. J — *Gaelic in the Colleges*

Ag feadóig an tsléiḃe do ċualaiḋ mé sgeul
Go gcuirfiḋear an Gaoḋal a n-áirde,
Luċt Béarla faoi ċeó a's faoi náire go deó,
Agus sonas a's sóġ ar ár gcáirdiḃ.

An Craoibhin.

MICHAEL O'MAHONY — Fáilte do'n Ċraoiḃín

Ann's an áird-teangaiḋ bí ag bárd agus saoi
Cuirim róṁaiḃ-se na naoi míle fáilte,
Roiṁ mór agus beag, roiṁ óg agus sean,
Roiṁ fear agus bean agus páiste.

An Craoibhin.

THE REV. F W. CLAMPETT, D. D. — *Remarks*

Mo láṁ duit, a ḃráṫair is tréine,
Le fásgaḋ teann téiṫ, mar is cóir;
'Gus tabair dam do láṁ, mar an gceudna,
Táid sgarta le fada go leor.

Padraic.

THE REV P. C. YORKE — *Ireland a Nation*

Riaġail Éireannaċ in Éirinn,
Sin an focal 's milis linn
Focal a ḃfuil éifeaċt géar ann
Focal bríoġmar, focal binn.

An Craoibhin.

3

Toasts given at Hyde Banquet at Palace Hotel, San Francisco, 21 February 1906 him, heard what he had to say. It is no small feat to speak, and be heard, in each of the four corners of that large hall.

Approaching one o'clock at night or well after twelve, as we all listened to Frank Sullivan, I think, speak, the lights suddenly went out and 500 people were plunged into darkness. We could not see our hands in front of our faces. We remained so, conversing with one another in the dark, until waiters arrived with candles. I recall well Fr Yorke's sage words to me that night: 'note how quickly our civilisation disintegrates.' Strike in the right spot and you disrupt it. It came to mind a couple of months later as San Francisco burned after the earthquake; because the 'city's civilisation' was struck in its vital organ. The water pipes burst and the city burned due to the lack of water and most of those fine, generous souls that gathered with me at that party were left without house or home, without bed or dinner. Of the wonderful Palace in which we gathered that night, only the walls stood.

The failure of the lights did not lessen our conversation and we did not depart until after two o'clock in the morning! The following day some people said the soup was cold and the squab poor, but as one paper said, soup cannot be heated for 457 plates, and served hot to everyone; nor can all 457 squabs be roasted to perfection.

The published banquet booklet contained 88 pages, including all the speeches and toasts with excellent pictures of the speakers (see p. 159). Last to speak was Fr Yorke and, in my opinion, he surpassed all the other speakers. But Ide Wheeler, the University President, Dr Clampett, and Fr Frieden[269] S. J., President of St Ignatius College[270], also spoke very well.

The twenty-second day. I was exhausted today with a headache from last night's dinner. A thief and a villain – I did not know he was such at the time – called with his wife and they took us to the Cliff House. There was a beautiful view out over the sea and the bay. This man, Robinson, is a miner. I would advise strangers to this country to avoid anyone involved in gold mining in this country: few of them are trustworthy.

The twenty-third day. I lectured students at St Ignatius College at half past two on 'The last three centuries of Irish literature.' Despite being early in the day, a large crowd, 2,000 people, turned up to listen. The Jesuits brought me to their house.

In the afternoon, we dined with Robinson[271], the miner. There was a nice young Englishman, Grimes, who worked for him there. We dined on three of the finest ducks in the world; 'canvas-backs' as they are known in English, and plenty of wine.

The twenty-fourth day. My wife and I visited San Rafael, a very beautiful place, a few miles from the city, where I lectured female students in San Dominic's Convent. The nuns were very nice to me and gave us a fine dinner. They have a very agreeable

REV. PETER C. YORKE, S. T. D.

place, situated in a beautiful spot. I was to have lectured at the university again today, but Fr Yorke postponed it for fear that it would affect a public talk I am scheduled to deliver in Oakland and, instead, I went to San Rafael. Many people called on me in the hotel.

The twenty-fifth day. Robinson, his wife and Grimes took us by train to the mountaintop called Tamalpais. The train has to twist, turn and wind its way up to the mountain peak, a journey of an hour and a half. When we reached the peak, it was the finest panorama I have ever seen. To the left was the Pacific Ocean, to the right San Francisco Bay, maybe fifty or sixty miles long, and twenty miles, perhaps, across. Tiny islands dotted the bay and on the south shore lay the city of San Francisco. The day was splendid, the view exquisite.

I dined with James Phelan at the Bohemian Club.[272] Mrs Brooks dined with us along with a legate from Chile or Peru, a very amusing and pleasant man. I had met him previously.

The twenty-sixth day. James Phelan, my wife and I set out in his large automobile to San José a journey of more than fifty miles. As the roads are in poor condition, it took us an hour and three quarters. We strolled in Alum Park[273], a charming valley in the district. Judge Whelan and attorney Campbell joined us for dinner. Afterwards, I addressed a group of around 1,000 people in the theatre. Frank Sullivan's wife[274] and several of her cousins from Boston were also present.

The following day we had hoped to continue with the Sullivans to Santa Cruz but it poured rain and were compelled to return to San Francisco.

The people in San Francisco tell me that it is never wet here and when a wet day does occur, with tears almost in their eyes, they wonder at such a day that they have not seen for a year and so forth. However, in my opinion the weather in San Francisco at this time of the year at any rate is as wet as the weather in Dublin during the winter.

In the afternoon, a constable or detective, arrived from the president of the city police with an order from the city administrators to take us on a guided tour of Chinatown and to show us its wonders i.e. the shops, the opium dens, the joss-houses and the place called the Palace of Arts, etc, etc. The detective was very pleasant and would accept no payment nor any token of appreciation from me. In one of the holes in which opium is smoked, we saw an old Chinese man stretched out on a poor old bed made of boards with a cat seated on his chest. The man blew the opium smoke under the cat's nose in order to make it sleepy. He said that the cat would not give him a moment's peace until it went into an opium-induced sleep. He was smoking opium for some 40 years and 'I'm not dead yet,' he said 'but I am velli tin,' i.e. very thin and,

BRITTON & REY, LITHOGRAPHERS, SAN FRANCISCO 562
Mountain Train leaving Mill Valley for Summit of Mt. Tamalpais, Cal., over crookedest road in the World.
We went in this train up the mountain.

Courtesy of Westmeath Libraries (Aidan Heavey Collection)

Courtesy of Westmeath Libraries (Aidan Heavey Collection)

indeed, he was bare bones. Later that night, the detective took us to places such as the Palace of Arts, which is of ill repute. The place brims with every type of picture, mainly daubs, and food and whiskey are sold there. Two German women, speaking a mixture of German and English, sat at the same table as us. One told a rude, funny story in German that I did not fully understand, but laughed as if I did. That did not satisfy them. 'Oh,' they said, 'You are laughing at a story you don't understand.' I left unsure of them. We had another supper around one o'clock in a restaurant that was once a church. We returned home around half past two exhausted by the in-depth view of the sights of San Francisco – thanks to the police! The following day, Fr Yorke and Mr Grimes visited us and we went out shopping.

The First day of March. I had a very good meeting in the theatre at Oakland tonight. I spoke for an hour and three quarters. Fr Yorke crossed the bay with me and we dined with Fr McCue.[275] I met a newspaperman. He had married a girl I had known in County Roscommon who, when poor, had run messages for us. She was now wealthy, and I drank a bottle of champagne with her husband.

The second day of March. The Board of Education invited me to give a lecture at the Tivoli Opera House[276] to all the city's public teachers and the high-school students. After the lecture, the Board presented me with five gold pieces for my own pocket; each piece was the size of a half-crown. Though early in the day, the theatre was full to capacity with hundreds outside on the street unable to gain entry. I addressed a group of 1,200 schoolteachers and a large group of the senior girls from the high schools. There were more than ten judges and distinguished people on stage as well. I spoke on folklore for an hour and a half and fearing that I may not be understood, I made it as simple as possible. Once the lecture concluded, they presented me with the five coins and I spent them the following day buying gifts to bring back to Ireland. Animal skins and furs were available at reasonable prices in the West. I bought the largest bear skin I ever saw for $65. A hunter killed it in Alaska and returned with it to San Francisco. The Chinese and Japanese also have many wonderful things on sale, and I bought knives and daggers made from bone and carved ivory. The Chinese occupy a large portion of the city, not too far from the city centre; the Japanese also have a section near them. Everyone respects the Chinese, but the people do not love them. They call him 'honest John Chinaman'[277] as nobody in America is as honest or as punctual as him when it comes to repaying debts. At the start of a new year, the Chinese will not commence trade until the last penny owed is paid. But the Japanese are different. If the Yank is treacherous, crooked and deceitful; the Japanese man is more treacherous, more crooked and more deceitful. The western people once feared that the Chinese were in competition with them and would take the bite out of their own mouths such was the low pay they required. A large, toxic struggle commenced several years ago to keep the Chinese out entirely. My friend James Phelan, who on three occasions served as Lord Mayor of San Francisco, was to the fore in the campaign against the Chinese. The strongest arguments against the Chinese, claimed their enemies, were that they were pagans who neither sent their children to school, dressed like other citizens, nor saved their money to spend it in this country where they had accumulated it. Rather they brought it back to China and, on dying, would not even allow themselves to be buried in America but had their bones returned to the land of their forefathers. These are strong arguments against the Chinese and only a small number are now admitted. Things were thus, until another group arrived from the East, the Japanese, but none of the previous arguments applied to them. They dressed as Americans; were willing to send their children to school and learn English, and other things taught there; they were fully prepared to erect houses for themselves and to spend their money in America, and they were ready to live and die in that country. Therefore, another reason was required to oppose the Japanese, as the Western whites were firmly opposed to allowing them entry. If America and Japan ever go to war, this will be the major cause. So similar were they that I could hardly recognise where the Chinese shops ceased, and where the Japanese shops commenced, but it was easy to recognise the Japanese themselves with their felt, round American hats in contrast to the Chinese whose ponytails hung down to their shoulder blades. The police feared entering the streets of Chinatown; and when they searched there, they routinely found nothing. But, after the great earthquake, when the city was flattened, a week or so after we departed, the people who were rebuilding the city found buried tunnels and long passages throughout the city, dug by the Chinese, with many white women imprisoned in them. Almost a new city of underground rooms and roads! Everyone in this underground city perished when the city collapsed on top of them.

After my lecture, I brought Mayor Schmitz back to the hotel with me. He had introduced me to the audience. Some members of the Board of Education also accompanied us and I provided them with warm cakes and a few bottles of champagne.

In the evening, we dined with Robinson and his wife and attended a lecture by Fr Yorke at the Emmet Club. Fr Yorke is the best speaker I have ever heard. He has a nice, sweet voice like a silver trumpet. The sound pleases the ear. He starts lightly and gently and entices the audience to laugh and listen carefully. He then proceeds cleverly, describing what he is addressing and at the conclusion, his voice gradually reaches its full capacity; and like a poet, he concludes his speech with a storm of poetic prose of

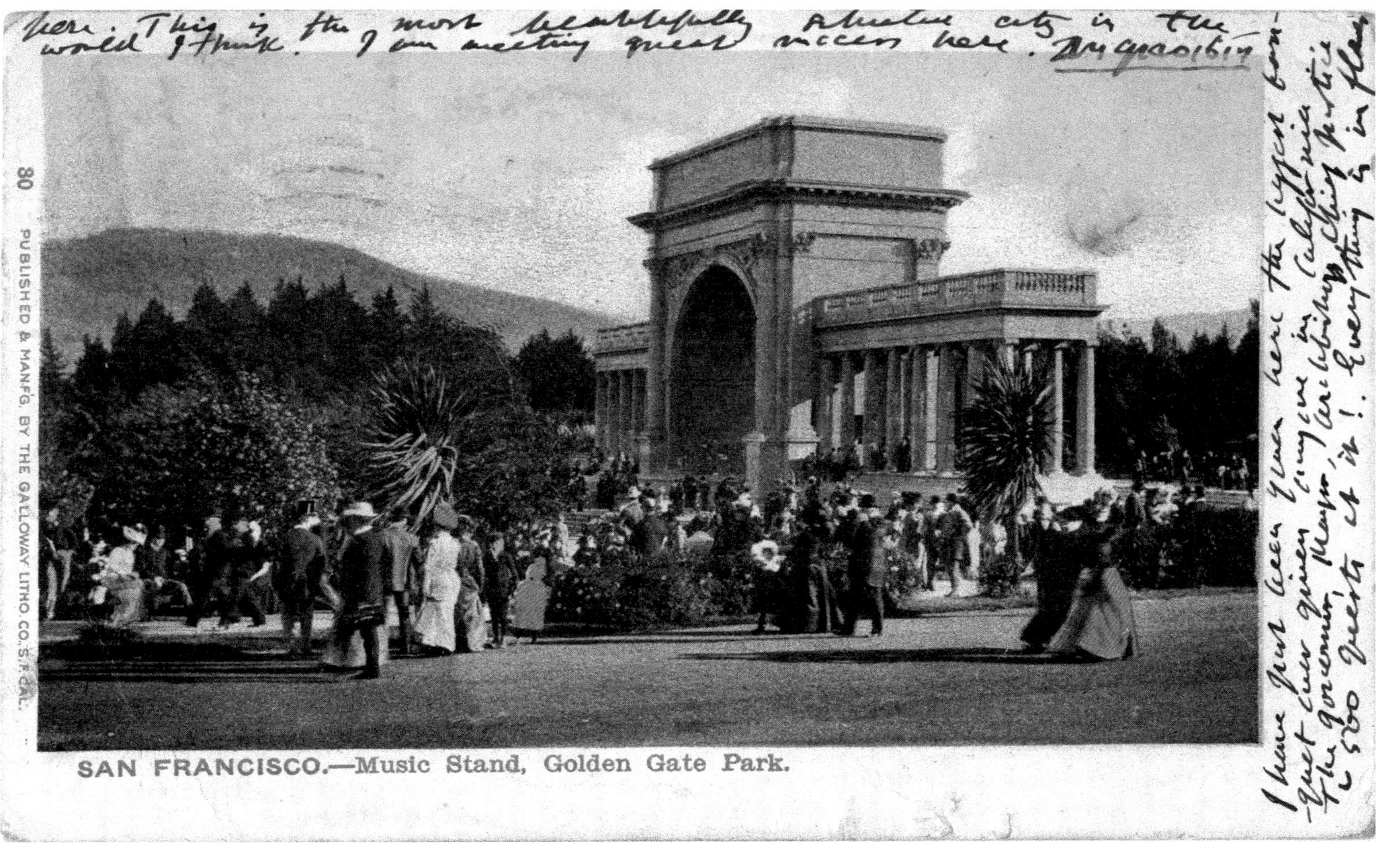

Le caoinchead Chnuasach Bhéaloideas Éireann, An Coláiste Ollscoile Baile Átha Cliath the cleanest and most beautiful kind I have ever heard. Without question, he is the best speaker and the most capable Irishman I have ever met. I returned home at one o'clock.

The third day of March. My wife and I crossed the bay again to the University of Berkeley, where I was to give my final lecture today. We lunched with Professor Miller and his wife. Fr Yorke attended the lunch, and one of the United States Commissioners who had been sent to the Philippines to report on the state of education in those islands. I do not recall the man's name but I considered him very narrow minded.

It was arranged that I would speak in the Greek Theatre, a unique venue in the United States or, perhaps, the world. A roofless, open-air, circular theatre; it has perhaps ten or twenty rows of seats extending around in three-quarters of the arena, each row slightly higher than another. There is a small hillock with trees to the rear; it is constructed so those in the seats can hear every word as if they were in a house. It is designed exactly on the plan of the ancient Greek theatres. Some donor gave it to the university. It was Benjamin Ide Wheeler who thought of building it. He attended each of the four lectures I delivered, and showed me this wonderful venue. But alas, the appointed day was wet and I could not attempt it; and we had to go into a large hall with protection from the rain. Fr Yorke, who is a university officer, chaired the meeting. I spoke on folklore and my speech pleased Fr Yorke so much that he took a copy of my talk and printed it in his own newspaper, *The Leader*.[278] We returned at six o'clock, reasonably tired.

Sunday, the fourth day of March. In the morning, I went to Dr Clampett's church[279], who spoke at the great reception. He is from Trinity College in Dublin but, of course, is a good Irishman. Fr O'Ryan arrived between two and three to take me out to the Park[280] to view a game of hurling and a game of football. I threw in the ball among the players and when the games finished, I made a brief speech: first to the hurlers and afterwards the footballers. I never saw hurling played as well as I saw that day. Many of the players were Munstermen and some had Irish. No game was ever played, even in Ireland, as keenly as that one. The gate of $325 was donated to the Gaelic League.

We dined with the Sullivans in the evening. They serve the finest dinners I ate in this country and, of course, the *unum porro*, the one thing necessary was not neglected. It is a word I heard from a cleric here, but had previously heard at home.

Every time we go to dinner, even if we go no further than three streets from the house, we have to pay four dollars, two going and two returning. The most expensive cabs in America are here.

The fifth day. Fr Yorke, Fr O'Ryan and the editor of Fr Yorke's paper – named Dreddy – visited us. When they departed, we went to the top of the Spreckels Building[281] from where we had a wonderful view of the city and the bay. The German Spreckels[282] is among the richest men in the West; James Phelan is almost as rich. We chanced on Frank Sullivan on our way home and he took us to see items belonging to the people who first came to this country: old flags and antique guns, old arms and clothes. We were looking at them until our feet almost buckled. Then he took us to the Pup[283], a restaurant and he supplied supper and a bottle of champagne. We went back early, very tired.

The sixth of March. I left the house in the morning to go to Sacramento. Fr Yorke met me at Oakland and, together, we went to Sacramento. The entire train boarded a large ferry to cross the water. Duck-hunting season is just over, but thousands and thousands of wild ducks, both 'canvas-backs' and others, were on every side of the train. The train travelled on a road constructed from wooden posts over the water. (After the earthquake several miles of this track disappeared). The ducks were as close as 20 yards to the train and displayed no fear. It was if they knew the hunting season was over. This is wet, low-lying land and most of the train journey passed through water, lakes and meadows. This place is much sought after by the ducks and wild geese. I saw a boy with five or six wild geese he had killed on his back. Except for waterfowl, I do not think this a healthy country.

Sacramento is the State capital, home to the parliament and some 20- to 30,000 people. Fr Ellis,[284] a fine young priest and the Irish-language mainstay in Sacramento, greeted us. He brought us to dinner with Dr Grace[285], the Bishop who hosted a reception for us and was very kind and generous. Many other guests attended, including Monsignor Capel.[286] He was a very capable man, and very renowned in his day. Disraeli includes his depiction in his novel, *Lothair*, under the false name Monsignor Catesby.[287] He converted the Third Duke of Bute[288] to Catholicism. I heard he fell out with Cardinal Manning[289] and was exiled to San Francisco. On reaching San Francisco, he proved himself a great opponent of the Irish and they knew that well. An old Irishman spied on him and reported him to the Archbishop; he was exiled, once again, to this place. He travelled to attend my lecture. He was wearing a badge on which was printed my image and a few words in Irish. This badge had been produced in San Francisco since I arrived there. The Monsignor was polite, pleasant and polished. It is a shame that such a person is stuck in such a remote outpost.

I had a fine meeting.[290] State Governor Pardee chaired the meeting and spoke very well. The Jewish Rabbi[291] was also present and the theatre was full to capacity. When

Courtesy of Westmeath Libraries (Aidan Heavey Collection)

I was ready, Fr Yorke delivered one of the finest lectures I have ever heard from him. He focused the audience's attention in a way I never before observed. We received $900 that night: an impressive amount when one considers how small this town is. We did not fare as well or any better anywhere else if we compare the size of the city. Fr Yorke and I spent the night in Sacramento in a hotel and we had a few bottles of wine that were badly needed after all our work. The word wine refers to champagne in this country. Nothing else is said, but 'wine.'

The seventh day of March. Fr Yorke and I spent the morning driving around Sacramento. I went to the Senate library and the first three items I pulled from the shelves were Irish-language manuscripts! Nobody knows how they ended up there. It was fate that I laid my hand on them. *Quae Regio in terris nostri non plena laboris.*[292]

We departed Sacramento at one o'clock and returned to Oakland at four, where I dined with Fr Yorke and his two curates. He paid me a great compliment. 'I heard you,' he said, 'giving that lecture on four occasions now, and on each occasion, it struck me in a different manner.' He went to San Francisco but I drove to the Christian Brothers' College where I lectured some 2,000 people. It was a mixed lecture, consisting of various parts of all my lectures. The Brothers brought me home with them, where we ate supper with plenty of wine. It was one o'clock in the morning when I reached San Francisco.

The eighth of March. My wife and I, after a poor night's sleep, left San Francisco at eight o'clock to travel south. It was late when I returned to the hotel last night. We had to pack all our clothes. We brought some with us and left the remainder at the hotel.

We were now heading south with the ocean on our right-hand side. We travelled three hundred miles and not a single moment of the journey lacked a spectacular view. In some places, it was the ocean; in others, it was hills, mountains and forests that contained every type of fruit, and groves of evergreen oak trees called *ilex*[293], a tree that thrives here. When the afternoon arrived, we had travelled as far as Santa Barbara on the way to Los Angeles.

We stopped in Santa Barbara and stayed at Potter's Hotel that overlooks a beautiful bay.[294] At night, this building was all alight. There is a lovely pathway to the sea with large palm trees on either side. This area is fashionable with millionaires, both male and female. I never saw so many people with so many clothes or ornaments. Despite the appearance of wealth, I thought there was a foul odour in the hotel. I considered the cause to be a lack of drainage. Despite the size, fashion and appearance, I found it uncomfortable.

Dr. Douglas Hyde Reception Committee

President - HON. FRANK J. SULLIVAN
Vice-President - REV. PHILIP O'RYAN
Secretary - MISS FRANCES X. BARR
Treasurer - HON. ROBERT J. TOBIN

HEADQUARTERS:
Room 22 Phelan Building
Telephone Main 3878

Cuiḋeaċta ċum an Ċraoiḃín Aoiḃinn d'ḟáiltiuġaḋ:

Uaċtarán—Proinnsias Ṁic Seáġain Ui Ṡúilliobáin.
Ar-Uaċtarán—an tAṫair Pilib Ua Riain.
Rúnaire—Proinnsias Ni Ġiollabáir.
Cisteóir—Riobárd Tóibín.

Áit Ġnóṫa
Oiffic 22 Teaċ Ui Ḟaoláin
Caṫair Naoiṁ Ṗroinnsiais.

SAN FRANCISCO, March 9th 1906

Mr. John Quinn,
120 Broadway,
New York, N. Y.

Dear Mr. Quinn:-

Providence is good to the Irish. By the merest accident I learned to-day that Mr. James Monahan of Spokane was in this City. I camped on his trail for about an hour until I found him. He leaves tonight for Spokane and has promised to do all in his power for the success of the Hyde Reception. He seems to think there will not be the slightest difficulty in guaranteeing $500. and he is certain that the leading Irish people there will enter into the project most heartily. Mr. Monahan is the gentleman to whom you wrote. He is the father of Lieutenant Monahan who was killed in Samoa some years ago.

Sacramento was a great success. Sacramento is proverbially slow. Perhaps the slowest town in California, but they had the most enthusiastic meeting. The lecture netted $900. so there will be no difficulty in raising it to One Thousand. The Governor spoke, Hyde delivered a great discourse and Father Yorke was so elated that he stood on his hind legs after Dr. Hyde's lecture and spoke most eloquently for almost an hour. He says it was one of the best meetings he ever attended - and he has attended some good ones.

Joe Scott dropped in last week. He was in Sacramento the day after Dr. Hyde lectured and was down with Father Yorke and Dr. Hyde on the train to this City. He has received in subscriptions $1100. I don't think Los Angeles will fall below the $2500. mark. Have you received the press clippings from Portland? They have done very well there.

Very truly yours,

P O'Ryan

Letter from Philip O'Ryan to John Quinn, 9 March 1906. Courtesy of the National Library of Ireland

Around half-past ten at night my old friend Lawrence Brannick[295], came from Los Angeles to see me, which greatly pleased me as my funds were running low and I feared that my cheques would not be honoured. He generously extended me a line of credit. As I mention money, I must say cash is a rarity here. They use gold and silver coins, but never copper. One day in San Francisco, a man from the East paid for his seat on the tram with five copper cents; as there was no room in his bag for copper, what did the trolleyman do, but derisively tossed the five small coins on the road.

LOS ANGELES

The ninth of March. We arose early and took the train to Los Angeles at about seven o'clock in the morning in the company of Brannick and Joe Scott.[296] When Fr Yorke and I returned from Sacramento, Scott was in the same carriage as us but I was too tired to converse with him and I left it to Fr Yorke. The train followed the coastline for some one hundred miles and I never took such a beautiful journey. There are two train routes from San Francisco to Los Angeles: one through central California, through the great San Joaquin (Uácin as it is pronounced here) Valley, and the other by the coast. On either side, we saw the little rabbits they call 'gophers' standing on their hind legs, squirrels and the occasional large rabbit. Above us were numerous turkey buzzards.

The welcome committee met us five miles out in a special trolley. Numerous photographs were taken, and finally we were allowed to make our way to the Alexander Hotel.[297] I spent the afternoon travelling around with Brannick and Joe Scott.

The tenth of March. We were taken in an automobile with Dr Jones[298], from Wales; Mrs O'Brien[299]; Miss Dillon[300] and Ford.[301] He is a very young Irishman and a lawyer. We were conveyed to Pasadena, a few miles outside the city. In the far distance Mount Lowe was visible and beyond, a sierra of beautiful mountains, and between them and the city lay Pasadena. Passing through Pasadena, I called on Michael Cudahy and his wife, the wealthy Chicago meat packer. The word 'packer' in America refers to someone who puts meat in small tin cans to sell. That is what happens to thousands and thousands of bullocks and pigs from the west. On hearing that I attended Pat Crowe's trial for kidnapping his nephew, he paid attention. That interested him. I said previously that he was seated beside me at the dinner Archbishop Riordan hosted for me and I don't know what influenced him - his chat with me or his friendliness with the Archbishop - but he donated 500 dollars for the meeting to be held in Los Angeles.

Courtesy of Westmeath Libraries (Aidan Heavey Collection)

Pasadena is home to the American millionaires. It is there that the finest houses and the most beautiful gardens are, full of palm trees, orange trees and pepper trees. The pepper tree is a very beautiful tree, with thin, slender branches like acacia flowing down. We had lunch at the Hotel Green, one of the largest such hotels I have ever seen.[302] We proceeded to a famous farm in the neighbourhood, owned by some Colonel[303] whose name I do not recall. He was in court recently for breaking his word, a breach of contract concerning a marriage proposal or something such, and his defence was that such was his poor reputation that nobody should have taken him at his word! We passed through numerous oranges groves and lemon groves. Some of the orange groves were four or five acres in size. I picked three or four oranges from the branch in a remote spot. They are so ubiquitous here that there is no harm for a passer-by to pick one anywhere as no metal fence protects them.

We returned just in time to change into evening attire to go to dinner with the Bishop, Dr Conaty.[304] This Bishop is a very gentle, caring soul and well-disposed to us. Two days prior to our dinner, thieves broke into his home and stole a great deal, including watches, rings, etc.

A large party attended the dinner and they were humorous, without any fault other than all we had to drink was water. The Bishop's niece, Lynch I believe, and Miss Reilly from Boston, and a great singer, named Karl were present. I later learned that the singer's name was O'Carroll. The Scots were present and others, and we had many songs.

The eleventh day of March. Today is Sunday. I had to rise very early to attend church[305] at half past seven as my organising committee had prearranged all. I had a quick breakfast and we departed Los Angeles at nine o'clock. Joe Scott, his wife, Brannick and Bodkin[306], an uncle of my friend Dr Costello[307] in Tuam, and some 20 others came with us. We were to go to Catalina, an island that is a few hours' journey away. Los Angeles is a strange city as it is not located on the coast. The Spaniards built it 20 or 30 miles inland so that the British fleet would not see it and attack from the sea. It is California's second city with almost 200,000 people. But it is not clear how the people make a living. Without any seaport and no international trade, nothing is manufactured here and it has no factories. As far as I can see, the city depends on its famed skyline and the beauty of the countryside. It was a 20-mile journey to the coast to get a boat for Catalina. We heard wonderful stories about the island; the water was so clear that the boatman could see the fish swimming ten or twenty fathoms beneath us, the boats have glass bottoms and the sharks and smaller fish, as large as a mackerel, were to be seen beneath us showing them the way. Such were the stories we had heard

Courtesy of Westmeath Libraries (Aidan Heavey Collection)

that we were very anxious to see this place above all others. But alas, it was not to be. A storm was brewing since morning. When we reached the sea[308], a gale was blowing and it was pouring rain. My wife and I took a cabin and lay down.[309] We sailed out on the rough sea and barely avoided sea-sickness. On reaching the island a few hours later, torrential rain occluded everything. As nothing could be seen, there was naught to do but sit in the hotel[310] and pass three miserable hours until the boat was ready to return to the mainland. We went aboard without seeing as much as a fish, a shark, a boat or even the island itself. We were fortunate to have a cabin to ourselves again as the sea was much rougher on the return journey than on the outward leg. On coming ashore, we ran to the trolley that was returning to Los Angeles. Not long afterwards, we noticed some commotion among our fellow passengers. It soon became apparent that water was seeping through the carriage. Before long, it was pouring in on us in a torrent and anyone having an umbrella opened it. This made it worse for those without umbrellas. It was almost as if the water was coming down on us through a sieve. It was clear to me from that experience that the regular weather here must be truly beautiful, truly fine as were such rain common, the carriages would have had appropriate covering. When we reached the city, the streets were flooded. Every street had become a river. They have no drainage to deal with the water and large planks had to be laid from side to side in the streets. My wife attempted to cross the street using one of these gangplanks and was wet to her ankles. Finally, we arrived at the hotel[311], almost dead, and soaked to the skin. It was so wet that nobody could call on us and we were left on our own for the remainder of the day for which we were grateful.

The twelfth day of March. It poured rain again today and this was the day arranged for my lecture. Every seat in the theatre[312] was sold, but when the appointed time came, it was still raining heavily. Many people travelled by trolley car to the theatre door but upon encountering a river between them and the theatre, returned home rather than enter with wet feet. Of those who attended, I am certain their shoes were wet. During my talk the water level, I later learned, rose six feet in the ground floor and a crew worked to bail the water. The theatre was not more than half full. Nonetheless, we collected a good sum of money. I spoke for an hour and three quarters. Bishop Conaty delivered an extremely fine speech, the best from any bishop yet. We went back for supper with the Scotts. Joe Scott's wife is half-Spanish.[313] They were very generous to us. We returned home at half past one o'clock.

The thirteenth day of March. I went to St Vincent's College[314] at two o'clock and spoke for an hour and a half on the last three centuries of Irish literature.[315] This is a large college run by Catholic priests. I had barely finished when I was ushered into a car and a delegation from the Ladies' club took me to their clubhouse. This Friday Morning Club[316], as it is called, is for some five or 600 of the most distinguished women in Los Angeles. I am certain that I shook hands with 300 or 400 of them, some of whom were young and pretty and some not. But those who were not, I noticed, did not allow those who were, to chat too long with me. After a period, I was brought into a great hall of the club to deliver my talk. I did not know in the slightest what I was to say. But someone whispered in my ear 'Say something about ... who died yesterday.'[317] I do not recall the name now and I never heard tell of her before or afterwards, who she was or what she did. I assumed a mournful disposition, and it appeared as if she was my own close relative. I said the city in which they lived was like Athens, without shipping, commerce or manufacturers, and it was the true Athens of all the American cities. I informed them that I had learned that American women were far more intellectual than their male counterparts. They enjoyed that greatly and it is probably also true. The woman in charge was Mrs Aubrey Davidson[318] and she was a true lady; I believe her to be capable and intellectual also. Of course, there were many of these women and I considered them very agreeable.

Having departed these ladies, I barely had time to change into my evening clothes when I was called to attend the Celtic Club[319], comprised of Irishmen, Scotsmen and Welshmen. This is the only city where I found the Celts from these three countries coming together. Malcolm MacLeod, a Scotchman,[320] was in charge of the dinner attended by eighty people.[321] A member of each of the three races spoke. I was amazed to see them cooperating so effortlessly as I did not think it possible that such a thing could occur. This is a new club but they hope to establish branches in San Francisco and other places. Of course, they sang 'The Bonny Bonny Banks of Loch Lomond' as if it were the native song of everyone there. Bishop Hamilton[322] from San Francisco was present. I think he is a Methodist and he introduced the only political note, giving thanks to God publicly that he was not an Anglo-Saxon and they all laughed. My name was proposed and accepted as the first honorary member of the first Celtic Club in America. The dinner suffered from the same flaw as the Bishop's – all we had to drink was water.[323] I asked about this afterwards and Fr Yorke explained that there were many Yanks in Los Angeles and they had a Puritan strain and a New England mentality. Far different from San Francisco – these people pretend not to drink but the entire world knows that as soon as the dinner concluded they all rushed to the bar to get a drink. That's false piety!

I encountered a man from my own place, a son of Nicholas Neary from Callow. He made a mint here selling clothes, or 'dry goods' as they call it. He gave me a 100 dollars

At the Cawston Ostrich Farm, South Pasadena, Cal.

Courtesy of Westmeath Libraries (Aidan Heavey Collection)

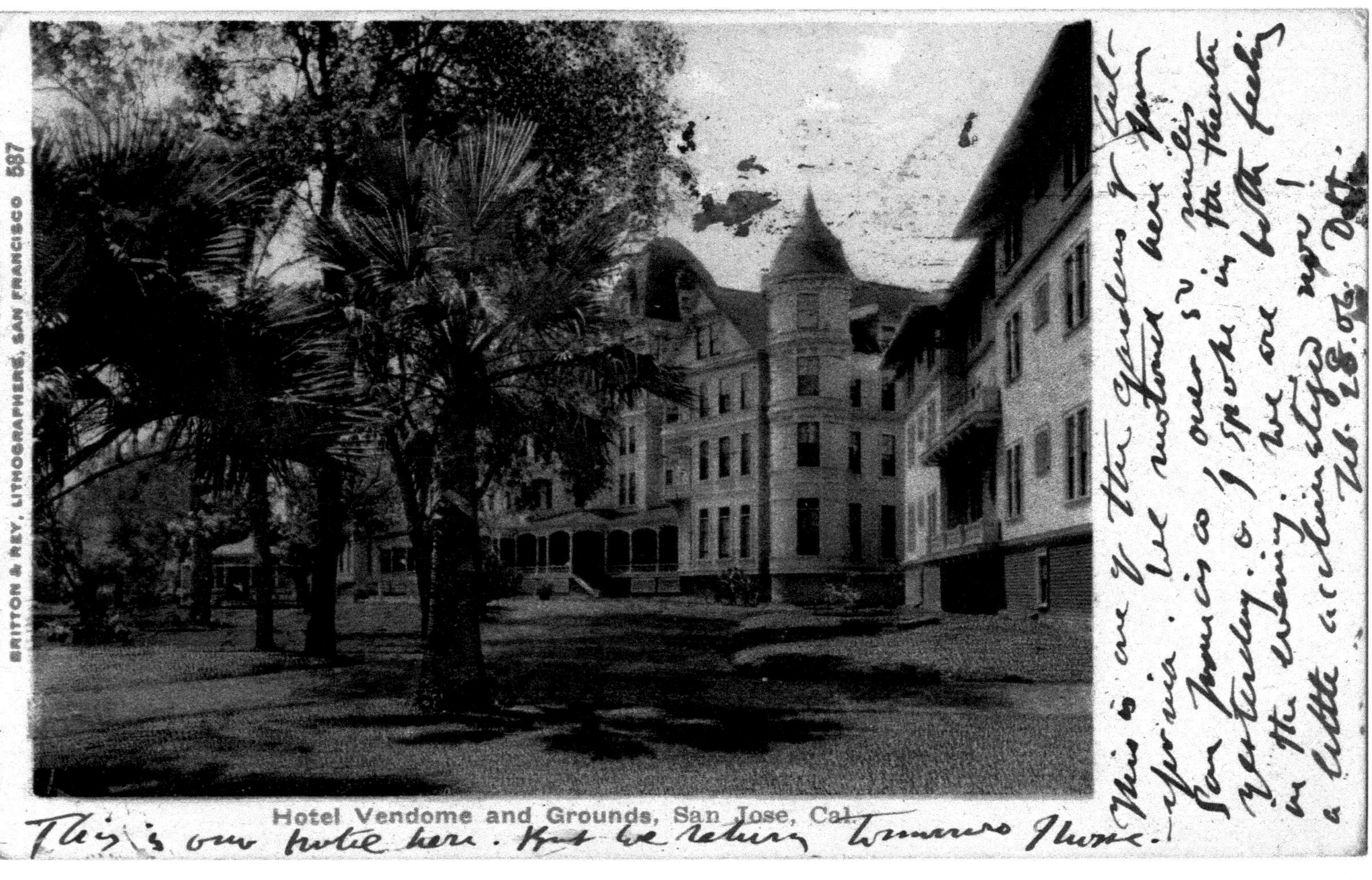

Le caoinchead Chnuasach Bhéaloideas Éireann, An Coláiste Ollscoile Baile Átha Cliath donation, and, something which I welcomed at that moment almost as much as the donation, a bottle of wine, when the official dinner was over.

The fourteenth day of March. We were to return to San Francisco today, but Joe Scott brought us to Chutes Park[324] to see the Indians from the Philippines. They are called *Ignarote*. There were 12 of them. They had the most beautiful skin I had ever seen, the colour of copper when light, hot and shiny. They wore no clothing other than a narrow cloth around their waist. They were head-hunters and they can also perform some metal work. They gave a performance, throwing spears, singing and so forth. He brought us back afterwards to the California Club[325] where he provided a good lunch and placed us abroad the train to return to San Francisco. Many people accompanied us to the station to bid us farewell. The generosity of the people of Los Angeles could not be bettered.

The fifteenth day of March. We travelled on the train all night and reached San Francisco at ten in the morning and returned again to the St Francis hotel. The flooding while we were in Los Angeles had greatly damaged the railway. It removed the earth beneath the rail track and we had to travel very slowly on a large part of the track. We came upon a train that had been wrecked a few hours beforehand. The engine lay on one side of the track and six broken carriages lay on the other side. We were fortunate not to have been aboard. Railway accidents are very common on this railroad, as it has only recently been constructed. Having changed our clothes, we headed for St Peter's Hall[326], owned by Fr Casey[327], a very kind man. I spoke there to around 1,000 people, nuns, teachers and high school students. Nuns do not hesitate to attend my lectures in this country. They sit among the regular people. They do not behave so in Ireland. Were I to speak in their own convent in Ireland, for example, some of them would only listen to me from behind some type of screen. Fr Yorke also spoke, and as usual, he spoke very well.

When I returned from Fr Casey, having received plenty to eat and drink, I had to change into evening clothes and run out to a large dinner hosted by the Knights of St Patrick. It was a fine dinner. 200 of the finest Irishmen in San Francisco were in attendance. I was accorded the first toast to speak on the 'the Day we are Extolling.' Phelan, Sullivan, Fr Yorke and Robinson, the miner, were also present. There were quite a lot of speeches and songs but it did not drag on too long and I was home by one o'clock. This dinner did not suffer from the fault of the two dinners in Los Angeles!

The sixteenth day. Frank Sullivan took me to San José which is forty or fifty miles south of San Francisco and onto the Jesuit College at Santa Clara.[328] I lectured there on Irish-language literature.[329] I had something to eat with the priests and there was plenty of talk and song, and we did not retire to our hotel in San José until two in the morning, tired and exhausted. Fr Gleeson is the College President.[330]

The seventeenth day of March. Today is St Patrick's day and I had to rise at seven o'clock in the morning to return to San Francisco with Sullivan: it was printed on the official programme of my trip that I would attend Fr Nugent's Church[331] with Frank Sullivan to hear a special sermon in Irish and to hear the rosary also in Irish.[332] The railway track, as usual, was poor, and the train slow, and we were an hour late walking into the church. Two look-outs were waiting for us outside the Church and did not lose a moment in ushering us in the church door among the congregation. They walked us through the church and deposited us at the altar railings like two fools in front of 2,000 pairs of watchful eyes. But, a priest, who was inside the railings, opened a small gate and offered two seats beside the altar. Frank and I sat there for the remainder of the High Mass and for the Irish-language sermon. I knew that everyone in the church was staring at us, beside the altar, and I was continually edging sideways until a portion of a cross was between me and those closest. As for the Irish sermon, the priest had his back to me with a soundboard overhead and I failed to hear a single word he said. But the rosary gladdened my heart the way the responses were given in Irish. In my opinion, nearly everyone present answered in Irish. Fr Nugent, as he told us, used for the first time, a rosary beads made of Connemara marble.

After a fine lunch with Fr Nugent, I was taken to a large hall of the Native Sons where I found a fine crowd and many speakers there before me. I spoke in Irish to them for 25 minutes. I did not utter a word in English. It was clear that most understood me. So worn out was I that I did not stay until the end. I went back to the hotel and threw myself on my bed for an hour. Then I had to rise and go to the Mechanics' Pavilion where 7,000 people waited me. This is a tormenting place for a public speaker. The hall is 500 yards long and appropriately wide! It has a wooden floor, as well as sidewalls made of wood. The echo would leave the Killarney echo[333] in the halfpenny place. It was a stand-alone building. There were dances to begin with, and afterwards a stage on wheels was brought out and positioned in the middle of the hall. Thousands gathered around it. Fr Yorke and I ascended the stage and I did my best to deliver a speech but it was in vain. I turned in every direction, north, south, east and west. I then spoke through a megaphone, I shouted, roared, screamed. I gesticulated so that I would be seen, if not heard, but I soon gave up. Fr Yorke attempted the same after me, but fared no better. Nobody, save those in the front, could hear what we had to say. I came home at half past twelve; never since I came west was I so exhausted.

The eighteenth day of March. I was to go to Oakland to dine with Fr Yorke today but my ribs were distressed and required iodine. My wife was also ill. Sullivan and Fr O'Ryan called. I went to bed early and slept well which allowed me to recuperate.

The nineteenth day of March. I lunched with Fr Yorke and went with him and Fr O'Ryan to the Cliff House in the Park. We shortened the road by attempting to converse in Latin – fools' Latin! Fr Yorke is an excellent companion, very humorous and I also like O'Ryan. In the evening, I dined with the Shea family. Judge Coffey and his nephew as well as others were there. I like the judge immensely. He returned to the hotel with me and we had a nightcap.

The twentieth day of March. Heavy rain again. It appears to me that every second or third day is wet. But, the people here will never admit as much. When a wet day arrives, they will state and swear that it is a complete exception; they never saw such a day for months, that it is very strange, and there is no place on earth as dry or as fine as this place. They impress that on you and I would believe them were it not for the fact that strangers who spent five or six months here, told me that the weather here is no better or worse than that I am experiencing and is no different from what they encountered since they arrived here.

In the evening, we went to dine with the City Mayor, Mayor Schmitz (See note p. 159). Fourteen people attended the dinner and others joined afterwards. The mayor sent his own car to collect us. San Francisco is full of hills; going up the hill on which the mayor lives, the automobile stalled halfway and began rolling backwards. We were frightened and jumped out. But the car was stopped and no damage occurred. It was at that dinner that I first saw a man about whom I had heard so much; a small Jew by the name of Ruef. He is said to be the real head of the city and that all Schmitz does is to put his name to the matters conducted by this man. He speaks several languages, German and Italian, and can give a good speech in both. He has a smart, quick mind. The workers support him. I heard this riddle posed in San Francisco: 'Why is San Francisco like a house?' The answer is 'because there is a Ruef over everything!'[334]

Schmitz's story is a peculiar tale. His father was German and his mother was Irish, a Logan. His wife is Irish, an O'Driscoll. Fiddling is his profession and he is a good player. The labour movement made him a leader initially and eventually he ran for Mayor. Every paper in San Francisco opposed him and attempted to bring about his defeat but the people elected him in spite of the papers. That I dine tonight with James Phelan, and tomorrow with the Mayor's sworn enemy is tribute to the organising committee's power and influence. Many Germans and Americans joined us after dinner when we sang and played music. He is a funny, homely man. He brought us upstairs to see his children asleep in their cots. He humorously said in jest that he would be glad to see me leave the city soon as he knew of nobody who would sooner pluck the joyful hand from him than me, and I might stand against him in the race for the mayorship! We came home at 12.30.

The twenty-first day of March. Today was fine and we called on Mrs Sullivan and went shopping. In the afternoon, I attended the annual meeting of the Gaelic League in California. Maybe I was a tad early arriving. Fr Yorke was addressing the delegates as I arrived and I knew immediately something was out of kilter. Fr Yorke requested two delegates escort me to a side room until I was called upon. I later asked him what the reason was and I understood that he was lambasting and castigating the delegates over petty jealousies and internal strife that has erupted among them but that he did not want to continue in my presence. Once he had concluded and all was pleasant again, I entered and made two speeches, one in Irish and the other in English. I brought Fr Yorke back with me to my hotel for supper.

The twenty-second day of March. We shopped in the morning in Chinatown, buying items unavailable elsewhere. In the afternoon, I spoke for an hour and twenty minutes to 600 or 700 people in St Peter's Hall and the money went to the Gaelic League. We had a fine dinner afterwards in the company of Fr Yorke and twelve other priests.

The twenty-third day of March. Heavy rain again today. When I called on James Phelan, he presented me with a small gold knife with my name on it as a memento and he gave my wife a gold brooch.

The twenty-fourth day. We arose at six o'clock in the morning and crossed the bay with Frank Sullivan. We boarded the train to Santa Cruz, which is sixty miles south of San Francisco. As is usual with the railway, the earth was eroded from the rails in places and we had to travel slowly. It took four hours to travel 60 miles. Some of the route passed through land with water and mountains on both sides of us. When we arrived in Santa Cruz, we lunched with Fr Fisher[335] and three or four other Irishmen whom Sullivan had invited. After lunch, we all – Sullivan, us, Fr Fisher and a veteran Irishman – piled into a carriage pulled by four horses to see the great trees. The rain had destroyed the direct road to the great trees and we had to take a detour of thirteen or fourteen miles. The countryside was wild and beautiful. To this very day, I cannot believe we survived without any damage or harm, such was the poor state of the roads; on occasions, the wheels sank to the axles in holes. We crossed rotten bridges with some of the planks hanging from them. I do not know how we did not overturn the carriage or put it upside down but we had a wonderful driver who masterfully steered the four horses. I do not know his name, but we all called him Colonel. That pleased him but he in no way resembled a soldier.

Finally, we arrived at these famous trees but before we were in their midst, we had to cross a bridge on foot that swayed from side to side. The planks were rotten; some gave way beneath our feet and the entire structure shook as if it were about to collapse into the river far beneath us. It frightened the priest and me, but I was too embarrassed to let on. The unfortunate priest froze midway: afraid to progress but similarly afraid to retreat, but when he saw the others cross safely he followed suit.

The trees, that we came so far to see, are truly wonderful. They are called Red Woods and are of a particular kind. The Californians say that they do not grow outside of the state and the many efforts made to plant them elsewhere all failed (and they often say it, but I am not sure it is true). They grow very slowly but once they mature, are very tall. They grow straight, without loop or bend, sixty or eighty, maybe even a hundred feet high, without any branches. Then the branches begin to sprout; not upwards but hanging downwards. Fellers knocked most of these trees in the state but this area was preserved. Many of the trees I saw were 45 feet in circumference at their base and 30 feet wide 4 yards off the ground. Some were 280 feet high. In addition, one or two were over three hundred feet. All rose straight up into the sky. Some bore scorch marks at the base from a much earlier fire, maybe hundreds of years ago but even though it burned some of the bases, it did not damage the wood nor halt its growth. The biggest of the trees are probably a couple of thousand years old. I read in some paper that they felled one of them and when they counted the rings, found 2,425; each ring marks a year's growth. Where we were, in a small area, stood 150 trees that were four yards across from side to side. We did not have much time to examine them thoroughly. It was becoming dark and we had to return. The return journey in the dark was worse than that going out. It was a miracle that we arrived home safely. We only barely caught the return train. That train brought us to a small town, the only place where I heard a word of Spanish spoken. We had to wait for another train then that did not arrive. The rail track, as usual, was broken. We did our best to find something to eat and finally found some bread and coffee. The train finally arrived and took us to San Francisco at one o'clock at night. Frank Sullivan took us to the Pup and gave us champagne and caviar that we badly needed. While we were eating, he said, we diced with death three or four times today, and he was right.

The twenty-fifth day of March. We were too tired to go out today, but Judge Coffey, his nephew and others called on us. At night, we dined with James Phelan.

Miss Jolliffe, the newspaperwoman who joined us on the train on the other side of the Sierra Nevada and six or more other also present. We came home early.

The time came to bid farewell to San Francisco. We are almost six weeks there now and such kindness and generosity I never before encountered. As regards to money, I think I collected as much here as in New York itself and I will never forget the good friends we made here. Little we thought on departing them today that they and their city would, in three weeks, be laid waste; that James Phelan's beautiful house, the house of the most generous Frank Sullivan and many other places in which we experienced such generosity and hospitality would go up in flames and their inhabitants left without a dry crust.

We packed today and finalised everything before heading northwards. Many people came to bid us farewell as we departed San Francisco at eight o'clock in the evening. Accompanying us across the bay came Fr Yorke, Frank Sullivan and his wife (who gave my wife a beautiful gold ornament), Judge Coffey, his two nephews, and six or seven others also came along. We boarded at 8.30. We bid farewell and began our 800-mile journey to Portland, Oregon.

The twenty-seventh day of March. I do not know what type of countryside we passed through during the night, but in the morning we were not too far from Mount Shasta, a large, beautiful mountain with a huge snowcap. It is over 14,000 feet high. The view was excellent. The mountains were taller and more beautiful than the Rockies and the Sierra Nevada. The track was dangerous in places. In one place, we halted on a mountain slope where a large tree had fallen on the track from the mountaintop, bending the tracks and a repair crew were busy at work. I alighted the train and observed them at work. The train itself was on the side of the mountain and there was a 1,000-foot slope under it, should it fall. As I watched them, I noticed the train's inside wheels were half an inch or an inch off the ground: they were not touching the rails at all. This is reputed to be the most dangerous area in the West. The train remained there teetering over the edge of the mountain valley. I do not think there was any danger but nonetheless it would frighten many! Several months later, I read of a train on the same mountain pass or a nearby mountain that left the rails and tumbled into a deep lake below. Nobody survived. Passengers and train remained in the lake never again to be seen or heard of.[336]

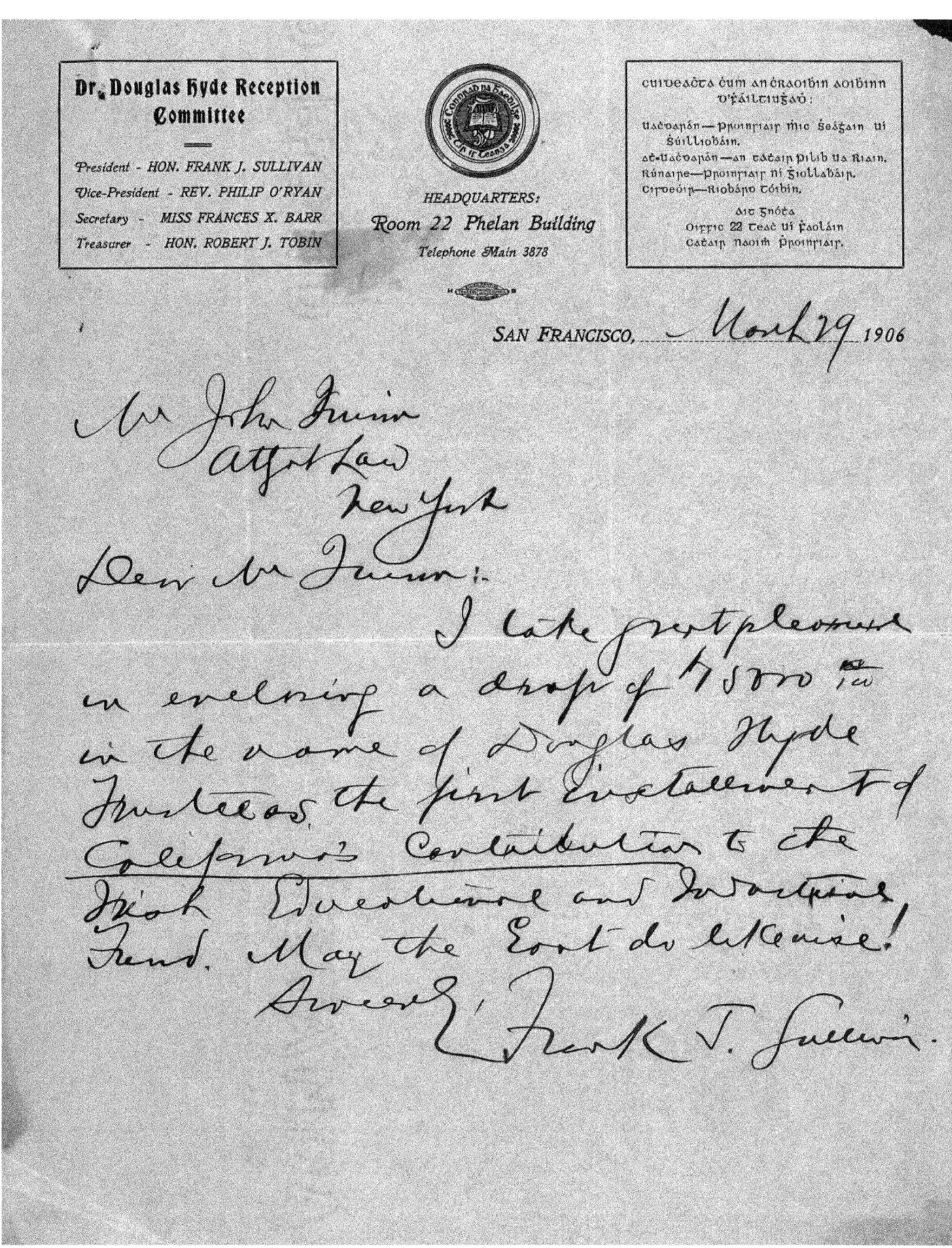

Dr. Douglas Hyde Reception Committee

President - HON. FRANK J. SULLIVAN
Vice-President - REV. PHILIP O'RYAN
Secretary - MISS FRANCES X. BARR
Treasurer - HON. ROBERT J. TOBIN

HEADQUARTERS:
Room 22 Phelan Building
Telephone Main 3878

Cuideachta chum an Chraoibhín Aoibhinn d'fháiltiughadh:
Uachtarán—Proinnsias mac Seághain Uí Shúilleabháin.
Ath-Uachtarán—an tAthair Pilib Ua Riain.
Rúnaire—Proinnsias Ní Ghiollabháin.
Cisteoir—Riobárd Tóibín.
Áit Gnótha
Oifig 22 Teach Uí Fhaoláin
Cathair Naoimh Proinnsias.

SAN FRANCISCO, March 29 1906

Mr John Quinn
Atty at Law
New York

Dear Mr Quinn:

I take great pleasure in enclosing a draft of $15000 to in the name of Douglas Hyde Trustees, the first instalment of California's Contribution to the Irish Educational and Industrial Fund. May the East do likewise!

Sincerely,
Frank J. Sullivan.

Letter to Frank J. Sullivan to John Quinn enclosing draft of $15,000. 29 March 1906. Courtesy of National Library of Ireland

PORTLAND

The twenty-eight day of March. We arrived in Portland at half-past seven in the morning. Tomás Bán had been there beforehand making arrangements, but he had since departed to lay the groundwork in Seattle, Spokane, Butte and Anaconda. A group came to welcome us and took us to the hotel.

After breakfast, we were taken in an automobile in the company of the Protestant cleric, Dr Morrison[337], his wife, and Dr Christie[338], the Catholic Archbishop, and others through the Park from where we saw one of the finest views in America. The city was beneath our feet with a light fog all around. On all sides were huge, towering mountains of which the smallest was 10,000 feet above sea level. The other mountains, including Mount Pitt, Mount Ranier, Mount St Helen, and others ranged from eighty miles to a hundred and twenty miles distant but the sky was so clear that they appeared close. The sky is wonderfully clear in the West. I heard of some Englishman who came out here and lodged in a hotel. The staff did not care for him. After breakfast, he said, 'I shall stroll out to the foothills of those mountains, how far away are they?' 'O,' said the hotelier, who could not abide the Englishman, 'two or three miles.' 'Just as I thought,' said the Englishman, 'I shall be back for lunch.' He found a companion to accompany him and he walked and walked but if he did, he appeared no closer to the hills. Finally, they reached a small stream but instead of leaping across, the poor man began to undress. 'What are you doing?' asked the other man. 'Going swimming,' said the Englishman, 'You never know how wide this is!' We visited the Catholic College with the Archbishop and Dr Morrison and I had a long chat with an old professor from County Mayo, whose name was Morrin.

The twenty-ninth day of March. It poured rain today. California was not dry but I believe it to be much wetter here. At two o'clock, I was taken to visit three or four clubs and was required to take a drink at each. At half past eight, I spoke in the theater[339] to approximately 900 people. It was the Archbishop himself who introduced me and Judge Munley[340] who introduced the Archbishop. I returned to the hotel after midnight.

SEATTLE

We rose today at six o'clock in the morning to catch the train to Seattle that is a few hundred miles further north in the State of Washington. Three or four accompanied

Courtesy of Westmeath Libraries (Aidan Heavey Collection)

us to the station and we were granted free passage on the railway by Fogarty[341], the rail company president. On reaching Tacoma, Henehan[342] and a man from Donegal, whose name I cannot now recall but who made his wealth gold mining, boarded the train and accompanied us to Seattle. We reached the place at 4.30. The welcoming committee greeted us and took us to the Butler Hotel.[343] The newspapermen swarmed in as usual. We dined at the hotel with Henehan.

Today is another very wet day. I purchased a large piece of beaver skin for 16 dollars. Henehan then took us out in his automobile but it rained so heavy that we could see little. We dined with Henehan, his wife, and two daughters. Their daughters were raised in New England, where they attended a Methodist University. Their father was very pleased when I said in jest that we have often heard that the dollar was the American God, but I think, I said, the cent is the American God in New England! The daughters did not find that amusing but their father greatly enjoyed it. The father is a princely Irishman and a fine Irish speaker from Tourmakeady in Mayo. He did not change his name to 'Bird,' as did many of his namesake in that county. There was a man in Liverpool long ago and he called himself Bird but says he, 'Sir, that is not my proper name, but I have learned that the English can't pronounce my name and call myself Bird.' O!, I said, 'you're a Henehan' 'No,' he said, 'Mac Canary (i.e. son of the shepherd) is my name.' Henehan was very generous to me and as I was leaving, he loaned me two fine Irish-language manuscripts that I returned to him once I found my way back to Ireland.

The First Day of April. There was a meeting in the Opera House[344] at three. Four or 500 attended. Judge Burke[345] requested subscriptions but did not do so in the proper manner and I believe little accrued from it. McGraw[346], who was once the governor, was not there but Bishop O'Dea chaired.[347] I shook hands with many people after the lecture. Besides my friend Henehan, I believe, the leading Irishmen in the city to be to be McGraw, Bishop O'Dea, Piggott, Gannon (a Donegal man who made his fortune in the Klondike) and Judge Burke.

Seattle is a strange city. It was mainly made by gold miners. Consequently, gold shops and jewel shops are more plentiful here than in any other city in which I have ever been. I presume the reason is that gold prospectors make their money overnight and, on becoming rich, do not know how to spend it. They rush to purchase watches, bracelets, gold chains and other ornaments hence so many gold shops. Seattle is not yet complete rather it is a city under construction. The labourer's wage is very high. Bricklayers earn as much as six dollars per day; carpenters earn $4.50 and so forth. The labourers' wage is a quarter to a third higher than anywhere else I have been. Four major railways serve Seattle and the price of land is skyrocketing. I saw the stumps of large trees that were felled to make way for new streets with sap still seeping from them. These trees, I believe, were almost as large as those I saw in Santa Cruz. I said to some of the citizens that they would soon regret felling such fine trees, without at least preserving some to ornament the city. They paid little heed to my comments. They cared for little but charging forward and building a great new city. Seattle is not on the coast but on a long inlet, that penetrates the State of Washington. Lake Washington, a beautiful lake some twenty miles in length, is near the city. This place is almost as wet as Ireland. They say that some 32 inches of rain fall every year. Many things in this region remind me of Ireland. It has boggy fields in which grow rushes, primroses, long grass and weeds, herbs and weeds of every type and above everything else there is the daisy. This is the only place since I came to America I have seen a daisy. If it were not for the great forests on all sides and the high mountains hidden in snow, I could believe I was in Ireland! They tell me that Chinese pheasants are common in the woods. A few were introduced a while back and they fared well as they are now plentiful.[348]

Wild animals are still common. I saw a wolf skin that was eight feet long. I saw a sea otter skin and was informed that it was worth 300 pounds. It was intended for Russia, where the most valuable pelts go.

SPOKANE

We have now travelled as far north as is possible to travel. We are almost in Canada. We must go east again and Spokane is the next stop.

We departed Seattle early in the morning at 7.30 to go to Spokane. Henehan came to the station to bid us farewell. I received a free ticket for the train. The first part of the journey went through forests with beautiful, tall trees, mostly excellent Oregon pine trees. As we travelled east, away from the ocean, the woods decreased and we journeyed through burnt wasteland and burnt woods. The rail track began to twist and turn like an eel as it ascended the mountains known as the Cascade Mountains, some 4,000 or 5,000 feet above sea level. It then entered the ground through a hole until it emerged on the far side.[349] For more than half the day, we had a view of Mount Ranier, the finest mountain of them all. After five hours of travelling, this mountain appeared no closer or no further from us. At eleven at night, we reached our destination and Monaghan, O'Shea and 20 other people greeted us and took us to the hotel.

I was going around the town buying skins as this place is like Seattle, full of skins and furs and very reasonably priced. I bought a polar bear skin from a man from

Courtesy of Westmeath Libraries (Aidan Heavey Collection)

Alaska. He said two Indians had killed it and one of them was about to decapitate it saying, 'this is my first bear and if I don't take the head off, it will return to haunt me.' However, his companion would not allow it as removing the head would reduce its value. They argued over it but finally the trader bought it with the head intact, and I bought it from him for 66 dollars. I bought more skins from the same man; on returning to New York, I regretted not buying much more as they are much, much more expensive there than in the west.

We had a good meeting in the afternoon at Gonzaga College[350], run by the Jesuits, only a few miles outside the city. After the meeting Monaghan[351], a kind old man of some 60 years, brought me home with him to his beautiful house. This was the man who brought me to Spokane. He is wealthy and has a fine home. He and his two daughters chatted with me and they were speaking on the telephone to fetch a car to take me to my hotel when I noticed that his face suddenly blanched; he slid off the chair and slumped on the floor. It was a shocking blow to us all. The two daughters with whom we had dined beforehand were present and almost lost their minds. The older girl, a beautiful young woman, thought him dead. I was of the same opinion. I ran up the stairs with the girls and we brought down a bed and placed him in it. I removed his coat, opened his shirt, and the girls summoned doctors. A doctor arrived after a while, but he was French and did not speak English, and the girls had no French. Few, very few, people in America have French. I had to pose the questions to the doctor and translate his answers into English for the unfortunate girls.[352] Other doctors arrived presently and I departed the house at three o'clock at night and went to my own hotel. My wife was there waiting; she was worried to death as she did not know what had delayed me. We had to depart Spokane at six in the morning and that only allowed us three hours. I was upset and worried on returning from Monaghan's house. After a few hours rest I was on the road again, departing Spokane and heading to Butte (Biút as it pronounced), Montana.

BUTTE

On leaving Spokane, we had a lovely journey through the Rocky Mountains. Around midday, we arrived at Lake Pend Oreille[353] and it is among the nicest places I have ever seen. We regretted the fall of night as it deprived us of the view. It was close to two o'clock in the morning when we reached Butte. O'Meara[354] and Tomás Bán greeted us at the station. When I was in California, Tomás was there with his brother and his

Courtesy of Westmeath Libraries (Aidan Heavey Collection)

family. I was pleased to see him again here. They brought us to the Thornton hotel[355], named for a man from County Galway, Ó Droighneáin.[356] The Ó Droighneáin people called themselves Thornton in this county.

The fifth day of April. Butte is not a large city. It has 40,000 or 50,000 people. I am certain it is the ugliest place I have ever seen. There is neither a tree, bush, plant nor even a blade of grass here or anywhere nearby. There are miles and miles of barren land on every side. The noxious smoke from the large chimneys in which Clark[357], the Senator from Montana, smelts his copper, kills and burns everything.[358] The arsenic in the smoke kills everything it comes into contact with. This is an almost Irish city. Most of the inhabitants are Irish. The Mayor is Irish and the Irish control everything. Nonetheless, I would not say that the state of the Irish here is satisfactory. They depend entirely on the mines. Were anything to happen to the mines, half of the Irish would be idle. They would be better off to have some land. It was Marcus Daly[359], an Irishman who died a short while ago, that made Butte. He had wanted to settle some Irish in a valley named Bitter Root Valley but, despite his best efforts, failed. Then a cluster of Yanks from Missouri arrived and settled in the glen the Irish had rejected. Today, you could not buy that valley for forty million dollars.

They brought me to show me the mines and begged me to enter but Quinn had warned me against doing so as he suffered terribly from having once done so. I therefore declined. They presented me with copper gifts of every type.

The evening arrived and we had a fine meeting. The theatre was filled to capacity.[360] Bishop Carroll[361] from Helena introduced me to the audience. O'Meara was in the chair. I spoke for more than two hours. There was no collection, but nonetheless I was promised 2,000 dollars. I returned at one o'clock. The sixth day of April. I spent the day until five o'clock greeting people who called on me.

ANACONDA

At five o'clock we went to Anaconda that is some 20 miles from Butte. One hundred and fifty people came to the station and Dr Spelman[362] brought me to the Montana Hotel.[363] It was Marcus Daly, (who also created Anaconda), that erected this fine hotel. It was the Doctor who arranged the meeting and it was Thurston, the editor of the *Standard*[364], who chaired it. The meeting was very good and when asked to donate, the audience subscribed 615 dollars. When it was over, I went back to the hotel where we drank and talked, as usual, until one o'clock!

The seventh day of April. We passed the entire day in the care of Captain Kelly[365] and Mr Mathewson[366], the mine's director, going through Anaconda and viewing the Washoe Smelter. This smelter makes Anaconda's wealth. It smelts most of the copper mined in Butte. Butte sits on a hill and is called 'the mile high town.' Anaconda is the same, with a hill, and the smelter sits on the hill. There is a big hole that draws the smoke upwards; this hole, dug out of the side of the hill, connects to a large chimney on the hilltop so the hole and chimney are one pipe. This chimney is 300 feet high and 27 feet wide at the mouth. That large voracity continuously belches forth large, heavy, black, poisonous clouds. Yet the smoke does not descend on the town; the hill is so high that the wind carries away the clouds of smoke, but they often sit above the town and its people. They must descend somewhere and the farmers in the locality intend to prosecute the smelter for ruining their land as nothing grows where the arsenic falls. I presume the Big Company that owns the smelter will have to purchase all the surrounding land; that would not be too expensive for the Company; this place is in the middle of the Rocky Mountains, the bare land is not worth much and there is only the occasional farmer. When an animal eats the arsenic grass, it grows fat for a month; but if it continues to eat, it becomes emaciated and finally dies. I said that Butte was in the middle of the Rocky Mountains; this is where the water flows on both sides: on this side of Butte, water flows into the Atlantic and on the other side, the water flows into the Pacific. The Americans call this the Great Divide: in English it is the Watershed and in German, *Wasserscheide*.

When copper is taken from the mines in Butte, it must first be crushed and finely-crushed, then melted. The first time it is melted, half the copper remains but after the second melting only pure copper remains. They must be very careful that the copper, after the first boiling, does not touch the water around the mould; if it did, a terrible explosion would result. Copper is not smelted again in this place; it is sent to the East and each ton of copper is valued at fifty dollars gold and silver.

Wages are high here. The ordinary worker, with neither trade nor specialist skill, earns thirteen shillings per day. The work force are well cared for. They have a place to hang their clothes; they have baths and a skilled nurse on standby in case anyone suffers an injury. I suppose there is copper in the chimney smoke; there was a hillock near the old smelter and they took the land from the hill and flattened it; the amount of copper recovered made it worthwhile.

Edward O'Dwyer, who was the Superintendent of Education, toured the area with us and, as a gift, gave me a book I never saw before or since. That was the *Leabhar Gabhála*, translated into French, and he also gave me three stone arrowheads he had found in the mountains where long ago the Indians killed wild ox or buffalo. He also gave me snakeskins, the type that make a warning noise with their heads before they strike. This Dywer was a lover of literature and I never saw a person more to be pitied than he. He returned with us to Butte after dinner. His place and position depend on the voice of the people and voters in their hundreds were arriving in the town that very day. The APA (American Protective Association)[367] supporters, as I understood it, opposed him. The APA movement is totally dead in the East, but still active in the West. The Scandinavians are mainly in charge and the Germans and the Jews were the only two groups not involved. But this poor Dwyer was not a fighter; he was a man better suited to a university position rather than going about seeking votes from ignorant people.

The eighth day of April. Today is Sunday and I went to the Rector's church.[368] He was a kind man who attended my own meeting. I noticed that he, like all the other clerics out here, on concluding the service hastened to the door and stood there shaking hands with people as they left.

I went afterwards to a meeting in the City Hall[369] where Tomás Bán and I established a branch of the Gaelic League, a branch that would assist us every year hereafter. Some 200 people attended. The work lasted two and a half hours. A Gaelic League branch was established, an executive elected and it was agreed to subscribe 700 dollars per year. (Which they did for several years afterwards.)

Afterwards O'Meara and his wife brought us out to where there were Indian cabins. The tribe is called *Cree*.[370] The place was filthy with much half-rotten meat hanging from ropes around the camp. I believe the meat was the remains of what the Butte butchers had slaughtered. These poor people, I suspect, survive on the city's leftovers. I entered a cabin and found a young girl reading a book that, at first, I thought was printed in shorthand. But, it was not so; rather it was a font devised by the French missionaries in which each letter has the sound of a syllable. It is often forgotten that the French were in America before the English and they left their mark, especially in the place names.

When night fell Kilroy, a young Irishman, visited me and we had a long conversation. He is now the editor of a newspaper here but was once a cowboy and spent a while among the Indians. He was unhappy with the state of Montana. It would frighten one to listen to him. According to him (and many others said the same), Standard Oil[371], the Big Oil Company and the other huge companies, corporations as they are called, control the large state of Montana. 'They succeeded,' he said 'in acquiring every source of wealth in advance: the mines, the wood on the hills, the water wells, every fertile

Form No. 1.

THE WESTERN UNION TELEGRAPH COMPANY.

INCORPORATED

24,000 OFFICES IN AMERICA. CABLE SERVICE TO ALL THE WORLD.

This Company **TRANSMITS** and **DELIVERS** messages only on conditions limiting its liability, which have been assented to by the sender of the following message. Errors can be guarded against only by repeating a message back to the sending station for comparison, and the Company will not hold itself liable for errors or delays in transmission or delivery of **Unrepeated Messages**, beyond the amount of tolls paid thereon, nor in any case where the claim is not presented in writing within sixty days after the message is filed with the Company for transmission.
This is an **UNREPEATED MESSAGE**, and is delivered by request of the sender, under the conditions named above.

ROBERT C. CLOWRY, President and General Manager.

NUMBER	SENT BY	REC'D BY	CHECK
9 Rep	Ut	Ht	10 Pd 1830

RECEIVED at the WESTERN UNION BUILDING, 195 Broadway, N. Y. Apr 1906

Dated San Francisco Calif 9

To Jno Quinn

120 Bway Newyork

Advise immedy whether draft fifteen thousand has been received yet

Francis Sullivan

Telegram from Frank Sullivan to John Quinn checking whether $15,000 had arrived from San Francisco, early April 1906. Courtesy of the National Library of Ireland valley and, of course, they control the newspapers. These papers are excellent but they do not pay for themselves. They require funding and the corporations come to their aid and are very careful in this regard – nothing will be published that will harm the corporations and if something detrimental must be published, they must dress it up; if it cannot be ignored, they distort it.' 'People,' he said, 'were becoming aware of the situation, and he believed that war would have occurred in Montana had Roosevelt not been elected president. Roosevelt inspired hope that the corporations would be opposed on legal grounds and their wings clipped.' But, he himself did not believe anything of the sort. He said at least 3,000 Irishmen in Butte were earning between three to four dollars per day but collectively they do not have $50,000 in the bank. The Scandinavians, that neither number a quarter of the Irish nor were as prominent, have half a million in the bank.

The ninth day of April. I rested the entire day and wrote letters. I told Tomás Bán my journey was almost complete and sent a cable home, stating I did not believe much more could be accomplished and that Tomás Bán would sail home in three weeks' time.

The tenth day of April. We departed Butte after midday. O'Meara, Daly and others escorted us to the station. Around four o'clock we arrived at a small place in the mountains where we were required to remain for three or four hours. We found something to eat in a small hotel. A Texan couple managed it. They said good hunting was to be had within twenty miles and their neighbour, the butcher's son, had shot three elk (the largest horned deer in America) a short while before that and one of them had the largest set of antlers they had ever seen. It is regrettable the manner in which these fine animals are being wiped out. When my brother-in-law[372] first went out to Wyoming, he often saw up to 1,000 of these fine creatures coming down from the mountains in a single herd. Now you could search for a week without sighting one. There is a certain organisation, scattered widely throughout America, that call themselves 'Elks' and it is a matter of pride among them to have elk teeth. The most distinguished members have teeth and the poor elks are in great demand to supply these teeth.

I went hiking alone to the top of the hill above the small town and had a fine view of the Rocky Mountains on all sides. It was like a panorama. The train arrived at nine o'clock at night and we slept aboard.

The eleventh day of April. We passed the day on the train taking in the view of North Dakota plains. This province is home to few people yet but I believe the land to be fertile and many people will soon move here. The landscape is bizarre: strange valleys, land like towers, land like castles, land like waves and so forth. There was a problem with the train's pipes; at various intervals, we were perishing with the cold or sweltering with the heat. I took out the Dante that Fr Zahm at Notre Dame gave me and translated the remainder of the fifth canto from the *Inferno* into Irish. I had not had a moment to attend to it, other than the few days travelling west to San Francisco and today.

The twelfth Day of April. We arrived in St Paul at eight in the morning and my friend John D. O'Brien greeted us and drove us to the Ryan Hotel.[373] What brought me back to St Paul the second time was the fact that we could not ascertain how much money had been collected the first time I spoke here three months earlier and I wanted to clarify the situation. My wife was exhausted and went to bed; I spent most of the day trying to speak on the telephone with Regan who was the chair when I delivered my lecture three months earlier and with Hagerty, the treasurer.

I spent the afternoon with O'Brien and his household, and had supper with them. His eldest daughter is very beautiful. There was thunder and lightning as I returned to the hotel.

The thirteenth day of April. I finally succeeded in speaking with Regan and Fr Harrington in Minneapolis and urged them to send on their money quickly and complete affairs. I lunched with O'Brien and visited an old Fenian who has a gun store. He was one of the five white men who supported Louis Riel when he rebelled against the government in Canada. I had been here previously and he gave me a shotgun that fired five bullets, one after the other. We departed St Paul at eight in the evening and slept aboard the train.

The fourteenth day of April. We reached Chicago at nine in the morning. I had promised the Chicagoans that I would spend a week with them on returning from the West, as I understood that the AOH were less than happy that nothing special be done for them given the assistance they had accorded me. I also hoped to establish a branch of the Gaelic League that would provide perpetual support. They promised to do so.

Young Hackett called and spent the afternoon with us. I spoke with McGarry and Keating on the telephone. Three journalists called to interview me and were reluctant to leave! I went to Marshall Field's department store[374] and walked through it to purchase some items to send to my sister in Wyoming.

The fifteenth day of April. Easter Sunday. I attempted to attend church but it was full, with up to one hundred people outside in a line. That surprised me, as Chicagoans tended not to take much interest in their churches. I bought the Sunday newspaper: the Sunday newspaper was usually three times larger than the weekly edition and had a fine picture of the Resurrection by one of the old masters, but on the other side of the page there was the image of a young girl and these words beneath: 'Champion Easter Bride.' She was only 23 and had just married her eighth husband!

In the afternoon, I went to a large Irish-language class with William Dillon[375], the brother of John Dillon, MP, with McGarry and Hagerty where I spoke Irish to them. I did not want to neglect a class taught by an old man named Raleigh for fear than he would think that I was being disrespectful. We had to walk up 166 steps to reach the class; and today being Sunday, the elevator was not working. When we finally reached the room, there was no class, just one student! Much tension existed between him and the rest of the Gaelic League; he complained bitterly how the others had removed him from the presidency and how they stole his students. His complaint did not greatly surprise me. He is a gentle old man but is said to be unkind and a miser who never gave much to the Gaelic League. He only began to learn Irish when he was fifty.

Hackett joined us for dinner in the evening as well as Fr Fielding and Fr Small, a friend of Fielding's and they remained, chatting and smoking, until late into the night.

The sixteenth day of April. I rose early and John Raleigh, Waldron from Ballyhaunis, Mrs Springer and others called on me. Then I drove with Fr Fielding to call on the Archbishop and had a long conversation with him.

At eight in the evening, we all gathered to establish a branch of the Gaelic League. Keating, McGarry, O'Donnell, the lawyer, O'Shaughnessy and old O'Sullivan (a fine Irish-speaker), Captain Kelly, Fr Judge and a few others were present. We established the Mid-West branch of the Gaelic League for the centre of the country and then we christened it! I returned home at midnight.

The seventeenth day of April. We went out with Murphy to his new house in Elmhurst[376], a little outside Chicago, the house I had named *Cúl na Craoibhe* and I lunched there with him and his household. I returned in time to attend a reception hosted for me by the Irish Fellowship Club. Ninety people attended the reception.[377] Several speeches were delivered. I spoke for half an hour. O'Shaughnessy[378] chaired. I sat near Colonel Finnerty and he was telling me about the Indians. He had been a reporter with the American troops in the Indian Wars. He was present at some battles with them and had the greatest respect for them: their intelligence as warriors, their bravery and courage. He knew some of their leading warriors personally. He said many believed the Indian would never show his body in battle, always fighting from behind a tree or rock. 'That is not the case,' he said, 'I saw them, a 100 times, fighting on the open plains.'

My old friend Kelly from Milwaukee came especially to attend the reception and spoke on the current state of Ireland. It was his opinion that the county's intelligent class went into the Church and any intelligent man who joined the church was lost to

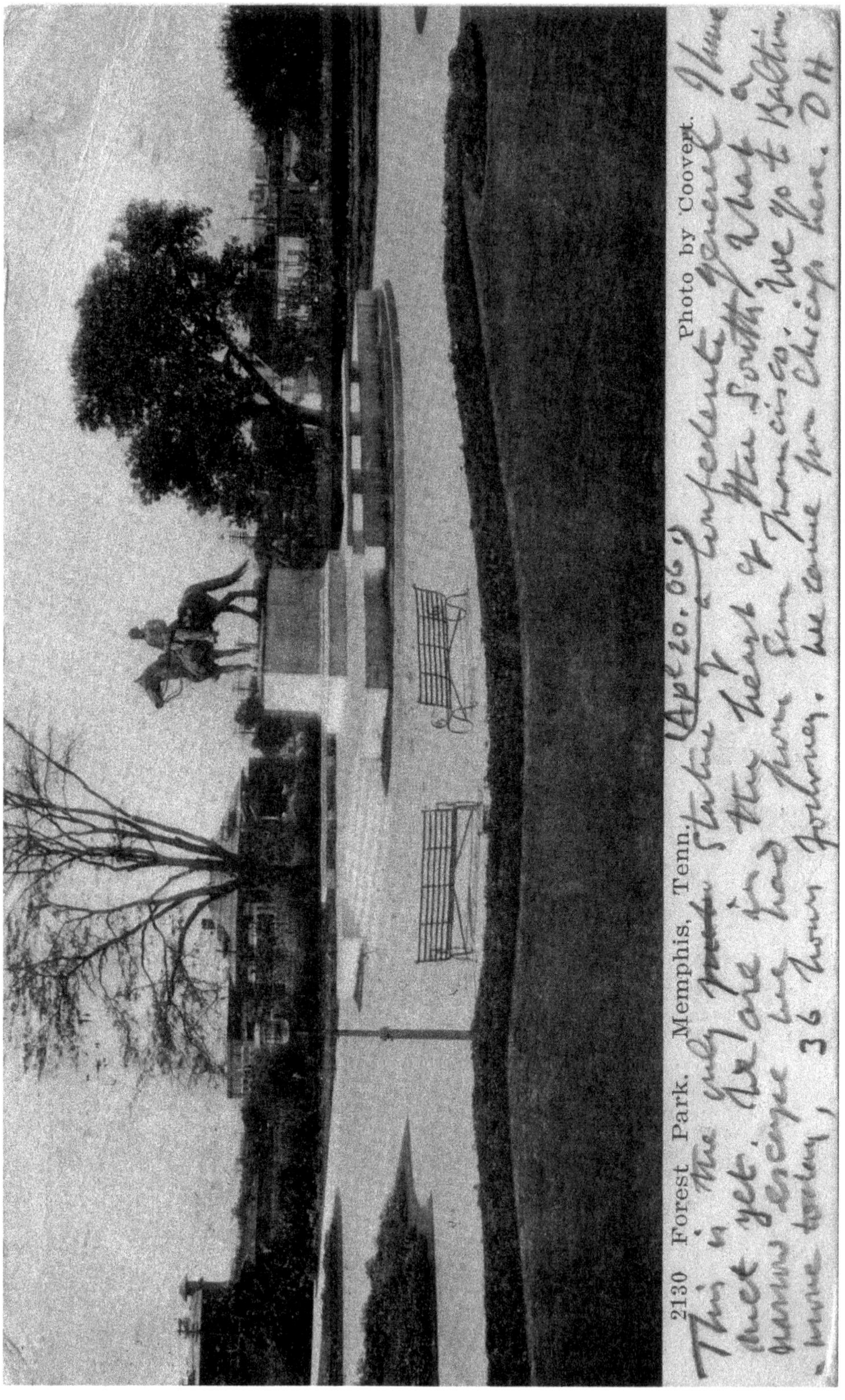

Courtesy of Westmeath Libraries (Aidan Heavey Collection)

Ireland because he left no descendants. *'Incedit per ignes, suppositos cineri doloso,'*[379] I said to myself. He was walking on the thinnest ice; I greatly feared it would give way beneath him and some cleric would challenge him.

Colonel Finnerty[380] was called upon to speak but he answered politely that it was best for him not to do so. Were he to speak, he said, he might say something with which we would not all agree. But, I believe, he knew that he had raised his elbow once too often and did not trust himself! The Colonel is a big handsome man but is a little red-faced. He is the editor of the *Chicago Citizen* and strongly favours the UIL and the MPs but John Devoy, the editor of the *Gaelic American*[381] is a Fenian and despises the parliamentarians and, alas, he and the Colonel hate one another! They show that in their respective papers. Poor Ireland when her fate rests in the hands of newspapermen!

On my left sat, I believe, a lawyer, a fine, handsome man named Hanecy.[382] I was told that he was opposing Dunne[383] for the city's mayorship; everyone thought he would defeat Dunne but an enemy went to where he had been born in Wisconsin and learned that he has been baptised 'Patrick' but changed his name to 'Elbridge'!

That reminds me of a story about one of the O'Briens in Boston. One man asked another 'How is O'Brien?', 'O,' said the other man, 'The O' spoiled his name as a fashionable man so he denied he has any O', and that ruined him as a politician!'

We had a very enjoyable dinner and the conversation was good as is usual. I came home at half-past one in the morning.

The eighteenth day of April. The time finally arrived to travel southwards, 500 miles or more to Memphis, Tennessee and we had to bid farewell to Chicago. We boarded the train at 10 in the morning; McGarry accompanied us to the station and then we were off to the South. As we travelled, everything became progressively greener. Hardly a green leaf was evident anywhere near Chicago, but before half the day had passed, most of the trees were in leaf. Gradually, the weather was warming and when we finally arrived at Memphis, after midnight, the cold was completely gone from the air. As night fell, while aboard the train, I saw a newspaper notice that San Francisco was burning. The news greatly disturbed me and I waited anxiously for more information. It worried my heart to think of those loyal people and good friends I had left behind there. No further information, however, was to be had that night nor any accurate information for several days.

Fr Larkin met us at the station after midnight and took us to the best hotel in the city. Nonetheless, it is a really filthy, untidy place in contrast to the fine hotels we frequented in the West, East and North. The lift never went the entire way up; it

Courtesy of Westmeath Libraries (Aidan Heavey Collection)

COPYRIGHT, 1906, BY AMERICAN-JOURNAL-EXAMINER.
San Francisco.
EARTHQUAKE RUINS IN MISSION STREET.

Courtesy of Westmeath Libraries (Aidan Heavey Collection)

always stopped three feet beneath the floor level and we had to haul ourselves up by hand! It was an athletic feat! I understood black people ran the place.

The nineteenth day of April. First thing in the morning, I bought every newspaper and read all the incredible news about San Francisco, how the Cliff House had fallen into the sea etc., etc., things that were all false. I sent one or two telegrams to San Francisco but they were never delivered, it seems.

In the afternoon, Malone[384], the city Mayor, a gentle old man, took us in an automobile to the races.[385] I found the Mayor very amusing. He is a Southerner, exactly as described in novels. He spoke slowly and was unable to pronounce the letter 'r'; he spoke much of his origins and the property they owned in Ireland 200 years ago. He said his family settled in Virginia 200 years ago. 'We were,' he said, 'this country's aristocracy before the war,' or as he would say it 'befo' the wah, suh.'

The horse races last three weeks here. They are all on flat courses with neither fence nor ditch. The races I observed were no longer than a mile or a mile and a quarter. The course was pleasant and plenty of bets were placed on the horses.

Returning from the racetrack, I went to a convent where a large number of nuns from various orders had gathered and I spoke to them for half an hour. The following morning, they kindly sent five dollars as a payment.

I had a good meeting in the theatre in the afternoon even though I do not think there are many Irish in the city. I met no true Irishmen, other than a young man named Walsh and Fr Larkin, from Limerick, I believe, a man who could be called 'the fair-haired priest' as he has long fair hair and everyone apparently likes him. Nevertheless, the meeting went well and I hope to receive 500 dollars as a result.

I think half of the people in Memphis are black. The large town is situated on the Mississippi and is the main centre for American cotton. The Mississippi overflows its banks here every year and I saw many trees standing in water as if growing there. Fr Larkin took me to see the large bales of cotton, compacted together by force of water, and ready in packed bags to be sent to the ends of the world! The river is a great lake here and steam ships go up and down constantly.

The twentieth day of April. I am not going to New Orleans or anywhere further south than Memphis and will have to travel northwards again. Baltimore, Maryland is the next destination I will head for now and that will take a few days to reach. Fr Larkin took us out in an automobile this morning. I saw woods on every side of the road and the mayor told me that they used to be full of millions of pigeons that arrived every year. The branches bent beneath their weight but they no longer appear. 'It is not that they were killed,' he said, 'You would not kill a hundredth of them, but for some reason they vanished, whatever happened.' Fr Larkin provided lunch and we left Memphis at one o'clock.

We were travelling the entire day, heading north-eastwards through Tennessee and Kentucky and finally, around two in the morning, the train halted at Louisville. We had to go to another station then and board another train at six in the morning to continue our journey.

The twenty-first day of April. We spent the day travelling through Kentucky and Virginia with nothing to do but look out the window as Spring arrived in the woods and the forests on both sides. Dog trees[386] with their white leaves and large patches of red or pink leaves brightened the woods on all sides. These were Judas trees.[387] I saw nothing prettier than them. They have no leaves, it appears, save the pink blossoms that cover them from top to bottom. It is said that Judas hanged himself on that tree, hence their name; but the trees I saw were too light and their branches too weak to hang anyone! These small trees are very common in the South, but I do not think they are found in the North.

As evening approached, we reached the Allegheny Mountains. They are not tall but are very pretty. Looking at the woods dressed in their spring dress, I observed that they appeared much more red than green. A very attractive river flowed along the mountain rim and it was not long until a summer lightning storm lit up the hills and the river about us for hours on end.[388]

BALTIMORE

The twenty-second day of April. Having travelled all night, we arrived in Baltimore at eight o'clock in the morning. Scully[389], Monahan and the welcome committee greeted us and brought us to the Kernan Hotel.[390] After breakfast, they took me in an automobile around the Park of which they are very proud. It has 700 acres and much of it consists of old natural wood with deer grazing among the trees. We had a fine meeting in the afternoon. The theatre[391] was full to capacity with some 1,800 people or so in attendance. They paid between one and two shillings admission. Cardinal Gibbons was in a box while I talked. I spoke for an hour and three quarters and believe I acquitted myself well having had a few days rest aboard the train. As ornamentation on the walls, in large letters, were these words: GINN FINN GINN FINN AMAIN FAILCE 7 SLAINCE 'Sinn Féin, Sinn Féin amháin, Fáilte agus sláinte' [i.e. 'Sinn

(Telegram)

New York, April 24, 1906.

Hon. Frank J. Sullivan,
Phelan Building,
San Francisco, California.

Overwhelmed with sorrow at the great calamity. Hope and trust you all have escaped any personal injury.

Douglas Hyde.

Draft of telegram from Douglas Hyde to Frank J. Sullivan, 24 April 1906. Hyde was shocked by the news of the San Francisco earthquake and immediately returned the money that had been collected there. Courtesy of the National Library of Ireland

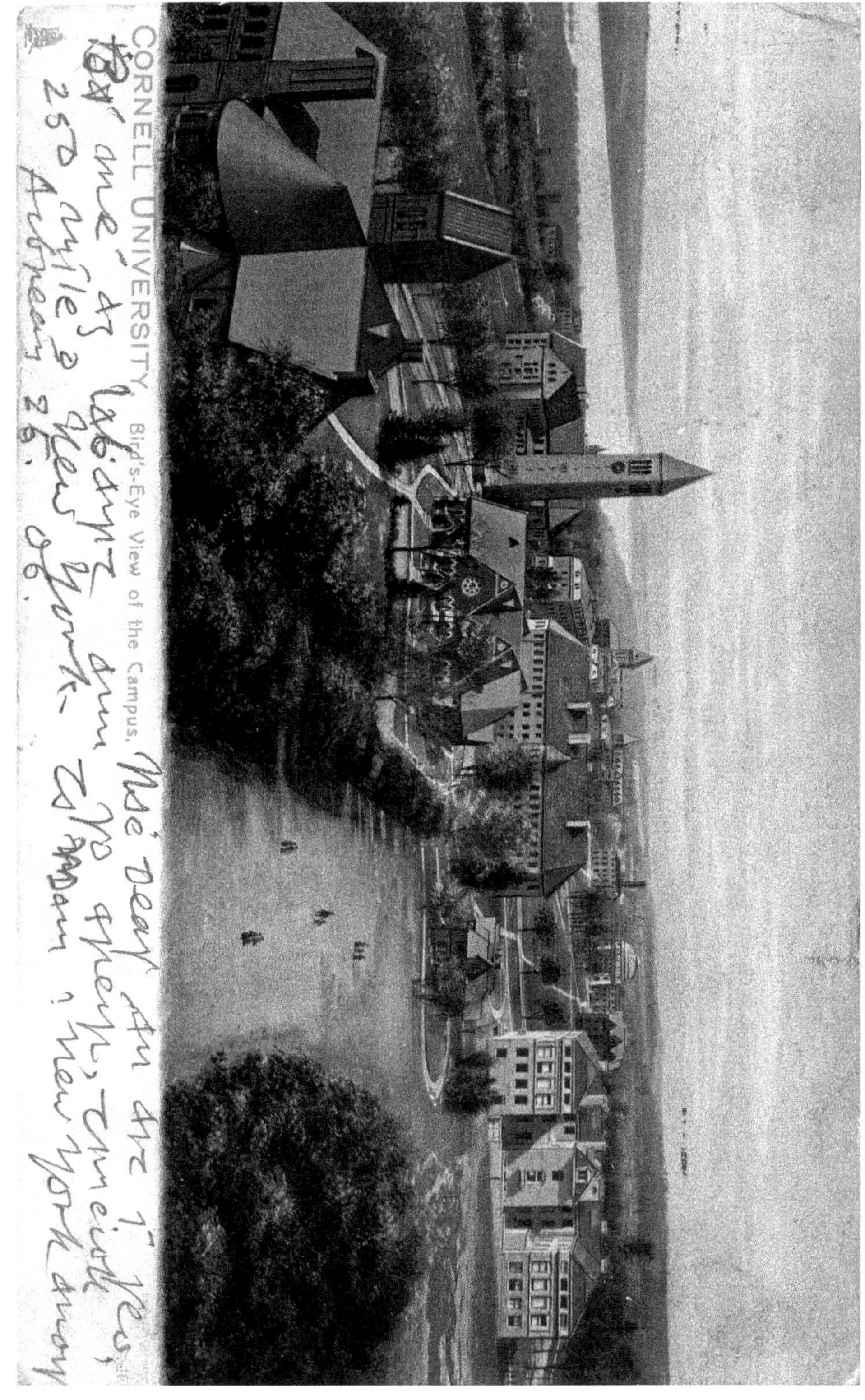

Courtesy of Westmeath Libraries (Aidan Heavey Collection)

Féin, Sinn Féin alone, Welcome and Health'], is, of course, what was meant. I suppose nobody noticed that it was meaningless – and if they did not, they were as well off!

The twenty-third day of April. We are to return to New York again today having been absent for three months and three weeks. We left Baltimore at midday and reached New York at six o'clock in the evening. I was delighted to see Quinn again but was disappointed that he was not looking well. His brother had died while I was absent. Visiting his house was almost a return home, to him and his clerk Curtin. Nonetheless, I did not delay too long with him, as I had to depart again the following day.

CORNELL

The twenty-fourth of April. I left New York at a quarter past nine in the morning. Quinn came with me on the ferry to Hoboken. I boarded the train to Ithaca where the University of Cornell is located, some one hundred miles outside New York but in the same state. Professor McMahon[392], a Trinity College man, met me at the train station and brought me to his own house. Only he and his wife were there.[393]

This is one of the Land Grant universities. Various states received sums of money to establish universities. Most of the states sold the land they received, but an old man Cornell[394] bought the land for himself and when the price of the land had greatly increased, sold it and gave it to the university. There is a law that this university and others must instruct students in soldiery. I saw students in uniform drilling everywhere. After the war, the government gave the money in the hope that the universities would provide officers if they were required. But Cornell also has an agricultural college, as well as colleges of construction, veterinary and engineering.

A good-sized crowd listened when I spoke in the afternoon on the Gaelic League's philosophy. It was the Dean, Dr Crane, who introduced me to the audience. He is married to McMahon's sister.

The twenty-fifth of April.[395] I spent the morning consulting the library's fine Dante collection as well as their good collection of books about Iceland and a Petrarch collection.

At three o'clock I gave a lecture about Irish poetry and then went with O'Connor to Elmira. Twenty-eight people attended a dinner in my honour; it commenced at ten o'clock and did not end until half past one. Moore[396], the editor of the *Telegraph*, chaired. It was half past two in the morning when I returned with O'Connor[397] to his home.

ELMIRA

In the morning, I went to the Ladies' College[398] at Elmira. This college is renowned as the first college in America founded for women. I believed the women there to be finer and more beautiful than anywhere else. They are said to excel at athletics. I spoke to them for half an hour and made them laugh. When the evening arrived, I made an error. I had a large meeting, some 1,200 people, but I failed to realise that not even a quarter were Irish and gave the same speech as I had in Carnegie Hall, in San Francisco and in Philadelphia. The girls from the college, in their caps and gowns, came to hear me. I did not understand in time that the audience was American and while I altered the talk slightly, it was too late. Moore was very unhappy with me about my 'mistake' as he called it, but I feel that most of the audience were not in agreement with him. Had I known in advance, I would have given a lecture on poetry or something else as I had done that morning to the college girls. Nevertheless, we did well in Elmira and received 600 dollars but O'Connor gave 150 dollars of that.

O'Connor took me home, uncorked a bottle of champagne and it was a long time before I went to bed. He is a wealthy timber man and among the wealthiest men in Elmira and is very knowledgeable about horses. He is also a friend of old Monaghan in Spokane and I told him of his accident.

SCRANTON

I left Elmira to go to Scranton at midday. Fr Hurst[399] from Scranton came the previous night and brought me with him. He was an old friend of mine who had stayed with me in Ratra once, and had served as a priest in Swinford, County Mayo for a period. O'Connor uncorked another bottle of champagne before we could depart and we had to drink it. As a result, I felt sleepy on board the train and barely kept my eyes open. I was less than pleased, therefore, when two men from Scranton entered the train seeking me when we were still 60 miles away. They were Casey, a millionaire from Scranton, and Dr O'Malley. There are two Caseys[400], the whiskey makers that come from Coolavin[401] or nearby, where my friend MacDermot lives. They were pleased when I told them that I knew Coolavin very well and often fished there in the Lung River and in Lough Gara. They named their whiskey from somewhere near Coolavin, but I do not recall the name now.

When we arrived at the station, the mayor sent his automobile for me bearing an Irish and an American flag. We had a fine meeting that afternoon, attended by 1,200 people and they paid between two and six shillings admittance.[402] The Bishop, Dr Hoban[403] and the mayor Dimock[404], a tall handsome man of Welsh descent, attended the meeting and were on the platform. The bishop spoke, but I do not recall who chaired the meeting. I spoke for two hours. Scranton is full of Irish people. They are miners and many come from Mayo. Fr Hurst informs me that more Irish is spoken in Scranton than any other city in the world. It is a large town with up to 170,000 people. Coalmines made Scranton rich and tunnels run beneath the city; I heard people say that someday the city will collapse into them! I met a good Irish-speaker from Connemara, named Griffin. He, along with the Caseys, Fr Hurst and Dr O'Malley are the main Irishmen I encountered in the city. On the Lackawanna rail line, one line goes to Scranton and it is called the Anthracite Road as it is all coal.

The twenty-eighth day of April. I rose at six in the morning to go to New York. I noticed that there are yet but few leaves on the trees here, but the willows are beginning to wear their green dress and the hard maples are starting to flower. These flowers are red when young and give the trees a yellow-reddish, rather than green appearance. Observing a wood that has dressed in spring attire, your eye will detect every shade: pale-green, dark-green, yellow-red, but little of that vivid green one finds in Ireland. The nicest aspect of the wood, in my opinion, is the willow.

I arrived in New York at one and went to Quinn's office. I lunched with him. Emmet, Cohalan and Conway from the Irish Volunteers were there.

I urged them to send 5,000 dollars to San Francisco as I was reluctant to do so without the Executive Committee's permission or, I should say, I could not do so without it, but I received their permission today, and Quinn sent it to Fr Yorke via telegram. After dinner, Quinn, his sister and I went to the Opera House, Lexington where they performed my play 'An Pósadh.'[405] The Kellys had a box there. I had to make a small speech in Irish to the audience. I met Graham, a Scotsman from Canada, and we had a drink together. He is a man who has seen much of the world, and I had a long, interesting conversation with him. It was late when I returned to Quinn's house.

The twenty-ninth day of April. Today is Sunday. I attended Church and then went for a stroll with Quinn. We saw French and American war ships on the river. I was idle today.

The thirtieth day of April. Another idle day. Quinn took me to lunch with Cohalan, Judge Keogh and others.

May Day. My wife and I left New York to go again to Philadelphia. A welcome committee met us at the station. Fr Coghlan[406], O'Kane, Fr O'Donnell, Daly - the treasurer - and others attended. We were brought to Fr Coghlan's house where we stayed. He provided a fine dinner with plenty of wine and so forth. Fr O'Donnell, his sister (they are relatives of Coghlin) and two other priests were there.

The second of May. We were taken in two carriages to view the Park. Dr Carroll[407], the old Fenian, was our guide and we had to examine carefully all the images and buildings. Then we drove out a beautiful road by the banks of the Wissahickon[408] River and then along the Schuylkill River. We returned at five o'clock and had dinner.

The third day of May, Dr Carroll called on us again. He showed us Independence Hall, where the Americans first signed the Declaration of Independence, Carpenter Hall where the first Congress convened, and City Hall that is as tall as the Washington Monument. We received special permission to take the lift to the top of Penn's statue which is nearly 500 feet high. From there we had an excellent view of all Philadelphia, including the Schuylkill River and the great docks. Afterwards, we went to the Freemasons' Hall and we had to enter every room and marvel at the wonderful styles! I thought my feet would give way. I think Carroll is both a Catholic and a Freemason, as well as being a Fenian to boot!

When night fell, there was a dinner for me in Dooner's Hotel.[409] Some forty attended and there were many speeches and talk. I asked them to establish a branch of the Gaelic League as is intended to happen in Chicago. I returned home at one o'clock but I did not go to bed until three as Fr Coghlan, Fr McLaughlin and Fr O'Donnell and I commenced a game of 25 that delayed us.

The fourth day of May. We departed Philadelphia. Fr Coghlan and all were very kind to us and, within a few hours, we were back in New York again. I lunched with Quinn and left him to go to Vassar College. It is located on the Hudson River, a few hours' journey from New York. The day was beautiful and the river looked very well. Miss Wylie[410], a professor of English literature, met me and took me to the college, where I dined in the common room among the professors and female students. Mrs Kendrick[411] is the College President and has around 1,000 students. I lectured on Irish-language Poetry to between 500 and 600 people. I held a reception for them afterwards and many came to shake my hand.

Afterwards, I was fortunate to observe a very strange but special event – the female students selecting their class tree. Each class selects a tree for themselves. The class that went to choose the tree employed every form of sorcery and dark arts. They dressed in the strangest clothes, such as the Goddess Juno on her deathbed and other goddesses etc. Electric lights shone on them as they marched and they recited unusual poems. It is very difficult, they admit, not only to create the costumes but hide them from the prying eyes of the younger class members who would tear them into strips if discovered.

The fifth day of May. I slept in Vassar last night. This morning I bade farewell to Miss Wylie and returned to New York in time to lunch with Quinn, Mrs Thursby, and Hackett at Delmonico's. In the afternoon, I attended a review by the Irish Volunteers at Grand Central Palace.[412] Judge Dowling[413], Quinn, Cohalan and Conway were there. I inspected the troops with one of the majors[414], examining them closely as a president would. They were a fine troop, between three and 400 men. I addressed them for about half an hour. The money is to go to San Francisco. If not for that and that the men were called out for charity, I do not think I would have attended; it is not wise for me to be present with a group of armed volunteers. In reality, I think they are all linked with Clan na nGael.[415]

After that, we had wine with the officers and Judge Dowling. Then I went to the Players' Club with Quinn and Graham, and did not return home until two o'clock.

The sixth day of May. Miss Coates[416], a dear friend of Quinn breakfasted with us. I had a headache from the previous night. I went with my wife on the train to New Rochelle, where Judge Keogh lives, for lunch. Mr Palén[417], director of the *Catholic Encyclopaedia* that is to be established, Temple Emmet and other people were there. I had a long chat with Palén and told him not to forget to devote much coverage and attention to the Irish and Ireland in his book when it appears. 'It is the Irish,' I told him 'who are the chief Catholics in this country.' I am almost certain that what I said had an impact, as Ireland was well served in his books. They drove us through Pelham Park[418] after spending a very enjoyable day with them.

The seventh day of May. I met Mrs Thursby[419] and her brother Brisbane[420] (editor of the *Evening Journal*), Mrs Cary from Buffalo and her daughters for lunch at Delmonico's. I had a long conversation with Brisbane.

Monsieur Janvier and his wife called on me in the afternoon. He is a large handsome man of French origin. He and his wife are writers and authors, and knew 'Fiona Mac Leóid'.

The eighth day of May. I dined with Quinn at Delmonico's. Judge Keogh and his son, and Cohalan were there. After dinner, we went upstairs to a quarterly meeting of the Friendly Sons of St Patrick. There were about one hundred there: all people who have succeeded in life, the cream of Irish society, in my opinion. Two men from San Francisco were there, a nephew of Judge Coffey and a cousin of James Phelan Clarke[421], the poet who wrote 'Kelly, Burke and Shea'[422], chaired. Crimmins was also there. As far as I could see, this is the only organisation patronised by the wealthy Irish. The affluent people gradually withdrew from the other Irish organisations. They encountered too much friction, disunity and fighting, and fearing they would be involved in the perpetual bickering and fighting which occurs among other groups, they left them all, almost, and joined this group which has no purpose other than to meet now and again, eat dinner and so forth. I am almost certain that the most competent, richest and most distinguished people are not found in the other groups. If a man of great ability is a president or is prestigious in another society and some chancer wants his position, it is said he makes a personal attack on that man by smearing him and if enough dirt is thrown, some will inevitably stick. Or if some dispute occurs among them, the same thing happens; it is no surprise that the wealthy men do not tolerate it. 'We are not obliged to join any of those societies,' they say. 'It is for the country's benefit and not our own benefit, nor for wealth or benefit or honour that we are in such societies and we suffer plenty by them. Why would we endure that? Let us quit them all!'

On the other hand, Cohalan says, 'it is scandalous the manner in which her best sons desert mother Ireland.' He says, 'that the leading Irish are betraying their own people.' 'If they wished to be of the people and to do their share, they would direct the Irish in the proper manner and would earn gratitude and honour for themselves.' Maybe he is partially correct but nonetheless, it is only natural that important people will not favour those who are certain to cause them conflict.

I believe this society has been in existence since Washington's era. I had to recount some of my adventures from having departed New York until my return; my tale of dinner in Columbus with Dr Thompson, and the funny story that Colonel Kilburn told made them laugh. I would have great store in these men if only their nationalism was fired up. But when an Irishman becomes wealthy, and has plenty of money to share on whatever he wishes, rarely does he endow Ireland or anything connected with Ireland. Most are very generous to the Church and give much to it.

The ninth day of May. I passed the day writing letters, and my wife and I dined with Monsieur and Madame Janvier. They were friendly with Sharpe, the Scotsman who writes under the penname 'Fiona Macleod.' They told me the truth that there never was a 'Fiona' and his own sister was 'Fiona Nic Leóid.' And Sharpe dictated everything for her. Janvier and his wife are Félibres[423] and charming people. We came home after midnight.

The tenth day of May. Miss Coates, a friend of Quinn, called and took my wife and me to the Museum of Art in Central Park and returned to have lunch with us.

In the afternoon, we dined with the Kelly family. Kelly's brother, Eugene and another man were at dinner. We went home after midnight.

The eleventh day of May. I lunched with Phelan, a cousin of James Phelan and O'Keefe.

In the afternoon, Quinn brought Miss Coates and us to the Hippodrome.[424] We saw seals there playing with a ball. They threw the ball in the air from seal to seal and would not drop it for five minutes. There was also a ballet featuring 170 dancers, the largest ballet, they say, in the world. We went home close to two.

BUFFALO

The twelfth day of May. After this holiday, we left New York again. This time we are to go north to Buffalo. We were eleven hours on the train and arrived there at seven o'clock. Ryan[425], Murphy and Wall met us and took us to the Iroquois Hotel.[426] Numerous people called: Judge Kenefick[427], O'Rourke, O'Connor[428] (who owns two newspapers here), Ryan of Clan na Gael, Murphy and many others and they were not gone until almost twelve at night. Many newspaper men also called.

The thirteenth day of May. Sunday. I lunched with the Careys who are related to Mrs Thursby and Mrs Stopford Green. It poured rain. I spoke in the afternoon at Shea's Theatre. There was about 1,200 people present. Bishop Colton[429] introduced me to the people and Judge Kenefick chaired. Fr Comyns from Roscommon was there also. He is collecting for a fine church to be erected in that town. I spoke for an hour and forty minutes. The Judge asked the people for money and we received 1,150 dollars.

The fourteenth day of May. After one, we took a tram to Niagara to see the great waterfall. Murphy, Ryan, Mrs Murphy and Mrs Wall were with us. We were taken to the powerhouse, where electricity is made. The people complained that the electricity had ruined Niagara but I do not believe that. As far as I was concerned, the waterfall appeared as fine and as wide as it was when I was there fourteen years ago. We went to the base of the waterfall and looked at the Brock Monument[430] on the Canadian side of the river, and went as far as to see Lake Ontario.

We then proceeded to Niagara College run by the Vincentian order. Fr Likly is its president. We had dinner there and of course it was badly needed. The women in our group had not eaten since breakfast and were weak with hunger, as was I. I then spoke to some 600 students about Irish-language literature. We returned to the hotel at 12.30 exhausted.

The fifteenth day of May. We lunched with Murphy. I think he is an insurance man. Ryan of Clan na Gael and Fr O'Sullivan (who said he came 200 miles to hear me) were also at lunch. Fr Comyns called and we chatted. He collected a lot of money in South America for his church.[431] Everyone was very tired today, after the day before, as

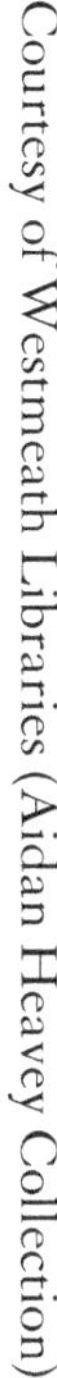

Courtesy of Westmeath Libraries (Aidan Heavey Collection)

we had not eaten anything from breakfast until dinner at six or seven in the evening. Today we dined on our own in comfort in the hotel. I visited Sweeney, a cloth merchant from County Leitrim who, after the meeting on Sunday, had given me a 100 dollars. 'It is not easy to get money from me,' he said, 'It you had not struck the right note, you wouldn't have got it!'

ROCHESTER

We both departed for Rochester on the 'Empire State Express,' the fastest train I have yet travelled on – it travels seventy miles in sixty-nine minutes. O'Grady, O'Connor the newspaper man, Bradley, a whiskey or beer maker, and Finucane who owns a large telephone plant accompanied us. Finucane brought us around the Genessee Valley in his automobile. I spoke in the evening to around a 1,000 people.[432] Bishop Hickey was present. A banquet[433] with speeches, wine and tobacco followed until three in the morning. There was a judge present, a Lynn[434], who spoke extremely well, as I thought, and a kind priest with a strange name, Fr Codyre.[435] He is a sworn enemy of O'Grady and I believe he is the man who most encouraged the others to bring me to them.

TORONTO

The seventeenth[436] of May. Now we are entering Canada – going among those who are unsupportive of anything Irish, among the real Orangemen or, as the old people used to say, the Lodgemen, among the Yellow men, among those who never forgot their vindictiveness towards the Irish – to Toronto!

The welcoming committee greeted us at the station, two carriage loads, and they drove us around. With me in the carriage was a Scotsman, named Fraser, a very gentle man. There was also Walsh, Hearn, a lawyer; and Hernon (a butcher, I think); they are the main Irishmen whom I met there.

We had a meeting[437] in the afternoon, but the wealthy Irish of the city were divided about attending. I was told many did not attend, as they did not understand what precisely I would speak about and, fearing there would be some trouble there, remained at home. I admit I was anxious and devised a scheme to avoid all trouble, as I had not forgotten the meeting in Ithaca. The Scots are strong in Toronto, as they

New York We saw this beautiful lake at Buffalo but
SUNSET ON LAKE ONTARIO had no time to sail on it - they are very
dangerous lakes as sudden storms arise quickly.
Warwick Bro's & Rutter, Limited, Publishers, Toronto S1296
May 19. 06

Courtesy of Westmeath Libraries (Aidan Heavey Collection)

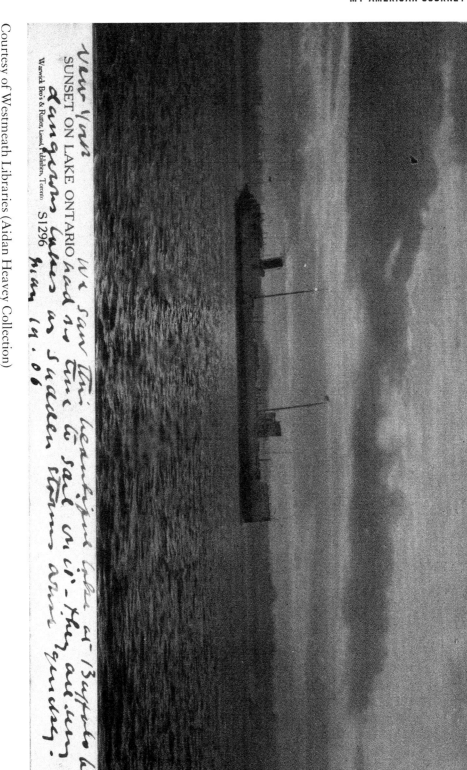

are throughout Canada; I intended to praise the Scots, pretending that I was speaking about the Gaelic-speaking Scots as well as the Irish in my talk. I said that it was the Scots that had put Canada on its feet, and that it was a scandal that there was a great university in Toronto and that not a word of the history or of the language of the people was taught in it. I continued to speak in that fashion and while it greatly pleased the Scots, the Irish were not unhappy with it. I said nothing that would allow the enemy an opportunity. There were about 1,000 people in attendance, and nobody could say whether I was advocating for the Irish-speakers of Ireland or the Gaelic-speakers of Scotland!

The eighteenth day of May. All the newspapers appeared today and contained favourable accounts of the meeting. I was very happy and it pleased the Irish greatly. More than any other city, the Toronto Irish were in my debt; they are more accustomed to insult and criticism. Today, not a word of such was heard.

I spent the morning sightseeing in the city. A large section burnt several years ago and is yet to be rebuilt. The Court House and the University are fine buildings. Based on what I saw, I considered the land here more fertile than in most of the cities in the States. I lunched with Hearn, Hernon and Walsh and they came to the station with us to board the train at five o'clock to return to New York.

The nineteenth day of May. We slept aboard the train and arrived in New York in the morning. I lunched with Quinn and Cohalan, and another man. I went with him and Miss Coates to see a light opera that featured Fritzi Scheff.[438] We went home after two.

WASHINGTON DC

The twentieth day of May. I departed New York with my wife for Washington. We reached there at five o'clock in the evening and met Dr Dunn and Dr Healy. They brought us to the hotel, the New Willard.[439] I was eating my dinner before leaving for the lecture when my back suddenly suffered acute rheumatism. The pain was fierce and left me almost devoid of feeling. I could neither breathe nor move my legs or hands. I attended the meeting despite the terrible pain. It had little impact on my talk but I was unable to gesticulate. I usually did so while talking, bending as if to pick up a piece of mud, but I thought I would die were I to bend over and omitted it entirely. I believe the pain resulted from sitting by an open window with a soft, warm, pleasant draught for four hours on the train.

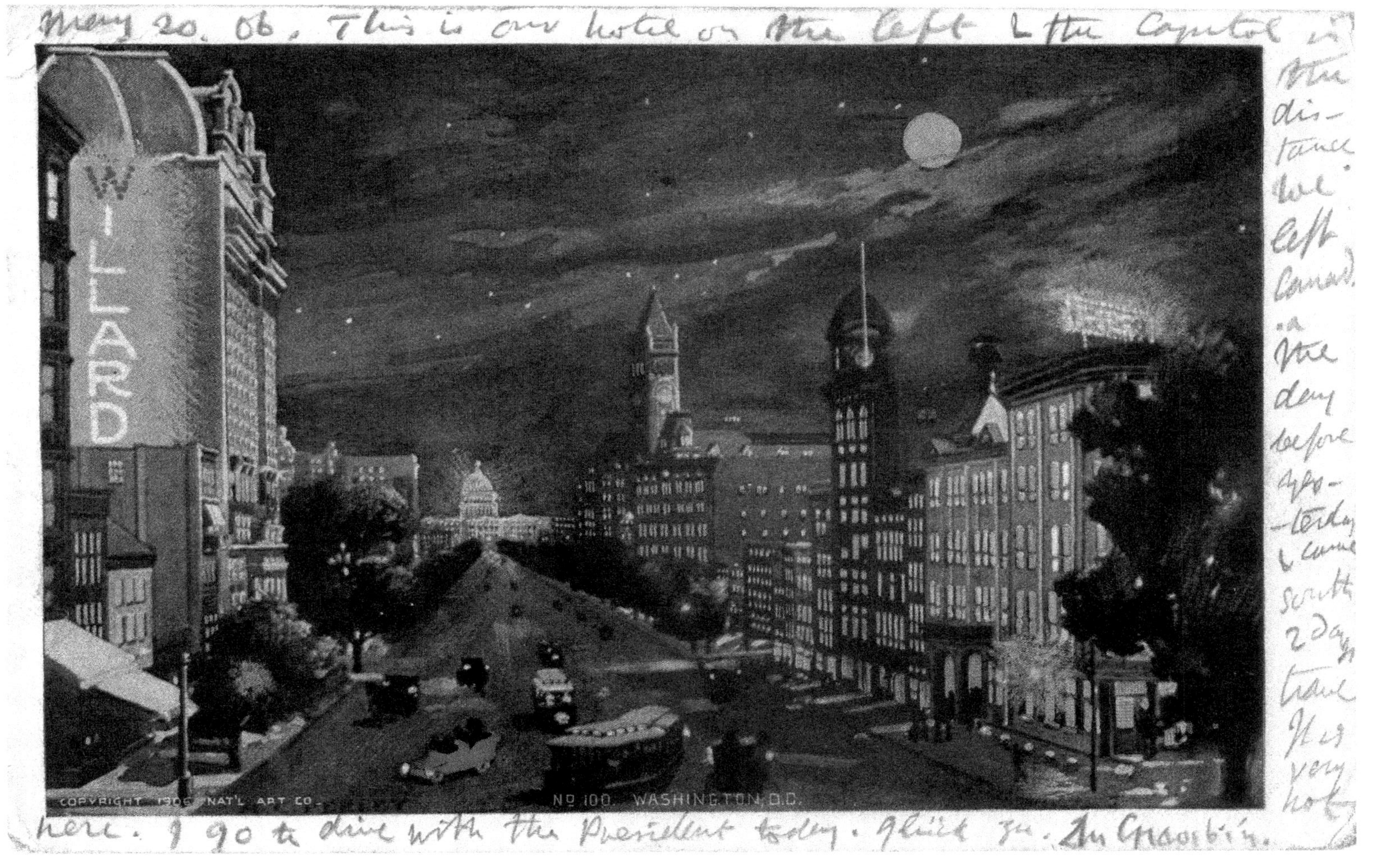

Courtesy of Westmeath Libraries (Aidan Heavey Collection)

The meeting[440] was small, around 400 people, but while small, it was productive. Uncle Joe Cannon[441], the House Speaker, and many other distinguished people attended. The great heat kept people away; it is too late in the season now for public meetings. I was in great pain throughout but nonetheless spoke well enough, I believe.

The twenty-first day of May. The pain is still intense. I was barely able to walk up to the White House for lunch with President Roosevelt.[442] Dunn, the Irish-language professor at the Catholic University, and Dr Egan[443], a small handsome man with a large beard and a friend of the president, accompanied me. 'In God's name,' said Egan, as we approached, 'don't give me away'. What he meant by that, I think, was not to reveal that he was not an Irish-speaker. 'Don't let me down,' he said in English. 'Have no fear,' I said, and found an opportunity during lunch to say to the president, 'my friend here is associated with one of the finest European scholarly families, the Egans from Ballymacegan in County Tipperary,' and that satisfied him immensely. We had a simple lunch. Admiral Cole[444] who married the president's sister, his own wife's sister and another woman joined us for lunch. The president had written an essay comparing an old-Irish story and a Scandinavian saga.[445] He said that when he wrote his letter shortly before that about the rates on the railways he knew that he would be denigrated about it throughout the country and, to take his mind off it, would write an essay on Irish poetry. He was very kind and generous, and if I say so, very friendly in a familial sense.

After lunch, I returned with Egan to the Cosmos Club[446] and had a Mint Julep. This is a common drink in these parts but not one I encountered anywhere else. Similar to a High Ball, it is poured in a large tall glass and garnished with mint leaves. To drink it, one places their nose and mouth in the mint, and inhales the herb's taste and scent. I was in a bad way with the pain when I took the initial drink but thought the pain lessened afterwards. Either way, I did not leave the club nor did Egan abandon me until we had had four each. Although I barely managed to make it to the White House, I was able to walk back home to the hotel reasonably well.

The twenty-second of May. A small group of us went up the river: Egan, Dr Dunn, Mrs Sullivan, Egan's two daughters, Campbell who has returned home from the Philippines and some others. We went to Mount Vernon, where Washington had his home. It is 11 miles up river. We went through his house, an old house of the type that used be in the America colonies. I noticed several large hawks – a combination of a hawk and a crow that they call a buzzard – circling and gliding high in the sky. They are nature's cleaners and there is a law against killing them. When something

Copyright 1906 by the Rotograph Co.
A 209 White House, Main Entrance, Washington, D. C.
May 23. 1906

Courtesy of Westmeath Libraries (Aidan Heavey Collection)

dies, it cannot escape them. They wait until the meat is sufficiently tender for them and then swallow it straight away. I did not see them clearly, until I came here. We saw Washington's tomb, the room in which he died and much more. I noticed the kitchen was a small, separate house as was the milking parlour; there was a separate hut for the gardener and separate houses for the black people. The garden was like an old English garden.

I went to the Catholic University in the evening where I lectured on the Gaelic League[447] and had a good conversation with the professors and Dr Shahan.[448] There were plenty of stories about the first Irish-language professor there, the Déise-man from Portlaw. I fear he made an enemy of the entire college. No one sided with him. I gave a good speech and returned home at midnight.

The twenty-third day of May. I went with my old friend James Mooney[449] to the Smithsonian Institute. He has written a large book[450] that he gave me a copy of previously[451] and I do not believe there is another man in America as knowledgeable as him about the Indians. He introduced me to many people concerned with the Institute's work and since they knew that I collected stories from the Canadian Indians, the *Maliseet* Indians[452] when I was there a dozen years earlier and published them in an American newspaper[453], they made me a member of the Institute. They were to send me every book they issued. The Institute holds the pictures Caltin[454] made, many bows and arrows, and everything else associated with the Indians from every part of America. (I acquire these fine books ever since as they appear in print. I have almost eighty of them and when I left Dublin in 1933, I presented them all to the Folklore Society). I cannot praise the government enough for this great project and what they have done to shed light on the old ways, and the history and culture of the Indians. It is England's disgrace that they did not do something similar in Australia among the aboriginal people before they all die.

I gave another lecture on Irish-language literature at the Catholic University. Mrs Sullivan took us in her carriage and I dined with Monsignor O'Connell[455], the university president; my wife dined with Dr O'Shea and others.

The twenty-fourth day of May. I attended the Senate to hear the proceedings. Nothing of importance was discussed, and it was a stale and stiff affair. I then went to the Lower House. There, everything was much livelier but I thought it lacked dignity. I saw three men on their feet at the same time not addressing the chairman, but each other. Uncle Joe was not in the chair, but the man who was, had to strike the table repeatedly with the gavel to impose some order. Afterwards we went to the Library of Congress that is very fine but, in my opinion, too fine and too ornate.

Courtesy of Westmeath Libraries (Aidan Heavey Collection)

In the afternoon, I went to the University again and spoke to a large crowd about folklore. I dined with Monsignor O'Connell and Dr Shahan. I came home at twelve.

The twenty-fifth day of May. We had to depart Washington today. It is a wonderfully fine city. It is in a beautiful setting, and has the Capitol, the finest building in America. The Library of Congress is like a forest of pillars with beautiful marble columns, but I thought the pitiable pictures on the walls and too many ornaments spoiled it. I think a Frenchman designed the city and, in my opinion, it is closer to Paris than any other city I visited. The Capitol, the city's main building, is a three-and-a-half acre site with fine large streets stretching outwards in an orderly and regular manner. Most of the streets are 30 to 40 feet wide. The Washington Memorial is made of marble and is 555 feet tall. No goods of any kind are manufactured in the city; it is only a place from where the states are ruled. The city itself is independent of any state, constructed in its own territory, called the District of Columbia. This small district is independent and self-ruled. Black people are about a third of the city's population. There are numerous universities as well as the Catholic University but I did not see them. The men associated with the Catholic University are among the broadest minded and sharpest men I have ever met. They are real Americans, without any trace of the Italian mentality; they spoke so independently about everything that it amazed me.

The heat was so great that we were not loath to leave this beautiful place. We boarded the train to New York at eleven o'clock in the morning and Dr Healy, Dr Dunn and James Mooney came to the station to bid farewell to us. We arrived in New York at five in the afternoon.

I was going for dinner with Quinn when a fire engine drove down the street; as it swept past a cinder from the engine went into my eye. It almost blinded me. Quinn took me to four doctors before he located one that would take the cinder out of my eye.

The twenty-sixth day of May. I lunched at Delmonico's with Quinn and Cohalan, Brisbane, Judge Keogh and Peter Finley Dunne whose name is well-known throughout America as 'Mister Dooley'. We sat down at one o'clock and did not leave the place until six. Such conversation I never heard before; everyone talking and telling stories. Dunne rose every quarter of an hour to speak on the telephone with someone to inform them that he would be back in a quarter of an hour, but one quarter followed another and he did not move! I was sitting beside him and had much conversation with him. He is connected, I believe, with Clan na Gael. His speech is not as humorous as his writing, and I think he was the least talkative of us at that party. Nonetheless, he is a kind gentle man.

It would not be easy, I believe, to bring together six similar men as we had at that lunch today.

BRIDGEPORT

My wife and I departed New York to go to Bridgeport. It is situated on Long Island. The island is not wide but is some 80 miles long. Mr Wren[456] met us at the station and took us to his home.[457] He is a whiskey-maker. He is a Catholic but nonetheless has been the President of the Board of Education here for 17 years. The city mayor, Hurley - a millionaire connected with the railroad - some general or other, and three or four others attended the dinner he had arranged for me, but no woman attended.

Then we had a big meeting in the theatre and I spoke to them for two hours, but I was hoarse and I am afraid I did not speak very well. I went to sleep at 12.30.

The twenty-eighth day of May. An elderly man, Sullivan, came in from Hartford to see me. He gave me a wonderful stick which had 12 kinds of wood in its handle. We left this place at eleven o'clock and we returned safely to New York.

PATERSON

No sooner had I arrived in New York than I left again to go to Paterson, New Jersey. It was pouring rain and very cold. Today was thirty degrees colder than yesterday. I reached Paterson at six o'clock. This is the main town for silk in America.

I had dinner at the Club[458] with Gourley[459], two judges and the sheriff. We then had a meeting in the theatre[460] but it was not a large meeting as the heavy rain scared the people. I spoke well, better than in Bridgeport. We all returned and we sat with our wine until half past one.[461]

The twenty-ninth day of May. Gourley is a lawyer who is doing well in life and he has a lovely place. He is unmarried and his sister lives with him. They took me out in their automobile to a place called Eagle Rock[462] and the Orange Mountains, above Newark and Orange; we were looking at New York in the distance, some 15 or 20 miles. Nonetheless, the large buildings near the Battery were clearly visible and we saw the cathedral[463] on 50th street and the other large buildings in the distance as if they were mountains. This district is one long series of lovely houses and nice pretty gardens with neither fence nor wall between them, but all side by side. Most people who reside here work in New York during the day and come here at night. Others live in New York during the winter and come out here in the summer. From atop Eagle Rock, I was looking at an area that contained the same number of people as all of Ireland. I boarded the 2.40 train that brought me to New York at 4.30, in time to see Wall and to conduct an interview with him for the papers.

Miss Worthington and Miss Merrington[464] i.e. the lady who gave me the sage advice about newspaper men while I was aboard the ship coming here, called.

The thirtieth day of May. This is Decoration Day[465] and my wife, Quinn and I lunched with Cohalane. His wife[466], his brother and his father[467] were also in attendance. I never heard a finer Irish-speaker than his father. From south County Cork, somewhere not far from Skibbereen, I believe. It was his father who told me that Cahalan and not Cohalan, was the correct surname and it means a 'man of battle.'[468]

The thirty-first of May. I had dinner with Mrs Worthington at the Arts Club. Miss Merrington was also there. Thieves broke into her room the previous night. There were some musicians and Quinn arrived late. We went home at midnight.

The first day of June. I went to Hollenbeck, the phonographer who gave me an apparatus to learn French, German and Spanish through his phonographs. I spoke Irish into one of the cylinders for the phonograph. I then visited young Hackett[469] and lunched with him.

Quinn gave a tea party attended by Mrs Worthington, Miss Merrington, Miss Coates and others.

The second day of June. I stayed indoors all-day writing letters and completing an essay for Scribner.[470]

The third day of June. My wife, Quinn and I went to Judge Keogh's house for lunch, and to inspect his new library.[471] Mrs Ford and another woman came to the judge's house and brought us to their home, a few miles from where we were, at Rye. They provided a fine dinner there. It was only us and a German doctor. We remained on the balcony, above the doorway until midnight, marvelling at the sea which comes up almost to the house.

The fourth day of June. The two women took us in an automobile to the station and we arrived safely back in New York. We attended a party at Mrs Worthington's; around 12 people attended. Mark Twain was to attend but failed to appear due to some accident. We dined in the evening with Quinn at Delmonico's and old O'Connor from Elmira was there.

The fifth day of June. I went to Scribner's and gave them the essay. Then I called on Gilder, the editor of *Century* and he brought me to the Actors' Club for lunch. I then called on Wessel[472], the book publisher, as I had heard that Fisher Unwin had sent him some of the *The Religious Songs of Connacht*. My wife and I dined with Phelan, a cousin of my friend James Phelan. The dinner was at the Yacht Club, overlooking the

Courtesy of Westmeath Libraries (Aidan Heavey Collection)

Hudson. The day was very hot but it was pleasant and fresh above the river and we remained there until half-past eleven.

The weather is becoming so hot, already, that it is not easy to stand it. We will return to Ireland as soon as possible. My work in this country is complete.

The sixth day of June. Miss Merrington hosted a party for us in another woman's rooms. Many interesting people attended, Mrs Choate, Mrs Jane Custer, Mrs Thursby and some others. After the party, Quinn took us and my friend, Mrs Thursby to dinner in Delmonico's. After dinner, my wife and I went to the theatre to a box offered by Miss Merrington to see Sothern[473] and Miss Marlowe.[474] The heat tormented us during the morning but at night it turned cold and wet. We did not return until one o'clock.

The seventh day of June. Early in the morning, I again called at the steamship company even though I despaired of securing a berth on a ship. I had often called on the same office but failed to secure a passage on any vessel. We went down today hoping that someone might, perhaps, have cancelled their room; and just five minutes before we arrived, someone did, and I took it there and then. The room cost $450, but regardless of the price we had to take it as we could no longer abide the New York heat and Quinn said that it would only become hotter. Had I arrived five minutes later, I might have lost the room. The ship is named the *Celtic* and she departs New York on the fifteenth.

We dined with Quinn and Miss Coates at the Majestic.[475] Gregg[476] arrived in the afternoon. I knew him, long ago, in Ireland. He works for a newspaper here and is doing well. We stayed talking and smoking until two in the morning. It was a great relief to me to secure a passage aboard at last.

The eighth of June. I sat at home all day practising how to use a typewriter. We dined with Quinn in the evening. Charles Johnston[477] and his wife called and spent the afternoon with us. I knew him in Ireland. His wife is a clever, gentle woman.

I stayed at home all morning making notes. That Robinson I saw in San Francisco spoke with me on the telephone and invited me to dinner with him at the Waldorf.[478] I went there and dined with him, his engineer, Lee and another man, named Todd. He summoned the Waldorf head-chef and introduced me to him; the head-chef[479] presented me with his big cookery book as a gift. (I gave it as a present to Mrs Stopford Green[480] when I returned home). He called the man in charge of drinks and ordered him to make us a cocktail like the rainbow. Robinson said that this man was the only one able to make it. The waiter took a tall slim glass and poured some liqueur into it. On top of which, he slowly poured another liqueur. The second liquid did not mix with the first but remained on top. He then slowly added a third liqueur and continued adding six or seven other liqueurs, none of which mixed; each retaining its own intrinsic colour: white, yellow, red, green or blue. Called a rainbow cocktail, when drunk, each liqueur is tasted consecutively in one drink and each liqueur is said to prepare the way for the subsequent taste! He drove me back to Quinn's home. He came in and stayed talking and reciting poetry until half-past one in the morning.

Quinn took an instant dislike to him and denied him any opportunity to establish a friendship with him. (How I chanced to meet him in Ireland is a long story as is how he took advantage of me and others.)

The tenth and eleventh day of June. We stayed at home until 4.30. We then lunched and ventured out to Sheepshead Bay.[481] We had a good dinner at Tappan Hotel and remained watching Coney Island bathed in light. It was like Tír na nÓg. In another portion of the sky, lightning of both types was flashing about Sandy Hook; the short-forked lightning, sharp flashes, and the slow wide lightning which lasted half a minute. Before we departed New York, there was a large dust and ash storm; then it rained as if the skies had opened. It caused great damage. The three of us, with Miss Smith[482], observed the storm from her balcony. We lodged in her house. We then rode the rides at the Coney Island amusements; racing downwards in a boat from the top of a hill into a lake, riding on two camels, etc, etc.

A day or two afterwards, Quinn took us to dinner at Delmonico's with Judge Dowling, Judge Keogh and his wife, William Temple Emmet, Mrs James Byrne, Mr Snyder and his wife, and two or three others.[483] I spent two or three days posting some hundred copies of *The Religious Songs of Connacht*[484] (2 volumes) to those who had most aided me everywhere I had visited. Fisher Unwin had sent them over to me beforehand and they arrived in time. In each book, I wrote my name, the recipient's name and, in most cases, included a letter. At the end, I was in such a hurry leaving New York that time did not allow me to bid farewell to America. Quinn, however, told me to do so and I wrote a letter, half in his room in the morning and the other half aboard ship; he took it with him and distributed it to every evening paper and again in the morning to the morning papers. This is the note Quinn wrote to me when I left the city:

> The sum of money collected during the Great Trip was deposited in the Trust Company of America.[485] The accounts were carefully maintained under the direction of a firm of accountants and I worked for three or four evenings until late at night examining the figures prior to your departure. A receipt was entered for every item, even the stamps, and every small expenditure that White paid out.[486] The accountant examined and

> approved every receipt. Two or three days after drawing the final check (He gave me a check for over ten thousand pounds to bring home) on the Trust Company - a check, according to the accounts, that exhausted the account – I received formal notification from the Trust Company that I had overdrawn by one cent! That shows how precise the accountants were and how carefully they calculated the figures!

I have nothing else to say, other than we arrived home safe and sound, and received a great welcome in Dublin. I deposited the check in the bank for 10,000 pounds (see note on page 160) on behalf of the Gaelic League and told the Executive Committee that I had promised the people in America I would not spend more than 2,000 every year!

That money brought the League direct to the door of the National University and the door opened – barely – when it was exhausted.[487]

This is my American journey thus far.

Page 8, line 1
It was Ellen, John O'Leary's sister, who requested that I compose this song. I did so in English and believe her to be pleased with it. Afterwards, I translated it into Irish. This, if I recall correctly, is the first verse:

Féach sinne, clann na hÉireann
    Rugadh ins an oileán so
Támaoid bailighthe ar ár sléibhtibh
    Mar ba ghnáthach linn, fad ó.
Féach na h-airm ar ár ngualain,
    Ní'l aon phíce in ár láimh,
M'anam d'fheicfí iad go luath linn
    Dá mbéadh Éire ina ngádh!

    Chorus
Ar son Éireann támaoid bailighthe,
    Támaoid cruinnighthe ar an sliabh,
Gan aon sgannradh gan aon fhaitcheas
    Gan aon eagla acht roimh Dhia. etc., etc.

Page 21, line 2
The Boston meeting did not succeed half as well as it should have. Politics and the spite which was among the Irish themselves saw to that. 'The poor spiritless people that never united.' Fr Sheerin sent a letter to John Quinn two months after my lecture, explaining why it did not succeed better. I don't believe that he is fully correct in what he says, nonetheless, I offer it here to demonstrate the strife that John Quinn saved me from in New York. I have no recollection of Fr Sheerin and do not recall if I ever encountered him:

East Boston, Feb. 5th, 1906.

Dear Mr Quinn,
I enclose checks for $1,783.83 representing the total proceeds of the lecture given by Douglas Hyde in Boston, December 3, 1905.

I regret very much that the amount is so small. I was hopeful that the 'Hub' would surely be a good second to New York in this work. Since the event I have had time to reflect on the conditions that led to failure, and as they unfold themselves to me I am rather amazed that we even got so much as we did. Discord and inability to amalgamate on behalf of the common cause was very markedly shown by the United I. Leaguers, Hibernians and Clan-na-Gael. Many of them pretended to be working for the cause whilst in reality they would rather block its success because they considered it took some of the water away from their own mill. Besides when Concannon first came to Boston he fell into the hands of some former friends who never exhibited any interest in the Gaelic cause previous to his arrival. These persons did not know the Gaelic workers of Boston. As a consequence in the preparatory meetings the natural allies and friends of Douglas Hyde and his cause were overlooked unintentionally. Many of them considered themselves ignored by this mishap and in consequence sat down and looked on, claiming that as John Redmond associated himself with his natural allies so should Douglas Hyde and Concannon.

Added to all this there was a bitter 'donnybrook-fair' political contest between the Irish people at the time, in the city of Boston, and both Concannon and Hyde were unwittingly made victims of it by small designing politicians.

As I see them, these were the conditions that led to the financial failure of said lecture. The worst feature that I see in the whole affair, is that instead of cementing the Gaelic Schools of Boston and vicinity, which should be Hyde's natural allies, into an amalgamated body to which he or his successors in the cause could appeal in future, they have been left in a more disintegrated state than they were in previous to his visit. Personally, therefore, on behalf of the cause, I would suggest that Hyde should not leave the US. Without taking some steps in New England to amalgamate and unify the efforts of Gaelic Leaguers for the future. Therefore, if you have a chance to do so, I would ask you to bring this matter to his attention before he quits the country.

Sincerely yours,
Rev. Daniel S. Sheerin.

Page 26, line 4
'The Groves of Blarney' was composed as a parody of 'Castle Hyde.' Most people know 'The Groves of Blarney,' but few now have heard the original. I heard it myself in County Roscommon when I was young and as it is not available in print as far as I know, I offer it here. The Hyde that resided in the Castle at that time did not reward the poor poet who composed the song despite the poet's expectation of a big prize. He amended the final verse and changed it thus: 'In all my thradin' and serenadin'; / I met no n*é*ager like Humpy Hyde.' He termed him 'humpy,' due to his hunchback. As a very young infant he was brought down stairs on the day of his christening, I presume, to be shown to the collected audience. A small girl pleaded keenly to be allowed hold him. She prevailed, but dropped him and he injured his back. On growing up, he fell in love with this girl but when he proposed, she callously replied 'I won't marry a hunchback!'

The 'Battle Mail Castle' or the 'Suit of Armour Castle' is the proper name in Irish of Castle Hyde as *éideach* means shield or armour. The phrase '*in airm agus in éide*' (viz. 'armed and equipped') is still frequent in Irish.

Sir Clarendon Hyde[488] in England had a copy of this song, but did not comprehend that it was composed in the Irish style and that the final word of the first line and the third line correspond aurally with a word in the middle of the second and fourth lines. I had to explain that to him. The Hydes came from Berkshire, England to Ireland initially, at the start of Queen Elizabeth's reign. I still possess an antique clock with a crown and *Fleur de lis* on it, that the Hydes always believed that the Queen presented to that first Hyde to go to Ireland. That may be true as he was a friend of the Queen's lover, that rogue Dudley.[489] They often played cards together and it was in my ancestors' home that Amy Robsart[490], Dudley's wife, spent her final day. The Hydes had their ancestral home in England until a few hundred years ago, but they all died. Sir

Clarendon then arrived, descended from the Irish Hydes, and bought the property back for himself and erected a fine house on the site of the old house.
This is the song as I heard it:

Castle Hyde

As I roved out of a summer's m*o*rning
    Down by the banks of Blackw*a*ter's side
To view the groves and the meadows ch*a*rming
    And the pleasant g*a*rdens of Castle Hyde.

It's there you'd hear the thrushes w*a*rbling
    The dove and p*a*rtridge I now describe,
Sporting there upon every m*o*rning
    All to ad*o*rn sweet Castle Hyde.

There are fine walks in those pleasant g*a*rdens,
    And seats more ch*a*rming in shady bowers,
The gladianthor[491] who is bowld and d*a*rin'
    Each night and m*o*rnin' to watch the flowers.

If noble princes from foreign n*a*tions
    Should chance to s*a*il to this Irish shore,
It is in this valley they should be féasted,
    Where often héroes had been before.

The wholesome *a*ir of this habit*a*tion
    Would recre*a*te your heart with pride,
There is no valley throughout this n*a*tion
    In beauty *ae*qual to Castle Hyde.

There are fine horses and stall-fed *o*xen,
    A den for f*o*xes to play and hide,
Fine mares for br*ee*ding and foreign sh*ee*p
    With snowy fl*ee*ces in Castle Hyde.

The richest groves throughout the n*a*tion
And fine plant*a*tions you would see there,
The rose, the tulip and the sweets of n*a*ture
All vieing with the lily f*a*ir.

The buck and doe, the fox and *a*igle,
Do skip and pl*a*y by the river's side
The trout and salmon are always pl*a*ying[492]
In the clear str*é*ams of Castle Hyde.

I roved from Blarney down to Barney (?)
From Thomastown to sweet Doneraile
And from Cillarmac (?) that joins Rathcormac
Besides Killarney and Abbeyfail.

The flowing Nore and the rapid Boyne,
The river Shannon and pleasant Clyde,
And in all my r*a*nging and recre*a*tion
No place could *ae*qual sweet Castle Hyde.

Page 66, paragraph 2, line 5
This is the song I transcribed from Casey in O'Keefe's tailor shop on 2 February 1906. It is obvious that the English is like Irish, attempting to replicate the tune, 'The Flowers of Edinburgh,' as Seán Lloyd did in his sweet song 'Cois leasa dham go huaigneach':

In a desert most seréne
I l*a*y a while bem*o*aning
The present lot and st*a*te
Of our country at large,
A damsel I saw séated
On a néat bed of r*o*ses,
And she bitterly bem*o*aning
The approach of the éir.[493]
Her *a*mber locks were h*a*nging d*ow*n
Upon her b*a*ck unto the gr*ou*nd
Which might engage a m*o*narch's cr*ow*n

So néatly compósed.
Her *fa*ce as if *pai*nted
By *na*ture such beauty yields
As left all my sécrets
Quite *na*ked, expósed.

Page 82, paragraph 4, line 2
'A Souvenir of the Dr Hyde Banquet held in the Palace Hotel in the City of San Francisco, February twenty-first, 1906.'

This book contains all the speeches in full and the names of all in attendance, a copy of the menu and each speaker's photograph. The following spoke: Judge Coffey, Archbishop Montgomery, James D. Phelan, Governor Pardee, Mayor Schmitz, Chief Justice Beatty, Hon. Frank J. Sullivan, John MacNaught, Benjamin Ide Wheeler, Very Rev. J. P. Frieden, S. J., Michael O Mahoney, Rev. F. W. Clampett, Rev. P. C. Yorke.

Page 105, paragraph 4, line 1
When I returned to Ireland, I was appointed to the Committee which was to investigate University Education in Ireland and to explore the issue of Trinity College.[494] In every enquiry undertaken into University Education in Ireland until then, Trinity College succeeded in excluding itself, but was unable to do so on this occasion, and in the course of the committee's investigation all affairs, including financial and other matters, regarding that place came to light. The Committee convened for almost a year and sat in London and Dublin. The Provost Dr Traill[495] allowed us to sit in his own house, the Provost's House, in the College when we were in Dublin.[496]

It happened that the rest of the committee members and I were meeting in the Provost's House examining evidence when a servant entered and whispered to me that two American gentlemen were outside and wished to speak with me. I went out to them and who was it but Mayor Schmitz and a friend of his. When speaking to them in the hall the Provost passed by and I introduced the Mayor to him. The Mayor told him that he and his friend were travelling Europe to see the great buildings and houses there as the people of San Francisco had to rebuild their city from scratch and he wanted to see the best buildings beforehand. The Provost offered to show them that house and did so, and all the innovations he installed.

But it was not to view buildings or anything of that sort that brought Schmitz abroad, rather San Francisco was too hot for him. As that man who had been kind and gentle until the city collapsed, he himself fell when it was being rebuilt as it was said that he accepted a bribe from people who wanted this place and that place to build shops and so forth. When he returned to San Francisco, he was convicted and sent to San Quentin[497] along with Ruef, as I heard. But the papers and the influential people were opposed to him, and they probably did not want to miss an opportunity against him.

Page 154, paragraph 2, line 2
I should set down here the amounts of money we received from the meetings we held. The following are cities in which Tomás Ua Coincheanainn and I worked (I took this information from the *Irish American* (23–6–1906) that provided me with great assistance, but Tomás Bán was also in San Francisco, Minneapolis and St Paul).

	$
Hartford	114.85
Boston	1,783.38
Manchester	150.00
Springfield, Mass.	292.00
Ansonia	101.50
Lowell	176.35
Waterbury	237.00
Providence	680.00
Philadelphia	4,624.77
Worcester	87.95
Lawrence	215.75
Chicago	6,782.11
Indianapolis	1,102.48
St Louis	1,400.00
San José	663.25
Oakland	500.00
Sacramento	1,000.00
Portland	1,021.80
Seattle	570.00
Spokane	800.00
Butte	2,212.60
Anaconda	650.00
	———
	25,165.79

Cities in which I alone worked

Brockton	176.00
Jersey City	226.19
New Haven	300.00
Pittsburg	972.50
Milwaukee	556.00
Cleveland	1,170.20
Columbus	528.05
Cincinnati	1,000.00
South Bend	130.00
St Paul	300.00
Minneapolis	338.00
Omaha	1,555.60
San Francisco	9,836.75
Los Angeles	1,500.00
San Francisco	1,500.00
(again, St Patrick's Day celebrations)	
Memphis	510.35
Baltimore	768.52
Elmira	600.00
Scranton	431.51
Bridgeport	350.00
Buffalo	1,090.00
Rochester	754.65
Washington	352.00
Paterson	75.00
In addition to that amount, through John Quinn himself in New York, was received	
From James Byrne	1,000.00
From the Hon. John D. Crimmins	1,000.00
From William Sheehan (per Donal Cohalan)	500.00
From T. F. Ryan (per the Hon. Martin Keogh)	500.00
Clarence H. Mackey (per ditto)	500.00
J. W. Daly (per ditto)	250.00
P. F. Collier (per ditto)	100.00

From the New York State Gaelic League	167.23
J. C. Lynch	100.00
Hugh Grant, the Hon.	100.00
Bourke Cockran, the Hon.	100.00
From James I. Phelan	100.00
From Thomas H. Kelly	100.00
Per others	365.00
	———
	4932.23

The following purchased boxes at Carnegie Hall when Cohalane auctioned them. The names and amount are:

John Goodwin	300.00
James Butler	300.00
Judge Dowling	250.00
John B. McDonnell	200.00
Judge Keogh, Hon.	150.00
Charles Murphy, Hon.	150.00
Henry McDonagh	150.00
Many other boxes were sold and earned	1,700.00
	———
	3,200.00
Pre-sold seats	862.50
Seats sold at the door	905.50
Total income from New York	9,303.53
The *Gaelic American* subscription fund for the language, which yielded	$4,000.00

I brought a check for £10,054 home with me and sent another 1,000 pounds to the League, 19 December 1905 and the Executive Committee in St Louis sent $1,400.00 directly to Dublin and the Executive Committee in Pittsburgh sent $972.50 directly to Dublin as well, and I gave 5,000 dollars back to San Francisco. I received that back from them a few years later. My journey therefore generated over £12,400 in total. That is the financial account thus far.

MO THURAS GO MEIRICEÁ

NÓ

I MEASC NA nGAEL SAN OILEÁN ÚR

Mí Lúnasa 1902[1] a casadh Seán Ó Cuinn orm ar dtús. Ba dhlíodóir Meiriceánach é as Nua-Eabhrac. Is cuimhin liom go maith an chéad uair a chonaic mé é. Bhí an Bhantiarna Greagóir, Eadbhard Mártain ó Thul Aighre, agus slua mór daoine bailithe le chéile i Reilig Chill Fhínín, an áit ar cuireadh suas, mar chuimhneachán ar Raiftearaí, an file, cloch bhreá agus scríbhinn uirthi i litreacha óir. Bhí mé féin thuas ar an ardán – bhí ardán breá déanta acu – agus mé ag labhairt chomh bríomhar agus a bhí ionam leis an bpobal i nGaeilge, nuair a thug mé faoi deara fear uasal, caol, ard, ina sheasamh i measc an tslua agus é ag éisteacht liom ar a dhícheall. Bhí an slua ag brú isteach ar an ardán, agus bhí seanfhear á dtiomáint ar ais, 'siar', 'gabh siar as sin,' a deireadh sé. Nuair a bhí an cruinniú thart agus na hóráidí críochnaithe, casadh an fear ard orm arís. Bhí caint agam leis, agus dúirt sé liom go raibh sé ar a laethanta saoire, ag siúl na hÉireann. Sílim go raibh sé ar aíocht leis an mBantiarna Greagóir. Ba í sin an bhean uasal a chuir faoi deara an tuama breá a thógáil do Raiftearaí, agus sílim gur thug sí Mac Uí Chuinn léi abhaile go Teach na Cúile, a háit chónaithe féin. Bhí caint agam leis an Meiriceánach agus bhí sé ag cur ceisteanna orm i dtaobh na Gaeilge in Éirinn. Is dóigh gur chuir sé suim sa mhéid a bhí le rá agam leis, óir fuair mé litir nó dhó uaidh nuair a chuaigh sé ar ais go Nua-Eabhrac, agus dúirt sé liom teacht go dtí an tOileán Úr dá bhféadfainn é, agus go bhfaighinn cúnamh uaidh féin agus ó dhaoine eile. Chuir sé an-suim i rud ar bith a bhain le healaíon, nó le litríocht, agus bhí na leabhair a scríobh mé féin léite aige cheana. 'Rinne sé rud nach ndearna éinne eile i Meiriceá, sílim,' dúirt an breitheamh Mac Eochaidh liom, 'léigh sé do *Literary History of Ireland* faoi dhó!' Bhí sé an-mhór leis an bhfile Yeats, freisin, agus thug sé amach go Meiriceá é cúpla bliain roimhe sin, agus stiúraigh sé ó chathair go cathair, agus ó

Ollscoil go hOllscoil. B'fhéidir go mba é an ní sin a chuir ina cheann iarraidh ormsa dul amach chuige mar a rinne Yeats. D'éirigh mé an-mhuinteartha leis, ach b'fhánach dó bheith ag iarraidh orm dul amach, go dtí an bhliain 1905. Fuair m'athair bás an bhliain sin agus d'fhág a bhás saor mé le dul thar lear. Bhí Conradh na Gaeilge ar aigne duine éigin a chur amach chun airgead a bhailiú dóibh, dá mb'fhéidir é, agus ní raibh éinne eile saor ach mé féin, agus ó bhí mise i m'Uachtarán ar an gConradh ó bunaíodh é, ní raibh, dar leo, aon duine níos oiriúnaí ná mé féin.

Bhí go leor litreacha, ansin, ar siúl idir mise agus Seán Ó Cuinn, agus gheall seisean go réiteodh sé an tslí romham, dá dtéinn chuige, ach fear a chur amach romham féin.

Toghadh Tomás Bán Ua Concheanainn le dul amach. Rugadh Tomás in Inis Meáin in Árainn, agus nuair a bhí sé seacht mbliana déag d'aois chuaigh sé amach go Meiriceá, agus ar nós na Meiriceánach féin chuaigh sé ó áit go háit. Chuaigh sé go Meiriceá Theas, go Meicsiceo tar éis tamaill, agus d'fhoghlaim sé an Spáinnis ansin. Tá a lán Éireannach san Airgintín. Dúirt Señor Bulfin liom, go bhféadfadh marcach dul ar chapall ar feadh seacht lá agus seacht n-oíche, gan talamh na nÉireannach a fhágáil. Dúirt an tAthair Ó Gramhnaigh, beannacht Dé lena anam, liom go mba ghnách leis na daoine a chónaigh ina thimpeall féin dul go Meiriceá Theas, mar a théann na daoine as áiteanna eile in Éirinn go dtí na Stáit; agus nuair a thagaidís abhaile tar éis fiche nó tríocha nó daichead bliain a chaitheamh ann, ní aithneofá ar a gcaint gur fhágadar Éire riamh. Ní hionann agus an drong a théann chun na Stát. Muna mbeadh ach coicís curtha isteach ag duine i Nua-Eabhrac nó i mBostún, cuireann sé athrach canúna air féin! Dúirt an tAthair Ó Gramhnaigh liom gur mhinic a chuala sé an Spáinnis dá labhairt sna margaí san Iar-Mhí. Nuair a tháinig Tomás Bán abhaile, 1898, fuair sé cumainn na Gaeilge faoi lánseol agus chuidigh seisean leis, agus ba é an chéad timire agus an taca ab fhearr a bhí againn é. Shiúil sé Éire, síos suas, ó thaobh go taobh ag timireacht dúinn agus ag craobhscaoileadh shoiscéal na Gaeilge.

Ar an ábhar sin bhí eolas maith aige ar Éirinn agus an t-eolas céanna aige ar na Stáit. Mar sin toghadh é le dul amach romhamsa. Bhí sé mar Réamh-Thimire nó *Advance Agent*, romham i gcuid mhór de na cathracha agus stáit san Oileán Úr. Murach an chrua-obair a rinne sé ní bheadh sé inár gcumas an oiread sin airgid a chnuasach do Chonradh na Gaeilge.

Ó Stáit Shasana Nua amach go dtí Stáit Mheánacha na tíre móire sin, chomh fada le Missouri agus Minnesota, bhí sé ag obair de réir clár ama a leag Seán Ó Cuinn amach. Réitigh Mac Uí Chuinn gach ní romham agus dhéanainn de réir mar a deireadh sé.

Ar shroicheadh San Francisco bhí Tomás ag oibriú i gCalifornia, Oregon, Washington agus Montana faoin Athair Yorke, Ceann-Treorach agus Comhairleoir na nGael sa chuid sin den Domhan Thiar.

Tomás Bán Ua Concheanainn. Le caoinchead Fhoras na Gaeilge

Níor dhóigh liom go raibh aon duine eile in Éirinn i measc na gConraitheoirí a raibh sé ina chumas an obair sin a dhéanamh chomh maith leis.

Sular tháinig Tomás amach, comóradh cruinniú de dhaoine measúla i Nua-Eabhrac le Seán Ó Cuinn, Mí Mheán Fómhair 29, 1905, agus chuir sé Coiste ar bun chun fáilte a chur romhamsa. Fuair sé daoine a raibh clú agus meas orthu ar fud na cathrach, daoine mar an Príomh-Bhreitheamh Mártain Mac Eochaidh, an breitheamh Ó Dúllaing, Temple Emmet, Domhnall Ó Cathaláin* (dlíodóir a bhí ann an uair sin), Seán Ó Dubhuí an sean-Fhínín, agus tharraing sé isteach uachtaráin mórán cumann lúth-chleasa, lucht ceoil, Conradh na Gaeilge, agus go leor eile nach iad. Fuair sé litreacha ag gealladh cúnta ón mBreitheamh Mac Gearailt, ón mBreitheamh Morgan Ó Briain, ón mBreitheamh Ó Gormáin, ón Recorder Mac Eochaidh**, ó Sheán D. Ó Croimín, ó Phádraig Mac Giollarnáth, Eagarthóir an *Irish World* agus ó thuilleadh. Ní dóigh liom go raibh éinne eile i Nua-Eabhrac a mbeadh sé ar a chumas na daoine seo a thabhairt le chéile ach amháin Seán Ó Cuinn.

Tháinig Tomás go Nua-Eabhrac i nDeireadh Fómhair agus thug Seán Ó Cuinn isteach ina theach féin é, agus thug aíocht dó, ag 120 Broadway. Chuir Conradh na Gaeilge imlitir amach go dtí Meiriceá á rá go raibh mise ag dul amach, agus ag iarraidh ar Ghaeil Mheiriceá fáilte a chur romham. Bhí ainmneacha an bheirt leas-Uachtarán .i. An tAthair Peadar Ó Laoghaire agus Eoin Mac Néill leis an litir seo, agus ina theannta sin ainm Phádraig Uí Dhálaigh an Rúnaí, agus ainm Stiofáin Bairéad an cisteoir a bhí againn.

Bhí amhras ar chuid de na daoine nuair a chonaiceadar na fir mhóra a bhí ag obair ar son an Ghaelachais, agus dúirt an *Irish World:* 'Is ait agus is aisteach mar atá an scéal i dtaobh 'na fáilte' i Nua-Eabhrac. Samhlaíonn sé go bhfuil an-obair ar fad idir lámha ag na daoine sin a bhí – tá a fhios acu féin cad chuige – deighilte amach ó gach gluaiseacht Ghaeilge, más fíor go bhfuil siad ag dul ag íoc sa deireadh cuid bheag de na fiacha náisiúnta atá sa mhullach orthu. Is fearr go mall ná go brách; cuirfidh sé lúcháir mhór ar Chonradh na Gaeilge, óir tá na Conraitheoirí ar nós na n-anam sa bhflaitheas os ár gcionn, .i. déanann siad lúcháir seacht n-uaire faoi fhilleadh na droinge a chuaigh amú, agus bíonn siad sásta ligean do na gnáthfhiréin dul tharstu gan aire a thabhairt dóibh… is maith is eol dár lucht léite ár dtuairim i dtaobh na nÉireannach saibhir agus i dtaobh na faille atá déanta acu, etc., etc.'

*Dúirt athair Dhomhnaill liom – labhair sé an Ghaeilge is fearr agus is blasta agus is cruinne dár chuala mé i Meiriceá – go mba é Ó Cathaláin a shloinne ceart, agus gur tháinig sé ón bhfocal "cath" .i. duine a bhí go maith chun cath a chur. Ach ba ghnáth leo ag labhairt Béarla Co-halon a rá, .i. "halon" ar aon fhuaim leis an ainm Fallon, i mBéarla.

**Goff i mBéarla.

Níor léir do mo chairde uile nach amháin chun an Ghaeilge agus an Gaelachas a chur ar aghaidh a tháinig mise go dtí na Stáit, ach ar thóir airgid freisin; agus ó tharla gurbh é an t-airgead a bhí uaim b'éigean dom dul go dtí na daoine a raibh an t-airgead acu; agus go dtí na háiteanna a raibh an t-airgead iontu. Is cuimhin liom go maith nuair nach raibh mé ach trí nó ceithre lá i Nua-Eabhrac agus mé fós gan tuiscint cheart ar aon rud, gur chuir Mac Uí Chuinn páipéar i mo lámh ag rá liom go mbeadh daoine a raibh míshástacht orthu ag teacht chugam le gearán a dhéanamh liom, agus scríobh sé an freagra a mhol sé féin domsa a thabhairt orthu. Ach bhí oiread eile gnótha ar m'aire gur chuir mé an páipéar i mo phóca gan a léamh. Sa tráthnóna tháinig seisear nó mórsheisear isteach go dtí an teach ósta le m'fheiceáil, agus gearán fada acu. Shílfeá, ar a n-aghaidheanna, go raibh an domhan ar fad ag titim as a chéile. Dúirt siad ansin liom, agus iad ag féachaint chomh gruama agus ab fhéidir, nach raibh an ghluaiseacht agus an 'Fháilte' faoi chúram na ndaoine cearta, nach ndearna lucht na 'Tuxedos'* gníomh fónta riamh ar son na hÉireann.

Ní raibh a fhios agam ar dtús cérbh iad, ach chuimhnigh mé ar an bpáipéar a thug Mac Uí Chuinn dom. Má chuimhníos bhí sé rómhall. Ní fhéadfainn a tharraingt amach as mo phóca ina láthairsean. Ach tar éis beagán cainte a dhéanamh leo lig mé orm gur chuala mé an guthán ag gliogarnaigh i mo sheomra codlata, agus dúirt mé de phreab 'tá an guthán bradach sin ag gliogarnaigh arís. A dhaoine uaisle, glacaigí mo leithscéal ar feadh nóiméid amháin go bhfeice mé céard é.' Rith mé isteach i mo sheomra agus labhair mé de ghuth ard ar an nguthán, ag ligean orm go raibh duine éigin ag caint liom, agus tharraing mé amach an páipéar a thug Mac Uí Chuinn dom, agus léigh mé é. Thuig mé ansin cérbh iad na daoine, agus an rud a bhí uathu, agus cé a bhí ag séideadh fúthu. Tháinig mé ar ais chucu agus dúirt mé leo go raibh mé an-bhuíoch díobh, ach go raibh mise le gach tairbhe ab fhéidir a fháil as lucht na 'Tuxedos,' agus a gcuid cairde, gur tháinig mé ar theachtaireacht go dtí na hÉireannaigh idir ard agus íseal, agus nach ndiúltóinn do chúnamh ó éinne. Labhair mé Gaeilge le fear nó beirt acu a raibh Gaeilge acu, agus thug mé deoch dóibh, agus tar éis mórán cainte d'fhágadar go buíoch beannachtach mé agus níor chuala mé aon scéal eile uathu.

Daoine cneasta macánta a bhí sna fir sin. Fir a sheas dom go maith in áiteanna eile, togha na nGael is dóigh, ach níor thuigeadar i gceart an chaoi a raibh an scéal i Nua-Eabhrac. Tá mé beagnach cinnte go raibh éad agus formad orthu nuair a chonaic siad na daoine a raibh mise faoina sciatháin, Mac Uí Chuinn agus a chairde; agus is dóigh gur shíleadar dáiríre nach dtiocfadh aon mhaith astu. Ach má shíleadar sin bhí dul amú mór orthu. Thuig mise go maith an rud a bhí le déanamh agam, .i. airgead a bhailiú!

*Cóta gearr tráthnóna.

Maidir liomsa, d'fhág mé féin agus mo bhean Baile Átha Cliath, Samhain 6, 1905, ar a seacht a chlog, tráthnóna, agus slua mór daoine i mo thimpeall. Tháinig an tArd-Mhaor ina chóiste oifigiúil go dtí an cruinniú. Dúirt sé san óráid a thug sé, 'Tá ceithre pháirtí déag i mBardas Bhaile Átha Cliath, - agus i gcúig cinn nó i sé cinn díobh sin níl ach duine amháin, agus mar sin bíonn gach páirtí acu siúd ar aon ghuth i gcónaí – ach nach mór an onóir don Chraoibhín é go rabhadar go léir ar aon fhocal ag fágáil slán croíúil aige, agus gur éiríodar go léir go fonnmhar as a n-obair le teacht anseo.' Bronnadh a lán dileagraí orm, ceann ón gCoiste Gnó, ceann ó chraobh Choilm Naofa Mhá Nuad, ceann ó Choiste Ceantair Fhine Gall, ceann ó Luimneach, ceann ón Uaimh, ceann ó Thír Amhlaidh, ceann ó Chumann Cleas-Lúith Bhaile Átha Cliath agus ceann ó Chumann Tráchtála Bhaile Átha Cliath. Nuair a bhí ormsa freagra a thabhairt orthu, dúirt mé gurbh fhíor an chaint a bhí ag an Ard-Mhaor nár Chumann polaitíochta Conradh na Gaeilge. 'Is fíor é sin,' arsa mise, 'agus sin díreach an fáth gurb é an Cumann polaitíochta is láidre in Éirinn é. Is í an chiall cheart atá leis an bhfocal 'polaitíocht' de réir na Gréigise, aon chumhacht a bhaineas go dlúth le gach cathraitheoir, agus is cumhachtach aon Chonradh a bhfuil greim aige ar na daoine, agus atá ag bailiú isteach chuige féin muintir na cathrach, agus ar an ábhar sin is cumann an-láidir polaitíochta é! Ach ní thaobhaíonn sé le dream amháin seachas an dream eile.' Dúirt mé tuilleadh i dtaobh na rudaí a chuir mé romham a dhéanamh san Oileán Úr. D'fhágamar an Gresham ansin agus chuamar trí na sráideanna a bhí plúchta le daoine, agus slua lucht chamáin inár dtimpeall, agus iad ag gabháil amhráin a cheapas féin dóibh blianta roimhe sin.* Ní raibh áireamh ar a raibh de charráistí inár ndiaidh, agus mháirseálamar go mall, síos cois na habhann, gur thángamar go dtí an stáisiún ag Droichead an Rí.[2] Nuair a bhíomarna imithe isteach go dtí an stáisiún céard a rinne siad siúd a lean mé ach cruinniú a chur ar bun taobh amuigh. Is ó chairde a chuala mé sin, óir ní raibh a fhios agam féin ach go raibh slua mór i mo thimpeall. D'imigh an traein agus bhíodh daoine eile romham ag gach stáisiún ar stop sí ann.

Bhí sé a haon a chlog san oíche nuair a thángamar go dtí crosbhóthar iarainn Luimnigh, áit a bhfuil teach ósta maith. D'fhanamar an oíche ansin. Ar maidin fuair mé sreangscéal ó mo sheanchara an Canónach Artúr Ó Riain, sagart paróiste Thiobraid Árann, ag iarraidh orainn lón a ithe leis, óir níl Tiobraid Árann ach trí mhíle nó mar sin ón gCrois. Chuamar chuige agus bhí lá pléisiúrtha againn agus tuilleadh dileagraí, ón gConradh féin, agus ó Chumann na gCleas-Lúith. Thángamar ar ais ansin go dtí an Chrois agus chuamar ar bord na traenach go Corcaigh ar a 6.20. Nuair a thángamar go Mala bhí cruinniú an-mhór ann agus b'éigean dom labhairt leo.

*Féach nóta ar amhrán lch 307.

Bainċéile an Ċraoiḃín

Lucy Cometina Hyde. Le caoinchead Fhoras na Gaeilge

Ach nuair a ráiníomar go Corcaigh is ansin a bhí an slua. Bhí an tArd-Mhaor féin i láthair agus thug sé mé féin agus an Róisteach agus Mac Uí Argáin leis ina chóiste go dtí Halla na Cathrach. Bhí na mílte daoine inár dtimpeall. Bhí teachtaireachtaí ó cheithre Chumann fichead ann agus bhí sé bhuíon cheoil ann. Tugadh cúig dhileagra dom agus rinne mé óráid, agus rinne mo chara an tAthair Aibhistín caint chomh maith agus a chuala mé riamh. Nuair a bhí gach rud thart chuaigh mé go teach an Uindéalaigh, mo sheanchara, Uachtarán an Choláiste, an áit a raibh mo bhean cheana, agus chaith mé an oíche ansin. An lá arna mhárach níor chorraigh mé as a theach ach d'fhanas ann agus ligeas mo scíth ina measc, óir ba sheanchairde dom iad.

Ar maidin, lá arna mhárach, amach linn go dtí an Cóbh ar a 9.50, agus cuireadh fáilte mhór romham arís ansin, agus bhí an tEaspag de Brún, Easpag Chluana ann. Ar bord an 'tender' linn agus mórán cairde inár bhfochair, gur cuireadh slán ar bord na loinge sinn, faoi dheireadh. B'shin críoch ar ár n-imeacht as Éirinn, nó ba chirte a rá ar mo chaithréim aisti. Bhí ministéir mór Protastúnach a chuaigh amach go dtí an long linn, agus bhí mé ag caint leis, mar bhí aithne agam air féin agus ar a bhanchéile, bean a tháinig as mo chontae féin. Bhí ainm an duine uasail seo sa pháipéar, an lá ina dhiaidh sin, i measc na ndaoine eile a tháinig amach chun na loinge, chun slán a fhágáil agamsa. Agus b'éigean don fhear bocht litir a chur chun an pháipéir á bhréagnú sin, agus ag rá, nach chun slán a fhágáil agamsa ach ag duine eile ar fad a tháinig sé amach; rud ab fhíor dó. Thuig sé, is dóigh, gur bheag an chreidiúint dó, onóir a dhéanamh do Chonradh na Gaeilge!

Chuamar i dtír i Nua-Eabhrac, Samhain 15, 1905, agus sular fhágamar an long ar chor ar bith thug lucht páipéar cuairt orainn agus chuireadar roinnt ceisteanna orainn. Caithfidh an 'tuairisceoir' Meiriceánach rud éigin a rá, agus ní ghoilleann sé air, ar uaire, an rud sin a cheapadh dó féin. Bhí ionadh orm an lá arna mhárach nuair a léigh mé go raibh croiméal 'beag' orm agus go raibh ceangal glasuaithne faoi mo bhráid. Ar ndóigh ní raibh aon rud glas ná uaithne orm. Bhí éadaí dubha orm chomh dubh leis an bpic, mar gheall ar bhás m'athar, ach dúirt fear an pháipéir gur *bottle green* a bhí mé a chaitheamh. Maidir le lucht na bpáipéar seo, is mór an buaireamh iad. Bhí mé ag caint ina dtaobh sular fhág mé an long, le bean uasal a raibh baint aici leis an amharclann, agus a chaith beagnach daichead bliain i Meiriceá, agus d'fhiafraigh mé di céard ab fhearr dom a dhéanamh leo. Thug sise ríchomhairle dom. 'Bí leo,' a dúirt sí, 'mar a bheifeá le duine ar bith eile, agus gheobhaidh tú amach go mbeidh siadsan go geanúil leatsa.' Ag dul trí Mheiriceá dom chuimhnigh mé ar an gcomhairle sin, agus is mar seo a dhéanainn, nuair a thiocfadh fear páipéir ag cur ceisteanna orm. Agus is iad a chuireadh na ceisteanna achrannacha crua ar dhuine! Ní raibh aon bhaile mór dá ndeachaigh mé ann nach bhfiafródh fear an pháipéir díom 'cad tá na feisirí a dhéanamh ar son na Gaeilge' agus mórán ceisteanna eile i dtaobh na bhfeisirí agus na parlaiminte. Ba ghnáth liomsa, nuair a chuirtí ceisteanna den sórt sin orm, stad ar feadh tamaillín, mo chás toitíní a tharraingt amach, toitín a dheargadh go mall dom féin, agus toitín a thairiscint don fhear a bhí ag caint liom, ag rá leis, san am céanna, 'Anois, a dhuine uasail, ba mhaith liom gach faisnéis a thabhairt duit, - cén chaoi a dtaithníonn mo thoitín leat? – ach tá a fhios agat, eadrainn féin, ar ndóigh, tá cúpla ceist ann, agus b'fhearr liom gan iad a chur orm, ach tuigeann tú féin sin chomh maith agus a thuigimse é.' Bhínn i gcónaí an-chúirtéiseach leo, agus is féidir liom a rá gur tháinig mé tríd an tír ar fad gan aon trioblóid uathu, ach in aon áit amháin.

Bhí áitín iargúlach amháin a raibh mé ann - ní cuimhin liom anois an t-ainm a bhí air - agus nuair a bhí mé tuirseach go leor de bharr bheith ag síorchaint, chuala mé, i lár na hoíche, cnag agus cnag eile ar an doras a bhí faoi ghlas. Níor thug mé aon aird air, i dtosach, ach bhris ar an bhfoighde agam sa deireadh, agus ní ligfinn an fear isteach. Dúirt mé cúpla focal tríd an doras amach, agus ar ndóigh ní hé mo bheannacht a thug mé dó! D'imigh mo dhuine agus scríobh sé alt ina pháipéar an lá arna mhárach, ag ligean air go raibh agallamh aige liomsa, agus go ndúirt mé go raibh socair agam cruinniú mór de na hÉireannaigh a chomóradh sa bhaile sin ag deireadh na bliana, agus go mba cheart do na hÉireannaigh tosú ar ullmhúchán a dhéanamh ina chomhair. B'éigean domsa sreangscéal a chur go dtí Nua-Eabhrac á rá nach raibh focal den fhírinne san alt sin, agus gan aon aird a thabhairt air. Má bhí mé go cúramach roimhe sin, bhí mé i bhfad níos cúramaí ina dhiaidh sin, chun gach ceart agus cóir a thabhairt do lucht na bpáipéar de ló is d'oíche!

Tháinig a lán daoine go dtí an long le fáilte a chur romham. Orthu siúd bhí Seán Ó Cuinn, a stiúraigh agus a leag amach an obair ar fad, agus Tomás Bán a bhí ag obair ar feadh míosa sa chathair, an breitheamh Mac Eochaidh agus go leor eile. Le hómós domsa níor iarr lucht an chustaim mo bhagáiste a oscailt ar chor ar bith, agus ligeadar isteach mé gan bacadh liom. Thug Seán Ó Cuinn mé go teach ósta mór an Manhattan, áit a raibh 'suite' de sheomraí ag fanacht linn, óir mar a dúirt sé féin 'ní bhíonn meas ar aon duine anseo, muna gcuireann sé faoi in áit mhaith.'

D'fhan mé ceithre lá sa Manhattan, agus lucht na bpáipéar ag teacht go síoraí agus ag cur ceisteanna orm. Níor mhór dom mo dhícheall a dhéanamh chun go mbeadh meas ag Nua-Eabhrac orm, óir leanann páipéir na tíre ar fad, nach mór, an rud a deir na páipéir i Nua-Eabhrac, nó muna leanann siad é cuireann siad suim mhór ann. Ar an ábhar sin bhí orm mo dhícheall a dhéanamh le go mbeadh na páipéir fábhrach dom. Nuair a bhí ceithre lá caite agam sa Manhattan thug Mac Uí Chuinn isteach go dtí a áit féin sinn, ag 120 Broadway. Bhí Tomás Bán (a bhí ag cur faoi ansin) imithe uaidh scaitheamh roimhe sin.* Bhí 'flat' ag Mac Uí Chuinn agus bhí seomra compordach ann dúinne.

Bhí orm an chéad phíosa cainte a dhéanamh ag Harvard, an Ollscoil is clúitiúla, b'fhéidir i Meiriceá, an 20ú den mhí. Chuaigh mé ó Nua-Eabhrac ar an traein go Bostún, an lá sin, agus casadh an Dochtúir Robinson, Ollamh na Ceiltise orm ag an stáisiún, agus an tAthair Ó Flannagáin. Thug Robinson go dtí a theach féin mé, agus ní raibh ann ach go raibh an t-am agam mo dhinnéar a ithe agus mo chuid éadaigh a athrú, nuair a tugadh mé go dtí Halla Léachta na hOllscoile, chun léacht ar bhéaloideas na hÉireann a thabhairt uaim. Ní raibh Elliot, Uachtarán na hOllscoile i láthair, ach bhí Briggs, an Déan, ann, an fear is gaire céim don Uachtarán féin. Bhí sé cúthail neirbhíseach, agus ag dul suas an staighre bhí sinn in achrann a chéile gan a fhios cé a rachadh isteach i dtosach, agus arís nuair a chuamar isteach ní raibh sé cinnte an ar a thaobh deas nó ar a thaobh clé ba cheart dom suí. Óir bíonn siad i bhfad níos cúramaí i Meiriceá i dtaobh rudaí beaga den sórt sin ná a bhítear in Éirinn. Ach chuamar isteach sa deireadh. Bhí tuairim is cúig chéad duine i láthair idir ollúna agus mhic léinn. Bhain mé gáire astu go minic agus mé ag labhairt agus dúirt gach éinne go raibh mo léacht 'informal' rud a thaitnigh leo, óir níl siad cleachtach ar a leithéid sin. Chuamar go léir abhaile go teach Robinson ansin agus bhí páirtí mór aige, timpeall seachtó duine, na hollúna agus a gcuid ban. Shíl mé gurbh iad na mná uaisle sin na mná ba dheise a chonaic mé go dtí sin, agus ba mhóide é mo mheas ar bhreithiúnas na n-ollamh!

Bhí sé an-déanach san oíche nuair a shín mé ar mo leaba. Ar maidin tháinig deartháir mná Robinson agus gluaisteán aige agus thug sé amach sinn go Concord, an áit ar scaoileadh an chéad urchar sa Chogadh Meiriceánach, 'a ndeachaigh a mhacalla ar fud an domhain.' Ar thaobh an bhóthair ba mhinic íomhá na 'minute men' le feiceáil. Ba iad sin na fir a dúirt go n-éireoidís chun na Sasanaigh a chur amach ach nóiméad amháin a thabhairt dóibh. Ní raibh míle dár chuireamar dínn nach raibh leacht le feiceáil a tógadh i gcuimhne na dtréanfhear, idir Phoncánaigh agus Éireannaigh, a thit, agus iad ag treascairt na Sasanach. Ní rófhada ó Concord a bhí teach Hawthorne, an t-úrscéalaí, agus ní fhaca mé riamh teach ba dhorcha agus ba dhoilíosaí le féachaint air ná é. Chonaic mé mar an gcéanna iníon Child, eagarthóir na ndán béaloideasa,

*Seo é an modh oibre a bhí aige: Nuair a thagadh sé go dtí cathair ba ghnách leis dul chuig gach duine a raibh aithne agus eolas aige orthu, agus chucu seo ar tugadh a n-ainmneacha dó mar dhaoine a bhí cairdiúil do ghluaiseacht na Gaeilge. Orthu seo bhí easpaig, sagairt, dochtúirí, dlíodóirí, fir mhóra gnótha, lucht páipéir nuachta, agus na Cumainn Ghaelacha; agus ba é a ghnó iad seo a thabhairt le chéile chun timireacht a dhéanamh ar na cruinnithe ina raibh mise le labhairt, agus féachaint le cabhair airgid a fháil, mar aon le cairdeas na bpáipéar agus neart fógraíochta a fháil uathu.

agus iníon Longfellow, agus chaitheas seal fada ag comhrá leo. Thángamar ar ais chun lóin, agus cé a bheadh romham ach Elliot, an fear is mó le rá, agus is mó a bhfuil meas air, b'fhéidir, i gcúrsaí oideachais, dá bhfuil sna Stáit, agus dáréag eile de na hollúna ina chuideachta. Ní raibh aon bhean ann. An fear is mó acu ar chuireas suim ann ba é Kittridge é. Sórt York Powell Meiriceánach é. Bhí a ladar aige i ngach cineál eolais, ach go mórmhór i mbéaloideas. D'fhanamar inár suí ag caint agus ag ól go raibh sé in am dom filleadh go Bostún.

Tháinig mé go Bostún tar éis turas uaire i gcarráiste, agus nuair a ráinigh mé é bhí Uachtarán an AOH, Maitiú Ó Coimín romham. Bhí beirt eile in éindí leis, Ó Conchúir agus Ó Murchú. D'fhanamar le chéile ag caint go dtí go raibh sé ina oíche, agus ansin thugadar leo timpeall na cathrach mé, chun cuairt a thabhairt ar thithe na bpáipéar, agus b'éigean dom fanacht ag féachaint orthu ag ullmhú na bpáipéar i gcomhair na maidine, ag cur isteach pictiúr agus eile. Scríobh mé litreacha Gaeilge do thrí cinn de na páipéir is mó, á rá le muintir Bhostúin go mbeinn ar ais ina measc go luath arís, agus ag guí beannacht orthu ó Chonradh na Gaeilge. Clóbhuaileadh macasamhail na dtrí litreach lá arna mhárach. Tháinig mé ar ais go dtí an teach ósta idir a haon is a dó a chlog san oíche. Ar maidin lá arna mhárach tháinig mé ar ais go Nua-Eabhrac, áit a bhí turas cúig uaire uaim, agus chaith mé féin agus Mac Uí Chuinn dinnéar le chéile i dteach bia sa chathair.

Bhí orm dul inniu go dtí an dara hollscoil is mó, b'fhéidir, dá bhfuil i Meiriceá, ba é sin Yale. Chuaigh mé ar bord na traenach go New Haven. Ráinigh mé an áit sin i gceann cúpla uair an chloig agus tháinig mé amach as an traein, ach ní raibh duine ar bith romham! D'fhan mé ansin agus mo sháith drochmhisnigh orm, ach, tar éis tamaill fhada, tháinig drong de na hÉireannaigh a bhí sa bhaile mór le fáilte a chur romham.

Bhí mé ag caint leo go meidhreach nuair a tháinig sórt ciúnais agus tosta orthu go tobann. Dhearc mé uaim agus chonaic mé fear beag neirbhíseach ag teacht faoinár gcomhair. Chuir sé é féin in aithne dom, Mr Hadley, Uachtarán na hOllscoile. Bhí ionadh ar mo chairde Gaelacha gur tháinig an fear mór go dtí an stáisiún i mo choinne. Dúirt siad nach ndearna sé a leithéid riamh le haon léachtaí eile. Chuir a shibhialta is bhí sé sórt scátha orthu. Nuair a d'imigh an tUachtarán tugadh go dtí teach ósta mé agus bhí rud le n-ithe agam. Agus tháinig an tUachtarán arís le mo thabhairt leis go dtí ionad mo léachta, agus, ó bhí sé róluath, shuigh sé liom ag caint agus ag cur ceisteanna faoi Éirinn orm ar feadh ceathrú uaire eile. Bhí sé an-lách. Thug mé léacht uaim ansin ar 'intinn agus fealsúnacht Chonradh na Gaeilge.' Chuaigh an tUachtarán i gceannas an chruinnithe, agus shuigh sé ag éisteacht liom go dtí an deireadh, agus

mac uí ṁurċaḋa

William W. Murphy. Le caoinchead Fhoras na Gaeilge

sílim gur chuir sé spéis sa mhéid a dúirt mé. Níor spáráil mé na Sasanaigh agus oideachas na Sasanach, ach ní raibh aon Sasanach ann, agus maidir leis na hollúna, níor tháinig aon duine acu ann, sílim, ach amháin an tUachtarán, agus ní raibh ach tuairim dáréag de na mic léinn i láthair, níorbh ionann é agus Harvard. Muna mbeadh gur tháinig na hÉireannaigh isteach ón mbaile mór ní bheadh lucht éisteachta ar bith agam. Líonfaidís sin an teach go bruach ach gur shíl siad nach dtaitneodh sin le lucht ceannais an choláiste. Dúradh liom nach raibh ach timpeall tríocha duine ag éisteacht leis an léachtaí a tháinig romhamsa, agus go raibh sé ar na cainteoirí ba mhó clú sna Stáit. Bhí timpeall céad duine ag éisteacht liomsa. Bhíodar go léir go han-bhuíoch den Uachtarán, Mr Hadley, faoi éisteacht liom go dtí an deireadh. Dúradar liom nach ndearna sé sin riamh roimhe sin le héinne.

Nuair bhí an léacht thart, thug na hÉireannaigh abhaile leo féin mé go dtí club a bhí acu sa bhaile mór. Casadh orm ansin scata seanlaoch agus seanghaiscíoch breá, saighdiúirí a throid sa Chogadh Cathartha. Chuadar sna Fíníní tar éis an chogaidh, agus chuadar go hÉirinn ag súil le cogadh ansin. Bhí fear acu, an Captaen Ó Briain, agus choinnigh sé sinn ar feadh uair an chloig ag éisteacht leis ag cur síos ar a chuid eachtraí in Éirinn, agus faoin gcaoi ar cuireadh i bpríosún i gCluain Meala é, agus ar éalaigh sé as. Dúirt sé go mba shiocair báis é d'uachtarán an phríosúin, mar gur lig sé air gurbh é an t-uachtarán féin a scaoil amach é. Is cuimhin liom mar a d'inis sé dúinn an chaoi a raibh sé i bhfolach faoi scáth sceiche, céadlá lámhaigh na bpatraiscí; agus ba bheag nach bhfuair na madraí a bhí ag cúpla gunnaire, amach é. Bhí sé an-ghreannmhar ar fad, agus b'fhearr liom ná rud ar bith gléas nó gramafón a bheith agam, lena chuid scéalta a chur síos.

Bhí an Captaen Ó Doinn i láthair, freisin, athair an Mhac Uí Dhoinn sin a lean De Hindeberg in ollúnacht na Gaeilge i Washington. Bhí fear, Ó Maidín, agus fear de na Súilleabhánaigh ann freisin. Seansaighdiúirí iad go léir a bhí in Éirinn sa bhliain '68, nó mar sin, agus bhí siad go léir eolasach ar dheochanna a mheascadh! Bhí sé tar éis a dó a chlog nuair a ligeadar uathu mé.

D'fhill mé go Nua-Eabhrac an lá arna mhárach, agus an oíche chéanna ar a haon déag chuaigh mé féin agus Mac Uí Chuinn ar bord na traenach a bhí ag dul go Washington. Bhí carráiste codlata fúinn, agus ráiníomar príomhstát Mheiriceá ar a seacht nó ar a hocht ar maidin. Bhí cuireadh againn ón Uachtarán Roosevelt féin lón a ithe leis. Chuaigh mise agus Mac Uí Chuinn go dtí an 'Teach Bán' ar a haon a chlog, agus chuir an tUachtarán fíorchaoin fáilte romhainn. Chuir sé sinn in aithne dá bhanchéile, bean uasal dheas a bhí inti, agus don dara hiníon (ní raibh Ailís an ceann is sine ar a dtugtaí an banphrionsa sa bhaile), do bhean a dhearthár, agus do na páistí eile, agus shuíomar chun lóin gan gothaí arda ar bith. Lón simplí a bhí ann, agus aon searbhónta gorm amháin ag freastal orainn. Cupán tae agus gloine seirise le n-ól. Úlla agus caora fíniúna glasa, a tógadh díreach as an mbairille agus a raibh an luaithreach timpeall orthu fós, a bhí againn ar an dara cúrsa. Bhí togha an eolais aige ar scéalta na hÉireann agus ar scéalta na Lochlannach, freisin, agus bhí sé ag déanamh comórtais eatarthu. Chaitheamar tobac i gcomhluadar a chéile tar éis an lóin, agus dúirt sé linn go mba bhanaltraí ó Éirinn a bhí aige féin agus é óg, agus go raibh eolas aige riamh ar ainmneacha Chú Chulainn agus Fhinn Mhic Cumhaill, i bhfad sula bhfaca sé ar pháipéar iad. Dúirt se gur bhanaltraí Éireannacha a bhí ag a chlann, freisin. Ba é a bharúil féin go raibh an iomarca 'coilíneachta' i Meiriceá fós, go mba náisiún é a raibh mórán náisiún eile fite le chéile ann, agus ó bhí an oiread sin Éireannach ina measc gur cheart do Mheiriceá gach rud maith nó fiúntach nó spéisiúil ar bith a bhí i mbeatha na nGael a ghlacadh uathu, agus a gcuid féin a dhéanamh de. Dúirt sé go raibh sé le alt a scríobh sa *North American Review*, ag moladh do na hÉireannaigh shaibhre i Meiriceá ollúnachtaí Gaeilge a chur ar bun sna coláistí. Chuaigh mé féin agus Mac Uí Chuinn ar ais ansin go dtí ár dteach ósta agus bhí Mac Uí Dhoinn, ollamh na Gaeilge i Washington, ansin romhainn. Ní féidir leis Gaeilge a labhairt go maith, mar is i Meiriceá a rugadh agus a tógadh é. Chuamar ar cuairt go dtí Eagarthóir an *National Hibernian*, agus go dtí Uachtarán an AOH sa chathair. Bhí aithne agam airsean cheana, óir shuigh an bheirt againn in aice a chéile ag Feis na Fainge i gcontae Luimnigh, an samhradh roimhe sin. Rinne sé óráid ardghlórach nár thaithnigh liom go mór, ar an ócáid sin, ach bhí sé an-lách inniu. Tháinig mé féin agus Mac Uí Chuinn ar ais go Nua-Eabhrac ar a deich a chlog nó mar sin, sa tráthnóna, agus bhí orainn dul timpeall na cathrach go dtí na páipéir mhóra le rá leo gan scéal a thugamar dóibh cheana a chlóbhualadh. Ba é an scéal é sin go raibh mise ag bronnadh cóipe de *Abhráin Diadha Chúige Connacht* ar Roosevelt.[3] Ach nuair a thuigeamar, an lá sin, cén sórt fir a bhí san Uachtarán, bhí náire orainn go rachadh a leithéid de scéal amach, ar eagla, dá bhfeicfeadh sé é go silfeadh sé go raibh sé róchosúil le fógra a dhéanamh dom féin agus go mba stocaireacht é, agus mar a deir an seanfhocal 'ní den stuaim an stocaireacht.' B'fhada an obair í ag dul timpeall go dtí na páipéir.

Anois tháinig an lá mór a raibh bua nó bris i ndán dom. Ba é sin an lá a raibh cruinniú mór le bheith agam sa Carnegie Hall. Bhí sé ullmhaithe le fada an lá roimh ré. Díoladh ar cantáil an chéad rang de na boscaí, roimhe sin, ag an Hoffman House, agus tugadh a lán airgid isteach.

A bhuíochas sin ar Mhac Uí Chuinn. Chruinnigh sé na daoine le chéile agus chuir sé Peadar Fionnalaigh Ó Doinn, fear a raibh aithne air ar fud Mheiriceá, mar 'Mister

Dooley,' ag díol na mboscaí. Ach nuair nár fhéad seisean teacht, fuaireadar fear mór eile lena ndíol. Tugadh suas le trí chéad dollar ar chuid de na boscaí. Bhí céad agus daichead leas-Uachtarán ann, daoine clúiteacha nó daoine saibhre iad go léir, agus bhí siad fial lena gcuid airgid ag ceannach na mboscaí. Ach an dara rang de na boscaí díoladh iad le fear a dúirt go raibh sé á gceannach ar son na gcontaetha, óir bíonn cumann speisialta di féin ag gach contae. Níor íoc an fear seo roimh ré, óir ní raibh duine ar bith in amhras air. Ach nuair a tháinig oíche an chruinnithe chuaigh sé siar ar a mhargadh, agus dúirt gur theip air na ticéid a dhíol, agus ina theannta sin thug sé ar ais céad go leith acu a bhí ceannaithe aige. Is dóigh gur d'aon turas, leis an gcruinniú a mhilleadh, a rinneadh é seo. Chífidh an léitheoir gur imríodh cleas den sórt céanna orm i mBostún. Tá a fhios agam go maith cé a d'imir an cleas orm sa bhaile sin, agus cad chuige ar imríodh é, ach níl a fhios agam i gceart cé a bhí ciontach leis i Nua-Eabhrac; arbh iad na daoine a raibh éad agus formad orthu le lucht na 'Tuxedos,' nó daoine a shíl nach raibh na Gaeil ag dul ar an mbealach ceart ag leanúint an Chonartha? 'Finn' an t-ainm a bhí ar an bhfear a cheannaigh na ticéid agus a bhris a mhargadh. Ach is dóigh nach raibh ann ach uirlis i lámha daoine eile. Ar chuma ar bith chuir sé stad leathuaire, nach mór, ar an gcruinniú. Bhí Seán Ó Cuinn ag stiúradh chuile shórt, agus é ina sheasamh ag an doras, agus nuair a tugadh ticéid na mboscaí ar ais dó, gan coinne aige leo, ar eagla go mbeadh na boscaí folamh agus an cruinniú millte, céard a rinne sé ach dul ar an bpointe boise agus na daoine nach raibh acu ach ticéid choitianta (dollar amháin a bhí orthu sin) a sheoladh isteach sna boscaí folmha. Bhí an amharclann lán ansin, agus níor thug éinne faoi deara gur tharla aon rud. Bhí an cruinniú le tosú ar a hocht a chlog, ach mar gheall ar ar thit amach bhí sé níos mó ná leathuair mall ag tosú. An Príomh-Bhreitheamh Mac Eochaidh a bhí i gceannas, agus ba é Búrcach Ó Cogaráin, fear saibhir, fear stáit agus Éireannach maith a labhair i dtosach le mé chur in aithne don slua. Cuireadh geasa air gan labhairt níos mó ná ceathrú uaire, agus gheall sé agus d'athgheall sé nach rachadh sé thairis sin, ach níor chomhlíon sé a gheallúint. Tá guth breá aige agus deirtear gurb é an fear óráidíochta is fearr sna Stáit é, agus creidim sin, óir nuair a bhain sé amach sa chaint agus slua mór daoine ag éisteacht leis, níor fhéad sé srian a chur lena theanga agus labhair sé ar feadh trí nóiméad déag ar fhichid - agus é ag caint an t-am go léir faoi cheist nach raibh aon eolas aige uirthi! Nuair a chríochnaigh sé ghabh mo chara Pádraig Ó Séaghdha an 'Maidrín Rua' agus 'Aililiú na Gamhna' go breá. Labhair an tArd-Bhreitheamh Ó Dúllaing agus thairg sé rún i bhfábhar na Gaeilge agus do ghlaoigh sé ormsa mo léacht a thabhairt uaim.

Thosaigh mé ansin, agus mo chroí ag bualadh agus ag preabarnaigh ionam le neart sceoin. Thosaigh mé i nGaeilge agus lean mé di ar feadh cúig nóiméad. Thuig cuid mhaith daoine mé ach bhí scanradh an domhain ar an gcuid is mó acu. Shíl siad go raibh mé ag dul ag labhairt Gaeilge ar feadh na hoíche. Thosaigh mé i mBéarla ansin agus thug mé *mutatis mutandis* beagnach an léacht chéanna a thug mé go rímhinic cheana sa bhaile, ar Dhí-Shacsanú na hÉireann. Labhair mé ar feadh uaire go leith, agus bhí na daoine go léir ag éisteacht go cúramach le gach focal dá ndúirt mé, agus ag gáire, agus do mo mholadh. Bhí siad go léir ar aon intinn liom, agus b'fhurasta sin a fheiceáil; agus thug sé sin croí agus misneach dom le mo chuid teagaisc a chraobhs-caoileadh go dána; agus rinne mé sin. Ag tosú dom i nGaeilge dúirt mé go rabhamar cruinnithe chun buille a bhualadh ar son na seanmhná boichte, 'ach, dar mo lámh,' arsa mise, 'ní seanbhean bhocht í anois, ach cailín óg croíúil a bhfuil na mílte agus na mílte ag titim i ngrá léi. Tá sí bocht go fóill, ach má tá féin, tá sí óg álainn deas dathúil, agus tá rudaí ann níos measa ná an bochtanas. Ach bocht nó saibhir is í ár nÉire féin í, agus táimid ag dul dá tógáil. Fuaireamar ár dtír,' arsa mise, 'dhá bhliain déag ó shin, ina cúige, – ní hea, ina contae de Shasana, ina rubaillín beag suarach, agus táimidne ag déanamh náisiúin di. Is le cur i gcéill agus i dtuiscint daoibh céard atáimid a dhéanamh in Éirinn a tháinig Tomás Bán agus mé féin anall anseo. Tá difir mhór idir an Éire a bhí againn dhá bhliain déag ó shin agus an Éire atá ann inniu. Ní raibh le feiceáil an uair sin in Éirinn ach an dá pháirtí amháin, na Tiarnaí agus na Tionóntaí ag bualadh ag léasadh agus ag plancadh a chéile. Ach buíochas le Dia tá an troid sin beagnach thart anois. Tá na daoine ag fáil seilbhe ar thalamh na tíre arís, agus tá na Tiarnaí ag éirí i bhfad níos Gaelaí ná a bhídís, ó scar siad lena gcuid talún.' Ag deireadh na cainte dúirt mé, 'Éire nach mbeadh inti ach teanga, ceol, spóirteannaí, rincí agus béasa na nGall, ba chuma liom ann nó as í, ba chuma liom in uachtar no in iochtar í, óir ní hí Éire a bheadh ann ach rubaillín de Shasana, agus b'fhearr liom bheith i mo chónaí i Sasana féin ná sa rubaillín sin.' Béarla do labhair mé ina dhiaidh sin.

Tar éis mo léachta, do thairg Diarmuid Ó Loingsigh, Uachtarán Chonradh na Gaeilge i Nua-Eabhrac, dileagra dom, agus ba dheas an dileagra é. Seo iad na focail dheiridh a bhí ann, - ní chuirfinn síos anseo iad ach gur tháinig siad fíor, nó beagnach fíor, buíochas le Dia - 'go dtugaidh Dia na glóire fad saoghail agus sláinte dhuit a phrionnsa na nGaedheal; agus ná tugadh Sé Chuige féin thú nó go mbeidh Éire saor ó ghéar-smacht an tSacsanaigh.' Cé a shílfeadh an uair sin go mbeadh an Sasanach imithe chomh luath sin as na Sé Chontae Fichead agus go nglacfaí leis an nGaeilge mar theanga náisiúnta!

An lá arna mhárach bhí cur síos ar an gcruinniú sna páipéir, agus bhí siad ar aon fhocal, á rá gur éirigh go breá leis, agus dúirt gach éinne nach raibh a leithéid de chruinniú d'Éireannaigh i Nua-Eabhrac ó aimsir Pharnell. Más fíor sin, is do Sheán

Ó Cuinn agus dósan amháin atá an chreidiúint ag dul. Ní fhéadfadh Tomás Bán agus mé féin an obair a dhéanamh go bráth gan a chúnamhsan.

Agus is anois ba chóir dom a rá go raibh, ní hé amháin na hÉireannaigh foghlamtha saibhre ar mo chúl - a bhuíochas sin ar Mhac Uí Chuinn - ach bhí an AOH liom mar an gcéanna, nó muna rabhadar, bhí Clann na nGael liom, ón gcéad lá riamh, agus bhí cuid díobh sin i gach slua den AOH agus ba iad sin 'an t-eireaball a bhain gluaiseacht as an madra.' Thuigeadarsan ar nós nár thuig daoine eile croí agus brí na hoibre a bhí ar láimh agamsa.

Bhí mé lánsásta, an lá arna mhárach, leis na páipéir agus leis na rudaí a chuala mé, óir bhí a fhios agam dá mbeadh fáilte romham i Nua-Eabhrac go n-éireodh liom in áiteanna eile, óir leanann, mar a dúirt mé cheana, cuid mhór de na páipéir ar fud na Stát aon rud a bhfuil branda agus séala Nua-Eabhrac air. Ach níor fhéad mé mo scíth a ligean. B'éigean dom dul, lá arna mhárach, go Hartford, Connecticut.

HARTFORD

Is baile mór é sin a bhfuil timpeall 100,000 duine ann, agus is Éireannaigh tuairim 30,000 díobh sin. I dTigh an Opera a bhí an cruinniú. Bhí slua maith mór i láthair, ach ní dhearnadh aon bhailiú airgid sa teach tar éis mo léachta, agus d'fhág sé sin an Conradh ar an gcaolchuid. $113.85 tairbhe an chruinnithe, agus ba bheag é an méid sin, óir níor tháinig isteach ach luach na dticéad a díoladh. Nuair a bhí deireadh ráite agam léigh sean-Éireannach, Cross a ainm, dán Gaeilge a rinne sé dom. Nuair a chonaic mé nár tháinig mórán airgid isteach dúirt mé liom féin nár mhór dom cuairt phearsanta a thabhairt ar na daoine is saibhre, lá arna mhárach, agus chuaigh mé ar dtús go dtí an Coirnéal Ó Donnchú, fear déanta biotáille, agus gheall sé cabhair dom, agus go dtí Iníon Uí Leannacháin agus go dtí fear arb ainm dó Mag Shamhráin, fear árachais. Gheall seisean dhá chéad dollar dom. Bhí fear eile, Ó Garbháin ab ainm dó, agus gheall seisean cúnamh dom freisin. Ach stop an coirnéal mo bhéal le buidéal champagne, agus chuir sé mé á ól gur tháinig mo thraein isteach. Ní raibh agam ach trí nó ceithre nóiméad lena ól! D'fhág mé an gnó ansin idir lámha Iníon Uí Leannacháin agus Mhac Uí Éigeartaigh, an rúnaí.* Tháinig mé ar ais go Nua-Eabhrac tráthnóna, agus slaghdán agus píochán orm, agus an lá arna mhárach níor fhág mé an teach. Cuireadh mo dhinnéar isteach chugam. An lá ina dhiaidh sin ba é 'Lá Breithe Buíochais' é, an

*Níor tháinig pingin den airgead seo a gealladh dom isteach riamh!

lá is mó dá bhfuil acu i Meiriceá, agus ní fhéadfainn aon obair a dhéanamh dá mbeinn ar fónamh féin.

BOSTÚN

Lá nó dhó ina dhiaidh sin d'fhág mo bhean agus mé féin Nua-Eabhrac go moch ar maidin le dul go Bostún. Bhí mé le bheith ann in am i gcomhair lóin a bhí fear ionaid an Ard-Mhaoir le tabhairt dom, ar son an Bhardais agus in ainm na cathrach. Fuair mé sreangscéal uaidh, agus mé ar an traein, á rá liom tuirlingt den traein ag Back Bay, óir, tá dhá stáisiún i mBostún. Rinne mé sin, agus casadh rúnaí an Mhaoir orm, agus thug sé leis mé go dtí an teach ósta, áit ar chuir mé aithne ar an Maor féin, agus ar scór, b'fhéidir, den lucht oideachais ba mhó le rá sa chathair, agus eagarthóirí páipéar etc. agus bhí mé ag dul ag suí síos chun lóin, agus mé go lánsásta ardaigeantach, nuair a ghlaoigh Tomás Bán orm ar an nguthán. Dúirt sé in ainm Dé gan lón a ithe muna bhfaighinn gealladh ón Maor nach sílfí go raibh sa chuairt seo a thug mé air ach cuairt phríobháideach. Dúirt Tomás go raibh Conradh na Gaeilge i mBostún briste cheana, i ngeall ormsa a bheith ag ithe lóin leis an Maor; agus go raibh fearg an mhí-áidh mhóir ar na daoine. Ar ndóigh, nuair a fuair mé an scéal sin ó Thomás cuireadh trína chéile go mór mé, agus ní raibh a fhios agam i gceart céard a dhéanfainn. Chuaigh mé ar fhód faoi leith leis an Maor, agus dúirt mé leis go príobháideach go raibh súil agam nach measfaí go raibh aon bhaint agamsa le polaitíocht na cathrach, mar gheall ar lón a ithe leis-sean; agus go raibh a fhios agam go raibh troid ar siúl i dtaobh Mhaoracht na cathrach, 'agus,' arsa mise, 'tá ciall cheannaithe agam, le fada an lá, gan leithscéal a thabhairt d'éinne chun a rá go raibh mé ar a thaobhsan seachas ar thaobh eile.' Rinne an Maor gáire agus d'inis sé dom nár thug sé cuireadh d'éinne ach amháin do lucht oideachais agus do lucht páipéar. Mar sin féin, níor bhain mé aon sásamh as an lón, agus goile ar bith a bhí agam milleadh orm é! Ag cuimhneamh dom ar an scéal seo ina dhiaidh sin, sílim gur cuireadh scanradh nach raibh gá leis ar Thomas Bán. Sílim gurb éard ba bhun leis an trioblóid ar fad nár thug an Maor cuireadh go dtí a lón don duine sin den AOH a bhí ina uachtarán ar an gcoiste a bhí chun fáilte a chur romham go Bostún; shíl seisean go mba tharcaisne dósan é, agus scanraigh sé Tomás Bán, agus scanraigh Tomás mise! Fuair mé amach ina dhiaidh sin go raibh coiste chun fáilte a chur romham ag fanacht liom ag an stáisiún eile, agus shíl siad go mba ghránna an cleas a imríodh orthu mé a thabhairt amach ag an gcéad stáisiún. Níor thuig mé riamh an cheist seo i gceart, ach chuala mé ina dhiaidh sin ó dhaoine creidiúnacha go raibh daoine a raibh baint acu le páirtí láidir polaitíochta ag fanacht liom ag an stáisiún eile, agus gurbh é Mac Uí Thuama, an fear ar leis *Donahoe's Magazine*, a smaoinigh ar an scéim sin, mise a thabhairt amach ag Back Bay, chun nach gcuirfí in achrann mé ina dhiaidh sin.

Bhí mo chara Robinson, fear Harvard, ag an lón, agus mórán eile de lucht oideachais, agus b'éigean dom beagán cainte a dhéanamh tar éis an lóin, sa dá theanga, ach níor labhair mé go maith, bhí mé chomh buartha sin.

Tugadh mé go dtí an Touraine ina dhiaidh sin, an teach ósta is sean-nósaí agus is compordaí dá raibh mé ann fós, agus d'fhan mé i mo shuí go raibh sé an-déanach san oíche ag cur fáilte roimh na fichidí a tháinig ar cuairt chugam.

An lá arna mhárach tháinig seandlíodóir clúiteach, Ó Dochartaigh ab ainm dó, agus thug sé go dtí an Teampall Protastúnach mé, agus chuir sé in aithne don easpag mé. Chaith mé féin agus mo bhean lón le Mac Uí Thuama agus lena mhnaoi! Bhí Tomás Bán ann, freisin, agus fear ó mo chontae féin arbh ainm dó Ó Gealbháin. Bhí an cruinniú mór le bheith agam ar a ceathair a chlog in Amharclann Bhostúin. Ba rí-olc an tráthnóna é, agus é ag stealladh báistí. Mar sin féin bhí i bhfad níos mó ná trí cheathrú den amharclann lán, agus is dóigh go mbeadh sé lán go dtí an doras ach gur clóbhuaileadh fógra i gceann nó dhó de na páipéir ar maidin ag rá nach san amharclann sin ach in amharclann eile a bheadh an cruinniú agam, agus nach san iarnóin ach sa tráthnóna a bheadh sé. Ní de dhearmad, ná le faillí, a thit sé sin amach, ach is cinnte go ndearnadh d'aon turas é chun an cruinniú a mhilleadh orm. Dúirt mórán daoine liom cé a rinne é. Fear é a bhí ina rúnaí don UIL Cuireadh an fear seo ar an gcoiste a bunaíodh le fáilte a chur romhamsa agus le honóir éigin a thabhairt dó rinneadh uachtarán de choiste na poiblíochta de. Dúradh liomsa go ndearna sé a dhícheall, ó thús go deireadh, gach uile rud tubaisteach a dhéanamh, agus bhí toradh ar a shaothar an mhaidin sin. Ach thug sé aire gan an fógra mícheart a chur ina pháipéar féin! Sin é an scéal mar a chuala mise, agus is dóigh gurb í sin an fhírinne, ach ar eagla nach í an fhírinne í, ní chuirfidh mé síos ainm an duine sin. Casadh orm féin é agus níor thaithnigh sé liom.

Is binn béal ina thost! Níor lig mé riamh orm gur imríodh cleas mar sin orm. Chuaigh mé trí Mheiriceá ar fad, agus níor inis mé an scéal sin d'éinne beo. Bhí sé an-chosúil leis an gcleas a imríodh orm i Nua-Eabhrac nuair a tugadh ar ais ticéid na mboscaí tar éis iad a bheith ceannaithe. Dúradh liom go raibh éad ar an bhfear seo i mBostún ar eagla go n-éireodh níos fearr leis an gcruinniú a bhí agamsa ná le cruinnithe a pháirtí féin.

Labhair mé ar feadh uair an chloig agus daichead nóiméad, agus sílim go ndeachaigh mo chuid cainte i bhfeidhm ar an lucht éisteachta, agus bhí na páipéir nuachta go léir go han-fhábhrach dom. Rinne siad rud a chuir iontas orm; d'oscail siad a gcolúin do shíntiúis ar mo shon sular tháinig mé ar chor ar bith, agus thug gach ceann acu féin céad dollar uaidh! Mar sin féin níor éirigh go rómhaith linn ó thaobh an airgid. Fágadh clúdach ar gach suíochán chun go gcuirfeadh an lucht éisteachta a gcuid airgid isteach ann, agus go mbaileofaí agus go dtabharfaí suas ar an ardán ansin é. B'fhearr go mór a d'éireodh linn dá n-éireodh triúr nó ceathrar ina seasamh ar an ardán agus dá dtabharfaidís sin síntiús uathu. Ansin d'fhéadfadh an cathaoirleach iarraidh ar an lucht éisteachta a gcuid síntiús féin a thabhairt suas. Ach ní raibh Seán Ó Cuinn agam i mBostún, agus nuair nár láimhseáladh ceist an airgid níos fearr, níor bailíodh ach b'fhéidir leath an mhéid a bhaileofaí dá ndéanfaí ar shlí eile é.*
Nuair a bhí deireadh leis an gcruinniú, ba bheag nár plúchadh mé leis an méid daoine a bhí ag teacht chun lámh a chroitheadh liom, agus d'fhan mé go raibh sé déanach san oíche ag cur fáilte roimh na daoine a tháinig ar cuairt chugam sa teach ósta.

MANCHESTER

An lá arna mhárach chuaigh mé go Manchester, New Hampshire, baile mór atá timpeall turas trí huaire an chloig ó Bhostún. Bhí sé tar éis sioc mór a dhéanamh agus bhí sneachta ar an talamh. Casadh sean-Ghael, Ó Dubhda, orm ag an stáisiún, fear a raibh an-eolas aige ar leabhair agus ar gach ní a bhain leis an nGaeilge, agus bhí fear eile ann ó Loch Tailt i gContae Shligigh a raibh togha na Gaeilge aige agus an-chuimse amhrán. Beirt an-dúthrachtach a bhí iontu. Bhí daoine eile ann freisin. Thugadar go dtí teach an easpaig mé, an Dochtúir Ó Dubhshláine. Is é easpag New Hampshire é, agus tá a fhairche chomh mór le hÉirinn ar fad. Fear óg a bhí ann, agus é an-lách, an-charthanach. Ní raibh gothaí arda ar bith ag baint leis. Casadh orm é an lá arna mhárach sa traein, agus hata coitianta billycock air, agus é ag caitheamh todóige dó féin. Mar a dúirt na daoine liom, 'is *citizen* maith an t-easpag.' Ní thugaidís 'Tiarna' air, ach oiread. 'Easpag' a deiridís i gcónaí. Chaith mé greim bia ina chomhluadar, agus ansin chuamar go léir go Teach an Opera. Is mór an baile cadáis é Manchester. Chuala mé go bhfuil cuid de na muilte cadáis is mó dá bhfuil sa domhan ann. Tharraing na

*$1,783.83 a frítheadh i mBostún, ach frítheadh $9,303.53 ar fad i Nua-Eabhrac. Féach Aguisín, lch 307.

muilte sin na mílte Francach isteach ann ó Cheanada. Chuala mé, freisin, go raibh, ar a laghad 18,000 Francach ann, agus beagán níos mó ná sin d'Éireannaigh. Bhí tabhairt amach mór againn ag dul síos go Teach an Opera. Bhí na 'Foresters' ann agus iad gléasta go breá, na 'Friendly Sons' agus cuid den AOH agus cath de mhílíste an Stáit, agus lucht tóirsí, agus faoi dheireadh mé féin agus an t-easpag i gcarráiste. Labhair mé ar feadh uaire agus daichead nóiméad. Bhain mé rud beag níos mó tairbhe as mo chaint ná mar a bhain mé in Hartford. Fuair mé 150 dollar.

D'fhill mé an lá arna mhárach go Bostún, agus chuaigh mé timpeall na cathrach go dtí cúig cinn de na tithe tráchtála is mó agus is saibhre, ag iarraidh síntiúis do Chonradh na Gaeilge. Diúltaíodh mé i gceann acu, ach dúradh liom sna cinn eile go ndéanfaí smaoineamh ar an gceist. Ní dóigh liom go bhfuair mé aon rud fónta uathu. D'imigh mo bhean inniu go dtí muintir Mhic Giolla Phádraig. Tá ceann de na háiteanna is mó i mBostún ag Mac Giolla Phádraig. Maidir liom féin, d'fhág mé an Touraine, agus chuaigh mé ar an traein go dtí South Hadley, Mass., go Coláiste Mount Holyoke. Coláiste ban é sin, agus ó tharla nach raibh mé riamh ina leithéid sin d'áit roimhe sin, chuir mé spéis faoi leith ann. Tháinig banollamh faoi mo choinne go dtí an stáisiún, agus scuab sí léi mé gan nóiméad a chailleadh isteach i gcóiste, agus thug sí go dtí an coláiste mé. Chaith mé dinnéar i gcomhluadar Miss Wooley, uachtarán an choláiste. Níor fhéad mé an coláiste a fheiceáil an oíche sin ach chonaic mé lá arna mhárach é. Tá céad acra talún ag gabháil leis, ceapaim, agus tithe móra anseo agus ansiúd a bhfuil na hiníonacha ina gcónaí iontu. Tugann siad an 'campus' air sin. Lasann siad aon sorn mór amháin gach lá, agus tugann sin teas do gach aon teach acu, cé go bhfuil siad go measartha fada óna chéile. Dóitear sé thonna guail gach lá sa sorn. Tá leabharlann, músaem, seomraí do na ranganna, seomraí léachta etc. san áit seo freisin.

Tar éis an dinnéir tháinig na cailíní go léir, oiread agus seacht gcéad acu, isteach sa halla mór, agus thug mise léacht dóibh ar 'Litríocht Fhileata na hÉireann.' Is minic a thug mé léacht ab fhearr ná é, ach sílim go raibh na cailíní an-sásta leis, agus thugadar an-bhualadh bos dom. Bhain mé gáire astu ag tosú dom. 'A mhná uaisle,' arsa mise, agus ansin stad mé, agus dúirt mé, 'ba ghnáth liom i gcónaí, 'a dhaoine uaisle' a rá i ndiaidh a mhná uaisle, ach ó nach bhfuil aon duine uasal ann, déarfaidh mé a mhná uaisle agus a Miss Wooley.' Bhí seanfhear thíos i gcúl an tí, a tháinig isteach ó Lowell le mo chloisteáil, agus chuir sé béic as nuair a dúirt mé nach raibh aon duine uasal ina measc, agus dúirt 'tá mise anseo!' Bhain sé sin tuilleadh gáire astu. Nuair bhí an léacht thart ní imeodh an seanfhear gan caint a dhéanamh liom, agus thug sé maide a ghearr sé i bhFlorida mar bhronntanas dom. Nuair a fuair mé an maide cheap mé gurbh é mo

T. Mac Giolla Pádraig

Thomas B. Fitzpatrick. Le caoinchead Fhoras na Gaeilge

scáth fearthainne féin a bhí i mo ghlac agam, agus d'fhág mé mo scáth i mo dhiaidh, agus thug mé an maide liom! Conchubhar Ó Súilleabháin ab ainm don seanfhear agus ba as Contae Chiarraí dó.

Lá arna mhárach, go moch ar maidin, tugadh mo bhricfeasta isteach chun mo sheomra, agus ar a hocht nó ar leathuair i ndiaidh a hocht b'éigean dom dul go dtí an séipéal go bhfeicfinn na cailíní agus iad cruinnithe le chéile, caipíní agus gúnaí coláiste ar an gcuid is mó acu, agus Miss Wooley féin mar a bheadh ardsagart nó easpag ann agus róba fada dubh uirthi ag léamh seirbhíse dóibh! Ba ghreannmhar an radharc domsa é, nach bhfaca aon rud dá shórt riamh go dtí sin.

D'fhág Miss Wooley mé i gcúram beirte de na banollúna ba dheise a bhí sa choláiste, chun an áit a thaispeáint dom. Chaith gach aon duine den bheirt uair an chloig liom do mo thionlacan timpeall na háite. Níor fhág siad ball den áit nár thaispeáin siad dom agus b'fhiú é a fheiceáil. D'ith mé lón le Miss Wooley i measc na gcailíní go léir. Ba iad na cailíní féin a rinne an freastal orainn. Ní fhaca mé ariamh, agus níor shíl mé go bhfeicfinn go deo, rud chomh cosúil leis an méid a léigh mé, fadó, sa *Princess* le Tennyson.

SPRINGFIELD

Tar éis dom lón a chaitheamh, d'imigh mé go Springfield, áit nach bhfuil rófhada ó Holyoke. Is ansin a casadh orm an Gael is fearr dár casadh orm in aon áit acu, Mac Uí Éigeartaigh ab ainm dó. Bhí cruinniú maith agam sa tráthnóna – bhí timpeall cúig chéad duine ann – agus chuir mé 292 dollar le chéile dá bharr.

Tar éis na léachta thug cuid de na hÉireannaigh go dtí an Club mé. Bhí triúr acu ann a tháinig in éineacht liomsa, agus Albanach. Chuir na hÉireannaigh seo déistin agus gráin orm, ach ar ndóigh níor lig mé tada orm. Ní raibh éinne ina measc ar cheart Gael a thabhairt air ach amháin an tAlbanach, agus bhíodh na daoine eile á phiocadh, á chiapadh agus ag déanamh magaidh faoi. Shílfeá orthu go raibh náire orthu deoir ar bith den fhuil Ghaelach a bheith iontu, agus tá mé cinnte nár thuig éinne acu ach an tAlbanach soiscéal an Chonartha. Sin é an rud a buaileadh isteach ar m'aigne an oíche sin, ar chuma ar bith. Bhain sé an misneach díom, ach b'fhéidir nach raibh an ceart agam. Dar liomsa ba iad na hÉireannaigh ba mheasa dár casadh fós orm iad.

Lá arna mhárach chuaigh mé ar cuairt go teach Mhic Uí Éigeartaigh. Tá clann aige, agus is í an Ghaeilge a labhraíonn siad i gcónaí lena n-athair is lena máthair. Tá faitíos orm go bhfuil an saol ag dul rite leo. Áit mhór chun airm rialtais a dhéanamh is ea

Springfield, agus is as an trácht sin a thagann mórán de shaibhreas an bhaile mhóir. Ní bhíonn ar na hoibrithe ach ocht n-uaire an chloig a chur isteach. Deir Mac Uí Éigeartaigh go bhfuil go leor bochtanais sa chathair, cé go mbreathnaíonn sé saibhir go leor ar an taobh amuigh. Ach buíochas le Dia tá a theach féin aige, agus déanann gach éinne a dhícheall chun a theach féin a cheannach. B'olc liom an Gael maith seo a fhágáil.

ANSONIA

Chuaigh mé go Ansonia, Connecticut, sa tráthnóna. Áit í a bhfuil go leor oibreacha iarainn agus práis ann. Tá 28,000 duine ann agus Éireannaigh is ea an chuid is mó acu sin. Fearghaill an t-ainm atá ar an Maor. Tháinig sé i mo choinne, go dtí an stáisiún, agus thug sé go dtí a theach féin mé. Fear óg oilte foghlamtha é, agus fear an-lách é ina theannta sin. Dúirt sé go raibh a mhuintir sa tír seo ó 1640 nó mar sin, ach níor cheap sé go raibh aon fhuil eile ina chuisleanna seachas fuil Nua-Shasanach nó Poncán. Mhínigh mise dó cérbh iad muintir Uí Fhearghaill ó cheart. Tá oibreacha móra iarainn aige féin, agus 800 duine ag obair iontu. Tá teach an-álainn aige. Bhí mór-roinn Mheiriceá, Sasana, agus mórchuid den Eoraip siúlta aige, agus, tríd agus tríd, ba é an fear ab oilte é dár casadh orm fós. Bhí cruinniú réasúnta maith sa tráthnóna agam, agus bhailigh mé 101 dollar.

Thug an Fearghailleach ina ghluaisteán mé timpeall na tíre sin. Tá learga áille inti, srutháin nó aibhneacha ag sní tríothu, agus is fíorchoirceog de gach saghas déantúis gach cnocán acu. Cuireadh muilte ar na haibhneacha i dtosach, agus anois féin, nuair is gal atá á n-oibriú in áit uisce, d'fhan na muilte agus an obair sa tseanáit chéanna.

D'fhill mé go Bostún sa tráthnóna mar bhí Seán Ó Cuinn le teacht amach chugam, agus bhíomar le dul le chéile go teach Mhic Giolla Phádraig, an áit a raibh mo bhean. Bhí mé i mo sheasamh liom féin ar ardán an bhóthair iarainn sa chathair, gan a fhios agam cá raibh mé, nó cén bealach a thiontóinn, agus ba léir d'éinne go raibh mé ag dul amú. Labhair sean-Éireannach liom agus dúirt sé gur aithin sé mé, agus go gcuirfeadh sé ar an mbealach ceart mé. Rugadh i gContae Chorcaí é i bhfoisceacht do Chaisleán de hÍde (nó do Charraig an Éide[4] má thugaim a ainm ceart Gaeilge air) agus thosaigh sé ansin, agus ghabh sé an t-amhrán sin go léir dom ó thús go deireadh!* Ansin chuir sé mé ar an eolas.

*Féach nóta, lgh 308-10.

D'aimsigh Mac Uí Chuinn mé, agus d'imigh an bheirt againn go teach Mhic Giolla Phádraig. Fear tostach fadcheannach é, agus eisean an t-aon Éireannach dá bhfaca mé i mBostún go bhféadfainnse 'fear saibhir' a thabhairt air, cé gur Éireannaigh níos mó ná leath na ndaoine atá i mBostún. Díolann sé ribíní agus mionéadaí agus tá siopa iontach mór aige. Is togha Éireannaigh é, agus bíonn sé réidh chun cúnamh a thabhairt d'aon ghluaiseacht a bhíonn ag dul ar aghaidh in Éirinn. Ach maidir liom féin, bhí sórt scátha air romham. Ní raibh a fhios aige i gceart cén tuairim pholaitíochta a bhí agam. Bhí eagla air go raibh mé in aghaidh, nó go raibh Conradh na Gaeilge in aghaidh lucht na Parlaiminte, ar bhealach. Nuair a mhínigh mé dó nach rabhamar ina n-aghaidh, a bheag ná a mhór, d'athraigh sé a intinn, agus thug sé céad dollar dom. Tá faitíos orm go raibh mórán daoine ar aon intinn leis, i measc na ndaoine saibhre, daoine a raibh amhras orthu fúinn; agus gach áit a ndeachaigh mé rinne mé mo dhícheall ar an drochbharúil sin a athrú. Tá teach deas aige, bean agus clann, agus fuair sé bonn óir ón bPápa. Nuair a bhí an lón caite againn d'fhág mé Bostún arís le dul go Lowell, turas uair an chloig ó Bhostún.

LOWELL

Bhí an sneachta go tiubh ar an talamh. Tháinig uachtarán na gconstáblaí, Joe Smith, i mo choinne. Thug sé go dtí teach ósta mé, agus d'ólamar buidéal fíona agus d'itheamar dinnéar maith le chéile. Is é an fear is mó a bhfuil fuath aige do na Sasanaigh dá bhfaca mé i Meiriceá, sílim. Bhí sé bacach ó aimsíodh le piléar sa chois é. Amuigh in iarthar Mheiriceá a tharla sin dó. D'inis sé dom an chaoi a d'éalaigh sé, agus é ag cromadh síos ar íochtar díge, as an áit a d'aimsigh an piléar é, go bhfuair sé féin gunna piléar, agus rop sé píosa luaidhe tríd an bhfear a chaith leis, gur mharaigh sé é. Chuamar go dtí an cruinniú ansin. Bhí timpeall is cúig chéad duine ann. Ach ní raibh seisean sásta leis, shíl sé go mbeadh i bhfad níos mó i láthair. Bhí suipéar againn ansin, agus nuair a d'imigh na daoine eile d'fhan fear de mhuintir Ghallchóir lena chur i gcéill domsa gurbh é Joe Smith féin a mhill an cruinniú, ach dá bhfágfadh sé é faoi na Cumainn Éireannacha ar fad, nó faoin nGallchórach féin, bheadh cruinniú an-mhór ann. Níor chreid mé é. Fuair mé $176 de bharr mo chainte.

D'fhill mé go Bostún lá arna mhárach, le dul go dtí Coláiste Wellesley, coláiste ban eile, nach bhfuil turas uair an chloig as an gcathair, agus bhí mé go díreach in am don 'Fháiltiú,' a chuir Miss Hazard,[5] uachtarán an choláiste, romham. Sílim go bhfuil an áit seo rud beag níos mó ná Holyoke, agus tá sé suite in áit díreach chomh deas leis. Cuireadh in aithne mé do shlua maith daoine agus b'éigean dom aithriseoireacht a dhéanamh dóibh! Chaith mé dinnéar i gcomhluadar Miss Hazard agus le seisear banollamh agus le fear amháin. Tá 110 ollamh ann, agus is mná iad go léir ach amháin timpeall dáréag acu. Ní hionann é agus Holyoke, níl fear ar bith acu san áit sin. Bhí cruinniú an-mhór de na hiníonacha léinn agam, os cionn seacht gcéad acu, agus thug mé an óráid chéanna faoi Chonradh na Gaeilge a thug mé ag Yale. Ní raibh taise agam ar lucht polaitíochta Shasana, ach ar ndóigh ba chuma leis an lucht éisteachta sin!

Dúirt bean uasal amháin liom go raibh sí i gcónaí i bhfábhar na hÉireann, ach nár chreid sí go raibh maith ar bith sa teanga nó gur chuala sí mise, agus gur athraigh mise a haigne. Is iontach an méid eolais a bhí acu ar chúrsaí na hÉireann agus an tsuim a chuir siad inár dtír. Is dóigh gurbh é an fáth a bhí leis sin, an chuairt a thug Yeats ar an áit cúpla bliain romhamsa.

BROCKTON

Tháinig mé ar ais go Bostún tar éis mo bhricfeasta agus chaith mé lón le muintir Mhic Giolla Phádraig, agus chuaigh mé amach as an áit sin go Brockton, baile mór a ndéantar bróga ann. Níl aon áit eile sna Stáit a ndéantar an oiread sin bróg inti. Tá tuarastal mór le fáil as déanamh na mbróg, agus ó bhí ceannach agus díol an-mhór orthu an t-am sin, bhí gach uile dhuine lánsásta. Tháinig chomh maith le hocht gcéad duine go dtí mo léacht. Tá timpeall 40,000 duine sa chathair, agus is Éireannaigh cuid mhór díobh. Tá dochtúir ansin, Mac Suibhne ó Mhaigh Chromtha, cainteoir breá Gaeilge, agus is é croí na gluaiseachta é, ach ní raibh mórán cainte agam leis. Mac Giolla Mhuire, *alderman*, a bhí i gceannas an chruinnithe, agus ó tharla nár díoladh aon sórt biotáille sa bhaile mór níor fhéad sé deoch a thabhairt dom tar éis na léachta. Is baile é seo a bhfuil cosc ar ólachán ann, ach fuair sé deoch i siopa poitigéara agus d'ól mé í sin i mo sheomra codlata! Is aisteach an rud é cosc a bheith ar an ól sa bhaile mór agus cead ag muintir Bhostúin, nach bhfuil ach turas uair an chloig nó mar sin ón áit seo, a rogha rud a ól. Is de bharr togha áitiúil nó 'local option' é. Chuaigh Bostún ar thaobh an óil, agus chuaigh an áit seo ina aghaidh. Thaithnigh muintir Brockton liom go mór. Shíl mé go mba iad na hÉireannaigh ba chroíúla dár casadh orm fós iad. Tháinig 170 dollar isteach de bharr mo chuid cainte.

Chuaigh mé ar ais go Bostún go moch ar maidin, agus d'fhág mé féin agus mo bhean an chathair sin le dul go Nua-Eabhrac. Chuamar go dtí teach Mhac Uí Chuinn mar ba ghnáth dúinn, agus chaitheamar dinnéar in éineacht leis ag an Manhattan. Bhí Mr Brisbane agus a dheirfiúr, Mrs Thursby, bean álainn a casadh orm i Londain

Shasana roimhe sin, ann, freisin. Bhí culaith bhaintrí uirthi inniu, mar sin is dóigh gur cailleadh a fear ó chonaic mé í. Is é Brisbane eagarthóir an *Evening Journal,* agus fear cumhachtach i measc lucht páipéar é. Deirtear gurb é an comhairleoir agus an fear taca atá ag W. R. Hearst an fear a bhfuil an oiread sin de pháipéir Mheiriceá faoina smacht. Tar éis an dinnéir chuamar go léir go dtí Coláiste Fordham, ollscoil atá faoi stiúradh Chumann Íosa. An tAthair Ó Coileáin an t-uachtarán atá air, ach is é an tAthair Ó Mathúna an fear is mó a raibh le déanamh aige i dtaobh mo léachta. Is ar fhilí na hÉireann a bhí mé le cur síos, ach nuair a chonaic mé an oiread sin sagart le chéile shíl mé go mb'fhearr dom labhairt ar Chonradh na Gaeilge leo, rud a rinne mé. Ní raibh mé sa bhaile tigh Mhac Uí Chuinn go dtí tar éis a haon a chlog san oíche.

WATERBURY

Lá arna mhárach chuaigh mé go dtí Waterbury, Connecticut, áit dhéanta uaireadóirí agus gach uile shórt seoid agus ornáide. Bhí súil ag na daoine go dtiocfainn ar a trí a chlog, agus bhí fleá réidh acu romham, ach níor tháinig mise go dtí an t-am a raibh an léacht le tosú san amharclann, agus mar sin chuireadar an fhleá siar go dtí an oíche. Agus ba phléisiúrtha an fhleá í. D'fhanamar inár suí, timpeall scór againn, go dtí a trí a chlog, ag ól, ag insint scéalta agus ag déanamh óráidí. Bhí neart le n-ithe agus le caitheamh againn, agus bhí gach uile dhuine againn níos croíúla ná a chéile. Fear arbh ainm dó Ó Loidigh croí agus anam don ghluaiseacht anseo. Tá sé an-chosúil le Mac Uí Éigeartaigh i Springfield agus le Mac Uí Dhubhda i Manchester ach gan na nósanna aisteacha aige atá ag an Dubhdach. Bhí sagart deas beag, Mac Uí Bhraonáin, agus Uachtarán na hArdscoile, Wilby, ann. Fear lách, greannmhar é Wilby, agus é an-Ghaelach ina aigne, bíodh nach bhfuil deoir den fhuil Ghaelach ann. Bhí sé le m'ais i rith na fleá. Bhí adhlacánach ann freisin, an fear ba mhó spórt agus greann dár casadh orm riamh de mhuintir na ceirde sin. Bhí seisean ina mháistir ar an bhfleá. Gach aon duine a bhí i láthair thugadar dollar dom agus rinneadh comhaltaí de Chonradh na Gaeilge díobh. Ba iad an drong b'oilte, ba dhea-bhéasaí agus ba láiche iad dár casadh orm ó tháinig mé go Meiriceá. Fuair mé anseo $237.

Lá arna mhárach bhí sé an-fhuar ar fad. Thiomáin mé le Mac Uí Loidigh agus leis an Athair Ó Braonáin tríd an mbaile agus chuamar ar cuairt go dtí Wilby, Uachtarán na hArdscoile. D'fhill mé go Nua-Eabhrac sa tráthnóna, agus lá arna mhárach chuaigh mé le Mac Uí Chuinn go dtí Club na nDlíodóirí, áit ar thug sé lón don Bhreitheamh Ó Dúllaing agus do Dhomhnall Ó Cathaláin. D'iarr mé go géar orthu seo bronntanas

Nollag de mhíle punt a chur abhaile go dtí an Conradh, agus d'aontaíodar sin a dhéanamh; 'Taispeánfaidh sé do na daoine,' arsa mise, 'go bhfuil mé ag obair!'

Rinne mé lá saoire de seo agus chuamar go léir go dtí an amharclann le Sarah Bernhardt a fheiceáil i bpíosa arbh ainm dó *Femme de Claude*. Bhí sí chomh grástúil agus chomh coséadrom agus a bhí sí riamh, agus bhí an áit lán. Casadh fear ansin orm de mo shloinne féin, fear a raibh a ainm in airde sna páipéir ó tháinig mé go dtí an tír seo, i ngeall ar scannal éigin a bhain le hárachas. Cuireann sé an-suim in oideachas Francach. Is é a thug an *Alliance Française* go Meiriceá. Fear réasúnta óg é atá an-saibhir. Chaitheamar suipéar ag na Beaux Arts, agus bhí sé a dó san oíche nuair a ráiníomar an baile.

PROVIDENCE

B'éigean dom dul go Providence, Rhode Island, lá arna mhárach, baile mór atá timpeall turas cúig uair an chloig ó Nua-Eabhrac. Sular fhág mé Nua-Eabhrac le dul ansin chuaigh mé go dtí dochtúir speisialta ar son scornach, agus nigh sé mo scornach le rud éigin, agus d'oibrigh sé gléas aibhléise uirthi. Ó bhí orm labhairt i bProvidence anocht agus i Philadelphia amárach bhí eagla orm nach seasfadh mo ghuth.

Ráinigh mé Providence ar a sé a chlog tráthnóna, agus chaith mé dinnéar le fear arbh ainm dó Mac Uí Ghormáin. Bhí níos mó ná dáréag de na daoine ba mhó gradam sa chathair ag an dinnéar. Thiomáineamar ansin go dtí Teach an Opera. Bhí an teach lán go doras, timpeall dhá chéad déag nó trí chéad déag duine ann, agus thug siad síntiúis mhaithe uathu freisin. Sílim go mba é seo an cruinniú ab fhearr a bhí agam taobh amuigh de Nua-Eabhrac agus de Bhostún. Tháinig mé ar ais go teach Mhac Uí Ghormáin agus bhí an tAthair Breatnach in éineacht liom. Is Éireannach maith é, ach is fearr an t-eaglaiseach é! Bhí deochanna againn agus chodlaíomar an oíche ansin.

Bhí mé ag obair i Sasana Nua i measc na bPoncán, sna bailte atá ar an taobh ó thuaidh de Nua-Eabhrac go dtí anois, ach inniu bhí orm den chéaduair dul ó dheas, go Philadelphia. Ach sular fhág mé Providence tháinig an tAthair Breatnach i gcóiste Mhac Uí Gormáin le mo thabhairt go teach dochtúra, Ó Súilleabháin ba shloinne dó, fear a bhfuil milliún dollar aige. Níor tháinig an dochtúir go dtí an cruinniú a bhí agam aréir, agus is dóigh nach gcuireann sé suim ar bith i gcúrsaí na Gaeilge, cé gur Gaeilgeoir maith é féin. Tá teach álainn aige, agus cosúlacht an tsaibhris ar gach taobh de. Níor iarramar aon síntiús airgid air, ach má dhéantar bailiúchán amach anseo, is cosúil go dtabharfaidh sé síntiús maith. Fuair mé amach, ó shin, idir an cruinniú agus na síntiúis, gur chuireamar 680 dollar le chéile i bProvidence.

PHILADELPHIA

D'fhág mé Providence ar a haon déag agus ráinigh mé Nua-Eabhrac ceathrú tar éis a trí. Casadh Mac Uí Chuinn orm, agus ar an bpointe boise, thiomáin sé mé go dtí an stáisiún. Bhí mé go díreach in am. Ráinigh mé Philadelphia ar a sé, nó mar sin, agus bhí timpeall deichniúr is fiche de na hÉireannaigh ba mhó le rá sa chathair ag an stáisiún romham. D'ardaigh siad leo mé go dtí an Bellevue, teach ósta, dar liomsa, atá chomh mór le haon teach dá shórt dá bhfuil i Nua-Eabhrac. Thug siad dinnéar dom ansin. B'aisteach ar fad an comhluadar a bhí agam ag an dinnéar seo. Ar thaobh díom bhí ministéir d'Eaglais Phrotastúnach na hOllainne, nó mar thug siad air i mBéarla *Dutch Reformed Church*, agus os mo choinne amach bhí ministéir eile agus é rud beag dúr searbh, agus blas Sasanach ar a chaint, mar a shíl mise. Bhain an fear seo leis an Eaglais Phrotastúnach Easpagach, nó 'Episcopalian.' Ar an taobh eile díom bhí an tAthair Ó Cochláin, seansagart lách séimh as Béal Easa i gContae Mhaigh Eo. I lár an dinnéir bhain an ministéir Ollannach geit asam, nuair a dúirt sé gur chreid sé nach raibh Meiriceánach ar bith eile ann, ach é féin, a scaoil gunnaí móra loinge le long chogaidh Shasana. B'fhíor dó é sin beagnach, mar a fuair mé amach ina dhiaidh sin. Bhí sé ina chaptaen ar na gunnaí ar bhord an *Jackmel*, agus dúirt sé gur thimpeallaigh sé Éire faoi thrí, agus dá bhrí sin gur chomhlíon sé tairngreacht Cholm Cille. Ní dúirt sé cén fáth nár chuir long chogaidh Shasana go tóin poill é! B'fhéidir gur éalaigh sé uathu sa cheo,* agus maidir le tairngreacht Cholm Cille níor chuala mise riamh í, ach ní dúirt mé sin leis. Maidir leis an ministéir dúr a bhí os mo choinne, Dochtúir Page an t-ainm a bhí air, mac iníne do Sheán Mistéil ab ea é, agus thug seisean an fuath céanna do Shasana a thug a sheanathair dó. B'Fhínín eile an tAthair Ó Cochláin. Bhí fear de mhuintir Dhálaigh ann, freisin, an cisteoir a bhí againn, fear saibhir, fear árachais, sílim.

Nuair a bhí an dinnéar caite againn chuamar go léir síos go dtí Acadamh an Cheoil, áit a raibh cruinniú an-mhór ar fad againn, timpeall 2,600 nó 2,700 duine.

*Níl aon chur síos ar an scéal seo sa phíosa *The Cruise of the Jackmel* a cuireadh i gcló sa bhliain 1868? Bhí siad ar an bhfarraige 107 lá, bhí siad ag dul timpeall na hÉireann ar feadh 24 lá, agus sheol siad ar fad 9,265 míle. Nuair a bhí siad naoi lá ar an bhfarraige d'ardaigh siad bratach nua, an Gal Gréine, agus scaoil siad a gcuid gunnaí in onóir di. Is dóigh gur air seo a bhí an ministéir ag cuimhneamh.

An tÁrd-easbog Ó Riain

Patrick John Ryan, Archbishop of Philadelphia. Le caoinchead Fhoras na Gaeilge

Bailíodh ceithre chéad dollar de shíntiúis tar éis mo chuid cainte gan bacadh leis an méid a tháinig isteach as díol na dticéad. Bhí an sean-Ardeaspag, Mac Uí Riain, ansin, i gceann de na boscaí, agus Maor na cathrach, Sasanach, agus go leor de dhaoine móra eile na cathrach. Ba é seo an cruinniú ab fhearr a bhí agam fós, taobh amuigh de Nua-Eabhrac. Bhí mo phictiúr sa pháipéar ba mhó clú sa chathair, lá arna mhárach, agus bhí na páipéir go léir go fábhrach dúinn.

Lá arna mhárach, bhí mé an-ghnóthach. Thug an Dochtúir Ó Cochláin, Mac Mhic Oireachtaigh, an Dochtúir Page (ua Sheáin Mhistéil), ár gcisteoir Mac Uí Dhálaigh, agus seisear nó mórsheisear eile, timpeall na cathrach mé, in dhá chóiste. Chuamar go dtí an tArdeaspag i dtosach, agus bhí sé go lách muinteartha linn, cé nár thug sé ach síntiús beag uaidh. Bhí daoine eile ag caint leis roimhe sin, mar a chuala mé, ar eagla go laghdódh sé a shíntiús don UIL Tar éis leathuair a chaitheamh leis chuamar go dtí an ardscoil, a bhfuil an Dochtúir Thompson ina uachtarán uirthi. Tá cúpla míle duine san ardscoil seo, agus téann timpeall céad go leith díobh sin isteach in ollscoil éigin, gach bliain. Tá gach uile chompord le fáil ag na buachaillí sa scoil seo. Maidir le compord níl aon chúis ghearáin acu! Chuamar ansin go dtí an ardscoil Chaitliceach, a bhfuil ceithre chéad buachaill inti. Labhair mé leo i dtosach i mBéarla agus dúirt mé beagán i nGaeilge freisin, agus ansin labhair mé leis na buachaillí Gearmánacha i nGearmáinis. Chuala mé riamh trácht ar *Pennsylvanian Dutch*, ach sílim nach gcloistear a leithéid sa chathair. Ba léir dom ar mo chairde a bhí in aice liom nár thuig siad cén uair a stad an Ghaeilge agus cén uair a thosaigh an Ghearmáinis! Mheall mé leathlá saoire do na buachaillí ón uachtarán. Maidir le Ellis Thompson, is fear é a bhfuil a chroí le cúis na saoirse i ngach aon tír, agus scríobh agus rinne sé go leor ar son na hÉireann.* Ansin thugamar cuairt ar an gClub Gaelach-Mheiriceánach. Sin é an príomháras atá ag Clann na nGael sa chathair. Bhí siad an-lách liom, agus thaispeáin siad an áit go léir dúinn. Bhí seanbhuachaill ó Ros Comáin ansin, Mac Uí Dhálaigh an t-ainm a bhí air, sílim, agus rinne sé aithriseoireacht dúinn, agus labhair sé mar dhea, le pictiúr Thomáis Phroinsias Uí Mheachair a bhí ar crochadh ar an mballa, agus shil sé deora le linn na cainte dó. Ach is é Mac Uí Chrosáin ceannaire agus croí Chlann na nGael anseo, 'Old Man Crossen' a thugtar air. Scoth na nÉireannach é, fear intleachtach, fadcheannach gan éirí in airde ar bith air. Tá sé an-chosúil le Seán Ó Dubhuí i Nua-Eabhrac. Bhí siad go léir ar aon intinn liomsa go gcaithfimid an Ghaeilge a shábháil, agus í a thabhairt ar ais. Tar éis uair nó dhó a chaitheamh ansin, thugamar cuairt ar an Athair Ó Cochláin, duine muinteartha le mo sheanchara Mac Uí Chochláin ó Bhéal Easa, Contae Mhaigh

*Is minic a scríobhadh sé alt fada in *The Irish World*.

Eo. Bhí dinnéar againn ina theach, agus bhí Mrs Page, iníon do Sheán Mistéil i láthair agus d'ólamar a sláinte. Bhí timpeall dáréag eile ann. Is é an tAthair Ó Cochláin croí agus anam Chonradh na Gaeilge i Philadelphia. Is ar éigean a lig sé dom a theach a fhágáil in am don traein a bhí le mo thabhairt ar ais go Nua-Eabhrac. Tháinig Mac Mhic Oireachtaigh ar ais an bealach go léir go Nua-Eabhrac liom. Níor stop sé i rith an turais ar fad, ach ag cur síos, i measc rudaí eile, ar a shaol féin, an chaoi ar tháinig sé go Meiriceá gan réal ina phóca, agus ar iompair sé mála do dhuine uasal ón long go dtí stáisiún an bhóthair iarainn, agus an chaoi ar fhiafraigh an duine uasal de cá raibh sé ag dul. Nuair a chuala an duine uasal nach raibh pingin i bpóca an stócaigh a cheannódh ticéad dó, cheannaigh sé féin dó é. Tá stór mór ólacháin aige faoi láthair, agus tá ag éirí go rímhaith leis. Is fear é a bhfuil meas air i measc Chlann na nGael, agus thug sé féin 500 dollar de shíntiús dom, ag súil go leanfadh na daoine eile a shampla, ach mo léan, níor lean siad! D'oibrigh Clann na nGael go maith ar mo shon ar feadh an ama a raibh mé i Meiriceá, agus mura mbeadh gur chuidigh siad liom i Philadelphia tá faitíos orm nach n-éireodh liom ansin ach go dona. Rinneadh iarracht ar an gcleas céanna a imirt orm ansin agus a imríodh orm i Nua-Eabhrac, nuair a tugadh na ticéid ar ais an nóiméad deiridh. Ach bhí Mac Oireachtaigh agus a chairde san airdeall orthu, agus theip ar lucht na cleasaíochta. Bhí deichniúr nó dáréag ar an gcoiste gnótha a bhí níos saibhre ná Mac Oireachtaigh, ach ní raibh éinne acu gar do bheith chomh flaithiúil lena chuid airgid is a bhí seisean. Bhíomar ag caint go ráiníomar Nua-Eabhrac ar an meán oíche, agus bhí Tomás Bán ansin romham, agus thug seisean Mac Oireachtaigh go dtí a theach ósta féin.

WORCESTER

Lá arna mhárach, mí na Nollag, 20, d'fhág mé Nua-Eabhrac arís, agus chuaigh mé go Worcester atá timpeall turas cúig uair an chloig ar an traein ó Nua-Eabhrac. Bhí mo sheanchara Duff, Ceanadach ó Albain, nó Albanach ó Cheanada, romham ansin, agus thug sé go dtí a theach féin mé. Bhí sé in éineacht liomsa fadó i New Brunswick. Chuamar go dtí an amharclann, an áit a raibh mé le léacht a thabhairt. Tháinig slua den AOH, ag máirseáil tharam agus a gcuid gunnaí agus claimhte acu. Ach mar sin féin ní raibh an amharclann ach measartha lán. Tar éis na léachta tugadh mé go dtí an Waldo a raibh fear arbh ainm dó Mac Uí Ruairí agus a bhean ina bhun. Bhí litreacha agam uathu sula ndeachaigh mé go Meiriceá, agus tháinig mórán daoine isteach le cuairt a thabhairt orm. D'fhill mé ar an meán oíche go teach mo charad, Duff.

Bhí sé fuar thar na bearta inniu, agus ba mhaith liom sin, óir níor cuireadh isteach orm beag ná mór, agus d'fhág sin go saor mé chun mo scíth a ligean agus seanchas beag a dhéanamh le Duff. Ar leathuair i ndiaidh a dó d'fhág mé Duff agus chuaigh mé amach le cuairt a thabhairt ar sheanchara liom, Risteárd Ó Floinn, Déiseach. Bhí an fear bocht ag fáil bháis nuair a shroich mé an teach, agus dúirt a mhac liom, 'Nuair a bhí tusa ag teacht thosaigh m'athair ag labhairt Gaeilge, rud nach ndearna sé le blianta, agus ní raibh a fhios aige go raibh tú sa chathair seo chor ar bith.' D'fhág an fear bocht a phíobaí ceoil le huacht agamsa, mar a chuala mé, ach ní fhaca mise riamh iad! D'fhág mé slán ansin ag Duff agus ag mo chairde ar an gcoiste gnótha, agus d'fhág mé an baile mór sin le dul go Lawrence.

LAWRENCE

Chun dul go Lawrence b'éigean dom dul ar ais trí Bhostún arís. Bhí ceathrar sagart sa chóiste liom a bhí ag dul go Lawrence ar shochraid sagairt d'ord San Agaistín. Tháinig duine acu, an tAthair Ó Mathúna go dtí mo léacht. Níorbh fhearrde mo chruinniú bás an tsagairt sin. An tAthair Ó Raghallaigh a bhí ina uachtarán ar an gcruinniú. Eisean a bhí in a cheann ar Ord Naomh Agaistín sa chathair. Labhair sé go breá i mo dhiaidhse agus d'iarr síntiúis, agus fuair sé cuid mhaith airgid. Chuireamar 215 dollar le chéile sa bhaile seo.

Tar éis an chruinnithe thug an Dochtúir Micheál Ó Súilleabháin abhaile leis féin mé. Tá cúigear Súilleabhánach ina ndochtúirí i Lawrence, agus insíodh dom go raibh timpeall caoga dochtúir agus timpeall daichead dlíodóir Gael-Mheiriceánach sa bhaile seo. Is iad na hÉireannaigh is mó atá ag gabháil don dlí agus don dochtúireacht, ach níl ag éirí go maith leis na hÉireannaigh sna muilte. Tá na Sasanaigh ag déanamh níos fearr ná iad sna háiteanna sin. Bhí páirtí deas ag an Dochtúir Ó Súilleabháin agus ar na daoine a bhí i láthair, bhí dochtúir arbh ainm dó Mac Gabhráin ó Chontae an Chabháin a labhair an Ghaeilge go maith. Bhí fear ann arbh ainm dó Mac Uí Chaochlaoich, freisin, fear a bhí i láthair ag an gcéad chruinniú a bhí agam i gCorcaigh, dhá bhliain déag ó shin, agus atá anois ina chonraitheoir a bhfuil meas mór air i Lawrence. Bhí sé tar éis a dó a chlog nuair a shín mé ar mo leaba.

Tháinig mé ar ais go Nua-Eabhrac lá arna mhárach, ag dul trí Bhostún dom, agus ní raibh agam ach an t-am chun culaith éadaigh eile a chur orm agus dul chun léacht a thabhairt uaim ag Coláiste Manhattan, atá faoi stiúradh na mBráithre Críostaí. Labhair mé ar an litríocht Ghaeilge a bhí ann le trí chéad bliain anuas. Chonaic mé

Tomás Ó Ceallaigh, mac d'Eoghan Ó Ceallaigh, an baincéir, nach maireann, i measc an lucht éisteachta. Fear an-saibhir is ea é. Ghnóthaigh a athair, an baincéir, a chuid airgid i gCalifornia, nuair a bhí gach rud nua ansin. Ar éigean báis a chuaigh sé féin agus beagán daoine eile thar na sléibhte go ráinigh siad an tír sin, nuair a frítheadh an t-ór inti den chéad uair. Ní raibh ach bruscán beag daoine i San Francisco an uair sin, mianadóirí óir an chuid ba mhó acu. D'oscail seisean stór nó siopa ann, agus d'éirigh leis. Adhmad a bhí sna tithe ar fad an t-am sin, agus bhí na daoine an-tugtha don ólachán, don chearrbhachas agus do gach sórt ragairne. Chonaic an Ceallach nach fada go ndófaí an baile, agus dúirt sé leis féin go bhfillfeadh sé soir arís agus go dtiocfadh sé ar ais le fuinneoga agus le doirse iarainn lena gcur ina stór, ar eagla go ndófaí é, dá dtiocfadh tine. D'fhág sé féin agus timpeall dáréag eile an baile faoi threorú cúpla Indiach, le dul thar na sléibhte arís.

D'éirigh leo go maith go raibh siad turas deich lá nó mar sin amach ar a mbóthar. Ansin thug siad faoi deara go raibh na hIndiaigh an-mhíshuaimhneach, corraithe, agus go raibh rud éigin ag cur as dóibh. D'fhiafraigh siad díobh céard é a bhí ag déanamh imní dóibh, agus d'fhreagair siadsan go raibh faitíos orthu go raibh sneachta ag teacht, 'agus má thagann sneachta,' ar siad, 'fágfaimid lorg ár gcos ar an machaire agus leanfaidh na hIndiaigh fhiáine sinn agus maróidh siad sinn.' Thit sé amach mar a dúirt siad, tháinig an sneachta anuas, agus bhí an machaire go léir faoi bhrat bán. Tháinig siad go léir timpeall na tine, agus ba é an chomhairle a cheap siad, dhá bhuíon a dhéanamh díobh féin, agus gan an bóthar céanna a leanúint. Shíl siad dá dtiocfadh na hIndiaigh ar an lorg a d'fhág dream acu go leanfaidís an lorg sin, agus go dtabharfadh an dream eile na cosa leo. Agus is mar sin a tharla. Rinne siad dhá chuid dá mbuíon, agus thug siad bóithre éagsúla orthu féin. Agus an dream a raibh Mac Uí Cheallaigh leo, tháinig siad slán, ach tásc ná tuairisc níor frítheadh riamh faoin dream eile; is dóigh gur mharaigh na hIndiaigh iad.

Maidir leis an gCeallach cheannaigh sé fuinneoga iarainn agus doirse iarainn, agus chuir sé ar mhuin miúile iad, agus chuaigh sé arís thar na sléibhte. Thóg sé teach cloiche agus chuir sé na fuinneoga agus na doirse nua ann. Ní raibh sé i bhfad tógtha nuair a tharla an rud a chonacthas dó roimh ré; bhris tine amach, dódh an baile ar fad, ach amháin a theachsan. Ní raibh san áit, as sin amach, ach a stór féin, agus is chuige a thagadh lucht na mianach go léir le gach rud a theastaigh uathu a cheannach. Tháinig an t-ór isteach chuige ina charnán, agus níorbh fada go raibh an Ceallach ina fhear saibhir. Cheannaigh sé cuid den talamh a bhí ar an taobh thall den bhá ar a dtugtar Oaklands inniu. Ní raibh ann ach fásach an uair sin. Ach, blianta ina dhiaidh sin, nuair a bhí San Francisco ag dul i méid, bhí sé ag tabhairt faoi shráideanna a dhéanamh agus tithe a chur suas in Oaklands, ach fuair sé amach go raibh an áit tógtha cheana ag daoine bochta a raibh botháin bheaga adhmaid curtha suas acu, agus níor éirigh leis iad a ruaigeadh as. D'fhág sé rófhada iad ina mbotháin, agus thug sin teideal dóibh ar an talamh. Muna mbeadh sin bheadh sé ina mhilliúnaí fá dhó nó fá thrí. Chuaigh sé ar ais go Nua-Eabhrac agus rinneadh baincéir de. Bhí sé an-saibhir agus bhí sé go fial flaithiúil le gluaiseacht ar bith a raibh baint aici le hÉirinn. Bhí sé ina chisteoir ar an *Land League* go bhfuair sé bás. D'fhág sé beirt mhac ina dhiaidh agus ba dhuine acu an Tomás a tháinig go dtí mo léacht.

Thug an tAthair Chadwick chun suipéir sinn. Bhí seisean ina shéiplíneach ar an long chogaidh sin an *Maine*, nuair a pléascadh sna spéartha í, ach tháinig seisean slán as an ngábh. Ba mhaith an scéalaí agus an cainteoir é. Ba ghreannmhar an fear é, freisin, agus má bhí ceann nó dhó dá chuid scéalta a chuir Rabelais i mo chuimhne níor lúide ár suim iontu! Bhí tart an domhain ormsa agus bhí fíon deas milis ar an mbord, agus creidim gur ól mé a lán de. Timpeall a dó dhéag chuaigh mé chun mo leapa, mar bhí mé sáraithe amach is amach tar éis an turais fhada ó Lawrence, agus tar éis a ndearna mé de chaint.

An lá dár gcionn bhí dinnéar agam ag an *Players' Club*. Seán Ó Cuinn agus fear arbh ainm dó Graham a thug an dinnéar dúinn. Cúig nó sé dhuine dhéag a bhí i láthair. Ní dhearnadh óráid ar bith, ach rinneadh go leor comhrá. B'éigean do gach duine scéal a insint. B'éigean domsa scéal Chonradh na Gaeilge a insint, agus an méid a bhí déanta aige. Bhí go leor daoine a bhain le páipéir i láthair: Pól Elmer Ó Mórdha, eagarthóir an *Evening Post*, Artúr Brisbane, eagarthóir *The Evening Journal*, S.I.C. Ó Cléirigh, eagarthóir an *Sunday Herald* a d'aithris dúinn a dhán nua, 'Kelly and Burke and Shea', Witter Bynner ó *McClure's Magazine*, agus Risteárd Watson Gilder, eagarthóir an *Century*. Bhí i láthair, freisin, Munró, fear a lean Tolstoy mar threoraí – Ó Maoileoin, seanléiritheoir drámaí, agus mo sheandalta féin Van Thorne, atá ag obair ar pháipéar i Nua-Eabhrac anois. Chuireamar an t-am tharainn go haoibhinn, ag caint, ag seanchas, agus ag scéalaíocht go dtí a trí a chlog ar maidin. Chaith mé níos mó todóg ná a chaith mé le tamall fada, agus d'ól mé cuid de na deochanna a dtugtar *high balls* orthu sa tír seo. Chuaigh mé abhaile ar a 3.30 nó mar sin.

Inniu an Domhnach, agus chuamar go dtí an teampall ba ghaire dúinn. Ach ba chosúla go mór le háit chuideachta ná le háit adhartha é. Maidir le deabhóideacht ní raibh a leithéid ann. An t-aon rud a raibh blas teampaill air, an pláta a cuireadh timpeall, agus carn mór de bhillí dollar air. Leathuair i ndiaidh a trí chuaigh mé le mo sheanchara, Diarmuid Ó Loingsigh, go dtí a chumann féin, an Philo-Celtic. Rinne mé óráid fhada i nGaeilge ansin. Bhí timpeall céad duine i láthair. As sin chuaigh mé go dtí Craobh Naomh Breandán. Bhí níos mó Gaeilgeoirí maithe ansin ná in aon áit eile ina raibh mé. Bhí, go speisialta, seanfhear de mhuintir Fheirtéir ann. Ní raibh geáitsí ar bith aige agus níor ardaigh sé a ghlór, ach scaoil sé chugainn sruth den Ghaeilge ba ghlaine agus ba bhinne dá bhféadfá a chloisteáil. Labhair mé i nGaeilge arís leo seo. Ansin thug mé cuairt ar Chumann Chontae Shligigh atá in aon teach leis an Philo-Celtic. Rinne mé beagán cainte ansin chomh maith. Bíonn a chumann féin ag gach contae i Meiriceá, agus níl a fhios agam an rud maith nó drochrud é. Deir daoine liom go gcoscann sé na baill ó theacht le chéile mar Éireannaigh, agus go ndealaíonn sé na Gaeil mhaithe óna chéile. Tá an nós céanna ag na mic léinn i Maigh Nuad in Éirinn, áit a mbíonn cumann ag muintir gach fairche faoi leith, agus ní mheascann siad le daoine as na fairchí eile. Thug an Loingseach agus ceathrar nó cúigear eile mé go teach ósta ansin agus thug siad dinnéar dom, agus thriallamar linn go léir amach go Brooklyn. Ráiníomar an áit sin idir a hocht agus a naoi a chlog, agus thug mé cuairt ar thrí chumann eile, agus labhair mé i mBéarla agus i nGaeilge ag gach ceann acu, agus chroith mé lámh le gach duine dá raibh i láthair, le ceithre chéad nó le cúig chéad duine ar fad, b'fhéidir. Bhí sé a haon a chlog san oíche nuair a tháinig mé abhaile. Níl rud ar bith is fear a thaitníonn liom, ná gabháil timpeall i measc na nGaeilgeoirí seo; daoine simplí cneasta macánta iad agus blas na bhfíor-Ghael orthu, agus d'fhéadfadh duine a anam a imirt orthu, cibé éad nó easaontas nó faltanas a bhíonn i measc a gcuid taoiseach ó am go ham ach ní chasaim leo ach amháin ar an Domhnach.

Inniu Lá Nollag. Bhíomar chomh tuirseach sin nár chorraíomar as an teach go dtí a seacht sa tráthnóna, nuair a chuaigh mé féin agus mo bhean amach chun dinnéir le Tomás Ó Ceallaigh agus a bhean. Mar a dúirt mé cheana chuireamar aithne ar an Tomás seo fadó in Éirinn. Ní thiocfadh Mac Uí Chuinn linn, agus ní raibh ann ach an bheirt againn. Ba é Eoghan Ó Ceallaigh, deartháir do Thomás, a thug an dinnéar dúinn ag an Metropolitan Club. Fear lách croíúil is ea an tEoghan seo. Tá sé pósta le Spáinneach ó Mheiriceá Theas, ach ní raibh sí in éineacht leis. Ní raibh ann ach an bheirt Cheallach agus bean Thomáis, bean uasal, ó Bretagne na Fraince, a fuair a cuid oiliúna ag Vassar, bean óg álainn a raibh eolas maith aici ar an nGréigis. Maidir le putóg na Nollag, thug Eoghan féin amach leis í ón Orleans Club i Londain Shasana san fhómhar! Ní pióg rómhaith a bhí inti, dar liomsa, ach shíl seisean go raibh sí ar fheabhas, fuair sé an oiread san dá dhua, is dóigh! Tar éis an dinnéir chuamar go léir go seomraí Eoghain, áit a raibh crann Nollag. Bhí puins an-mhaith ar thug sé 'Barbadoes Punch' air, ansin aige. Rinne sé as a stuaim féin é, tar éis blianta a chaitheamh ag meascadh agus ag blaiseadh! Bhí an puins sin chomh maith le n-ól fuar, as an mbuidéal, agus a bheadh sé lena ól te. Bhí a shliocht ormsa an mhaidin ina dhiaidh sin, ar chuma ar bith. Ní raibh ann ach an cúigear againn.

Ba é an Tomás Ó Ceallaigh seo a thug seomra in aisce do Scoil Fhoghlaim na Gaeilge ar feadh tamaill fhada i mBaile Átha Cliath, agus ba é a ghríosaigh Pádraic Colum chun leanúint den litríocht. Ach sílim nár thug sé ach síntiús beag domsa!

Lá 'le Stiofáin an lá inniu ach níl trácht ar dhreoilíní anseo! Thug an príomhbhreitheamh Mac Eochaidh leis mé le cuairt a thabhairt ar Aindriú Carnegie. Shíleamar go bhféadfaimis a thabhairt air spéis a chur i gcúrsaí Chonradh na Gaeilge. Tá an cháil air go bhfuil sé ar an mbeirt fhear is saibhre i Meiriceá. Nuair a thángamar go dtí a theach níor fhéadamar a fheiceáil go ceann tamaill fhada, óir bhí sé gnóthach, ag réiteach imreas tráchtála éigin. Ach nuair a bhí an obair sin críochnaithe aige tháinig sé chugainn agus chuir sé míle fáilte roimh an mbreitheamh, fear a bhfuil ardmheas ag gach éinne air. Bhí sé an-mhuinteartha liomsa chomh maith. Fear beag gearr é, féasóigín liath air, agus ar ndóigh níl sé sciamhach. Agus níl aon chuimse lena bhfuil de mheas aige ar a chlú féin! D'inis sé a lán scéalta dúinn na thaobh féin. Seo ceann acu. Dúirt sé go raibh sé tar éis litir a fháil ó mhisinéir sa tSeapáin. Bhí sé lánsásta leis an litir agus léigh sé amach dúinn í. Dúirt fear scríofa na litreach go raibh sé ina shuí faoi scáth ardchrainn, nuair a tháinig Seapánach óg chuige, agus chun ócáid a thabhairt dó féin ar Bhéarla a labhairt, thosaigh sé mar seo i mBéarla. 'Is Críostaí thú.' 'Sea!' arsa an misinéir. 'Ní maith an creideamh é sin,' arsa an Seapánach. 'Ná bac leis sin,' arsa an misinéir, 'ach inis dom an méid seo, nach ndéanfaidh tú a admháil go bhfuil daoine móra maithe taobh amuigh de do thír féin?' 'Admhaím sin,' arsa an Seapánach. 'Tá go maith,' arsa an misinéir, 'ní raibh éinne riamh ba mhó ná ní b'fhearr ná Íosa Críost, agus deirim é seo cé nach as mo thír féin é, ach gur rugadh sa Phalaistín é.' 'Ach,' arsa an Seapánach óg, 'tá fear mór maith agamsa, freisin, agus ní bhaineann seisean le mo thír féin, ach oiread.' 'Agus cé hé sin?' arsa an misinéir. 'Aindriú Carnegie' a d'fhreagair an Seapánach.

'Ó bhó,' arsa an breitheamh, agus bhuail sé a lámh ar a shliasta, 'Tá a fhios agam cén fáth a ndúirt sé sin,' agus shíl mise gurb amhlaidh a dúirt an breitheamh é sin, mar gheall ar na síntiúis mhóra a thug Carnegie do leabharlanna agus do theagasc na ndaoine. Ach ní mar sin a thuig Carnegie é. 'Bhuel, sea,' ar seisean, 'nuair a aistríodh an leabhar deiridh a scríobh mé go Seapáinis, bhí níos mó díol air, ná ar aon leabhar dár aistríodh riamh sa teanga sin!'

Bhí comhrá fada againn agus thug sé leabhar beag dom a raibh clúdach páipéir air a scríobh sé féin, nuair a bhí mé ag imeacht. Bhí mé chun é a chur i mo phóca, ach dúirt sé 'lig dom ar dtús é a dhéanamh luachmhar duit,' agus scríobh sé a ainm ann! Maidir le Conradh na Gaeilge níor thaispeáin sé go raibh aon mheas aige air, gur scinn ainm Hórais Pluincéid amach. Chuir sé cluas air féin ansin. Lean sé go dtí an doras mór sinn, agus d'iarr orm teach ar cuairt chuige arís, tar éis dom teacht ar ais ón Iarthar. 'B'fhéidir,' arsa mise liom féin, 'go dtiocfaidh rud éigin as an gcuairt seo fós, má bhíonn an t-ádh orm!' Ach ní fhaca mé arís é.

Lá arna mhárach chuaigh mé chun lóin leis an mbreitheamh, agus le Séarlas DeKay, ag Teacht Ósta Delmonico. Scríobh DeKay, atá ina uachtarán ar Chlub na nEalaíon, leabhar léannta le cruthú agus le dearbhú go mba éanacha Déithe na Gréige ar dtús! Bhí Fionn Mac Cumhaill ina éan, freisin, agus Cú Chulainn ina éan, agus b'ionann Fionn agus Faunus! Dúirt sé go bhfuair sé lorg na nDéithe a bhí ina n-éanacha, sa Ghréig, in Éirinn agus i dTír na bhFionlannach, ach gur scriosadh gach lorg den fhírinne seo sna tíortha eile san Eoraip leis na hArianaigh. Bhí díospóireacht againn faoin teagasc seo agus chaitheamar cúpla uair le chéile ag seanchas. Portáin bheaga a bhí againn ag an lón, agus ní raibh aon cheann acu níos mó ná beach mhór. Taobh istigh d'oisrí a chónaíonn na portáin, agus níl siad le fáil ach in oisrí atá beo. Nuair a róstar iad is bia iad a gcuireann na Meiriceánaigh suim mhór ann. Ní fhaca mise riamh iad, agus níor chuala mé trácht orthu, go dtí sin.

NEW JERSEY

An t-ochtú lá fichead de mhí na Nollag atá ann inniu. Chuaigh mé le mo bhean go dtí an Battery chun Íomhá na Saoirse a fheiscint, ach ní dheachaigh mé amach chuige i mbád. Chuaigh mé go dtí Jersey City sa tráthnóna le Mac Uí Chuinn. Ar an taobh eile den Hudson atá an chathair sin, agus cé go bhfuil sí gar do Nua-Eabhrac ní sa stát céanna atá sí. Bhí fear maith ansin arbh ainm dó Pádraig Ó Meára, fear de Chlann na nGael, agus chuir sé an cruinniú seo ar bun, gan cabhair gan cuidiú ó aon duine, beagnach. Ba é sin an cruinniú ba lú a bhí agam go dtí seo. Bhí timpeall 250 duine ann. Mar sin féin nuair a d'iarr an tAthair Ó Lochlainn a bhí ina chathaoirleach ar an gcruinniú síntiús orthu tar éis na hóráide a rinne mise, bhí siad fial tabhartasach, agus thug siad $250 suas ar an ardán dom. Bhí suipéar agam le Mac Uí Mheára, agus tháinig sé trasna na habhann liom, ar ais go Nua-Eabhrac. Bhí sé i bhfad tar éis an mheán oíche nuair a shroich mé an teach.

Lá arna mhárach, níor fhág mé an teach go dtí an tráthnóna, nuair a chuaigh sinn féin agus Mac Uí Chuinn chun dinnéir chuig Seán D. Ó Croimín. Tá teach deas aige agus cuid mhaith de sheoda luachmhara ann, agus ina measc tá roinnt de sheanlitreacha suimiúla. George Washington féin a scríobh ceann acu seo. Faoi chúnna mac tíre a bhí sé ag scríobh. Sa bhliain 1788 a scríobhadh an litir seo, agus dúirt an tÉireannach a d'fhreagair í go raibh a fhios aige go raibh cú mac tíre baineann i ndeisceart na hÉireann, agus cú fireann sa tuaisceart, ach nach raibh a fhios aige cá mbeadh an dá cheann acu le fáil in éineacht. Sílim gur ó Lafayette a theastaigh na cúnna, agus gur scríobh sé go dtí Washington fúthu, agus scríobh Washington ansin go dtí duine éigin in Éirinn. Thrácht an duine seo ar uasal éigin a raibh na cúnna seo aige chun na mic tíre a scanrú agus a ruaigeadh as a dhúiche, ach ní dóigh liom go raibh ach fíor-chorr-mhac tíre le fáil in Éirinn sa bhliain 1788. Bhí dhá litir luachmhara eile aige de chuid Burns, an file Albanach. Bhí Burns ag cur na seacht mallacht ar mháthair duine dá leannáin iomdha. Bhí cúpla lámhscríbhinn Ghaeilge aige freisin. Tá iníon leis pósta, Mac Sheoinín* ainm a fir. Thug siad sinn go léir go dtí damhsa mór ina theachsan. Cailíní saibhre Caitliceacha a bhí i láthair. Dúradh gurbh fhiú tríocha milliún dollar eatarthu iad. Bhí siad go léir gléasta go galánta ach ní raibh éinne ina measc a bhféad-fadh duine a rá go raibh sí rósciamhach. Bhí iníonacha an Chroimínigh féin ar na daoine ab fhearr acu. Bhí sé tar éis a haon a chlog nuair a thángamar ar ais.

NEW HAVEN

Lá arna mhárach d'fhan mé sa teach ag scríobh litreacha agus an lá ina dhiaidh sin, lá deiridh na bliana, d'fhág mé Nua-Eabhrac ar a ceathair a chlog le dul go New Haven, turas cúpla uair an chloig de shiúl ó Nua-Eabhrac féin.

Tá 120,000 duine san áit seo, agus is dóigh go bhfuil dhá scór míle díobh sin ina nÉireannaigh. Tháinig slua go dtí an stáisiún le fáilte a chur romham, agus thug siad leo mé go teach ósta a bhí ag Gaeilgeoir éigin. Bhí an Ghaeilge a bhí ag a mháthair i bhfad níos fearr ná an Béarla a bhí aici. Seanbhean as Contae Chiarraí a bhí inti, agus bhí sí ina tionónta, tráth, do Dhónall Ó Conaill, agus bhí comhrá go minic aici leis nuair a bhí sí ina girseach. Bhí cruinniú maith againn san amharclann, timpeall cúig chéad duine, ach bhí siad ar na daoine ba mheasúla agus ba ghéanúla a bhí sa chathair. Níor labhair mé riamh níos fearr ó tháinig mé go dtí an tír seo, óir tar éis mo scíth a ligean, beagán, i rith na Nollag, tháinig tuilleadh nirt agus fuinnimh ionam. Ach níor tógadh síntiúis ón lucht éisteachta, agus tá faitíos orm gur fhág sin an oíche ar bheagán tairbhe. Fuair mé amach ina dhiaidh sin gur chuireamar trí chéad dollar le chéile tar éis an chruinnithe.

Chuaigh mé ar ais go dtí an teach ósta agus mo phócaí lán de thodóga a thug daoine dom mar chomhartha muintearais! Bhí dinnéar breá mór leagtha amach romhainn,

*Jennings i mBéarla.

agus bhí timpeall tríocha duine i láthair. Shuigh mise ag ceann boird in éineacht le Maor na cathrach, agus bhí Mac Uí Mhuircheartaigh ar an taobh eile díom. Tháinig seisean isteach ó Waterbury le mé a chloisteáil den dara huair, óir chuala sé cheana mé. Tháinig an sean-Chaptaen Ó Briain sin a d'éalaigh as príosún Chluain Meala in Éirinn isteach le mé a chloisteáil arís, freisin. Bhí sé ina mharcach faoin Sirideánach, ag greadadh leis trí Ghleann Shenandoah sa Chogadh Cathartha. Tháinig an Captaen Ó Doinn, athair Ollamh na Ceiltise, faoi dhó, chomh maith. Bhí duine eile ann ach theip orm a ainm a fháil. Ba as Contae Mhaigh Eo é, ach bhí ocht mbliana déag caite aige i bpríosún i Sasana mar gheall ar iarracht a rinne sé ar Theach na bhFeisirí i Londain a phléascadh. Bhí go leor dochtúirí agus daoine measúla eile ann. Nuair a tháinig an meán oíche léim siad go léir ar a gcosa agus chuir siad fáilte roimh an mbliain nua, ag gabháil amhráin a raibh baint aige, mar a shíl mise, le Yale. Chan siad go leor amhrán ansin, ach ba mhó an bhaint a bhí acu le Yale ná le hÉirinn! Rinne an fear bocht a bhí i bpríosún i Sasana píosa beag cainte i nGaeilge agus beagán eile i mBéarla. Ba thruamhéalach an cruth a bhí air, agus é brúite briste, cosúil le fear nach raibh a mheabhair ar fad aige. Chuala mé gur thug an Maor post éigin sa chathair dó, mar chúiteamh beag ar ar fhulaing sé. Bhí Súilleabhánach ann, dlíodóir, agus ba é croí an chruinnithe é. Gheall sé mórán cúnaimh dúinn, ach níor cruinníodh síntiús ar bith. Mar sin féin d'éirigh go hálainn le chuile shórt, agus shíl mé gur cruinniú iontach a bhí ann agus í ina hoíche dheiridh den bhliain. Bhí sé thar leathuair tar éis a dó nuair a shín mé ar mo leaba.

1906 – LÁ COILLE

D'fhill mé go Nua-Eabhrac agus tháinig an Captaen Ó Briain liom go dtí an stáisiún. Sa tráthnóna chuaigh mé féin agus Seán Ó Cuinn go páirtí mór a thug Séarlas DeKay. Mar a dúirt mé cheana, is é uachtarán Chlub na nEalaíon é, agus tá sé pósta le deirfiúr do Gilder, eagarthóir *The Century*. Bhí coire mór agus é lán den deoch sin a dtugtar *egg-nog* uirthi, agus bláthfhleasc mhór fite timpeall air, i lár an bhoird. Bhí bean an tí gnóthach ag líonadh gloiní do gach aon a bhí sa seomra. Bhí brú mór daoine ann, agus bhí baint acu go léir ar shlí éigin, le litríocht nó leis na healaíona. Níor chuir mise spéis in éinne acu, ach amháin in Mrs Worthington, bean a raibh aithne agam uirthi cheana. Ní raibh an páirtí seo cosúil le haon pháirtí eile dá ndeachaigh mé ann, i ngeall air nach raibh ceol ná amhráin ar bith ann, agus i ngeall ar a raibh de *egg-nog* ann!

D'fhan mé sa teach, lá arna mhárach, ag obair go dtí an tráthnóna, nuair a chuamar go léir chun dinnéir go dtí Mac Uí Bhroin, an dlíodóir, agus a bhean. Bhí Emmet óg agus a bhean, agus cailín arbh ainm di Mistéil ann, agus bhí dinnéar an-mhaith agus an-phléisiúrtha againn, agus thángamar abhaile um meán oíche.

An lá ina dhiaidh sin bhí sé ag stealladh báistí. Chaith mé lón le Mrs Thursby, bean a raibh aithne agam uirthi cheana i Londain Shasana. Níor chuir mé mo shrón amach sa tráthnóna.

Bhí mé ag scríobh agus ag pacáil agus ag fáil faoi réir le bheith ag imeacht inniu, óir tháinig an t-am anois le dul siar, agus slán a fhágáil ag Seán Ó Cuinn, óir ní raibh mé lena fheiceáil arís go dtí go dtiocfainn ar ais san earrach. Mar sin féin, bhí gach rud agus gach áit a raibh mé le labhairt ann leagtha amach aigesean roimh ré. Bhí mé faoina stiúradh agus faoina threorú go rachainn trasna na sléibhte agus isteach go California cúpla míle míle ó Nua-Eabhrac. Ba é Seán Ó Cuinn bunúdar agus ceann urra mo thurais. Rinne sé gach rud, shocraigh sé gach rud, níor dhearmad sé rud ar bith, chaith sé a chuid ama agus a chuid airgid go fial liomsa, agus rinne sé an méid sin go léir le teann muintearais liom. Ní fhéadfainn a bheith róbhuíoch de. Is ina theach a bhí mé féin agus mo bhean ag cur fúinn ó thángamar go Meiriceá agus is leis a théimis amach chun dinnéir gach oíche, agus is é a chuir in aithne mé do na daoine ba mhó clú agus saibhreas sa chathair. Agus anois bhíomar lena fhágáil, ag gluaiseacht siar agus gan a fhios céard a bhí romhainn.

PITTSBURGH

An ceathrú lá d'Eanáir d'fhág mé féin agus mo bhean Nua-Eabhrac, agus chaitheamar an oíche go léir ar an traein. Bíonn pasáiste ag dul tríd an traein, agus leapacha ar thaobh an phasáiste sin, agus cuirtíní éadroma ar crochadh rompu. Bíonn dhá leaba i ngach aireagal, ceann acu os cionn an chinn eile, agus ní mór don té a bhfuil an leaba uachtair aige dul suas inti ar dhréimire beag. B'fhéidir, amanna, gur bean a bheadh sa leaba uachtair agus fear a bheadh sa leaba íochtair. Ar maidin, nuair a dhúisíonn searbhónta na traenach – fir ghorma iad go léir – na daoine, gan amhras is orthu a bhíonn an droch-chruth tar éis na hoíche. Dá bhféadfaidís iad féin a fheiscint bheadh náire orthu le chomh míshlachtmhar is a bhíonn siad ag breathnú! Is i Stát Pennsylvania atá Pittsburgh, ach tá sé timpeall trí chéad míle ó Chathair Philadelphia. Is í an chathair is salaí agus is duibhe i Meiriceá í, dar liomsa, óir is ann atá na hoibreacha móra iarainn agus cruach. Tá sé suite idir dhá abhainn, an Allegany agus an Monongahela, agus is sa dá ghleann atá ar bhruacha na n-aibhneacha atá na hoibreacha móra iarainn le feiceáil. Éiríonn an deatach in airde uathu ina néal mór, agus nuair a shoilsíonn an ghrian orthu ag dul faoi di, is cosúil le lasair mhór an deatach sin. Ní fhaca mise aon rud cosúil leis riamh. Dúirt Francach éigin, a chonaic é den chéad uair, go mba 'ifreann é, gan chumhdach.' Is san áit seo a shaothraigh Carnegie a chuid airgid. Tá timpeall 300,000 duine sa chathair. Níl a fhios agam cé mhéad acu sin atá ina nÉireannaigh, ach is Slóvacaigh 50,000 díobh. Tugann siad Slóvacaigh ar na daoine as an gCróit, as an Liotuáin, agus ar shliocht eile nár chuala mé trácht orthu riamh cheana i.e. na Kreimers. Dúirt an Dochtúir Ó Ceanndubháin, an t-easpag, liom, gur craobhscaoileadh an Soiscéal i dtrí theanga dhéag gach Domhnach sa chathair.

Tháinig slua go dtí an stáisiún le fáilte a chur romham, Seán Mac Cárthaigh, Alderman Mártain – Iúistís atá ar leathláimh – agus Micheál Ó Máille, cainteoir breá Gaeilge. Thaithnigh an Cárthach go mór liom féin. Thug siad go dtí teach ósta mé agus d'fhan mé ansin i rith an lae go léir, ag cur fáilte roimh na daoine a tháinig le cuairt a thabhairt orm. Tháinig daoine ó chúig pháipéar nuachta chugam, le ceisteanna a chur orm. Tar a éis sin tháinig dream ó Mhic Phádraig chugam agus dileagra acu dom. Tá trí chéad duine sna Mic Phádraig seo, agus is Pádraig an t-ainm baiste atá ar gach duine acu. Ní náire atá ar na daoine seo Pádraig a bheith baiste orthu, ach tá siad bródúil as, agus rinne siad club díobh féin. Is é seo an chéad chomhartha dá bhfaca mise go raibh meas ag na hÉireannaigh orthu féin, óir ní dóigh liom go bhfeictear a leithéid i measc na bPoncán san oirthear.

Chaith mé dinnéar le fear arbh ainm dó Mac Uí Abhartaigh agus le Mac Uí Lochlainn. Is dlíodóir óg fear acu, agus tá baint ag an bhfear eile le Clann na nGael, agus chuir an fear seo a lán trioblóide air féin ag déanamh réitigh romham.

Lá arna mhárach chaith mé an mhaidin ag cur fáilte roimh na daoine a tháinig le cuairt a thabhairt orm. Ansin tugadh isteach mé i dtram – nó *trolley car*, mar a thugtar orthu anseo – a bhronn Comhlacht na dTram in aisce orainn. Ba é an rud a chuir an Coiste Gnótha a bhí agam rompu, cuid de na hÉireannaigh shaibhre a thabhairt amach liomsa sa charr seo, chun go bhfeicfimis áiteanna sonracha na cathrach le chéile. Ní raibh an t-ádh air mar phlean. Thosaigh na hÉireannaigh shaibhre, ar nós na droinge sa Soiscéal, ag déanamh leithscéil. Ach is dóigh liom nach raibh aon am acu le caitheamh ag dul thart faoin gcathair mar sin go díomhaoin. Ar chuma ar bith níor tháinig siad. Ach tháinig an tAthair Ó Talchair*, an tAthair Prís, an tAthair Ó hEithir, Iníon Uí Ógáin agus tuairim is dáréag eile liom. Bhí an aimsir an-fhuar ar fad, agus bhainfeadh an ghaoth an tsrón de dhuine. Chuamar go garraí na n-ainmhithe, áit a bhfacamar

*Toler.

scata de leoin bhreátha, ach is beag nach rabhamar reoite ag siúl go dtí iad! Thug siad go dtí an rinc sleamhnaithe ansin mé, an rinc is mó den sórt sin atá i Meiriceá. Bhí timpeall 1,800 duine i láthair ag sleamhnú ar leac oighir, faoi chumhdach aon tí amháin, agus banna ag seinm ceoil dóibh. Chomh luath agus a bhuail mise isteach sheinn an banna 'The Wearing of the Green'.

Bhí mé ag caint leis an Iúistís, 'Squire Martin' a thugann siad air. Íoctar é de réir an mhéid oibre dhéanann sé, as an jab. Uaireanta bíonn suas le 4,000 cúis aige sa bhliain.

Bhí cruinniú an-mhór againn sa tráthnóna ach ní fhaca mé riamh áit ba mheasa ná an halla cúng fada a raibh sé ann. Bhí timpeall 2,500 duine i láthair ach bhí siad go léir ina suí ar an aon leibhéal amháin. Ní raibh mé féin ach beagán níos airde ná iad agus chonacthas dom go raibh na suíocháin deiridh a raibh an lucht éisteachta ina suí orthu caoga slat uaim. Ghlaoigh mé, bhéic mé, scread mé, ag súil go gcloisfeadh an slua mé, rinne mé geáitsí, bhuail mé ar an ardán le mo chosa agus rinne mé gach rud ab fhéidir lena n-intinn a dhíriú ar an rud a bhí mé a rá. Bhí an t-easpag, an Dochtúir Ó Ceannubháin, i gceannas an chruinnithe, agus labhair seisean chomh maith. Mar sin féin níor chruinníomar ach 350 dollar.*

Ba bheag nár cailleadh mé i bPittsburgh. Chuaigh mé amach i ngluaisteán le Mac Uí Ghacháin, uachtarán an AOH, agus fear arbh ainm dó Mag Uinseannáin ag tiomáint an ghluaisteáin. Bhí sé ag dul róthapa ar fad, b'fhéidir 40 míle san uair, nuair a casadh orainn capall agus bugaí. Cheap mé féin nach raibh ach orlach nó dhó idir clocha an chabhsa ar thaobh, agus an bugaí ar an taobh eile. I bPittsburgh a chuir mé eolas den chéad uair ar dheoch nua, ar a dtugann siad *rock and rye*, i.e. uisce beatha seagail, agus *candy* ann. Chuir sé pian croí orm.

CHICAGO

An seachtú lá d'Eanáir. Thriallamar ar feadh na hoíche ar an traein agus ráiníomar Chicago ar a 8.50. Bhí coiste gnótha deisiúil ann le fáilte a chur romham. Bhí Tomás Ua Concheanainn, bhí Liam deartháir do Sheán Diolún, Seán Mag Fhearaigh, an Dochtúir Mac Conchra, Seán T. Mac Céitín, de Barra agus go leor daoine eile. Thug siad go dtí an teach ósta, an Auditorium, sinn, atá os coinne an locha, agus le cineáltas dúinn d'fhág siad sinn chun ár scíth a ligean go dtí a ceathair a chlog. Ansin tháinig níos mó ná dáréag de lucht páipéir, agus

*Ach ní in aisce a labhair mé. Thug Pittsburg 972 dollar ar fad dúinn.

an tAthair Mac an Bhreithiún a bhí, tráth, ina ollamh i Maigh Nuad isteach chugam. Bhí an cruinniú san Auditorium ar a hocht a chlog. Bhí sé beagnach chomh maith de chruinniú leis an gceann mór i Nua-Eabhrac. Bhí mé cinnte nach mbeadh aon ghlór fágtha agam tar éis na hoíche aréir i bPittsburgh, ach buíochas le Dia, agus de bharr na scíthe a lig mé ar maidin, tháinig mo ghuth ar ais chugam go maith, agus labhair mé ar feadh uair an chloig agus daichead nóiméad. Bhí an Auditorium beagnach lán. Dúirt na páipéir go raibh prealáidí, scoláirí, lucht gnó, agus mórán teachtairí ó chumainn Éireannacha sa teach, agus nuair a tháinig mise amach gur léim siad go léir in airde ar a gcosa, ag croitheadh ciarsúr agus ag cur gártha áthais astu. An Dochtúir Ó Coigligh, Ard-Easpag Chicago, agus Maor na Cathrach, Mac Uí Dhoinn, a bhí i gceannas an chruinnithe. Dúirt an páipéar gur leag mé mo mhéar ar chuisle na sean-Ghael a bhí i láthair nuair a thosaigh mé ag labhairt Gaeilge leo, agus nuair a thosaigh mé ar an mBéarla a labhairt glaodh orm as gach taobh den amharclann leanúint den Ghaeilge, agus bhí an-bhualadh bos ann. I lár na cainte dúirt mé go raibh páipéir Shasana ag cur miúile in áit inchinne i gceann na ndaoine, agus d'éirigh mo sheanchara an tAthair Ó Ficheallaigh ina bhosca agus ghlaoigh sé amach, 'Seo céad dollar chun an mhiúil a throid,' agus fuair sé, sílim, síntiús mór – ó dheich go dtí caoga dollar – ó gach sagart i Chicago, beagnach. D'iarr an Maor ar na daoine a bheith fial lena gcuid síntiús agus labhair sé go han-bhríomhar. Seo é an rud a dúirt an páipéar nuachta faoi, lá arna mhárach, 'Ag deireadh na hóráide níor chloígh an Maor, Eadbhard F. Ó Doinn, go dlúth le clár an chruinnithe, agus d'iarr sé ar an lucht éisteachta airgead a thabhairt don chúis. D'éirigh fir agus mná ar a gcosa i ngach áit den amharclann, agus gheall siad go dtabharfadh siad síntiúis ó dhollar amháin go céad dollar. Scaipeadh roinnt clúdach i measc an lucht éisteachta, agus líonadh na céadta díobh le billí airgid. Frítheadh 4,488 dollar sna clúdaigh a osclaíodh ar an ardán, agus níor osclaíodh iad go léir. Scríobhadh ar cheann de na clúdaigh na focail 'Ó Chailín Éireannach' agus chuir an slua a bhí i láthair liú áthais astu.'

Tháinig an tAthair Ó Ficheallaigh agus daoine eile ar ais liom, agus chuaigh mé chun mo leapa idir a haon agus a dó, agus mé lánsásta le hobair na hoíche. Tá mé le príomháit a dhéanamh de Chicago anois, agus gabhfaidh mé go dtí na bailte móra atá ina thimpeall, díreach mar a rinne mé nuair a bhí mé i Nua-Eabhrac. Ar an ábhar sin bhí an t-ádh orm gur éirigh liom chomh maith sin i Chicago, agus go raibh na páipéir go léir fábhrach dom.

An t-ochtú lá d'Eanáir. Chaith mé an mhaidin le daoine a bhí ag déanamh grianghraf díom i gcomhair na bpáipéar nuachta, agus ag fáiltiú roimh na daoine a tháinig le cuairt a thabhairt orm. San iarnóin thug an Dochtúir Mac Conchra amach sinn ina charráiste. Thug sé isteach sinn chun gléas múchta tine a thaispeáint dúinn. Bhíomar

an taṫair ó fiṫċeallaiġ

Fr Fielding. Le caoinchead Fhoras na Gaeilge

istigh ag féachaint ar na capaill, nuair a baineadh an clog a thaispeáin go raibh tine in áit éigin. Thit na húmacha uathu féin ar na capaill, bhí na fir ina gcuid suíochán agus bhí na hinnill glanta amach as a n-áiteanna, taobh istigh de leathnóiméad ó buaileadh an clog. Ní fhaca mé riamh aon rud a bhí chomh gasta leis. Ó is gur d'adhmad atá an chuid is mó de thithe sna Stáit déanta ní mór dóibh gléas an-mhaith a bheith acu le tine a mhúchadh. Táthar bródúil as an ngléas atá acu agus ní hionadh ar bith é go bhfuil. Is Éireannaigh naonúr as gach deichniúr acu, agus is é an t-aon roinn amháin, nach mór, nach bhfuil faoi smacht polaitíochta. Is gnách don rialtas an t-ardcheannphort a cheapadh, ach fágtar na daoine eile go léir gan chorraí, is cuma cén rialtas a bhíonn ann. Sa tráthnóna tháinig an tAthair Tomás Mac an Bhreithiún – eagarthóir an *New World* – agus thug sé fear leis le mo chuid freagraí ar a chuid ceisteanna féin a chur síos i ngearrscríbhinn. Chaith sé timpeall dhá uair an chloig ag cur ceisteanna orm. Clóbhuaileadh an comhrá seo ina pháipéar féin agus i gcuid de na páipéir eile, focal ar fhocal, idir cheisteanna agus fhreagraí. Is ábalta intleachtach an fear an sagart seo agus togha cainteora é. As Baile an Mhóta dó. Labhair sé go breá ag an gcruinniú a bhí agam san Auditorium ag iarraidh airgid dom. Nuair a bhí mé réidh leis an Athair Mac an Bhreithiún tháinig an tAthair Ó Fitheallaigh, Mag Fhearaigh, an Céitíneach, agus daoine eile, agus d'fhan cuid acu go dtí an dó dhéag san oíche.

MILWAUKEE

An naoú lá d'Eanáir. D'fhág mé Chicago le dul go dtí Milwaukee i Wisconsin. Ráinigh mé an baile mór sa tráthnóna, agus tháinig slua le fáilte a chur romham. Bhí orthu seo Mac Uí Cheallaigh, Mac Uí Ruacháin agus Mac Uí Chonchúir. Tháinig siad seo tríocha míle amach as an gcathair le fáilte a chur romham. Nuair a thángamar go dtí Milwaukee féin bhí Gobharnóir an Stáit ag fanúint liom. Lochlannach as an Iorua is ea é, arb ainm dó Davidson. Bhí sirriam na cathrach ansin freisin, agus seanfhear arbh ainm dó Mac Uí Chuinn, a bhí ina Fhínín ina óige, agus níor mhaith sé riamh don Eaglais a ndearna siad don ghluaiseacht Fhíníneach. Labhair mé san amharclann sa tráthnóna. Bhí an tArd-Easpag Messmer as an Eilbhéis, agus Gobharnóir an Stáit, agus timpeall 800 duine i láthair.

An Wisconsin seo a bhfuil mé ann faoi láthair, is Stát leath-Lochlannach é. Deirtear go bhfuil daichead Lochlannach ann in aghaidh gach céad duine dá bhfuil sa Stát. Ach mar sin féin níl sé chomh Lochlannach leis an stát ar a thaobh ó thuaidh, Minnesota, áit a bhfuil beagán níos mó na leath na ndaoine ina Lochlannaigh. Dúradh liom nach mbeidh aon ghobharnóir feasta ag ceachtar den dá stát seo ach Lochlannach, óir má ainmnítear Lochlannach[6] le bheith ina ghobharnóir gheobhaidh an fear sin, ní hé amháin guthanna a pháirtí féin, ach mórán guthanna ó na páirtithe eile, mar gheall ar é a bheith ina Lochlannach. Ar an ábhar sin ní mór don dá pháirtí Lochlannach a ainmniú. Thogh na Lochlannaigh seanadóir le labhairt go speisialta ar a son féin. Ach Éireannach ar bith dá bhfuil ar an Seanad, ní mar Éireannach a toghadh é ach mar Mheiriceánach. Cathair mhór is ea Milwaukee. Tá timpeall 350,000 duine inti, agus Gearmánaigh is ea beagnach a leath acu sin. Is áit mhór déanta leanna é, agus Pabst ainm an fhir is mó a dhéanann é. Is cosúla go mór an leann a dhéantar ann le *lager* na nGearmánach ná leis an leann a dhéantar i Sasana agus in Éirinn. Tá Gearmáinis á múineadh i ngach scoil sa chathair. Labhair go leor de na daoine a tháinig ar cuairt chugamsa Gearmáinis, nuair a fuair siad amach gur thuig mé an teanga sin. Is féidir le go leor Éireannach í a labhairt, chomh maith. Mar sin féin tá an bás i ndán di, agus déarfainn go mbeidh deireadh léi go luath, óir chuir mé cluas orm féin le fáil amach cén teanga a bhí á labhairt ag na daoine óga eatarthu féin ar an tsráid. Béarla ar fad a bhí acu. Ach dúradh liom gur Gearmáinis an teanga is mó a labhraídís cois teallaigh.

Thug Mac Uí Cheallaigh agus Mac Uí Ruacháin amach i gcarráiste mé, agus thugamar cuairt ar an Ard-Easpag, ach ní fhacamar é, óir bhí seisean ag teacht ar cuairt chugamsa, san am céanna. Chuaigh an chaint a rinne mé aréir chomh mór sin i bhfeidhm air gur thug sé 50 dollar dom. B'fhéidir gur bogadh é nuair a labhair mé beagán Gearmáinise agus mhol mé na Gearmánaigh sa chaint dom. Cé gur Eilvéiseach a bhí ann bhí sé i bhfad níos féile ná Ard-Easpag Pittsburgh, an Dochtúir Ó Ceannubháin. Ach tá cáil na féile agus an chroí mhóir ar an Dochtúir Messmer, chuile áit.

An deichiú lá d'Eanáir. Tháinig mé ar ais go Chicago sa tráthnóna, agus labhair mé ag an Twentieth Century Club, i dteach fir arbh ainm dó Dochtúir Turck. Bhí timpeall sé scór duine i láthair, agus labhair mé i dtaobh na hÉireann ar feadh uair an chloig. Bhí suipéar an-bhreá againn ina dhiaidh sin, agus bronnadh fleasc i bhfoirm cláirsí de lile na ngleanntán orm. Ráinigh mé mo leaba ar cheathrú tar éis an dó a chlog.

An t-aonú lá déag d'Eanáir. Thug an Dochtúir Mac Conchra amach ina charráiste sinn, ach ní raibh aon chur síos ar chomh fuar is a bhí sé. Bhí meallta móra de leac oighir ar bhruach an locha (Michigan), agus bhí an loch féin reoite. Bhí an ghloine mórán céimeanna faoi bhun *zero*, agus chuaigh an fuacht isteach inár gcnámha. Sa tráthnóna thug fear arbh ainm dó De Barra dinnéar mór dom ag club an *Union League*, an club is fearr san iarthar más fíor a ndeirtear. Bhí Mac Uí Chuidithe, an pacálaí saibhir feola ó Chicago, le bheith ann, ach chuir sé scéala chugainn tar éis dúinn suí síos ag gabháil leithscéil faoi nár fhéad sé teacht. Eagla a bhí air, is dóigh, go mbainfinnse airgead de, óir níor tháinig éinne de clann Chuidithe chugam in aon chathair fós. Ach bhí mórán daoine saibhre eile ann. Gheall fear acu, Loingseach ab ainm dó, cúig chéad dollar dom tar éis an dinnéir seo. Tá sé ina uachtarán ar cheann de na bainc sa chathair. Bhí an dinnéar go han-ghalánta ar fad, agus rinneadh go leor óráidí. Is cuimhin liom ceann acu. Mhol fear arbh ainm dó Mac Uí Chaomhánaigh go ndéanfadh an breitheamh óráid agus tar éis sin mhol an fear céanna go dtabharfadh an tArd-Aturnae óráid eile. Sílim go mba Dhónallach an tArd-Aturnae, agus dúirt sé san am céanna gur thuill Mac Uí Dhónaill a bheith ina bhreitheamh freisin. Is dóigh gur chuir sé sin míshásamh mór ar Mhac Uí Dhónaill, óir chuala mé go mba dhlíodóir mór é, agus go bhfuil sé ag saothrú mórán airgid. Mar seo a thosaigh sé a óráid: 'Bhfuil fhios ag éinne agaibh cén fáth ar cosúil dlíodóir le fear imeartha *baseball*?' Is é an freagra a thug sé, *When he fails to make a hit he's sent to the bench!* Dá bhfeicfeá an aghaidh a bhí ar an mbreitheamh! Ach scairt an chuideachta go léir ar gháirí.

An dóú lá déag d'Eanáir. Tháinig duine uasal inniu arbh ainm dó Payne le mo thabhairt amach go dtí an Ollscoil atá timpeall ocht míle ón áit seo. Thug mé léacht uaim ansin do 800 nó do 900 mac léinn ar fhilí na hÉireann. Labhair mé ar feadh uaire agus ceathrú. Bheadh an cruinniú níos mó mura mbeadh go bhfuair uachtarán na hOllscoile, an Dr Harper, bás an lá roimhe sin. B'fhear suimiúil é. Bhí mé féin ag scríobh chuige agus ag fáil litreacha uaidh ceithre bliana déag roimhe sin.

Chaith mé an tráthnóna le Mac Uí Néill, uachtarán na bpóilíní, tráth, agus atá ar pinsean anois. Ba é an tAthair Ó Ficheallaigh a thug amach mé. Gach uile phíobaire nó veidhleadóir, nó ceoltóir ó Éirinn a thagadh go Chicago, gheobhadh Mac Uí Néill greim air, agus dhéanfadh sé póilín de, agus i gcionn tamaill d'fhaigheadh sé a gcuid fonn agus ceoil uathu seo. Rinne sé cúpla leabhar mór de na foinn a fuair sé ó na ceoltóirí Éireannacha seo. Anocht bhí lucht rince, lucht amhrán, lucht píobaireachta, agus ceoltóirí eile, cruinnithe aige, agus lean an slua den rince agus den cheol ar feadh dhá uair an chloig nó trí. Ba Ghaeilgeoirí an chuid ba mhó acu, agus bhí na rinceoirí ar fheabhas. Bhronn sé leabhar mór fonn orm a bhí clóbhuailte aige. Tháinig mé abhaile ar leathuair tar éis a haon déag.

An tríú lá déag d'Eanáir. Thug mé léacht do mhuintir na hOllscoile arís ar bhéaloideas na hÉireann. Bhí timpeall trí chéad duine i láthair. Labhair mé ar feadh uair an chloig agus fiche nóiméad. Ar éigean a bhí mo léacht thart nuair a tugadh mé go dtí an Sherman House, go dtí *Memorial Luncheon* an *Fellowship Club*. Bhí deichniúr agus trí fichid nó mar sin i láthair, agus rinneadh an-chuid cainte. Labhair mé féin ar feadh fiche nóiméad!

Tháinig mé ar ais, d'fhág mé an Auditorium agus thug mé mo bhean agus ár gcuid bagáiste go dtí an Virginia Hotel, áit a gcuirfidh sí fúithi go mbeidh na bailte móra siúlta agamsa. Chuaigh mé féin ar bord na traenach go Cleveland, Ohio, leathuair i ndiaidh a deich san oíche.

CLEVELAND

Tar éis oíche a chur tharam ar an traein tháinig mé go Cleveland ar a hocht ar maidin, agus tháinig slua le fáilte a chur romham, agus thug siad leo mé go dtí an Hollenden House. Cathair mhór í Cleveland, agus tá timpeall leathmhilliún duine inti. B'fhéidir go mbeadh caoga míle Éireannach orthu sin, ach tá siad scaipthe go mór ó chéile. Tá gual agus iarann sa chathair, agus is beag rud nach ndéantar ann. Is iontach an áit í chun gach uile shórt earraí a dhéanamh. Casadh cuid mhaith daoine anseo orm a chónaigh tráth in aice le m'áit féin i gContae Ros Comáin. Casadh orm mar an gcéanna fear arbh ainm dó Mac Uí Mhadagáin. Tá an oifig is fearr sa chathair aige ach ceann amháin eile; oifig an mhaoir an ceann sin. Nuair a bhíomar ag caint le chéile dúirt sé gur shíl sé go raibh mé ag déanamh áibhéile, agus nach raibh Éire ag éirí Gaelach mar a dúirt mise. 'Agus cén áit in Éirinn a dtagann tú féin as?' arsa mise. 'As Faing i gContae Luimnigh domsa,' ar sé. 'Tá aithne agat ar na Monteagles mar sin,' arsa mise. 'Tá go cinnte, tuige nach mbeadh?' ar seisean. 'D'eile!' arsa mise, 'Dá dtaispeánfainn litir a scríobhadh i nGaeilge, duit, litir a fuair mé ó Mháire Spring Rís, iníon an tiarna, an gcreidfeá go raibh athrú ag teacht ar an tír?' Tharraing mé amach as mo phóca an litir a fuair mé uaithi an lá roimhe sin. Ádhúil go leor bhí ainm an tí, Mount Trenchard, clóbhuailte ar cheann an pháipéir, agus rinne sé féin iarracht ar Mháire Spring Rís a léamh i nGaeilge. D'iompaigh a líth ann, agus dúirt 'chuaigh sin go croí ionam, cibé rud a déarfaidh tú feasta, creidfidh mé thú.' Bhí cruinniú measartha maith againn san amharclann, bhí timpeall ocht gcéad duine i láthair, agus bhailíomar sé chéad dollar, ach is ón AOH a frítheadh an chuid is mó den airgead, sílim.

Bhí an tEaspag Horstmann agus an tAthair Mac Héil ann, mar chathaoirleach. Gnás i Meiriceá é, an cathaoirleach a chur in aithne don slua ar dtús, agus ansin cuireann an cathaoirleach an léachtaí nó an cainteoir in aithne don slua, agus deir sé beagán faoi. Bhí óráidín deas réidh ag an Athair Mac Héil, ach bhí óráid an Easpaig go han-fhada agus níor thug sé aon ócáid don sagart bocht a raibh réidh aige féin a rá. Ach dhíol sé an chóir leis an easpag ag deireadh na scríbe. Nuair a bhí deireadh ráite agamsa agus nuair a bhí seisean ag iarraidh síntiús ar an lucht éisteachta, chuir sé na daoine go léir sna tríthí gáire ag lochtú an easpaig. 'Sin anois faoi dhó a d'imir sé an cleas céanna orm,' ar seisean, 'ach an t-am seo bhain sé as mo bhéal an óráid is fearr bhí mé le déanamh choíche.' Chuir sé greann agus áthas ar an lucht éisteachta go léir – ach amháin ar an Easpag, is dóigh – agus mheall sé na daoine lena chuid grinn chun a bheith níos flaithiúla lena gcuid airgid.

Sin rud a thug mé faoi deara go minic, nach bhfuil aon chaoi níos fearr chun síntiúis a fháil ná gáire a bhaint as na daoine nuair a bhítear ag bailiú!

An cúigiú lá déag d'Eanáir. Chaith mé an mhaidin ag scríobh litreacha agus ag cur fáilte roimh dhaoine a tháinig ar cuairt chugam, agus chaith mé dinnéar leis an Athair Mac Héil sa tráthnóna. Bhí an Madagánach agus naonúr sagart ann. Ba bheag nár shíl mé go raibh mé sa bhaile arís! Bhí sagart óg ann, fear de na Paoracha, a bhí an-dúthrachtach faoi chúis na Gaeilge, agus ghabh sé cúpla amhrán breá dúinn.

Chuala mé a lán, nuair a bhí mé sa chathair seo, faoi chumann ar tugadh na *Knights of Equity* orthu. Ba chumann é, mar a thuig mise, chun tráchtáil agus siopadóireacht na nÉireannach a choimeád i measc na nÉireannach féin. Chuala mé go ndearna sé a lán maitheasa an fad a sheas sé, ach gur throid na Ridirí eatarthu féin, agus gur briseadh an Cumann. Is i gCleveland a bhíodh ceannáras an chumainn, ach is i gcathair éigin eile bhí sé faoi láthair. An pholaitíocht a bhris é. Is an-doiligh an pholaitíocht a choinneáil amach as gnó mar sin! Is ar an gcarraig seo na polaitíochta a bhristear gach loingeas, luath nó mall.

An séú lá déag d'Eanáir. Thug mé cuairt ar an Easpag ar maidin, agus thug sé leathchéad dollar dom. D'fhág mé Cleveland ansin, agus tháinig mé go hOberlin sa tráthnóna. Coláiste mór clúiteach atá anseo, agus timpeall 1,800 mac léinn ann. Níl aon ollscoil eile sa tír chomh cúng agus chomh searbhasach leis, tá sé in aghaidh an ólacháin agus an ghrinn. An tOirmhinneach Mr King an t-uachtarán atá air, agus thug sé aíocht domsa ina theach féin. Thug sé leis mé chun éisteacht le ceathrar a sheinn ar théada *smetano* éigin, agus ar eagla nach dtuigfeadh na daoine an chiall a bhí leis an gceol bhí duilleog chlóbhuailte fágtha ar gach suíochán. De réir na duilleoige seo bhí ciall speisialta le gach nóta den cheol, agus ciall i bhfad níos iontaí ná an chiall a bhí le baint as an nod a rinne Lord Burleigh sa dráma úd a cheap an Sirideánach. Labhair mé faoi bhéaloideas sa tráthnóna, agus bhí timpeall seacht gcéad i láthair idir ollúna agus mhic léinn. Tar éis sin chuir mé fáilte roimh na daoine a tháinig le lámh a chroitheadh liom, agus labhair mé leis na hollúna faoi Chonradh na Gaeilge, agus d'fhreagair mé na ceisteanna iomdha a cuireadh orm. Tháinig mé ar ais idir a haon déag agus a dó dhéag agus mé an-tuirseach. Chuir an t-uachtarán coinneal lasta i mo lámh, agus d'fhiafraigh sé díom 'ar mhaith leat aon rud?' Sin ceist a cuireadh orm go mion minic roimhe sin, agus ní raibh ach an aon chiall amháin léi i.e. 'céard a ólfaidh tú?' Rinne mise dearmad ar fad ar cháil na hOllscoile agus gan smaoineamh orm féin, dúirt mé go simplí, 'Bhuel braoinín beag seagail,* má tá sé agat.' Níor thuig mé an botún a bhí déanta agam go bhfaca mé a aghaidh. Ach dúirt sé ansin go raibh máthair a chéile nó duine éigin eile sa teach a bhí á chaitheamh mar leigheas, agus go bhfaigheadh sé dom é, rud a rinne.

COLUMBUS

Bhí an t-uachtarán agus a bhean go han-lách liom agus lig siad dom codladh go dtí idir a naoi agus a deich a chlog ar maidin. Is annamh a thiteann a leithéid sin amach sa tír seo. Dar liomsa bíonn gach éinne ina shuí agus ag dul i mbun a chuid oibre ar a seacht a chlog. D'fhág mé slán aige, agus chuir sé a rúnaí féin liom chomh fada le Wellington, agus níor fhág sé mé gur chuir sé mé ar bord na traenach go Columbus, príomhchathair an Stáit Ohio. Ráinigh mé Ohio mall sa tráthnóna, agus chuir mé fúm leis an Dochtúir Thompson, Uachtarán na hOllscoile ansin. Fuair mé amach go luath go mb'Éireannach é, ach ní raibh a fhios sin ag éinne sa chathair gur tháinig mise. Sílim gurb as Cúige Uladh a tháinig sé. Tá timpeall 150,000 duine sa chathair seo, agus Éireannaigh, b'fhéidir, 15,000 duine díobh sin. Gach fiche slat, nó mar sin, tá áirse iarainn ag dul trasna na príomhshráide agus bíonn na céadta lóchrann beag áibhléiseach ceangailte de na háirsí, agus nuair a lastar iad san oíche ba dhóigh le duine go raibh na céadta droichead tine ag dul thar chúpla míle den tsráid. Ní fhaca mé aon rud cosúil leis in aon áit eile, agus is mór an slacht a chuireann sé ar an gcathair san oíche.

Bhí cruinniú mór againn san amharclann. Bhí suas le míle duine i láthair. Bhí easpag na cathrach i.e. an Dochtúir Hartley, Coirnéal Kilburn a bhí ina sheansaighdiúir sa chogadh, agus go leor daoine eile ann. Labhair an Dochtúir Thompson go maith agus ba ghreannmhar an óráid a rinne sé nuair a chuir sé in aithne do na daoine mé, ach ní raibh aon bhailiú airgid ann.

An t-ochtú lá déag d'Eanáir. Taispeánadh an phríomhchathair dom inniu, agus teach na parlaiminte. Sa chuid is mó de na stáit a raibh mise iontu, ní thagann *Congress* le chéile ach uair amháin gach dhá bhliain, agus ansin ní shuíonn sé ach ar feadh cúpla mí. Tagann faitíos agus sórt critheagla ar an gcuid is mó de na daoine sa stát nuair a bhíonn congress ina shuí, óir ní fios dóibh ó lá go lá cad é an sórt amaidí a dhéanfaidh

*Déantar uisce beatha den seagal sa tír sin. Tá cineál uisce beatha ann freisin *Bourbon* a dhéantar de ghrán Indiach, ach níor thaithnigh sé riamh liom, cé go ndúirt Ó Néill Ruiséal liom (agus thuig seisean an cheist) go mba é ab fhearr.

sé, nó cén sórt mí-áidh a thiocfaidh as! Mar sin is fada leo go gcuirtear ar athló arís é. Ní mar sin a bheadh an scéal in Éirinn, sílim. Dá mbeadh parlaimint againne agus cead cainte acu, an dóigh le héinne go mbeimis sásta le cúpla mí as gach dhá bhliain? Ach níl aon mheas ag lucht an Oileáin Úir ar chaint; bíonn siad róghnóthach ag iarraidh airgead a dhéanamh, agus ní le caint a dhéantar sin.

Thug iníon an Dr Thompson, a bhí díreach tar éis céim a fháil, timpeall na hollscoile mé. Tá 1,800 duine san ollscoil, agus is mná trí chéad acu sin. Tá coláiste breá talmhaíochta ag dul leis an ollscoil, agus déantar milseoga ansin ó na crainn mhailpe. Tagann timpeall pionta síoróipe as gach crann. Chun pionta amháin den tsíoróip a dhéanamh ní mór 40 pionta de shú. Cuirtear mórán poll sa chrann i dtosach ach gan aon cheann acu níos doimhne ná orlach, agus sileann an sú amach as na poill seo.

Thug an Dochtúir Thompson lón dom ag club éigin, agus thug sé cuireadh don Easpag Hartley, don Choirnéal Kilburn, do Mhac Uí Riain, Rúnaí an Stáit, tráth, d'fhear de mhuintir Sheoighe, agus do thuairim is deichniúr eile. Bhíomar go sásta ag ithe, ag ól agus ag caint, agus cibé rud a tharraing anuas an t-ábhar cainte sin, bhí mé féin ag tagairt don chaoi a sheas Conradh na Gaeilge in aghaidh an ólacháin, agus dúirt mé gur beag duine a bhí sa Chonradh a d'ól aon deoir, ach mé féin. 'Á!' arsa an coirnéal – agus gan aon bhlas Meiriceánach ar a chaint, agus é gléasta mar dhuine a shiúlfadh amach as club éigin i Londain – 'cuireann an rud sin a deir tú scéal i gcuimhne dom.' Anois is dóigh go raibh mé féin ag ól níos lú ná aon duine eile ag an mbord, ach trí mhí-ádh éigin tharla an t-am sin gur os mo chomhairse amach a bhí an chuid is mó de na buidéil a bhí ar an gclár, cruinnithe. D'fhéach an coirnéal ar na buidéil sin agus chaoch sé a shúil, 'cuireann sé sin scéal i gcuimhne dom a tharla sa bhaile beag ar rugadh agus tógadh mé féin ann. Ní raibh mórán todóg ann an uair sin, agus nuair a chaitheadh fear ceann acu theilgeadh sé bun na todóige uaidh ar an tsráid, agus léimeadh duine de na gasúir a bhíodh ag díol páipéar air, agus lasadh sé an bun dó féin. Ach i gceann tamaill ní raibh siad sásta leis sin, agus dúirt siad go ndéanfaidís club díobh féin, agus go gceannóidís todóg cheart dóibh féin, go mbeadh a fhios acu cén blas a bhí ar cheann úr. Tháinig dáréag acu le chéile agus thug siad dhá *cent* an duine agus cheannaigh siad todóg mhaith ar an airgead sin. Thogh siad uachtarán dóibh féin ansin, agus chuir siad é ina shuí i gcathaoir, agus chuir siad an todóg ina bhéal go mbeadh an chéad ghal aige as. Nuair a bhí trí nó ceithre ghal aigesean, thosaigh siad ag rá go mba leor dó é sin, agus a thabhairt do ghasúr eile. 'Ní hé sin an margadh a rinneadh,' arsa an t-uachtarán. 'Ba é an margadh a bhí ann,' ar seisean, 'go n-ólfadh an t-uachtarán an tobac agus go mbeadh cead ag an gcuid eile an seile a chaitheamh!' Leis sin chaoch an coirnéal a shúil arís ar na buidéil a bhí romhamsa. D'fhág an coirnéal gan focal mé. Ní raibh de fhreagra agam air ach a rá go bacach 'nach raibh aon cháil ag duine nár dhuine den cháil sin mé.' Nuair a tháinig mé ar ais go Nua-Eabhrac tamall fada ina dhiaidh sin, d'inis mé an scéal seo do Ridirí Phádraig Naofa, lá a raibh mé ina measc, agus bhain sé gáire astu!

Nuair a bhí an lón caite againn thug mé cuairt ar an *Catholic Columbian* a bhfuil Mac Uí Chearúill ina eagarthóir air. Is é an Cearúllach rúnaí an AOH i Meiriceá. Bhí fear as Contae Mhaigh Eo in éineacht leis, ab ainm dó Mac an Bhearshúiligh i.e. Varley. Rinne mé mo dhícheall a chur i gcéill don Chearúllach chomh héifeachtach agus chomh bríomhar agus a bhí Conradh na Gaeilge agus an gá a bhí lena leithéid, agus an obair mhór náisiúnta a bhí á déanamh aige. Thuig mé gur beag fear i Meiriceá d'fhéadfadh an méid céanna a dhéanamh dúinn a d'fhéadfadh seisean a dhéanamh dúinn, dá mba mhaith leis é. Bhí sé fábhrach dom, agus gheall cúnamh dúinn. Caithfidh mé a rá anseo go raibh an AOH ar mo thaobh sa chuid is mó de na stáit, go mórmhór, sílim, sna stáit láir agus na stáit thiar.

INDIANAPOLIS

D'fhág mé Columbus ar leathuair tar éis a cúig agus ráinigh mé Indianapolis, Indiana, idir a haon déag agus a dó dhéag san oíche. Bhí daoine romham chun mé a thabhairt go dtí teach ósta.

An naoú lá déag. Chuaigh mé ar maidin ar cuairt go dtí ministéir Meitidisteach ó Sciobairín arbh ainm dó de Bhulbh, cara don ollamh Gaeilge Goodman a bhíodh i gColáiste na Tríonóide.

Sílim gurb é Mac Mhic Shuibhne an fear is láidre ar thaobh na Gaeilge atá sa bhaile mór seo. Bhíodh sé ina mhúinteoir scoile, tráth, ach tá sé ina fhear saibhir anois. Tá bean Ghearmánach aige agus labhraíonn sé an Ghearmáinis go rímhaith. Bhí sé i mbaol an bháis beagán bliain ó shin. Bhí an díleá go dona aige agus leigheas sé é féin, agus rinne fear láidir de féin arís, trí chúpla lán béil de bhran a ithe gach maidin roimh a bhricfeasta. An méid seile a dhéantar sa bhéal sular féidir leis an bpíobán an bran a shlogadh siar, is leigheas é don díleá is measa ar bith. Dúirt sé liom gur leigheas sé mórán daoine ar an tslí chéanna. Bhí beirt eile ann, a bhí go maith, freisin, i.e. Mac Uí Chuinn, fear árachais, agus fear arbh ainm dó Mac Uí Dhonnaile a bhfuil teach ósta mór aige. Bhí Gaeilgeoir breá ó na Creaga i ndeisceart Chontae Ros Comáin, agus dúirt sé liom go raibh cúig mhíle duine, idir óg agus aosta, tamall beag amach ó

Indianapolis a labhraíonn an Ghaeilge, ach mo léan géar ní bhfuair mé an t-am le dul amach chucu. Bhí Gael maith eile, Mac Uí Mhathúna, ball de Chlann na nGael, ach níl seisean saibhir mar atá na daoine eile. Casadh Éireannach saibhir eile orm, fear a chonaic mé cheana i mBaile Átha Cliath. Fear mór ard a phós bean ó Ghort Inse Guaire. Ach cé go bhfuil sé an-saibhir níor thug sé ach deich ndollar dom.

Bhí daoine ag teacht ar cuairt chugam ar feadh an lae, agus bhí cruinniú mór againn sa tráthnóna, ach b'olc agus ba rí-olc an áit í chun labhairt ann. Bhéic mé agus scread mé chomh hard is ab fhéidir liom ar feadh dhá uair an chloig, le dhá mhíle nó le dhá mhíle go leith duine. Ach sílim go raibh siad sásta. Ní raibh mé i mo leaba go dtí a dó a chlog ar maidin.

An fichiú lá. D'fhan mé istigh ar feadh na maidine agus tháinig gach uile shórt duine ar cuairt chugam. Thug an coiste gnótha fleá dom a mhair ó leathuair i ndiaidh a dó go dtí leathuair i ndiaidh a cúig sa tráthnóna. Bhí trí dhuine dhéag ann, agus rinne gach duine acu óráid. An Suibhneach an fear ab fhearr acu.

Chuamar go léir, nó an chuid is mó againn, ar cuairt ansin go dtí an file mór Séamus Whitcomb Ó Raghallaigh, óir nuair a ráinigh mé mo theach ósta arú inné fuair mé beart mór de rósanna áille ansin romham. Eisean a chuir chugam mar bhronntanas iad. Thug na daoine ar an ardán cláirseach mhór de rósanna dom aréir. Bhí an chláirseach os cionn ceithre troithe ar airde agus bhí lilí na ngleanntán measctha trí na rósanna. Dúirt mé leis an gcoiste go mba chóir an bhláthfhleasc seo a thabhairt dósan. Chuireamar an chláirseach isteach i gcarráiste agus chuamar ar thóir an fhile. Fuaireamar é ina leaba, agus todóg mhór ina bhéal, agus a dhochtúir in éineacht leis. Bhí sé tar éis teacht ó chuairt a thug sé ar a dhaoine muinteartha sa deisceart, agus is é mo dhóigh gur rómhaith an fháilte a chuir siad roimhe! Ar chuma ar bith dúirt mé leis gur thug mé an chláirseach sin chuigesean de bhrí nach raibh aon fhear in Indianapolis a d'fhéadfadh seinm uirthi ach é féin! B'Éireannach a athair nó a sheanathair, níl fhios agam cé acu, agus tá braon beag d'fhuil na hOllainne measctha leis an bhfuil Ghaelach. Fear an-lách cóir simplí é, agus go leor grinn ann. Mar sin féin is maith an fear gnó é, agus deirtear go bhfuil a lán airgid aige curtha i dtaisce i dtalamh agus i dtithe. Ba ghnáth leis a lán airgid a fháil ó na léachtaí grinn a thugadh sé, freisin.

Nuair a d'fhágamar é ní raibh ann ach go raibh mo sháith ama agam le filleadh don teach ósta agus éadaí tráthnóna a chur orm féin le dul go dtí an Athenaeum Club, áit a raibh mé le léacht a thabhairt uaim ar bhéaloideas. Tháinig cuid mhaith de na Gaeil liom, an Suibhneach, Mac Uí Chuinn agus eile, le mé a chloisteáil. Bhí 'fáiltiú' ag an gclub tar éis na léachta, agus soláthraíodh sólaistí, uachtar reoite, tae, agus eile dúinn.

Tá an Loingseachánach in Indianapolis. Rinne Sasana a lándícheall greim a fháil air, ach tháinig na hÉireannaigh go léir le chéile agus bhuaigh siad ar an iarracht a rinne Sasana ar a fháil. Rinne siad sin le faltanas agus le fuath do Shasana, agus is cosúil nár thuig siad gur ropaire de chladhaire a bhí ann. Dúirt an bithiúnach féin, 'Nuair a chaillfear mé beidh Indianapolis scríofa ar mo chroíse,' agus ar ndóigh níor mhór dó a bheith buíoch de lucht na cathrach sin. Bhí sé ar an ardán agus mé ag labhairt, agus tháinig sé chun lámh a chroitheadh liom, agus é go leathnáireach faoi theacht in aice liom. Níor thuig mé ar dtús i gceart cé bhí ann, ach dúirt mé leis i nGaeilge, 'chuala mé caint ortsa roimhe seo,' agus d'iompaigh mé uaidh.

Bhí sé tar éis a haon déag nuair a thángamar, mé féin, Mac Uí Chuinn, an Suibhneach, Mac Uí Dhonnaile, agus Mac Uí Mhathúna ar ais go dtí an teach ósta. Bhíomar ag caitheamh tobac, agus ag ól dí, nuair a dúirt duine éigin – níl a fhios agam cén fáth – an focal 'taibhse.' Sin rud nár tháinig i mo cheann ó ráinigh mé Meiriceá, agus chomh fada agus d'fhan mé i Meiriceá níor chuala mé an focal arís. Ní áit do phúcaí ná do thaibhsí na Stáit! Ar an ábhar sin ba mhór é m'iontas nuair a fuair mé amach nach raibh éinne de na hÉireannaigh a bhí i láthair nach raibh baint aige, tráth, le rudaí ón saol eile. Agus bhí gach éinne acu chomh cinnte sin ina thaobh nach raibh aon ghar a bheith ag argóint leis faoi. Agus ní d'aon sórt ná d'aon chosúlacht na rudaí a chonaic siad.

Dúirt an Mathúnach gur éirigh sé go moch nuair a bhí sé ina ógánach, agus gur shiúil sé féin agus buachaill eile ceithre mhíle slí chun breith ar choiníní idir an aill agus an fharraige, le héirí na gréine. Scar siad óna chéile agus d'imigh duine acu le bheith idir na coiníní agus an aill, agus bhí an fear eile chun na coiníní a ruaigeadh. Nuair bhí an Mathúnach ag siúl tríd an raithneach ard dhúisigh sé coinín a bhí, dar leis, chomh mór le capall. Rith an fheithide sin chun na farraige agus léim sé isteach inti. Ba bheag nár thit sé i laige. Bhí sé tinn ar feadh tamaill mhaith ina dhiaidh sin.

Maidir le Mac Uí Chuinn, dúirt sé go raibh sé ina sheasamh, tráthnóna, taobh amuigh de dhoras tí a mháthar le breathnú ar an oíche, agus chonaic sé bodóg nó bó bhán in aice leis. Níor chuir sé suim ar bith inti go bhfaca sé ag éirí sa spéir í agus ag dul as amharc uaidh.

Bean bhán a chonaic an Suibhneach ar bhóthar amach roimhe. Chuaigh sí de léim thar an gclaí, agus d'imigh as amharc. Dúirt sé gur minic a chonaic daoine eile í san áit chéanna.

B'aisteach an scéal a bhí ag an Donnallach. Nuair a bhí sé óg bhí duine uasal ag fáil bháis sa chomharsanacht, a raibh an scéal amuigh air go raibh bean sí ag a bhunadh.

Cheap Mac Uí Dhonnaile agus cúigear nó seisear de bhuachaillí eile go rachaidís ag faire timpeall an tí go mbeadh a fhios acu an dtiocfadh an bhean sí. Maidir leis féin chuaigh sé i bhfolach i lár toim labhrais a bhí ar an tslí isteach go dtí doras mór an tí. Chuaigh na buachaillí eile i bhfolach in áiteanna eile timpeall an tí. Ní raibh siad i bhfad ag fanúint nuair a chuala siad go soiléir an bhean sí agus í ag teacht aníos chuig an doras, agus í ag gol agus ag caoineadh agus ag bualadh bos. Chuala sé féin í ag dul thairis, agus ba bheag nár bhain a héadach leis, agus í ag scuabadh isteach an doras mór. Bhí sé scanraithe agus rith sé ar ais go dtí na buachaillí eile, agus nuair a tháinig siad le chéile thug gach duine acu a mhionna gur chuala sé an bhean sí ag dul amach thairis féin ar an nós céanna. Ba é sin go díreach an uair a fuair an fear a bhí tinn bás. Chomh fada agus a bhí mé i Meiriceá níor chuala mé aon chur síos ar rudaí den sórt seo ach amháin an oíche sin. B'ait an scéal é, dar liomsa, óir níor shíl mé go bhfaighinn duine as céad sa tír seo a chreidfeadh rudaí mar iad sin. Ach bhí ceathrar agam anseo agus daoine gnó fadcheannacha, saibhre – milliúnaithe ab ea beirt acu – iad go léir.

CINCINNATI

D'fhág mé Indianapolis inniu cé gurbh olc liom a fhágáil, agus chuaigh mé go Cincinnati, Ohio. Ráinigh mé sin ar a ceathair sa tráthnóna. Tháinig an Captaen Mac Suibhne, Mac Conraoi agus cúpla duine eile i mo choinne. Bhí dinnéar agam le fear de mhuintir Chaomhánach, agus labhair mé san oíche in amharclann mhór. Bhí dhá mhíle nó dhá mhíle go leith duine i láthair. Labhair mé ar feadh dhá uair an chloig, agus nuair a bhí mé réidh tugadh beart mór de rósanna dom.

Is féidir cathair Ghearmánach a thabhairt ar Cincinnati. Tá 400,000 duine inti, agus Gearmánaigh 300,000 duine acu sin. Dá bhrí sin níorbh é mo dhearmad na Gearmánaigh a mholadh go mór ar son a dtréithe, a scoláireacht agus eile. Dá gcloífeadh an tÉireannach agus an Gearmánach le chéile (agus baineann an bheirt acu sochar agus dochar as na rudaí céanna) ansin ní fada go bpléascfaí an bholgóid Angla-Shasanach. Tá siad an-mhuinteartha lena chéile go minic, agus is breá an chlann a bhíonn acu. Ach chuala mé bean á rá nár mhaith léi go bpósfadh a hiníon Gearmánach, óir, ar sise, b'fhéidir go maródh sé é féin. Tá féinmharú seacht n-uaire níos coitianta i measc na nGearmánach ná i measc na ndaoine eile, agus is annamh ar fad a thiteann a leithéid amach i measc na nGael. Chuir Chamberlain fear óg intleachtach cliste go dtí an tír seo chun a chreideamh polaitíochta féin a scaipeadh inti, agus casadh Mac Uí Mhurchú i mBuffalo leis. Dúirt Mac Uí Mhurchú leis an Sasanach, 'Éirigh as,' ar seisean, 'níl aon ghar duit a bheith ag féachaint comhcheangal Angla-Shasanach a chur i bhfeidhm, nó dlí a dhéanamh chun gach conspóid a fhágáil faoi bhreithiúnas daoine áirithe. Buaifimidne ort gach uile uair.' 'Agus cén chaoi a dhéanfas sibh sin?' arsa an Sasanach. 'Tá slí shimplí lena dhéanamh,' arsa Mac Uí Mhurchú, 'Bhaineamar triail as agus tá sé fíor. Scríob Gearmánach agus gheobhaidh tú namhaid do Shasana.' Ní chreidim féin sin!

An dóú lá fichead. Tugadh mé trasna na habhann inniu, agus anonn go Kentucky atá ar an taobh eile. Deirtear gurb ionann Kentucky agus 'an talamh dorcha fuilteach,' i dteanga na nIndiach.

Nuair a tháinig mé ar ais tugadh isteach go Seomra na Tráchtála mé agus níor mhór dom labhairt leis na baill. Bhí timpeall céad duine ann, seandaoine an chuid ba mhó acu, agus ó bhí mé beagnach cinnte go mba Ghearmánaigh a bhformhór mhol mé a gcine agus a gcathair, mhol mé a gcuid bád, mhol mé a n-abhainn mhór, agus chuir mé a gcuid talún i gcomparáid leis an 'talamh dorcha fuilteach' ar a raibh mé an mhaidin sin, agus labhair mé beagán Gearmáinise leo. Shásaigh sé sin iad, agus chuala mé gur cluineadh fir nár labhair Gearmáinis os ard le fada, gur cluineadh iad á labhairt le chéile chomh luath agus d'fhág mise an seomra.

Nuair a d'fhág mé an lucht gnó seo thug triúr Éireannach, Mac Cionaoith, Mac Uí Chaomhánaigh agus Mac Conraoi amach go dtí an ollscoil mé. Bhí bean álainn mhodhúil ann, a chuir fáilte romhainn thar cionn na hollscoile, agus shuigh ag ceann an bhoird. Chuala mé ina dhiaidh sin go mba Pholannach í, ach labhair sí Béarla, chomh maith sin gur shíl mise go mba Éireannach í. Bhí páirtí an-deas acu, agus chuir siad fáilte chroíúil romham. Bhí Francach éigin – ní cuimhin liom an t-ainm bhí air – a tháinig chun léacht a thabhairt ar son an *Alliance Française*, ina chomh-aoi liom ag an bhfáiltiú.

Nuair a thángamar ar ais ón ollscoil chuamar go léir go dtí teach álainn Mhic Conraoi. Is fear díolta troscáin é, agus tá siopa mór aige in St Louis, freisin. Tá sé ar na hÉireannaigh is fearr, agus is intleachtaí a casadh orm fós, ach níl mé ag rá nach mbeadh sé, b'fhéidir rud beag contráilte. Thug sé fíon dúinn, agus nuair a d'fhágamar é chuamar go dtí mo theach ósta, áit ar thugadar fleá dom. Ní raibh an fhleá thart go dtí tar éis a naoi a chlog, nuair ab éigean dom iad a fhágáil le dul go dtí St Louis. Bhí eagarthóir páipéir nuachta a dtugtaí *Men and Women* air ag iarraidh orm 'agallamh' a thabhairt dá pháipéar i gcomhair Lá Fhéile Pádraig, agus thug sé gearrscríbhneoir leis lena chur síos, ach ní raibh a fhios aige féin cén sórt ceisteanna a chuirfeadh sé orm, agus níor fhéad sé cuimhneamh ar aon cheist. Mar sin chuireas féin na ceisteanna orm féin, agus d'fhreagair mé iad, chomh maith. Cailín óg Gearmánach a scríobh síos an chaint, agus labhair sí an Ghearmáinis go maith. D'fhiafraigh mé di an labhraíodh siad an teanga sin ina dteach féin. Dúirt sí nár labhair, riamh, ach nuair a labhródh an t-athair nó an mháthair leo í. Bhí cúpla Éireannach maith eile a casadh orm anseo, Mistéalach, Táilliúrach, Mac Uí Mhaoilmhichíl agus Mac Uí Airt. Is ait an rud é go bhfuil an aimsir breá bog anseo an tráth seo den bhliain, agus chonaic mé daoine inniu ag obair gan a gcuid casóg orthu.

ST LOUIS

An tríú lá fichead. Chodail mé sa traein agus ráinigh mé St Louis, Missouri, ar a hocht ar maidin. Is cathair an-mhór í seo, tá timpeall 700,000 duine inti agus is Gearmánaigh timpeall 200,000 duine, agus Éireannaigh is ea tuairim is 100,000 duine den chuid eile. Bhí an talamh faoi shneachta agus bhí an ghloine daichead céim níos ísle ná a bhí sí i Cincinnati inné! Tugadh mé go dtí teach ósta Jefferson agus tugadh seomraí breátha dom. Ba é Mac Uí Dhúill, fiaclóir, an fear ba ghnóthaí i measc lucht m'fháiltithe. Ba é an Bráthair Barnairdín an cathaoirleach. Labhair mé an tráthnóna sin san Odeon. Bhí an tArdeaspag Mac Giolla Fhionnáin sa chathaoir agus labhair sé go rímhaith. Bailíodh timpeall 500 dollar, ach ní mór le rá an méid sin do chathair mhór mar St Louis. Chonaic mé a lán daoine as mo chomharsanacht féin, i gContae Ros Comáin, ó Chlogarnach, ó Lios an Choirce, ón gCeathrú Gharbh, agus ó Bhealach an Doirín. Tháinig fear gaoil dom .i. Oldfield Cubbage isteach ó Moberly, 100 míle as seo, le mo chloisteáil. Bhí sé a dó a chlog nuair a bhain mé mo leaba amach.

An ceathrú lá fichead. Thug an Dochtúir Ó Dúill, an fiaclóir, amach leis mé i ngluaisteán, agus thugamar cuairt ar cheathrar daoine, agus ansin chaith mé lón leis an Ardeaspag, an tArdeaspag is óige i Meiriceá, sílim. Níl sé ach trí bliana is daichead. Fear ard dathúil, an-ghreannmhar é. Bhí mórán cainte agam leis. Dúirt sé féin liom gur Mac Ghiolla Fhionnáin a ainm ceart. Tá cáil mhór air i St Louis, agus taithníonn sé go mór le muintir na cathrach go léir. Cosúlacht na galántachta ar dhuine is ea aithne a bheith aige air.

Nuair d'fhág mé an tArdeaspag chuaigh mé go dtí an 'Wednesday Club' mar a thugtar air, chun labhairt le ceithre chéad bean uasal ar bhéaloideas, agus nuair a tháinig mé ar ais bhí fleá mhór réidh romham sa teach ósta. Shuigh ceithre dhuine dhéag agus ceithre fichid ag an mbord. Óladh go leor 'sláintí,' agus ó tugadh na sláintí do chainteoirí speisialta roimh ré, bhí na hóráidí – mar is gnách – go han-mhaith. Shuigh mise idir an Bráthair Barnairdín agus an breitheamh Ó Néill Ó Riain. Rinne an breitheamh caint fhíochmhar ghéar shearbh in aghaidh na Sasanach, agus bhí eagla orm go ndéanfadh a chuid cainte dochar. D'iarr mé os íseal ar an gcathaoirleach a iarraidh orm beagán a rá arís, nuair a bheadh na sláintí go léir thart. Rinne sé sin, agus lig mise orm gur chuir sé iontas orm gur iarradh orm labhairt faoi dhó. B'fhéidir gurb é an fáth a rinneadh sin le deis a thabhairt dom le slán a fhágáil arís ag mo chairde. Leis sin, rinne mé tagairt do cheist na polaitíochta agus mhínigh mé dóibh go raibh gach uile shórt polaitíochta sa Chonradh, agus dá mhéad difríocht a bhí eadrainn i bpolaitíocht go rabhamar go léir ar aon intinn i dtaobh na teanga. Rinne mé é sin gan aon mhíshásamh a chur ar éinne. Níor thug an breitheamh aon ní faoi deara. Is fear an-bheag é, glanbhearrtha, cloigeann cruinn air, agus na beola druidte go dlúth ar a chéile. Cuireann sé fuinneamh lena chuid cainte. Is é an fear is mó cumhacht atá ag Clann na nGael sa taobh seo tíre é. Tá cáil mhór air ar son a chneastachta agus a intleachta agus tá gach uile dhuine fábhrach dó.

An cúigiú lá fichead. Shocraigh an fiaclóir, an Dochtúir Ó Dúill, go mbeadh lón speisialta ar mo shon i dteach ósta Jefferson, agus thug sé cuireadh do sheisear nó do mhórsheisear de na daoine ba mhó saibhreas sa chathair. Bhí Wade agus Drew, Mag Uinseannáin agus Breathnach, agus cúpla Gearmánach ina measc. Níor chuir an chuideachta ach amháin na Gearmánaigh, mórán suime in aon rud. Má bhí súil ag an Dúilleach go dtiocfadh aon rud tairbheach as a lón, mealladh é, óir mhill sé féin é. Tharraing sé chuige na bóithre iarainn mar ábhar cainte, rud a raibh fios i bhfad níos fearr ag na Gearmánaigh ná aigesean air. Agus leis sin, labhair sé in aghaidh Shasana agus na Sasanach chomh borb agus chomh míréasúnta sin nach ndeachaigh an chuid eile dá chaint i bhfeidhm ar an gcuideachta. Thaispeáin sé go róshoiléir an rud a bhí ina intinn; agus cuireann sé sin faitíos agus ar uaireanta déistin ar dhaoine. Is an-ait an fear é, agus níor thuig mé féin é.

Nuair a bhí an lón thart chuaigh mé go teach Mrs Bailley le casadh ar mo shean-chara Mrs Worthington, agus uathu sin chuaigh mé chun dinnéir leis an mBreitheamh Ó Néill Ó Riain ag a chlub. Bhí an Dochtúir Ó Catháin, sean-Fhínín, an Bráthair Barnairdín, agus an fiaclóir ann. Nuair a bhí an dinnéar thart chuaigh mé go Coláiste na mBráithre Críostaí agus thug mé léacht do thimpeall cúig chéad duine, ar litríocht na Gaeilge ar feadh na dtrí chéad bliain a chuaigh thart. Bhí sé tar éis a dó san oíche nuair a bhí mé i mo leaba.

An séú lá fichead. D'fhág mé St Louis ar a naoi a chlog ar maidin, agus tháinig an breitheamh go dtí an stáisiún le slán a fhágáil agam. Bhíomar ag caint le chéile agus bhí mise á rá leis go ndearna mé mo dhícheall chun na Gearmánaigh agus na hÉireannaigh a tharraingt le chéile. 'Ó!' ar seisean, 'Is Talleyrand thusa!' Leis sin ligeadh an fhead agus thosaigh an traein ag gluaiseacht, agus níor fágadh am agam le hinsint dó gur de mo shinsir féin ar thaobh mo sheanmháthar, an Talleyrand céanna. Ní bhfuair mé an ócáid an uair sin ná ó shin, ach gur chuir mé scéala chuige le cara, má fuair sé riamh é!

Bhí traein thapa agam, agus ní raibh mé ach naoi n-uaire an chloig ag filleadh go Chicago. Tá an tír cothrom idir an dá áit, gan cnoc gan cnocán. Ní cheiltear an t-amharc ar aon taobh ar feadh nóiméid amháin trí bhanc nó cnocán ar bith a bheith ar thaobh an bhóthair iarainn. Is iontach an talamh i gcomhair barr arbhair Indiaigh í. Tá an talamh go léir, nach mór, faoi churaíocht. Maidir leis na bóithre, tá siad go han-dona ar fad, sna bailte féin. Tá siad cosúil le lorg a dhéanfadh eallach. Is iad na bóithre na rudaí is measa i Meiriceá, sílim.

Ar theacht dom in aice le Chicago chonaic mé, mar a shíl mé, ar mo thaobh clé na chéad chnoic a chonaic mé ó d'fhág mé St Louis. Bhí an tír ar fad chomh cothrom sin gur shíl mé ar dtús gur sléibhte a bhí ann. Ach níorbh ea. Ba iad na clocha móra, an chréafóg agus na carraigeacha a pléascadh as an díog mhór a bhfuil camraí agus salachar Chicago ag dul amach inti. Pléascadh an díog ábhalmhór seo as na carraigeacha, agus fágadh oscailte gan dúnadh í ar feadh daichead éigin míle, agus tugtar an t-iomlán isteach in abhainn bheag éigin, agus sílim go scuabtar sa deireadh é isteach sa Mississippi, ach triomaítear agus súitear an salachar go léir, nach mór, i bhfad sula dtagann sé chomh fada sin. Súitear cuid mhór de isteach sa talamh fhliuch trína sníonn sé ar feadh cuid dá chúrsa. Deirtear gurb é seo an píosa draenála is iontaí sa domhan, ach ní raibh aon dul as acu ach sin a dhéanamh, óir ní fhéadfadh siad Loch Michigan, as a bhfaigheann siad a gcuid uisce, a shalú. Ar an taobh eile den chathair tá páirceanna loma gainimh, nach fiú dada iad. Ach thóg Rockefeller roinnt díobh agus rinne sé dabhcha móra dá chuid ola iontu.

Nuair a tháinig mé ar ais go Chicago arís d'itheas dinnéar le Clann Mhurchú. Bhí siad an-lách le mo bhean fad is a bhí mé as láthair. Fear déanta uisce beatha é, agus tá sé an-saibhir. Tá triúr iníonacha aige, cailíní deasa. Bhí mo bhean imithe amach nuair a tháinig mé. Bhí sí ag tabhairt cuairte ar Miss Adams, an bhean is mó a dhéanann maith do dhaoine, dá bhfuil sa chathair. Dúirt an Sasanach, Seán Burns, gurbh iad an dá rud is fearr a fuair sé i Meiriceá Miss Adams agus a gcuid pióg úll!

SOUTH BEND, INDIANA

B'éigean dom an chathair a fhágáil arís, agus dul go South Bend, Indiana, atá timpeall ceithre fichid míle ó Chicago. Tháinig Aodh Ó Néill atá ina ollamh ann i mo choinne, agus bhí Mag Fhearaigh agus fear eile, Súilleabhánach as Cúige Mumhan, a bhfuil go leor Gaeilge aige in éineacht leis. Chuaigh mé go hAcadamh Naomh Muire, a bhfuil siúracha na Croise Naofa[7] ina bhun, agus labhair mé le cúig chéad cailín ar litríocht na Gaeilge. Ní raibh aon rud le n-ithe agam ó mhaidin, agus bhí mé lag leis an ocras. Bhí sé tar éis a sé a chlog nuair a chríochnaigh mé, agus fuair mé blúire beag bia ó na Siúracha agus bhí orm rith liom ansin go dtí Notre Dame chun léacht a thabhairt uaim ar bhéaloideas do chúig chéad buachaill. Nuair a bhí sin thart bhí caint fhada agam leis an Uachtarán, an tAthair Ó Caomhánaigh, agus le cuid eile de na hollúna. Bhí mé an-tuirseach tar éis dhá léacht a thabhairt uaim – uair go leith gach ceann acu – agus gan ach cúpla uair an chloig eatarthu, agus mé i mo throscadh.

Thug an tAthair Ó Caomhánaigh leaba dom sa choláiste, agus lig sé dom codladh go dtí a haon dhéag. Bhí lón agam ar a haon, agus ansin tugadh mé ar cuairt chuig an Athair Zahm, a bhfuil an cnuasach is mó i Meiriceá aige, is dóigh, de leabhair a bhaineann le Dante. Seanfhear an-lách atá san athair, agus bhronn sé cóip bheag dheas de Dante orm, agus d'iarr sé go géar orm cuid de a chur i nGaeilge. Dúirt sé go raibh sé tiontaithe i ngach aon teanga nach mór, ach amháin an Ghaeilge. Gheall mé go ndéanfainn rud air, dá bhféadfainn.*

Is iad Sagairt na Croise Naofa atá i mbun Ollscoil Notre Dame, agus is iad Siúracha na Croise Naofa atá i mbun Acadamh Naomh Muire. Níl siad ach trí mhíle óna chéile, ach níl aon bhaint eatarthu, ach amháin an t-ainm. Indiaigh a bhíodh anseo trí fichid bliain ó shin, agus is dóigh go bhfuil cuid dá sliocht ann fós. Sa tráthnóna thug mé léacht uaim ag South Bend, an baile a bhfuil Ollscoil Notre Dame inti. Tá timpeall leathchéad míle duine ann, agus is mór an áit í chun céachta agus gléasanna fuála a dhéanamh. 'Oliver' a thugtar ar na céachtaí, agus chonaic mé iad i ngach áit i Meiriceá. Tá timpeall seacht gcéad dalta san Ollscoil, agus mórán acu ina bProtastúnaigh, ach téann siad go minic chun Aifrinn leis na daltaí eile. Ba é mo chruinniú i South Bend an ceann ba lú a bhí agam fós. Ní raibh níos mó ná dhá chéad duine ann, agus ní dhearnadh aon bhailiú airgid.

An naoú lá fichead. D'fhill mé go Chicago inniu. Bhí drochthinneas cinn orm ar feadh an lae. Thug Mac Uí Mhurchú dinnéar breá dúinn inniu, chun go mbaistfinn a theach nua dó; tá sé tar éis a theach a thógáil, amach ón mbaile mór. 'Cúl na Craoibhe' an t-ainm a thug mise air. Bhí an tAthair Ó Ríordáin deartháir don Ardeaspag, Dr Gueron, a raibh aithne aige ar Fhíona Nic Leóid (i.e. Liam Sharp), na hAogánaigh, Iníon Uí Mhóráin, agus roinnt daoine eile i láthair.

*Rinne mé sin ag dul thar na Sléibhte Carraigeacha dom nuair a bhí cúpla lá saor agam féin sa traein.

MADISON, WISCONSIN

An deichiú lá fichead. D'fhág mé Chicago ar a naoi ar maidin, le dul go Madison, Wisconsin, via Milwaukee. Ráinigh mé an áit sin ar a trí. Chuir an cléireach sa teach ósta amú mé, óir threoraigh sé an tslí fhada mé, agus mura mbeadh sin bheinn ann i bhfad roimh an trí. Is cathair í seo a bhfuil timpeall leathchéad míle duine inti. Tá a lán Gearmánach sa chathair, ach tá i bhfad níos mó Fionn-Lochlannach inti. Níl ach an t-aon ollscoil amháin sa stát, agus is anseo atá sí. Casadh orm an tOllamh de Brún, seandalta Dr Robinson. Scríobhaimis litreacha chuig a chéile faoi scéalta Artúir nuair a bhí mé sa bhaile. Chaith mé lón leis, agus ansin thug sé mé go teach Van Hise, an tUachtarán. Ní raibh aon duine sa teach, ach thaispeáin cailín aimsire seomra codlata dom, agus chaith mé mé féin ar an leaba agus thit mé i mo chodladh. Níor dhúisigh mé go raibh sé mall san oíche. D'fhág mé mo sheomra agus bhí mé ag dul amach ar an staighre nuair a casadh iníon an Uachtaráin orm, agus ó tharla nach raibh a fhios aici go raibh éinne sa teach shíl sí ar dtús gur robálaí mé! Bhí muintir an tí ag ithe a ndinnéir agus bhí dinnéar agam leo. Dúirt Van Hise liom go bhfuil muintir an stáit réidh agus toilteanach lena gcuid airgid a thabhairt don ollscoil, óir tugann an ollscoil trína teagasc ar churadóireacht, agus ar rudaí den sórt sin, i bhfad níos mó ar ais don slua ná mar a chaitheann an slua uirthise. Dúirt sé go ndearna sé a dhícheall riamh an ollscoil agus na daoine a thabhairt le chéile, agus coláiste fíor-*democratach* a dhéanamh. Bhí an Dochtúir Mahaffy ó Bhaile Átha Cliath ann, scaitheamh beag romhamsa, ach níor thaithnigh sé le héinne. Ní raibh focal maith aige le rá i dtaobh aon rud i Meiriceá. Is sampla breá d'ollscoil náisiúnta í seo. Thug mé léacht ar Bhéaloideas do thimpeall sé chéad duine, agus shiúil mé ar ais leis an mBrúnach go dtí a sheomraí féin. Bhí cuid dá chairde ansin roimhe. Bhí an oíche go han-fhuar, agus bhí mionsneachta tirim ag síobadh ar an ngaoth, agus b'éigean dom seomraí compordacha an Bhrúnaigh a fhágáil ar a haon a chlog san oíche. Ní raibh carr ná cóiste le fáil, agus b'éigean dom siúl agus mo mhála féin a iompar. Tháinig an Brúnach bocht in éineacht liom. Bhí cúpla míle le siúl againn go dtí an stáisiún, agus níor stad an sneachta ná an ghaoth. Chuaigh siad isteach i mo chluasa agus rinne siad bodhar mé. Ní dóigh liom gur leigheasadh ar fad an bhodhaire sin riamh. Nuair a ráinigh mé an stáisiún (nó an *depot* mar a thugtar air anseo), ní raibh aon traein le fáil, agus b'éigean dom fanacht ar feadh cúpla uair an chloig gur tháinig ceann.

ST PAUL

Bhí an traein cúpla uair an chloig mall ag teacht isteach go St Paul. Shíl mise go mbeinn istigh ar a naoi a chlog, agus níor itheas aon ní ar an traein, ach bhí sé leathuair tar éis a haon déag nuair a ráinigh sé an chathair. D'fhéach mé thart thimpeall ansin ach ní fhaca mé éinne a raibh aithne aige orm. Chuaigh mé isteach i gcarráiste agus dúras leis an tiománaí mé a thabhairt go dtí teach ósta maith, ach thug sé mé go dtí áit shalach dhorcha. Tháinig slua le fáilte a chur romham agus fuaireadar ansin mé agus thugadar leo mé go teach ósta eile, go dtí teach Mhac Uí Riain. Ansin ní ligfidís dom aon rud a ithe go dtógfaí mo phictiúr. Ach nuair a bhí an obair sin críochnaithe, bhí seomra an bhia sa teach ósta dúnta agus níor osclaíodh é go ceann cúpla uair an chloig ina dhiaidh sin! Níl aon chur síos ar an bhfuacht atá anseo, tá an ghloine ag *zero*, nó faoina bhun agus tá dhá throigh de leac oighir ar an Mississippi. Ach deirtear liom gurb í seo an bhliain is boige a bhí acu le blianta!

Is mór an chathair í seo, tá timpeall 200,000 duine inti. Is Gearmánaigh cuid mhaith acu seo agus is Caitlicigh trí cheathrú díobh. Ach tá 25,000 nó 30,000 Éireannach ina measc. Tá dhá chathair in aice lena chéile anseo, St Paul agus Minneapolis. Níl ach a ceathair nó a cúig de mhílte eatarthu agus ba chóir dóibh bheith ina n-aon chathair amháin. Ach bíonn éad mór orthu lena chéile. Tá St Paul ag barr na Mississippi, an áit a dtosaítear seoltóireacht uirthi, agus is í an tairbhe mhór a thagann de sin a rinne cathair éifeachtach di. Is féidir le bád dul síos ó St Paul go béal na Mississippi ag Orleans. Ach is i Minneapolis atá na muilte móra plúir – is í an áit is mó plúr i Meiriceá í. Tá go leor Lochlannach inti. Lochlannaigh is ea beagán thar leath na ndaoine atá i Stát Minnesota. Tá gruaig ar dhath an luaithrigh ar thrí ceathrú nó ar dhá dtrian ar a laghad de na mná a fheictear sa chathair.

Bhí cruinniú ábhalmhór agam sa tráthnóna. Is ar éigean a bhí áit le seasamh ag na daoine. Déarfainn go raibh ar an laghad 2,800 duine ann. Bhí an tArdeaspag de Irleónt .i. Ireland, ar an ardán, agus mar sin ba eisean ba cheart a bheith i gceannas an chruinnithe, ach chuaigh S. Ó Riagáin atá ina Uachtarán ar an AOH i gceannas air. As Mainistir na Búille é. Ba mhaith le Mac Uí Chuinn go ngabhfadh an tArdeaspag sa chathaoir, ach thóg an chomhairle sin, mar a chuala mé, stoirm mhór i measc lucht polaitíochta an AOH.

Cruinniú poiblí a bhí ann agus ligeadh na daoine isteach in aisce, agus ní dhearnadh aon bhailiú airgid. Labhair mé ar feadh níos mó ná dhá uair an chloig.

Casadh daoine ó m'áit féin i gContae Ros Comáin orm anseo, ó Chartún agus ó Ráth Chiara, ach ba é Seán Ó Briain an fear ba láiche agus ba mhó a thaithnigh liom díobh go léir. Ba eisean an t-aon fhear amháin a casadh riamh orm a mharaigh lachain fhiáine le bogha agus le saighead. Ní bhíodh pointe ná barr géar ar bith ar an saighead, dúirt sé, ach cnapán measartha mór adhmaid. Bhí sé ina dhlíodóir anois, ach rugadh agus tógadh é ar oileán i gceann de na locha móra, i measc na nIndiach, agus labhair sé Chippewa go líofa. Thug sé abhaile go dtí a theach féin mé agus bhí mórán cainte agam leis. Bhí sé an-ghéarintinneach. D'fhaigheadh sé an *Leader*, páipéar an Mhóránaigh, gach seachtain. Bhíodh aiste Gaeilge ag an Athair Ó Duinnín ann, agus d'iarr sé orm Béarla a chur ar aiste na seachtaine sin dó, óir ní raibh aon Ghaeilge aige féin. Bhí an aiste – mar ba ghnách leis an Athair Ó Duinnín – spéisiúil agus ciallmhar, agus chuir sin iontas ar an mBrianach, óir shíl sé go dtí sin nach raibh sa Ghaeilge ach sórt dalladh púicín! Bhí cuimhne aige ar an am nach raibh i Stát Minnesota ar fad ach 2,200 duine. Bhí sé féin le linn a óige ina mháistir poist i St Paul, agus b'fhurasta dó litreacha na cathrach go léir a chur ar aon charr amháin.

An chéad lá d'Fheabhra. Bhí lón agam leis an Ardeaspag de Irleónt. Bhí naonúr nó deichniúr eile i láthair. Tá an tArdeaspag an-lách agus an-ghreannmhar agus bhí mórán scéalta maithe á n-insint inár measc. Is Meiriceánach breá leathanintinneach é, chomh leathan sin nach dtaithníonn sé leis an dream atá níos caolaigeanta ná é féin. Rinne sé a dhícheall chun na hÉireannaigh a mhealladh go dtí an tIarthar, an áit a mbíodh talamh le fáil beagnach in aisce ag gach éinne an uair sin. Dá n-éireodh leis, bheadh cuid mhór de thrí nó de cheithre stát mhóra ag na hÉireannaigh dóibh féin inniu. Ach bhí na sagairt in Oirthear na tíre ina aghaidh, agus lucht na polaitíochta Democrataí 'na aghaidh, óir bhí vótaí na nÉireannach ag teastáil uathu sin, mar ba *Democrat* gach Éireannach, agus b'fhearr leis na sagairt agus leosan go bhfanfadh na hÉireannaigh sna cathracha móra nuair a thagaidís amach go Meiriceá. Dúirt an tArdeaspag liom gur chuir sé dhá choilíneacht ar bun, ceann acu d'Éireannaigh agus an ceann eile do Phoncánaigh. Thug sé Avondale ar an gceann Éireannach. Nuair a thagadh strainséir ag cur thuairisc na háite, ag féachaint an mbeadh sé feiliúnach dó féin le cur faoi inti, thosaíodh na hÉireannaigh, agus sórt ceann faoi orthu, ag maslú na háite agus ag déanamh beag is fiú di, agus ag tabhairt na cáile is measa ar bith uirthi. Dá bhfiafródh an strainséir cén fáth ar fhanadar ina leithéid sin d'áit, is é rud a deiridís, 'Och, muise, níl a fhios agam; is orm a bhí an mí-ádh agus a theacht amach anseo riamh!' ach dá rachadh an strainséir cúpla míle eile agus go dtiocfadh sé go háit na bPoncánach agus go gcuirfeadh sé na ceisteanna céanna orthu siúd, is é rud a deiridís leis, 'Nach bhfeiceann tú le do dhá shúil cinn féin cén sórt tíre é seo, gurb é parthas Dé é. Féach na páirceanna, féach an ithir, féach an t-amharc. Má ligeann tú thart í gan cur fút inti beidh aithreachas go brách ort.' 'Sin é,' arsa an tArdeaspag, 'an difríocht, nó cuid di, atá idir an tÉireannach agus an Poncánach.'

Rinneadh iarracht láidir timpeall na bliana 1866, mar a chuala mé, chun na hÉireannaigh a bhí ag brú isteach an uair sin ina bhfichidí de mhílte, a threorú go dtí an tIarthar. Tionóladh cruinniú mór i Nua-Eabhrac i dtaobh an scéil, agus bhí an chuid is mó de na hEaspaig agus de thaoisigh na nGael i bhfabhar sin a dhéanamh, gur éirigh an tArdeaspag Mac Aodha agus go ndearna sé óráid chumhachtach ina aghaidh, á rá go gcaillfidís na Gaeil a gcine agus a gcreideamh dá bplandálfaí thiar iad. Sílim gur mhór an trua é sin. Chaill cuid mhór acu a gcine agus a gcreideamh gan trácht ar a sláinte sna cathracha san Oirthear, ach dá dtéidís an uair sin amach ar na machairí móra san Iarthar, bheadh seilbh acu inniu ar chuid mhór de leathdhosaen Stát, agus bheadh siad saibhir agus neamhspleách. Rinne an tArdeaspag de Irleónt agus an tEaspag Spalding a ndícheall, ach níor éirigh go rómhaith leo. Síleadh an uair sin gur fhásach neamhthairbheach cuid mhór de na Stáit seo san Iarthar, ach is é a mhalairt ar fad a thit amach. Nuair a bhristí an talamh bhán – agus bhristí, abair, ceithre mhíle go leith talún sa bhliain – lean an fhearthainn an briseadh. Sin é an scéal a chuala mise, ach is dóigh gurb í an fhírinne í gur shúigh an talamh bhriste an fhearthainn isteach inti, ar nós nach ndéanadh sí nuair a bhí sí ina machaire, agus go ndearnadh talamh mhaith den áit sin a raibh cáil uirthi bheith ina drochthalamh go dtí gur briseadh í. Labhair Seán Ó Briain go láidir in aghaidh an bhotúin a rinneadh gan na hÉireannaigh a mhealladh le cur fúthu ar an talamh seo. Chuala mé, ach ní cuimhin liom anois an ó Sheán Ó Briain a chualas é, gur mhian leo sa Róimh, na *Knights of Labour* a dhaoradh mar chumann rúnda. Tháinig an tArdeaspag de Irleónt agus an tArdeaspag Ó Ríordáin agus an tEaspag Spalding go dtí an Cairdinéal Mac Giobúin i mBaltimore agus d'iarradar air a ainm a chur lena n-ainm féin ar pháipéar in aghaidh dhaoradh an chumainn. Níor thaithnigh sin leis an gCairdinéal, ach nuair a cuireadh go crua air, scríobh sé a ainm, ag rá san am céanna, 'A dhaoine uaisle, tá mé millte agaibh.' Ach in áit dochar ar bith a dhéanamh dó, tharraing an gníomh sin meas agus grá na ndaoine air, agus bhí sé níos cumhachtaí ná riamh. Tá Cairdinéal ón Róimh i Meiriceá faoi láthair ag tabhairt aire speisialta do chúrsaí na hEaglaise sa tír sin.

MINNEAPOLIS

Tar éis dom a theacht ar ais ón lón a chaith mé leis an Ardeaspag, thug Gearaltach éigin agus fear eile amach go Minneapolis mé ar an *trolley car*. Má bhí cruinniú mór

Patrick Carmody Heafey. Le caoinchead Fhoras na Gaeilge

agam i St Paul ba mhó ná sin an ceann a bhí agam i Minneapolis. Sílim go raibh os cionn trí mhíle duine ann. Labhair mé ar feadh dhá uair an chloig agus deich nóiméad, ach ó bhí an áit go holc chun éisteachta b'éigean dom béiceadh in ard mo chinn agus mo ghutha. Ba shagart óg agus Éireannach maith – an tAthair Ó hArrachtáin – a bhí i gceannas an chruinnithe. Ba mhaith an fear, leis, an sean-Ghearaltach. Cúpla nóiméad sular thosaigh mé ag caint, cuireadh litir i mo lámh ó 'Frederick Stuart' ag tairiscint $25,000 dom ar son Chonradh na Gaeilge. Dúirt sé gur an-deacair an rud é 'trustee' a fháil dó, ach faoi dheireadh gur aontaigh Carnegie dul ina bhun. Chuir mé tuairisc i dtaobh an duine seo agus dúradh liom go raibh fear ag fanacht liom tamall fada sular tháinig mé isteach, agus gur thug sé 'Frederick Stuart' air féin. Ach dá mba mhian leis mé a fheiceáil bhí ócáid mhaith aige, óir d'fhan mé scaitheamh maith fada ar an ardán tar éis na léachta, ag croitheadh lámh leis na daoine, agus d'fhéadfadh sé labhairt liom dá mba mhian leis é. Chuardaigh mé an *Directory* ach ní raibh aon duine den ainm sin ann. Mar sin, is dóigh gur 'bhrionglóid píopa' é, focal atá acu anseo ar speabhraídí den sórt sin. Bhí sé a dódhéag nuair a tháinig mé ar ais go dtí an teach ósta i Minneapolis.

Chaith mé cuid mhaith den mhaidin le Gearmánach nó Lochlannach, táilliúir a bhfuil siopa aige faoin teach ósta, cothrom leis an tsráid. Bhí beirt Chiarraíoch, Mac Uí Leannacháin agus Mac Uí Chathasaigh, ag obair sa siopa aige. Bhí cúpla amhrán Gaeilge ag an gCathasach agus scríobhas uaidh iad. Ansin thug sé píosa Béarla dom, ar bhain mé úsáid as go minic ó shin, ag cur síos dom ar fhilíocht na Gaeilge.*

Tháinig mé ar ais go St Paul ar a ceathair a chlog agus amach go Teach Sheáin Uí Bhriain chun dinnéir. Tá bean lách agus beirt iníonacha áille aige. Go cinniúnach chonaic mé fógra a chuir siopadóir éigin go dtí an cailín is sine acu 'An Dualgas atá ar an Áille,' ab ainm don fhógra seo. Dúradh sa scríbhinn go raibh sé de dhualgas ar an té a bhí álainn, páipéar agus clúdaigh dá réir, a bheith aici, agus nach raibh siad sin le fáil ach ag na daoine a chuir amach an fógra seo! Ag sin mar a dhéantar gnó i Meiriceá!

Tar éis mo dhinnéir chuaigh mé go Scoil Naomh Lúcás agus thug mé léacht ar bhéaloideas. Bhí an tArdeaspag ar an ardán, agus triúr nó ceathrar de bhreithiúna, agus daoine móra eile, is é an tAthair Tornóir an sagart atá i gceannas na scoile, agus is dearthair é do mo sheanchara féin, an *Redemptorist* in Éirinn.

Tháinig mé ar ais go teach an Bhrianaigh agus mé an-fhuar ar fad. Rinne mé gloine puins dom féin ar eagla go bhfaighinn slaghdán. Níor bhlais mé puins mar dheoch ó tháinig mé amach go Meiriceá. Ní óltar sa tír seo é, agus níl fios a dhéanta ag éinne!

*Féach nóta, lch 311.

An cúigiú lá d'Fheabhra. Bhí lá fuar eile againn lá arna mhárach, agus is annamh a fuair mé fuacht mar í. Shiúil mé amach le Mac Uí Bhriain go dtí Fort Shelling[8] ag ceann na Mississippi. D'fhág mé an áit seo le filleadh go Chicago ar a 7.30 sa tráthnóna, cé gur leasc liom scaradh leis na Brianaigh. Chodail mé ar an traein, agus ráinigh mé Chicago slán agus chaith mé an oíche le muintir Mhurchú. Ba é seo an chéad lá saor a bhí agam féin, le tamall maith.

Ba é an lá ina dhiaidh sin an lá deiridh i Chicago agam, agus chaith mé an chuid is mó de ag scríobh litreacha. Scríobh Iníon Uí Mhurchú agus Proinsias Haicéad cuid acu dom ar an gcló-inneall. Is fear óg an Haicéadach agus rinne sé a dhícheall ar mo shonsa ó tháinig mé. Sílim gur eagarthóir ar pháipéar tráthnóna é. Is as Cill Chainnigh a tháinig a mhuintir. Tá sé an-lách. D'fhágamar Chicago le dul go hOmaha, ar ár mbealach go San Francisco. Cheannaigh an tAthair Fielding[9] ticéid dúinn ar leath an ghnáthairgid. Tháinig sé féin agus an Haicéadach linn go dtí an traein. Táimid le dul siar go ceartlár Mheiriceá anois.

OMAHA, NEBRASKA

Thángamar go hOmaha ar a haon déag ar maidin. Bhí romhainn ag an stáisiún T. P. Réamann, fear dathúil glanbhearrtha a bhfuil ceann de na háiteanna is mó sa chathair aige, agus C. S. Smyth, fear dathúil eile a bhfuil gruaig bhán air. Cé nach fear aosta é, bhí sé ina Ardaturnae do Stát Nebraska. Bhí Mac Uí Éafaigh ann, freisin, adhlacóir, agus Iníon Uí Eideáin. Chuamar amach sa tráthnóna chun dinnéir leis na hEideánaigh. Bhí Count Creighton ann, seanghaiscíoch breá a raibh féasóg bhán air, agus scéalaí maith lena chois sin. Eisean a chuir suas an chéad sreangscéal idir Salt Lake City agus Omaha, nuair a bhí na hIndiaigh in airde sa tír sin. Is iontach an fear déanta maitheasa é. Thóg sé coláiste agus ospidéal agus níl a fhios agam cé mhéad rud eile in Omaha. Tá sé an-saibhir. D'inis sé scéalta agus ghabh sé amhrán. Bhí dinnéar maith againn.

An t-ochtú lá d'Fheabhra. Chuaigh mé féin agus mo bhean chun lóin leis an Easpag Ua Scannaill. Corcaíoch é a bhfuil flúirse Gaeilge aige.* Chuamar ann, in éineacht le Mr Smyth. Ansin chuaigh an bheirt againn go dtí an Clochar agus as sin go dtí an coláiste a thóg Count Creighton. Tá an coláiste faoi stiúir Chumann Íosa. Bhí an Count féin ansin romhainn, agus thug sé deochanna dúinn go léir, agus chuir sé cnapán siúcra i ngach gloine acu. Nós é sin sa tír seo. Thug mé óráid do na cailíní sa chlochar i nGaeilge agus chuir an tEaspag Béarla air! Bhí comhrá fada agam leis

*Deir siad Scan-ell i mBéarla, agus brí an ghutha ar an dara siolla; an chaoi chéanna le Mor-an.

Count Creighton

Count John A. Creighton. Le caoinchead Fhoras na Gaeilge

na sagairt. Bhí fear acu ann a tháinig ó chomharsanacht Bhealach an Doirín, Stritch ab ainm dó. Tá timpeall 150,000 duine in Omaha, agus is Éireannaigh timpeall 25,000 díobh sin. Casadh fear arbh ainm dó Conn Ó Donnabháin orm agus thaispeáin sé leabhar mór Gaeilge dom, lámhscríbhinn a raibh timpeall ceithre fichid seanmóir ann. Dúirt mé leis an Easpag gur cheart an leabhar seo a shábháil ar shlí éigin, nó go gcaillfí é go cinnte. Níl a fhios agam céard a bhain dó. Ní scarfadh an Donnabhánach leis. Bhí fear eile ansin, dlíodóir, Holmes ab ainm dó. Rugadh agus tógadh é sa tír seo, ach mar sin féin bhí togha na Gaeilge aige.

Sa tráthnóna bhí cruinniú breá againn san amharclann. Labhair an tEaspag go han-mhaith i nGaeilge agus i mBéarla. Bhí Smyth, fear a bhí ina Ardaturnae, tráth, sa chathaoir.

Nuair a bhí an cruinniú thart chuamar go dtí teach ósta, idir mhná uaisle agus dhaoine uaisle, suas le tríocha duine againn, agus bhí suipéar againn. Thosaíodar ansin ar scéalta a insint. Is iontach na scéalaithe iad, agus táthar i bhfad níos tugtha don scéalaíocht de réir mar a théann tú siar sna Stáit.

An naoú lá d'Fheabhra. Thug Mac Uí Éafaigh amach sinn i gcarráiste a raibh péire álainn de chapaill dhubha aigeantacha faoi. Sular scar sé linn thug sé dúinn leabhar a raibh gach litir agus gach sreangscéal a fuair sé nuair a d'éag a bhean clóbhuailte ann. Ba leabhar réasúnta mór a bhí ann. Ní fhacas aon rud cosúil leis riamh mar chuimhneachán ar mharbh! Bhí sé féin, nó a athair, ina thionónta don Ghinearál Ó hÍcí i gContae Thiobraid Árann, sílim. Mhol sé a sheantiarna talún go mór. Bhí sé go han-lách linn. Ansin thug an tArdaturnae isteach i gcúirt a bhí ar siúl sinn. Bhí cúis éifeachtach á plé inti. Ligeadh mé féin agus mo bhean isteach mar strainséirí cáiliúla, agus tugadh dhá chathaoir dúinn in aice leis na giúistísí. Beirt díobh sin a bhí ann. Mionnaíodh coiste an dáréag agus bhí ionadh orm go raibh beirt choisteoirí gorma air. Fear a raibh droch-cháil air, mar a chuala mé, arbh ainm dó Cró, a ciontaíodh i ngeall ar gur ghoid sé buachaill nach raibh ach tuairim is dhá bhliain déag d'aois, agus gur choinnigh sé i mbotháinín beag suarach é gur díoladh oiread seo dollar as – tríocha míle, sílim. Ní raibh aon rud sa chúirt a chuirfeadh cúirt in Éirinn nó i Sasana i gcuimhne duit. Shiúil daoine isteach is amach ar doras mór. Sílim gur chaitheadar tobac, freisin. Daoine an-choitianta a bhí ar an gcoiste. Bhí siad go léir bocht de réir cosúlachta agus bhí Cró féin gléasta níos fearr agus níos geanúla ná an chuid is mó acu. Ba léir dom, tar éis tamaillín, go saorfaí Cró, ba chuma cén fhianaise a bhí ina aghaidh, óir b'fhollas go raibh áthas orthu go léir, idir choiste agus lucht éisteachta, gur éirigh le héinne an t-airgead sin a bhaint den mhilliúnaí, duine de na deartháireacha an-saibhre sin na Cuidithigh, ó Chicago. Saoradh é, freisin.

Táimid tagtha anois go ceartlár Mheiriceá, óir tá Omaha leath bealaigh idir an dá fharraige, idir San Francisco agus Nua-Eabhrac. Bhí na cathracha in Oirthear Mheiriceá siúlta agam anois, agus labhair mé i ngach cathair ar iarradh orm léacht a thabhairt inti, agus i ngach áit eile dá raibh socraithe ag Mac Uí Chuinn agus ag Tomás Bán go dtiocfainn inti. Ach is stáit nua na Stáit eile, na cinn atá idir Omaha agus California, agus níl mórán daoine ná cathracha móra iontu. Mar sin de, bhí orainn dul díreach anois go California, go San Francisco, áit a raibh an tAthair Mac Conchearca, (.i. Father Yorke) le mo threorú in áit Mhac Uí Chuinn. Bhí Tomás Bán Ua Conċheanainn imithe romhainn cheana ó St Louis, chun scíth bheag a ligean lena dheartháir agus le lámh chúnta a thabhairt don Athair Yorke sa taobh sin den tír. Bhí orainne é a leanúint tar éis Omaha a fhágáil. Mar sin de d'fhágamar Omaha, inniu, an deichiú lá d'Fheabhra le dul siar go dtí an t-aigéan ar an taobh eile de Mheiriceá. Tháinig Mac Uí Éafaigh agus cuid mhaith daoine eile go dtí an stáisiún agus ní shásódh aon rud Mac Uí Éafaigh ach go gceannódh sé ticéid i gcomhair cathaoireacha dúinn.

Ar feadh an lae bhíomar ag dul trí thír a mbíodh tithe móra feirme inti thall is abhus. Ach ní raibh siad iomadúil. Bhí na feirmeacha an-mhór ar fad. Seo cuid den tír ar cheart na hÉireannaigh a bheith suite inti. Tá slua beag d'Éireannaigh, mar a chuala mé, i measc na bhfeirmeacha seo, ach sna háiteanna a raibh feirmeacha maithe acu, féin, níl siad chomh líonmhar anois agus a bhídís, óir dhíolaidís na feirmeacha agus théidís go dtí na bailte móra. Ar feadh na hoíche is dócha gur tríd an sórt céanna tíre a bhíomar ag dul.

An t-aonú lá déag. Lá arna mhárach, bhíomar ag dul trí na Sléibhte Carraigeacha, agus bhí fásach agus fiántas agus fuacht ar gach taobh. Bhí muineacha ísle sáiste ag fás tríd an alcalí, agus fíorchorr mharcach le feiceáil. Bhí an tír bán leis an alcaile agus ní raibh teach ná téagar ná curaíocht le feiceáil. Tharla gurbh é seo an chéad scíth a bhí agam, agus chaith mé an lá ag cur Gaeilge ar an gcanto sin a scríobh Dante faoi Phaolo agus Francesca, mar a gheall mé don Athair Zahm. Scríobh mé i d*terzetti* Gaeilge é, agus ní dóigh liom gur baineadh úsáid riamh as an meadaracht sin i nGaeilge roimhe seo. Bhíomar ag dul trí Stát Wyoming ar feadh an lae agus trí Rawlins, áit a bhfuil feirm mhór ag mo dheirfiúr. Nuair a d'fhágamar Wyoming thángamar go hUtah, an Stát a rinne na Mormannaigh. Ba mhór an míshásamh a chuir sé orm nuair a ráiníomar Ogden sa tráthnóna, atá ar bhruach an Locha Mhóir Salainn, gur tháinig beirt isteach chugam ó pháipéir nuachta i San Francisco. Chuir na páipéir iad míle míle le caint a dhéanamh liom, agus le scéala a chur rompu trí shreangscéal ar a raibh fúm a dhéanamh agus a rá. Ba bhean uasal shaibhir duine acu, a ghabh leis an gceird sin mar chaitheamh aimsire dí féin – Miss Jolliffe a hainm. Ba sheanfhear an duine eile, Pop

Risteárd ua Scanail, easbog Omaha.

Richard Scannell, Bishop of Omaha. Le caoinchead Fhoras na Gaeilge

Céil* a thugadar air. Chuaigh an traein amach thar an Loch Salainn ar chabhsa a bhí crochta ar phostaí agus ar shaileanna a tiomáineadh síos sa ngaineamh. Tá an cabhsa seo timpeall trí fichid míle trasna an Locha. Chuamar thairis go han-mhall, chomh mall le duine a bheadh ag coisíocht.

Lá arna mhárach, an dóú lá déag d'Fheabhra, bhíomar i Stát Nevada, agus ag dul tríd an *Sierra Nevada*. Ba bhreátha go mór na sléibhte seo ná na Sléibhte Carraigeacha. Bhí an sneachta ar gach taobh dínn, agus ar eagla go ndéanfadh titim an tsneachta dochar don traein nó go stopfadh sé an bóthar iarainn, bhí dídean nó ballaí cumhdaithe déanta de phostaí agus d'adhmad ar an taobh is airde den bhóthar, agus d'fhág sin nár fhéadamar na radhairc is fearr a fheiceáil. Bhí an dídean seo le hais an bhóthair iarainn ar feadh na bhfichidí agus na bhfichidí de mhílte, gur dhóigh leat ar uaireanta gur ag dul trí pholl a bhíomar.

Anois thosaigh na crainn ar thaobh an bhóthair arís, agus tar éis scaithimh eile thángamar go dtí áiteanna a raibh adhmad breá ard ag fás iontu. Chuamar gan mhoill amach le cois cuid de na mianaigh is saibhre sa domhan, gur thángamar faoi deireadh go Sacramento. Tá sé seo timpeall turas dhá uair an chloig ó San Francisco, agus is é príomhchathair Chalifornia é, mar is ann atá an Pharlaimint agus na cúirteanna, cé gur áit bheag í. Ar an nós céanna ní hé Nua-Eabhrac príomhchathair an Stáit sin, ach Albany, baile beag atá suite níos faide thuas ar an Hudson. Tháinig an tAthair Yorke agus Proinsias Ó Súilleabháin amach faoinár gcoinne go Sacramento, agus tamaillín ina dhiaidh sin chuaigh an traein mhór fhada a rabhamar uirthi, ar bord sórt soithigh – deirtear gurb é an soitheach is mó den sórt sin sa domhan é – agus chuaigh an soitheach agus an traein air, trasna an chuain, gur thángamar go Cathair San Francisco. Bhí fáilte mhór romhainn ansin, agus rinneadh pictiúir agus grianghraif go rabhamar sáraithe. Ansin tugadh go dtí an teach ósta, an St Francis, sinn, ceann de na tithe ósta is fearr dá bhfuil i Meiriceá.

An tríú lá déag. Tháinig go leor daoine ó na páipéir agus go leor cuairteoirí, agus lucht déanta grianghraf. Níor stopadar seo san oíche féin; tháinig siad agus las siad púdar éigin le solas a dhéanamh dóibh féin, go raibh an seomra dubh leis an deatach. Bhí páirtí againn féin sa tráthnóna, agus chuireamar fáilte roimh na daoine a tháinig. Bhí timpeall dhá chéad duine ann. Bhí an tArdeaspag Montgomery, agus mórán ban uasal i láthair. Ba é Séamas Ó Faoláin, Maor na Cathrach, tráth, agus duine de na fir is saibhre sa chathair, a chuir in aithne mé do na daoine, agus labhair mé féin ar feadh ceathrú uaire, nó mar sin, ag tabhairt freagra air. Bhí Craobh Uí Ghramhna de Chonradh na Gaeilge agus teachtairí ón AOH ann freisin.

*Pap[a] Cahill?

proinsias ó súilleabáin

Frank Sullivan. Le caoinchead Fhoras na Gaeilge

An ceathrú lá déag d'Fheabhra. Thug Proinsias Ó Súilleabháin mé trasna an chuain go teach an Dochtúra Benjamin Ide Wheeler, Uachtarán ollscoil California, nó Ollscoil Berkeley, mar tugtar an dá ainm air.

Deirtear go raibh an mhuintir a chuir an ollscoil ar bun ag caint is ag cúiteamh cén t-ainm a bhéarfaidís air, nuair a labhair duine acu an véarsa seo a rinne Berkeley, an tÉireannach clúiteach, Easpag Chluana, *Westward the Course of Empire takes its way*, agus bhíodar ar aon intinn, ansin, Berkeley a thabhairt ar an Ollscoil.

Thug an tUachtarán páirtí in onóir dom. Bhí timpeall 120 duine i láthair agus soláthraíodh babhla mór den phuins fuar is fearr dár ól mé riamh. D'iarr sé orm rud éigin a scríobh ina leabhar agus scríobh mé ar an nóiméad rann as laoi Oisín.

Is í an tír is aoibhne le fáil,
Is mó cáil anois faoin ngréin,
Crainn ag cromadh fá thorthaí a's bláth,
A's duilliúr ag fás go barr na ngéag.

Agus b'fhíor é sin, freisin. Bhíomar tar éis teacht ó gheimhreadh go samhradh, nuair a thángamar trasna an Sierra Nevada. Bhí duilliúr ar na crainn, bhí rósanna faoi bhláth, bhí na mílte bláth de gach saghas le feiceáil, agus ba chosúil le cleas draíochta é an chaoi a ndearnadh samhradh den gheimhreadh taobh istigh de chúpla lá. Bhí an Dochtúir Wheeler an-mhuinteartha ar fad liom, go mór mór ó bhí sé féin ag déanamh staidéir ar an tSean-Ghaeilge, ar mhór-roinn na hEorpa, nuair a bhí sé óg, faoi Zimmer nó Thurneysen, ní cuimhin liom cé acu. D'fhan mé leis chun dinnéir, agus ansin labhair mé ar 'intinn Chonradh na Gaeilge i taobh an Oideachais,' i láthair sé chéad duine nó mar sin. Bhí sé ag stealladh fearthainne ar feadh an lae, agus b'éigean dom dul ar ais san oíche trasna an chuain liom féin, agus ó bhí mo chuid éadaigh fliuch, tháinig slaghdán orm.

Lá arna mhárach thug Séamas Ó Faoláin amach sinn ina ghluaisteán mór, a bhfuil 45 cumhacht capaill ann, go bruach na farraige, go Teach na hAille.[10] Tá an teach seo ar bharr carraige móire, agus amharc álainn uaidh ar an aigéan mór atá sínte amach fúithi. Timpeall leathmhíle, nó míle, amach ó Theach na hAille tá carraigeacha loma ag éirí aníos ón bhfarraige, a bhfuil acra nó dhó iontu, agus bhí siad seo folaithe leis na hainmhithe is iontaí ar bith. Bhí rónta móra orthu ach ba iad na leoin farraige a chuir an t-iontas ar fad orm. Bhí cuid de na leoin seo chomh mór leis an mbó is mó dá bhfaca mé riamh. Ba ghreannmhar an t-amharc é a bheith ag breathnú orthu agus iad ag iarraidh dul in airde ar na carraigeacha, ag dreapadóireacht leo, as an bhfarraige. Bhí

James Phelan. Le caoinchead Fhoras na Gaeilge

fadradharcán againn agus chonaic sinn go han-soiléir iad, agus b'fhéidir go raibh siad níos faide amach uainn ná a shíleamar, ach chualamar go soiléir iad ag screadaíl. Bhí seacht nó ocht gcinn de na leoin ar an gcarraig, agus rónta an-mhóra measctha tríothu. Chaitheamar lón ag Teach na hAille, agus ansin chuamar timpeall na Páirce chun an mathúin mór *grisli*, a fheiceáil. Gabhadh beo é le haghaidh páipéar mór nuachta éigin, agus tugadh don Pháirc é mar fhógra don pháipéar, chun a ainm a chur in airde.

Nuair a tháinig an tráthnóna chuaigh mé trasna an chuain arís. An Geata Óir a thugann siad ar an gcaol seo den fharraige. Téann sé isteach daichead míle sa tír, agus tá Oakland agus an Ollscoil agus mórán eile ar an taobh thall de, ach tá cathair San Francisco ar an taobh seo. Nuair a bhí na Sasanaigh lena gcuid loingis ag seoladh thairis, ag iarraidh bailte na Spáinneach a shlad, in aimsir Eilíse, theip orthu an cuan seo a fheiceáil, agus sheoladar thairis, gan creach ar bith a dhéanamh.

Chuaigh mé chun dinnéir leis an Ollamh Schilling agus a bhean, daoine an-lácha. Is Gearmánach é féin, agus dúirt sé liom go ndearna sé a dhícheall na Gearmánaigh a thabhairt le chéile chun nach ligfidís dá litríocht féin, dá dteanga agus dá sean-nósanna dul ar ceal uathu. D'éirigh leis ar feadh tamaill, agus ansin cuireadh ina leith gur cleas polaitíochta a bhí á imirt aige, agus thit a iarracht ar lár. Dúirt sé liom gur daoine gan eolas, daoine ainbhiosacha, an chuid is mó de na Gearmánaigh sin a chuir mórán airgid le chéile i Meiriceá, mar Claus Spreckels i San Francisco féin. Níor chuir siad suim i litríocht ná i dteanga ná i rud ar bith ach in airgead.

Tar éis an dinnéir, labhair mé le 1,200 duine ar na 'Trí chéad bliain deiridh de litríocht na Gaeilge,' agus tháinig mé abhaile liom féin arís, ar an meán oíche trasna an Chuain. Tá sé a trí nó a ceathair de mhílte sílim ó thaobh go taobh.

Lá arna mhárach chuaigh mé féin agus mo bhean trasna an Chuain arís, agus bhí dinnéar againn leis an ollamh Gayley agus a bhean. Is Éireannach é, agus bhí sé ag obair go dian faoi Pharnell nuair a bhí sé óg. Tar éis an dinnéir thug mé léacht uaim do níos mó ná míle duine, Éireannaigh ó Oakland, an chuid is mó acu, ar na 'Baird Ghaelacha.' Nuair a bhí an léacht thart tugadh mé go Club na nOllúna, áit a bhfuair mé leann le n-ól. Ní ligtear dóibh aon deoch eile a bheith acu sa chlub. Tháinig mé abhaile arís trasna an Chuain ar an meán oíche, agus bhí píobán nimhneach tinn orm.

An seachtú lá déag. Bhí socair agam dul trasna an chuain agus labhairt arís ag Berkeley inniu, ach bhí faitíos orm. Bhí sé ag stealladh fearthainne ar feadh an lae, agus bhí an tinneas píobáin chomh dona sin orm gurbh éigean dom fanacht sa teach agus mo bhéal a choinneáil oscailte os cionn soithigh uisce a bhí ar fiuchadh, ag ligean don ghal dul síos sa scornach. Rinne mé gach rud a bhí ar mo chumas, chun go mbeinn réidh i gcomhair an chruinnithe mhóir a bhí le bheith ann amárach – an chéad uair a labhair mé i San Francisco féin.

An t-ochtú lá déag. Dé Domhnaigh. Lá an chruinnithe mhóir. Buíochas le Dia go bhfuair mé mo ghuth ar ais, go réasúnta maith. Labhair mé ar feadh uaire agus daichead nóiméad. Ar an gceathrú tar éis a dó bhí an cruinniú agam sa Tivoli Opera House. Ní raibh suíochán nár tógadh, agus nár díoladh as. Díoladh na boscaí ar $1,400, an *parquet* – gach uile shuíochán dá raibh ann – ar dhá dhollar an suíochán agus na háiléir uachtair ar dhollar an suíochán. Thug Proinsias Ó Súilleabháin an síntiús is mó a fuair mé i Meiriceá, roimhe nó ina dhiaidh, 1,200 dollar – dom, agus sular fhág mé California fuair mé 1,000 dollar ó Shéamas Ó Faoláin. Ach ní raibh an tsuim chéanna i gcúrsaí na hÉireann ag an bhFaolánach agus a bhí ag Mac Uí Shúilleabháin. Chaitheamar lón le Mac Uí Fhaoláin féin roimh an léacht, agus bhí Mrs Brooks ann, bean uasal atá pósta le coirnéal Sasanach. De shliocht Sheoirse III, rí Shasana agus a bhean Mrs Fitzherbert í. Bhí guth iontach aici. Casadh í orm i Londain Shasana ina dhiaidh sin. Bhí Proinsias Ó Súilleabháin i gceannas an chruinnithe, agus bhí an tArdeaspag Montgomery ar an ardán. Maidir leis an lucht éisteachta, ba iad na daoine ba chroíúla iad ar labhair mé leo riamh. Sa tráthnóna chuaigh mé féin agus mo bhean go dtí dinnéar mór a thug Proinsias Ó Súilleabháin dúinn.

An naoú lá déag. Bhí mé lánsásta go bhfuair mé mo ghuth ar ais agus gur éirigh chomh maith sin liom inné. Tháinig go leor de lucht na bpáipéar nuachta agus daoine eile isteach chugam i rith na maidine. Tar éis an lóin chuaigh mé thart in éineacht leis an Athair Ó Riain, fear óg geanúil Gaelach atá ina chúntóir ag an Athair Yorke, agus atá ar aon intinn leis faoi chúis na Gaeilge. Chuamar i ngluaisteán ar cuairt go dtí Maor Schmitz, agus chuamar thart go bhfeicfinnse cuid den chathair. Bhí an chathair seo an-Ghaelach tamall beag sular tháinig mise. Ainmneacha Gaelacha a bhí ar an gcuid is mó de na siopaí móra a bhí sa phríomhshráid. Ach chuala mé nár thaithnigh obair a n-aithreacha lena gclanna, agus go raibh na siopaí móra, sea, agus na sráideanna féin, ag dul go luath as seilbh na nÉireannach agus go raibh na Giúdaigh ag tógáil seilbhe orthu.

Sa tráthnóna thug an tArdeaspag dinnéar mór breá, an-chostasach, dom, rud nach ndearna sé, mar a chuala mé, d'aon neach riamh. Bhí timpeall fiche duine ag an dinnéar, agus b'fhiú leathchéad milliún dollar iad le chéile. Cuireadh mise i mo shuí taobh le taobh le Mícheál Ó Cuidithe, duine de cheathrar deartháireacha. Ba mhaith liom bualadh uime, óir shleamhnaigh sé féin agus a dheartháireacha go cliste as mo líon nuair a bhí mé i Chicago, i St Louis, agus i Milwaukee. Ba é a dheartháir, sílim, ar goideadh a mhac uaidh in Omaha. Cloisim gur dlúthchara don Ardeaspag é, agus is dóigh gurbh é sin an fáth nár dhiúltaigh sé do theacht. Deirtear gur ag an bhfear seo atá intleacht Mhuintir Chuidithe go léir, agus creidim sin, óir labhair sé go han-chiallmhar i dtaobh gach aon rud. D'inis sé dom gur as Callainn i gContae Chill Chainnigh a thángadar ar dtús go Meiriceá, agus iad ag teitheadh ón nGorta i mbliain an drochshaoil. Ní raibh náire ar bith air a admháil. Bhain mé tairbhe as mo chuid cainte leis, ina dhiaidh sin, óir nuair a tháinig mé go Los Angeles, áit a bhfuil áras aige, thug sé cúig chéad dollar uaidh don bhailiú a rinneadar ann domsa.

An fichiú lá. Chuaigh mé go Coláiste na mBráithre Críostaí, Bráithre an Chroí Naofa, agus labhair mé ansin os cionn dhá uair an chloig ar 'na trí chéad bliain dheireanach de litríocht na Gaeilge.' Bhí slua ábhalmhór i láthair, os cionn dhá mhíle duine, agus bhí mórán bualadh bos. Thug na bráithre abhaile leo mé agus thugadar neart le n-ithe agus le n-ól dom, agus tháinig mé abhaile leathuair tar éis an mheán oíche, óir bhí na bráithre go fial flaithiúil, agus ní ligfidís uathu mé níos túisce.

An t-aonú lá fichead. Tugadh an fhleá is mó a tugadh riamh do dhuine príobh-áideach (nó d'fhéadfainn a rá do dhuine ar bith) ar an gcósta seo domsa anocht. Bhain mé an blúirín seo a leanas, as an bpáipéar mór laethúil, an *Chronicle*, lá arna mhárach. 'Shuigh chun boird aréir in éineacht le Dubhglas de hÍde, ag teach ósta an Pháláis, os cionn 450 de na cathróirí is geanúla i San Francisco, agus is dóigh go mba í an fhleá is mó a tugadh sa chathair seo riamh in onóir do dhuine príobháideach. Ní raibh creideamh, ná aicme, ná náisiún nach raibh ionadaí uaidh ag an bhfleá, agus ní raibh ach an t-aon chuspóir amháin acu go léir, is é sin meas na nÉireannach orthu féin a thabhairt ar ais arís, agus cúis a thabhairt dóibhsean, freisin, a bheith bródúil as an eolas go raibh tír a sinsir taobh thiar díobh, fearacht na nGearmánach, na bhFrancach agus na náisiún eile. Shuigh ag an mbord céanna an tArdeaspag, Seoirse Montgomery agus cuid eile den chléir, an tOirmhinneach F. W. Clampett ó Eaglais Phrotastúnach Easpagóideach na Tríonóide, Rabbi Jacob Voorsanger agus Rabbi Nerto, Gobharnóir Pardee, an tArdmhaor Schmitz, an Dr Benjamin Ide Wheeler ó Berkeley, an Dr Dáithí Starr Iordan ó Stanford (Ollscoil), An Príomh-Ghiúistís Beatty ón Ard-Chúirt agus cuid eile de na breithiúna. Bhí scaipthe tríd an halla fir a raibh clú mór orthu ó thaobh na scoláireachta, ó thaobh an airgid nó ó thaobh na tráchtála, agus chuireadar go léir gártha áthais astu faoi gach focal dá ndúradh i dtaobh aiséirí na hÉireann. Níor fhéad na Gearmánaigh a gcuid teangacha a chasadh timpeall na bhfocal 'Sláinte na nGael,' ach d'fhreagraídís le 'Gut Heil!' agus bhuail gach uile dhuine a ghloine féin in aghaidh ghloine a chomharsan. Ba é an príomh-bhreitheamh Séamus V. Ó Cofaigh a bhí ina mháistir ar na 'sláintí,' agus bhí bratach na Stát Aontaithe agus bratach na hÉireann crochta taobh thiar den mháistir. Sheinn na ceoltóirí foinn Ghaelacha ar feadh an tráthnóna, agus ar uaireanta bhí an comhluadar go léir ag déanamh curfá leo. Ar lámh dheas an mháistir a shuigh an t-aoi onórach, an Dochtúir Dubhglas de hÍde, in aice le Séamas Ó Faoláin, agus ina aice sin bhí an Gobharnóir Pardee. Ar lámh chlé an mháistir a shuigh Proinsias S. Ó Súilleabháin, Príomh-Ghiúistís Beatty, an tArd-Mhaor agus Benjamin Ide Wheeler. Bhí an *menu* clóbhuailte i mBéarla agus i nGaeilge, agus tar éis gach sláinte acu bhí suaitheantas Gaeilge, agus léigh an máistir na blúiríní seo i mBéarla.'

Mhol na páipéir go léir an fhleá freisin, agus mhol siad mo mhisean.

Bhí rud amháin cearr leis an bhfleá seo. Thug mé an rud céanna faoi deara go minic i bhfleánna eile. Is é sin go raibh go leor fíona i dtosach na hoíche, agus neart le n-ól, ach, amach san oíche, nuair a bhíodh tart ar na daoine ón gcaint nó ón tobac, d'fhág an lucht freastail iad gan fliuchadh a mbéal a thabhairt dóibh. Ba mhór an dearmad é sin, óir ní bheadh ón gcuideachta ach buidéal den fhíon saor coitianta, bán nó dearg, chun a gcuid scornach a fhliuchadh, ó am go ham, ach ní raibh sé le fáil.

Bhí trí 'sláintí' déag agus triúr cainteoirí déag ann, agus labhair an Príomh-Bhreitheamh Ó Cofaigh féin, roimh gach sláinte acu. Fear an-lách an-uasal é an breitheamh seo, agus tá grá ag gach duine i San Francisco dó – ach amháin na dlíodóirí! Ach tá guth beag caol aige, agus níor chuala na daoine, ach amháin iad seo a bhí i ngar dó, céard a bhíodh sé a rá. Óir níor bheag an gaisce é do dhuine labhairt sách ard le go gcloisfí i ngach cúinne den halla mór sin é.

Tarraingt ar a haon a chlog san oíche, nó tamall maith tar éis an dó dhéag, nuair a bhí Proinsias Ó Súilleabháin, sílim, ag caint, agus sinne go léir ag éisteacht leis, múchadh an solas go tobann agus fágadh cúig chéad duine sa dorchadas. Ní fhéadfadh éinne acu a lámh a fheiceáil. D'fhanamar mar sin ag comhrá le chéile sa dorchadas gur tháinig lucht freastail isteach le coinnle. Is cuimhin liom go maith focal ciallmhar a dúirt an tAthair Yorke liom an oíche sin. 'Féach,' ar seisean, 'chomh furasta agus tá sé ár sibhialtacht do mhilleadh. Buail san áit cheart í agus cuireann tú as gléas í.' Tháinig sé sin i mo cheann cúpla mí ina dhiaidh sin, nuair a dódh San Francisco tar éis an chreatha talún, de bhrí gur buaileadh 'sibhialtacht na cathrach' sa bhall marfach. Briseadh na píopaí a dtagadh an t-uisce tríothu, agus dódh an chathair cheal uisce, agus an chuid ba mhó de na daoine breátha fiala fairsinge a bhí cruinnithe i mo thimpeall ag an bhfleá sin fágadh gan teach gan téagar, gan leaba gan lón iad. An pálás mór a rabhamar cruinnithe ann an oíche sin, níor fhan de ach cuid de na ballaí!

Níor chuir mí-ádh sin an dorchadais deireadh leis an gcaint, agus níor scoireamar go dtí tar éis an dó a chlog san oíche! Bhí cuid de na daoine á rá lá arna mhárach go raibh an anraith fuar, agus nach raibh na coilm óga go maith, ach mar a dúirt ceann de na páipéir ní féidir anraith a bhruith do 457 pláta, agus é a bheith go te do gach éinne, ná 457 colm óg a róstadh agus iad go léir a bheith ar fheabhas.

Clóbhuaileadh agus tugadh amach leabhar den fhleá, a raibh na hóráidí agus na sláintí agus pictiúir an-mhaithe de na cainteoirí ann. Bhí 88 leathanach* sa leabhar. Ba é an tAthair Yorke an fear deiridh a labhair, agus dar liomsa sháraigh sé na cainteoirí eile go léir. Ach do labhair Ide Wheeler, Uachtarán na hOllscoile, an Dochtúir Clampett, agus an tAthair Frieden, S. J., Uachtarán Choláiste Iognáid Naofa go han-mhaith, freisin.

An dóú lá fichead. Bhí mé an-tuirseach inniu agus tinneas cinn orm tar éis an dinnéir aréir. Tháinig gadaí agus bithiúnach – ní raibh fhios agam an uair sin go mba ghadaí agus bithiúnach é – lena bhean, agus thugadar sinn amach go Teach na hAille. Bhí amharc aoibhinn againn ar an bhfarraige agus ar an gcuan. Is mianadóir an fear seo, Mac Roibín a ainm. Agus aon duine a bhfuil baint aige le mianaigh óir, sa tír seo, ní mholfainn do strainséir cairdeas a dhéanamh leis, óir is beag acu ar iontaoibh iad.
An tríú lá fichead. Thug mé léacht uaim do mhic léinn Choláiste Iognáid Naofa ar a leathuair i ndiaidh a dó, ar na 'Trí chéad bliain dheireanach de litríocht na Gaeilge.' Bíodh go raibh sé luath sa lá, bhí slua mór, os cionn dhá mhíle duine, ag éisteacht liom. Thug muintir Chumann Íosa abhaile leo mé.

Sa tráthnóna chuamar chun dinnéir leis an mianadóir Mac Roibín. Bhí Sasanach óg lách ann, Grimes a ainm, a bhí ag obair faoi. Bhí trí cinn de na lachain is fearr sa domhan, ar a dtugtar i mBéarla *canvas-backs*, agus neart fíona aige.

An ceathrú lá fichead. Chuaigh mo bhean agus mé féin go dtí San Rafael, áit an-álainn, beagán de mhílte ón gcathair, agus thug mé léacht d'iníonacha léinn Chlochar San Doiminic. Bhí na mná rialta an-lách liom agus thugadar dinnéar breá dúinn. Tá áit an-deas acu, suite ar bhall aoibhinn.

Bhí ceaptha agam léacht eile a thabhairt uaim ag an ollscoil inniu. Ach chuir an tAthair Yorke siar é, ar eagla go ndéanfadh sé dochar don chaint phoiblí atá mé le tabhairt uaim ag Oakland, agus chuaigh mé go San Rafael ina áit. Tháinig go leor daoine ar cuairt chugam sa teach ósta.

An cúigiú lá fichead. Thug Mac Roibín agus a bhean agus Mr Grimes sinn leo ar an mbóthar iarainn, go barr an tsléibhe ar a dtugtar Tamal Pias. Ní mór don bhóthar iarainn casadh agus athchasadh, agus lúibíní agus snaidhmeanna a dhéanamh di féin, le dul suas go barr an tsléibhe, turas uair go leith an chloig. Ach nuair a thángamar go

*Féach nóta lch 311

dtí an barr, sílim go bhfaca mé an radharc ba bhreátha dá bhfaca mé riamh. Ar ár lámh chlé bhí an tAigéan Mór, agus ar ár lámh dheas bhí Bá San Francisco, a bhí leathchéad nó trí fichid míle ar fad, agus fiche míle, b'fhéidir, ar leithead. Bhí an bhá breactha le hoileáiníní, agus cathair San Francisco suite ar an gcladach theas. Bhí an lá ar fheabhas agus an radharc go ró-álainn.

D'ith mé dinnéar le Séamas Ó Faoláin ag an Bohemian Club. Bhí Mrs Brooks ag an dinnéar linn, agus ambasadóir ón tSile nó ó Pheiriú, fear mór grinn agus fear an-lách; casadh orm roimhe sin é.

An séú lá fichead. Thug Séamas Ó Faoláin, mé féin, agus mo bhean amach ina ghluaisteán mór go San José, turas níos mó ná leathchéad míle. Uair agus trí cheathrú a thóg sé orainn dul ann, óir níl na bóithre go maith. Chuamar ag siúlóid i bPáirc Alum, gleann álainn atá sa chomharsanacht. Tháinig an breitheamh Ó hAoláin agus an tAturnae Caimbéal chun dinnéir linn agus tar éis an dinnéir labhair mé le timpeall míle duine san amharclann. Bhí bean Phroinsias Uí Shúilleabháin agus cúpla col ceathrar di ó Boston i láthair freisin.

Lá arna mhárach bhí súil againn dul ar aghaidh leis na Súilleabhánaigh go Santa Cruz, ach bhí sé ag stealladh fearthainne agus b'éigean dúinn dul ar ais go San Francisco.

Deir muintir Chalifornia féin nach mbíonn sé fliuch anseo, agus nuair a thagann lá fliuch, deir siad, agus na deora beagnach ina súile, gurb iontach leo ar fad an lá seo, nach bhfacadar a leithéid le bliain, agus mar sin de; ach is í mo thuairim féin go bhfuil an aimsir i San Francisco – an tráth seo de bhliain ar chuma ar bith – chomh fliuch leis an aimsir a bhíonn i mBaile Átha Cliath sa gheimhreadh.

Sa tráthnóna tháinig constábla, nó bleachtaire, ó Uachtarán na bPóilíní sa chathair, agus ordú ó lucht stiúrtha na cathrach aige sinne a thabhairt trí Bhaile na Síneach agus gach rud aisteach a thaispeáint dúinn .i. na siopaí, na prochlaisí ina gcaitear *opium*, na Joss-houses, agus an áit a dtugann siad uirthi Pálás na hEalaíon, etc., etc. Bhí an bleachtaire an-lách, ní ligfeadh sé dom aon rud a íoc, agus ní ghlacfadh sé féin aon rud uaimse. I gceann de na poill a gcaitear opium iontu chonaiceamar sean-Síneach sínte siar ar dhrochleaba a bhí déanta de chúpla clár. Bhí cat ina luí ar a ucht, agus an fear ag séideadh gal an opium faoi shrón an chait, chun a chur ina chodladh. Dúirt sé nach dtugadh an cat síocháin ná suaimhneas dó go gcuirfeadh sé ina chodladh leis an *opium* é. Bhí sé ag caitheamh opium ar feadh daichead bliain, nach mór, agus 'níl mé marbh fós' ar sé, 'ach tá mé *velli tin*' .i. an-tanaí, agus ar ndóigh ní raibh pioc ar a chnámha. Amach san oíche thug an bleachtaire sinn go dtí áiteanna mar 'Pálás na hEalaíon,' áit a bhfuil droch-cháil uirthi. Tá an áit lán de gach uile shórt pictiúr, dábanna an chuid is mó acu, agus díoltar bia agus uisce beatha ann. Shuigh beirt bhan Ghearmánacha a bhí ag labhairt Gearmáinise agus Béarla measctha ar a chéile, ag an mbord céanna linn. D'inis duine acu scéal grinn gáirsiúil i nGearmáinis, ach níor thuig mé é i gceart, ach rinne mé gáire chomh maith is dá dtuigfinn. Níor shásaigh sin iad, 'Och,' ar siad, 'tá tú ag gáire faoin scéal agus ní thuigeann tú é, ní thuigeann tú é!' D'fhág mé iad gan a dtuiscint. Bhí suipéar eile againn timpeall a haon a chlog i dteach bia, áit a bhí ina theampall, tráth. Thángamar abhaile timpeall leathuair i ndiaidh a dó agus sinn tuirseach go leor tar éis radharcanna San Francisco a bheith feicthe go maith againn – trí chúirtéiseacht na bpóilíní!

Lá arna mhárach, tháinig an tAthair Yorke agus Mr Grimes ar cuairt chugainn, agus chuamar féin amach ag siopadóireacht.

An chéad lá de Mhárta. Bhí cruinniú an-mhaith agam san amharclann in Oakland anocht. Labhair mé ar feadh uaire agus trí cheathrú. Tháinig an tAthair Yorke trasna an chuain liom, agus chaitheamar dinnéar leis an Athair Mac Aodha. Casadh fear páipéir orm a bhí pósta le cailín a raibh aithne agam uirthi sa bhaile i gContae Ros Comáin, nuair a bhí sí ag gabháil an bhóthair ag déanamh teachtaireachta dúinn agus í an-bhocht. Bhí sí saibhir anois, agus d'ól mé buidéal *champagne* lena fear.

An dara lá de Mhárta. Fuair mé cuireadh ó Bhord an Oideachais léacht a thabhairt uaim sa Tivoli Opera House do mhúinteoirí poiblí na cathrach go léir, agus do mhic léinn na n-ardscoileanna. Thug Bord an Oideachais cúig phíosa óir dom, le cur i mo phóca féin, tar éis na léachta agus gach píosa díobh chomh mór le leathchoróin. Cé nach raibh sé ach luath sa lá bhí an amharclann lán go doras, agus bhí na céadta eile ar an tsráid nach raibh slí dóibh istigh. Labhair mé le dhá chéad déag de mhúinteoirí scoile agus le slua mór de na cailíní is sine ó na hardscoileanna. Bhí níos mó ná deichniúr de bhreithiúna agus go leor daoine móra oirirce eile ar an ardán freisin. Labhair mé ar bhéaloideas ar feadh uaire go leith, agus ar eagla nach dtuigfí mé labhair mé chomh simplí agus ab fhéidir liom. Nuair a bhí mo léacht críochnaithe cuireadh na cúig bhonn i mo lámh, agus chaith mé lá arna mhárach iad ag ceannach rudaí le tabhairt ar ais go hÉirinn liom. Bhí craicne ainmhithe agus fionnadh le fáil saor go leor san Iarthar. Cheannaigh mé an craiceann mathúna is mó a chonaic mé riamh ar $65. Fear seilge a mharaigh é in Alasca agus a thug ar ais leis é go San Francisco. Tá rudaí iontacha ag na Sínigh agus ag na Seapánaigh le díol, freisin, agus cheannaigh mé sceana agus miotóga cnáimh nó eabhair shnoite uathu. Tá cuid an-mhaith den chathair ag na Sínigh, áit nach bhfuil rófhada ó lár na cathrach, agus tá áit eile ag na Seapánaigh in aice leo.

Bíonn meas ag gach éinne ar an Síneach ach níl aon ghrá ag na daoine dóibh. Tugann siad 'Seán Síneach cneasta' air, óir níl éinne i Meiriceá chomh cneasta ná chomh poncúil leis ag íoc a fhiacha. Nuair a thagann an bhliain nua ní thosóidh an Síneach ag tráchtáil nó go mbeidh an phingin dheireanach dá bhfuil air íoctha aige. Ach ní mar sin don Seapánach. Más fealltach, cam, cleasach, an Poncán, is fealltaí, is caime agus is cleasaí an Seapánach. Bhíodh faitíos an Domhain ar mhuintir an Iarthair, go mbeadh na Sínigh ag dul i gcomórtas leo, agus go mbeadh siad ag baint an greim as a mbéil féin faoi rá is gur beag an luach saothair a theastaigh uathu. Cuireadh troid an-mhór, an-nimhneach ar siúl beagán de bhlianta roimhe sin ag iarraidh na Sínigh a choinneáil amach ar fad. Bhí mo chara, Séamas Ó Faoláin, a bhí ina Ard-Mhaor ar San Francisco trí huaire, i lár na troda in aghaidh na Síneach. Ba iad na hargóintí ba láidre a bhí ag naimhde na Síneach, go mba phágánaigh iad nach gcuirfeadh a gcuid clainne chun scoile, nach ngléasfadh iad féin ar nós na gcathróirí eile, nach gcruinníodh siad a gcuid airgid lena chaitheamh sa tír inar ghnóthaíodar é, ach go dtéidís abhaile go dtí an tSín arís leis, agus tar éis bháis dóibh nach ligidís oiread agus a gcnámha a chur i Meiriceá, ach go gcaithfidís a n-iompar ar ais go tír a n-aithreacha. Argóintí láidre iad sin i gcoinne na Síneach agus ní ligtear isteach ach uimhir bheag acu anois. Bhí go maith agus ní raibh go holc gur tháinig dream eile ón Oirthear, na Seapánaigh, agus níor oir aon argóint de na hargóintí thuas dóibhsean. Ghléasaidís iad féin ar nós na Meiriceánach, bhí siad lántoilteannach a gcuid clainne a chur chun scoile ag foghlaim Béarla agus na rudaí eile a mhúintear inti, bhí siad lánréidh chun tithe a chur suas dóibh féin agus chun a gcuid airgid a chaitheamh i Meiriceá, agus bhí siad réidh chun maireachtáil agus chun bás a fháil sa tír sin. B'éigean, mar sin, argóintí eile a fháil in aghaidh na Seapánach, óir bhí daoine bána an Iarthair go daingean ina n-intinn nach ligfí isteach iad. Má thagann sé choíche chun cogaidh idir an tSeapáin agus na Stáit, is é seo an t-ábhar cogaidh is mó a bheas eatarthu. Is ar éigean a d'aithin mise an áit ar stop na siopaí Síneacha agus ar thosaigh na siopaí Seapánacha, bhí siad chomh cosúil lena chéile, ach b'fhurasta na Seapánaigh féin a aithint, lena gcuid hataí cruinne feilte Meiriceánacha, thar na Sínigh a mbíodh a gcuid eireaball cúil ag sileadh síos ar a slinneáin acu. Bhíodh sórt scátha ar na póilíní a mbealach a dhéanamh trí na sráideanna Síneacha, agus nuair a chuardaídís iad ní fhaighidís tada. Ach nuair a tháinig an crith mór talún, agus nuair a leagadh an chathair, seachtain nó mar sin tar éis dúinne a fhágáil, fuair na daoine a bhí ag tógáil na cathrach arís go raibh bealaí agus pasáistí fada faoin gcathair tochailte amach ag na Sínigh, agus cuid mhaith de mhná bána ina bpríosúnaithe iontu. Bhí seomraí agus bóithre faoin talamh ar nós cathrach nua! Fuair gach aon duine a bhí sa chathair-faoi-thalamh seo bás nuair a leagadh an chathair orthu.

Tar éis mo léachta thug mé an Maor, Schmitz, ar ais go dtí an teach ósta liom. Eisean a chuir in aithne don lucht éisteachta mé. Tháinig cúpla duine de Bhord an Oideachais in éindí linn freisin, agus thug mé bonnóga teo agus cúpla buidéal *champagne* dóibh.

Sa tráthnóna chaitheamar dinnéar le Mac Roibín agus a bhean, agus chuamar go dtí léacht a thug an tAthair Yorke don Emmet Club. Is é an tAthair Yorke an cainteoir is fearr dár chuala mé riamh. Tá glór deas binn aige ar nós stoc airgid, a dtaithníonn a fhuaim le do chluasa. Tosaíonn sé go mall éadrom agus cuireann sé fonn gáire agus mian éisteachta ar a bhfuil i láthair. Ansin labhraíonn sé go han-chéillí leo ag cur síos ar an rud atá i gceist aige, agus ag deireadh a chainte méadaíonn a ghlór de réir a chéile, agus é ag labhairt ar nós file, agus críochnaíonn sé a óráid le stoirm den phrósfhilíocht is glaine agus is áille dár chuala cluas ariamh. Gan aon amhras is é an cainteoir is fearr agus an tÉireannach is ábalta dár casadh orm riamh é. Tháinig mé abhaile ar a haon a chlog.

An tríú lá de Mhárta. Chuaigh mé féin agus mo bhean trasna an chuain arís go dtí Ollscoil Berkeley, áit a raibh mé leis an léacht dheireanach a thabhairt uaim inniu. Bhí lón againn leis an Ollamh Miller agus a bhean. Bhí an tAthair Yorke ag an lón, agus duine de Choimisinéirí na Stát Aontaithe a cuireadh go dtí na hOileáin Fhilipíneacha chun cuntas a thabhairt abhaile ar cheist an oideachais sna hOileáin sin. Ní cuimhin liom ainm an fhir seo, ach shíl mé go raibh sé go han-chaolintinneach.

Bhí socair go labhróinn san Amharclann Ghréagach, áit nach bhfuil a mhaca-samhail eile sna Stáit, nó b'fhéidir sa domhan. Amharclann chiorclach amuigh faoin spéir atá ann, gan aon díon air. Tá b'fhéidir deich nó fiche líne de shuíocháin ag dul timpeall trí cheathrú den chiorcal, gach line díobh rud beag níos airde ná a chéile. Tá cnocáinín beag agus crainn ar a chúl, agus tá sé tógtha ar shlí ar féidir leis na daoine ar na suíocháin gach rud a chloisteáil, chomh maith agus dá mbeidís i dteach. Tá sé déanta go díreach ar lorg agus ar nós sean-amharclann Ghréagach. Duine éigin a bhí ina chúntóir don Ollscoil a thug dóibh é. Ba é Benjamin Ide Wheeler, an tUachtarán, a chuimhnigh ar a dhéanamh. Tháinig sé féin go dtí na ceithre léacht a thug mé uaim, gach aon cheann acu, agus thaispeáin sé an áit iontach seo dom, ach faraor! Tháinig an lá fliuch, agus níor fhéad mé triail a bhaint as, óir b'éigean dúinn go léir dul isteach sa halla mór as an bhfearthainn. Bhí an tAthair Yorke i gceannas an chruinnithe, óir is duine de lucht stiúrtha na hOllscoile é. Bhí timpeall dhá chéad déag duine i láthair. Labhair mé ar bhéaloideas agus thaithnigh mo chuid cainte chomh mór sin leis an Athair Yorke go bhfuair sé cóip den óráid uaim, agus gur chlóbhuail sé ina pháipéar féin an *Leader* é. Thángamar ar ais ar a sé a chlog, tuirseach go leor.

Dé Domhnaigh, an ceathrú lá de Mhárta. Chuaigh mé ar maidin go hEaglais an Dochtúra Clampett, an fear a labhair ag an bhfleá mhór. Is ó Choláiste na Tríonóide i

an taṫair YORKE

Father Peter Yorke. Le caoinchead Fhoras na Gaeilge

mBaile Átha Cliath é, ach gan amhras tá sé ina Éireannach maith. Tháinig an tAthair Ó Riain idir a dó agus a trí le mo thabhairt amach go dtí an Pháirc chun cluiche iománaíochta agus cluiche peile a fheiceáil. Chaith mise an liathróid isteach i measc an lucht imeartha, agus nuair a bhí na cluichí críochnaithe rinne mé beagán cainte, ar dtús le lucht na gcamán agus ina dhiaidh sin le lucht na peile. Ní fhaca mé riamh iománaíocht ab fhearr ná a chonaic mé an lá sin. As Cúige Mumhan cuid mhór den lucht imeartha agus bhí an Ghaeilge ag cuid acu. Níor imríodh riamh, in Éirinn féin, cluiche ba ghéire ná é sin. An t-airgead a fuaireadar ag an ngeata, 325 dollar, tugadh é go léir do Chonradh na Gaeilge.

Chuamar chun dinnéir leis na Súilleabhánaigh sa tráthnóna. Is iad a thugann na dinnéir is fearr dár ith mé sa tír seo, agus ar ndóigh ní dhéantar dearmad ar an *unum porro* – 'an t-aon rud atá riachtanach.' Focal é sin a chuala mé ó chléireach anseo, ach chuala mé cheana sa bhaile é.

Gach uair a dtéimid amach chun dinnéir, cuir i gcás nach mbeimis ag dul ach trí shráid ón teach ósta, caithfimid ceithre dhollar a íoc, dhá cheann ag dul ann agus dhá cheann ag teacht ar ais. Tá na cóistí is costasaí i Meiriceá anseo.

An cúigiú lá. Tháinig an tAthair Yorke, an tAthair Ó Riain agus eagarthóir pháipéar an Athar Yorke – Ó Dreada ab ainm dó – ar cuairt chugainn. Nuair a bhíodar imithe chuamar suas go barr an Spreckels Building, agus bhí radharc álainn againn uaidh, ar an gCathair agus ar an gcuan. Tá an Gearmánach Spreckels ar na daoine is saibhre san Iarthar, agus tá Séamas Ó Faoláin beagnach chomh saibhir leis. Casadh Proinsias Ó Súilleabháin orainn ag dul abhaile, agus thug sé sinn leis chun rudaí a bhí ag na daoine a tháinig chun na tíre seo ar dtús a thaispeáint dúinn. Bhí seanbhratacha ann agus seanghunnaí agus seanairm agus seanéadaí, agus bhíomar ag féachaint orthu, beagnach go dtí gur lúb na cosa fúinn. Ach ansin thug sé go dtí an Pup sinn, teach bia atá aige, agus thug buidéal *champagne* agus suipéar dúinn. Chuamar ar ais go moch, agus bhíomar go han-tuirseach.

An séú lá de Mhárta. D'fhág mé an teach ar maidin le dul go Sacramento. Casadh an tAthair Yorke orm ag Oakland, agus chuamar le chéile go Sacramento. Chuaigh an traein iomlán ar bord soithigh mhóir ag dul trasna an uisce. Tá an séasúr chun lachain a mharú go díreach thart anois, ach bhí na mílte agus na mílte lachan fiáin, idir *canvas backs* agus eile, ar gach taobh den traein. D'imigh an traein ar bhóthar a bhí tógtha ar phostaí adhmaid os cionn an uisce.* Bhí na lachain i bhfoisceacht fiche slat don traein, agus níor cuireadh scanradh ar bith orthu. Shílfeá go raibh a fhios acu go raibh an

*Nuair a tháinig an crith talún d'imigh cúpla míle den bhóthar seo as amharc ar fad.

séasúr thart. Tír fhliuch íseal í seo, agus téann an chuid is mó den bhóthar iarainn trí uisce agus locha agus léanta. Tá an-tóir ag na lachain agus ag na géanna fiáine ar an áit seo. Chonaic mé buachaill agus cúig nó sé cinn de ghéanna fiáine a mharaigh sé aniar ar a dhroim aige. Ní dóigh liom gur tír shláintiúil an tír seo, ach amháin d'éanlaith uisce.

Is é Sacramento príomhchathair an Stáit agus is ann a bhíonn an Pharlaimint ina suí. Tá idir fiche agus tríocha míle duine ann. Tháinig an tAthair Ellis inár gcoinne, sagart breá óg agus príomhthaca na Gaeilge i Sacramento. Thug sé sinn chun dinnéir leis an Dochtúir de Grása, an tEaspag. Bhí fleá bhreá aigesean dúinn agus bhí sé go lách cineálta linn. Bhí mórán aíonna eile aige, agus ina measc bhí Moinsíneoir Capel. B'fhear an-ábalta agus an-chlúiteach lena linn an fear seo. Tá a phictiúr tugtha ag Disraeli san úrscéal, *Lothair*, faoi ainm bréige Moinsíneoir Catesby. Ba é a rinne Caitliceach den tríú Marcas de Baoithe. Chuala mé gur tháinig imreas éigin idir é féin agus an Cairdinéal Manning, agus gur díbríodh chun San Francisco é. Nuair a tháinig sé go San Francisco thaispeáin sé é féin bheith ina namhaid mhór do na hÉireannaigh, agus bhí a fhios sin go maith acusan. Rinne seanfhear acu spíodóireacht air agus thug sé a scéala don Ard-Easpag agus díbríodh arís é go dtí an áit seo. Tháinig sé isteach le bheith i láthair ag an gcruinniú a bhí agamsa. Bhí sé ag caitheamh cnaipe a raibh mo dhealbhsa agus cúpla focal Gaeilge buailte air. Rinneadh an cnaipe seo in San Francisco ó tháinig mise ann. Bhí an Moinsíneoir go cúirtéiseach, go greannúil agus go líofa. Is mór an trua é duine mar eisean a bheith sáite in áitín iargúlta mar seo.

Bhí cruinniú breá agam. Bhí Pardee, Gobharnóir an Stáit, sa chathaoir agus labhair sé go han-mhaith. Bhí an Rabbi Giúdach ann chomh maith, agus bhí an amharclann lán go doras. Nuair a bhí mise réidh thug an tAthair Yorke ceann de na hóráidí is fearr uaidh dár chuala mé riamh, agus thóg sé aigne na ndaoine ar shlí nach bhfaca mé go dtí sin. Fuaireamar 900 dollar an oíche sin. Is mór an tsuim airgid í sin má chuimhnítear ar chomh beag agus atá an baile. Ní dhearnamar níos fearr, ná chomh maith féin, in aon áit eile, má chuirtear méid an airgid i gcomórtas le méid an bhaile mhóir. Chaith mé féin agus an tAthair Yorke an oíche i dteach ósta i Sacramento, agus bhí cúpla buidéal fíona againn a bhí ag teastáil uainn go mór tar éis ár n-oibre. Nuair a deirtear an focal 'fíon' san tír seo, *champagne* an chiall a bhíonn leis. Ní deirtear aon rud eile ach 'fíon.'

An seachtú lá de Mhárta. Chaith mé féin agus an tAthair Yorke an mhaidin ag tiomáint timpeall Sacramento. Chuaigh mé isteach sa leabharlann a bhí ag an Seanad, agus na trí leabhar tosaigh a tharraing mé amach ó na cláir, cad a bhí iontu ach trí lámhscríbhinn Gaeilge! Ní raibh a fhios ag éinne cad a thug ansin iad. Trí chinniúint a chuir mise mo lámh orthu. *'Quae Regio in terris nostri non plena laboris,'* arsa mise.

D'fhágamar Sacramento ar a haon a chlog agus thángamar ar ais go hOakland ar a ceathair, áit ar chaith mé dinnéar leis an Athair Yorke agus lena bheirt séiplíneach. Thug sé moladh mór domsa. 'Chuala mé thú,' ar seisean, 'ag tabhairt na léachta sin uait ceithre huaire anois, agus níl aon uair dár chualas thú nár bhuail sé in áit nua mé.' D'imigh sé leis go San Francisco, ach thiomáin mise go dtí Coláiste na mBráithre Críostaí, agus thug mé léacht uaim do thimpcall dhá mhíle duine. Sórt léachta measctha a thug mé dóibh, a raibh giotaí inti as mo léachtanna go léir. Thug na Bráithre abhaile leo mé, agus bhí suipéar agus neart fíona acu. Bhí sé a haon a chlog san oíche nuair a ráinigh mé San Francisco.

An t-ochtú lá de Mhárta. D'fhág mé féin agus mo bhean San Francisco ar a hocht ar maidin le dul ó dheas, tar éis drochoíche chodlata, óir bhí sé déanach nuair a tháinig mise go dtí an teach ósta aréir. B'éigean dúinn ár gcuid éadaigh go léir a phacáil, agus thugamar cuid de linn agus d'fhágamar an chuid eile sa teach ósta.

Bhíomar ag dul ó dheas anois, agus an fharraige ar thaobh na láimhe deise dínn. Chuamar trí chéad míle agus ní raibh nóiméad den turas sin nárbh fhiú féachaint ar an amharc álainn. Bhí an t-aigéan ann in áiteanna, agus in áiteanna eile bhí cnocáin agus sléibhte, agus coillte a raibh gach uile shórt measa orthu agus garráin den dair shíorghlas ar a dtugtar *ilex*, crann a bhfuil fás breá faoi anseo. Nuair a tháinig an tráthnóna bhíomar chomh fada le Santa Barbara, ar ár mbealach go Los Angeles.

Stadamar ag Santa Barbara agus chuireamar fúinn i dteach ósta Potter, atá tógtha ar bhá fhíorálainn. San oíche bhí an teach mór seo in aon lasair sholais amháin. Tá cosán álainn go dtí an fharraige ann, agus tá pailmeacha móra ag fás ar thaobh gach cosáin acu. Áit í seo a bhfuil tóir uirthi ag lucht na milliún, idir fhear agus bhean. Ní fhaca mé riamh an oiread sin daoine a raibh an oiread éadaigh agus an oiread ornáidí orthu. Ach cé go raibh cosúlacht an tsaibhris ar an áit cheap mise go raibh drochbholadh le fáil sa teach go léir. Easpa draenála, mar a shíl mise, ba chionsiocair leis. In ainneoin mhéid agus ghalántacht agus bhreáthacht na háite bhí sí go míchompordach.

Timpeall leathuair i ndiaidh a deich san oíche tháinig mo sheanchara, Labhrás Breannóc, amach ó Los Angeles chugam, rud a chuir áthas orm, óir bhí mo chuid airgid ag teacht gearr, agus bhí eagla orm nach nglacfaí seiceanna uaim. Fuair mé mo sháith airgid ar iasacht uaidhsean. Ó tharla mé bheith ag trácht ar airgead, ní mór dom a rá nach bhfeictear páipéar ach go hannamh amuigh anseo. Baineann siad úsáid as ór agus as airgead geal, ach ní fheictear copar ar chor ar bith. Chonaic mé, lá, i San Francisco, fear ón Oirthear ag íoc as a shuíochán ar an tram le cúig cent copair, agus toisc nach raibh aon áit ina mhála do chopar céard a rinne fear an chairr ach na cúig phíosa bheaga a chaitheamh amach ar an mbóthar arís go tarcaisneach.

Joe Scott. Le caoinchead Fhoras na Gaeilge

An naoú lá de Mhárta. D'éiríomar go moch ar maidin, agus chuamar ar an traein go Los Angeles, timpeall a seacht a chlog ar maidin, in éineacht leis an mBreannócach agus le Joe Scott. Nuair a bhí mé féin agus an tAthair Yorke ag teacht abhaile ó Sacramento bhí Scott sa charráiste céanna linn, ach bhí mise róthuirseach chun caint a dhéanamh leis, agus d'fhág mé faoin Athair Yorke é. Chuaigh an traein le cois an chósta timpeall céad míle, agus ní raibh mé riamh ar thuras a bhí chomh hálainn leis. Tá dhá líne de bhóithre iarainn ag dul ó San Francisco go Los Angeles, ceann acu trí lár California, tríd an ngleann mór San Joaquin, ('Uácin' a deirtear sa chaint), agus an ceann eile cois na farraige. Chonaiceamar ar gach taobh na coiníní beaga a dtugann siad *gopher* orthu ina seasamh in airde ar a gcosa deiridh, agus ioraí rua, agus corrchoinín mór. Os ár gcionn bhí a lán de bhultúir thurcacha.

Tháinig Coiste an Fháiltithe cúig mhíle amach faoinár gcoinne, agus bus tralaí speisialta acu. Ansin tógadh grianghraif dínn arís agus arís eile, agus faoi dheireadh ligeadh síos ag teach ósta Alexander sinn. Chaith mé an tráthnóna ag dul timpeall na háite leis an mBreannócach agus le Joe Scott.

An deichiú lá de Mhárta. Tugadh sinn amach inniu i ngluaisteán leis an Dochtúir Jones, ón mBreatain Bheag, Bean Uí Bhriain, Iníon Dhiolúin, agus Mac Giollarnáth. Fear óg an-Ghaelach é seo; dlíodóir atá ann. Tugadh amach sinn go Pasadena, cúpla míle taobh amuigh den chathair. I bhfad uainn bhí Mount Lowe le feiceáil agus *sierra* de shléibhte áille ar a chúl, agus eatarthu sin agus an chathair bhí Pasadena. Ag dul trí Pasadena dom bhuail mé isteach ar cuairt chun Micheáil Uí Chuidithe agus a bhean, an pacaire saibhir ó Chicago. Is é an chiall atá leis an bhfocal pacaire i Meiriceá, duine a chuireas feoil i gcáis bheaga dhlútha stáin lena ndíol. Sin é an rud a dhéantar i Chicago leis na mílte agus na mílte bológ agus muc ón Iarthar.

Nuair a chuala sé go raibh mé i láthair ag triail Phat Cró faoi mhac a dhearthár a ghoid, chuir sé cluas air féin. Ba shuimiúil an scéal sin leis. Dúirt mé cheana go raibh sé ina shuí le m'ais ag an dinnéar a thug an tArd-Easpag Ó Ríordáin dom, agus níl a fhios agam cé acu a d'oibrigh air, a chaint liomsa, nó a mhuintearas leis an Ard-Easpag, ach thug sé cúig chéad dollar don chruinniú a bhí in Los Angeles.

Is i bPasadena atá na milliúnaithe Meiriceánacha le fáil. Is ann atá na tithe is breátha, agus na gairdíní is áille. Tá an áit lán de chrainn phailme, de chrainn oráistí, agus de chrainn phiobair. Is an-álainn an crann é an crann piobair, lena chuid craobhacha tanaí caomha ar nós acáise ag sileadh anuas as. Chaitheamar lón ag teach ósta Green, ceann de na tithe ósta is mó den sórt seo dá bhfaca mé. Ansin d'imíomar romhainn ar cuairt go feirm chlúiteach éigin a bhí sa chomharsanacht. Bhí sé i seilbh choirnéil éigin, ní cuimhin liom an t-ainm a bhí air. Bhí a chúis dá plé sna cúirteanna tamall ó shin de

an tÁrd-easbog ó Ríoġḃardáin

Archbishop Patrick William Riordan of San Francisco. Le caoinchead Fhoras na Gaeilge bhrí gur bhris sé a fhocal. Gealladh pósta nó rud éigin den sórt sin a bhí i gceist, agus is é an leithscéal a rinne seisean dá chosaint féin, go raibh an oiread sin droch-cháile air, gurbh amaideach a rá gur chreid aon duine eile a fhocal!

Chuamar trí go leor garrán oráiste agus garrán líomóide. Bhí ceithre nó cúig acra i gcuid de na garráin nó coillte beaga oráiste. Bhain mé trí nó ceithre cinn de na horáistí de chrann in áit iargúlta. Tá siad chomh coitianta anseo nach aon dochar é don duine a bhíonn ag dul thar bráid ceann acu a bhaint, áit ar bith nach bhfuil cumhdach cosanta de shreang iarainn ina thimpeall.

Thángamar ar ais díreach in am le héadaí tráthnóna a chur orainn féin, le dul chun dinnéir leis an Easpag, an Dochtúir Ó Connachtaigh nó Conaty. Fear an-gheanúil an-lách an tEaspag seo, agus fear é atá an-fhábhrach dúinne. Dhá lá sular chaitheamar dinnéar leis, bhris gadaithe isteach ina theach agus goideadh a lán rudaí uaidh, uaireadóirí agus fáinní, etc.

Bhí páirtí mór aige ag an dinnéar, agus páirtí an-ghreannmhar, gan aon locht air ach nach raibh aon rud le n-ól againn ach uisce. Bhí iníon dheirfiúr an Easpaig, Loingseach a hainm, agus Iníon Uí Raghallaigh ó Bhostún, agus cantaire mór amhrán, ar a dtugadh Karl, i láthair – fuair mé amach ina dhiaidh sin gur Cearúill ainm dílis an amhránaí. Bhí na Scotaigh agus daoine eile ann, agus bhí a lán amhránaíochta againn.

An t-aonú lá déag de Mhárta. Inniu an Domhnach. B'éigean dom éirí go han-mhoch le dul chun an teampaill ag leathuair i ndiaidh a seacht, óir bhí gach uile rud socair roimh ré dom ag an gCoiste Gnótha a bhí agam.

Bhí bricfeasta faoi dheifir againn agus d'fhágamar Los Angeles ar a naoi a chlog. Bhí Joe Scott agus a bhean, agus an Breannócach agus an Bóidicíneach, uncail do mo chara an Dochtúir Ó Coisdeala i dTuaim, agus timpeall fiche duine eile linn. Bhíomar le dul go Catalina, oileán atá turas cúpla uair an chloig amach san fharraige. Is aisteach an chathair í Los Angeles, óir níl sí suite ar an bhfarraige. Thóg na Spáinnigh í fiche nó tríocha míle isteach ón bhfarraige ag súil nach bhfeicfeadh an loingeas Sasanach í, agus nach bhféadfaidís í a scrios ón muir. Is í an dara cathair i gCalifornia í, agus tá beagnach dhá chéad míle duine inti. Ach ní léir conas a mhaireann na daoine inti. Níl aon loingeas ag teacht isteach inti, ná aon tráchtáil á déanamh aici le háiteanna thar lear, agus níl aon earra á dhéanamh inti, ná aon mhonarcha inti, agus, chomh fada agus is léir domsa, is ar cháil a spéire agus ar áilleacht na tíre ina timpeall atá an chathair ag brath. Bhí fiche míle againn le dul go dtí an cósta chun long a fháil go Catalina. Chualamar scéalta iontacha i dtaobh an oileáin seo, go raibh an t-uisce chomh glan sin go bhféadfadh an bádóir na héisc a fheiceáil agus iad ag snámh deich nó fiche feá faoi, go raibh íochtar gloine sna báid, agus go bhfeicfí na siorcanna fúthu agus

an teasbog ó connaċtaiġ

Thomas James Conaty, Bishop of Los Angeles. Le caoinchead Fhoras na Gaeilge éiscíní beaga, timpeall chomh mór le scadán, amach roimh a sróna ag déanamh an eolais dóibh. Sin iad na scéalta a chualamar go raibh bruith laidhre orainn an áit thar áiteanna seo a fheiceáil. Ach ní mar a shíltear a bhítear. Bhí stoirm ag tuar ó mhaidin. Nuair a shroicheamar an fharraige tháinig sé ina ghála agus ina chlagarnach báistí orainn. Fuair mé féin agus mo bhean cábán agus luíomar síos. Sheolamar amach ar an bhfarraige gharbh, agus is ar éigean a thángamar slán gan tinneas. Nuair a ráiníomar an t-oileán tar éis cúpla uair an chloig bhí an áit go léir múchta faoi smúid báistí. Ní raibh aon rud le feiceáil ná aon rud le déanamh ach suí sa teach ósta agus trí huaire a chaitheamh ann go hanróiteach, go raibh an bád ag dul ar ais go dtí an mhórthír arís. Chuamar isteach inti gan iasc ná siorc ná bád ná an t-oileán féin a fheiceáil. Ach bhí an t-ádh orainn go bhfuaireamar cábán dúinn féin arís, óir má bhí an fharraige go garbh ag gabháil amach dúinn ba sheacht measa í ag dul abhaile. Nuair a tháinig an long chun tíre ritheamar linn go dtí an tram a bhí ag filleadh go Los Angeles. Ach ní fada a bhíomar inti seo gur thugamar faoi deara gluaiseacht agus corraí i measc na muintire a bhí istigh. I gcionn tamaillín ba léir dúinn an fáth. Thosaigh an t-uisce ag teacht isteach orainn trí chumhdach an chóiste. I gceann tamaillín bhí an fhearthainn ag titim orainn ina tuile, agus éinne a raibh scáth fearthainne aige d'oscail sé suas é. Rinne sin an scéal níos measa do na daoine nach raibh scáth acu. Déarfá go raibh an t-uisce ag teacht anuas orainn trí chriathar. Ba léir dom, uaidh sin, go mba fhíorbhreá, fhíorálainn, gnáthaimsir na háite seo, óir dá mba rud coitianta an fhearthainn seo, bheadh cumhdaigh ar na carranna nach ligfeadh an t-uisce tríothu. Nuair a thángamar isteach go dtí an chathair bhí tuile ar na sráideanna romhainn. Bhí gach sráid ina habhainn. Níl aon draein acu chun an t-uisce a thabhairt leis, agus b'éigean dóibh cláir mhóra a leagan trasna gach sráide ó thaobh go chéile. D'iarr mo bhean dul trasna na sráide ar cheann acu seo, agus fliuchadh go dtí na rúitíní í. Ach faoi dheireadh thángamar go dtí an teach ósta, beagnach marbh, agus fliuch go craiceann. Bhí sé chomh fliuch sin nár fhéad éinne teacht in aice linn, agus fágadh fúinn féin sinn an chuid eile den lá, agus bhíomar go buíoch mar gheall air sin!

An dara lá déag de Mhárta. Bhí sé ag stealladh fearthainne arís inniu, agus seo é an lá a bhí socraithe i gcomhair mo léachta. Bhí gach suíochán san amharclann díolta, ach nuair a tháinig an t-am bhí sé ag clagarnach báistí fós. Tháinig mórán daoine ar na carranna go dtí an doras, ach nuair a fuaireadar abhainn eatarthu féin agus an amharclann, b'fhearr leo dul abhaile arís ná teacht isteach agus a gcosa fliuch. Na daoine a tháinig, tá mé cinnte go raibh an t-uisce os cionn a gcuid bróg. Nuair a bhí mé ag labhairt d'éirigh an t-uisce, mar a chuala mé, sé troithe sa bhunurlár, agus bhí slua daoine á thaoscadh amach. Ní raibh an amharclann níos mó ná leathlán, ach mar sin féin cruinníodh cuid mhaith airgid. Labhair mé féin uair agus trí cheathrú. Thug an tEaspag Ó Connachtaigh óráid fhíorbhreá uaidh, an óráid is fearr a chuala mé ó aon Easpag fós. Chuamar ar ais chun suipéir le muintir Scott. Is leath-Spáinneach bean Joe Scott. Bhí siad an-lách linn. Thángamar ar ais leathuair tar éis a haon a chlog.

An tríú lá déag de Mhárta. Chuaigh mé go Coláiste San Vincent ar a dó agus labhair mé ar feadh uair go leith ar na trí chéad bliain deiridh de litríocht na Gaeilge. Is coláiste mór é seo, atá faoi stiúir na sagart Caitliceach. Ar éigean a bhí deireadh ráite agam nuair a sádh isteach i ngluaisteán mé, agus thug toscaireacht ban ó Chlub na mBan amach mé go dtí Teach an Chlub. 'Club Mhaidin Dé hAoine' is ainm dó, agus tá baint ag timpeall cúig nó sé chéad de na mná uaisle is fearr i Los Angeles leis. Tá mé cinnte gur chroith mé lámha le trí nó ceithre chéad acu. Bhí cuid acu ann a bhí óg álainn, agus cuid eile nach raibh. Agus iadsan nach raibh thug mé faoi deara nár fhágadar iadsan a bhí i bhfad ag caint liom. Tar éis tamaill tugadh mé isteach san halla mór a bhí sa chlub, chun caint a dhéanamh leo. Ní raibh a fhios agam ar thalamh an domhain cad a déarfainn. Ach chuir duine éigin cogar i mo chluais 'Abair rud éigin faoi.....a cailleadh inné.' Ní cuimhin liom an t-ainm anois, agus níor chuala mé trácht riamh uirthi, roimhe sin nó ina dhiaidh, cérbh í féin nó céard a rinne sí. Mar sin féin chuir mé brat bróin mar dhea i mo thimpeall agus shílfeadh duine go mba bhean ghaoil dom féin í. Dúirt mé go mba chosúil an chathair a raibh siad ina gcónaí inti le Cathair na hAithne, nach raibh loingeas ná tráchtáil ná lucht déanta earraí ina gcathair agus go mba fhíor-Aithin é thar chathracha eile Mheiriceá. Dúirt mé go bhfuair mé amach go raibh mná uaisle Mheiriceá i bhfad níos intleachtaí ná a gcuid fear. Thaithnigh sé sin go mór leo agus is dóigh gur fíor é, leis. Mrs Aubrey Davidson ab ainm don bhean uasal a bhí i gceannas, agus b'fhíorbhean uasal í, agus sílim go raibh sí ábalta intleachtach, chomh maith. Agus ar ndóigh bhí mórán de na mná seo agus is dóigh liom go raibh siad go han-deas.

Is ar éigean a bhí an t-am agam, tar éis na mná uaisle seo a fhágáil, chun mo chuid éadaigh tráthnóna a chur orm, nuair a glaodh orm dul go dinnéar an Chlub Cheiltigh. Éireannaigh, Albanaigh agus Breatnaigh atá sa Chlub seo. Is í seo an t-aon chathair amháin a bhfuair mé na Ceiltigh ag teacht le chéile as na trí thír seo. Maolcholaim Mac Leóid, Albanach, a bhí i gceannas an dinnéir, agus bhí ceithre fichid duine i láthair. Labhair daoine de gach cine de na trí cinn. B'iontach liom iad a fheiceáil ag obair as lámh a chéile mar sin, óir níor shíl mé go bhféadfadh oiread sin aontaithe a bheith eatarthu. Is club nua é seo ach tá súil acu brainsí a bhunú i San Francisco agus in áiteanna eile. Ar ndóigh ghabhadar le chéile *The Bonny Bonny Banks of Loch Lomond*, amhail agus dá mba é a fhonn dúchasach féin ag gach duine acu é. Bhí an tEaspag

Hamilton ó San Francisco i láthair, Meitidisteach sílim, agus thug seisean isteach an t-aon nóta polaitíochta amháin; thug sé buíochas do Dhia go poiblí nár Angla-Shacsanach é, agus chuireadar go léir gáir áthais astu. Cuireadh m'ainm féin i láthair an chlub, agus toghadh mé i mo chéad bhall onórach den chéad Chlub Ceilteach i Meiriceá. Bhí an locht céanna ar an dinnéar seo a bhí ar dhinnéar an Easpaig – nach raibh le n-ól againn ach uisce. Chuir mé ceist ina thaobh seo ina dhiaidh sin, agus mhínigh an tAthair Yorke dom go raibh a lán Poncán i Los Angeles, agus go raibh a lán de mhianach na bPiúratánach agus d'intinn Shasana Nua iontu. Níorbh ionann é sin agus San Francisco – daoine ag ligean orthu nach n-ólfaidís, agus a fhios ag an domhan gur rith gach éinne acu amach go dtí an beár, tar éis an dinnéir, chun deoch a fháil dó féin. Cráifeacht bhréige í sin!

Casadh fear as m'áit féin orm anseo, mac do Nioclás Ó Náraigh ón gCaladh. Rinne sé carn airgid dó féin anseo ag díol éadaigh, nó *dry goods*, mar a thugann siad orthu. Thug sé céad dollar de shíntiús dom, agus, rud a thaithnigh liom an nóiméad sin beagnach chomh mór leis an síntiús, buidéal fíona, nuair a bhí an dinnéar oifigiúil críochnaithe.

An ceathrú lá déag de Mhárta. Bhíomar le dul ar ais go dtí San Francisco inniu. Ach thug Joe Scott amach sinn go dtí Chutes Park, chun Indiaigh ó na hOileáin Fhilipíneacha a fheiceáil. Ignarote an t-ainm a bhí orthu. Bhí dáréag acu ann. Bhí na craicne ab áille dá bhfaca mé riamh orthu ar dhath copair agus é éadrom te soilseach. Ní raibh aon éadaí orthu ach banda beag caol timpeall a láir. Lucht seilge ceann a bhí iontu agus is féidir leo beagán obair mhiotail a dhéanamh, freisin. Thug siad taispeántas uathu, ag caitheamh gath, ag seinm amhrán, etc. Thug sé sinn ar ais ina dhiaidh sin go dtí Club California, agus thug lón maith dúinn, agus chuir ar bord na traenach sinn le filleadh go San Francisco. Tháinig go leor daoine chun an stáisiúin linn le slán a fhágáil againn. Níorbh fhéidir cineáltas mhuintir Los Angeles a shárú.

An cúigiú lá déag de Mhárta. Bhíomar ag taisteal sa traein ar feadh na hoíche. Ráiníomar San Francisco ar a deich ar maidin agus chuamar ar ais go dtí teach ósta St Francis arís. Rinne an tuile mhór bháistí a bhí ann nuair a bhíomar ag Los Angeles dochar mór don bhóthar iarainn. Ghlan sí amach an chréafóg a bhí faoi na ráillí, agus b'éigean dúinn snámhaíocht ar chuid mhór den bhóthar, go mall mall. Fuaireamar traein romhainn a scriosadh beagán uair an chloig romhainne. Bhí an t-inneall ina luí ar thaobh an bhóthair, agus bhí sé charráiste briste ina luí ar an taobh eile. Bhí an t-ádh orainne nach rabhamar féin inti. Tá timpistí an-choitianta ar an mbóthar iarainn seo, óir ní rófhada ó cuireadh suas é.

Nuair a bhí ár gcuid éadaigh athraithe againn, rinneamar ar Halla Naomh Peadar. Is leis an Athair Ó Cathasaigh é, fear an-lách. Labhair mé ansin le timpeall míle duine, mná rialta, múinteoirí agus scoláirí na n-ardscoileanna. Ní bhíonn scrupall ar bith ar na mná rialta teacht go dtí mo chuid léachtaí sa tír seo. Suíonn siad i measc na ndaoine eile. Ní dhéanann siad sin in Éirinn. Dá labhróinn, cuir i gcás, ina gclochar féin in Éirinn, ní éistfeadh cuid acu liom ach ar chúl scátha éigin. Labhair an tAthair Yorke, chomh maith, agus labhair sé go breá mar is gnáth leis.

Nuair a tháinig mé ar ais ón Athair Ó Cathasaigh tar éis neart a fháil le n-ithe agus le n-ól, b'éigean dom éadaí tráthnóna a chur orm agus rith amach arís go dtí dinnéar mór a thug Ridirí Naomh Pádraig. Ba bhreá an dinnéar é. Bhí dhá chéad de na hÉireannaigh is fearr i gcathair San Francisco i láthair. Tugadh an chéad tósta domsa le labhairt ar 'An lá atáimid a mhóradh.' Bhí an Faolánach, an Súilleabhánach, an tAthair Yorke, agus Mac Roibín an mianadóir, i láthair freisin. Bhí cuid mhaith óráidí agus cuid mhaith amhrán, ach níor síneadh amach é go rófhada, agus bhí mé ar m'ais ar a haon a chlog. Ní raibh an locht céanna ar an dinnéar seo a bhí ar an dá dhinnéar eile a bhí agam in Los Angeles!

An séú lá déag. Thug Proinsias Ó Súilleabháin leis mé go San José, atá daichead nó caoga míle ó dheas de San Francisco, agus as sin go Coláiste Chumann Íosa, Santa Clara. Thug mé léacht ar litríocht na Gaeilge uaim ansin. Bhí rud le n-ithe againn leis na sagairt agus bhí go leor amhránaíochta agus cainteoireachta ann, agus níor thángamar ar ais go dtí ár dteach ósta i San José go dtí a dó san oíche, agus ba mé a bhí tuirseach traochta. Is é an tAthair Ó Gliasáin uachtarán an Choláiste.

An seachtú lá déag de Mhárta. Lá Fhéile Pádraig atá ann inniu, agus b'éigean dom éirí ar a seacht a chlog ar maidin le dul ar ais go San Francisco leis an Súilleabhánach: óir clóbhuaileadh é ar chlár oifigiúil mo thurais go raibh mé le dul in éineacht le Proinsias Ó Súilleabháin go teampall an Athar Mag Uinseannáin, chun éisteacht le seanmóir speisialta i nGaeilge, agus leis an gCoróin Mhuire i nGaeilge. Bhí an bóthar iarainn, mar ba ghnáth leis, go lag, agus bhí an traein go mall, agus bhíomar uair an chloig mall nuair a shiúil an Súilleabhánach agus mé féin go doras an teampaill. Bhí beirt ag faire ag fanacht linn taobh amuigh den teampall agus níor chaill siad sin nóiméad, ach sheoladar isteach tríd an doras sa teampall sinn, i measc na ndaoine. Shiúlamar síos leo, trí lár an teampaill, agus níor stopadar gur fhágadar sinn inár seasamh ag ráillí na haltóra, mar a bheadh beirt amadán ann, agus bhí súile dhá mhíle duine greamaithe ionainn. Ach d'oscail sagart a bhí taobh istigh de na ráillí doras beag agus thug dhá chathaoir dúinn le hais na haltóra, agus shuigh Proinsias agus mé féin ansin ar feadh an chuid eile den Ard-Aifreann, agus ar feadh na seanmóra Gaeilge. Bhí a fhios agam go raibh gach éinne sa teampall ag breathnú go grinn orainne, cois na haltóra, agus bhí mé ag corraí i ndiaidh a chéile gur chuir mé cuid de chrois a bhí ann, idir mé féin agus na daoine ab fhoisce dom. Maidir leis an tseanmóir Ghaeilge bhí cúl an tsagairt liom, agus clár torannach os a chionn, agus theip orm oiread agus focal amháin a chloisteáil. Ach maidir leis an gCoróin Mhuire chuir sé gliondar ar mo chroí mar a tugadh na freagraí i nGaeilge. D'fhreagair, dar liomsa, beagnach gach duine a bhí sa teampall i nGaeilge. Rinne an tAthair Mag Uinseannáin úsáid, den chéad uair, mar a dúirt sé linn, de phaidrín de chlocha marmair ó Chonamara.

Tar éis lóin bhreá a chaitheamh leis an Athair Mag Uinseannáin, rugadh mé go halla mór na *Native Sons*, agus fuair mé slua mór daoine agus mórán cainteoirí ansin romham. Labhair mé féin Gaeilge leo ar feadh cúig nóiméad fichead. Níor labhair mé focal Béarla leo. Ba léir dom gur thuig a bhformhór mé. Níor fhan mé go dtí an deireadh, bhí mé chomh sáraithe sin. Chuaigh mé ar ais chun an tí ósta agus chaith mé mé féin ar mo leaba ar feadh uair an chloig. Ansin b'éigean dom éirí agus imeacht go dtí an *Mechanics' Pavilion*. Bhí seacht míle duine i láthair romham. Is áit chéasta í seo do chainteoir poiblí. Tá an halla cúig chéad troigh ar fad agus tá sé leathan dá réir! Urlár clár atá ann. Taobh-bhallaí déanta d'adhmad air. Macalla ann nach gcuirfí macalla Chill Airne i gcomparáid leis! Áras ann féin a bhí ann. Bhí rincí ar siúl i dtosach, ach tar éis tamaill tugadh amach stáitse ar rothaí, agus tiomáineadh isteach i lár an halla é. Chruinnigh na mílte ina thimpeall ar ball. Chuaigh mé féin agus an tAthair Yorke in airde air, agus rinne mé mo dhícheall óráid a dhéanamh, ach b'fhánach mo ghnó dom. Chas mé thart i ngach aird, soir, siar, thuaidh, agus theas. Labhair mé trí mheigeafón ansin. Bhéic, liúigh, scread mé. Rinne mé geáitsí i gcaoi go bhfeicfí mé nuair nár cloiseadh mé, ach d'éirigh mé as, go luath. Rinne an tAthair Yorke iarracht i mo dhiaidh, ach níor éirigh leis-sean níos fearr ná liomsa. Ní féidir gur chuala éinne ach na daoine a bhí thart orainn céard a bhíomar a rá. Tháinig mé abhaile ag leathuair tar éis a dó dhéag agus ní raibh mé chomh sáraithe sin ó tháinig mé go dtí an tIarthar. An t-ochtú lá déag de Mhárta. Bhí mé le dul amach go hOakland chun dinnéir leis an Athair Yorke inniu, ach bhí mo chliathán do mo phianadh agus b'éigean dom iaidín a chur air. Bhí mo bhean breoite freisin. Tháinig an Súilleabhánach agus an tAthair Ó Riain chugainn. Chuaigh mé go luath chun mo leapa agus bhí codladh fada agam a chuir biseach orm.

An naoú lá déag de Mhárta. Chuaigh mé chun lóin leis an Athair Yorke, agus chuaigh mé amach leis féin agus leis an Athair Ó Riain go Teach na hAille sa Pháirc. Bhíomar ag giorrú an bhealaigh, ag iarraidh Laidin a labhairt eadrainn féin – Laidin na gcábóg! Is compánach fíormhaith fíorghreannmhar é an tAthair Yorke agus is maith liom an Rianach, freisin.

Chuaigh mé chun dinnéir le muintir Shé sa tráthnóna. Bhí an breitheamh Ó Cofaigh agus mac a dhearthár agus daoine eile i láthair. Taithníonn an breitheamh go han-mhaith liom. Tháinig sé ar ais chun an teach ósta liom, agus bhí deoch againn le chéile.

An fichiú lá de Mhárta. Fearthainn throm arís. Dar liomsa tagann gach dara lá nó gach tríú lá fliuch. Ach ní admhódh muintir na tíre seo sin. Nuair a thagann lá fliuch déarfaidh siad leat agus, dearbhóidh siad duit, gur eisceacht ar fad an lá seo, nach bhfaca siad a leithéid de lá le míonna, gurb an-aisteach é, agus nach bhfuil spéir faoin ngrian níos breátha nó níos tirime ná an spéir atá acusan, agus mar sin de. Cuireann siad sin ina luí chomh maith sin orm go gcreidfinn iad, sílim, ach go n-abrann strainséirí liom, a chaith cúig nó sé mhí anseo, nach fearr agus nach measa an aimsir atá mise a fháil ná an aimsir a fuaireadar féin ó tháinig siad ann.

Chuamar amach sa tráthnóna chun dinnéar a ithe le Maor na Cathrach, Maor Schmitz.* Bhí ceithre dhuine dhéag ag an dinnéar, agus tháinig daoine eile isteach ina dhiaidh sin. Chuir an Maor a ghluaisteán féin faoinár gcoinne. Tá San Francisco lán de chnoic agus ag dul suas dúinn ar an gcnoc a raibh an Maor ina chónaí air, sheas an gluaisteán leath bealaigh, agus thosaigh sé ag cúlú síos le fána arís. Cuireadh scanradh orainn agus léimeamar amach. Ach cuireadh cosc ar an ngluaisteán agus ní dhearnadh aon dochar dó. Is ag an dinnéar sin do chonaic mé ar dtús duine beag ar chuala mé trácht air roimhe sin, Giúdach beag arbh ainm dó Ruef. Deirtear gurb é fíoruachtarán na cathrach é, agus nach bhfuil de ghnó ag Schmitz ach a ainm a chur faoi na rudaí a dhéanas an fear eile. Labhrann sé cuid maith teangacha, an Ghearmáinis agus an Iodáilis agus is féidir leis óráid mhaith a dhéanamh sa dá cheann acu. Tá intinn ghlic thapa aige. Tá an lucht oibre taobh thiar de. Chuala mé an tomhas seo dá chur 'cén fáth a bhfuil San Francisco cosúil le teach?' Agus ba é an freagra a tugadh 'de bhrí go bhfuil "Ruef" os a chionn!'

Is ait an scéal é, scéal Schmitz. Ba Ghearmánach a athair agus b'Éireannach a mháthair, Bean de na Lógánaigh. Tá bean Éireannach aige de mhuintir Dhrisceoil. Is í an veidhleadóireacht a cheird agus is fidléir maith é. Ba iad na Cumainn Oibre a fuair amach mar shórt taoisigh é ar dtús, agus faoi dheireadh thug sé faoin maoracht, ní raibh páipéar i San Francisco nár scríobh ina aghaidh, agus nach ndearna a dhícheall chun é a bhualadh, ach thogh na daoine é gan buíochas do na páipéir. Cruthú láidir ar fheabhas mo choiste gnótha é go mbím ag dinnéar inniu le Séamas Ó Faoláin agus amárach lena dheargnamhaid an Maor. Tháinig cuid mhaith Gearmánach agus Meiriceánach isteach tar éis an dinnéir agus bhí ceol agus amhránaíocht againn. Is fear greannmhar tíúil é. Thug sé suas an staighre sinn go bhfeicfimís a chuid clainne ina

*Féach nóta lch 312.

gcuid cliabhán. Dúirt sé trí ghreann gur mhaith leis mé bheith ag imeacht go luath as an gcathair, óir nárbh eol dó féin éinne is luaithe a bhéarfadh an lámh lúcháireach uaidh ná mise, agus b'fhéidir go seasfainn ina aghaidh sa mhaoracht! Thángamar abhaile ar a 12.30.

An t-aonú lá fichead de Mhárta. Bhí an lá go breá inniu agus chuamar ar cuairt go bean an tSúilleabhánaigh, agus ag siopadóireacht. Chuaigh mé sa tráthnóna go dtí Comhdháil Bhliantúil Chonradh na Gaeilge i gCalifornia. B'fhéidir go raibh mé rud beag róluath ag teacht. Bhí an tAthair Yorke ag labhairt leis na Teachtaí nuair a tháinig mé isteach, agus ba léir dom ar an nóiméad go raibh rud éigin bunoscionn. D'iarr an tAthair Yorke ar bheirt de na teachtaí mise a threorú de leataobh go seomra eile, go nglaofaí orm. D'fhiafraigh mé de ina dhiaidh sin cad ba chiall dó sin, agus thuig mé go raibh sé ag sceimhliú agus ag scóladh agus ag sciúrsáil na dteachtaí mar gheall ar imreas agus éad a bhris amach eatarthu, agus níor mhaith leis leanúint dó, a fhad is a bhí mise i láthair. Nuair a bhí sé críochnaithe, agus iad go léir umhal arís, tháinig mise agus rinne mé dhá óráid, ceann acu i nGaeilge agus ceann i mBéarla. Thug mé an tAthair Yorke ar ais liom chun suipéir go dtí an teach ósta.

An dóú lá fichead de Mhárta. Ag siopadóireacht a bhíomar ar maidin i mBaile na Síneach, ag ceannach rudaí nach bhfuil le fáil in aon áit eile. Sa tráthnóna labhair mé ar feadh uaire agus fiche nóiméad le sé nó seacht gcéad duine i Halla Naomh Peadar, agus tugadh an t-airgead don Chonradh. Bhí dinnéar maith againn ina dhiaidh sin, an tAthair Yorke agus dáréag sagart eile.

An tríú lá fichead de Mhárta. Fearthainn mhór throm arís inniu. Nuair a chuaigh mé ar cuairt chuige thug Séamas Ó Faoláin scian bheag óir dom, mar chuimhneachán, agus m'ainm uirthi, agus thug dealg óir do mo bhean.

An ceathrú lá fichead. D'éiríomar ar a sé a chlog ar maidin, agus chuamar trasna an chuain, le Proinsias Ó Súilleabháin. Chuamar isteach sa traein le dul go Santa Cruz, atá trí fichid míle ó San Francisco, ó dheas. Mar is gnáth leis an mbóthar iarainn, bhí an chréafóg imithe ó na ráillí in áiteanna, agus b'éigean dúinn gluaiseacht go mall. Bhíomar ceithre huaire an chloig ag cur na dtrí fichid míle dínn. Bhí cuid den bhóthar ag dul trí uisce, agus sléibhte ar an dá thaobh dínn. Nuair a ráiníomar Santa Cruz chaitheamar lón leis an Athair Fisher agus le triúr nó ceathrar d'Éireannaigh a fuair cuireadh ón Súilleabhánach. Tar éis an lóin, isteach linn – an Súilleabhánach, sinn féin, an tAthair Fisher agus sean-Éireannach eile – i gcarráiste a raibh ceithre chapall faoi, ar ár mbealach chun na crainn mhóra a fheiceáil. Milleadh agus scriosadh an bóthar díreach go dtí na crainn leis an bhfearthainn agus b'éigean dúinn dul timpeall, trí nó ceithre mhíle dhéag. B'álainn agus b'fhiáin an tír í, agus ní féidir liom a thuiscint, anois féin, conas a thángamar saor gan dochar gan damáiste. Chuamar thar bhóithre a bhí chomh holc sin gur minic a bádh na rothaí síos go dtí an t-acastóir sna poill; thiomáineamar thar dhroichid lofa a raibh cuid den adhmad ag titim astu. Níl a fhios agam cén chaoi nár iompaíodh an carráiste nó nár cuireadh bunoscionn é; ach bhí tiománaí iontach maith againn. B'iontach é mar a stiúraigh sé a cheithre chapall. Níl a fhios agam cén t-ainm a bhí air, ach thugamar go léir 'Coirnéal' air. Thaithnigh sin leis, ach ní raibh aon rud ag baint leis a chuirfeadh saighdiúir i mo cheann!

Faoi dheireadh thiar thall thángamarna go dtí na crainn chlúiteacha seo, ach sular thángamar isteach ina measc bhí orainn dul ag coisíocht thar dhroichead a bhí ag luascadh ó thaobh go taobh. Bhí na cláir lofa agus thit cuid acu faoinár gcosa agus chroith agus luasc an t-iomlán ar nós go mba dhóigh leat go dtitfeadh sé san abhainn a bhí i bhfad thíos fúinn. Bhain sé scanradh as an sagart, agus asamsa, ach bhí náire orm aon cheo a ligean orm. D'fhan an sagart bocht leath bealaigh, níor fhéad sé dul ar ais agus bhí faitíos air dul ar aghaidh, ach nuair a chonaic sé go ndeachaigh na daoine eile slán thairis, tháinig seisean, chomh maith.

Is iontach ar fad na crainn mhóra seo ar thángamar chomh fada sin lena bhfeiceáil. Crainn dhearga nó *red wood* a thugtar orthu, agus is cineál faoi leith iad. Deir muintir California nach bhfásann siad taobh amuigh den stát sin, gur minic a rinneadh iarracht iad a phlandú in áiteanna eile, agus nár éirigh leo (ach cé go n-abrann siad sin go minic níl a fhios agam an bhfuil sé fíor, ní dóigh liom go bhfuil). Fásann na crainn seo go han-mhall. Bíonn airde iontach iontu nuair a thagann siad chun aoise. Fásann an crann go díreach gan cam gan claonadh trí fichid nó ceithre fichid nó b'fhéidir, céad troigh, gan craobh gan géagán as. Ansin tosaíonn na craobhacha a theacht amach, agus ní suas a fhásas siad ach iad ag claonadh anuas. Ghearr lucht leagtha crann na crainn bhreátha seo go léir sna Stáit, beagnach, ach sábháladh an áit seo. Bhí go leor de na crainn a chonaic mé anseo cúig troithe is daichead timpeall orthu ag a mbun, agus tríocha troigh timpeall orthu, ceithre shlat ón talamh. Bhí cuid acu 280 troigh ar airde, agus ceann nó dhó os cionn trí chéad troigh. Chuaigh gach ceann acu suas sa spéir go colgdhíreach. Bhí lorg tine ag bun cuid acu, tine a bhí ann i bhfad ó shin, b'fhéidir na céadta bliain ó shin, ach cé gur dódh cuid de na bunanna níor mhill sé an t-adhmad agus níor stop sé an fás. Is dóigh go bhfuil na crainn is mó acu cúpla míle bliain d'aois. Léigh mé i bpáipéar éigin gur leagadh ceann acu agus gur comhairíodh na fáinní a bhí ann, agus bhí 2,425 acu ann, agus is ionann gach fáinne agus bliain. San áit a rabhamar ann, bhí, taobh istigh de bheagán acraí, 150 crann ina seasamh a raibh ceithre shlat iontu trasna ó thaobh go taobh. Ní raibh mórán ama againn chun scrúdú ceart a dhéanamh orthu. Bhí sé ag éirí dorcha agus b'éigean dúinn filleadh. Bhí an turas ar ais tríd an dorchadas níos measa ná an turas ag teacht. Ba mhíorúilt é gur thángamar slán abhaile. Is ar éigean a bhíomar in am le breith ar an traein a bhí ag dul ar ais. Thug an traein sin go dtí sráidbhaile beag, an t-aon áit ar chuala mé focal Spáinnise á labhairt inti. B'éigean dúinn fanacht le traein eile ansin, ach níor tháinig sé. Bhí an bóthar briste mar ba ghnáth. Rinneamar ár ndícheall chun beagán a fháil le n-ithe agus faoi dheireadh fuaireamar píosa aráin agus cupán caife. Faoi dheireadh tháinig traein a d'fhág sinn ag San Francisco ar a haon a chlog san oíche. Thug Proinsias Ó Súilleabháin sinn go dtí an 'Pup' agus thug champagne agus caviar dúinn, agus bhí siad ag teastáil uainn. Dúirt sé féin nuair a bhíomar ag ithe, 'Bhíomar ar bhruach an bháis trí nó ceithre huaire inniu,' agus bhí an fhírinne aige.

An cúigiú lá fichead de Mhárta. Bhíomar róthuirseach le dul amach inniu ach tháinig an breitheamh Ó Cofaigh agus mic a dhearthár agus daoine eile isteach ar cuairt chugainn. Chuamar chun dinnéir le Séamas Ó Faoláin san oíche. Bhí Miss Jolliffe, an bhean óg a tháinig ón bpáipéar, ar bord an traein i mo choinne an taobh eile den Sierra Nevada, agus seisear nó mórsheisear eile i láthair ag an dinnéar. Thángamar abhaile go luath.

Tháinig an t-am anois dúinn chun San Francisco a fhágáil. Táimid beagnach sé sheachtain ann anois, agus a leithéid de mhuintearas agus de dhúthracht níor casadh orm riamh, agus maidir leis an airgead, sílim gur chuir mé le chéile an oiread de anseo agus a bhailíos i Nua-Eabhrac féin, agus ní dhéanfaimid dearmad go deo ar na cairde maithe a rinneamar. Is beag an smaoineamh a bhí againn ar imeacht uathu inniu, go mbeadh siad féin agus a gcathair ar lár i gceann trí sheachtain; agus go rachadh teach álainn Shéamais Uí Fhaoláin agus áras fial flaithiúil Phroinsias Uí Shúilleabháin agus mórán de na háiteanna eile a bhfuaireamar cineáltas agus aíocht iontu, go rachadh siad suas ina ndaighear dhonn lasrach, agus na daoine a bhí iontu go mbeadh siad gan lán a mbéil den arán tur féin acu.

Bhíomar ag pacáil inniu agus ag cur deise ar gach rud roimh imeacht ó thuaidh dúinn. Tháinig go leor daoine le slán a fhágáil againn, agus d'fhágamar San Francisco ar a hocht a chlog sa tráthnóna. Tháinig linn, dár dtionlacan trasna an chuain, an tAthair Yorke, Proinsias Ó Súilleabháin agus a bhean (thug sise ornáid álainn óir do mo bhean), an breitheamh Ó Cofaigh, agus beirt mhac a dhearthár, agus seisear nó mórsheisear eile. Chuireadar isteach ar an traein sinn ar a 8.30. D'fhágamar slán acusan, agus siúd ar ár mbóthar go Portland Oregon sinn, turas ocht gcéad mile.

An seachtú lá fichead de Mhárta. Níl a fhios agam cén sórt tíre a rabhamar ag dul tríd san oíche, ach ar maidin ní rabhamar rófhada ó Shliabh Shasta, sliabh mór álainn a raibh clóca mór sneachta anuas air. Tá sé os cionn 14,000 troigh ar airde. Bhí an t-amharc go hálainn ar fad. Bhí na sléibhte níos airde agus níos áille ná na Sléibhte Carraigeacha agus ná an Sierra Nevada. Bhí an bóthar iarainn contúirteach in áiteanna. In aon áit amháin stopadh an traein ar learg sléibhe. Crann mór a thit ar an mbóthar ó bharr an tsléibhe a chas agus a cham na ráillí, agus bhí meitheal gnóthach á ndeisiú arís. Chuaigh mé féin amach as an traein agus bhí mé ag féachaint orthu ag obair. Bhí an traein féin ar thaobh an tsléibhe agus bhí míle troigh d'fhána faoi, dá dtitfeadh sé. Nuair a bhí mé ag féachaint ar an lucht oibre, súil dár thug mé ar an traein, chonaic mé go raibh na rothaí a bhí ar an taobh istigh, go rabhadar leathorlach nó orlach tógtha den talamh. Ní raibh siad ag teagmháil leis na ráillí a bheag ná a mhór. Deirtear gurb í seo an áit is contúirtí san Iarthar. Bhí an traein ar crochadh mar sin ar bhruach an ghleanna sléibhe. Is dóigh nach raibh aon chontúirt ann, ach mar sin féin scanródh sé duine gan eolas! Léigh mé cúpla mí ina dhiaidh seo faoi thraein a bhí ag rith thar cham an tsléibhe chéanna nó sléibhe in aice leis, agus d'fhág sé na ráillí agus thug léim isteach i loch gan tóin a bhí faoi. Ní fhacthas an traein ná éinne a bhí inti arís riamh; bhí idir thraein agus phaisinéirí in íochtar an locha.

PORTLAND

An t-ochtú lá fichead de Mhárta. Ráiníomar Portland ag leathuair tar éis a seacht ar maidin. Bhí Tomás Bán ansin ag réiteach romham, ach bhí sé imithe chun an rud céanna a dhéanamh dom i Seattle, Spokane, Butte, agus Anaconda. Tháinig slua le fáilte a chur romhainn agus tugadh sinn go dtí teach ósta.

Nuair a bhí an bricfeasta caite againn tugadh sinn amach i ngluaisteán in éineacht leis an gcléireach Protastúnach an Dr Morrison, agus a bhean, agus leis an Dr Mac Críosta, an tArd-Easpag Caitliceach, agus le daoine eile tríd an bpáirc. Bhí amharc álainn againn ón bpáirc, ceann de na hamhairc is fearr i Meiriceá. Bhí an chathair fúinn ag ár gcosa, agus ceo éadrom ina timpeall. Ansin bhí ag éirí suas ar gach taobh dínn, sléibhte áibhéile móra, agus bhí an ceann ba lú acu deich míle troigh ar airde. Bhí Sliabh Pitt, Sliabh Ranier, Sliabh St Helen, agus cúpla ceann eile ó cheithre fichid míle go dtí céad agus fiche míle, uainn, ach bhí an spéir chomh soiléir sin go mba dhóigh le duine go raibh siad i bhfogas dó. Is iontach é glaine na spéire san Iarthar. Chuala mé scéal faoi Shasanach a tháinig amach an taobh seo, agus chuir sé faoi i dteach ósta sa dúiche. Níor thaithnigh sé le lucht an tí. Dúirt sé tar éis a bhricfeasta: 'Siúlfaidh mé amach go dtí na bunchnoic ag cois an tsléibhe úd, cá fhad uainn iad?' 'Ó,' arsa fear an tábhairne, óir níor fhéad sé an Sasanach a sheasamh, 'cúpla míle nó trí.' 'Is mar sin a cheapas féin,' ar seisean, 'beidh mé ar m'ais chun lóin.' Fuair sé compánach le dul leis, agus bhí sé ag siúl agus ag síorshiúl, ach má bhí, ní raibh sé ag teacht níos gaire do na cnoic. Faoi dheoidh thángadar go dtí sruthán beag agus in áit léimnigh thairis thosaigh an fear bocht ag baint a chuid éadaigh de. 'Céard atá tú a dhéanamh?' arsa an fear eile. 'Dul á shnámh,' arsa an Sasanach, 'cá bhfios dom cén leithead é!'

Thugamar cuairt ar an gColáiste Caitliceach leis an Ard-Easpag agus leis an Dr Morrison, agus bhí caint fhada agam le seanollamh as Contae Mhaigh Eo, Ó Muirín an t-ainm a bhí air. Chaitheamar dinnéar sa tráthnóna leis an Dr Morrison, lena bhean agus lena iníonacha. Is as Baile Átha Cliath dó, agus is maith an tÉireannach é.

An naoú lá fichead de Mhárta. Bhí sé ag stealladh fearthainne inniu. Ní raibh sé tirim i gCalifornia, ach creidim go bhfuil sé i bhfad níos fliche anseo. Tugadh amach mé ar a dó a chlog ar cuairt go dtí a trí nó a ceathair de chlubanna agus b'éigean dom deoch a ól ag gach club acu. Ar a leathuair i ndiaidh a hocht labhair mé san amharclann le tuairim is naoi gcéad duine. Ba é an tArd-Easpag féin a chuir in aithne do na daoine mé, agus an breitheamh Ó Maonaile a chuir an tArd-Easpag in aithne dóibh. Tháinig mé ar ais chun an tí ósta tar éis an mheán oíche.

SEATTLE

D'éiríomar inniu ar a sé a chlog ar maidin, le breith ar an traein go Seattle atá cúpla céad míle níos faide ó thuaidh i Stát Washington. Tháinig triúr nó ceathrar go dtí an stáisiún chun slán a fhágáil againn, agus bhí saorchead againn ar an mbóthar iarainn. Ón uachtarán a bhí ar an líne, Mac Uí Fhógartaigh, a frítheadh an cead sin.

Nuair a shroicheamar Tacoma, tháinig Mac Uí Éidhneacháin agus fear as Dún na nGall nach cuimhin liom a ainm anois, fear a rinne carn airgid as tochailt óir, isteach sa traein agus thángadar linn go dtí Seattle.

Ráiníomar an áit sin ar 4.30. Tháinig coiste an fháiltithe inár gcoinne agus thugadar sinn go dtí Teach Ósta an Bhuitléaraigh. Bhrúigh lucht páipéar isteach orainn mar is gnách. D'itheamar dinnéar sa teach ósta le Mac Uí Éidhneacháin.

Lá an-fhliuch eile atá ann inniu. Cheannaigh mé píosa mór de chlúmh béabhair ar shé dhollar déag. Thug Mac Uí Éidhneacháin amach sinn i ngluaisteán ach bhí an bháisteach chomh trom sin nach raibh pioc le feiceáil. Chaitheamar dinnéar le Mac Uí Éidhneacháin, lena bhean agus lena bheirt iníonacha. Tógadh na hiníonacha seo i Sasana Nua, chuadar go hOllscoil Mheitidisteach ann. Thaithnigh sé go mór lena n-athair nuair a dúirt mé leo trí mhagadh gur chualamar go minic gurb é an dollar Dia na Meiriceánach, ach sílim, arsa mise, gurb é an *cent* Dia na bPoncán i Sasana Nua! Níor

Martin Henehan. Le caoinchead Fhoras na Gaeilge

thaithnigh sin leis na hiníonacha, ach thaithnigh sé go mór leis an athair. Is rí-Ghael an t-athair agus cainteoir breá Gaeilge é, as Tuar Mhic Éadaigh i gContae Mhaigh Eo. Ní dhearna sé *Bird* dá ainm mar a rinne cuid mhór de mhuintir Éidhneacháin sa chontae sin. Bhí fear i Learpholl agus thug sé *Bird* air féin, ach ar seisean, 'a dhuine uasail, ní hé sin an t-ainm ceart atá orm, ach fuair mé amach nár fhéad na Sasanaigh m'ainm ceart a rá agus thug mé *Bird* orm féin.' 'Ó!' arsa mise, 'Is fear de na hÉidhneachánaibh thú.' 'Ní hea, muise!' ar seisean, 'Mac Canary (i.e. Mac an Aodhaire) is ainm dom!' Bhí Mac Uí Éidhneacháin an-lách ar fad liom, agus nuair a bhí mé ag imeacht thug sé dhá lámhscríbhinn bhreátha Gaeilge ar iasacht dom, agus chuir mé ar ais chuige arís iad nuair a tháinig mé go hÉirinn.

An chéad lá d'Aibreán. Bhí cruinniú i dteach an opera ar a trí. Bhí ceithre nó cúig chéad duine ann. D'iarr an breitheamh de Búrca airgead orthu, ach níor iarr sé go ceart é, agus ní dóigh liom gur tháinig mórán isteach dá bharr. Ní raibh Mag Raith, an fear a bhí ina Ghobharnóir tráth, ann, ach bhí an tEaspag Ó Deá sa chathaoir. Chroith mé lámh le go leor daoine tar éis na léachta. Taobh amuigh de mo chara Mac Uí Éidhneacháin is dóigh gurb iad na príomh-Ghaeil sa chathair Mac Mhig Raith, an tEaspag Ó Deá, an Piogóideach, Mac Mhig Fhionnáin (Conallach, ó Dhún na nGall a rinne saibhreas ag Klondyke) agus an breitheamh de Búrca.

Is aisteach an chathair í Seattle. Lucht tochailte óir is mó a rinne é. Ar an ábhar sin tá siopaí óir agus siopaí seod níos iomadúla ann ná atá in aon áit eile dá raibh mé riamh ann. Is dóigh gurb é an fáth atá leis sin go ndéanann lucht tochailte an óir a gcuid airgid go tobann, agus, nuair a gheibheann siad saibhreas ní bhíonn a fhios acu céard air a gcaithfidh siad é. Ritheann siad chun uaireadóirí, práisléid, slabhraí óir agus ornáidí eile a cheannach, agus sin é an fáth a bhfuil an oiread sin siopaí óir ann. Ní cathair chríochnaithe Seattle fós, ach cathair atá á déanamh. Tá tuarastal na ndaoine oibre an-ard inti. Tá lucht brící a chur ag fáil suas le sé dhollar sa lá an duine, tá saoir adhmaid ag fáil $4.50, agus mar sin de. Tá na pánna a gheibheas lucht oibre ceathrú nó trian níos airde ná atá sna háiteanna a raibh mé iontu cheana. Tá ceithre bhóthar mhóra iarainn ag tarraingt ar Seattle, agus tá costas talún ag léimnigh in airde. Chonaic mé stumpaí na gcrann mór a leagadh chun sráideanna nua a dhéanamh agus an sú ag sileadh astu fós. Bhí na crainn seo dar liomsa, beagnach chomh mór leis na cinn mhóra a chonaic sinn ag Santa Cruz. Dúirt mé le cuid de na cathróirí go mbeadh aithreachas orthu gan mhoill faoi na crainn bhreátha sin a leagan, gan ar a laghad, cuid acu a spáráil mar ornáid mhór don chathair. Níor chuireadar aon suim ina ndúras. Ba chuma leo ach réabadh rompu agus cathair mhór nua a chur suas! Ní ar an bhfarraige féin atá Seattle, ach ar ghabhal fada mara atá ag brú isteach i Stát Washington. Tá

Loch Washington, loch álainn atá fiche míle éigin ar fad, in aice leis an gcathair. Tá an áit seo beagnach ar aon fhliche le hÉirinn. Deir siad go dtiteann timpeall dhá orlach déag ar fhichid d'fhearthainn sa bhliain. Tá mórán rudaí sa tír seo a chuireas Éire i mo chuimhne. Tá páirceanna fliucha inti agus luachair ag fás iontu, tá bainne bó bleachta inti, tá féar fada agus fiailí ag fás inti, tá luibheanna agus luibhearnach de gach uile shórt inti, agus thar gach aon rud eile tá an nóinín. Is í seo an t-aon áit amháin a bhfaca mé an nóinín inti ó tháinig mé go Meiriceá. Muna mbeadh na foraoisí móra atá ar gach taobh agus na sléibhte arda a bhfuil sneachta á bhfolach, d'fhéadfainn a chreidiúint gur in Éirinn a bhí mé! Deir siad liom go bhfuil piasúin Shíneacha coitianta sna coillte. Tugadh beagán acu isteach tamall ó shin, agus d'éirigh leo go maith, óir tá siad go líonmhar anois.

Tá ainmhithe fiáine coitianta fós. Chonaic mé craiceann mic tíre a bhí ocht dtroithe ar fad. Chonaic mé craiceann dobharchon farraige, agus dúradar gurbh fhiú trí chéad punt é. Bhíothas chun a churtha go dtí an Rúis, an áit is mó a dtéann gach clúmh luachmhar ann.

SPOKANE

Táimid imithe chomh fada ó thuaidh agus is féidir. Táimid beagnach i gCeanada. Tá orainn anois dul soir arís agus Spokane an chéad áit eile atá romhainn.

D'fhágamar Seattle go moch ar maidin ar 7.30 le dul go Spokane. Tháinig Mac Uí Éidhneacháin go dtí an stáisiún chun slán a fhágáil againn. Thugadar ticéad in aisce ar an traein dom féin. Ar an gcéad chuid den turas chuamar trí fhoraoisí a raibh adhmad ard álainn agus crainn thar barr iontu, giúis Oregon an chuid is mó díobh. De réir mar a bhíomar ag dul soir ón bhfarraige bhí na crainn ag dul i laghad, agus thriallamar trí fhuíll-each tinte, agus trí choillte dóite. Thosaigh an bóthar iarainn ag casadh agus ag lúbadh ar nós eascainne ag dul suas go barr na sléibhte ar a dtugtar Sléibhte Cascade, ceathair nó a cúig de mhílte os cionn na farraige. Ansin chuaigh sé isteach sa talamh trí pholl gur tháinig sé amach anuas ar an taobh eile. Ar feadh níos mó ná leath an lae bhíomar ag féachaint ar Shliabh Ranier, an sliabh is breátha acu go léir. Thar éis cúig uair de thaisteal a dhéanamh dúinn níor fhéach an sliabh níos faide uainn ná níos foisce dúinn. Ar a haon déag san oíche bhaineamar an ceann scríbe amach, agus tháinig Mac Uí Mhanacháin, Mac Uí Shé agus fiche duine eile inár gcoinne, agus thugadar sinn go dtí teach ósta.

Bhí mé ag dul timpeall an bhaile mhóir agus ag ceannach craicne, óir tá an áit seo ar nós Seattle lán de chraicne agus de chlúmh agus tá siad an-saor. Cheannaigh mé craiceann mathúna bháin ó fhear as Alasca. Dúirt sé gur mharaigh beirt Indiach é, agus go raibh fear acu leis an gcloigeann a bhaint de, óir dúirt sé, 'Is é mo chéad mhathúin é agus muna mbainfidh mé an ceann de tiocfaidh a thaise ar ais le mo bhuaireamh.' Ach ní ligfeadh a chomrádaí dó sin a dhéanamh, óir dúirt sé go laghdódh sé luach an chraicinn an ceann a bhaint de. Throideadar ansin, ach faoi dheireadh cheannaigh an ceannaí é, agus an cloigeann air, agus cheannaigh mise uaidhsean é ar shé dollar agus trí fichid. Cheannaigh mé craicne eile ón bhfear céanna, agus nuair a ráinigh mé Nua-Eabhrac arís b'olc liom nár cheannaíos i bhfad níos mó, óir bhí siad i bhfad is i bhfad níos daoire ann ná san Iarthar.

Bhí cruinniú maith againn sa tráthnóna ag Coláiste Gonzaga, faoi Chumann Íosa, atá cúpla míle taobh amuigh den chathair. Nuair a bhí an cruinniú thart thug Mac Uí Mhanacháin, seanfhear lách timpeall trí fichid bliain d'aois, abhaile leis sinn, go dtí a theach álainn féin. Ba é seo an fear a thug go Spokane mé. Tá sé saibhir agus áit bhreá aige. Bhí sé féin agus a bheirt iníonacha ag caint agus ag comhrá liomsa agus bhí siad go díreach ag labhairt ar an nguthán ag glaoch ar charr le mo thabhairt go dtí mo theach ósta, nuair a thug mé faoi deara gur bánaíodh a aghaidh go tobann, agus ansin shleamhnaigh sé anuas den chathaoir agus thit sé go mall ar an urlár. Ba thubaisteach an buille dúinn go léir é sin. Bhí an bheirt iníonacha a rabhamar ag ithe dinnéir leo tamall beag roimhe sin i láthair, agus ba bheag nár baineadh an mheabhair díobh. Shíl an iníon is sine, cailín óg álainn, go raibh sé marbh. Shíl mé féin an rud céanna. Rith mé suas an staighre leis na cailíní agus thugamar leaba anuas agus chuireamar ina luí ar an leaba é. Bhain mé an cóta de, d'oscail mé a léine agus chuir na cailíní fios ar dhochtúirí. Tháinig dochtúir tar éis tamaill, ach ba Fhrancach é, agus ní raibh aon Bhéarla aige, agus ní raibh aon Fhraincis ag na hiníonacha. Is beag agus is an-bheag duine i Meiriceá a bhfuil an Fhraincis aige. B'éigean domsa ceisteanna a chur ar an dochtúir, agus Béarla a chur ar a chuid freagraí do na cailíní bochta.* Tháinig dochtúirí eile ansin, faoi dheireadh, agus d'fhág mé an teach ar a trí a chlog san oíche, agus chuaigh mé ar ais go dtí mo theach ósta. Bhí mo bhean ansin romham agus imní an domhain uirthi mar ní raibh a fhios aici céard a bhí ag cur moille orm, óir bhí orainn Spokane a fhágáil ar a sé ar maidin, agus níor fhág sin ach trí huaire an chloig agam. Bhí mé go brónach agus m'intinn buartha ag filleadh dom ó theach na Manachánach. Tar éis cúpla uair de scíth a ligean bhí mé ar an mbóthar arís, ag fágáil Spokane le dul go Butte ('Biút' a deirtear sa chaint) Montana.

*Blianta ina dhiaidh sin tháinig Mac Uí Mhanacháin agus a bheirt iníonacha agus cara leo go Baile Átha Cliath chugamsa. Dúirt siad gur tháinig sé chuige féin tar éis tamaill, agus níor ghoill a thinneas tobann air. Chuir mé ceist orthu i dtaobh an dochtúra Fhrancaigh. Fear mórchlú a bhí ann, agus d'fhág sé an Fhrainc go tobann mar gheall ar pholaitíocht. Ní raibh sé ach tamall gearr in Spokane an uair sin, agus sin é an fáth nach raibh Béarla aige.

BUTTE

Nuair a d'fhágamar Spokane bhí turas álainn againn trí na sléibhte Carraigeacha. Timpeall an mheán lae thángamar go Loch Pend Oreille, agus tá sé sin ar na háiteanna is deise dá bhfaca mé riamh. B'olc linn nuair a tháinig an oíche, óir níor fhéadamar an radharc a fheiceáil. Bhí sé gar don dó a chlog san oíche nuair a ráiníomar Butte. Tháinig Mac Uí Mheára agus Tomás Bán go dtí an stáisiún faoinár gcoinne. Nuair a bhí mise i gCalifornia bhí Tomás ag cur faoi lena dhearth//air ansin, agus lena mhuintir féin. Ba mhaith liom é a fheiceáil arís anseo. Thugadar sinn go dtí Teach Ósta Thornton – teach ósta a fuair a ainm ó fhear as Contae na Gaillimhe, Mac Uí Dhroighneáin. Tugann muintir Dhroighneáin 'Thornton' orthu féin sa chontae sin.

An cúigiú lá d'Aibreán. Ní cathair mhór í Butte. Tá daichead nó caoga míle duine inti. Tá mé cinnte gurb í an áit is gránna dá bhfaca mé riamh. Níl crann, níl sceach, níl luibh, níl oiread agus tráithnín féir inti ná in aice léi. Tá na mílte agus na mílte spáis ar gach taobh di gan fás ann. Tá gach rud dóite agus ite ag an deatach nimhneach a thagann ó na simléirí móra ina leánn Mac Uí Chléirigh an Seanadóir ó Montana a chuid copair. Tá arsanaic sa deatach, agus maraíonn sin gach aon rud a thagann ina bhealach. Cathair Éireannach í seo, beagnach. Is Éireannaigh iad an chuid is mó de na daoine atá inti. Is Éireannach an Maor, agus tá stiúradh gach rud ar lámh na nÉireannach. Mar sin féin, ní abróinn gur sásúil í staid na nÉireannach anseo. Tá a seasamh ar fad ar na mianaigh. Dá dtitfeadh aon rud amach a mhillfeadh na mianaigh bheadh a leath de na hÉireannaigh díomhaoin. B'fhearr dóibh go mór beagán talún a bheith acu. Ba é Marcas Ó Dálaigh, Éireannach a fuair bás tamall beag ó shin, a rinne Butte. Ba mhian leis cuid de na hÉireannaigh a shuí i ngleann a dtugtar *Bitter Root Valley* uirthi, ach theip air, d'ainneoin a dhíchill. Ansin tháinig bruscán de Phoncánaigh ó Missouri, agus chuireadar fúthu sa ghleann, an ní nach ndéanfadh na hÉireannaigh, agus ní fhéadfá an gleann seo a cheannach inniu ar dhaichead milliún dollar!

Thugadar mé go dtí na mianaigh lena dtaispeáint dom, agus d'iarradar go géar orm dul síos iontu, ach fuair mé rabhadh ó Mhac Uí Chuinn gan dul síos, óir chuaigh sé féin síos tráth, agus d'fhulaing sé go leor iontu. Mar sin, dhiúltaigh mé dóibh. Thugadar bronntanais chopair dom de gach sórt ansin.

Nuair a tháinig an tráthnóna bhí cruinnú breá againn. Bhí an amharclann lán go béal. An tEaspag Ó Cearúill ó Helena a chuir mé in aithne do na daoine. Bhí Mac Uí Mheára sa chathaoir. Labhair mé ar feadh níos mó ná dhá uair an chloig. Ní raibh aon bhailiú airgid ann, ach gealladh dhá mhíle dollar dom. Tháinig mé ar ais ar a haon a chlog.

S. Ó MEAḊRA

John J. O'Meara. Le caoinchead Fhoras na Gaeilge

An séú lá d'Aibreán. Chaith mé an lá go dtí a cúig sa tráthnóna ag fáiltiú roimh na daoine a tháinig ar cuairt chugam.

ANACONDA

Chuamar ar a cúig a chlog go dtí Anaconda atá timpeall fiche míle ó Butte. Tháinig céad go leith duine go dtí an stáisiún, agus thug an Dochtúir Spelman go dtí an teach ósta Montana mé. Ba é Marcas Ó Dálaigh (a rinne Anaconda freisin) a chuir suas an teach ósta breá seo. Ba é an dochtúir a chuir an cruinniú ar bun, agus ba é Thurston, eagarthóir an *Standard,* a bhí i gceannas an chruinnithe. Bhí an cruinniú go han-mhaith, agus nuair a iarradh airgead ar an lucht éisteachta thugadar 615 dollar dúinn. Nuair a bhí sé thart chuaigh mé ar ais chun an teach ósta agus chaitheamar go dtí tar éis a haon ag ól agus ag caint, mar ba ghnách!

An seachtú lá d'Aibreán. Chaitheamar an lá iomlán faoi threorú Chaiptín Ó Ceallaigh agus Mr Mathewson, stiúrthóir na háite, ag dul trí Anaconda, agus ag féachaint ar an Washoe Smelter. Is é an *Smelter* seo a dhéanann saibhreas Anaconda. Leáitear ann an chuid is mó den chopar a thógtar i mButte. Tá Butte féin suite ar ardán. Tugtar 'an baile atá míle ar airde' air. Tá Anaconda mar an gcéanna. Tá cnoc ansin agus tá an *Smelter* ar bharr an chnoic. Tá poll mór a dtarraingítear an deatach suas ann, agus tá an poll seo tollta amach ar thaobh an chnoic, suas go dtí an barr, agus ansin tá an simléar mór ar bharr an phoill, i gcaoi gur píob amháin an poll agus an simléar. Tá an simléar seo trí chéad troigh ar airde, agus tá béal an tsimléir 27 troigh trasna. Bíonn na néalta móra troma dubha nimhiúla ag síorbhrúchtadh amach as an gcraos áibhéil mór sin. Ach ní thagann an deatach anuas ar an mbaile mór; tá an cnoc chomh hard sin go séideann an ghaoth na néalta deataigh ar shiúl léi, ach bíonn siad scaitheamh maith os cionn an bhaile agus na ndaoine. Caithfidh siad teacht anuas in áit éigin, agus tá na feilméaraí sa chomharsanacht ag dul chun dlí le lucht an *Smelter* faoina gcuid talún a mhilleadh, óir ní fhásann aon rud san áit a dtiteann arsanaic inti. Is dóigh go mbeidh ar an gCumann Mór a bhfuil an Smelter acu an talamh go léir timpeall na háite a cheannach, ach ní bheidh sin ródhaor ar an gCumann, óir is i gceartlár na Sléibhte Carraigeacha atá an áit seo, agus ní fiú mórán an talamh lom, agus níl ach corrfheilméara ann. Nuair a itheann beithíoch an féar a bhfuil an arsanaic ann, ar feadh míosa, éiríonn sé go ramhar beathaithe, ach má leanann sé de níos faide ná sin éireoidh sé tinn tanaí agus gheobhaidh sé bás. Dúirt mé go bhfuil Butte i gceartlár na Sléibhte Carraigeacha, óir seo í an áit a bhfuil an t-uisce ag titim le dhá fhána, an méid uisce atá ar an taobh seo de Butte ritheann sé go dtí an fharraige Atlantach, agus an méid atá ar an taobh eile téann sé isteach san Aigéan Thiar. Tugann lucht Mheiriceá an *Great Divide* air seo, *Watershed* i mBéarla, agus *Wasserscheide* i nGearmáinis.

Nuair a thógtar an copar as na mianaigh i mButte caithfear a bhrú agus a mhion-bhrú ar dtús. Ansin leáitear é. An chéad uair a leáitear é fágtar a leath den chopar ann, ach nuair a thugtar an dara leá dó ní bhíonn fágtha ach an copar glan. Caithfidh siad a bheith go han-aireach nach mbainfidh an copar tar éis an chéad leá leis an uisce atá thart timpeall na múnlaí, óir, dá mbainfeadh, bheadh pléascadh áibhéil ann. Ní leáitear an copar arís san áit seo, cuirtear é chun an Oirthir chun sin a dhéanamh, agus baintear luach caoga dollar d'ór agus d'airgead as gach tonna copair.

Tá an tuarastal go hard anseo. An gnáthfhear oibre nach mbíonn ceird ná eolas speisialta ar bith aige, faigheann sé trí scillinge déag sa lá. Tugtar an-aire don lucht oibre. Bíonn áit the acu lena gcuid éadaigh a chrochadh, bíonn fothragthaí acu, agus bíonn banaltra chliste i gcónaí in aice leo ar eagla go ngortófaí duine acu.

Is dóigh go bhfuil copar sa deatach a thagann ón tsimléir, óir bhí cnocán in aice leis an sean-*smelter* agus bhaineadar an talamh den chnoc agus leádar é agus an méid copair a bhí ann d'íoc sé go maith iad.

Tháinig Eadbhard Ó Duibhir, a bhí ina Cheannphort ar Oideachas, timpeall na háite linn, agus thug sé mar bhronntanas dom leabhar nach bhfaca mé riamh roimhe sin ná ó shin. Ba é sin an *Leabhar Gabhála* agus é aistrithe i bhFraincis, agus thug sé dom trí rinn chloiche de thrí shaighead a fuair sé féin sna sléibhte in áit ar mharaigh Indiaigh an damh fiáin nó an *buffalo,* anallód. Thug sé craiceann nathrach nimhe dom freisin, an sórt a dhéanann torann lena cheann mar rabhadh sula mbuaileann sé. Ba dhuine a thug grá don litríocht an Mac Uí Dhuibhir seo, agus ní fhaca mé riamh díol trua ba mhó ná é. Tháinig sé ar ais linn go Butte tar éis dinnéir sa tráthnóna. Tá a áit agus a phost ag brath ar ghuthanna na ndaoine, agus bhí lucht na vótaí ag teacht isteach ina gcéadta sa bhaile mór an lá sin féin. Lucht an APA a bhí ina aghaidh mar a thuig mise. Tá gluaiseacht an APA marbh ar fad san Oirthear ach tá sí beoga go leor fós san Iarthar. Is iad na Lochlannaigh is mó atá ina bhun, agus ba iad na Gearmánaigh agus na Giúdaigh na haon daoine amháin nach raibh baint ar bith acu leis. Ach níorbh fhear troda an Duibhireach bocht, b'fhear é ar cheart dó post a bheith aige in Ollscoil éigin agus gan a bheith air bheith ag gabháil thart ag iarraidh vótaí ar dhaoine ainbhiosacha.

An t-ochtú lá d'Aibreán. Inniu an Domhnach agus chuaigh mé chun an teampaill a bhí ag an Rector. B'fhear lách é a tháinig go dtí mo chruinniú féin. Thug mé faoi deara go ndearna seisean, fearacht na gcléireach uile amuigh anseo, deifir amach go dtí doras an teampaill, tar éis na seirbhíse a chríochnú, agus gur sheas sé ansin ag croitheadh lámh leis na daoine ag dul amach dóibh.

Chuaigh mé ina dhiaidh sin go dtí cruinniú i Halla na Cathrach gur chuir Tomás Bán agus mé féin craobh de Chonradh na Gaeilge ar bun, craobh a bhéarfadh cabhair dúinn gach bliain feasta. Bhí timpeall céad duine i láthair. Mhair an obair dhá uair go leith, cuireadh an chraobh ar bun, toghadh coiste gnótha, agus d'aontaíodar seacht gcéad dollar sa bhliain a thabhairt dúinn.*

Ina dhiaidh sin thug Mac Uí Mheára agus a bhean amach sinn go háit a raibh cábáin Indiacha, *Cree* an t-ainm atá ar an treibh. Bhí an áit go léir salach agus mórán feola leathlofa crochta ar théada timpeall an champa. Sílim gur fuílleach na mbeithíoch a mharaigh na búistéirí i mButte a bhí san fheoil. Sílim go dtagann na daoine bochta seo beo ar fhuílleach na cathrach. Chuaigh mé isteach i gcábán acu agus fuair mé cailín óg ag léamh leabhair a bhí mar a shíl mé ar dtús, clóbhuailte i ngearrscríbhinn. Ach níorbh ea, ach sórt cló a fuair na misinéirí Francacha amach, a bhfuil fuaim siolla iomláin ag gach litir. Is minic a dhéantar dearmad go raibh na Francaigh i Meiriceá sular tháinig na Sasanaigh, agus d'fhág siad a lorg ina ndiaidh go mórmhór ar ainmneacha na n-áiteanna.

Nuair a tháinig an oíche thug Éireannach óg, Mac Giolla Rua, cuairt orm, agus bhí seanchas fada againn le chéile. Eagarthóir é ar pháipéar anseo anois, ach bhí sé ina bhuachaill bó tamall, agus tamall eile i measc na nIndiach. Ní raibh sé sásta le staid Montana. Scanródh sé duine a bheith ag éisteacht leis. De réir an mhéid a dúirt seisean (agus dúirt mórán daoine eile an rud céanna) tá Montana, an stát mór sin, idir anam agus chorp, i seilbh an Chumainn Mhóir Ola, *Standard Oil,* agus na gCumann mór eile, *corporations* a thugtar orthu. 'D'éirigh leo,' a deir sé, 'gach bunfhréamh, arbh fhéidir saibhreas a tharraingt as, a cheannach dóibh féin roimh ré: na mianaigh, an t-adhmad ar na cnoic, buntoibreacha an uisce, gach gleann a bhfuil talamh maith inti, agus ar ndóigh is acusan atá na páipéir nuachta. Tá na páipéir seo ar fheabhas, ach ní íocann siad astu féin. Bíonn easpa airgid orthu, ach tagann na Cumainn Mhóra i gcabhair orthu, agus tugann siad síoraire don ní seo – nach gclóbhuailfidh na páipéir aon rud a dhéanfadh dochar do na Cumainn Mhóra féin, agus más éigean rud a chlóbhualadh a bheadh damáisteach dóibh, caithfidh siad craiceann bréige a chur air, mura b'fhéidir a cheilt ar fad.' Dúirt sé go raibh na daoine ag tosú ar fhios a fháil ar an scéal, agus shíl sé go mbeadh cogadh i Montana mura mbeadh gur toghadh Roosevelt ina Uachtarán. Thug Roosevelt dóchas dóibh go gcuirfí in aghaidh na gCumann Mór seo de réir an dlí, agus go mbainfí na cleití astu, ach maidir leis féin níor chreid seisean aon ní dá

*Agus thug, gach bliain go ceann tamaill.

shórt. Dúirt sé go raibh ar a laghad trí mhíle Éireannach i mButte ag saothrú ó thrí go cheithre dhollar gach lá, agus níl, ar seisean, 50,000 dollar sa bhanc eatarthu go léir. Ach na Lochlannaigh nach bhfuil an ceathrú cuid chomh líonmhar ná chomh mór le rá leo, tá leathmhilliún acu sin sa bhanc.

An naoú lá d'Aibreán. Lig mé mo scíth ar feadh an lae agus scríobh mé litreacha. Dúirt mé le Tomás Bán go raibh mo thuras ionann agus críochnaithe anois, agus chuir mé cábla-scéal abhaile á rá gur shíl mé nach bhféadfainn mórán eile a dhéanamh agus go rachadh Tomás Bán ar bord loinge i gceann trí seachtaine.

An deichiú lá d'Aibreán. D'fhágamar Butte tar éis an mheán lae. Tháinig Mac Uí Mheára, Mac Uí Dhálaigh agus daoine eile go dtí an stáisiún linn.

Timpeall a ceathair a chlog thángamar go háit bheag i lár na sléibhte, agus bhí orainn fanacht ar feadh trí nó ceithre uaire an chloig inti. Bhí teachín beag ósta ann, agus fuaireamar rud le n-ithe. Lánúin ó Texas a bhí ina bhun. Dúirt siad go raibh seilg mhaith le fáil i bhfoisceacht fiche míle dóibh, agus gur mharaigh mac an bhúistéara, comharsa dóibh, trí Elcs (na fianna móra beannacha is mó atá i Meiriceá) tamall beag roimhe sin, agus go raibh na hadharca is mó dá bhfacadar riamh ar cheann acu. Is mór an trua an chaoi a bhfuil na hainmhithe breátha seo á scriosadh amach. Nuair a chuaigh céile mo dheirfféar amach go Wyoming ar dtús d'fheiceadh sé go minic suas le míle de na créatúir bhreátha seo ag teacht anuas na sléibhte in aon tréad amháin. Anois d'fhéadfá dul ar a lorg ar feadh seachtaine agus b'fhéidir nach bhfeicfeá ceann acu. Tá cumann áirithe scaipthe go forleathan trí Mheiriceá a dtugann siad na 'Elcs' air, agus is comhartha onóra ina measc fiacail eilce a bheith acu. Bíonn fiacla ag na daoine is mó gradam sa chumann, agus bíonn an-tóir ar na fianna bochta chun na fiacla seo a fháil.

Chuaigh mé liom féin ag dreapadh suas go barr an chnocáin a bhí os cionn an bhaile bhig, agus bhí amharc álainn agam ar na Sléibhte Carraigeacha ar gach taobh; ba chosúil le panorama é. Tháinig an traein ar a naoi a chlog sa tráthnóna agus chodlaíomar ann.

An t-aonú lá déag d'Aibreán. Chaitheamar an lá ag féachaint as an traein ar mhachairí Dakota Thuaidh. Proibhinse é nach bhfuil ach corrdhuine ann fós, ach sílim go bhfuil an talamh go maith, agus gur gearr go mbeidh go leor daoine ag cur fúthu ann. Tá cruthanna agus foirmeacha aisteacha ar an talamh, gleannta aisteacha, talamh ar nós toir, talamh ar nós caisleáin, talamh ar nós tonnta na farraige, agus mar sin de. Bhí rud éigin cearr leis na píobaí sa traein, agus ar an ábhar sin bhíomar sioctha le fuacht ar feadh tamaill nó dóite leis an teas tamall eile. Tharraing mé amach an Dante a thug an tAthair Zahm dom ag Notre Dame agus chuir mé Gaeilge ar an gcuid eile den chúigiú *Canto den Inferno*. Ní raibh nóiméad agam chun sin a dhéanamh, ach an cúpla lá a bhí agam agus mé ag dul siar go San Francisco, agus an lá inniu.

An dóú lá déag d'Aibreán. Ráiníomar St Paul ar a hocht ar maidin, agus tháinig mo chara Seán D. Ó Briain faoinár gcoinne, agus thiomáin sé don Óstán uí Ríain sinn. Is é rud a thug go dtí St Paul mé an dara huair ná seo, toisc nár fhéadamar aon scéal ná aon fhaisnéis a fháil ar an méid airgid a rinne mé nuair a labhair mé anseo trí mhí ó shin, agus ba mhaith liom scéal éigin a fháil ina thaobh. Bhí mo bhean go tuirseach traochta agus chuaigh sí chun a leapa, agus chaith mise an chuid is mó den lá ag iarraidh labhairt ar an nguthán le Mac Uí Riagáin a bhí ina chathaoirleach nuair a thug mé an léacht trí mhí ó shin agus le Mac Uí Éigeartaigh a bhí ina chisteoir.

Chaith mé an tráthnóna le Mac Uí Bhriain agus lena líon tí, agus bhí suipéar agam leo. Tá an iníon is sine an-sciamhach. Bhí toirneach agus tintreach ann agus mé ag filleadh go dtí an teach ósta.

An tríú lá déag d'Aibreán. D'éirigh liom faoi dheireadh dul chun cainte le Mac Uí Riagáin agus leis an Athair Ó hArrachtáin i Minneapolis, agus bhrostaigh mé iad a gcuid airgid a chur isteach chugainn go tapa agus an obair a chríochnú. Bhí lón agam le Mac Uí Bhriain agus chuaigh mé ar cuairt go dtí sean-Fhínín a bhfuil siopa gunnaí aige. Bhí sé ar an gcúigear duine bán a bhí ar chúl Louis Riel nuair a d'éirigh sé amach i gCeanada in aghaidh an Rialtais. Nuair a bhí mé anseo cheana thug sé gunna gránurchar dom a scaoileadh cúig urchar i ndiaidh a chéile. D'fhágamar St Paul ar a hocht sa tráthnóna, agus chodlaíomar ar an traein.

An ceathrú lá déag d'Aibreán. Ráiníomar Chicago ar a naoi ar maidin. Bhí geallta agam do mhuintir Chicago go gcaithfinn seachtain leo ar fhilleadh dom ón Iarthar, óir thuig mé nach raibh an AOH róshásta gan rud speisialta éigin a dhéanamh dóibh agus an cúnamh a thugadar domsa. Bhí súil agam, freisin, craobh de Chonradh na Gaeilge a chur ar bun, a bhéarfadh síorchúnamh dúinn. Ghealladar go ndéanfaidís sin.

Tháinig an Haicéadach óg chun an tráthnóna a chaitheamh linn. Labhair mé le Mag Fhearaigh agus leis an gCéitíneach ar an nguthán. Tháinig triúr de lucht páipéar ag cur ceisteanna orm, agus níor mhaith leo imeacht!

Chuaigh mé go dtí mórshiopa Marshall Field, agus shiúil mé tríd le beagán earraí a cheannach agus a chur go dtí mo dheirfiúr in Wyoming.

An cúigiú lá déag d'Aibreán. Domhnach Cásca. Rinne mé iarracht ar dhul chun an teampaill, ach fuair mé go raibh sé lán agus suas le céad duine taobh amuigh de, ina n-eireaball. Chuir sin iontas orm, óir ní gnách le muintir Chicago mórán suime a chur ina gcuid teampall. Cheannaigh mé páipéar an Domhnaigh. Is gnách an páipéar Domhnaigh a bheith trí huaire níos mó ná páipéir na seachtaine, agus bhí pictiúr breá den Aiséirí ó cheann de na seanmháistrí air, ach ar an taobh eile den duilleog bhí deilbh chailín óig agus na focail seo faoina deilbh: '*Champion Easter Bride.*' Ní raibh sí trí bliana fichead agus bhí sí tar éis a hochtú fear a phósadh!

San iarnóin chuaigh mé le Liam Diolún, deartháir Sheáin Díolúin, feisire, le Mac Mhig Fhearaigh agus le Mac Uí Éigeartaigh go dtí rang mór Gaeilge, agus labhair mé i nGaeilge leo. Níor mhaith liom, ansin, gan dul chomh fada leis an rang a mhúin seanfhear arbh ainm dó Rálaigh, ar eagla go sílfeadh sé go raibh mé ag déanamh leathchuma air. B'éigean dúinn céad agus sé Lch choiscéim ar thrí fhichid a shiúl suas sular ráiníomar an áit a raibh sé, óir, ó tharla gurbh é an Domhnach a bhí ann, ní raibh an gléas tógála ag obair. Nuair a bhaineamar amach an seomra, faoi dheireadh, ní raibh sa rang aige ach scoláire amháin! Bhí faltanas mór idir é féin agus an chuid eile de Chonradh na Gaeilge agus rinne sé gearán go searbh liom i dtaobh an chaoi ar dhíbir an drong eile as a uachtaránacht é, agus i dtaobh an chaoi a ghoideadar a chuid daltaí uaidh. Ní mór an t-ionadh a chuir a ghearán orm. Is seanfhear cneasta é ach deirtear go bhfuil sé go han-sprionlaithe, agus gur stiocaire é, a thug fíorbheagán don Chonradh. Níor thosaigh sé ar an nGaeilge a fhoghlaim go raibh leathchéad bliain slánaithe aige.

Tháinig an Haicéadach chun dinnéir linn sa tráthnóna, agus an tAthair Ó Ficheallaigh agus an tAthair Smál, cara don Fhicheallach, agus d'fhanadar go raibh sé mall san oíche ag caint agus ag caitheamh tobac.

An séú lá déag d'Aibreán. D'éirigh mé go moch ar maidin, agus tháinig Seán Rálaigh, Mac Bhaildrín ó Bhéal Átha hAmhnais, Mrs Springer agus daoine eile ar cuairt chugam. Ansin thiomáin mé leis an Athair Ó Ficheallaigh chun cuairt a thabhairt ar an Ard-Easpag agus bhí comhrá fada agam leis.

Ar a hocht sa tráthnóna thángamar go léir le chéile chun craobh de Chonradh na Gaeilge a chur ar bun. Bhí an Céitíneach, Mac Mhig Fhearaigh, Mac Uí Dhónaill an dlíodóir, Mac Uí Sheachnasaigh, an sean-Súilleabhánach (cainteoir maith Gaeilge), Caiptín Ó Ceallaigh, an tAthair Mac an Bhreithiún, agus roinnt daoine eile i láthair. Chuireamar craobh de Chonradh na Gaeilge ar bun do lár na tíre, .i. Middle West, agus bhaisteamar é! Abhaile liom tar éis sin ar an meán oíche.

An seachtú lá déag d'Aibreán. Chuaigh sinn amach le Mac Uí Mhurchú go dtí a theach nua ag Elmhurst, tamall amach ó Chicago, an teach ar bhaist mé *Cúl na Craoibhe* air, agus chaith mé lón ansin leis féin agus lena líon tí.

Tháinig mé ar ais in am le dul go dtí fleá mhór a thug an 'Irish Fellowship Club' dom. Bhí deichniúr agus ceithre fichid ag an bhfleá. Rinneadh cuid mhaith cainte ann. Labhair mé féin ar feadh leathuaire. Bhí Mac Uí Sheachnasaigh sa chathaoir. Shuigh mise in aice leis an gCoirnéal Ó Fionnachta agus bhí sé ag insint dom i dtaobh na nIndiach. Bhí sé ina fhear páipéir in éineacht leis na trúpaí Meiriceánacha sa chogadh Indiach. Bhí sé i láthair ag fiche éigin de throideanna leo agus bhí meas an domhain aige orthu, ar a gclisteacht mar lucht troda, ar a gcalmacht agus ar a misneach. Bhí aithne phearsanta aige féin ar chuid dá bpríomhghaiscígh. Dúirt sé gur cheap go leor daoine nach dtaispeánfadh an tIndiach a chorp i gcogadh, ach gur throid sé i gcónaí ar chúl crainn nó carraige. 'Ní mar sin atá,' a dúirt sé, 'chonaic mé céad uair iad á dtaispeáint féin sa mhachaire.'

Tháinig mo sheanchara Mac Uí Cheallaigh ó Milwaukee go speisialta chun a bheith ag an bhfleá seo, agus labhair seisean ar staid na hÉireann faoi láthair. Ba é a bharúil go ndeachaigh intleacht uile na tíre isteach san Eaglais, agus aon fhear cliste a chuaigh isteach san Eaglais cailleadh don tír é, óir, níor fhág sé a shliocht ina dhiaidh.

Incedit per ignes
Suppositos cineri doloso,

arsa mise liom féin. Bhí sé ag siúl ar an leac oighir is tanaí, agus bhí eagla mhór orm go mbrisfeadh sí faoi, agus go bhfreagródh cléireach éigin é.

Iarradh ar an gCoirnéal Ó Fionnachta labhairt, ach d'fhreagair seisean go lách cneasta gurbh fhearr dó gan labhairt. Dá labhródh sé, dúirt sé, go mb'fhéidir go n-abródh sé rud éigin nach mbeimis go léir ar aon intinn ina thaobh. Ach sílim go raibh a fhios aige gur 'ardaigh sé a uillinn' go rómhinic cheana, agus ní raibh aon iontaoibh aige as féin! Tá an Coirnéal ina fhear mór dathúil, agus aghaidh rud beag dearg air. Tá sé ina eagarthóir ar an *Chicago Citizen* agus tá sé go láidir i bhfábhar an UIL[12] agus na bhfeisirí. Ach is Fínín Seán Ó Dubhuí, eagarthóir an *Irish American,* agus is gráin leis lucht na Parlaiminte, agus is gráin lena chéile eisean agus an Coirnéal, agus faraor! Taispeánann siad sin ina gcuid páipéar. Mo thrua Éire nuair a sheasann a cosaint ar lucht páipéar!

Ar an taobh clé díom shuigh fear a bhí ina dhlíodóir, sílim, fear breá dathúil, Hanecy a ainm. Insíodh dom go raibh sé ag dul in aghaidh Mhac Uí Dhoinn sa chomórtas ar son Mhaoracht na Cathrach, agus gur shíl gach éinne go mbuailfeadh sé Mac Uí Dhoinn, ach go ndeachaigh namhaid éigin go dtí an áit a rugadh é, i Wisconsin, agus fuair sé amach gur Pádraig an t-ainm a baisteadh air agus gur athraigh sé féin go Elbridge é!

Cuireann sé sin scéal i mo chuimhne i dtaobh duine éigin de na Brianaigh a bhí i mBostún. D'fhiafraigh fear d'fhear eile 'Cén chaoi a bhfuil Ó Briain.' 'Och,' arsa an fear eile, 'mhill an tÓ atá ina shloinne é mar fhear fhaisin, agus ansin shéan sé go raibh aon Ó aige, agus mhill sin mar fhear polaitíochta é!'

Bhí an dinnéar an-phléisiúrtha agus bhí an chaint go maith mar is gnách. Tháinig mé abhaile leathuair tar éis a haon san oíche.

An t-ochtú lá déag d'Aibreán. Tháinig an t-am faoi dheireadh le dul ó dheas, cúig chéad míle nó níos mó, go Memphis, Tennessee, agus b'éigean dúinn Chicago a fhágáil. Chuamar ar bord na traenach ar a 10 ar maidin, agus tháinig Mac Mhig Fhearaigh linn go dtí an stáisiún, agus siúd sinn ar ár mbealach ó dheas. De réir mar a bhíomar ag gluaiseacht bhí gach ní ag éirí níos glaise. Is ar éigean má bhí duilleog ghlas le feiscint ar aon chrann in aice le Chicago, ach sula raibh leath an lae caite againn bhí duilliúr ar an gcuid is mó de na crainn. De réir a chéile bhí an aimsir ag éirí níos teo agus nuair a thángamar faoi dheireadh go dtí Memphis, tar éis an mheán oíche, bhí an fhuacht imithe as an aer ar fad. Nuair a bhí sé ag éirí dorcha agus mé ar an traein chonaic mé fógra ar pháipéar nuachta go raibh San Francisco dóite. Chuir an scéal scanradh áibhéil orm, agus d'fhan mé go neamhfhoighdeach go gcloisfinn tuilleadh. Chuaigh sé go croí ionam nuair a smaoinigh mé ar na daoine dílse agus ar na cairde maithe a d'fhág mé i mo dhiaidh ansin. Ach ní raibh aon scéal eile le fáil an oíche sin, ná aon scéal beacht go ceann cúpla lá eile.

Casadh an tAthair Ó Lorcáin orainn ag an stáisiún tar éis an mheán oíche, agus thug sé go dtí an teach ósta is fearr a bhí sa bhaile sinn. Ach áit shalach chiotach ghioblach amach is amach í, i gcomórtas leis na tithe ósta a chleachtamar san Oirthear, san Iarthar agus sa Tuaisceart. An gléas tógála, nó an lift a bhí againne ní dheachaigh sé riamh suas an bealach ar fad ach stadadh sé i gcónaí timpeall trí troithe níos ísle ná urlár an tseomra, agus b'éigean dúinn sinn féin a tharraingt in airde le neart ár lámh agus ár ngéag! Cleas aclaíochta a bhí ann! Daoine gorma a bhí i mbun na háite, mar a thuig mé.

An naoú lá déag d'Aibreán. Cheannaigh mé na páipéir go léir, an chéad rud ar maidin, agus fuair mé scéalta áibhéile faoi San Francisco, mar a slogadh Teach na hAille san fharraige, etc., etc., rudaí nach raibh fíor. Chuir mé sreangscéal nó dhó go dtí San Francisco, ach níor frítheadh iad is dóigh.

Sa tráthnóna thug Mac Uí Mhaoileoin, maor na cathrach, seanfhear lách, i ngluaisteán go dtí na rásaí sinn. Bhain mé greann mór as an maor. Deisceartach, go díreach cosúil leo seo a bhfuil cur síos orthu sna húrscéalta ab ea é. Labhraíodh sé go mall, agus ní raibh sé ina chumas an litir 'r' a rá agus bhí mórán cainte aige i dtaobh a bhunaidh agus i dtaobh na dúiche a bhí acu in Éirinn dhá chéad bliain ó shin. Dúirt sé go raibh a mhuintir suite i Virginia le dhá chéad bliain. 'Ba sinne,' ar seisean, 'seanuaisleacht na tíre roimh an gcogadh,' nó mar a deireadh seisean é, 'befo' the wah, suh.'

Maireann na rásaí capall ar feadh trí seachtaine anseo. Is ar thalamh cothrom a bhíonn siad go léir, gan aon chlaí ná aon sconsa. Na cinn a chonaic mise, ní raibh siad níos faide ná míle nó míle agus ceathrú. Bhí an cúrsa go deas, agus cuireadh go leor geall ar na capaill.

Ar theacht ar ais ó na rásaí chuaigh mé go clochar a raibh mórán ban rialta ó oird éagsúla inti, agus labhair mé ar feadh leathuair an chloig leo. Ar maidin lá arna mhárach chuireadar cúig dhollar chugam go cineálta mar luach saothair.

Bhí cruinniú maith agam san amharclann um thráthnóna, cé nach dóigh liom go bhfuil mórán Éireannach sa chathair. Níor casadh fíor-Éireannaigh ar bith orm ach amháin an tAthair Ó Lorcáin, as Luimneach sílim, fear a bhféadfá 'sagart na cúile báine' a thabhairt air, óir tá gruaig fhionn fhada air, agus taithníonn sé de réir dealraimh le gach éinne – agus Éireannach óg arbh ainm dó Breathnach. Mar sin féin bhí an cruinniú go maith, agus tá súil agam le cúig chéad dollar dá bharr.

Sílim gur daoine gorma leath na ndaoine atá i Memphis. Tá an baile mór suite ar abhainn na Mississippi, agus is í is príomháit do chadás Mheiriceá. Snámhann an Mississippi amach thar a bruacha gach bliain anseo, agus chonaic mé mórán crann ina seasamh san uisce, amhail agus dá mbeidís ag fás ann. Thug an tAthair Ó Lorcáin leis mé go bhfeicfinn na hualaí móra cadáis teannta le chéile le cumhacht uisciúil, agus iad ina málaí pacáilte, réidh lena gcur go deireadh an domhain! Loch mór atá san abhainn anseo, agus téann longa gaile go síor suas síos, síos suas uirthi.

An fichiú lá d'Aibreán. Níl mé ag dul go Nua-Orleans ná go dtí aon áit níos faide ó dheas ná Memphis, agus beidh orm dul ó thuaidh feasta. Is é Baltimore, Maryland, an chéad áit ar a mbuailfidh mé anois, agus tógfaidh sé cúpla lá orm dul ansin. Thug an tAthair Ó Lorcáin amach i ngluaisteán sinn ar maidin. Chonaic mé coillte ar gach taobh den bhóthar, agus dúirt an maor liom go mbíodh na coillte sin go léir folaithe leis na milliúin colm a thagadh iontu gach bliain. Bhíodh na géaga dá lúbadh fúthu. Ní thagann siad anois. 'Ní hé gur maraíodh iad,' ar seisean, 'ní fhéadfá an céadú cuid acu a mharú, ach d'imigh siad ar ceal, ar nós éigin, cibé rud a tharla dóibh.' Thug an tAthair Ó Lorcáin lón dúinn, agus d'fhágamar Memphis ar a haon a chlog p.m.

Bhíomar ag gluaiseacht ar feadh an lae ag dul soir ó thuaidh, trí Tennessee, agus trí Kentucky, agus faoi dheoidh, timpeall a dó san oíche, stad an traein ag Louisville. B'éigean dúinn dul go stáisiún eile ansin agus ar bord traenach eile ar a sé a chlog ar maidin, agus leanamar dár dturas.

An t-aonú lá fichead d'Aibreán. Bhíomar ag taisteal ar feadh an lae trí Kentucky agus trí Virginia, agus gan le déanamh againn ach féachaint amach ar na fuinneoga ar

An tAṫair Ó Lorcáin

Fr Larkin. Le caoinchead Fhoras na Gaeilge

an earrach ag teacht isteach, ar na coillte agus ar na foraoisí ar gach taobh den bhóthar. Bhí an crann madra nó *dog tree* ag gealú na gcoillte lena bhláth bán, agus bhíodh paistí móra dearga nó bándearga le feiscint ar gach taobh. B'in iad na crainn Iúdáis. Ní fhaca mé aon rud níos áille ná iad. Ní bhíonn duilleoga orthu ach amháin, de réir cosúlachta, na bláthanna bándearga a chlúdaíos iad féin ó bhun go barr. Deirtear gur chroch Iúdás é féin ar an gcrann sin, agus gur thug sé a ainm dóibh, ach na crainn a chonaic mise bhí siad ró-éadrom agus bhí na géaga rólag chun éinne a chrochadh orthu! Tá na crainn bheaga seo an-fhairsing sa Deisceart, ach ní dóigh liom go bhfuil siad le fáil sa Tuaisceart.

Nuair a bhí an tráthnóna ag teacht bhuaileamar Sléibhte Allegheny. Níl siad ard, ach tá siad go hálainn. Thug mé faoi deara, ag féachaint ar na coillte ag cur a mbrait earraigh umpu, go raibh i bhfad níos mós de dheirge iontu ná a bhí de ghlaise. Bhí abhainn an-deas ag dul cois na sléibhte, agus níorbh fhada gur thosaigh tintreach shamhraidh ag taitneamh inár dtimpeall, ag lasadh na gcnoc agus na habhann ar feadh uaireanta an chloig.

BALTIMORE

An dóú lá fichead d'Aibreán. Tar éis a bheith ag siúl ar feadh na hoíche thángamar go Baltimore ar maidin ar a hocht a chlog. Tháinig Mac Uí Scolaí, Mac Uí Mhanacháin agus coiste fáilte chugainn, agus thugadar sinn go dtí Teach Ósta Mhic Thiarnáin. Thugadar amach i ngluaisteán mé tar éis an bhricfeasta, agus timpeall na Páirce, áit a bhfuil siad mórálach aisti. Tá seacht gcéad acra inti agus cuid mhaith den seanadhmad nádúrtha, agus bíonn fianna ag iníor i measc na gcrann. Bhí cruinniú breá againn sa tráthnóna. Bhí an amharclann lán go béal, bhí 1800 duine nó mar sin i láthair agus d'íocadar dhá scilling go scilling ar dhul isteach. Bhí an Cairdinéal Mac Giobúin i mbosca nuair a bhí mé ag labhairt. Labhair mé ar feadh uaire agus trí cheathrú, agus sílim gur chruthaigh mé go maith tar éis na scíthe breátha a lig mé ar an traein. Bhí mar ornáid ar an mballa, i litreacha móra, na focail seo: GINN FINN GINN FINN AMAIN FAILCE 7 SLAINCE 'Sinn Féin, Sinn Féin amháin, Fáilte agus sláinte' na focail a bhí i gceist acu, is dóigh!

Is dóigh nár thug duine ar bith faoi deara nach raibh aon chiall leo! – agus munar thug, bhí siad chomh maith leis an rud ceart!

An tríú lá fichead d'Aibreán. Táimid le dul ar ais go Nua-Eabhrac arís inniu tar éis sinn a bheith imithe as ar feadh ráithe agus trí seachtaine. D'fhágamar Baltimore ar an meán lae, agus ráiníomar Nua-Eabhrac ar a sé a chlog sa tráthnóna. Bhí áthas mór orm Mac Uí Chuinn a fheiceáil arís ach b'olc liom nach raibh sé ag féachaint níos fearr. Cailleadh a dhearthháir fad a bhí mé imithe. Ba chosúil le dul abhaile mo theacht go dtí a theachsan arís, é féin agus an Cuirtíneach, a chléireach. Mar sin féin níorbh fhada a d'fhan mé leis, óir bhí orm é a fhágáil an lá arna mhárach.

CORNELL

An ceathrú lá fichead d'Aibreán. D'fhág mé Nua-Eabhrac ag ceathrú tar éis a naoi ar maidin. Tháinig Mac Uí Chuinn liom go dtí bád an chalaidh go Hoboken. Ansin chuaigh mé ar bord na traenach a bhí le dul go hIthaca, an áit a bhfuil ollscoil Cornell. Tá an áit sin cúpla céad míle amach as Nua-Eabhrac ach is sa stát céanna é. Tháinig an tOllamh Mac Mathúna, fear as Coláiste na Tríonóide go dtí an traein, agus thug sé mé ar ais leis go dtí a theach féin. Ní raibh ann ach é féin agus a bhean.

Ceann de na hollscoileanna a dtugtaí *Land Grants* orthu atá san ollscoil seo. Tugadh suim airgid do stáit éagsúla chun ollscoileanna a chur ar bun. Dhíol an chuid is mó de na stáit an talamh a fuaireadar. Ach cheannaigh an seanfhear seo, Cornell, an talamh dó féin, agus nuair a ardaíodh go mór luach na talún dhíol sé é agus thug sé don ollscoil é. Tá dlíthe ann go gcaithfidh an ollscoil seo, agus ollscoileanna eile, saighdiúireacht a mhúineadh do na mic léinn. Chonaic mé féin na mic léinn agus cultacha saighdiúir orthu, ag déanamh a gcuid aclaíochta ar fud na háite. Bhí súil ag an Rialtas nuair a thugadar an t-airgead, i ndiaidh an chogaidh, go mbeadh oifigigh le fáil sna hollscoileanna seo, dá mbeadh gá leo. Ach tá coláiste curaíochta ag Cornell, freisin, coláiste foirgníochta, coláiste tréad-leighis agus coláiste innealtóireachta.

Bhí slua maith ag éisteacht liom nuair a labhair mé sa tráthnóna ar fhealsúnacht Chonradh na Gaeilge. Ba é an Déan, an Dr Ó Carráin, a chuir mé in aithne don slua. Tá sé pósta le deirfiúr don Mhathúnach.

An cúigiú lá fichead d'Aibreán. Chaith mé an mhaidin ag breathnú ar an leabharlann bhreá atá acu faoi Dante, agus tá cruinniú breá de leabhair acu faoin Íoslainn, agus cruinniú eile faoi Phetrarc.

Ar a trí a chlog thug mé léacht faoi fhilíocht na hÉireann, agus d'imigh mé ansin le Mac Uí Chonchúir ó Elmira go dtí an áit sin. Thugadar fleá dom ansin, a raibh ocht nduine fichead i láthair aici, agus thosaigh sí ar a deich a chlog agus ní raibh sí thart go dtí leathuair tar éis a haon. Bhí Moore, eagarthóir an *Telegraph,* sa chathaoir. Bhí sé

James J. O'Connor. Le caoinchead Fhoras na Gaeilge

leathuair i ndiaidh a dó san oíche nuair a tháinig mé ar ais le Mac Uí Chonchúir go dtí a theach féin.

ELMIRA

Chuaigh mé ar maidin go Coláiste na mBan uasal ag Elmira. Tá sé de cháil ar an gcoláiste seo gurbh é an chéad choláiste i Meiriceá é a cuireadh ar bun do na mná. Agus shíl mé go raibh na cailíní a bhí ann níos breátha agus níos áille ná in aon áit eile. Deirtear go bhfuil siad ar fheabhas chun aclaíochta. Labhair mé leo ar feadh leathuaire agus bhain mé mórán gáire astu. Ach nuair a tháinig an tráthnóna rinne mé botún. Bhí cruinniú mór agam, timpeall 1,200 duine ach níor thuig mé nach raibh an ceathrú cuid ina nÉireannaigh agus thug mé uaim an chaint chéanna a thug mé uaim sa Carnegie Hall agus i San Francisco agus i Philadelphia. Tháinig na cailíní ón gcoláiste gona gcuid caipíní agus gúnaí le mo chloisteáil. Ach níor thuig mé in am gur Mheiriceánaigh an lucht éisteachta a bhí agam agus cé gur thug mé casadh don chaint, rud beag, bhí sé rómhall. Bhí Moore go han-mhíshásta liom ar fad faoin 'mbotún' seo, mar a thug sé air, ach sílim nach raibh an chuid is mó den lucht éisteachta ar aon intinn leis. Dá mbeadh a fhios agam in am bhéarfainn léacht ar fhilíocht nó ar rud éigin eile dóibh, mar a bhí tugtha agam ar maidin do chailíní an choláiste. Mar sin féin rinneamar go maith as Elmira óir fuaireamar sé chéad dollar as, ach thug Mac Uí Chonchúir féin 150 dollar de sin.

Thug Mac Uí Chonchúir abhaile leis mé, bhain sé corc as buidéal champagne, agus b'fhada sula raibh mé i mo leaba. Is fear saibhir adhmaid é. Tá sé ar na daoine is saibhre in Elmira, agus is maith an t-eolas atá aige ar chapaill. Is cara é mar a gcéanna don tsean-Mhanachánach i Spokane, agus d'inis mé dó i dtaobh na timpiste a tharla dó.

SCRANTON

D'fhág mé Elmira le dul go Scranton um meán lae. Tháinig an tAthair Hurst ó Scranton an oíche roimhe sin agus chuaigh sé ar ais liomsa. Ba sheanchara dom féin é, óir d'fhan sé liom i Ráth Treágh uair amháin, agus bhí sé ina shagart i mBéal Átha na Muice i gContae Mhaigh Eo, ar feadh tamaill. Bhain Mac Uí Chonchúir an corc as buidéal eile champagne sula ligfeadh sé dúinn imeacht, agus b'éigean dúinn a ól. Tháinig fonn codlata dá bharr orm sa traein, agus is ar éigean a d'éirigh liom mo dhá shúil a choinneáil gan dúnadh. Mar sin ní mó ná go measartha a thaithnigh sé liom nuair a tháinig beirt ó Scranton isteach sa traein chugam, nuair a bhíomar fós trí fichid míle amach ón áit sin. Ba iad sin Mac Uí Chathasaigh, milliúnaí ó Scranton, agus an Dochtúir Ó Máille. Tá beirt Chathasach ann, lucht déanta uisce beatha, agus is as Cúil Ó bhFinn nó as áit in aice leis, mar a bhfuil mo chara Mac Diarmada ina chónaí a thagann siad. Bhí áthas orthu nuair a dúirt mé leo go raibh togha na haithne agam ar Chúil Ó bhFinn agus go raibh mé go minic ag iascach in Abhainn na Loinge agus i Loch Uí Ghadhra. Thugadar ainm ar an uisce beatha a dhéanann siad, ó áit éigin in aice le Cúil Ó bhFinn, ach ní cuimhin liom anois cén t-ainm é. Nuair a ráiníomar an stáisiún chuir Maor na Cathrach a ghluaisteán féin, agus bratach Éireannach agus bratach Meiriceánach ceangailte thart air, faoi mo choinne. Bhí cruinniú breá againn sa tráthnóna, 1,200 duine, agus d'íoc siad ó dhá scilling go dtí sé scillinge an duine. Tháinig an tEaspag, an Dr Ó hÚbáin, agus an Maor Dimock, fear ard dathúil de shliocht Breatnach, go dtí an cruinniú, agus bhíodar ar an ardán. Labhair an tEaspag ach ní chuimhním cé a bhí sa chathaoir. Labhair mé féin ar feadh dhá uair. Tá Scranton lán de Ghaeil; mianadóirí iad. Tagann go leor acu as Contae Mhaigh Eo. Deir an tAthair Hurst liom go bhfuil níos mó Gaeilge á labhairt i Scranton ná in aon chathair eile sa domhan. Is mór an baile é, agus tá suas le 170,000 duine inti. Mianaigh ghuail a rinne saibhreas do Scranton, agus tá mianaigh tochailte faoin gcathair féin, agus chuala mé daoine á rá go dtitfeadh an chathair isteach orthu lá éigin! Casadh Gaeilgeoir maith orm ó Conamara, Mac Mhic Grífín a ainm. Is é féin agus na Cathasaigh, an tAthair Hurst agus an Dr Ó Máille na príomh-Éireannaigh a bhuail umam sa chathair. Ar bhóthar iarainn Lackawanna a théitear go dtí Scranton, agus tugtar an 'Bóthar *Anthracite*' air, óir is gual ar fad é.

An t-ochtú lá fichead d'Aibreán. D'éirigh mé ar a sé ar maidin le dul go Nua-Eabhrac. Thug mé faoi deara nach bhfuil ach fíorbheagán duilliúir ar na crainn anseo fós, ach tá na saileoga ag tosú ar a gculaith ghlas a chur orthu féin, agus tá bláthanna ag teacht ar na mailpeanna crua. Bíonn na bláthanna seo dearg nuair a bhíonn siad óg, agus cuireann sin cosúlacht bhuídhearg in áit cosúlacht ghlas ar na crainn. Ag féachaint duit ar choill atá tar éis a culaith earraigh a chur uirthi féin, gheobhaidh do shúil gach sórt scáile inti, glasbhán, glasdorcha, buídhearg, ach fíorbheagán den ghlasuaine sin a fheictear in Éirinn. An rud is deise sa choill is iad na crainn saileog, sílim.

Tháinig mé go Nua-Eabhrac ar a haon, agus chuaigh mé go hoifig Mhac Uí Chuinn, agus chaith mé lón leis. Bhí Mr Emmet, an Cathalánach agus Mac Uí Chonbhuí ó na hÓglaigh Éireannacha ann.

D'iarr mé go géar orthu cúig mhíle dollar a chur go San Francisco, óir bhí leisce orm a dhéanamh gan cead ón gCoiste Gnótha, nó ba chóir dom a rá níor fhéadas a dhéanamh, ach fuair mé cead uathu inniu agus chuir Mac Uí Chuinn trí shreangscéal go dtí an tAthair Yorke é. Tar éis an dinnéir chuaigh mé féin agus Mac Uí Chuinn agus a dheirfiúr, go dtí Teach an Opera, Lexington, an áit ar léiríodar mo 'Phósadh.' Bhí bosca ag na Ceallaigh ann. B'éigean domsa óráid bheag a dhéanamh don lucht éisteachta, i nGaeilge. Casadh Graham, Albanach as Ceanada, orm, agus bhí deoch againn le chéile. Is fear é a chonaic mórán, agus bhí caint fhada spéisiúil agam leis. Bhí sé mall go leor nuair a d'fhill mé go teach Mhac Uí Chuinn.

An naoú lá fichead d'Aibreán. Inniu an Domhnach. Chuaigh mé chun an teampaill, agus ansin ag spaisteoireacht le Mac Uí Chuinn. Chonaiceamar longa cogaidh na bhFrancach agus na Meiriceánach san abhainn. Bhí mé díomhaoineach inniu.

An deichiú lá fichead. Lá díomhaoineach eile. Thug Mac Uí Chuinn leis mé chun lóin leis an gCathalánach, leis an mBreitheamh Mac Eochaidh, agus le daoine eile.

Lá Bealtaine. D'fhág mé féin agus mo bhean Nua-Eabhrac le dul go Philadelphia arís. Tháinig lucht fáiltithe go dtí an stáisiún romhainn. Bhí an tAthair Ó Cochláin, an Catháнach, an tAthair Ó Dónaill, Mac Uí Dhálaigh, an cisteoir, agus daoine eile i láthair. Tugadh sinn go teach an Athar Ó Cochláin, agus chuireamar fúinn ann. Thug sé dinnéar breá dúinn agus neart fíona, etc. Bhí an tAthair Ó Dónaill agus a dheirfiúr, (is gaolta don Chochlánach iad), agus beirt shagart eile ann.

An dara lá de Bhealtaine. Tugadh amach sinn in dhá charráiste tríd an bPáirc. Ba é an Dochtúir Ó Cearúill an sean-Fhínín ár dtreoraí, agus b'éigean dúinn breathnú go dlúth ar na híomhánna agus ar na foirgnimh uile. Ansin thiomáineamar linn amach bóthar an-álainn cois abhainn na Wissahickon agus ansin suas cois aibhne na Schuylkill. Thángamar ar ais ar a cúig a chlog, agus bhí dinnéar againn.

An tríú lá de Bhealtaine. Tháinig an Dochtúir Ó Cearúill arís. Thaispeáin sé dúinn Independence Hall, áit ar chuir Meiriceánaigh a n-ainmneacha ar dtús faoi Chairt na Saoirse, agus Carpenter Hall, áit an chéad Congress, agus Halla na Cathrach atá ar aon airde le cuimhneachán Washington. Fuaireamar cead speisialta le dul suas sa ghléas tógála go barr íomhá Penn, atá suas le cúig chéad troigh ar airde. Agus as an áit sin bhí amharc thar barr againn ar Philadelphia go léir, ar abhainn na Schuylkill, agus ar na dugaí móra. Ansin chuamar go dtí Halla na Saormháisiún agus níor mhór dúinn bualadh isteach i ngach seomra a bhí acu, agus iontas a dhéanamh de na stíleanna éagsúla a bhí orthu! Shíl mise go dtitfeadh na cosa fúm. Sílim gur Caitliceach agus Saormháisiún an Cearúllach, agus é ina Fhínín in éineacht leis sin! Nuair a tháinig an oíche tugadh fleá dom ag Teach Ósta Mhac Uí Dhúnabhra. Bhí timpeall daichead i láthair agus rinneadh mórán cainte ag an bhfleá. D'iarr mise orthu Craobh den Chonradh a chur ar bun, mar táthar le déanamh i Chicago. Tháinig mé ar ais ar a haon, ach ní raibh mé i mo leaba go dtí a trí, óir thosaigh an tAthair Ó Cochláin, an tAthair Ó Lochlainn, an tAthair Ó Dónaill agus mé féin ar chluiche 'cúig-ar-fhichid,' a chuir moill orainn.

An ceathrú lá de Bhealtaine. D'fhágamar Philadelphia. Bhí an tAthair Ó Cochláin, agus iad go léir an-lách ar fad linn, agus i gceann cúpla uair an chloig nó trí bhíomar ar ais i Nua-Eabhrac arís. Bhí lón agam le Mac Uí Chuinn agus d'fhágas é le dul go Coláiste Vassar. Tá sé suite turas cúpla uair an chloig ó Nua-Eabhrac ar an Hudson. Bhí an lá go hálainn agus d'fhéach an abhainn go rídheas. Tháinig Miss Wylie, ollamh le litríocht Bhéarla, faoi mo choinne go dtí an stáisiún, agus thug sí mé go dtí an coláiste, áit a raibh dinnéar agam sa seomra coitianta, i measc na nollúna agus na n-iníonacha léinn. Mrs Kendrick uachtarán an choláiste, agus tá timpeall míle dalta aici. Thug mé léacht dóibh ar Fhilíocht na nGael, agus bhí idir a cúig agus a sé chéad duine ag éisteacht liom. Chuir mé fáilte rompu ansin, agus tháinig go leor acu agus chroitheadar lámh liom.

Ina dhiaidh sin bhí d'ádh orm ócáid aisteach speisialta a fheiceáil – na hiníonacha léinn ag toghadh crainn dá rang féin. Toghann gach rang crann dóibh féin. An rang a chuaigh ag toghadh an chrainn, tharraing siad chucu féin gach uile shórt astralaíochta agus rúndiamhrachta. Gléasadh iad sna cultacha is aistí, mar an bandia Iúnó ag fáil bháis, agus bandéithe eile, etc. Caitheadh soilse aibhléiseacha orthu sa siúl dóibh, agus bhí siad ag gabháil dánta neamhghnácha. Tá sé an-deacair, deir siad féin, sa chéad áit na cultacha a dhéanamh, agus sa dara háit iad a chur i bhfolach ó shúile na ranganna is óige, óir dá bhfaighidís seo amach iad réabfaidís ina mionsraoilleanna iad!

An cúigiú lá de Bhealtaine. Chodail mé i Vassar aréir. Ar maidin inniu d'fhág mé slán ag Miss Wylie agus d'fhill mé go Nua-Eabhrac in am chun lón a bheith agam le Mac Uí Chuinn, le Mrs Thursby, agus leis an Haicéadach, ag Teach Delmonico. Sa tráthnóna chuaigh mé go dtí taispeántas na nÓglach Éireannach, ag an Grand Central Palace. Bhí an breitheamh Ó Dúllaing, Mac Uí Chuinn, an Cathalánach agus Mac Uí Chonbhuí ansin. Shiúil mé thart ag scrúdú na saighdiúirí le ceann de na majors, ag féachaint go géar orthu mar uachtarán. Slua breá iad, idir trí agus ceithre chéad acu. Labhair mé leo ar feadh leathuaire. Tá an t-airgead le dul go San Francisco. Muna mbeadh sin, agus gur ar son déirce a tarraingíodh amach na fir, ní dóigh liom go mbeinn i láthair, óir ní críonna an bheart liom bheith i láthair le slua óglach faoi airm. Óir dáiríre baineann siad go léir, sílim, le Clann na nGael.

Tar éis an mhéid sin bhí fíon againn leis na hoifigigh agus leis an mBreitheamh Ó Dúllaing. Ansin chuaigh mé go Club na nAisteoirí le Mac Uí Chuinn agus le Graham agus níor tháinig mé abhaile go dtí a dó a chlog.

An séú lá de Bhealtaine. Tháinig Miss Coates, cara mór do Mhac Uí Chuinn, chun bricfeasta. Bhí tinneas cinn ormsa tar éis na hoíche aréir. Chuaigh mé amach le mo bhean ar an traein go New Rochelle, an áit a bhfuil an breitheamh Mac Eochaidh ina chónaí, chun lóin. Bhí Mr Palén, stiúrthóir an *Catholic Encyclopedia*, atáthar le cur ar bun, Temple Emmet agus daoine eile i láthair. Bhí caint fhada agam le Palén agus dúirt mé leis gan dearmad go leor slí agus spás a thabhairt do Ghaeil agus d'Éirinn ina leabhar nuair a thiocfadh sé amach 'óir is iad na hÉireannaigh,' arsa mise, 'príomh-Chaitlicigh na tíre seo.' Tá mé beagnach cinnte gur tháinig toradh maith as an méid a dúirt mé leis, óir fuair Éire cothrom maith ina chuid leabhar. Thiomáineadar sinn ar ais trí Pháirc Pelham, tar éis lá an-phléisiúrtha a chaitheamh leo.

An seachtú lá de Bhealtaine. Casadh Mrs Thursby agus a deartháir Brisbane (eagarthóir an *Evening Journal*), Mrs Cary ó Buffalo agus a cuid iníonacha orm, ag lón i dTeach Delmonico. Bhí caint fhada agam le Brisbane.

Tháinig Monsieur Janvier agus a bhean ar cuairt chugam sa tráthnóna. Is fear mór dathúil é, de bhunadh Francach. Scríbhneoirí agus údair é féin agus a bhean agus bhí aithne acu ar 'Fhíona Mac Leóid.'

An t-ochtú lá de Bhealtaine. Bhí dinnéar agam le Mac Uí Chuinn i dTeach Delmonico. Bhí an breitheamh Mac Eochaidh agus a mhac, agus an Cathalánach ann. Tar éis an dinnéir chuamar suas an staighre go cruinniú ráithiúil 'Mac Carthanach N. Pádraig.'[13] Bhí timpeall céad ball acu ann. Daoine iad seo go léir ar éirigh an saol go maith leo, togha agus rogha, dar liomsa, den chine Éireannach iad. Bhí beirt as San Francisco ann, mac dearthár don Bhreitheamh Ó Cofaigh, agus col ceathrar do Shéamas Ó Faoláin. Bhí Mac Uí Chléirigh, an file a scríobh 'Kelly, Burke and Shea', sa chathaoir. Bhí Mac Uí Chroimín ann freisin. Chomh fada agus is léir domsa, is é seo an t-aon chumann Gaelach a bhfuil aon bhaint ag na hÉireannaigh shaibhre leis. I ndiaidh a chéile d'éirigh na daoine saibhre as na cumainn Ghaelacha eile. Fuair siad an iomarca easaontais, faltanais, agus troda iontu, agus ar fhaitíos go mbeadh siad féin measctha sna síordhíospóireachtaí agus imreasáin a bhíos i measc lucht na gcumann eile d'éirigh siad astu ar fad, nach mór, ach tagann siad isteach sa chumann seo, nach bhfuil de chuspóir aige ach teacht le chéile anois agus arís, dinnéir a ithe, agus a leithéid. Tá mé beagnach cinnte nach bhfuil na daoine is ábalta agus is saibhre agus is mó le rá, le fáil sna cumainn eile. Má bhíonn fear mór ábalta ina uachtarán nó go hard i ngradam in aon chumann acu, agus gur maith le scraiste nó stangaire éigin bheith ina áit, deirtear go ndéanann an scraiste ionsaí pearsanta ar an bhfear eile, agus go gcaitheann sé salachar leis, agus má chaitear go leor salachair greamóidh cuid de.

Nó má thagann easaontas nó imreasán ar bith ina measc, déanfar an rud céanna, agus ní hionadh nach gcuireann na daoine saibhre suas leis sin. 'Níl aon cheangal orainne bheith in aon chumann ar bith acu,' a deir siad. Is chun tairbhe na tíre, agus ní ar ár son féin, ná ar son saibhris ná tairbhe ná onóra dúinn féin atáimid sna cumainn seo, agus táimid ag fulaingt go leor uathu. Cén fáth a ndéanfaimis sin? Éirímis astu ar fad!'

Ar an lámh eile a deir Mac Uí Chathaláin 'gur scannalach an chaoi a dtréigeann na mic is fear a máthair Éire.' Deir sé 'go bhfuil na hÉireannaigh mhóra ag déanamh feille ar a ndaoine féin.' 'Dá mba mhian leo,' a deir sé, 'bheith páirteach leis na daoine, agus an cion ba dhual dóibh a dhéanamh, threoróidís na hÉireannaigh sa tslí cheart, agus thuillfidís buíochas agus onóir dóibh féin.' B'fhéidir go bhfuil cuid den cheart aige, ach mar sin féin, níl sé ach de réir nádúir nach rachadh daoine móra i gcomhluadar aon dreama a mbeadh siad cinnte go dtarraingeodh an dream sin trioblóid orthu féin.

Sílim go bhfuil an Cumann seo ann ó aimsir Washington anuas. B'éigean domsa cuid de m'eachtraí a insint dóibh, ó d'fhág mé Nua-Eabhrac gur tháinig mé ar ais, agus bhain mo chur síos i dtaobh an lóin a thug an Dr Thompson dom ag Columbus, agus an scéal greannmhar a d'inis Coirnéal Kilburn gáire astu. Bheadh iontaoibh mhór agam as na daoine seo dá bhféadfaí a gcuid náisiúntachta a chorraí. Ach nuair a éiríonn Éireannach saibhir agus go mbíonn neart airgid aige le bronnadh ar aon rud is maith leis, is annamh gur ar Éirinn ná ar aon rud a bhfuil baint aige le hÉirinn a bhronnas sé é. An chuid is mó acu tá siad an-fhial leis an Eaglais, agus bronnann siad a lán uirthi sin.

An naoú lá de Bhealtaine. Chaith mé an lá ag scríobh litreacha agus chaith mé féin agus mo bhean dinnéar le Monsieur agus le Madame Janvier. Bhí siad an-mhór le Sharpe, an tAlbanach a scríobhas faoin ainm chleite 'Fiona Macleod.' D'inis siad an fhírinne dom nach raibh aon 'Fhíona' ann riamh, agus gurbh í a dheirfiúr féin 'Fíona Nic Leóid' agus go ndeachtaíodh Sharpe gach ní di. Is *Felibres*[14] Janvier agus a bhean, agus is daoine an-gheanúla iad. Thángamar abhaile uathu tar éis an mheán oíche.

An deichiú lá de Bhealtaine. Tháinig Miss Coates, cara do Mhac Uí Chuinn, ar cuairt chugainn, agus thug sí mé féin agus mo bhean go dtí Halla na bPictiúr i Central Park, agus tháinig sí ar ais linne chun lóin.

Sa tráthnóna bhí dinnéar againn le muintir Cheallaigh. Bhí deartháir an Cheallaigh, Eoghan, agus fear eile ag an dinnéar. Chuamar abhaile tar éis an mheán oíche.

An t-aonú lá déag de Bhealtaine. Bhí lón agam le Mac Uí Fhaoláin, col ceathrar do Shéamas Ó Faoláin agus le Mac Uí Chaoimh.

Sa tráthnóna thug Mac Uí Chuinn sinne agus Miss Coates go dtí an Hippeadróm. Chonaiceamar rónta ansin, agus iad ag imirt le liathróid. Chaithidís an liathróid suas san aer ó rón go rón, agus ní ligidís dó titim ar an talamh ar feadh cúig nóiméad. Bhí ballet ann freisin, a raibh 170 duine ann, an ballet is mó, deir siad, sa domhan. Chuamar abhaile ag teacht ar an dó.

BUFFALO

An dóú lá déag de Bhealtaine. Tar éis na laethanta saoire seo, d'fhágamar Nua-Eabhrac arís. Is le dul ó thuaidh atáimid an t-am seo, go dtí Buffalo. Bhíomar aon uair déag ar an traein, agus ráiníomar Buffalo ar a seacht a chlog. Tháinig Mac Uí Riain, Mac Uí Mhurchú agus De Bhál faoinar gcoinne, agus tugadh sinn go dtí an teach ósta Iroquois. Tháinig go leor daoine ar cuairt chugam, an breitheamh de Ciniféic, Mac Uí Ruairc, Mac Uí Chonchúir (fear ar leis dhá pháipéar nuachta anseo), Mac Uí Riain de Chlann na nGael, Mac Uí Mhurchú, agus cuid mhaith eile, agus ní raibh siad uile imithe go dtí teacht ar an dó dhéag san oíche. Tháinig go leor de lucht páipéar, chomh maith.

An tríú lá déag de Bhealtaine. Dé Domhnaigh. Bhí lón agam le muintir Chiardha atá gaolmhar le Mrs Thursby agus gaolmhar le Mrs Stopford Green. Bhí sé ag steall-adh fearthainne. Labhair mé sa tráthnóna ag amharclann Uí Shé. Bhí timpeall dhá chéad déag duine i láthair. An tEaspag Colton a chuir mé in aithne do na daoine, agus an breitheamh de Ciniféic a bhí sa chathaoir. Bhí an tAthair Ó Comáin ó Ros Comáin ann, freisin. Tá sé ag bailiú airgid i gcomhair an teampaill bhreá atá sé ag dul a chur suas sa bhaile sin. Labhair mise ar feadh uaire agus daichead nóiméad. D'iarr an breitheamh airgead ar na daoine, agus thógamar 1,150 dollar.

An ceathrú lá déag de Bhealtaine. Tar éis a haon, chuamar ar thram go Niagara go bhfeicfimis an tEas Mór. Bhí Mac Uí Mhurchú agus Mac Uí Riain linn agus Bean Mhac Uí Mhurchú agus Bean de Bhál. Tugadh sinn go teach na cumhachta, áit a ndéantar an leictreachas. Bhí gearán mór i measc na ndaoine go raibh Niagara millte ag lucht an leictreachais, ach ní chreidim gur fíor é sin. Dar liomsa bhí an tEas Mór díreach chomh breá agus chomh forleathan agus a bhí sé nuair a bhí mé ansin ceithre bliana déag ó shin. Chuamar síos go bun an easa, agus bhreathnaíomar ar chuimhneachán Brock ar thaobh Cheanada den abhainn, agus chuamar chomh fada sin go bhfacamar Loch Ontario.

Chuamar ansin go dtí Coláiste Niagara atá faoi stiúradh lucht Naomh Uinseann. An tAthair Likly an t-uachtarán atá air. Bhí dinnéar againn ansin agus ar ndóigh theastaigh sé go géar uainn. Níor ith na mná a bhí linn aon bhlas óna mbricfeasta, agus bhíodar lag leis an ocras, fearacht mé féin.

Labhair mé ansin le tuairim is sé chéad mac léinn ar litríocht na nGael. Thángamar ar ais go dtí an teach ósta ar a 12.30, agus bhíomar an-sáraithe amach is amach.

An cúigiú lá déag de Bhealtaine. Bhí lón againn le Mac Uí Mhurchú. Sílim gur fear árachais é, agus bhí Mac Uí Riain de Chlann na nGael agus an tAthair Ó Súilleabháin (a dúirt gur tháinig sé dhá chéad míle le mo chloisteáil) ag an lón freisin. Tháinig an tAthair Ó Comáin ar cuairt chugam agus bhí caint agam leis. Chruinnigh sé a lán airgid i Meiriceá Theas ar son a theampaill.* Bhí gach uile dhuine an-tuirseach inniu tar éis an lae inné óir ní bhfuaireadar aon ní le n-ithe óna mbricfeasta go dtí a ndinnéar, ar a sé nó a seacht a chlog sa tráthnóna. Chaitheamar dinnéar inniu linn féin ar ár suaimhneas ag an teach ósta. Chuaigh mé ar cuairt go Mac Suibhne, fear díolta éadaigh ó Chontae Liatroma, a thug céad dollar dom tar éis an chruinnithe a bhí agam Dé Domhnaigh. 'Ní furasta airgead a fháscadh asamsa,' ar seisean, 'agus mura mbeadh gur aimsigh tú san áit cheart mé, ní bhfaighfeá é!'

ROCHESTER

D'imíomar araon go Rochester, ar an traein is luaithe dá raibh mé inti fós. Tugtar 'Empire State Express' air, agus rith sé seachtó míle i naoi nóiméad agus trí fichid. Tháinig Mac Uí Ghráda, Mac Uí Chonchúir fear páipéarachta, Mac Uí Bhrolcháin fear déanta uisce beatha nó leanna, agus Mac Uí Fhionmhacáin a bhfuil mórghléas teileafónachta aige in éineacht linn. Thug Mac Uí Fhionmhacáin sinn timpeall Ghleann Genessee, ina ghluaisteán. Labhair mé sa tráthnóna le timpeall is míle duine. Bhí an tEaspag Ó hÍcí i láthair. Ansin bhí fleá agus óráidí, fíon agus tobac, go dtí a trí a chlog ar maidin. Bhí breitheamh i láthair, Mac Uí Loinn, a labhair go han-mhaith ar fad, mar a shíl mise, agus sagart lách a raibh ainm aisteach air, an tAthair Codyre. Is deargnamhaid é do Mhac Uí Ghráda, agus sílim gurbh é an fear is mó a ghríosaigh na daoine eile chun mé a thabhairt chucu.

TORONTO

An seachtú lá déag de Bhealtaine.[15] Táimid le dul isteach go Ceanada anois, i measc daoine nach bhfuil fábhrach d'aon rud Gaelach, i measc na bhFear Oráiste nó na

*Agus tá a rian ar a theampall álainn i Ros Comáin inniu, an teampall is ornáidí dá bhfuil i gConnachta, sílim.

'bhFear Lóiste' mar a deireadh na seandaoine, i measc na bhFear Buí, nár dhearmad riamh a bhfaltanas leis na Gaeil – go Toronto!

Tháinig lucht fáiltithe go dtí an stáisiún, dhá charráiste acu, agus thiomáineadar sinn timpeall na háite. Bhí Albanach arbh ainm dó Frisealach in éineacht liomsa sa charráiste, fear an-lách ab ea é. Bhí ansin freisin fear de na Breathnaigh, Mac Uí Earáin,* dlíodóir, agus Mac Uí Iarnáin (búistéir, sílim); sin iad na príomh-Éireannaigh a casadh ormsa ansin.

Bhí cruinniú againn sa tráthnóna, ach má bhí, ní raibh Éireannaigh shaibhre na cathrach ar aon intinn ina thaobh. Dúradh liom nár tháinig mórán acu mar nach raibh a fhios acu i gceart céard a bhí fúm a rá, agus bhí faitíos orthu go mbeadh trioblóid éigin ann, agus d'fhanadar sa bhaile. Admhaím go raibh sórt eagla orm féin, agus cheap mé slí chun gach trioblóid a sheachaint, óir níor dhearmad mé an cruinniú a bhí agam in Ithaca. Tá na hAlbanaigh go láidir i dToronto, mar atá siad i ngach aon áit i gCeanada, agus chuir mé romham na hAlbanaigh a mholadh, ag ligean orm gur thar ceann Ghaeil na hAlban, chomh maith le thar ceann na nÉireannach a bhí mé ag caint. Dúirt mé gurbh iad na hAlbanaigh a chuir Ceanada ar a bhoinn agus go mba scannalach an scéal é go raibh ollscoil mhór i dToronto, agus nach raibh focal de sheanchas ná de theanga na ndaoine sin á múineadh inti. Lean mé den chaint ar an mbealach sin, agus thaithnigh sí go mór leis na hAlbanaigh, agus ní raibh na hÉireannaigh míshásta léi. Ní dúirt mé focal ar bith a bhéarfadh faill don namhaid. Bhí timpeall míle duine i láthair, agus ní fhéadfadh duine a rá an ar son Ghaeil na hÉireann nó ar son Ghaeil na hAlban a bhí mé ag labhairt!

An t-ochtú lá déag de Bhealtaine. Tháinig na páipéir nuachta go léir amach inniu, agus bhí aistí iontu fábhrach don chruinniú. Bhí an-áthas ormsa agus thaithnigh sé thar barr leis na hÉireannaigh. Chuir mé Éireannaigh Toronto faoi chomaoin agam, níos mó ná in aon chathair fós, óir is ar an maslú agus ar an gcáineadh is mó atá siad cleachtach. Ní bhfuaireadar focal de inniu!

Chaith mé an mhaidin ag dul tríd an gcathair. Dódh paiste mór den chathair cúpla bliain ó shin agus níl sí atógtha fós. Áiteanna móra breátha is ea Teach na Cúirte agus an Ollscoil. Shíl mise ón méid a chonaic mé go raibh an ithir níos fearr ná atá sí timpeall an chuid is mó de chathracha na Stát. Bhí lón againn le Mac Uí Earáin, le Mac Uí Iarnáin agus leis an mBreathnach agus tháinig siad go dtí an stáisiún linn ar a cúig a chlog le dul ar ais go Nua-Eabhrac.

An naoú lá déag de Bhealtaine. Chodail sinn ar an traein agus thángamar go Nua-Eabhrac ar maidin. Bhí lón agam le Mac Uí Chuinn agus leis an gCathalánach

*Hearn i mBéarla.

agus le fear eile. Chuaigh mé leis-sean agus le Miss Coates chun opera éadrom a fheiceáil, a raibh Fritzi Scheff ann. Chuamar abhaile tar éis a dó.

WASHINGTON

An fichiú lá de Bhealtaine. D'fhág mé Nua-Eabhrac le mo bhean, le dul go Washington. Ráiníomar an áit sin ar a cúig a chlog sa tráthnóna, agus casadh orainn an Dochtúir Ó Doinn agus an Dochtúir Ó hÉilí. Thugadar go dtí teach ósta, an New Willard, sinn. Bhí mé ag ithe mo dhinnéir roimh dhul amach go dtí an cruinniú dom, nuair a tháinig géarscoilteacha go tobann i mo dhroim, chuaigh an phian go croí ionam. Ba bheag nár fhág sé gan mhothú gan arann mé. Níor fhéad mé m'anáil a tharraingt, ná mo rítheacha ná mo lámha a shíneadh amach. Chuaigh mé go dtí an cruinniú cé go raibh pian mhillteach orm. Ní dhearna sé sin mórán dochair don chaint, ach amháin nach raibh sé ar mo chumas geáitsí ar bith a dhéanamh. Ba ghnách liom le linn dom bheith ag caint cromadh chun píosa láibe a thógáil den tsráid, mar dhea, ach shíl mé go bhfaighinn bás dá gcromfainn, agus d'fhág mé amach ar fad é. Sílim gurbh é rud ba chionsiocair leis na pianta seo, mé a bheith i mo shuí os coinne fuinneoige oscailte sa traein ar feadh ceithre uaire an chloig, agus an ghaoth bhogthe thaitneamhach ag séideadh isteach orm.

Bhí an cruinniú beag, timpeall ceithre chéad duine, ach má bhí sé beag bhí sé go maith. Bhí Uncail Joe Cannon Cathaoirleach an Tí ann, agus mórán daoine uaisle eile. Ba é an t-ainteas a bhí ann a choinnigh níos mó daoine ó bheith i láthair, sin agus go bhfuil an séasúr ag éirí rómhall do chruinnithe poiblí feasta. Bhí pian mhór ag gabháil dom ar feadh an ama ach mar sin féin labhair mé maith go leor, sílim.

An t-aonú lá fichead de Bhealtaine. Tá na pianta go dona fós, agus is ar éigean a bhí sé ar mo chumas siúl suas go dtí an Teach Bán le lón a chaitheamh leis an Uachtarán Roosevelt. Tháinig Mac Uí Dhoinn, Ollamh na Gaeilge san Ollscoil Chaitliceach in éineacht liom, agus an Dochtúir Mac Aogáin, fear beag dathúil a raibh féasóg mhogallach ghearr air, cara don Uachtarán. 'In ainm Dé,' arsa an tAogánach liom, agus sinne ag dul suas le chéile, 'ná sceith orm.' Is é rud a chiallaigh sé leis sin, is dóigh, ná lig ort nach Gaeilgeoir mé. *Don't let me down*, ar seisean i mBéarla 'Ná bíodh faitíos ort,' arsa mise, agus fuair mé ócáid in imeacht an lóin a rá leis an Uachtarán, 'Baineann mo chara anseo le ceann de bhunaidh mhóra scolártha Iarthar na hEorpa, Mic Aogáin ó Bhaile Mhic Aogáin i gContae Thiobraid Árann,' agus ar ndóigh is é a bhí sásta. Bhí

bainċéile an tsúilleaḃáiniġ

Alice Phelan, wife of Frank Sullivan, sister of James Phelan. Le caoinchead Fhoras na Gaeilge lón simplí againn. Bhí Admiral Cole a phós deirfiúr an Uachtaráin, agus deirfiúr a mhná féin agus bean eile ag an lón linn. Bhí an tUachtarán tar éis aiste a scríobh ag déanamh comórtais idir an seanscéal Gaeilge agus an sága Lochlannach. Dúirt sé nuair a scríobh sé a litir scaitheamh beag roimhe sin faoi na rátaí ar na bóithre iarainn go raibh a fhios aige go bhfaigheadh sé masla mar gheall uirthi ar fud na tíre, agus chun a intinn a chur ó smaoineamh air sin a scríobh sé aiste ar fhilíocht na nGael. Bhí sé an-lách an-chúirtéiseach, agus dá n-abróinn é, muinteartha linn.

Tar éis an lóin d'fhill mé le Mac Mhic Aogáin go dtí an Cosmos Club, agus d'ól mé *Mint Julep* leis. Deoch choitianta san áit seo í sin, ach ní fhacas í in aon áit eile. Is cosúil é le *High Ball* agus é líonta amach i ngloine mhór ard, agus béal na gloine dúnta le pósae de mhiontas. Chun an deoch a ól cuireann duine a bhéal agus a shrón sa mhiontas, agus tarraingíonn sé isteach blas agus cumhracht na luibhe. Bhí mé go dona leis na pianta nuair a d'ól mé an chéad deoch agus shíl mé gur tháinig biseach orm dá bharr. Ar chuma ar bith níor fhág mé an club agus níor lig Mac Mhic Aogáin uaidh mé go raibh ceithre cinn ólta againn beirt. Cé gur ar éigean a d'éirigh liom mé féin a tharraingt go dtí an Teach Bán, bhí ar mo chumas siúl ar ais go dtí an teach ósta go réasúnta maith.

An dóú lá fichead de Bhealtaine. Chuamar suas ar an abhainn, buíon againn, Mac Mhic Aogáin, an Dochtúir Ó Doinn, Bean Uí Shúilleabháin, beirt iníonacha an Aogánaigh, Caimbéalach atá tar éis teacht abhaile ó na hOileáin Fhilipíneacha, agus roinnt daoine eile. Chuamar go dtí Mount Vernon áit a raibh áras Washington. Tá sin aon mhíle dhéag suas ar an abhainn. Chuamar trína theach, seanteach den chineál bhíodh acu an uair sin nuair a bhí Meiriceá ina choilíneacht. Thug mé faoi deara go raibh go leor seabhac mór, éan atá idir seabhac agus préachán, a dtugann siad *buzzard* air, ag foluain agus ag gabháil thart go hard sa spéir. Is iad lucht glanta na háite iad sin, agus tá dlí ann in aghaidh a maraithe. Nuair a gheibheann aon rud bás ní féidir a cheilt orthusan. Fanann siad go mbeidh an fheoil bog go leor dóibh, agus ansin slogann siad í ar an bpointe boise. Ní fhaca mé i gceart iad gur tháinig mé anseo. Chonaiceamar tuama Washington, an seomra ina bhfuair sé bás, agus mórán eile. Thug mé faoi deara go mba theachín ar leith a bhí sa chisteanach agus theachín ar leith eile i dteach an bhainne, bothán ar leith eile ag fear an ghairdín, agus tithe ar leith ag na daoine gorma. Ba chosúil le seanghairdín Sasanach an gairdín.

Chuaigh mé go dtí an Ollscoil Chaitliceach sa tráthnóna agus thug mé léacht dóibh ar Chonradh na Gaeilge, agus bhí cuid mhaith cainte agam leis na hollúna agus leis an Dochtúir Ó Séacháin. Bhí siad ag cur síos go flúirseach ar an gcéad ollamh Gaeilge a bhí acu, an Déiseach ó Phort Lách. Tá eagla orm go ndearna sé naimhde den choláiste ar fad. Ní raibh aon duine acu páirteach leis. Rinne mé óráid mhaith agus tháinig mé abhaile ar an dó dhéag.

An tríú lá fichead de Bhealtaine. Chuaigh mé in éineacht le mo sheanchara Séamas Ó Maonaigh go dtí an Smithsonian Institute. Tá leabhar mór scríofa aigesean a thug sé dom roimhe seo,* agus ní dóigh liom go bhfuil fear eile i Meiriceá a bhfuil oiread eolais ar na hIndiaigh aige agus atá aigesean. Chuir sé mé in aithne do mhórán de na daoine atá gnóthach ar obair na hInstitiúide agus ó bhí a fhios acu gur chruinnigh mé féin scéalta i measc na nIndiach i gCeanada, na Mailisítigh, nuair a bhí mé ann, dosaen de bhlianta roimhe sin, agus gur chuir mé i gcló iad i bpáipéar Meiriceánach, rinneadar ball den Institiúid díom. Bhí siad le gach leabhar a thagann amach uathu a chur chugam. Tá na pictiúir a rinne Catlin acu san Institiúid agus mórán boghanna agus saighead agus gach rud eile a bhain le hIndiaigh i ngach aon áit i Meiriceá.** Ní fhéadaimid an iomarca molta a thabhairt don Rialtas faoin obair mhór seo agus faoin méid a rinneadar chun solas a ligean isteach ar sheanbhéasa agus ar stair agus ar chultúr na ndaoine Rua. Is náire do Shasana nach ndearna sí rud éigin den sórt céanna san Astráil i measc na ndaoine gorma sula gcailltear iad go léir.

Thug mé léacht eile ar Litríocht na nGael don Ollscoil Chaitliceach. Thug Bean an tSúilleabhánaigh léi ina carráiste sinn, agus bhí dinnéar agamsa le Moinsíneoir Ó Conaill, Uachtarán na hOllscoile, agus chuaigh mo bhean chun dinnéir leis an Dochtúir Ó Sé agus daoine eile.

An ceathrú lá fichead de Bhealtaine. Chuaigh mé go dtí an Seanad, go gcloisfinn iad. Ní raibh aon rud tábhachtach ar siúl, agus ba righin spadalach an scéal é. Chuaigh mé go dtí an Teach Íochtarach ansin. Bhí gach rud i bhfad níos beoga ann, ach shíl mise go raibh easpa mórgachta orthu. Chonaic mé triúr fear ar a gcosa san am céanna, agus ní leis an gcathaoirleach a labhair siad, ach ag tiontú chun a chéile. Ní raibh Uncail Joe sa chathaoir, agus b'éigean don fhear a bhí ina áit an bord a bhualadh arís agus arís eile lena chasúirín chun ordú éigin a chur orthu. Ina dhiaidh sin chuamar isteach i leabharlann na Comhdhála, atá go han-bhreá, go róbhreá mar a shíl mise, agus go ró-ornáideach.

Chuaigh mé sa tráthnóna go dtí an ollscoil arís, agus labhair mé le slua mór daoine ar Bhéaloideas. Chaith mé dinnéar le Moinsíneoir Ó Conaill agus leis an Dr Ó Séacháin. Tháinig mé abhaile ar an dó dhéag.

**Myths of the Cherokee*, 576 leathanach, agus mórán pictiúr ann.

**Tá mé ag fáil na leabhar breá seo riamh ó shin, de réir mar a thagann siad amach. Tá beagnach ceithre fichid ceann agam díobh, agus nuair a d'fhág mé Baile Átha Cliath, i 1933, bhronn mé iad go léir ar an gCumann le Béaloideas.

An cúigiú lá fichead de Bhealtaine. Tá orainn Washington a fhágáil inniu. Is iontach breá an chathair í. Tá suíomh álainn uirthi, agus tá an foirgneamh is breátha i Meiriceá, an Capitol, inti. Tá leabharlann na Comhdhála mar a bheadh coill de philéir agus de cholúin áille marmair ann, ach shíl mise go raibh sé millte ag na drochphictiúir a bhí ar crochadh ar na ballaí agus leis an iomarca ornáidíochta. Sílim gur Francach a leag amach an chathair agus dar liomsa tá sí níos cosúla le Páras ná le haon chathair eile dá raibh mise inti. Tá trí acra go leith faoi phríomháras na cathrach, an Capitol, agus tá sráideanna móra breátha leathana sínte amach uaidh sin go deas agus go rialta. Tá an chuid is mó de na sráideanna ó thríocha go daichead slat ar leithead. Is de mharmar atá an cuimhneachán do Washington féin, agus tá sé 555 troigh ar airde. Ní dhéantar aon sórt earraí sa chathair, níl inti ach an áit a rialaítear na Stáit aisti. Ní bhaineann an chathair féin le haon stát faoi leith ach tá sí tógtha ar phíosa talún di féin, a dtugtar District of Columbia air. Tá an ceantar beag seo neamhspleách, agus rialaíonn sé é féin. Daoine gorma is ea timpeall trian de na cathróirí. Tá cúpla ollscoil eile ann chomh maith leis an ollscoil Chaitliceach, ach ní fhaca mise iad. Tá na fir a bhaineas leis an ollscoil Chaitliceach ar na daoine is leithne agus is léire intinn dár casadh orm fós. Is fíor-Mheiriceánaigh iad, gan blas d'Iodálachas ina measc, agus labhair siad chomh neamhspleách sin faoi gach rud gur chuir sé iontas orm. Bhí an teas chomh mór sin nár leasc linn an áit álainn seo a fhágáil. Chuamar ar bord na traenach go Nua-Eabhrac ar a haon déag ar maidin, agus tháinig an Dr Ó hÉilí, an Dr Ó Doinn agus Séamas Ó Maonaigh go dtí an stáisiún, le slán a chur linn. Ráiníomar Nua-Eabhrac ar a cúig sa tráthnóna.

Bhí mé ag dul amach chun dinnéir le Mac Uí Chuinn nuair a tiomáineadh gléas múchta tine síos an tsráid, agus ar scuabadh tharainn dó léim splaincín beag as an inneall agus chuaigh sé i mo shúil. Ba bheag nár dalladh mé. Thug Mac Uí Chuinn go dtí ceathrar dochtúirí mé sula bhfuair sé duine acu a bhainfeadh an splanc as mo shúil.

An séú lá fichead de Bhealtaine. Chuaigh mé chun lóin ag Tigh Delmonico le Mac Uí Chuinn, Mac Uí Chathaláin, Brisbane, an breitheamh Mac Eochaidh agus Peadar Fionnalaigh Ó Doinn a bhfuil a ainm in airde ar fud Mheiriceá go léir mar 'Mister Dooley.' Shuíomar chun lóin ar a haon a chlog agus níor fhágamar an áit go dtí a sé. A leithéid de chaint níor chuala mé ariamh, gach uile dhuine againn ag caint agus ag scéalaíocht. D'éiríodh Mac Uí Dhoinn gach ceathrú uaire le labhairt ar an nguthán le duine éigin á rá go mbeadh sé ar ais i gceann ceathrú uaire eile, ach d'imigh ceathrú uaire i ndiaidh ceathrú uaire, agus níor chorraigh sé! Bhí mise i mo shuí lena ais agus bhí mórán cainte agam leis. Tá baint aige, sílim, le Clann na nGael. Níl a chaint leath chomh greannmhar lena scríbhneoireacht, agus sílim gurbh é an duine againn ba lú caint ag an gcóisir é. Mar sin féin is lách geanúil an fear é.

Níorbh fhurasta é, sílim, seisear fear eile a tabhairt le chéile cosúil leis an seisear a bhí againn inniu, ag an lón seo.

BRIDGEPORT

D'fhág mé féin agus mo bhean Nua-Eabhrac le dul go Bridgeport. Tá sé suite ar Long Island. Níl an t-oileán leathan, ach tá sé timpeall ceithre fichid míle nó mar sin ar fad. Tháinig Mr Wren go dtí an stáisiún faoinár gcoinne, agus thug sé dá theach féin sinn. Is fear déanta uisce beatha é. Caitliceach é, ach mar sin féin tá sé le seacht mbliana déag ina uachtarán ar Bhord an Oideachais anseo. Bhí Maor na Cathrach, Mac Uí Mhurthuile, milliúnaí a raibh baint aige leis an mbóthar iarainn, Ginearál éigin, agus triúr nó ceathrar eile ag an dinnéar a thug sé dom, ach ní raibh bean ar bith i láthair.

Ansin bhí cruinniú mór againn san amharclann agus labhair mé ar feadh dhá uair an chloig leo, ach bhí piachán orm agus tá faitíos orm nár labhair mé go rómhaith. Chuaigh mé a chodladh ar a 12.30.

An t-ochtú lá fichead de Bhealtaine. Tháinig seanfhear, Mac Uí Shúilleabháin, isteach le m'fheiceáil ó Hartford. Thug sé maide iontach dom a raibh dhá shórt déag d'adhmad sa cheann. D'fhágamar an áit seo ar a haon déag a chlog agus thángamar ar ais slán go dtí Nua-Eabhrac.

PATERSON

Ach ní luaithe a ráinigh mé Nua-Eabhrac ná a d'fhágas arís é, le dul go Paterson, New Jersey. Bhí sé ag stealladh fearthainne, agus bhí sé an-fhuar. Bhí an lá inniu deich gcéim fichead níos fuaire ná an lá inné. Ráinigh mé Paterson ar a sé a chlog. Is é seo an baile is mó i gcomhair síoda i Meiriceá.

Bhí dinnéar agam ag club, le Mag Thoirealaigh,* beirt bhreithiúna, agus an Sirriam. Bhí cruinniú ansin againn san amharclann ach ní cruinniú mór a bhí ann óir scanraigh an tromfhearthainn na daoine. Labhair mé go maith, níos fearr ná ag Bridgeport, agus thángamar go léir ar ais agus shuíomar os cionn ár bhfíona go dtí leathuair tar éis a haon.

An naoú lá fichead de Bhealtaine. Is dlíodóir Mag Thoirealaigh a bhfuil an saol ag éirí go maith leis, agus tá áit álainn aige. Níl sé pósta agus tá a dheirfiúr ina cónaí

*Gourley i mBéarla.

leis. Thug an bheirt acu amach mé i ngluaisteán go dtí áit a dtugtar Carraig an Iolair air, agus go dtí na Sléibhte Oráiste, os cionn Newark agus Orange, agus bhíomar ag féachaint ar Nua-Eabhrac i bhfad uainn, cúig mhíle déag nó fiche míle. Mar sin féin bhí na foirgnimh mhóra atá in aice leis an mBattery le feiceáil go soiléir, agus chonaiceamar an t-ard-teampall ar Shráid 50, agus na foirgnimh mhóra eile uainn mar a bheadh sléibhte ann. Tá an ceantar seo ar fad ina aon sraith de thithe áille agus de ghairdíní deasa gleoite, agus gan claí ná balla eatarthu, ach iad go léir le taobh a chéile. An chuid is mó de na daoine a chónaíos iontu, bíonn siad ag obair i Nua-Eabhrac ar feadh an lae agus tagann siad amach anseo i gcomhair na hoíche. Daoine eile, cónaíonn siad i Nua-Eabhrac sa gheimhreadh agus tagann siad amach anseo sa samhradh. Ó bharr Charraig an Iolair bhí mé ag féachaint ar cheantar a raibh oiread daoine ann agus atá in Éirinn go léir. Ráinigh mé an traein ar a 2.40, agus thug sí go Nua-Eabhrac mé ar a 4.30, in am leis an Bhálach* a fheiscint, chun agallamh a bheith agam leis ar son na bpáipéar.

Tháinig Mrs Worthington agus Miss Merrington .i. an bhean uasal a thug an dea-chomhairle dom i dtaobh lucht páipéarachta nuair a bhí mé ar bord na loinge ag teacht, ar cuairt chugainn.

An deichiú lá fichead de Bhealtaine. Tugann siad 'Decoration Day' ar an lá seo, agus chuaigh mé féin, mo bhean agus Mac Uí Chuinn chun lóin le Mac Uí Chathaláin. Bhí a bhean, a dheartháir agus a athair ag an dinnéar chomh maith. Níor chuala mé riamh cainteoir Gaeilge ní b'fhearr ná a athair. Ó dheisceart Chontae Chorcaí dó, ó áit éigin nach bhfuil rófhada ón Sciobairín, sílim. Ba é an t-athair a dúirt liom nach é Cothalán ach Cathalán an sloinne ceart, agus gur 'fear catha' an chiall atá leis.

An t-aonú lá déag ar fhichid de Bhealtaine. Bhí dinnéar againn le Mrs Worthington ag Club na nEalaíon. Bhí Miss Merrington ann freisin. Bhris gadaithe isteach ina seomra an oíche roimhe sin. Bhí cúpla ceoltóir ann agus tháinig Mac Uí Chuinn, isteach mall. Chuamar abhaile ar an dó dhéag.

An chéad lá de Mheitheamh. Chuaigh mé go Hollenbeck, an fónagrafóir a thug gléas dom chun Fraincis, Gearmáinis agus Spáinnis a fhoghlaim trína fhónagraf. Labhair mé Gaeilge isteach i gceann de na píobaí i gcomhair an fhónagraif.

Chuaigh mé ar cuairt ansin chuig an Haicéadach óg agus chaith mé lón leis.

Thug Mac Uí Chuinn páirtí tae, agus bhí Mrs Worthington, Miss Merrington, Miss Coates agus daoine eile i láthair.

An dara lá de Mheitheamh. D'fhan mé istigh i rith an lae ag scríobh litreacha agus ag críochnú aiste do Scribner.

*Wall i mBéarla.

An tríú lá de Mheitheamh. Chuaigh mé féin agus mo bhean agus Mac Uí Chuinn go teach an Bhreithimh Mac Eochaidh chun lóin, agus lena leabharlann nua a fheiceáil. Tháinig Bean Mhic Giollarnáth agus bean eile go teach an Bhreithimh agus thugadar sinn go háit beagán mílte amach as an áit a rabhamar, go dtí a dteach féin, ag Rye. Thugadar dinnéar breá dúinn ansin. Ní raibh ann ach sinn féin agus dochtúir Gearmánach. D'fhanamar ar an áiléar nó *balcony* os cionn an dorais go dtí a dó dhéag san oíche ag déanamh iontais den fharraige atá ag teacht suas, beagnach, go dtí an teach.

An ceathrú lá de Mheitheamh. Thug an bheirt bhan sinn i ngluaisteán go dtí an stáisiún agus thángamar ar ais slán go Nua-Eabhrac. Chuamar go páirtí ag teach Mrs Worthington: bhí timpeall dáréag i láthair. Bhí Mark Twain le bheith ann ach theip air trí thimpiste éigin. Bhí dinnéar againn sa tráthnóna le Mac Uí Chuinn ag Teach Delmonico agus bhí an sean-Chonchúrach as Elmira ann.

An cúigiú lá de Mheitheamh. Chuaigh mé go Teach Scribner, agus thug mé an aiste dóibh. Ansin chuaigh mé ar cuairt go dtí Gilder, eagarthóir an *Century*, agus thug sé leis mé go Club na nAisteoirí chun lóin. Ansin chuaigh mé go Wessel, an foilsitheoir leabhar, óir chuala mé gur chuir Fisher Unwin cuid d'*Abhráin Diadha Chúige Connacht* chuige. Bhí dinnéar agam féin agus ag mo bhean le Mac Uí Fhaoláin, col ceathrar do mo chara Séamas Ó Faoláin. Ag Club na mBád Seoil, os cionn na Hudson, a bhí an dinnéar. Bhí an lá an-te ar fad, ach bhí sé go deas fionnuar ar an abhainn, agus d'fhanamar ann go dtí leathuair tar éis a haon déag.

Tá an aimsir ag éirí chomh te sin, cheana féin, nach furasta a seasamh. Rachaimid ar ais go hÉirinn chomh luath agus is féidir linn. Tá m'obair críochnaithe sa tír seo.

An séú lá de Mheitheamh. Thug Miss Merrington páirtí dúinn i seomraí mná eile. Bhí mórán daoine suimiúla ann, Mrs Choate, Mrs Sinéad Custer, Mrs Thursby, agus roinnt eile.

Tar éis an pháirtí thug Mac Uí Chuinn sinne agus mo chara Mrs Thursby chun dinnéir i dTeach Delmonico. Nuair a bhí an dinnéar thart chuaigh mé féin agus mo bhean go dtí an amharclann, go bosca a thug Miss Merrington dúinn, chun Sothern agus Miss Marlowe a fheicsint.

Bhíomar cráite leis an teas ar maidin, ach thiontaigh sé fuar fliuch san oíche. Níor thángamar ar ais go dtí a haon a chlog san oíche.

An seachtú lá de Mheitheamh. Chuaigh mé arís go moch ar maidin go dtí Comhlacht na Long Gaile, óir bhí éadóchas orm i dtaobh aon long a fháil. Chuaigh mé síos go minic cheana go dtí oifig na long ach theip orm slí a fháil in aon cheann acu. Chuamar síos inniu le súil, b'fhéidir, go gcuirfeadh duine éigin suas dá sheomra féin, agus díreach cúig nóiméad sular thángamar isteach chuir duine éigin suas don seomra a bhí tógtha aige, agus ghlac mise ar an bpointe é. 450 dollar a bhí ar an seomra, ach cibé airgead a bhí air b'éigean dúinn a ghlacadh, óir níor fhéadamar an teas a sheasamh níos faide i Nua-Eabhrac, agus dúirt Mac Uí Chuinn gur ag dul in olcas a bheadh sé. Dá mbeinn cúig nóiméad níos déanaí b'fhéidir go gcaillfinn mo sheomra. An *Celtic* is ainm don long, agus fágann sí Nua-Eabhrac an cúigiú lá déag.

Bhí dinnéar againn ag an *Majestic* le Mac Uí Chuinn agus le Miss Coates. Tháinig Gregg isteach sa tráthnóna. Bhí aithne agam air, fadó, in Éirinn. Tá sé ag obair ar pháipéar nuachta anseo, agus tá ag éirí go maith leis. D'fhanamar ag caint agus ag caitheamh tobac go dtí a dó a chlog. Ba mhór an suaimhneas a thug sé do m'intinn áit a fháil ar bord loinge faoi dheireadh.

An t-ochtú lá de Mheitheamh. D'fhan mé sa teach ar feadh an lae ag cleachtadh conas úsáid a bhaint as cló-inneall. Chaitheamar dinnéar le Mac Uí Chuinn sa tráthnóna. Tháinig Séarlas Mac Seáin agus a bhean isteach, agus chaitheadar an tráthnóna linn. Bhí aithne agam air in Éirinn. Is bean lách chliste a bhean.

D'fhan mé istigh ar feadh na maidine ag cur síos nótaí. Labhair an Mac Roibín sin a chonaic mé in San Francisco liom ar an nguthán, agus d'iarr orm dinnéar a chaitheamh leis ag an Waldorf. Chuaigh mé chuige agus bhí dinnéar agam in éineacht leis féin agus lena innealtóir Lee agus le fear eile, Todd a ainm. Ghlaoigh sé ar ard-chócaire an Waldorf agus chuir sé mise in aithne dó, agus thug an t-ard-chócaire a leabhar mór cócaireachta mar bhronntanas dom.* Ghlaoigh sé ar an bhfear a bhí os cionn an ólacháin agus thug sé air *cocktail* ar nós an stua-fhearthainne a dhéanamh dúinn. Dúirt Mac Roibín gurbh é seo an t-aon fhear amháin a bhí in ann a dhéanta. Thóg an fear freastail gloine fhada chaol agus dhoirt sé *liqueur* éigin isteach inti. Anuas air sin dhoirt sé *liqueur* eile go mall. Níor mheasc an dara ceann leis an gcéad cheann, ach d'fhan ar a uachtar. Ansin chuir sé *liqueur* eile isteach, agus rinne sé sin le sé nó seacht gcinn de *liqueuraí*, agus níor meascadh iad le chéile, agus bhí a dhath dílis féin, bán, buí, dearg, glasuaine nó gorm ar gach aon acu. Tugtar *rainbow cocktail* air sin. Nuair a óltar é, óltar gach *liqueur* acu i ndiaidh a chéile in aon deoch amháin, agus deirtear go n-ullmhaíonn gach *liqueur* acu an tslí roimh an gceann a leanas é! Thiomáin sé ar ais mé go teach Mhac Uí Chuinn, agus tháinig sé féin isteach, agus d'fhan sé ag caint agus ag aithriseoireacht go dtí leathuair i ndiaidh a haon a chlog.

Thug Mac Uí Chuinn fuath dó ar an bpointe, agus níor lig sé dó aon sórt muintearais a dhéanamh leis.**

*Thug mise mar bhronntanas do Mrs Stopford Green é nuair a tháinig mé abhaile.
**Scéal fada é an chaoi ar casadh orm é trí chinniúint in Éirinn, agus an chaoi a bhfuair sé faill ar fheall a dhéanamh ormsa, agus ar dhaoine eile.

An deichiú agus an t-aonú lá déag de Mheitheamh. D'fhanamar istigh sa teach go dtí a 4.30. Bhí lón againn ansin agus chuamar amach le dul go Bá Sheepshead. Bhí dinnéar maith againn ag teach ósta Tappan, agus d'fhanamar ag faire ar Coney Island, agus é go léir faoi bhrat solais. Ba chosúil le Tír na nÓg é. In aird eile den spéir bhí tintreach den dá shórt ag spréacharnaigh thar Sandy Hook, bhí an tintreach ghearr ghabhlach ann, spící géara, agus an tintreach mhall leathan a mhaireadh ar feadh leathnóiméid. Sular fhágamar Nua-Eabhrac bhí stoirm mhór luaithrigh agus deannaigh ann, agus tháinig an fhearthainn anuas amhail agus dá n-osclófaí an spéir. Rinne sé damáiste mór. Shuigh an triúr againn le Miss Smith ar áiléar a tí-se ag breathnú ar an stoirm. Chuireamar fúinn ina teachsa. Bhaineamar triail ansin as caitheamh aimsire Coney Island, ag rith anuas i mbád ó bharr cnoic isteach i loch, ag marcaíocht ar dhá chamall, etc.

Lá nó dhó ina dhiaidh sin thug Mac Uí Chuinn dinnéar dúinn ag Teach Delmonico, agus bhí an breitheamh Ó Dúllaing, an breitheamh Mac Eochaidh agus a bhean, Liam Temple Emmet, Bean Shéamais Uí Bhroin, Mr Snyder agus a bhean, agus beirt nó triúr eile ann. Chaith mé dhá lá nó trí ag cur chun bealaigh timpeall céad cóip de *Abhráin Diadha Chúige Connacht* (2 imleabhar) go dtí na daoine is mó a chuidigh liom i ngach áit a raibh mé. Chuir Fisher Unwin anonn chugam iad roimh ré, agus thángadar in am. Scríobh mé m'ainm i ngach leabhar acu agus ainm an té ar ar bhronn mé iad, agus litir leis an gcuid is mó acu. Bhí an oiread sin deifre orm ag fágáil Nua-Eabhrac faoi dheireadh, nach raibh an t-am agam focal a scríobh chun slán a fhágáil ag Meiriceá, ach dúirt Mac Uí Chuinn liom sin a dhéanamh, agus scríobhas a leath ina sheomrasan ar maidin, agus an leath eile ar bhord na loinge, agus thug seisean ar ais leis í, agus thug í go dtí gach páipéar tráthnóna agus arís ar maidin go dtí na páipéir mhaidine.

Ag seo nóta a scríobh Mac Uí Chuinn dom nuair a d'fhágas an chathair:

'An méid airgid a bailíodh i rith an Turais Mhóir cuireadh i dtaisce é sa Trust Company of America. Coinníodh na cuntais go cúramach, faoi stiúradh oifige de lucht cuntais, agus d'oibrigh mé féin ar feadh trí nó ceathair d'oícheanta, nó go raibh sé déanach san oíche, ag dul tríd na figiúir sular imigh tusa. Cuireadh isteach admháil ar son gach ní, ar son stampaí féin, agus gach mionairgead a d'íoc an Faoiteach.* Scrúdaíodh gach admháil leis an bhfear cuntais, agus dúirt sé go raibh siad go léir ceart. Dhá lá no trí tar éis an tseic dheiridh** ar an Trust Company a tharraingt amach dom, – seic a ráinigh, de réir lucht an chuntais, tóin an airgid, – fuair mé scéal foirmiúil ón Trust Company go raibh aon cent amháin sa bhreis tarraingthe amach agam! Taispeánann

*Rúnaí Mhac Uí Chuinn.
**Seic ar os cionn deich míle punt a thug sé dom le tabhairt abhaile liom.

sé sin chomh poncúil agus a bhí na cuntasóirí, agus chomh cúramach agus a bhíodar ina bhfigiúir!'

Níl aon rud eile le rá agam, ach gur thángamar slán abhaile, agus gur cuireadh fáilte mhór romhainn i mBaile Átha Cliath. Chuir mé an deich míle punt* sa bhanc ar son Chonradh na Gaeilge, agus dúirt mé leis an gCoiste gur gheall mé do lucht Mheiriceá nach gcaithfinn níos mó ná dhá mhíle de gach bliain!

Thug an t-airgead sin an Conradh go díreach go doras na hOllscoile, agus d'oscail an doras – ar éigean – nuair a bhí deireadh leis.

Mo thuras go Meiriceá go nuige sin.

*Féach nóta, lch 313.

NÓTAÍ

Leathanach 168
Ba í Eibhlín, deirfiúr Sheáin Uí Laoghaire, a d'iarr orm an t-amhrán seo a cheapadh. Rinne mé sin di i mBéarla agus sílim go raibh sí sásta leis. Ina dhiaidh sin chuir mé Gaeilge air. Seo é an chéad rann más cuimhneach liom i gccart é:

Féach sinne, clann na hÉireann
Rugadh ins an oileán seo
Támaoid bailighthe ar ár sléibhtibh
Mar ba ghnáthach linn, fad ó.
Féach na h-airm ar ár ngualain,
Ní'l aon phíce in ár láimh,
M'anam d'fheicfí iad go luath linn
Dá mbéadh Éire in a ngádh!

Curfá.
Ar son Éireann támaoid bailighthe,
Támaoid cruinnighthe ar an sliabh,
Gan aon sgannradh gan aon fhaitcheas
Gan aon eagla acht roimh Dhia, srl, srl.

Leathanach 182
Níor éirigh leis an gcruinniú mór i mBostún leath chomh maith agus ba chóir dó. Cúrsaí polaitíochta agus an faltanas a bhí i measc na nÉireannach féin is mó faoi deara sin. 'An dream bocht silte nár chuir lena chéile.' Chuir an tAthair Ó Sírín litir go Seán Ó Cuinn dhá mhí i ndiaidh mo léachta, ag míniú dó cad chuige nár éirigh liom níos fearr. Ní chreidim ar fad go bhfuil an ceart aige ina n-abrann sé, ach mar sin féin cuirim síos anseo é, óir taispeánfaidh sé an t-achrann ar ár shábháil Seán Ó Cuinn mé i Nua-Eabhrac. Níl aon chuimhne agam ar an Athair Ó Sírín, agus níl a fhios agam ar casadh orm riamh é:

East Boston, Feb. 5th, 1906

Dear Mr Quinn,
I enclose checks for $1,783.83 representing in total proceeds of the lecture given by Douglas Hyde in Boston, December 3, 1905.

I regret very much that the amount is so small. I was hopeful that the 'Hub' would surely be a good second to New York in this work. Since the event I have had time to reflect on the conditions that lead to failure, and as they unfold themselves to me, I am rather amazed that we even got so much as we did. Discord and inability to amalgamate in behalf of the common cause was very markedly shown by the United I. Leaguers, Hibernians and Clan-na-Gael. Many of them pretended to be working for the cause whilst in reality they would rather block its success because they considered it took some of the water away from their own mill. Besides when Concannon first came to Boston he fell into the hands of some former friends who never exhibited any interest in the Gaelic cause previous to his arrival. These persons did not know the Gaelic workers of Boston. As a consequence in the preparatory meetings the natural allies and friends of Douglas Hyde and his cause were overlooked **unintentionally.** Many of them considered themselves ignored by this mishap and in consequence sat down and looked on, claiming that as John Redmond had associated himself with his natural allies so should Douglas Hyde and Concannon.

Added to all this there was a bitter 'donnybrook-fair' political contest between the Irish people at the time, in the city of Boston, and both Concannon and Hyde were unwittingly made victims to it by small designing politicians.

As I see them, these were the conditions that led to the financial failure of the said lecture. The worst feature that I see in the whole affair, is that instead of cementing the Gaelic Schools of Boston and vicinity, which should be Hyde's natural allies, into an amalgamated body to which he or his successors in the cause could appeal in the future, they have been left in a more disintegrated state than they were in previous to his visit.

Personally, therefore, in behalf of the cause, I would suggest that Hyde should not leave the US without taking some steps in New England to amalgamate and unify the efforts of Gaelic Leaguers for the future. Therefore, if you have a chance to do so, I would ask you to bring this matter to his attention before he quits the country.

Sincerely yours,

Rev. Daniel S. Sheerin.

Leathanach 186

Scríobhadh 'The Groves of Blarney' mar aithris mhagaidh ar 'Castle Hyde.' Tá aithne ag formhór na ndaoine ar 'The Groves of Blarney,' ach is beag duine anois a chuala an bunamhrán. Chuala mé féin é i gContae Ros Comáin nuair a bhí mé óg, agus ó nach bhfuil sé le fáil i gcló, chomh fada agus is eol domsa, cuirfidh mé síos anseo é.

Níor thug an hÍdeach a bhí sa Chaisleán an uair sin aon duais don bhard bocht a rinne an t-amhrán, ach bhí súil ag an bhfile le duais mhór. Thiontaigh sé an véarsa deiridh ansin, agus chuir sé cruth nua air. Dúirt sé:

> 'In all my thradin' and serenadin'
> I met no n*é*ager like Humpy Hyde.'

Thug sé 'humpy' air de bhrí go raibh cruit air. Nuair a bhí sé ina naíonán an-óg tugadh anuas an staighre é, lá a bhaiste, is dóigh, lena thaispeáint don chuideachta. Bhí gearr-chaile beag ann agus d'iarr sí go géar é a iompar. Tugadh di é agus thit sé uaithi, agus loiteadh a dhroim. Tharla nuair a d'éirigh an bheirt acu suas gur thit sé i ngrá leis an gcailín seo, ach nuair a d'iarr sé uirthi é a phósadh, is é a dúirt sí go tarcaisneach 'Ní phósfaidh mise cruiteachán!'

'Carraig an Éidigh, nó Éadaigh' is ainm i nGaeilge do 'Castle Hyde', agus is ionann éideach agus sciath nó *armour.* Is focal coitianta i nGaeilge fós ' in airm is in éide.'

Bhí cóip den amhrán seo ag Sir Clarendon de hÍde i Sasana, ach níor thuig sé gur ar an nós Gaelach a rinneadh é, agus go raibh focal deiridh na chéad líne agus an tríú líne ag déanamh comhfhuaime le focal éigin i lár an dara líne agus an cheathrú líne. B'éigean dom sin a chur i gciall dó. Is ó Berkshire i Sasana a tháinig na hÍdigh go hÉireann ar dtús, i dtosach aimsir na Banríona Eilís, agus tá seanchlog an-ársa agam fós a bhfuil coróin agus *Fleur de lis* air, agus creideadh i gcónaí i measc na nÍdeach gur bhronntanas é a thug an Bhanríon don Ídeach sin a chuaigh ar dtús go hÉirinn. B'fhéidir gur fíor é sin, mar ba chara é do leannán na Banríona, an ropaire sin Dudley. Bhídís ag imirt cártaí go minic le chéile, agus is i dteach mo shinsir a chaith Amy Robsart, bean Dudley, a lá deiridh ar an saol seo. Bhí a n-áit bhunaidh ag na hÍdigh i Sasana go dtí cúpla céad bliain ó shin, ach d'éagadar go léir. Ansin tháinig Sir Clarendon a shíolraigh ó na hÍdigh in Éirinn agus rinne sé an dúiche a athcheannach dó féin agus teach breá a chur suas ar lorg an tseantí.

Seo é an t-amhrán mar a chuala mise é:

CASTLE HYDE
As I roved out of a summer's m*o*rning
Down by the banks of Blackw*a*ter's side
To view the groves and the meadows ch*a*rming
The pleasant g*a*rdens of Castle Hyde

It's there you'd hear the thrushes w*a*rbling
The dove and p*a*rtridge, I now describe,
Sporting there upon every m*o*rning
All to ad*o*rn sweet Castle Hyde

There are fine walks in those pleasant g*a*rdens,
And seats more ch*a*rming in shady bowers,
The gladianthor* who is bowld and d*a*rin'
Each night and m*o*rnin' to watch the flowers.

If noble princes from foreign n*a*tions
Should chance to s*a*il to this Irish shore,
It is in this valley they should be f*é*asted.
Where often h*é*roes had been before.

The wholesome *a*ir of this habit*a*tion
Would recre*a*te your heart with pride,
There is no valley throughout this n*a*tion
In beauty *ae*qual to Castle Hyde.

There are fine horses and stall-fed *o*xen
A den for foxes to play and hide
Fine mares for br*ee*ding and foreign sh*ee*p
With snowy fl*ee*ces in Castle Hyde.

The richest groves throughout the n*a*tion
And fine plant*a*tions you would see there,
The rose, the tulip and the sweets of n*a*ture
All vieing with the lily f*a*ir.

The buck and doe, the fox and *a*igle
Do skip and pl*a*y by the river's side
The trout and salmon are always pl*a*ying**
In the clear str*é*ams of Castle Hyde

*Sin "gladiator" is dóigh, íomhá a bhí sa ghairdín?
**"Sporting," mar a chuala mise é.

I rode from Blarney down to Barney (?)
From Thomastown to sweet Doneraile
And from Cillarmac (?) that joins Rathcormac
Besides Killarney and Abbeyfail.

The flowing Nore and the rapid Boyne
The river Shannon and pleasant Clyde
In all my r*a*nging and recre*a*tion
No place could *ae*qual sweet Castle Hyde.

Leathanach 229
Seo é an t-amhrán a scríobh mé ó bhéal Mhac Uí Chathasaigh a bhí i siopa táilliúireachta Mhac Uí Chaoimh, Feabhra 2, 1906. Is follas go bhfuil an Béarla ar nós na Gaeilge, ag iarraidh aithris a dhéanamh ar an bhfonn sin 'Blátha Dhún Éideann,' mar a rinne Seán Llid[16] ina amhrán binn, 'Cois leasa dom go huaigneach':

In a desert most ser*é*ne
I l*a*y a while bem*o*aning
The present lot and st*a*te
Of our country at large,
A damsel I saw s*é*ated
On a n*é*at bed of roses,
And she bitterly bem*o*aning
The approach of the *é*ir.*
Her *a*mber locks were h*a*nging d*ow*n
Upon her b*a*ck unto the gr*ou*nd
Which might engage a m*o*narch's cr*ow*n
So n*é*atly comp*o*sed.
Her f*a*ce as if p*ai*nted
By n*a*ture such beauty yields
As left all my s*é*crets
Quite n*a*ked, exp*o*sed

Leathanach 243
'A Souvenir of the Dr HYDE BANQUET held in the Palace Hotel in the City of San Francisco, February twenty-first, 1906.'

*Heir nó air?

Tugann an leabhar seo na hóráidí go hiomlán, agus tugann sé ainm gach duine a bhí i láthair, macasamhail an *menu*, agus pictiúr gach cainteora. Is iad seo na cainteoirí a labhair: Judge Coffey, Archbishop Montgomery, James O Phelan, Governor Pardee, Mayor Schmitz, Chief Justice Beatty, Hon. Frank J. Sullivan, John MacNaught, Benjamin Ide Wheeler, Very Rev. J. P. Frieden, S. J., Michael O Mahoney, Rev. F. W. Clampett, Rev. P. C. Yorke.

Leathanach 262

Nuair a tháinig mé ar ais go hÉirinn cuireadh mé ar an gCoiste a bhí le fiafraí i dtaobh Ard-Oideachas na hÉireann, agus le dul isteach i gceist Choláiste na Tríonóide. I ngach scrúdú a rinneadh ar Ard-Oideachas in Éirinn go dtí sin, d'éirigh le Coláiste na Tríonóide í féin a tharraingt siar as, ach níor fhéad sí í féin a shaoradh an t-am seo, agus frítheadh amach sa scrúdú a rinne an Coiste gach ní idir airgead agus eile a bhain leis an áit sin. Mhair an Coiste beagnach bliain, agus shuigh sí i mBaile Átha Cliath agus i Londain. Lig an Probhast, an Dochtúir Tráill, dúinn suí ina theach féin, teach an Phrobhaist, sa choláiste nuair a bhíomar i mBaile Átha Cliath.[17]

Tharla go raibh mé féin agus an chuid eile den Choiste inár suí i dteach an Phrobhaist ag cruinniú fianaise, nuair a tháinig fear freastail isteach agus dúirt sé liom i gcogar go raibh beirt dhuine uasal ó Mheirceá taobh amuigh, agus gur mhaith leo labhairt liomsa. Chuaigh mé amach chucu agus cé a bheadh ann ach Maor Schmitz agus cara leis. Nuair a bhí mé ag caint leo sa halla, ghabh an Probhast thart, agus chuir mé an Maor in aithne dó. Dúirt an Maor leis go raibh sé féin agus a chara ag taisteal ar fud na hEorpa go bhfeicfeadh sé na tithe móra agus na foirgnimh a bhí ann, óir bhí ar mhuintir San Francisco an chathair a thógáil as an nua, agus ba mhaith leis féin na foirgnimh is fearr a fheiceáil roimh ré. Dúirt an Probhast go dtaispeánfadh sé an teach sin dóibh, agus thaispeáin sé dóibh é, agus gach rud nua a rinne sé féin ann.

Ach ní foirgnimh a fheiceáil ná aon rud den sórt sin a thug Schmitz thar lear, ach bhí San Francisco róthe dó, óir an fear sin a bhí go cneasta macánta go dtí gur leagadh an chathair, thit sé féin nuair a bhíothas dá tógáil arís, óir dúradh gur ghlac sé breab ó dhaoine ar mhaith leo a leithéid seo nó a leithéid sin d'áit a bheith acu chun siopaí agus eile a thógáil uirthi. Nuair a chuaigh sé ar ais go San Francisco daoradh é agus cuireadh go San Quentin* é, agus Ruef in éineacht leis, mar a chuala mé. Ach bhí na páipéir agus na daoine móra ina naimhde dó, agus is dóigh nárbh olc leo faill a fháil air.

*Príosún mór San Francisco, mar Sing-Sing i Nua-Eabhrac.

Leathanach 306
Ba cheart dom a chur síos anseo na suimeanna airgid a fuaireamar ó na cruinnithe a bhí againn.

Cathracha a raibh Tomás Ua Concheanainn agus mé féin ag obair iontu.*

	$
Hartford	114.85
Boston	1,783.38
Manchester	150.00
Springfield, Mass	292.00
Ansonia	101.50
Lowell	176.35
Waterbury	237.00
Providence	680.00
Philadelphia	4,624.77
Worchester	87.95
Lawrence	215.75
Chicago	6,782.11
Indianapolis	1,102.48
St Louis	1,400.00
San José	663.25
Oakland	500.00
Sacramento	1,000.00
Portland	1,021.00
Seattle	570.00
Spokane	800.00
Butte	2,212.60
Anaconda	650.00
	25,165.79

*Is as an *Irish-American* (23-6-1906) a thug cúnamh mór dom, a bhaineas é seo, ach bhí Tomás Bán i San Francisco, Minneapolis, agus St Paul mar an gcéanna.

CATHRACHA A RAIBH MÉ FÉIN IONTU

	$
Brockton	176.00
Jersey City	226.19
New Haven	300.00
Pittsburgh	972.50
Milwaulkee	556.00
Cleveland	1,170.20
Columbus	528.05
Cincinnati	1,000.00
South Bend	130.00
St Paul	300.00
Minneapolis	338.00
Omaha	1,555.60
San Francisco	9,836.75
Los Angeles	1,500.00
San Francisco	1,500.00
arís, ceiliúradh Phádraig Naofa	
Memphis	510.35
Baltimore	768.52
Elmira	600.00
Scranton	431.51
Bridgeport	350.00
Buffalo	1,090.00
Rochester	754.65
Washington	352.00
Paterson	75.00

In éineacht leis an méid sin, tháinig isteach trí Sheán Ó Cuinn féin, i Nua-Eabhrac:

Ó Shéamas Ó Broin	1,000.00
Ó Sheán D. Ó Croimín, Onórach	1,000.00
Ó Liam Ó Síocháin (trí Dhomhnall Ó Cathaláin)	500.00
Ó T. F. Ó Riain (trí Mhártain Mac Eochaidh, Onórach)	500.00
Clarence H. Mackey (trí ditto)	500.00
J. W. Ó Dálaigh (trí ditto)	250.00
P. F. Collier (trí ditto)	100.00
Ó Chonradh na Gaeilge, Stát Nua-Eabhrac	167.23
J. C. Ó Loingsigh	100.00
Aodh Grant, Onórach	100.00
Ó Bhúrcach Ó Cogaráin, Onórach	100.00
Ó Shéamas L. Ó Faoláin	100.00
Ó Thomás H. Ó Ceallaigh	100.00
Trí dhaoine eile	365.00
	————
	4,932.23

Cheannaigh na daoine seo a leanas boscaí ag Carnegie Hall, nuair a dhíol Mac Uí Cathaláin trí cheant iad, agus thugadar orthu:

Seán Goodwin	300.00
Séamas Builtéar	300.00
An breitheamh Ó Dúllaing	250.00
Seán B. Mac Dónaill	200.00
An breitheamh Mac Eochaidh, Onórach	150.00
Cathal Ó Murchú, Onórach	150.00
Enrí Mac Donnchú	150.00
Ceannaíodh cuid mhór boscaí eile a bhfuarthas orthu	1,700.00
	————
	3,200.00
Suíocháin a díoladh roimh ré	862.50
Suíocháin díolta ag an doras	905.50
Fágann sé sin gur tháinig isteach ó Nua-Eabhrac ar fad	9,303.53
Ghlac an *Gaelic American* síntiúis don teanga, agus tháinig isteach tríothu sin	$4,000.00

Thug mé seic ar son £10,054 abhaile liom, agus chuir mé na mílte punt eile go dtí an Conradh, Mí na Nollag 19, 1905, agus chuir an coiste Gnótha i St Louis $1,400,00 abhaile go díreach go Baile Átha Cliath, agus chuir an coiste Gnótha i bPittsburgh $972.50 díreach go Baile Átha Cliath, freisin, agus thug mé cúig mhíle dollar ar ais do San Francisco. Fuair mé sin ar ais uathu i gceann cúpla bliain eile. Sin os cionn £12,400 ar fad a tháinig isteach ó mo thuras.

Scéal an airgid go dtí sin.

NOTAÍ

1 '1900' an dáta a tugadh sa chéad eagrán, trí dheamad.
2 Stáisiún Heuston an lae inniu.
3 *Dánta Diadha Chúige Connacht* a bhí sa chéad eagrán, trí dhearmad.
4 'Carraig an Éidigh', de réir Logainm.ie.
5 'Hagard' an leagan den sloinne a bhí in eagrán 1937, trí dhearmad.
6 Baineadh amach an frása 'duine ar bith seachas' a bhí roimh 'Lochlannach' sa chéad eagrán ar mhaithe leis an mbrí a shlánú.
7 'Siúracha an Spioraid Naoimh' atá in eagrán 1937, trí dhearmad.
8 'Fort Snelling' an t-ainm ceart.
9 Ainm Béarla an Athar Ó Ficheallaigh.
10 'Teach na hÁille' a bhí in eagrán 1937, ach 'Cliff House' an áit a bhí i gceist.
11 The American Protective Association, cumann rúnda frith-Chaitliceach, a bunaíodh sa bhliain 1887.
12 United Irish League.
13 The Friendly Sons of St Patrick.
14 Baill de chumann a thacaigh leis an Ocsatáinis i bProvence na Fraince.
15 An seachtú lá a luaitear in eagrán 1937, trí dhearmad.
16 Lúid agus Lloyd a thugtar mar shloinne air chomh maith.
17 Is ar lch 180 roimh an gcuntas ar 'A Souvenir of the Dr HYDE BANQUET' a foilsíodh an t-alt seo in eagrán 1937, sa tslí nach raibh ord an ábhair i gceart.

NOTES

INTRODUCTION

1 Finnín Ní Chonceanainn and Ciarán Ó Coigligh, *Tomás Bán* (Baile Átha Cliath, 1996), p. 126.

2 Janet Eglseon and Gareth W. Dunleavy, *Douglas Hyde: A Maker of Modern Ireland* (Berkeley and Los Angeles, 1991), p. 256.

3 John Quinn to Douglas Hyde, 27 Oct. 1905, National Library of Ireland (hereafter NLI) MS 17,299.

4 Ibid.

5 The Ancient Order of Hibernians (hereafter AOH), an Irish Catholic fraternal organisation, founded in New York City in 1836 to protect Catholic churches from anti-Catholic forces and assist immigrants who faced discrimination.

6 An Irish-American republican organisation, successor to the Fenian Brotherhood and a sister organisation to the Irish Republican Brotherhood.

7 Sean O'Casey, *Drums under the Windows* (New York, 1960), p. 164.

8 Douglas Hyde to Lady Gregory, 29 Nov. 1905, NLI MS 18,253 (2) (3).

9 *New York Times*, 27 Nov. 1905, p. 6.

10 Douglas Hyde to Lady Gregory, 29 Nov. 1905, NLI MS 18,253 (2) (3).

11 Letter from Francis Hackett to J. Quinn, 11 Feb. 1906. Letters to John Quinn, NLI PC190 Box 6 / USA / 1906.

12 Letter from John O'Callaghan to John Redmond, 21 Nov. 1905, NLI MS 15,213/7/9.

13 Letter from O'Callaghan to Redmond, 15 Dec. 1905, NLI MS 15,213/7/12.

14 Ibid. O'Callaghan was evidently not enthused by Hyde or his mission. Of the man himself he states in the same letter: 'I had less than three minutes conversation with him and have not gone to the trouble of seeing him since, although he has been back and forth to Boston while speaking in adjacent places ever since.'

15 Another example is the letter dated 3 Jan. 1906, which Hyde sent to his friend George Coffey, Harcourt Terrace, Dublin, NLI MS 46,291 (6) (2).
16 NLI MS 28,909 (2) (8) contains the first letter from Ní Bhriain to Hyde, the other seven are in MS 18,252 (3) (10)–(16).
17 Unsigned letter to John Quinn from Office of the Vice-President, The State Life Insurance Company, Indianapolis, Indiana, 22 Jan. 1906, NLI MS 18,253 (3) (1).
18 Francis Hackett, *American Rainbow: Early Reminiscences* (New York, 1971), p. 180.
19 The typed record of the question and answer session is contained in NLI MS 17,299. The first page is on the headed paper of Hollenden Hotel, Cleveland. The names of the journalist and newspaper in question are not given.
20 Diary, 22 Jan. 1906.
21 Dubhghlas de hÍde, *Mise agus an Connradh (go dtí* 1905*)* (Baile Átha Cliath, 1937). This was an account of Hyde's role in the Gaelic League from its inception to 1905.
22 Úna Ní Bhroiméil, *Building Irish Identity in America* 1870–1915*: The Gaelic Revival* (Dublin, 2003), p. 67.
23 Letter from John Quinn to Fr Peter Yorke, *c.* 26 Dec. 1905, NLI MS 18,253 (3) (3), p. 7.
24 Letter from Fr Philip O'Ryan to John Quinn, 23 Feb. 1906, NLI PC 190.
25 See Douglas Hyde, *Language, Lore and Lyrics*, in Breandán Ó Conaire (ed.) (Dublin, 1986). Originally published in *The Revival of Irish Literature* (London, 1894).
26 Typescript of lecture, undated, NLI MS 18,253 (2) (6), p. 1.
27 Ibid.
28 Ibid., p. 2.
29 Ibid., pp 16–17.
30 Letter from O'Callaghan to Redmond, 15 Dec. 1905, NLI MS 15,213 (7) (12), Dec.
31 For an Irish perspective, see Ann Wilson, 'A young woman's life in Edwardian Dublin', in *History Ireland* 22:6 (Nov./Dec. 2014). For the general international context, see David Prochaska and Jordana Mendelson (eds), *Postcards: Ephemeral Histories of Modernity* (Pennsylvania, 2010).
32 Hyde was the recipient rather than the sender of most of the cards in the UCD collection.
33 Eoin Mac Néill's papers, NLI MS 10,874 (15) (4).
34 Letter from Lucy C. Hyde to Mrs Hutton, 15 Feb. 1900, NLI MS 46,777.
35 Mrs Mary Hutton in Belfast was sent a card in Irish (of Post Office, Chicago, Ill.) by Hyde from Omaha, Nebraska written on 8 Feb. 1906, and postmarked the following day, informing her that he was on his way to San Francisco, that both he and Lucy were well, and that his trip was going successfully (NLI 8,611/9/1). A post card which Mrs Hutton had received from *An Craoibhín* (Douglas Hyde) – presumably the same one – is mentioned by Siobhán Ní Chruitín in a letter in Irish to Mrs Hutton, dated 2 Mar. 1906, NLI MS 8,611/9/3.
36 The picture is the same as that sent to Eoin Mac Néill: see note 33.
37 Letter from John Quinn to Hyde, 27 Oct. 1905, NLI MS 17,299 p. 4.
38 Letter from Quinn to Yorke, NLI MS 18,253 (3) (3), *c.* 24 Dec. 1905 p. 10.

39 Letter from Lucy C. Hyde to Miss O'Farrelly (Ní Fhaircheallaigh), 15 Dec. 1905, NLI MS 10,874 (15) (1).
40 Letter from Úna Ní Fhaircheallaigh to Eoin Mac Néill, 27 Dec. 1905, NLI MS 10,874 (15) (2).
41 Letter from Eoin Mac Néill to Miss O'Farrelly, 3 Jan. 1906, NLI MS 110,874 (15) (3).
42 Letter from Quinn to Hyde, 30 Mar. 1906, NLI MS 17,299.
43 Letter from Quinn to Hackett, 25 Apr. 1906. NLI PC 190 Box 6 / USA / 1906.
44 See Ní Chonceanainn and Ó Coigligh, *Tomás Bán*, pp 128–9.
45 Letter from Hyde to Ua Concheanainn, 16 Apr. 1906, quoted in ibid., p. 142.
46 Cable telegraph message from James Shehan to Douglas Hyde, 30 Apr. 1906, NLI MS 118,252 (5) (3).
47 Letter from J. V. Coffey to Mrs Dr Hyde, 22 May 1906, NLI MS 18,253 (1) (1).
48 Letter from Martan. P. Mac. an Báird. (Martin P. Ward) to Douglas Hyde, 15 Feb. 1906, NLI MS 18,253 (1) (11).
49 Letter from J. F. Sullivan to Douglas Hyde, 9 Aug. 1906, NLI MS 18,253 (1) (9).
50 Letter from M. J. Henehan (M. I. Ua h-Éidhneacháin) to Douglas Hyde, 12 July 1906, NLI MS 18253 (1) (3).
51 William Jenkins, *Between Raid and Rebellion: The Irish in Buffalo and Toronto, 1867–1916* (Montreal, 2013), pp 323–4, p. 441.
52 24 May 1906. See Janis and Richard Londraville (eds), *Too Long a Sacrifice: The Letters of Maud Gonne and John Quinn* (Selinsgrove, 1999), pp 34–6.
53 13 July 1906. See Alan Himber, *The Letters of John Quinn to William Butler Yeats* (Ann Arbour, 1983), pp 76–80.
54 File on Douglas Hyde in The National Archives, (UK) CO 904/204/5 File 199.
55 Sackville St did not officially become O'Connell St until after independence, although it was popularly called the latter for the previous 50 years.
56 Letter from Hyde to Quinn, 24 July 1906. See B. L. Reid, *The Man from New York: John Quinn and his Friends* (New York, 1968), p. 42.
57 The Irish phrase 'Sinn Féin' literally means 'Ourselves' but is often taken to mean 'Ourselves alone'. At first sporadically used, it became increasingly common in otherwise English-language discourse, where it emphasised Irish self-reliance. Máire de Buitléir is credited with prompting Arthur Griffith's adoption of the phrase as the name for the political party he founded in Dublin in late 1905.

MY AMERICAN JOURNEY

1 John Quinn (1870–1924), an Irish-American New York lawyer and patron of the arts.
2 Corrected from 1900 in the 1937 Irish-language edition.
3 Lady Isabella Augusta Gregory (1852–1932), cofounder of the Irish Literary Theatre and the Abbey Theatre,
4 Edward Martyn (1859–1923), a playwright and the first president of Sinn Féin.
5 Near Craughwell, Co. Galway.

6 Antaine Raiftearai / Anthony Raftery (1779–1835), a blind Irish-language poet. Hyde edited and published two volumes of Raftery's poems (1903).
7 The Gregory family home, near Gort, Co. Galway.
8 Martin J. Keogh (1855–1928), a judge of the New York Supreme Court.
9 Douglas Hyde, *A Literary History of Ireland from Earliest Times to the Present Day* (New York, 1899).
10 William Butler Yeats (1869–1939), first came to New York in Nov. 1903.
11 Rev. Arthur Hyde (1819–1905), whose family originally came from Castlehyde, Fermoy, Co. Cork.
12 Tomás Bán Ua Concheanainn (1870–1961).
13 William Bulfin (1863–1910).
14 Eugene O'Growney / Eoghan Ó Gramhnaigh (1863–99), an early founding member of Conradh na Gaeilge / Gaelic League and author of the best-selling series, *Simple Lessons in Irish.*
15 Fr Peter Yorke (1864–1925), based in San Francisco, he became the editor of *The Monitor* and later of *The Leader*. Peter Yorke Way in San Francisco is named after him. A Regent of University of California, he established a branch of the Gaelic League in San Francisco in 1905.
16 Robert Temple Emmet (1854–1936), his great-grandfather, Thomas Addis Emmet, was Robert Emmet's elder brother.
17 Daniel Florence Cohalan (1867–1946).
18 John Devoy (1842–1928), an exiled Irish rebel, owner and editor of the *Gaelic American* weekly newspaper.
19 Possibly James Fitzgerald (1851–1922). Born in Ireland, he served as President of the Friendly Sons of St Patrick and was a prominent member of the Democratic and Manhattan Clubs in New York.
20 Morgan Joseph O'Brien (1852–1937), a New York Supreme Court judge.
21 Possibly James Aloysius O'Gorman, Sr (1860–1943).
22 John William Goff, Sr (1848–1924), prominent in the rescue of six Fenian rebels from Australia in 1876.
23 Patrick Ford (1837–1913), he established the *Irish World*, Irish-America's main newspaper.
24 Peadar Ó Laoghaire (1839–1929), foremost literary author of the language revival.
25 Eoin Mac Néill (1867–1945), co-founder of Conradh na Gaeilge/Gaelic League.
26 Pádraig Ó Dálaigh (1873–1932).
27 Stiofán Bairéad (1867–1921).
28 Lucy Cometina Kurtz (1861–1938), born West Derby, Lancashire, England. She married Hyde in 1893.
29 An Craoibhín Aoibhinn (The Charming Little Branch), Hyde's pen name.
30 Established in 1817 on 21–2 Sackville Street (now O'Connell Street).
31 Stáisiún Heuston / Dublin Heuston, known as Kingsbridge Terminus until 1966.

32 Possibly Ryan's Station Hotel, Limerick Junction.
33 Alderman Joseph Barrett.
34 John J. Horgan, solicitor.
35 Professor Bertram C. A. Windle, President of Queen's College Cork and its successor University College Cork (1904–19).
36 Robert Browne (1844–1935), uncle of Francis Browne S. J., the famous photographer.
37 Possibly the Rev. William Daunt, Rector of Queenstown (Cobh).
38 A 14-story hotel, the Hotel Manhattan was built between 1895–6 in the style of a French chateau. It stood on the northwest corner of Madison Avenue and 42nd Street near Grand Central Terminal until 1961.
39 Fred Norris Robinson (1871–1966).
40 Charles William Eliot (1834–1926), Harvard University President (1869–1909).
41 LeBaron Russell Briggs (1855–1934).
42 Francis James Child (1825–96), Harvard Professor, scholar and folklorist.
43 George Lyman Kittredge (1860–1941), Harvard Professor of English Literature.
44 Matthew Cummings (1863–?).
45 Arthur Twining Hadley (1856–1930), Yale University President (1899–1921).
46 Lampson Hall.
47 Theodore Roosevelt Jr (1858–1919), the 26th US President.
48 Alice Lee Roosevelt Longworth (1884–1980).
49 They included Mary Ledwith ('Mame').
50 Founded in Boston in 1815 by Nathan Hale, the *North American Review* was the first US literary magazine.
51 The Willard InterContinental Washington, located at 1401 Pennsylvania Avenue, two blocks east of the White House, in Washington, DC, opened in 1901.
52 Newspaper of the Ancient Order of Hibernians (hereafter AOH), edited by Patrick J. Haltigan.
53 Edited and published by Hyde in 1906.
54 Located on Broadway, between 24th and 25th Streets.
55 Finley Peter Dunne (1867–1936). An American humourist from Chicago, he authored the nationally syndicated Mr Dooley sketches.
56 William Bourke Cockran (1854–1923), served as Democratic Representative from New York.
57 Patrick O'Shea, an Irish tenor.
58 Diarmuid Lynch (1878–1950).
59 AOH, an Irish Catholic fraternal organisation, founded in New York City in 1836 to protect Catholic churches from anti-Catholic forces and assist immigrants who faced discrimination.
60 An American-Irish republican organisation, successor to the Fenian Brotherhood and a sister organisation to the Irish Republican Brotherhood.

HARTFORD

61 Possibly Patrick Donaghue of 21 State Street, Hartford, Conneticut.

BOSTON

62 Michael P. Curran.

63 Opened in 1899.

64 Lenox Hotel, built in 1900 and located at the corner of Boylston and Exeter Street.

65 Daniel Aloysius Whelton (1872–1953). The first native-born Irish-Catholic Mayor of Boston. Whelton served as Chairman of the Board of Aldermen in 1905, and, during Mayor Patrick Collins's long illness, was acting mayor. Following Collins' death, Whelton became Mayor of Boston.

66 Daniel P. Toomey (1862–1916). Born in Kenmare, Co. Kerry, he came to Boston in 1873.

67 A general magazine aimed at a Catholic readership. It ran from about 1878 to 1908.

68 Hotel Touraine (1897–1966) located on the corner of Tremont Street and Boylston Street, near Boston Common.

MANCHESTER

69 John Bernard Delaney (1864–1906).

70 Thomas B. Fitzpatrick.

71 Founded in 1837 by Mary Lyon as Mount Holyoke Female Seminary, it became Mount Holyoke College in 1893.

72 Mary Emma Woolley (1863–1947).

SPRINGFIELD

73 Pádraig Ó hÉigeartaigh (1871–1936), employed by Charles F. Lynch Clothing Company, resided at 66 Cleveland Street, Springfield, Mass. Author of 'Ochón! a Dhonncha' (nó 'An Leanbh Báite'), lamenting the tragic death of his young son.

74 Reception hosted at Cooley Hotel, opposite R. R. Depot, Springfield, Mass., on 7 Dec. between 3.00–5.00pm

75 Held in the Court Square Theatre. Opened in 1892 and demolished in 1956, the theatre was located directly across from City Hall.

ANSONIA

76 He married Catherine Ward (1869–1955) and raised three daughters and four sons.

77 Alton Farrel (1879–1934).

78 Castlehyde / Carraig an Éidigh.

LOWELL

79 Joseph Smith, clerk of the board of police.
80 Rollaway Skating Rink.
81 Founded in 1870, a private women's liberal arts college, located in the town of Wellesley, west of Boston.
82 Caroline Hazard (1856–1945), president of Wellesley College (1899–1910).

BROCKTON

83 Edward Gilmore (1867–1924), US Representative from Massachusetts; President of the Brockton Board of Aldermen (1901–1906).
84 Arthur Brisbane (1864–1936), by the time of his death, reputed to be the highest paid newspaper writer in the world.
85 Alice Thursby (1853–1959), the daughter of Albert Brisbane, formerly of Kansas City, married in 1888.
86 William Randolph Hearst Sr (1863–1951).
87 St John's College, officially founded in 1841, renamed Fordham University in 1907.
88 John J. Collins (1856–1934), served as President of Fordham University (1904–6).
89 Possibly Fr Michael J. Mahoney, S. J.

WATERBURY

90 Poli's Theater, 145 East Main Street, Waterbury, opened on 19 Dec. 1897 next to the Broadway Casino, which later became the site of the State Theatre.
91 Hyde stayed at the Elton Hotel, located on West Main Stree, built in 1904.
92 Timothy F. Luddy, President of Patrick Sarsfield Club, dedicated to preserving Irish culture and the Irish language.
93 Possibly Rev. C. W. Brennan.
94 Mr Stephen Wilby, Crosby High School Principal (1896–1917).
95 The Lawyers' Club, 120 Broadway.
96 Sarah Bernhardt (1844–1923), a French stage actor.
97 James Hazen Hyde (1876–1959).
98 80 West 40th Street.

PHILADELPHIA

99 The Bellevue–Stratford Hotel, constructed in 1904, located at 200 South Broad Street at the corner of Walnut Street in Centre City.
100 Possibly Gerald P. Coghlan.

101 On 12 Apr. 1867, a party of some 40 to 50 men left NY aboard the *Jackmel* for Ireland hoping to assist in a Fenian rising. The *Jackmel* was renamed the *Erin's Hope* during the voyage.
102 Published by A. M. Sullivan, Abbey Street, Dublin in 1868.
103 Mary Mitchell married a Colonel Page.
104 Patrick John Ryan (1831–1911), an Irish-born Catholic prelate.
105 Joseph Hampton Moore (1864–1950).
106 The Roman Catholic High School of Philadelphia, also known as Boys' Catholic High School, opened in 1890, located at the intersection of Broad and Vine Streets in Philadelphia city centre.
107 Hyde had studied German at Trinity College Dublin, gaining first-class honours in his first year.
108 Robert Ellis Thompson (1844–1924), born in Lurgan, Co. Down, this Presbyterian clergyman taught at the University of Pennsylvania. In 1894, he took over the presidency of Central High School in Philadelphia.
109 Born Strabane, Co. Tyrone.

WORCESTER

110 Richard O'Flynn (1829–1905), born in Newtown, Waterford, Ireland, married Annie O'Neil who died in 1875 in Worcester.

LAWRENCE

111 Possibly Dr Michael F. Sullivan.
112 Located in the Bronx, New York City, established in 1853 by the De La Salle Christian Brothers.
113 Thomas Hughes Kelly, son of American banker Eugene Kelly.
114 Eugene Kelly (1807–94), born Frellick, Co. Tyrone, established the Donohoe–Kelly Banking Company.
115 John P. Chadwick (?–1935).
116 Launched in 1889 as an armoured cruiser, the *USS Maine* was a second-class pre-dreadnought battleship whose sinking by an explosion, either internal or by a mine, on 15 Feb. 1898, killing 266, precipitated the Spanish–American War.
117 The Players' Club, located at 16 Gramercy Park.
118 Paul Elmer More (1864–1937).
119 Established in 1801, the *New York Evening Post* was a respected broadsheet.
120 Joseph I. C. Clarke, 'The fighting race', in Edmund Clarence Stedman (ed.), *An American Anthology,* 1787–1900 (Boston, 1900), p. 1102.
121 Witter Bynner (1881–1968), assistant editor of *McClure's Magazine.*

122 Located at 324 West 47th Street, New York.

123 Presumably Patrick Ferriter from the Dingle peninsula, Co. Kerry, whom Hyde says elsewhere he met in America, and who bequeathed his collection of some 40 Irish language manuscripts to University College Dublin, in recognition of the fact that Irish was made an essential matriculation subject for entry to the National University in 1913.

124 Founded in 1903 by Kuno Meyer. R. I. Best served as the School's Honorary Secretary. Among the first students were Osborn Bergin and T. F. O'Rahilly. In 1904 it instituted the scholarly journal *Ériu*. The Royal Irish Academy incorporated the School in 1926.

125 Charles DeKay, literary and art critic for *The New York Times*, he founded the National Arts Club in 1898.

126 Located on the southern border of Lenox Hill at 502 Park Avenue Manhattan, New York City and designed by Goldner and Goldner, the building was originally the Viceroy Hotel but later renamed as the Cromwell Arms and as the Hotel Delmonico. The former skyscraper hotel is now a residential condominium owned by Donald Trump.

127 See Charles DeKay, *Bird Gods, With Accompaniment of Decorations by George Wharton Edwards* (New York, 1898).

NEW JERSEY

128 St Peter's Hall, St Peter's Roman Catholic Church, 144 Grand Street.

129 William T. McLaughlin, St Augustine's R. C. Church, Union Hill.

NEW HAVEN

130 Captain Lawrence O'Brien.

131 Dr Joseph Dunn (1872–1951), Professor of Celtic Languages and Literature, Catholic University of America.

132 Possibly Edmond O'Brien Kennedy (alias Timothy Featherstone) of 150 Franklin Street, New Haven, Connecticut. On 'Dynamite Saturday,' (25 Jan. 1885), the Fenians attempted to blow up a number of locations in central London, including London Bridge, the House of Commons and the Tower of London.

1906 – NEW YEAR'S DAY

133 Helena de Kay (1846–1916), founder of the Art Students' League and Society of American Artists. She modelled for the painter Winslow Homer who suffered from an unrequited love of her.

134 First published in 1881, *The Century Magazine* succeeded *Scribner's Monthly Magazine*. It ceased publication in 1930.

PITTSBURGH

135 Archbishop John Francis Regis Canevin (1853–1921).
136 John A. Martin (1870–?).
137 The Gardens, built in 1890, renamed the Duquesne Gardens (1896), had the world's largest indoor ice rink.

CHICAGO

138 Located at the northwest corner of South Michigan Avenue and Congress Street (now Congress Parkway), President Grover Cleveland laid the cornerstone on 5 Oct. 1887. When completed in 1889, it was the largest skyscraper in the US and the tallest in Chicago, and included a multi-use complex, including offices, a theatre and a first-class hotel.
139 'Nearly 8,000 descendants of the Gaelic race met at the Auditorium last night to listen to Dr Douglas Hyde …', in *The Oakland Tribune* (California), 8 Jan. 1906.
140 James Edward Quigley (1854–1915).
141 Edward Fitzsimmons Dunne (1853–1937).
142 'From an Irish girl.'
143 Thomas E. Judge (1865–1907).
144 *The Catholic New World*, now *Chicago Catholic*.

MILWAUKEE

145 James Ole Davidson (1854–1922).
146 Jeremiah Quinn, self-confessed 'State centre of the Fenian Brotherhood of Wisconsin since 1858.'
147 (Pabst Theatre), The Captain Frederick Pabst Theatre, located at 144 East Wells St.
148 Sebastian Gebhard Messmer (1847–1930), Archbishop of Milwaukee, Wisconsin.
149 Fenton B. Turck, resided at 151 Rush Street.
150 Mercury-in-glass thermometer.
151 Patrick Cudahy Jr (1849–1919).
152 Walter A. Payne, (1865–1941), 'recorder and examiner' of the University of Chicago.
153 University of Chicago.
154 Mandel Hall, located within the Reynolds Club, at 1131 East 57th Street.
155 William Rainey Harper (1856–1906), helped establish the University of Chicago and Bradley University, served as the first president of both.
156 Francis O'Neill (1848–1936), Chicago Chief of Police (1901–1905).
157 The Sherman House was one of the 'Big Four' of the post-fire hotels. Opened in 1873, it closed in 1910. Located at North-West corner of North Clark and West Randolph Streets.
158 Located at 78 Rush Street, North Side.

CLEVELAND

159 The Hollenden Hotel, a luxury hotel in downtown Cleveland, Ohio, opened in 1885.
160 Mary Ellen Spring Rice (1880–1924).
161 Mount Trenchard House, ancestral seat of the Rice, and subsequently Spring Rice, family, located near Foynes, Co. Limerick.
162 The 1,472-seat Colonial Theatre, located on Superior Avenue near East 9th Street, opened in 1903.
163 John McHale, Pastor of St Malachi's parish, nephew of Archbishop McHale of Tuam.
164 The Knights of Equity (KOE), established in Cleveland, Ohio in 1895, in reaction to the American Protective Association (APA), an anti-Catholic secret society established in 1887.
165 A private liberal arts college in Ohio, founded in 1833, the oldest co-educational liberal arts college in US
166 Henry Churchill King (1858–1934).
167 Thomas O'Neill Russell (1828–1908).

COLUMBUS

168 William Oxley Thompson (1855–1933), the fifth President of the Ohio State University.
169 James Joseph Hartley (1858–1944).
170 Daniel Joseph Ryan (1855–1923).
171 *The Catholic Columbian*, a newspaper that ran from 1875–1939.
172 James C. Carroll.

INDIANAPOLIS

173 Rev. George David Wolfe, pastor of the First Methodist church.
174 James Goodman (1828–1896), Professor of Irish at Trinity College Dublin.
175 Tomlinson Hall, northeast corner Delaware & Market Streets.
176 James Whitcomb Riley (1849–1916), writer, poet, and best-selling author, known as the 'Hoosier Poet' and 'Children's Poet' for his dialect works and his children's poetry respectively. His famous works include 'Little Orphan Annie' and 'The Raggedy Man.'
177 Das Deutsche Haus, opened in 1898, renamed the Athenaeum after WW1.
178 James Lynchehaun attacked and disfigured Agnes MacDonnel on Achill Island, Co. Mayo in 1894. The incident is the basis for J. M. Synge's play *The Playboy of the Western World*.
179 'I heard talk of you previously.'

CINCINNATI

180 '22 Jan. 1906 – Dr Douglas Hyde, of Ireland, who is visiting in the United States on behalf of an Irish National Movement, the principal object of which is to awaken interest in the

study of Irish and its advantages in an industrial sense, was a visitor to the Chamber of Commerce this day.' *Cincinnati (Ohio) Chamber of Commerce and Merchant's Exchange*, 1907 Annual Report, Vol. 58, p. 43.

181 The University of Cincinnati.

ST LOUIS

182 Located at 415 North Tucker Blvd. Opened in 1904 to facilitate visitors to the Louisiana Purchase Exposition.

183 Located at Grand and Finney Avenues.

184 John Joseph Glennon (1862–1946).

185 Founded in 1890 by women to continue their intellectual growth, stay abreast of the times and contribute to the community. Located at the corner of Westminster Place and Taylor Street.

186 Located as 415 North Tucker Blvd, the Hotel Jefferson opened in 1904 to serve visitors to the Louisiana Purchase Exposition. See 183 above.

187 Possibly Brother Bernardine Peter (John Robinson) (1856–1930).

188 Founded in 1850 by three French-speaking Christian Brothers from Montréal, Québec. Between 1882 and 1916, it was located in north St Louis on the northeast corner of Easton Avenue and North Kingshighway, where it served as a primary, secondary, and college boarding school for boys.

189 Charles Maurice de Talleyrand-Périgord (1754–1838).

190 The Calumet Region, including Gary, East Chicago and Hammond.

191 Michael W. Murphy (?–1931). 'Delaney & Murphy,' located it at 10–12 Wabash Avenue, produced Ben Franklin Rye. In 1871, Murphy married Mary J. Synon who died in 1879, leaving four young children, a boy and three girls.

192 Jane Addams (1860–1935), known as the 'mother' of social work.

SOUTH BEND, INDIANA

193 In 1843 the Sisters of the Holy Cross opened a school in Bertrand, Michigan, and in 1855 moved to the school's present site in South Bend, first becoming St Mary's Academy and eventually St Mary's College.

194 John W. Cavanaugh (1870–1935), President of the University of Notre Dame (1905–19).

195 John Augustine Zahm (1851–1921).

196 The Pokagon Band of the Potawatomi Indians lived in southwestern Michigan and north-eastern Indiana

197 Located in Mishawaka, Indiana, James Oliver established the Oliver Chilled Plow Works in 1853.

198 Daniel J. Riordan, the Archbishop's brother.

199 Patrick William Riordan (1841–1914).

MADISON, WISCONSIN

200 Arthur Charles Lewis Brown (1869–1946).
201 Charles Richard Van Hise (1857–1918), University of Wisconsin (Madison) President (1903–1918).
202 John Pentland Mahaffy (1839–1919) clashed with Hyde when he disparaged Irish-language literature in his public testimony to the 1899 Royal Commission on Intermediate Education.

ST PAUL

203 The Ryan Hotel, located at the northeast corner of the Robert and 6th Street intersection, opened 2 July 1885, demolished in 1962.
204 The People's Church, located at Pleasant Avenue and Chestnut Street, St Paul.
205 John Ireland (1838–1918).
206 James J. Regan.
207 Chippewa (also known as Southwestern Ojibwa) is an Algonquian language spoken from upper Michigan westward to North Dakota.
208 David Patrick Moran (1869–1936).
209 Patrick Stephen Dinneen / Pádraig Ua Duinnín (1860–1934).
210 Minnesota Irish Immigration Society, established 1864 and Catholic Colonisation Bureau, established 1876.
211 Between 1876 and 1881, Bishop Ireland established ten rural villages and farming communities in Minnesota (DeGraff, Clontarf, Graceville, Minneota, Ghent, Currie, Avoca, Iona, Fulda and Adrian) spread through five western Minnesota counties (Swift, Big Stone, Lyon, Murray and Nobles).
212 Avoca.
213 John Joseph Hughes (1797–1864).
214 Martin John Spalding (1810–72).
215 Noble and Holy Order of the Knights of Labor, founded in 1869 by Uriah Stephens. The Knights of Labor promoted workers' social and cultural uplift, rejected socialism and anarchism and demanded an eight–hour working day.
216 Patrick William Riordan (1841–1914).
217 John Lancaster Spalding (1840–1916).
218 James Gibbons (1834–1921).

MINNEAPOLIS

219 *Minneapolis City Directory.*
220 William Turner (1871–1936).
221 Founded by the US Army in 1819, troops commanded by Colonel Josiah Snelling constructed the original Fort Saint Anthony from 1820–1824. On completion in 1825, the Army renamed it Fort Snelling.

222 Francis Hackett (1883–1962), literary editor of *Chicago Evening Post*, Chicago's genteel evening paper.

OMAHA, NEBRASKA

223 Constantine Joseph Smyth (1859–1924).

224 Colonel Patrick C. Heafey (1861–1921), born Ballylongford, Co. Kerry, President of Power-Heafey Power Company, and Director of Heafey & Heafey Mortuary.

225 Count John A. Creighton (1831–1907).

226 Richard Scannell (1845–1916).

227 Creighton College, founded in 1878, by Mary Lucretia Creighton in memory of her husband, Edward Creighton. Edward's brother, Count John A. Creighton fostered the university.

228 Poor Clares Convent. In 1904, a new building was finished at 1310 North 29th Street.

229 M. I. Stritch, S. J.

230 George Holmes (1861–?), fluent Irish-speaker, later judge.

231 Boyd's Theatre, located at 1621 Harney Street.

232 Minor criminal, Pat Crowe's small butchering business was bankrupted by the Cudahy's expanding business empire. Crowe was also fired from his position in a Cudahy store for theft. Crowe, subsequently, kidnapped 16–year-old Edward Cudahy, Jr on 18 Dec. 1900. Nebraska had no kidnapping statute. When arrested, Crowe was charged with shooting a policeman, but the jury acquitted Crowe after only 80 minutes deliberation. A new charge of grand larceny sent Crowe to trial in Feb. 1906. The jury again acquitted Crowe.

233 The Overland Route, operated by the Union Pacific Railroad and the Central Pacific Railroad / Southern Pacific Railroad, between Council Bluffs, Iowa / Omaha, Nebraska, and San Francisco opened on 10 May, 1869.

234 The route crossed the Continental Divide at Creston. At Green River passengers encountered two spectacular rock formations (Man's Face and Castle Rock). The route entered Utah with its unusual and spectacular rock formations.

235 In the 2nd Circle (Canto 5) of Dante's *Inferno*, Francesca da Rimini and Paolo Malatesta suffer together in hell for their adultery.

236 Annette (Anne) Hyde, (1865–1952) married John Cambreth Kane (1844–1932) and lived in Snake River Valley, Rawlins, Wyoming until World War 1. 'Four years ago, Mr J. Cambreth Kane, an Irish ranchman, who had lived in the valley twelve years, was, in some way, brought back to his early religious life, and determined to start religious services. For, strange to say, although the valley is so well settled and the people are, in general, so prosperous, it does not contain a single church building, nor was there a religious work of any kind until Mr Kane undertook his religious mission. He began by holding services himself, as a lay reader. Then, obtaining a guarantee of salary from the people, he appealed to Bishop Talbot when Bishop of Wyoming and Idaho, for help. A lay-reader was sent out from New York City, who, it would seem, was a minister of some other

denomination, who was waiting the canonical time before entering our ministry. After his arrival, he found many of the people suspicious of our Church, and one morning calmly announced that he was now a Methodist minister. His character, as revealed by this action, gradually showed itself, in business matters, and he was compelled to withdraw.' *In the Sage Brush Country: Being an Account of the Snake River Valley Mission in the district of Laramie*, Episcopal Church. Domestic and Foreign Missionary Society (1902). 'Mr Kane an Irishman, who returned to the old sod was an early day settler and at one time ran six hundred head of cattle.' Mildred McIntosh, 'Some pioneer residents along the snake river', in *The Steamboat Pilot*, 11 Apr. 1930, p. 5.

237 Ogden, approximately 10 miles east of the Great Salt Lake, 40 miles north of Salt Lake City, was a major passenger railroad junction owing to its location along major east–west and north–south routes. The motto of the local chamber of commerce claimed, 'You can't get anywhere without coming to Ogden.'

238 The largest salt-water lake in the Western Hemisphere and the eighth-largest terminal lake in the world.

239 Frances Jolliffe.

240 Originally established in 1902–4 by the Southern Pacific Rail Company as two independent rock causeways extending from each shore, with a 12-mile wooden trestle bridge in the middle.

241 Two types of barriers were in use: Snow sheds, consisting of wooden galleries with roofs that followed the slope of the mountain, which ensured avalanches would pass over the tracks without dumping their heavy load. The second type consisted of large stonewalls, built across ravines, these barriers prevented the snow sheds from taking a direct hit from slides. 37 miles of tunnel was constructed.

242 Frank J. Sullivan, attorney and former candidate for mayor. Born in 1852, possibly a son of John Sullivan, survivor of the Donner Party.

243 On re-routing the Sacramento-Oakland segment of the Transcontinental Railroad in 1876, the Central Pacific established a ferry across the Carquinez Strait. The *Solano*, the world's largest ferryboat, and later the *Contra Costa*, carried whole trains of up to 48 freight cars or 24 passenger cars with their locomotives.

244 Located on Powell and Geary Streets on Union Square in San Francisco. Opened 21 Mar. 1904. The Hydes lodged in suite 309 on the 3rd floor.

245 George Thomas Montgomery (1847–1907).

246 James Duval Phelan (1861–1930), Mayor of San Francisco (1897–1902); US Senator (1915–21).

247 Built in 1900 and designed by architect Edgar A. Mathews, this private residence, a brown-shingle box, was located at 1820 Scenic Avenue, north of the campus.

248 Benjamin Ide Wheeler (1854–1927) served as President of the University of California (1899–1919).

249 George Berkeley (1685–1753).

250 The Lay of Oisín.

251 Heinrich Friedrich Zimmer (1851–1910).

252 Eduard Rudolf Thurneysen (1857–1940).

253 The Cliff House, at Point Lobos Avenue, on the headland above the cliffs at north of Ocean Beach, in the Outer Richmond neighbourhood of San Francisco.

254 The famous Monarch Bear, the last Californian wild grizzly bear, was captured in the Ojia Valley, Ventura Co., near Los Angeles and brought to San Francisco on 3 Nov. 1889. Refused by the Menagerie (zoo) at Golden Gate Park, Hearst placed it on exhibit at Woodward's Gardens in San Francisco. On opening day (10 Nov. 1889) over 20,000 people visited.

255 Hugo K. Schilling, President of German-American League. Resigned from Harvard in 1901 to accept the head professorship of German language and literature at the University of California.

256 See the National German-American Alliance / Deutschamerikanischer National-Bund, founded in Philadelphia, Pennsylvania on 1901, to promote and preserve German culture in America.

257 Claus Spreckels (1828–1908).

258 Charles Mills Gayley (1858–1932), professor of English, the Classics, and Academic Dean of the University of California at Berkeley (1889–1932).

259 Incorporated in 1902, as a private, mutual benefit corporation.

260 70 Eddy Street, corner of Eddy and Mason, San Francisco. Hyde's comments on Trinity College were critiqued in *Gleanings and Memoranda: A Monthly Record of Political Events and Current Political Literature*, 27, p. 2, when Hyde was appointed to a Royal Commission of Inquiry into Trinity College in June 1906.

261 Philip O'Ryan (1869–1920). Born in Co. Tipperary, educated at Thurles College for Holy Orders, ordained for the priesthood on 18 June 1893, the year he came to America and entered the Catholic University at Washington, where the degree of S. T. L. was conferred upon him in 1895. On his arrival in San Francisco in 1895, he was appointed assistant to St Mary's Cathedral. In 1896 he was made associate editor of the *Monitor*, the official organ of the Catholic Diocese of San Francisco, and assisted the editor, the Rev. P. Yorke.

262 Sacred Heart Cathedral 'Preparatory,' located in the Cathedral Hill neighbourhood of San Francisco. Founded in 1852, Sacred Heart Cathedral is San Francisco's oldest Catholic secondary school.

263 Rabbi Jacob Voorsanger (1852–1908).

264 George Cooper Pardee (1857–1941), Governor of California (1903–7).

265 Eugene Edward 'Handsome Gene' Schmitz (1864–1928), Mayor of San Francisco (1902–7).

266 David Starr Jordan (1851–1931), educator and eugenicist, president of Indiana University. Founding president of Stanford University.

267 William Henry Beatty (1838–1914), Chief Justice of California (1889–1914).

268 James Vincent Coffey (1846–1919).

269 John P. Frieden, S. J. (1896–1908). Superior of the Jesuit Mission in California. College President (1896–1908).

270 St Ignatius College Preparatory, originally located on Market Street, opened in 1855, moved to Hayes and Van Ness in 1883.
271 Possibly William J. Robinson, an Irish-born gold miner.
272 The Bohemian Club, incorporated 1872, as an 'association of gentlemen connected professionally with literature, art, music, the drama, and those having appreciation of the same.'
273 Alum Rock Park. Founded in 1872, California's oldest municipal park. Located in the Diablo Range foothills in eastern San José.
274 Alice Sullivan, (residence 201 Laurel Street), sister of James D. Phelan, was born in San Francisco on 24 Mar. 1860, and married in 1882 to Frank J. Sullivan. Her children included Mrs Frederick Lawrence Murphy; Sister Agnes (Ada Sullivan); Gladys Sullivan and Noel Sullivan.
275 Patrick McHugh (1872–?) studied for priesthood at All Saints in Dublin. Ordained in 1898, he was sent three years later to the Archdiocese of San Francisco California. In 1910 he was transferred to the parish of San Antonio, Oakland to serve as vicar under Fr Yorke.
276 Located at the southwest corner of Eddy and Mason, San Francisco.
277 'John Chinaman', the stock caricature of a Chinese labourer.
278 Established in 1902.
279 Rev. Frederick W. Clampett (1859–1929), Rector at Trinity St Peter's Episcopal Church; founded in 1849, it is the oldest Episcopal Church on the West Coast. Erected on the corner of Bush and Gough Streets in San Francisco in 1893.
280 Located at 8th Street and Market Street, Recreation Park/Central Park, had a seating capacity of 15,000. Opened in 1884, it operated until 1906.
281 Located at Market Street and Third Street in San Francisco.
282 John Diedrich Spreckels (1853–1926).
283 The Pup, located at Stockton and Market Streets; reputed to be among the city's dozen or so 'French restaurants.' It also served as Abe Ruef's informal political headquarters
284 John H. Ellis (1876–?).
285 Thomas Grace (1841–1921), Born in Co. Wexford.
286 Thomas John Capel (1836–1911). In 1868, Capel was named private chamberlain to Pope Pius IX, with the title of monsignor, and in 1873 became domestic prelate. He received into the Catholic Church the Marquess of Bute and many high-profile Anglicans.
287 In Disraeli's *Lothair* (1870), Capel figures as 'Monsignor Catesby.'
288 John Patrick Crichton-Stuart, 3rd Marquess of Bute (1847–1900).
289 Henry Edward Manning (1808–92), Archbishop of Westminster (1865–92).
290 Clunie Theatre, part of the Clunie hotel building, on K Street, between 8th and 9th Street.
291 Possibly Rabbi S. Gerstman.
292 'What region of the earth is not full of our calamities?', from Virgil's *Aeneid*, Book 1, Line 460.
293 *Quercus ilex*, a large evergreen oak native to the Mediterranean region.
294 'The opening of the Potter Hotel off West Beach in 1903 was a milestone in Santa Barbara tourism. The Potter soon eclipsed the Arlington Hotel as the top hostelry in the city and

in a short time, wealthy industrialists from the Midwest and East Coast were choosing to spend their winters within the opulent confines of the Potter. The hotel, with almost 600 guest rooms, was truly magnificent. The impeccably groomed grounds boasted a zoo and a rose garden with thousands of bushes ... The hotel came to enjoy a reputation international in scope.' Michael Redmond, *Santa Barbara Independent*, 3 Aug. 2006.

295 Lawrence T. Brannick, a graduate of Maynooth College and responsible for the return of O'Growney's body to Ireland in 1903.

LOS ANGELES

296 Joseph Scott (1867–1958) aka 'Mr Los Angeles.'

297 Opened on 12 Feb. 1906 less than a month prior to Hyde's arrival, the Hotel Alexandria was located at the southwest corner of Spring and 5th Street in downtown Los Angeles.

298 Dr J. W. Jones.

299 Mrs P. P. O'Brien.

300 Fannie Dillon.

301 W. Joseph Ford.

302 The Hotel Green, built in 1893 by George Gill Green, and later expanded in 1898 and again in 1903, it was the home of the Valley Hunt Club and the Tournament of Roses Association.

303 Elias Jackson 'Lucky' Baldwin (1828–1909). In 1885, the 'licentious 55-year-old millionaire persuaded 16-year-old Louise Perkins to accompany him on a trip, which spawned a $500,000 lawsuit for breach of promise.' See http://articles.latimes.com/1999/sep/05/local/me-7136.

304 717 South Burlington Avenue.

305 St Paul's Pro-Cathedral.

306 Possibly John Joseph Bodkin or, his son, Henry Grattan Bodkin.

307 Possibly Thomas Bodkin Costello (1864–1956).

308 San Pedro.

309 The vessel was *The Cabrillo*.

310 Hotel Metropole. George Shatto, having purchased Catalina Island in 1887 for $200,000, immediately built the Hotel Metropole on the shoreline.

311 Hotel Alexandria.

312 Mason Opera House.

313 Bertha Lucille Roth.

314 Established in 1865, by the Vincentian Fathers, St Vincent's College for boys was originally located in the Lugo Adobe House at the southeast corner of Alameda and Beirut Streets. The school later moved to a location at Grand Avenue and Washington Boulevard where it remained until being folded into the newly founded Los Angeles College in 1911. St Vincent's College became Loyola College – now Loyola Marymount University – in 1918.

315 Fr Meyer Memorial Hall, in memory of Aloysius J. Meyer, C. M., the first pastor of St Vincent's Parish.

316 Founded in 1891 by Caroline Severance with other women in Hollenbeck Hotel's reading room. Later relocated to Second Street and Broadway.

317 Susan B. Anthony (1820–1906) died on 13 Mar. 1906.

318 Rosetta Harben, daughter of William and Mary Harben, married Gilbert Aubrey Davidson in 1894.

319 Established on 6 Feb. 1906. *Los Angeles Times*, 7 Feb. 1906, 21, describes it as 'an organisation that embraces members of the six branches of the Celtic race Scotch, Irish, Welsh, Manx, Cornish and Bretons, and which was founded for the purpose of preserving the beautiful old traditions of these peoples, especially those which deal with music, poetry and art.'

320 Malcolm Macleod (1851–1914), founder and first president of the Celtic Club of Los Angeles.

321 Al Levy's restaurant. Levy (1860–1941) was born in Liverpool, England, but raised and educated in Dublin. Arriving in California, aged 16, he opened several restaurants before moving to Los Angeles where he opened his restaurant, at 3rd Street and Main Street, that became a centre of fashionable night life in 1906.

322 John William Hamilton, (1845–1934), bishop of the Methodist Episcopal Church.

323 Levy's Café.

324 Chutes Park, a 35-acre amusement park bounded by Grand Avenue on the west, Main Street on the east, Washington Boulevard on the north and 21st Street on the south, in Los Angeles, began as a trolley park in 1887.

325 Established in 1888 in downtown Los Angeles and the second-oldest such club in Southern California, the California Club is a members-only private social club. In 1904, it relocated to the northwest corner of 5th and Hill Streets in Los Angeles. A popular adage claimed: 'The people who "run" Los Angeles belong to The Jonathan Club; the people who "own" Los Angeles belong to The California Club.'

326 St Peter's Catholic Church, 1292 Alabama Street, San Francisco.

327 P. S. Casey.

328 Santa Clara College, founded in 1851, became the University of Santa Clara in 1912.

329 'Play for charity. The proceeds of the game next Sunday between the Prune Pickers and Santa Clara College will be devoted to the purposes of the Gaelic League, of which Dr Douglas Hyde is the president. Manager Mayer will play his strongest team as this is the last game before the opening of the regular league season on Apr. 8…', in *The Evening News*, 29 Mar. 1906, p. 2.

330 Richard A. Gleeson (1861–?)

331 St Francis's Church. Possibly St Francis of Assisi Church at 610 Vallejo Street on Columbus, North Beach. Dedicated as a parish church on 17 Mar. 1860. The twin towers and walls survived the 1906 Earthquake and fire, but the interior was gutted. The parish built a new church within the surviving walls and rededicated it on 2 Mar. 1919. The National Conference of Catholic Bishops named it the National Shrine of St Francis of Assisi in 1999.

332 Possibly St Rose's Church at North Brannan & Fifth Streets, San Francisco. Constructed in 1878. The Reverend John F. Nugent served as Rector during the 1906 earthquake and lived at 532 Brannan Street. Ordained in the church of St John Lateran at Rome in 1872, he came to St Brendan's Parish, San Francisco in 1879.

333 'The Killarney Echo,' famously described in Alfred Lord Tennyson's poem 'The Splendour Falls,' refers to the celebrated echo that resounds off the mountains and lakes of Killarney, Co. Kerry.

334 Abraham Ruef (1864–1936), corrupt political boss behind the administration of Mayor Schmitz.

335 Rev. P. J. Fisher (?–1918). 'Monsignor P. J. Fisher Pastor of Holy Cross Church is called to his Reward…', in *Santa Cruz Evening News*, 3 Dec. 1918.

336 Possibly a reference to the crash involving the engine, express car and smoking car of the westbound Great Northern fast train, that fell in the deep waters of Diamond Lake, one and a half miles east of Camden, about 30 miles from Spokane in July 1906. See *The Duluth News Tribune*, 25 July 1906.

PORTLAND

337 Dr A. A. Morrison, rector of Trinity Church.

338 Alexander Christie (1848–1925).

339 Marquam Grand Hotel, (renamed the Orpheum Theatre in 1908) existed from 1890 until 1912. It stood eight stories tall at 335 Morrison Street, currently 621 South West Morrison.

340 M. O. Munley.

SEATTLE

341 F. H. Fogarty, assistant general freight agent for the Northern Pacific railway.

342 Martin J. Henehan (1857–?) built up an extensive trade. He acquired his early education in the national and Franciscan schools of Ireland and subsequently pursued a course of study in the University of Notre Dame at Notre Dame, Indiana. As well as being the President and sole owner of The Seattle Frog & Switch Co., a manufacturer of railway supplies, he served as director of the German American Mercantile Bank and was widely recognized as a prosperous, enterprising and representative business man of the city. In 1891, he married Mary Alice Gormly, 'a daughter of John and Elizabeth (Cuffe) Gormly. Her father is a descendant of one of the leaders in the Irish rebellion. Among their children were Bess, (wife of R. M. Evans); Martina; Vincent; Ulic; and Kevin. See Clarence Bagley, *History of Seattle from the Earliest Settlement to the Present Time*, 3 (Chicago, n.d.), p. 33.

343 Butler Hotel, located at Second Avenue and James Street, Seattle.

344 Constructed 1898–1900, the Grand Opera House was located at Third Avenue and Cherry Street and had a capacity of 2,200 people.

345 Thomas Burke (1849–1925), chief justice of the Washington State Supreme Court.

346 John Harte McGraw (1850–1910), served as second Governor of Washington state (1893–7).

347 Edward John O'Dea (1856–1932).

348 Virginia C. Holmgren, *Chinese Pheasants, Oregon Pioneers* (Portland, 1964).

SPOKANE

349 The tunnel, 2.6 miles long, was completed on 20 Dec. 1900.

350 Gonzaga College (1887–1912), now Gonzaga University.

351 James Monaghan (1839–1916), born Belturbet, Co. Cavan. John Robert Monaghan, a graduate of the US Naval Academy and the eldest of the family's six children, was killed in a skirmish between Samoans and the German navy in 1899. A statue in downtown Spokane, unveiled in 1906, honours him.

352 Footnote in 1937 edition: Years later Monaghan and his two daughters and a friend of theirs came to see me in Dublin. They said he recovered after a while, and that his sudden illness had not affected him. I asked them about the French doctor. He was a famous man, and he left France hurriedly because of his politics. He had only been in Spokane a short while at that time, and that was the reason he did not speak English.

BUTTE

353 Lake Pend Oreille, the largest lake in Idaho.

354 J. J. O'Meara, Manager of the Montana Provision, Butte.

355 65 East Broadway.

356 J. C. C. Thornton (John Caldwell Calhoun 'Coon' Thornton (1834–87), a Confederate recruiter sent behind federal lines in Missouri in the winter of 1863–4 to round up and sign up as many southern men as possible.

357 William Andrews Clark Sr. (1839–1925).

358 The West Stewart Mine at Centerville.

359 Marcus Daly (1841–1900), born Derrylea, Ballyjamesduff, Co. Cavan.

360 The Margaret Theater, built in 1897 and named after Marcus Daly's wife, held 1,246 seats.

361 John Patrick Carroll (1864–1925).

ANACONDA

362 James Francis Spelman, physician and surgeon for the Anaconda Copper Mine. Born in 1868 in NYC, he married Isabelle Coburn of New York in 1895.

363 Montana Hotel, located at Park Street and South Main Street.

364 *The Anaconda Standard.*

365 William M. Kelly (1860–?).

366 Edward Frances Mathewson, Superintendent, Washoe Smelter.

367 The American Protective Association, founded in 1887, was an American anti-Catholic secret society.

368 Possibly Rev. E. R. Dodds, St Mark's German Lutheran Church.

369 401 East Commercial Street, Anaconda.

370 'In the vicinity of Butte the *Cree Indian* village must occupy a place of decided interest. Most Butte people going for a drive out on the flat give the *Cree Indian* camp a wide berth…', in *The Anaconda Standard*, 27 May 1906.

371 Established in 1870 by John D. Rockefeller, this corporation was the largest oil refinery in the world of its time. In 1911 the US Supreme Court ruled that Standard Oil held an illegal monopoly.

372 Annette (Anne) Hyde, (1865–1952) married John Cambreth Kane (1844–1932) and lived in Rawlins, Wyoming until World War I. See note 236.

373 Built in 1882, the Ryan Hotel was originally located at Robert Street North and 6th Street.

374 Built in 1891–2, the Marshall Field and Company Building was the flagship location of the Marshall Field and Company, and Marshall Field's chain of department stores. Located in the Chicago 'Loop' area of the downtown business district, it occupies the entire city block bounded by North State Street, East Randolph Street, North Wabash Avenue, and East Washington Street.

375 William Dillon (1850–1935).

376 A western suburb of Chicago, the city of Elmhurst sits in DuPage County and Cook County, Illinois.

377 De Jonghe's Hotel and Restaurant, 12 East Monroe Street.

378 James O'Shaughnessy, Founder and President of Irish Fellowship Club. 'James O'Shaughnessy's father had grown up in sight of Thoor Ballylee (now called Yeats' Tower), but fled Co. Galway during the Great Famine and settled in Missouri. By 1917, James was a very successful advertising agent, becoming one of the highest paid in the US. He had earlier been a star journalist on the *Chicago Tribune*, covering the Spanish-American conflict in Cuba and the last outright battle between Native Americans and the US army … One of James O'Shaughnessy's brothers was Thomas, also known as "Gus". He became the leading practitioner of Gaelic Revival art in the United States. Perhaps the best surviving example of his work consists of the windows and interiors of Chicago's "Old St Pat's Church," which is reputedly that city's oldest continuously used public building.' Colum Kenny, 'Uncle Sam's PR man – An Irishman's diary on James O'Shaughnessy, the US and the first World War', in *The Irish Times,* 22 Apr. 2017.

379 'He is treading on fires hidden under a treacherous crust of ashes.' (after Horace).

380 Col John F. Finnerty (1846–1908).

381 Corrected from *Irish American* in the 1937 edition.

382 Elbridge Hanecy (1852–1925), a Judge Circuit Court of Cook County, Illinois (1893–1903); Superior Court Judge (1903–4) and Republican nominee for Mayor of Chicago (1901).

383 Edward Fitzsimmons Dunne (1853–1937), 38th Mayor of Chicago (1905–7) and Governor of Illinois (1913–17).

384 James H. Malone (1851–1929), Mayor of Memphis (1906–10).

385 Montgomery Park Race Track.

386 *Cornus florida*.

387 *Cercis siliquastrum*.

388 Possibly the Conemaugh River.

BALTIMORE

389 D. J. Scully.
390 Hotel Kernan (Congress Hotel), built in 1903.
391 Ford's Opera House, located on West Fayette Street between North Howard and Eutaw Streets, opened in 1871.

CORNELL

392 James McMahon (1856–1922), Born in Co. Armagh, he was one of the two most prominent Cornell mathematicians of the early period. He married Katharine Crane and they leased the Oliver Cottage, located at 7 Central Avenue, from the University.
393 See *The Cornell Alumni News*, 8, p. 374.
394 Ezra Cornell (1807–74).
395 'Douglas Hyde regards Los Angeles as the most intellectual of all the cities he has visited in America, not excepting Boston – *Los Angeles Times*. He probably spent much of his time in the society of the editor of our sprightly California contemporary', in *The New York Herald*, 25 Mar. 1906.
396 John Moore.
397 James J. O'Connor.

ELMIRA

398 Elmira Female College.

SCRANTON

399 P. C. Hurst.
400 Born in Co Sligo, five of the Casey family, all boys, came to America. First to arrive were Lawrence, and Timothy Casey, about 1870 and settled in Lackawanna County (Scranton) and worked for M. Gilbin, a relative who involved in the local liquor trade. After working for Gilben & Madden the Caseys took over the liquor business and expanded the business, finally moving into a four-story building at 216 Lackawanna Avenue.
401 A barony in South Co Sligo.
402 The Lyceum Theatre, opened in 1894, by Arthur Frothingham. Destroyed by fire in 1916. Located at 210–12 Penn Avenue, after a fire, the Miles was rebuilt on the site in 1916, and became the Capitol in 1923.
403 Michael John Hoban (1853–1926).
404 Joseph Benjamin Dimmick (1858–1920). His name is given as 'Dimock' in the 1937 edition.
405 'The Philo-Celtic Society will produce Dr Hyde's *An Pósadh*. The dramatic section of the New York Philo-Celtic Society will produce, in Gaelic, on Saturday evening, *An Pósadh* at the Lexington Avenue Opera House. It is a one-act drama by Dr Douglas Hyde.

President of the Gaelic League, who is now lecturing in this country in the interests of the Irish literary revival. The English name of the piece is "The Marriage." It deals with the wanderings of Raferty, the blind minstrel of Connaught, in the days of O'Connell. The drama shows the Irish people in their everyday life. New dances, or at least old ones revived by the Gaelic League, will be introduced. Dr Hyde, who is now in Chicago, has sent word to the society that he will be present to witness the production. Tickets may be had at any time at the Philo-Celtic Society. 341 West Forty-Seventh Street, or at the Opera House', in *The New York Times*, 24 Apr. 1906, p. 11.

406 Gerald P. Co(u)ghlan (1848–?).

407 William Carroll (*c.* 1836–*c.* 1926).

408 Wissahickon Creek is a tributary of the Schuylkill River.

409 Located at 23–9 South, 10th Street in Philadelphia, PA, it opened in 1883 and closed in 1924. Women, allegedly, were forbidden to enter even if accompanied by their husbands.

410 Laura Johnson Wylie (1855–1932), one of the first women to receive, in 1894, a Ph.D. from Yale; she returned to Vassar in 1895 as an English instructor. She chaired the English Department from 1897–1921.

411 J. Ryland Kendrick (1821–89) became a trustee of Vassar College in 1875, and served as acting president in 1885. Kendrick's wife, Georgia Avery Kendrick (1848–1922), began a close connection with Vassar after his death. In 1891, she became Lady Principal, a position she held for 22 years. As social head of the college, Mrs Kendrick worked very closely with President Taylor.

412 The Grand Central Palace, Lexington Avenue and 43rd Street. Opened in 1893, this building was razed to make way for improvements to the tracks leading into the new Grand Central Terminal completed in 1913.

413 Victor James Dowling (1866–1934). Supreme Court Justice (1905–31).

414 Major J. C. Crowley.

415 *The Gaelic American* New York, 3:19, 12 May 1906.

416 Dorothy Coates, alleged to be Quinn's mistress.

417 Condé Benoist Pallen (1858–1929).

418 Pelham Bay Park is New York City's largest park, three times the size of Manhattan's Central Park.

419 Alice Brisbane (1859–1953), who married Charles R. Thursby.

420 Arthur Brisbane (1864–1936).

421 Joseph Ignatius Constantine Clarke (1846–1927).

422 'The fighting race', available at http://www.bartleby.com/248/1102.html.

423 Members of Félibrige, the organisation founded by Frederic Mistral in 1854 to preserve the Provençal language.

424 Located on Sixth Avenue between West 43rd and West 44th Streets, the New York Hippodrome opened as a theatre in New York City in 1905. Featuring circus animals, diving horses, opulent sets, and 500-member choruses. It closed in 1939.

BUFFALO

425 John T. Ryan.

426 Established 1889 and demolished 1940, located on Eagle Street and on Main and Washington Streets.

427 Daniel Joseph Kenefick (1863–1949), Justice Supreme Court of New York (1898–1906), and Trustee University of Buffalo.

428 Joseph O'Connor (1841–1908).

429 Charles Henry Colton (1848–1915).

430 A 56-metre column in Queenston, Ontario, dedicated to Major General Sir Isaac Brock, a Canadian hero in the War of 1812.

431 Footnote in 1937 edition: And it shows today in his fine church in Roscommon, the most ornate Church, I believe, in Connacht.

ROCHESTER

432 Colonial Hall. Located at 62nd Paul Street, Rochester.

433 Genesee Valley Club, established in 1885, relocated in 1889 to the northwest corner of East Avenue and Gibbs Street.

434 Possibly, William F. Lynn.

435 John L. Codyre.

TORONTO

436 The date is incorrectly given as the 'seventh' in the 1937 edition.

437 Massey Hall.

438 Fritzi Scheff (1879–1954) starred as Fifi in *Mlle. Modiste* that ran at the Knickerbocker Theatre, from 25 Dec. 1905 to 16 June 1906.

WASHINGTON

439 Washington's first skyscraper. Completed in 1904, it was located at 1401–09 Pennsylvania Avenue.

440 The New National Theatre, located three blocks from the White House.

441 'Uncle Joe,' Joseph Gurney Cannon (1836–1926). Leader of the Republican Party and served as Speaker of the US House of Representatives (1903–11).

442 'Social and Personal Prominent Men Are Guests of President at Luncheon … Among guests at the luncheon given by the President yesterday were Dr Douglas Hyde, Dr Maurice Francis Egan, and Dr Dunne', in *The Washington Post,* 22 May 1906, p. 7.

443 Maurice Francis Egan (1852–1924). A Professor of English at the University of Notre Dame (1888–96), and Professor of English at the Catholic University of America, (1896–1907), he was an associate editor of the ten-volume *Irish Literature* (1904). Roosevelt appointed him Ambassador to Denmark.

444 Rear Admiral William Sheffield Cowles (1846–1923) married Anna Roosevelt (1855–1931), Theodore Roosevelt's older sister, in 1896.

445 In 1907, *The Century Magazine* published an essay entitled, 'The ancient Irish sagas' that deals with the Ulster Cycle in the context of North-European literature and compares it with Norse Sagas and Arthurian Romances.

446 Located at 2121 Massachusetts Avenue, NW, the Cosmos Club, incorporated in 1878, is a private social club for women and men distinguished in science, literature, the arts, or public service.

447 Cardinal James Gibbons of Baltimore, dedicated McMahon Hall, the second-oldest building on campus, in 1889.

448 Rev. Thomas J. Shahan, served as rector of the Catholic University of America (1909–28). Denis Joseph O'Connell (1849–1927) previously served (1903–9).

449 James Mooney (1861–1921).

450 James Mooney, *Myths of the Cherokee: From Nineteenth Annual Report of the Bureau of American Ethnology* 1897–98, *Part I* (1900).

451 Footnote in 1937 edition: *Myths of the Cherokee*, 576 pages with many pictures.

452 The Maliseet/Malecite are an Algonquian-speaking First Nation of the Wabanaki Confederacy. The indigenous people of the St John River Valley and its tributaries, their territory extends across the current borders of New Brunswick and Quebec in Canada, and parts of Maine in the US.

453 Douglas Hyde, 'On some Indian folklore', in Breandán Ó Conaire (ed.), *Language, Lore and Lyrics: Essays and Lectures*, (Dublin, 1986), pp 135–44; see also editor's introduction, pp 43–4.

454 George Catlin (1796–1872), an American painter, the first white painter to depict Plains Indians in their native territory.

455 Denis Joseph O'Connell (1849–1927), served as president of the Catholic University of America (1903–9).

BRIDGEPORT

456 Peter W. Wren (1847–1928), member of the wholesale wine and spirit house of McMahon & Wren, in Bridgeport, the largest firm in that business in the State.

457 484 State Street, Bridgeport.

PATERSON

458 The Hamilton Club, located at 32 Church Street in Paterson, New Jersey, opened in 1897 as an exclusive gentlemen's club. Named for Alexander Hamilton, the first US Secretary of the Treasury and a founder of Paterson, NJ.

459 Willam B. Gourley (1856–1917), born Co. Down.

460 Lyceum Theatre.

461 'United Irish Societies of Passaic County – Lecture by Dr Douglas Hyde, at Lyceum Theatre, 28 Mar. 1906', in *Paterson NJ Morning Call*, 14 May, 1906, p. 6.

462 A bare rock mountain in Eagle Rock Reservation, it marks the boundary between the towns of Montclair and West Orange, NJ.

463 St Patrick's Cathedral located on Fifth Avenue and 50th Street.

464 Marguerite Merington (*c.* 1861–1951).

465 Decoration Day was an earlier name for Memorial Day. Memorial Day become the more common name after World War II and was declared the official name in the US in 1967.

466 Hanna O'Leary.

467 Timothy E. Cohalan.

468 Cathalán – 'the little brave warrior.'

469 See note 224.

470 Henry McCarter, with explanatory notes by Douglas Hyde, L. L. D., 'Scenes from the early history of Ireland', in *Scribner's Magazine*, 40:6 (Dec. 1906), pp 685–92.

471 338 Pelham Road, New Rochelle, NY.

472 A. Wessels & Company was established as publishing house in New York in 1900 and liquidated in 1911.

473 Edward Hugh Sothern (1859–1933), American actor renowned for romantic and Shakespeare roles.

474 E. H. Sothern and Julia Marlowe.

475 The Hotel Majestic, located in the Upper West Side, between the 71st Street and 72nd Street, and Central Park West.

476 John Robert Gregg (1867–1948), inventor of Gregg Shorthand. Born on 1867 in Co. Monaghan, he emigrated to Liverpool in 1887 and began to develop his own shorthand system. In 1893 he came initially to Boston and later Chicago. In 1898, he published *Gregg Shorthand* and two years later established the Gregg Publishing Company in Chicago. He moved the headquarters to New York City in 1907.

477 Charles Johnston (1867–1931). Born Co. Down, he became famous as a Sanskrit scholar and translator of Hindu texts. He married Vera Vladimirovna de Zhelihovsky.

478 Built in 1893, the original Waldorf-Astoria stood on Fifth Avenue, Manhattan. It was razed in 1929 to make way for construction of the Empire State Building. The current Waldorf Astoria is on Park Avenue.

479 Possibly, Oscar Tschirky (1866–1950), aka 'Oscar of the Waldorf,' the Waldorf Astoria's maitre d'hotel from 1893–1943. In 1896, the Werner Company published *The Cook Book by "Oscar" of The Waldorf*.

480 Alice Stopford Green (1847–1929).

481 A bay dividing Brooklyn from eastern Coney Island.

482 Possibly Miss Ada Smith.

483 'Hyde Refuses Personal Gift. Departs for Ireland With Fifty Thousand Dollars to Aid the Gaelic League, New York, June 16. Dr Douglas Hyde, president of the Gaelic League in Ireland, and Mrs Hyde sailed for their home in Ireland yesterday on the White Star liner

Celtic. Dr Hyde took back with him a check for $50,000 to aid the cause of the Gaelic League in Ireland. This sum was raised at public meetings that Dr Hyde addressed during his visit of seven months. Before sailing Dr Hyde said: 'I have found nothing except a generous welcome in America. I have traveled over 10,000 miles, visited over sixty cities and explained the cause of the Irish language to perhaps 86,000 persons. I have not heard a single word that was not favorable to our cause. I understand now as never before how great is this country, and how numerous, strong and powerful are the Irish in it. I have expressed my thanks to the many friends whom I have met, but there are many others to whom I have had no time to send letters. I shall ask them to accept this excuse from me. There is a great likeness between the people of Ireland and those of this country, I would sooner have the good will of this country than anything else in the struggle to bring back the language, music and customs of Ireland.' A number of Dr Hyde's friends here raised $2,500 to buy him a motor car for use in his work in Ireland. This fund was to have been presented to Dr Hyde on Thursday, but he declared he could not depart from the rule of his life not to accept any personal reward for his services to the Gaelic League and in behalf of Irish unity. The contributions were returned to the contributors', in *San Francisco Chronicle*, 17 June 1906.

484 *Abhráin Diadha Chúige Connacht or The Religious Songs of Connacht*, published by T. Fisher Unwin, London, and M. H. Gill and Son Ltd, Dublin, in 1906.

485 Founded in 1899, absorbed by the Colonial Trust Company in 1907.

486 Footnote in 1937 edition: Quinn's secretary.

487 Soon after his return, Dublin Corporation decided to confer the Freedom of the City on Dr Hyde: 'Conferring the Freedom of the City. A special meeting of the Dublin Corporation was held yesterday in the City Hall for the purpose of considering a proposal to confer the freedom of the city on Dr Douglas Hyde, president of the Gaelic League, on the occasion of his return from America, and in recognition of his magnificent and untiring services on behalf of the restoration of our national language.' The Lord Mayor presided, and there were about two dozen members present. None of the Unionist members attended. Mr John Kelly, having delivered a speech in Irish, afterwards proposed a resolution, the object of which was to confer the freedom of the city on Dr Hyde. He said it was an honour to have been asked to propose the resolution. There was no great necessity for bringing under their notice the work which Dr Douglas Hyde had done and was doing for the Irish language and Irish industries. It was for the purpose of acknowledging in some measure the work that he had done that they were proposing to confer this honour upon him. Since the foundation of the League, some thirteen years ago, Dr Hyde had been its president, and no man could possibly do more to promote its object than he had done. He had done not merely one man's part, but the work of ten men, to secure the success which the League had attained. Lately he went on an organizing tour to the United States, where he travelled some 20,000 miles organizing and working in the interest of the Irish language and Irish industries, and when he returned to this country he brought with him some ten thousand pounds. Although the League had received the benefit of his services for thirteen years

this was the first occasion on which a suitable opportunity had offered for recognizing his services. He (Mr Kelly) had pleasure in moving the adoption of the resolution. Mr Rooney seconded the resolution, stating that the freedom of the city had been conferred on some eminent Irishmen, but none deserved it more than Dr Douglas Hyde. He (Dr Hyde) was the president of the one organisation which knew no politics, and which was bringing all classes of Irishmen together for the good of the country. Their action in conferring the proposed honour on Dr Douglas Hyde would be ratified by the great majority of Irishmen regardless of politics. Alderman Irwin wished to associate himself with the sentiments expressed by the mover and seconder of the resolution, remarking that he was not in accord with some of the methods of the Gaelic League, and he was not in accord with some of the harassing methods of the other side. The League had, however, immensely benefited the material interests of the country in recent years. The honour now proposed had not been conferred during his time on anyone who deserved it better than Dr Douglas Hyde. Alderman Corrigan also supported the resolution. He said the League had done much to stimulate small industries, and revive some that had become extinct, and Alderman Doyle who also associated himself with the mover and seconder of the resolution, said the League was stamping out bigotry and bringing together in a spirit of good fellowship men of all classes and creeds. The Lord Mayor, in putting the resolution to the meeting, said their action would have the effect of strengthening the hands of those who were trying to obtain the same privileges and financial aid for the teaching of the Irish language as was given for the teaching of foreign languages, which were not more advantageous to the people of this country. The resolution was adopted unanimously and the meeting adjourned. It was agreed, in accordance with the terms of the resolution, to confer the freedom of the city on Dr Douglas Hyde on the 7th of August next', in *The Irish Times*, 30 June 1906, 4.

488 Sir Clarendon Golding Hyde (1858–1934).

489 Robert Dudley (1532–88).

490 Amy Dudley (née Robsart) (1532–60).

491 Footnote in 1937 edition: That is 'gladiator', probably a statue in the garden?

492 Footnote in 1937 edition: 'Sporting,' as I heard it.

493 Footnote in 1937 edition: *heir* or *air*?

494 Royal Commission on Trinity College, Dublin and the University of Dublin, chaired by Sir Edward Fry published in 1907.

495 Anthony Traill (1838–1914), Provost of Trinity College, Dublin; appointed Commissioner of National Education in 1901.

496 This paragraph was printed out of sequence in the first edition, before the piece on 'A Souvenir of the DR HYDE BANQUET'.

497 Footnote in 1937 edition: San Francisco's large prison, similar to Sing-Sing in New York.

INDEX

INNÉACS

96 ӡo ᴅcí an Ƭeac

agus ċuir an t-

ṗóṁainn. Do ċuir

Bain-ċéile, bean-uasal

ingin Cní nach Ailis

~~le~~ do ṁnaoi a ḋearbr

eile, agus ṡuiḋeamar

geáfrí. Goí ṡír

sgearbḟoġanta dubh

cuirscín tae agus

agus caora-ḟíneaim

x bairille agus an ~~De~~ ina

an dara cúrsa.

sgéaltaibh na h-Éir

Loċlannaċ, leir, agus

-tais eacorra. Do

tar éis an Lóin,